Deposit God's Word in ~~~
and you will draw i~~~

Author of quote un~~~

What others are saying about BIBLE IN A NUTSHELL:

"As an active pastor for many, many years, I longed for my people to be students of the Book of Books and to obtain a good overview of the Bible into which to put particular studies. I have encouraged folk to store in their heads and hearts memorized Scriptures for personal nurture and use all through their lives.
<u>*Bible in a Nutshell*</u> *would have been an excellent, practical, and usable resource for me to suggest for such purposes. I gratefully recommend it now!"*
— **Lloyd E. Batson, Th.D, D.D.**

"The Bible commands great respect and allegiance in our culture. Ironically, many are illiterate when it comes to knowledge of the actual content of the various books of the Bible. This guide is an excellent tool for becoming familiar with the content of the Bible and thereby gaining an appreciation of the scope and grandeur of the Biblical story."
— **Dr. Calvin Mercer, Associate Professor of Religion, East Carolina University**

"This work enables the reader to experience the Bible as 'living Word' in a simple, forthright manner, hopefully leading to further in-depth study. The author's approach is uncomplicated, yet thorough. It is free from superfluous detail, yet inclusive of the entire Biblical message."
— **Rev. Tom M. Jones, retired Director of Missions, Piedmont Baptist Association, Easley, SC**

"The hardest part of any journey seems to be the beginning. So here is good news, starting a journey through the Bible is easier and more memorable through this wonderful book. Concise introductions to each book of the Bible as well as a sincere, down-to-earth approach to remembering scripture will help the reader begin life-changing steps to put the Word into their heart. Some publications come from personal experience, some from passionate dedication, and some from a powerful desire to help others; <u>*Bible in a Nutshell*</u> *springs from all three sources. What a great way to begin a journey through the Bible!"*
— **Rev. James M. Tippins, Pastor, Summit Heights Baptist Church, Easley, SC**

THIS BOOK IS DEDICATED TO:

My loving parents, John and Martha Vickery,
who, from my childhood, have shown and taught me
God's love and the value of His Word;

And to my loving husband, supporter, encourager,
and best friend, Doug.

BIBLE IN A NUTSHELL
KEY SCRIPTURE, GENESIS TO REVELATION,
TO HIDE IN YOUR HEART AND LIGHT YOUR PATH

THY WORD HAVE I HID IN MINE HEART,
THAT I MIGHT NOT SIN AGAINST THEE.

PSALM 119:11 KJV

THY WORD IS A LAMP UNTO MY FEET,
AND A LIGHT UNTO MY PATH.

PSALM 119:105 KJV

Christmas 2002

Dear Brother Eugene,
I couldn't have written this without you! Thanks for being such a wonderful brother! With love,
Sarah Martha

Compiled by Sarah V. Tinsley

Co-Publishers:
HIS LIGHT Publications
Easley, SC USA

TP TRAFFORD Publishing, Inc.
New Bern, NC USA & Victoria, BC Canada

BIBLE IN A NUTSHELL

KEY SCRIPTURE, GENESIS TO REVELATION, TO HIDE IN YOUR HEART AND LIGHT YOUR PATH

Compiled by Sarah V. Tinseley

Copyright © 2002 by Sarah V. Tinsley

The Holy Bible, New International Version © 1973, 1978, 1984 by the International Bible Society

Published by:

HIS LIGHT Publications
Post Office Box 1666
Easley, S.C. 29641
URL http://www.BibleInANutshell.com

Note: See QUICK ORDER FORM in the back. E-BOOK orders and ALL orders by bookstores, distributors, wholesalers, or other resale purchasers should be directed to Trafford Publishing.

Printed in Victoria, B.C. Canada

Edition One

National Library of Canada Cataloguing in Publication

Tinsley, Sarah V., 1956-
    Bible in a nutshell : key scripture, Genesis to Revalation, to hide in your heart and light your path / Sarah V. Tinsley.
Includes bibliographical references and index.
ISBN 1-55395-105-0
    I. Title.

BS418.T55 2002   220.6'1   C2002-904574-6

TRAFFORD

This book was published *on-demand* in cooperation with Trafford Publishing.
On-demand publishing is a unique process and service of making a book available for retail sale to the public taking advantage of on-demand manufacturing and Internet marketing.
On-demand publishing includes promotions, retail sales, manufacturing, order fulfilment, accounting and collecting royalties on behalf of the author.

Suite 6E, 2333 Government St., Victoria, B.C. V8T 4P4, CANADA
Phone   250-383-6864   Toll-free   1-888-232-4444 (Canada & US)
Fax   250-383-6804   E-mail   sales@trafford.com
Web site   www.trafford.com   TRAFFORD PUBLISHING IS A DIVISION OF TRAFFORD HOLDINGS LTD.
Trafford Catalogue #02-0819   www.trafford.com/robots/02-0819.html

10   9   8   7   6   5   4   3   2   1

TABLE OF CONTENTS

Bible in a Nutshell
KEY SCRIPTURE, GENESIS TO REVELATION,
TO HIDE IN YOUR HEART AND LIGHT YOUR PATH

**Page numbers for Key Notes and Key Memory Verses
are listed for each Bible book on the following page:**

Page numbers for each Bible book are listed below. The first page numbers after each book are for the KEY NOTES which include an introduction, key contents, and key verses. The page numbers in parentheses are for KEY MEMORY VERSES repeated in the back of the book for easy study.

II TIMOTHY 2:15:

STUDY TO SHEW THYSELF APPROVED UNTO GOD, A WORKMAN THAT NEEDETH NOT TO BE ASHAMED, RIGHTLY DIVIDING THE WORD OF TRUTH.

ACKNOWLEDGEMENTS: I have been blessed with many wonderful friends and family members who have been most supportive and helpful in the writing of this book. I would like to extend special thanks to the following:

— Dr. Lloyd E. Batson for always being available to share his Biblical knowledge and helpful suggestions. I consider Dr. Batson my "lifetime pastor" as he has been my pastor throughout my childhood and into my adult life, even officiating my wedding;
— Rev. Jim Tippins, my pastor at Summit Heights Baptist Church, for his invaluable guidance, recommendations, and constant support;
— Dalene Parker, an author and English teacher, whose editing and suggestions have been very beneficial;
— Dr. David Vickery, Professor of Psychology at Union University, for guidance and marketing ideas;
— Eugene R. Vickery, whose expertise in computers has been very helpful throughout the writing of this book;
— Dr. Calvin Mercer, Professor of Religion at East Carolina University, for his added Biblical knowledge, and his wife, Dr. Susan Mercer, for her useful ideas and editing;
— Mike Hamer, Professor of English at East Carolina University, for helpful suggestions and editing;

And I note a special thank you to my husband, Doug Tinsley, who has been endlessly helpful and supportive, and to my parents, John and Martha Vickery, and in-laws, Harold and Rachel Tinsley, who have given much encouragement and support.

Front cover photo: Sunrise at Hilton Head Island, South Carolina — This picture is symbolic. The sun's rays leading to the sun illustrate the path of light leading to God, the author of light and life. All other paths lead to darkness. Jesus said, *"...I am the light of the world: he that followeth me shall not walk in darkness, but shall have the light of life"* (see John 8:12).

Disclaimer: Every effort has been made to make *BIBLE IN A NUTSHELL* as complete and as accurate as possible. However, there may be mistakes, both typographical and in content. This book should be used only as a companion guide to *THE BIBLE*, and by no means as a substitute for *THE BIBLE* itself.

A NOTE FROM SARAH

Like many others, I learn more quickly when information is simply stated and presented "in a nutshell." I have always found it hard to grasp completely *THE BIBLE's* key contents and key verses because of its vastness. Several years ago, I decided to briefly summarize the key contents and key verses of each chapter in *THE BIBLE* to familiarize myself with the scripture. Time and time again, I have referred to this resource which has helped establish God's Word in my heart and mind. I felt this resource would also be helpful to others. I encourage your using *BIBLE IN A NUTSHELL* to easily gain an overview of *THE BIBLE,* and your studying more extensively from *THE BIBLE* the passages that capture your attention. In each Bible book, you will find a brief introduction followed by the key contents and key verses of the book's chapters. I have written mostly in the present tense and have purposefully avoided writing commentary. The main goals of *BIBLE IN A NUTSHELL* are to imprint scripture in your heart and mind, let the scripture speak for itself, and have *THE BIBLE* be more understandable for you. Hopefully, you will find yourself memorizing many, or perhaps all, of the 1000 key memory verses! **Even if you cannot quote verses word for word, the most important aspect of scripture is to hold its meaning in your heart and mind as you apply it to your everyday life!**

As I brainstorm on ways to use *BIBLE IN A NUTSHELL*, I have the following suggestions:

— **Bible study classes can study the key contents and key verses of *THE BIBLE* in a year.** The teacher can announce which pages to review for the following Bible study. Also, the teacher may want to designate which areas of the text to study more thoroughly from *THE BIBLE* for discussion. Use the numbered days, from 1-365, to begin the study anytime during the year or use the dates to begin the study in January.

— **Youth groups can be challenged to memorize the key memory verses.** Bible drills can be held using *BIBLE IN A NUTSHELL* as the study text.

— **Families can use this book for daily devotions.** Members of a family can also choose to memorize certain verses and quote these verses to each other.

— **Individuals can use this book as a study guide.** If studying through *BIBLE IN A NUTSHELL* in a year's time, follow the dates or numbered days found on the memory verses. For example, if you begin at January 1, Day 1, you will read till you reach January 2, Day 2, for that day's study. Most days will have only one page to review, while some days will have two or three pages. If you want to review only the memory verses without the key notes, simply turn to the back section, "1000 Key Memory Verses,"and study the one to four verses listed for that day.

— **Anyone studying this book can mark certain verses to memorize throughout the year** and add more verses each following year.

— **Schools including colleges and universities can use *BIBLE IN A NUTSHELL* as a textbook** for students to easily learn the key contents and key verses of *THE BIBLE*.

— **Churches can use *BIBLE IN A NUTSHELL* for fundraisers.** Larger discounts are offered when purchasing 50 or more books from HIS LIGHT Publications.

— **Please let me know of other ways you have used *BIBLE IN A NUTSHELL*.** You can contact me at the website, www.Bibleinanutshell.com.

The more I learn, I learn there is so much more to learn. Don't worry if you can't figure out everything in life — none of us can! I think God made the world and universe so large that we can never explore or understand it all. *THE BIBLE* is like that, too. Each time you read God's Word, God can show you something new, even if you have already read it 100 times! I hope you enjoy *BIBLE IN A NUTSHELL*, and I would love to hear from you. I would also enjoy visiting your area for book-signings. Just contact HIS LIGHT Publications to make arrangements. Both myself and HIS LIGHT Publications can be contacted at the website www.Bibleinanutshell.com. See more publisher information on the copyright page or back order form.

You may want to list your favorite Bible verses in "Personal Notes" in the back of the book. Below are verses which have been most special in my life.

Psalm 19:14:

LET THE WORDS OF MY MOUTH, AND THE MEDITATION OF MY HEART,
BE ACCEPTABLE IN THY SIGHT, O LORD, MY STRENGTH, AND MY REDEEMER.

Psalm 51:10:

CREATE IN ME A CLEAN HEART, O GOD;
AND RENEW A RIGHT SPIRIT WITHIN ME.

Proverbs 16:24:

PLEASANT WORDS ARE AS AN HONEYCOMB,
SWEET TO THE SOUL, AND HEALTH TO THE BONES.

Luke 1:37:

FOR WITH GOD NOTHING SHALL BE IMPOSSIBLE.

John 3:16:

FOR GOD SO LOVED THE WORLD, THAT HE GAVE HIS ONLY BEGOTTEN SON,
THAT WHOSOEVER BELIEVETH IN HIM SHOULD NOT PERISH,
BUT HAVE EVERLASTING LIFE.

Romans 8:28:

AND WE KNOW THAT ALL THINGS WORK TOGETHER FOR GOOD
TO THEM THAT LOVE GOD...

Ephesians 4:32:

AND BE YE KIND ONE TO ANOTHER, TENDERHEARTED, FORGIVING ONE ANOTHER,
EVEN AS GOD FOR CHRIST'S SAKE HATH FORGIVEN YOU.

Philippians 4:6:

BE CAREFUL FOR NOTHING;
BUT IN EVERY THING BY PRAYER AND SUPPLICATION WITH THANKSGIVING
LET YOUR REQUESTS BE MADE KNOWN UNTO GOD.

I Thessalonians 5:16-18:

16. REJOICE EVERMORE.

17. PRAY WITHOUT CEASING.

18. IN EVERYTHING GIVE THANKS:...

I Peter 5:7:

CASTING ALL YOUR CARE UPON HIM; FOR HE CARETH FOR YOU.

I John 4:7-8:

7. BELOVED, LET US LOVE ONE ANOTHER: FOR LOVE IS OF GOD;...
8. ... GOD IS LOVE.

I Chronicles 22:19:

Now set your heart and your soul to seek the Lord your God; ...

INTRODUCTION

Would you like to know and/or recite more Bible scripture? *BIBLE IN A NUTSHELL* gives you a concise and simple way of imprinting in your heart and mind key Bible verses and passages. If you are familiar with *THE BIBLE*, the listed key scripture will refresh your memory. If you are not familiar with *THE BIBLE*, you can quickly acquaint yourself with its key scripture. In our busy lives, most of us do not read *THE BIBLE* as much as we desire. We are often overwhelmed when studying the Bible, such a large and seemingly mysterious book. In *BIBLE IN A NUTSHELL*, you can view highlights of each of the 66 Bible books in just one or a few pages. As you become familiar with the contents, finding scripture in *THE BIBLE* will be easier. *BIBLE IN A NUTSHELL* should spur your interest to delve more deeply into *THE BIBLE* itself.

BIBLE IN A NUTSHELL is a reference book for the Bible's key scripture providing, in a nutshell, key notes for each of the 66 books in *THE BIBLE*. Key notes for each Bible book consist of a brief introduction on the authorship, date, and purpose of the book, and key contents listed by chapters. The key contents of each chapter include key topics and themes in bold lettering, key verses in italic lettering, and key memory verses in boxed text. Notations state the references for all quoted verses. The key contents also show you the context in which verses are found. There are a total of 1000 key memory verses listed for the 66 Bible books.

For quick review, *BIBLE IN A NUTSHELL* repeats the 1000 key memory verses separately after the section on key notes. Each line of a memory verse is centered and carries a complete phrase (or phrases) of the verse, making study and memorization easier. Dates and numbered days are found on one to four of the key memory verses for study each day (for example, the first memory verse has January 1, Day 1). You can begin on January 1st or anytime you choose when using the numbered days. You will also see dates on the memory verses in the key notes which allows you to easily find and study the surrounding scripture for the daily verses. In a year's time, you will have studied all 1000 memory verses. Maybe some day you will have memorized all 1000 verses! This is "The 1000 Challenge!" Page 10 explains more about memorization.

Having a study Bible with you as you read *BIBLE IN A NUTSHELL* will allow your studying the scripture more closely. To better understand any scripture, you should refer to *THE BIBLE*, the scripture's context, and commentaries. Many wonderful study Bibles which include commentary are available. See "Resources" for suggested study Bibles and other resources. Many of these resources were helpful in writing this book. In *BIBLE IN A NUTSHELL*, commentary is avoided; the main goals are to provide an easy way to imprint *THE BIBLE's* key scripture in your heart and mind, allow the scripture to speak for itself, and have God's Word come alive for you.

Psalm 119:11 tells how hiding God's Word in our heart can keep us from sin, and Psalm 119:105 says God's Word is a lamp to our feet and a light to our path. As you become more and more familiar with this book, studying and perhaps memorizing much of it, key Bible verses and passages will come to mind more quickly. It is always a blessing to be able to quote a verse for yourself or others in times of special need and when praising and worshipping God.

Scripture verses in this book are listed in the King James Version (KJV) because of its wide use and poetic nature. Some verses have in parentheses parts of the New International Version (NIV) when it helps clarify the meaning. Key memory verses were chosen by one or more of the following criteria: their inspirational and life-applicable qualities, their ability to stand alone without explanation, their common familiarity with both clergy and laity, and their relevance to important themes found in the Bible books. You can use the page margins or the "Personal Notes" section to add additional key scripture and notes important in your life. **May you be blessed as you study and apply God's Word to your life.**

THE GREATEST LOVE STORY EVER

Quoted Scripture is from the King James Version

The Bible tells the greatest love story ever! It is the story of God (the creator of the world, the whole universe, and all things), who in His infinite love, created humanity with whom to share His love and creation.

True love allows one to have freedom. God in His infinite wisdom allows all people the freedom to choose whether or not to follow God; unfortunately, many turn from rather than to God. Even in God's created spiritual world, He allows this free choice. Satan, envious of God's power, has chosen to rebel against God **(see Isaiah 14:12-15)**. How could Satan hurt God more than by causing God's loved creation, humankind, to turn away from God? The cycle repeats over and over, God and Satan's battle for humanity's allegiance. Choosing to follow the ways of Satan rather than God and His commandments is sin.

True love also allows a way of forgiveness. God allows each person to unite with Him when having a truly repentant heart of his/her sins and asking God into his/her life. In the Old Testament (old covenant), God chose the Hebrew people to preserve a race that followed God. Even the Hebrew people disappointed God time after time, but God always forgave them when they repented of their sin and desired to return to Him. He gave them laws to follow including "The Ten Commandments." When they sinned, they could receive forgiveness when showing their sincere repentance by offering the blood of unblemished sacrificed animals. The animal, a substitute sacrifice, died instead of the sinner who deserved the death.

In the New Testament (new covenant), God came to earth in human form as His Son, Jesus Christ. **John 3:16** says, *"For God so loved the world, that he gave his only begotten Son, that whosoever believeth in him should not perish, but have everlasting life."* Jesus was the perfect man who shed His innocent blood and died on the cross as the ultimate unblemished substitute sacrifice for our sins. He then conquered death by rising from the grave. Sin causes death; therefore, death could not hold Jesus because He is 100% righteous (without sin). People no longer need animal sacrifices to show their repentant hearts since Jesus Christ is now the ultimate sacrifice for those who believe; see **Hebrews 7:26-27 and 9:12-14.** Jesus says in **John 14:6,** *"I am the way, the truth, and the life: no man cometh unto the Father, but by me."*

Each and everyone of us can ask God into our lives. God only asks that we be repentant of our sins and believe Jesus Christ is God's son. God indwells us through His Holy Spirit when we become Christians (believers in Christ). This 100% righteous spirit is the believer's passport to heaven; without the Holy Spirit, sin separates us from God. **Romans 3:23** tells us, *"For all have sinned, and come short of the glory of God."* **I John 1:9** promises, *"If we confess our sins, he is faithful and just to forgive us our sins, and to cleanse us from all unrighteousness."* **Romans 10:9** says, *"That if thou shalt confess with thy mouth the Lord Jesus, and shalt believe in thine heart that God hath raised him from the dead, thou shalt be saved."*

God has provided His Word, *THE BIBLE*, to help show all people His love. God chose many people throughout the ages to write His message. We do not always know exactly who wrote each book of *THE BIBLE* or exactly when it was written. But we do know God has a purpose for each of these books being a part of *THE BIBLE* **(see II Timothy 3:15-17)**. Anyone sincerely seeking God, will find God and can hear Him speak through His Word. It is each person's choice whether or not to be a child of God. If you do not know God, hopefully you will ask Him into your life, even at this moment, and become part of God's family.

WHAT SHALL IT PROFIT A MAN?

Author Unknown

What **shall it profit a man if he be a great artist,**

And know not Jesus, the one who is altogether lovely?
What shall it profit a man if he be a great architect,
And know not Jesus, the chief cornerstone?
What shall it profit a man if he be a great baker,
And know not Jesus, the living bread?
What shall it profit a man if he be a great banker,
And know not Jesus, the priceless possession?
What shall it profit a man if he be a great biologist,
And know not Jesus, the giver of life?
What shall it profit a man if he be a great builder,
And know not Jesus, the sure foundation?
What shall it profit a man if he be a great carpenter,
And know not Jesus, the door?
What shall it profit a man if he be a great doctor,
And know not Jesus, the great physician?
What shall it profit a man if he be a great educator,
And know not Jesus, the teacher?
What shall it profit a man if he be a great farmer,
And know not Jesus, the great Lord of the harvest?
What shall it profit a man if he be a great florist,
And know not Jesus, the Rose of Sharon and Lily of the Valley?
What shall it profit a man if he be a great geologist,
And know not Jesus, the Rock of Ages?
What shall it profit a man if he be a great astronomer,
And know not Jesus, the Bright and Morning Star?
What shall it profit a man if he be a great jeweler,
And know not Jesus, the pearl of great price?
What shall it profit a man if he be a great lawyer,
And know not Jesus, the great advocate?
What shall it profit a man if he be a great sculptor,
And know not Jesus, the living stone?
What shall it profit a man if he be a great student,
And know not Jesus, the incarnate truth?
What shall it profit a man if he be a great philanthropist,
And know not Jesus, the unspeakable gift?
What shall it profit a man if he gain the whole world,
And lose his own soul ?

— See Matthew 16:26 and Mark 8:36 —

BIBLE EVENTS IN A NUTSHELL
(Listed in Biblical Order and Outline Form)

OLD TESTAMENT
(God's Old Covenant Made through the Hebrew People)

Books of the Law (Genesis to Deuteronomy): The first five books of the Old Testament are known as the Pentateuch, a word from Greek meaning five scrolls — In the beginning, God creates the heavens and the earth — God creates humanity (Adam and Eve) — Humanity sins by disobeying God — Story of Noah and the flood — Story of the Tower of Babel — Story of Sodom and Gomorrah — God calls Abram (later named Abraham) to be the father of the Jewish Hebrew nation — Abraham obeys God by offering his son Isaac as a sacrifice, but an angel prevents the sacrifice — Isaac and Rebekah have twins, Esau and Jacob — Esau sells his birthright to Jacob — Jacob and his two wives, Rachel and Leah, have twelve sons and one daughter — The twelve tribes of the Israelites are named for and are descendants of the twelve sons — Jacob's favored son Joseph (known for his coat of many colors) is sold into slavery by his jealous brothers — After being in an Egyptian prison, Joseph becomes a ruler in Egypt by gaining the favor of the Pharaoh through his ability to interpret dreams — Joseph helps his family by moving them to Egypt during a great famine — A new evil Pharaoh in Egypt makes slaves of the Jews and commands the Jewish baby boys to be killed — Miriam hides her baby brother Moses in the bulrushes of the Nile to keep him from being killed — Pharaoh's daughter finds Moses and raises him as her son — God speaks to Moses through a burning bush and calls him to lead His chosen people, the Jews, out of bondage — Moses first runs from God and then agrees to lead the Jews out of Egypt — The Pharaoh will not let the Jews leave Egypt even after nine of the ten plagues are brought upon Egypt — The Pharaoh finally allows the Jews' departure only after the tenth plague, when at the Passover, the firstborn son of every Egyptian family is killed by the Lord — As the Jews leave Egypt, the Pharaoh changes his mind and sends his army after the Jews — God parts the Red Sea, allowing the Jews to pass, but closes the sea as the Egyptians are crossing — The Jews wander in the desert for 40 years before being allowed to enter Canaan — God provides manna and quail for food in the wilderness — God gives Moses the Ten Commandments at Mount Sinai during the beginning of the Israelites' wandering in the wilderness — Moses is helped by his brother Aaron.

Books of History (Joshua to Esther): Joshua succeeds Moses as the Israelites' leader and leads them into the land of Canaan, conquering many of the Canaanite tribes — Joshua leads the battle of Jericho — Israel is ruled by judges — Samson rules as one of the judges — Story of Samson and Delilah — Story of Ruth — The Jews decide to be ruled by kings — Story of Israel's first three kings in I and II Samuel — The priest Eli raises Samuel from childhood — Samuel anoints Saul and then David as kings — The life of King Saul — The life of King David (stories include David and Goliath, David and Bathsheba, and David's son, Absalom, revolting against him) — The life of King Solomon (God chooses David's son, Solomon, who is known for his wisdom, to build the temple in Jerusalem) — I and II Kings and I and II Chronicles tell of Israel's first three kings and the kings of the divided kingdom of Israel — In 931 B.C., Israel divides into two kingdoms, the northern kingdom known as Israel and the southern kingdom known as Judah — The northern kingdom is ruled by 20 kings and the southern kingdom is ruled by 19 kings and one queen before their falls — Prophets Elijah and Elisha minister to the northern kingdom of Israel — In 722 B.C., the northern kingdom of Israel falls to Assyria — In 586 B.C., the southern kingdom of Judah falls to Babylon ruled by King Nebuchadnezzar; the temple in Jerusalem is destroyed, the city is burned, and many are taken captive to Babylon — After conquering Babylon, the Persian king Cyrus decrees in 538 B.C. the Jews can return to Jerusalem; the new temple in Jerusalem is completed in 515 B.C. — The books of Ezra and Nehemiah tell how the Jews are freed after Persia conquers Babylon; they also tell about the Jews returning to Jerusalem to rebuild its temple and walls — Story of Esther.

Books of Poetry (Job to Song of Solomon): Job addresses human suffering — Psalms is known as the Jewish hymn book — Proverbs is a collection of wisdom verses — Song of Solomon is a love story — Ecclesiastes discusses the purpose of life.

Books of the Major Prophets (Isaiah to Daniel): Isaiah prophesies judgment on Israel, Judah, and many nations — Jeremiah prophesies the falls of Judah and other nations, and describes the Babylonians' capture of Jerusalem — Lamentations mourns Jerusalem's destruction — Ezekiel prophesies before, during, and after the Babylonian exile — Daniel prophesies to the Jews held captive in Babylon, and the book of Daniel also contains a message for the Jews after the exile — Daniel includes the stories of the fiery furnace and the lions' den.

Books of the Minor Prophets (Hosea to Malachi): These prophets are called "minor" since their books are shorter than those of the "major" prophets — Hosea prophesies to the northern kingdom of Israel — Joel prophesies to the southern kingdom of Judah — Although a native of Judah, Amos prophesies mainly to Israel — Obadiah prophesies to Edom and Judah — The book of Jonah prophesies to Ninevah and contains a message for Jews as well; this book includes the story of Jonah and the great fish — Micah prophesies to the common people of Judah and also warns of Israel's fall — Nahum prophesies to both Ninevah and Judah — Habakkuk and Zephaniah prophesy to Judah — Haggai, Zachariah, and Malachi prophesy to the Jews after the Babylonian exile.

Note: Many places in the poetic and prophetic books also contain prophesies of the future Messiah and the new covenant.

NEW TESTAMENT
(God's New Covenant for All People through Jesus Christ)

Books of The Gospels (Matthew to John): The Gospels emphasize Jesus Christ's birth, ministry, teachings, death, and resurrection — The ministry of John the Baptist and the twelve apostles are also included in the four Gospels.

Book of History (Acts): The coming of the Holy Spirit, Paul's missionary journeys, and the church's beginnings are emphasized in Acts.

Books of Letters (Romans to Jude): Romans to Jude are letters (epistles) mainly written to encourage new believers, both Jews and Gentiles — The suggested authors of these letters include Paul (the primary suggested author for the books of Romans to Hebrews), James, Peter, John, and Jude (suggested authors for the books of James to Jude).

Book of Apocalyptic Writing (Revelation): John's vision while on the island of Patmos.

KEY BIBLE PASSAGES
(Listed in Biblical Order)

OLD TESTAMENT:

In the Beginning, God Created	Genesis 1:1
God's Call of Abram	Genesis 12:1-3
The Ten Commandments	Exodus 20:3-17, Deuteronomy 5:6-21
Love Thy Neighbor	Leviticus 19:18, Matthew 22:39, Mark 12:31, Luke 10:27, Romans 13:9, Galatians 5:14, James 2:8
The Priest's Prayer of Blessing	Numbers 6:24-26
Love the Lord Thy God	Deuteronomy 6:5, 10:12-13, Matthew 22:37, Mark 12:30,33, Luke 10:27
Whither Thou Goest, I Will Go	Ruth 1:16
David's Song	II Samuel 22, I Chronicles 16:7-36
The Prayer of Jabez	I Chronicles 4:9-10
God Will Heal Their Land	II Chronicles 7:14
The Heavens Declare the Glory of God	Psalm 19
The Lord is My Shepherd	Psalm 23
Make a Joyful Noise unto the Lord	Psalm 100
The Virtuous Woman	Proverbs 31:10-31
To Everything There is a Season	Ecclesiastes 3
For Unto Us a Child is Born	Isaiah 9:6-7
With His Stripes We Are Healed	Isaiah 52:13-53:12 (see 53:5)
God Like a Potter	Jeremiah 18-19
The New Covenant Foretold	Jeremiah 31:31-34
Israel Compared to Dry Bones	Ezekiel 37:1-14

NEW TESTAMENT:

The Sermon on the Mount	Matthew 5-7, Luke 6:20-49
The Beatitudes	Matthew 5:1-14
The Lord's Prayer	Matthew 6:9-13, Luke 11:2-4
The Golden Rule	Matthew 7:12, Luke 6:31
The Greatest Commandment	Matthew 22:37-40, Mark 12:29-31
Meaning of the Lord's Supper	Matthew 26:26-29, Mark 14:22-25, Luke 22:15-20
The Great Commission	Matthew 28:19-20, Mark 16:15-16
Pulling an Ox out of a Pit on the Sabbath	Luke 14:5
In the Beginning Was the Word	John 1
For God so Loved the World	John 3:16-18
Christ the Good Shepherd	John 10:1-21
New Commandment	John 13:34-35
Jesus' Prayer for All Believers for All Time	John 17:1-26
The Roman Road to Salvation	Romans 3:10,23; 5:8; 6:23; 10:9,13
The Love Chapter	I Corinthians 13
We are New Creatures in Christ	II Corinthians 5:17
Fruit of the Spirit	Galatians 5:22-23
By Grace are You Saved	Ephesians 2:8-9
I Can Do All Things Through Christ	Philippians 4:13
By Him All Things Consist	Colossians 1:17
Pray without Ceasing	I Thessalonians 5:17
The Love of Money is the Root of All Evil	I Timothy 6:10
All Scripture is Inspired by God	II Timothy 3:16
Jesus Our Great High Priest	Hebrews 4:14-16
The Faith Chapter	Hebrews 11
Casting All Your Care upon Him	I Peter 5:7
God is Love	I John 4:8
Love One Another	II John 1:5
A New Heaven and a New Earth	Revelation 21

KEY BIBLE STORIES
(Listed in Biblical Order)

OLD TESTAMENT:

Creation Story	Genesis 1
Garden of Eden	Genesis 2:4 -3:24
Story of Cain and Abel and the Murder of Abel	Genesis 4
Noah and the Flood	Genesis 6-9
Tower of Babel	Genesis 11:1-9
Sarah Laughs at Having a Child	Genesis 18:1-19
Sodom and Gomorrah and Their Destruction	Genesis 18:20-19:30
An Angel Rescues Hagar and Ishmael	Genesis 21:9-21
Abraham Offers Isaac as a Sacrifice	Genesis 22:1-19
Isaac Marries Rebekah	Genesis 24
Esau Sells His Birthright to Jacob	Genesis 25:19-34
Jacob Deceives Isaac to Receive Esau's Blessing	Genesis 27
Jacob's Dream at Bethel	Genesis 28:10-22
Jacob Marries Leah and Rachel	Genesis 29:1-30
Jacob Flees Laban	Genesis 31
Jacob Wrestles with an Angel	Genesis 32:24-32
Jacob and Esau Make Peace	Genesis 33
Joseph is Sold into Slavery	Genesis 37
Joseph Interprets the Baker's and Butler's Dreams	Genesis 40
Joseph Interprets the Pharaoh's Dream	Genesis 41
Joseph's Brothers Travel to Egypt	Genesis 42-45
Joseph's Family Moves to Egypt	Genesis 46
Baby Moses is Hidden in the River Bulrushes	Exodus 2:1-10
Moses and the Burning Bush	Exodus 3
Ten Plagues on Egypt	Exodus 7-12
The Passover	Exodus 12
Parting of the Red Sea	Exodus 14
The Lord Provides Quail	Exodus 16, Numbers 11
The Golden Calf	Exodus 32
Aaron and Miriam's Leprosy	Numbers 12
Spies are Sent to Canaan	Numbers 13
Aaron's Rod Blossoms	Numbers 17
Moses' Bronze Serpent	Numbers 21:4-9
Balaam's Talking Donkey and Blessings for Israel	Numbers 22-24
Parting of the Jordan River	Joshua 4
Joshua and the Walls of Jericho	Joshua 6
The Sun and Moon Stand Still at Gibeon	Joshua 10:1-15
Gideon's Prayer for Dry Fleece and Wet Fleece	Judges 6:33-40
Gideon Chooses an Army by Who Laps Water	Judges 7
Jephthah's Offering of His Daughter	Judges 11
Samson and His Riddle	Judges 14
Samson and Delilah, Samson and the Philistines	Judges 16
Story of Ruth	Ruth 1-4
Hannah's Prayer for a Son Is Answered	I Samuel 1
The Lord Calls Samuel	I Samuel 3
Samuel Anoints Saul to be King	I Samuel 9
Samuel Anoints David Who Plays His Harp for Saul	I Samuel 16
David and Goliath	I Samuel 17
Jonathan Warns David with Arrows	I Samuel 20
David Spares Saul's Life	I Samuel 24 & 26
Saul Consults a Medium	I Samuel 28
Saul's Death	I Samuel 31, II Samuel 1, I Chronicles 10

David Commits Murder and Adultery	II Samuel 11
Nathan's Story of a Rich Man and Poor Man	II Samuel 12:1-14
David and Bathsheba's First Baby Dies	II Samuel 12:15-24
Absalom's Hair is Caught in Battle	II Samuel 18
Solomon's Request for Wisdom	I Kings 3:2-15, II Chronicles 1:1-13
Two Women Claim the Same Child	I Kings 3:16-28
Construction of Solomon's Temple	I Kings 7, II Chronicles 3-4
Queen of Sheba Visits Solomon	I Kings 10:1-13, II Chronicles 9:1-12
Elijah and the Drought (Widow's Food & Son)	I Kings 17
Elijah Challenges Baal Prophets on Mount Carmel	I Kings 18
Ahab and Jezebel Take Naboth's Vineyard	I Kings 21
Elijah and the Chariot of Fire	II Kings 2
Elisha and the Widow's Oil	II Kings 4:1-7
The Shunammite's Son is Raised from the Dead	II Kings 4:8-37
Naaman Washes in the Jordan Seven Times	II Kings 5
Elisha Recovers an Axe Head from the Jordan	II Kings 6:1-7
The Dogs Eat Jezebel's Flesh	II Kings 9
Josiah Reads the Found Book of the Covenant	II Kings 23:1-30, II Chronicles 34
Story of Esther	Esther 1-10
God Allows Satan to Test Job	Job 1:1-2:10
Jeremiah in a Muddy Cistern	Jeremiah 38
Jeremiah's Sinking Scroll	Jeremiah 51:60-64
Ezekiel's Call (Honey-Flavored Scroll)	Ezekiel 3
Daniel and Friends Refuse to Eat the King's Food	Daniel 1
Daniel Interprets Nebuchadnezzar's Dreams	Daniel 2 & 4
The Fiery Furnace	Daniel 3
Handwriting on the Wall at Belshazzar's Feast	Daniel 5
Daniel in the Lions' Den	Daniel 6
Story of Jonah and the Great Fish	Jonah 1-4

NEW TESTMENT:

Note: Many parables are given throughout the Gospels; only a few are mentioned in this list.

Angel Appears to Joseph	Matthew 1:18-25
The Christmas Story of Jesus' Birth	Matthew 2:1-12 (The Wise Men), Luke 2:1-20 (The Shepherds)
John the Baptist Baptizes Jesus	Matthew 3:13-17, Mark 1:9-11, Luke 3:21-22
Jesus is Tempted in the Wilderness	Matthew 4:1-11, Mark 1:12-13, Luke 4:1-13
Jesus Calls the First Disciples	Matthew 4:18-22, Mark 1:16-20, Luke 5:1-11
Jesus' Story of a Wise Man Building on Rock	Matthew 7:24-27, Luke 6:47-49
Jesus Calms the Sea	Matthew 8:18-27, Mark 4:35-41, Luke 8:22-25
Jesus Casts Demons into Swine	Matthew 8:28-34, Mark 5:1-20, Luke 8:26-39
Jesus Heals Paralytic Lowered through the Ceiling	Matthew 9:1-8, Mark 2:1-12, Luke 5:17-26
Jesus Heals a Man's Shriveled Hand on the Sabbath	Matthew 12:9-14, Mark 3:1-6, Luke 6:6-11
Parable of the Sower	Matthew 13:1-23, Mark 4:1-20, Luke 8:4-18
Parables of the Kingdom of Heaven	Matthew 13:1-52, Mark 4:1-34
Feeding the 5000	Matthew 14:13-21, Mark 6:30-44, Luke 9:10-17, John 6:1-14
Jesus Walks on Water	Matthew 14:22-33, Mark 6:45-52, John 6:15-21
Feeding the 4000	Matthew 15:21-38, Mark 8:1-9
Mount of Transfiguration	Matthew 17:1-13, Mark 9:2-13, Luke 9:28-36
Simon Fetches Coin from Fish's Mouth	Matthew 17:24-27
Parable of One Lost Sheep	Matthew 18:11-14
Rich Ruler Asks How to Inherit Eternal Life	Matthew 19:16-26, Mark 10:17-31, Luke 18:18-30
Jesus' Entry into Jerusalem on a Colt	Matthew 21:1-11, Mark 11:1-11, Luke 19:28-44, John 12:12-19
Jesus Cleanses the Temple	Matthew 21:12-17, Mark 11:15-19, Luke 19:45-46, John 2:13-25

Parable of the Talents	Matthew 25:14-30
Jesus is Anointed by Mary	Matthew 26:6-13, Mark 14:3-9, John 12:1-8
Garden of Gethsemane	Matthew 26:30-46, Mark14:26-42, Luke 22:39-46 John 18:1-11
Judas Betrays Jesus	Matthew 26:47-56, Mark 14:43-52, Luke 22:47-53, John 18:1-11
Peter's Denial of Christ	Matthew 26:57-75, Mark 14:66-72, Luke 22:54-62, John 18:16-27
Jesus' Trial and Crucifixion	Matthew 26:57-27:56, Mark 15:1-32, Luke 22:63-23:49, John 18:12-19:37
Jesus' Resurrection	Matthew 28, Mark 16:1-18, Luke 24:1-49,John 20-21
The Widow's Two Mites	Mark 12:41-44, Luke 21:1-4
The Lord's Supper	Mark 14:12-25, Luke 22:7-22, John 13:1-20
Jesus' Ascension into Heaven	Mark 16:19-20, Luke 24:50-53, Acts 1:1-11
An Angel Appears to Mary	Luke 1:26-38
Jesus in the Temple at Twelve Years Old	Luke 2:41-52
A Woman Anoints Jesus' Feet	Luke 7:36-50
Parable of the Good Samaritan	Luke 10:25-37
Jesus Speaks about the Kingdom of God	Luke 13:18-30
Parables of Lost Sheep, Lost Coin, and Prodigal Son	Luke 15
Parables of the Steward & the Rich Man and Lazarus	Luke 16
Ten Lepers are Healed	Luke 17:11-19
Parable of the Persistent Widow	Luke 18:1-8
Parable of the Pharisee and Publican	Luke 18:9-14
Zaccheus Climbs a Sycamore Tree	Luke 19:1-10
Miracle of Water to Wine at Wedding in Cana	John 2:1-11
The Samaritan Woman	John 4:4 -42
Lazarus is Raised from the Dead	John 11:1-44
Jesus Washes Apostles' Feet at "The Lord's Supper"	John 13:1-20
Jesus Asks Peter if He Loves Him	John 21:15-25
Holy Spirit Comes at Pentecost	Acts 2
Stephen's Sermon and Death by Stoning	Acts 6:8-7:60
Saul's Conversion	Acts 9
Peter and Cornelius	Acts 10
An Angel Leads Peter out of Prison	Acts 12:1-19
Philippian Jailer Believes	Acts 16:11-40
Paul's Speech in Athens	Acts 17
Silversmith Demetrius Causes an Uproar	Acts 19
Eutychus Falls from a Third Floor Window	Acts 20:7-12
Paul's Shipwreck	Acts 27
Paul is Snake Bitten	Acts 28:1-6

JOHN 21:25:

AND THERE ARE ALSO MANY OTHER THINGS WHICH JESUS DID, THE WHICH, IF THEY SHOULD BE WRITTEN EVERY ONE, I SUPPOSE THAT EVEN THE WORLD ITSELF COULD NOT CONTAIN THE BOOKS THAT SHOULD BE WRITTEN. AMEN.

MEMORIZING SCRIPTURE, THE 1000 CHALLENGE

The King James Version of the Bible has 31,101 verses! Of these verses, 23,144 are in the Old Testament and 7,957 are in the New Testament. *BIBLE IN A NUTSHELL* quotes 1000 key Bible memory verses using the King James Version. Many other verses are also quoted in the key contents of each Bible book.   If you are familiar with *THE BIBLE*, you will already be acquainted with many of these verses. The "Introduction" (see page 1) lists the criteria used in choosing the key memory verses.   Portions of the New International Version, NIV, are quoted when clarifying a verse. Just think, if you can memorize or at least know the content of these 1000 memory verses, you will know approximately 3% of *THE BIBLE's* verses! This knowledge is an awesome resource to have readily available in your heart and mind!

In *BIBLE IN A NUTSHELL,* each line of a memory verse is centered and carries a complete phrase (or phrases) of the verse making memorization easier.   When memorizing scripture, it is helpful to say each line aloud.   First memorize the reference of the verse (for example, John 3:16). Next memorize the verse one line at a time. After you have memorized the reference with the first line, begin memorizing the second line. Be able to quote the reference and the first two lines before memorizing the third line, and so forth. At the end of the verse, quote its reference again.

BIBLE IN A NUTSHELL's first section, pages 11-254, has key notes for each of the 66 Bible books. The key notes consist of a brief introduction to each Bible book and key contents by chapters which include the key memory verses. Within the key contents, you will be able to see the context in which the memory verses are found. The latter section, pages 255-351, repeats the 1000 key memory verses for easy review and study. Also, a yearly date and a numbered day, from 1-365, are listed on one to four of these memory verses for your study on that day. This allows you to begin a yearly study on January 1st or any day you choose when using the numbered days. In a year's time, you will have studied all 1000 verses.   You may want to challenge yourself to memorize all 1000 verses.   This is "The 1000 Challenge!" The ultimate challenge is to see if you can quote the verses by only looking at the index for the key memory verses.   You will notice the memory verses in the key notes also have the study dates listed.   This allows your studying the surrounding scripture of the memory verses listed for that day.

You may want to write the memory verses on index cards. By carrying a card with you during the day, you can review it when you have a moment (for example, while waiting in the grocery line). Or you can post the card somewhere to review it each time you see it (perhaps on the refrigerator or near your computer screen). Maybe your spouse or a friend would like to recite the verses with you each day or each week. Begin using the verses in your prayer life and draw upon God's strength.

Of course, not everyone will want to memorize all 1000 memory verses. You can simply mark the ones to memorize, and just review and study the others. You will probably find other verses important in your life that may not be listed in this book. You can write these in the page margins or in the "Personal Notes" section in the back of this book. **Enjoy taking "The 1000 Challenge," and may God bless you in His Word!**

THE OLD TESTAMENT KEY NOTES, GENESIS TO MALACHI

Quoted Scripture is from The King James Version, KJV.
The New International Version, NIV, is quoted when clarifying some of the verses.

If you choose to study through *BIBLE IN A NUTSHELL* in a year, simply read each day to the following day's date. Begin January 1st or follow the numbered days to begin anytime of the year. Most days will have only one page to review while some days will have two or three pages. You can mark verses you choose to memorize and simply review the other memory verses. In following years of study, you can mark more verses to memorize. The key notes surrounding the memory verses will help you understand the verses' context. Just remember, even if you cannot quote verses word for word, the most important aspect of scripture is to hold its meaning in your mind and heart, and apply it to your life!

GENESIS

Introduction: Genesis, which means origin, is a book about beginnings: the heaven and the earth, humanity, sin, etc. The first five books of the Bible are known as the Pentateuch, a word derived from Greek which means writings divided into five scrolls. Traditionally, authorship of these five books is attributed to Moses. Sometime between 1450-1400 B.C. during the Israelites' 40 years of wanderings is a likely date for the writings of Moses. As believed by Julius Wellhausen in 1875, many scholars agree the work of the following four sources comprise the Pentateuch: "J" (for Jahweh/Yahweh), "E" (for Elohim), "D" (for Deuteronomic), and "P" (for Priestly) sources written sometime during the 1000's to 400's B.C. Genesis has 50 chapters.

Key Contents and Key Memory Verses with Study Dates

<u>Genesis 1-2:</u> **The creation story** — Seven days of creation (see 1:1-2:3).

January 1 (Day 1), Memory Verse # 1
<u>**Genesis 1:1:**</u>

IN THE BEGINNING, GOD CREATED THE HEAVENS AND THE EARTH.

January 1 (Day 1), Memory Verses #2 & #3
<u>**Genesis 1:27-28:**</u>

27. SO GOD CREATED MAN IN HIS OWN IMAGE, IN THE IMAGE OF GOD CREATED HE HIM;
MALE AND FEMALE CREATED HE THEM.

28. AND GOD BLESSED THEM, AND GOD SAID UNTO THEM,
BE FRUITFUL, AND MULTIPLY, AND REPLENISH THE EARTH, AND SUBDUE IT:
AND HAVE DOMINION OVER THE FISH OF THE SEA, AND THE FOWL OF THE AIR,
AND OVER EVERY LIVING THING THAT MOVETH UPON THE EARTH.

— *"And God saw every thing that he had made, and behold, it was very good. And the evening and the morning were the sixth day"* (see 1:31) — **God rests on the seventh day of creation.**

January 1 (Day 1), Memory Verse #4
<u>**Genesis 2:3:**</u>

AND GOD BLESSED THE SEVENTH DAY, AND SANCTIFIED IT:
BECAUSE THAT IN IT HE HAD RESTED FROM ALL HIS WORK WHICH GOD CREATED AND MADE.

— *"**And the Lord God formed man of the dust of the ground,** and breathed into his nostrils the breath of life; and man became a living soul.   And the Lord God planted a garden eastward in*

Eden; and there he put the man whom he had formed" (see 2:7-8) — *"And the Lord God commanded the man, saying, Of every tree of the garden thou mayest freely eat: But of the tree of the knowledge of good and evil, thou shalt not eat of it: for in the day that thou eatest thereof thou shalt surely die. And the Lord God said, It is not good that the man should be alone; I will make him an help meet for him"* (see 2:16-18) — **Adam names every living creature — God makes a woman using one of Adam's ribs.**

January 2 (Day 2), Memory Verse #5
Genesis 2:24:

THEREFORE SHALL A MAN LEAVE HIS FATHER AND MOTHER,
AND CLEAVE UNTO HIS WIFE; AND THEY SHALL BE ONE FLESH.

Genesis 3: Adam and Eve disobey God by eating from the tree of good and evil knowledge, and they are driven from the garden of Eden.

Genesis 4: Adam and Eve have two sons, Cain and Abel — Jealous Cain kills Abel and must leave his family — Cain's descendants — Adam and Eve have another son, Seth.

Genesis 5: Genealogy of Adam to Noah (see 5:1-32) — *"And Enoch walked with God: and he was not; for God took him"* (see 5:24) — Enoch's son, Methuselah, lived 969 years (see 5:27).

Genesis 6-9: Story of Noah and the flood — *"And God saw that the wickedness of man was great in the earth, and that every imagination of the thoughts of his heart was only evil continually. And it repented the Lord that he had made man on the earth, and it grieved him at his heart"* (see 6:5-6) — God commands Noah to build an ark; God tells Noah, *"And behold, I, even I, do bring a flood of waters upon the earth, to destroy all flesh, wherein is the breath of life, from under heaven; and every thing that is in the earth shall die. But with thee will I establish my covenant; and thou shalt come into the ark, thou and thy sons, and thy wife, and thy sons' wives with thee. And of every living thing of all flesh, two of every sort shalt thou bring into the ark, to keep them alive with thee; they shall be male and female"* (see 6:17-19) — God covenants with man not to destroy the earth again with a flood, and God sends the rainbow as a sign of this covenant (see 9:11-13).

Genesis 10: Descendants of Noah's three sons (Japheth, Ham and Shem).

Genesis 11: Tower of Babel — *"Therefore is the name of it called Babel; because the Lord did there confound the language of all the earth: and from thence did the Lord scatter them abroad upon the face of all the earth"* (see 11:9) — **Genealogy of Shem** — Abram is a descendant of Shem — **Abram marries Sarai, and they move to Ur with Abram's father, Terah.**

Genesis 12: Abram's call from God:

January 2 (Day 2), Memory Verses #6 to #8
Genesis 12:1-3:
(God's Call of Abram)

1. **NOW** THE LORD HAD SAID UNTO ABRAM, GET THEE OUT OF THY COUNTRY,
AND FROM THY KINDRED, AND FROM THY FATHER'S HOUSE,
UNTO A LAND THAT I WILL SHEW THEE:

2. **AND** I WILL MAKE OF THEE A GREAT NATION,
AND I WILL BLESS THEE, AND MAKE THY NAME GREAT;AND THOU SHALT BE A BLESSING:

3. **AND** I WILL BLESS THEM THAT BLESS THEE, AND CURSE THEM THAT CURSETH THEE:
AND IN THEE SHALL ALL FAMILIES OF THE EARTH BE BLESSED.

— Abram, Sarah, Lot, and their attendants journey to Egypt because of a famine — The Egyptian Pharaoh is given a plague for taking Sarai who is pretending to be Abram's sister — The Pharaoh sends them out of Egypt.

<u>Genesis 13</u>: **Abram and his nephew Lot go separate ways since their herdsmen have quarreled** — *"And Abram said to Lot, Let there be no strife, I pray thee, between me and thee, and between my herdmen and thy herdmen; for we be brethren"* (see 13:8) — **Lot chooses to live in the plain of the Jordan near Sodom.**

<u>Genesis 14</u>: **Abram rescues Lot from captivity after Sodom and Gomorrah are defeated in battle by several kings who joined as allies against these cities** — *"And Melchizedek king of Salem brought forth bread and wine: and he was the priest of the most high God. And he blessed him, and said, Blessed be Abram of the most high God, possessor of heaven and earth: And blessed be the most high God, which hath delivered thine enemy into thy hand. And he gave him tithes of all"* (see 14:18-20).

<u>Genesis 15</u>: **God makes a covenant with Abram** — *"After these things the word of the Lord came unto Abram in a vision, saying, Fear not Abram: I am thy shield, and thy exceeding great reward"* (see 15:1) — **God promises Abram a child although Sarai is barren** — *"And he brought him forth abroad, and said, Look now toward heaven, and tell the stars, if thou be able to number them: and he said unto him, So shall thy seed be. And he believed in the Lord; and he counted it to him for righteousness"* (see 15:5-6).

<u>Genesis 16</u>: **Sarai persuades Abram to have a child by her maid Hagar**, but Sarai regrets this decision when Hagar is pregnant — Hagar flees from Sarai into the wilderness, but the angel of the Lord encourages Hagar to return and give birth to **Abram's child, Ishmael** — *"And the angel of the Lord said unto her, I will multiply thy seed exceedingly..."* (see 16:10).

<u>Genesis 17</u>: **God states His covenant with Abraham** — *"And when Abram was ninety years old and nine, the Lord appeared to Abram, and said unto him, I am the Almighty God; walk before me, and be thou perfect. And I will make my covenant between me and thee, and will multiply thee exceedingly. And Abram fell on his face: and God talked with him saying, As for me, behold, my covenant is with thee, and thou shalt be a father of many nations. Neither shall thy name any more be Abram, but* **thy name shall be Abraham; for a father of many nations have I made thee**" (see 17:1-5) — **Covenant of circumcision** — *"And God said unto Abraham, As for Sarai thy wife, thou shalt not call her name Sarai, but Sarah shall her name be. And I will bless her, and give thee a son also of her: yea, I will bless her, and she shall be a mother of nations; kings of people shall be of her. Then Abraham fell upon his face, and laughed, and said in his heart, Shall a child be born unto him that is an hundred years old? And shall Sarah, that is ninety years old bear?"* (see 17:15-17) — **"And God said, Sarah thy wife shall bear thee a son indeed; and thou shalt call his name Isaac: and I will establish my covenant with him for an everlasting covenant, and with his seed after him"** (see17:19).

<u>Genesis 18</u>: **The Lord appears to Abraham and tells him Sarah will have a child** (see mention of three men, one thought to be the Lord and two thought to be angels) — Sarah laughs at the thought of having a child since *"...Abraham and Sarah were old and well stricken in age; ..."* (see 18:11) — The Lord says to Abraham:

January 3 (Day 3), Memory Verse #9
<u>Genesis 18:14</u>:

IS ANYTHING TOO HARD FOR THE LORD?...

— The Lord tells of Sodom and Gomorrah's future destruction due to their wickedness — Abraham bargains with the Lord to spare Sodom and Gomorrah if ten righteous people are found there.

Genesis 19:   Two angels appear to Lot in Sodom warning of Sodom and Gomorrah's destruction — The angels tell Lot to leave with his family — *"...Escape for thy life; look not behind thee, neither stay thou in all the plain; escape to the mountain, lest thou be consumed"* (see 19:17) — **Sodom and Gomorrah's destruction —** Lot's wife looks back as Sodom and Gomorrah are destroyed by *"...brimstone and fire from the Lord out of heaven"* (see 19:24), and *"...she became a pillar of salt"* (see 19:26).

Genesis 20: Abraham tells King Abimelech that Sarah is his sister rather than his wife since he is afraid he would be slain by others who want Sarah for their wife (Sarah is actually Abraham's half-sister) — **King Abimelech takes Sarah to be his wife —** God warns Abimelech in a dream about Abraham's lie — **Abimelech returns Sarah to Abraham with gifts.**

Genesis 21:   The Lord's prophecy comes true when Sarah and Abraham have a son named Isaac — Hagar and Ishmael are cast into the wilderness by Sarah and Abraham, but the angel of God rescues them and supplies water — The angel tells Hagar, *"Arise, lift up the lad, and hold him in thine hand; for I will make him a great nation"* (see 21:18) — **Abimelech, Phichol of the Philistines, and Abraham make a covenant of peace at Beersheba.**

Genesis 22: God tells Abraham to offer Isaac as a burnt offering in the land of Moriah — On the journey to Moriah, Isaac asks, *"...where is the lamb for a burnt offering? And Abraham said, My son, God will provide himself a lamb for a burnt offering:...And they came to the place which God had told him of; and Abraham built an altar there, and laid the wood in order, and bound Isaac his son, and laid him on the altar upon the wood.. And Abraham stretched forth his hand, and took the knife to slay his son. And the angel of the Lord called unto him out of heaven, and said, Abraham: and he said, Here am I. And he said, Lay not thine hand upon the lad, neither do thou any thing unto him: for now I know that thou fearest God, seeing thou hast not withheld thy son, thine only son from me"* (see 22:7-12) — *"...for because thou hast done this thing, and hast not withheld thy son, thine only son: That in blessing I will bless thee, and in multiplying I will multiply thy seed as the stars of the heaven, and as the sand which is upon the sea shore; and, thy seed shall possess the gate of his enemies; And in thy seed shall all the nations of the earth be blessed; because thou hast obeyed my voice"* (see 22:16-18).

Genesis 23:   Sarah dies at age 127, and Abraham acquires the cave of Machpelah for a burial sepulcher.

Genesis 24:   Abraham sends his servant to the city of Nahor in Mesopotamia to find Isaac a bride of his own kindred — The servant prays for God to show him the one who is to marry Isaac by having the future wife offer him and his camels a drink at a well in Nahor — Rebekah, who is kindred of Abraham's family, is the one who offers the water — **Rebekah returns with the servant to marry Isaac.**

Genesis 25:   Abraham takes another wife, Keturah — Abraham dies at age 175 and is buried with Sarah at the cave of Machpelah — Ishmael's descendants (see 25:12-18) — **Ishmael dies at age 137 — Isaac prays to God for a child, and then Isaac and Rebekah have twin sons, Jacob and Esau —** *"And the Lord said unto her, Two nations are in thy womb, and two manner of people shall be separated from thy bowels; and the one people shall be stronger than the other people; and the elder shall serve the younger"* (see 25:23) — **Jacob tricks Esau, the firstborn, when he is very hungry into giving his birthright to Jacob in exchange for** *"...bread and pottage of lentils; ..."* (see 25:34).

Genesis 26: During a famine, the Lord instructs Isaac to stay in the Philistine's land — Isaac pretends Rebekah is his sister rather than his wife, and when King Abimelech discovers this lie, he commands, *"...He that toucheth this man or his wife shall surely be put to death"* (see 26:11) — Abimelech is afraid of God's punishment if anyone takes another man's wife — **Many of Isaac's wells are destroyed by the Philistines, so Isaac travels to Beersheba and settles there — Isaac and Abimelech make a peace covenant.**

Genesis 27: Pretending to be Esau, Jacob goes to Isaac, who has failing eyesight, to receive Esau's blessing — Isaac blesses Jacob by saying, *"Therefore God give thee of the dew of heaven, and the fatness of the earth, and plenty of corn and wine: Let people serve thee, and nations bow down to thee: be lord over thy brethren, and let thy mother's sons bow down to thee: cursed be every one that curseth thee, and blessed be he that blesseth thee"* (see 27:28-29) — **Rachel fears Esau will kill Jacob.**

Genesis 28: With Rachel's persuasion, Isaac blesses Jacob and sends him to find a wife in Haran where Rachel's brother Laban lives — Esau marries Ishmael's daughter — Jacob has a dream on his way to Haran — *"And he dreamed, and behold a ladder set up on the earth, and the top of it reached to heaven: and behold the angels of God ascending and descending on it. And behold, the Lord stood above it, and said, I am the Lord God of Abraham thy father, and the God of Isaac: the land whereon thou liest, to thee will I give it, and to thy seed; And thy seed shall be as the dust of the earth, and thou shalt spread abroad to the west, and to the east, and to the north, and to the south: and in thee and in thy seed shall all the families of the earth be blessed"* (see 28:12-14) — **Jacob creates a stone pillar to God and calls the place Bethel.**

Genesis 29: Jacob meets the shepherdess Rachel who is Laban's daughter — Jacob bargains to serve Laban seven years if he can marry Rachel after the seven years — **Laban tricks Jacob by giving him his daughter Leah** and requiring Jacob to work an additional seven years for Rachel — Leah bears four sons: **REUBEN, SIMEON, LEVI,** and **JUDAH.**

Genesis 30: Rachel's maid Bilhah bears two sons by Jacob: **DAN** and **NAPHTALI** — Leah's maid Zilpah bears two sons by Jacob: **GAD** and **ASHER** — Leah bears two more sons and a daughter: **ISSACHAR, ZEBULON** and **DINAH** — Rachel bears a son: **JOSEPH** — **Jacob tells Laban,** *"Send me away, that I may go unto mine own place, and to my country"* (see 30:25) — Laban promises certain livestock to Jacob.

Genesis 31: Taking all their family and possessions, Jacob, Rachel, and Leah flee from Laban to return to Canaan — Laban pursues and catches up with Jacob at Mount Gilead; God had told Laban in a dream to speak neither bad nor good to Jacob — Rachel had secretly taken Laban's images of gods, but Laban cannot find them in his search of her possessions — Jacob and Laban make a peace covenant, build a stone pillar, and offer a sacrifice — ***"And Laban said, This heap is a witness between me and thee this day...*** (see 31:48)**:**

January 4 (Day 4), Memory Verse #10
<u>Genesis 31:49</u>:

...THE LORD WATCH BETWEEN ME AND THEE,
WHEN WE ARE ABSENT ONE FROM ANOTHER.

Genesis 32: Jacob sends messengers to Esau to tell of his coming and desire to make peace — Jacob wrestles a man (referred to as an angel in Hosea 12:4) all night; *"...the hollow of Jacob's thigh was out of joint..."* (see 32:25) — Jacob will not stop wrestling until the man blesses him — **Jacob receives his blessing from this man who says, *"... Thy name shall be***

called no more Jacob, but Israel: for as a prince hast thou power with God and with men, and hast prevailed. And Jacob asked him, and said, Tell me, I pray thee, thy name. And he said, Wherefore is it that thou dost ask after my name? And he blessed him there. And Jacob called the name of the place Peniel: for I have seen God face to face, and my life is preserved" (see 32:28-30).

Genesis 33: Esau and Jacob make peace — *"And Esau ran to meet him, and embraced him, and fell on his neck, and kissed him: and they wept"* (see 33:4) — **Jacob (Israel) returns to Canaan and builds an altar at Shechem** — *"And he erected there an altar, and called it El-elohe-Israel"* (see 33:20) which means mighty is the God of Israel.

Genesis 34: Dinah is raped by Shechem, son of Hamor — Shechem is told he can marry Dinah if he and his men are circumcised — But Simeon and Levi slaughter the men while they are in pain after circumcision.

Genesis 35: God tells Jacob (Israel) to go to Bethel where God reaffirms His covenant — The Lord tells Jacob, *"And the land which I gave Abraham and Isaac, to thee I will give it, and to thy seed after thee will I give the land"* (see 35:12) — Jacob makes a pillar of stone to God — **Rachel dies while giving birth to BENJAMIN and is buried in Bethlehem — Reuben lays with Bilhah — Isaac dies at age 180.**

Genesis 36: Esau's descendants — Esau is called *"...the father of the Edomites"* (see 36:43).

Genesis 37: Joseph is sold into slavery by his brothers — Joseph's brothers are jealous of him since Jacob (Israel) favors Joseph and *"...made him a coat of many colours"* (see 37:3) — The brothers are also angered at Joseph for telling of his dreams where his family bows down to him — Jacob sends Joseph to check on his brothers who are tending Jacob's flock, but the brothers conspire to kill Joseph — Thinking he can rescue Joseph later, Reuben persuades his brothers to throw Joseph in a pit rather than kill him — But while Reuben is gone, the brothers sell Joseph into slavery to the Midianites who in turn sell him *"...into Egypt unto Potiphar, an officer of Pharaoh's, and captain of the guard"* (see 37:36) — The brothers pour goat's blood on Joseph's coat of many colors and tell Jacob he has been killed by a beast — Jacob mourns greatly, thinking Joseph is dead.

Genesis 38: Judah marries the daughter of Shuah, a Canaanite — Their firstborn son, Er, marries Tamar, but Er *"...was wicked in the sight of the Lord; and the Lord slew him"* (see 38:7) — Because Er's brother, Onon, will not be Tamar's husband, the Lord *"...slew him also"* (see 38:10) — Judah promises his son, Shelah, to Tamar when Shelah is old enough to marry — Judah's wife dies and he backs out on his promise to Tamar — Tamar disguises herself as a harlot and lays with Judah; Tamar gives birth to twins.

Genesis 39: Joseph is made overseer of Potiphar's house — When Joseph refuses to lie with Potiphar's wife, she accuses Joseph of trying to rape her — **Potiphar places Joseph in prison** — Joseph becomes the overseer of prisoners while in prison.

Genesis 40: The Egyptian king's chief butler and chief baker are put in prison — Joseph interprets the butler's and the baker's dreams as follows: the butler will be restored to his job with the king in three days, but the baker will be killed by the king in three days — The dreams come true, and when the butler is released from prison, he does not remember Joseph.

Genesis 41: The butler finally remembers Joseph when the Pharaoh needs his dream interpreted — **Joseph interprets Pharaoh's dream of seven fat cows and seven lean cows:** *"...What God is about to do he sheweth unto Pharaoh. Behold, there come seven years of great plenty throughout all the land of Egypt: And there shall arise after them seven years of famine; and all the plenty shall be forgotten in the land of Egypt; and the famine shall consume the land;"* (see 41:28-30) — **The Pharaoh appoints Joseph second only to him as ruler in Egypt and has Joseph prepare for the famine** — During the time of the famine, *"...all countries came into Egypt to Joseph for to buy corn; because that the famine was so sore in all lands"* (see 41:57).

Genesis 42: **Jacob (Israel) sends his sons to Egypt to buy corn** — Joseph's brothers do not recognize him, so he is able to accuse them of being spies — They deny the accusation, but Joseph says he will keep Simeon as a prisoner until they return with their youngest brother, Benjamin, to prove they are not spies — Joseph also hides bundles of money for each brother to find when they return home — Although fearful something will happen to Benjamin, Jacob allows him to travel back to Egypt with the brothers.

Genesis 43: **The brothers return to Egypt** with Benjamin, gifts, and money — Joseph invites them to dine with him and gives them much food and money to carry back to Canaan.

Genesis 44: **Joseph instructs his steward to hide his silver cup in Benjamin's goods** — The steward follows the brothers after they have left for Canaan, and finding the cup with Benjamin, the steward takes Benjamin back to Joseph — The brothers also return and plead to let one of them stay in Egypt in place of Benjamin.

Genesis 45: **Joseph reveals his identity to his brothers** — *"Now therefore be not grieved, nor angry with yourselves, that ye sold me hither: for God did send me before you to preserve life"* (see 45:5) — *"Moreover he kissed all his brethren, and wept upon them:..."* (see 45:15) — Joseph sends for all his family to move to Egypt where he can provide for them.

Genesis 46: **Joseph's family journeys to Egypt** — God speaks to Jacob (Israel) in visions telling him not to be afraid to go to Egypt — List of Jacob's descendants.

Genesis 47: **During the famine, Joseph trades food for Egyptian livestock and land, accumulating much wealth for the Pharaoh — Joseph swears to Jacob (Israel) that he will bury him in Canaan.**

Genesis 48: **Jacob (Israel) becomes sick and blesses Joseph's sons, Ephraim and Manasseh** — *"And he blessed them that day, saying, In thee shall Israel bless, saying, God make thee as Ephraim and as Manasseh: and he set Ephraim before Manasseh"* (see 48:20).

Genesis 49: **Jacob (Israel) blesses his sons, requests to be buried in the cave of Machpelah, and dies.**

Genesis 50: **Jacob (Israel) is embalmed and is buried in the cave of Machpelah — Joseph deals kindly with his brothers — Joseph dies at age 110 and is placed in an Egyptian coffin** (see Joshua 24:32 where the Israelites carry Joseph's bones to Canaan from Egypt to be buried where Jacob had purchased burial land).

GENESIS 1:1: IN THE BEGINNING, GOD CREATED THE HEAVENS AND THE EARTH.

EXODUS

Introduction: Tradition attributes authorship of Exodus to Moses. The date of Moses' writing is thought to be during 1450-1400 B.C. Some who support the traditional view of Mosaic authorship believe Exodus may have been written later around 1290 B.C., depending on the actual date of the Jews' departure from Egypt. See the introduction to Genesis for more authorship notes. Exodus comes from the Greek word for "exit." Exodus tells about God delivering His chosen people, the Israelites, out of Egypt and His developing a special covenant relationship with them (see Exodus 6:6-8). God chose Moses who was helped by his brother, Aaron, to lead the Israelites. Also, God gave "The Ten Commandments" and a system of laws to the Israelites and directed them in building the tabernacle. The theme of liberation from an oppressive life offers hope to individuals and groups of people who endure suffering by trusting God through difficult circumstances. Exodus has 40 chapters.

Key Contents and Key Memory Verses with Study Dates

<u>**Exodus 1:**</u> **Jacob (Israel) moves his family to Egypt because of the famine** — Israel and all his twelve sons die over time, yet have many descendants — **A new Egyptian king, who did not know Joseph, appoints taskmasters who force the Israelites to work hard for the Pharaoh** — Fearful of the increasing number of Israelites, the king commands the midwives to kill Hebrew male children, but the midwives fear God and disobey this order — The Pharaoh commands all the people, *"...Every son that is born ye shall cast into the river, and every daughter ye shall save alive"* (see 1:22).

<u>**Exodus 2:**</u> **A family of the house of Levi hides their newborn son, Moses, in a basket in the river's bulrushes** — Pharaoh's daughter finds baby Moses and decides to raise Moses as her son, first allowing Moses to stay a while with his family to be nursed — **As an adult, Moses kills an Egyptian who is** *"smiting a Hebrew"* (see 2:11) — **The Pharaoh seeks to kill Moses, so he flees to Midian** — In Midian, Moses helps the seven daughters of a priest water their flock — The priest gives Moses his daughter, Zipporah, to marry, and they have a son, Gershom.

<u>**Exodus 3:**</u> *"Now Moses kept the flock of Jethro his father in law, the priest of Midian: and he led the flock to the backside of the desert, and came to the mountain of God, even to Horeb. And the angel of the Lord appeared unto him in a flame of fire out of the midst of a bush: and he looked, and behold, the bush burned with fire, and the bush was not consumed"* (see 3:1-2) — *"And when the Lord saw that he turned aside to see,* **God called unto him out of the midst of the bush, and said, Moses, Moses. And he said, Here am I.** *And he said, Draw not nigh hither: put off thy shoes from off thy feet, for the place whereon thou standest is holy ground"* (see 3:4-5) — **The Lord tells Moses He wants him to lead the Israelites out of their bondage in Egypt.**

January 5 (Day 5), Memory Verse #11
<u>**Exodus 3:14:**</u>

AND GOD SAID UNTO MOSES, **I AM THAT I AM:**
AND HE SAID,
THUS SHALT THOU SAY UNTO THE CHILDREN OF ISRAEL,
I AM HATH SENT ME UNTO YOU.

<u>**Exodus 4:**</u> **Moses tells the Lord that the Israelites will not believe he is called by God — The Lord gives Moses three signs he can perform:** 1) casting a rod on the ground to become a snake, and picking up the snake to become a rod again; 2) putting his hand in his bosom and getting leprosy, and then placing his hand back on his bosom to remove the leprosy; and

3) changing water to blood when pouring water from the Nile onto the land — **Moses says he is "slow of speech"** (see 4:10) — The Lord says *"go, and I will be with thy mouth, and teach thee what thou shalt say"* (see 4:12) — The Lord is angry when Moses is still reluctant to obey God — **The Lord says he will use Aaron, Moses' brother, to help Moses speak** — *"And Moses and Aaron went and gathered together all the elders of the children of Israel: And Aaron spake all the words which the Lord had spoken unto Moses, and did the signs in the sight of the people. And the people believed: and when they heard that the Lord had visited the children of Israel, and that he had looked upon their affliction, then they bowed their heads and worshipped"* (see 4:29-31).

Exodus 5: *"Moses and Aaron went in, and told Pharaoh, Thus saith the Lord God of Israel, Let my people go…"* (see 5:1) — **Instead of letting the Israelites go, Pharaoh increases the labor of the Israelites** — The Pharaoh commands, *"Ye shall no more give the people straw to make brick, as heretofore: let them go and gather straw for themselves"* (see 5:7).

Exodus 6: **The Lord tells Moses, *"Wherefore say unto the children of Israel, I am the Lord, and I will bring you out from under the burdens of the Egyptians,*** *and I will rid you out of their bondage, and I will redeem you with a stretched out arm, and with great judgments: And I will take you to me for a people, and I will be to you a God: and ye shall know that I am the Lord your God, which bringeth you out from under the burdens of the Egyptians. And I will bring you in unto the land, concerning the which I did swear to give it to Abraham, to Isaac, and to Jacob; and I will give it you for an heritage: I am the Lord. And Moses spake so unto the children of Israel: but they hearkened not unto Moses for anguish of spirit, and for cruel bondage"* (see 6:6-9).

Exodus 7: **Moses and Aaron use the sign of a rod turning into a snake** — The magicians of Egypt perform the same sign, only *"…Aaron's rod swallowed up their rods"* (see 7:12) — **But the Pharaoh refuses to let the Israelites leave Egypt even through the following nine plagues** — First plague: The waters of Egypt become **BLOOD.**

Exodus 8: Second plague: **FROGS** — Third plague: **LICE** (gnats, NIV) — Fourth plague: **FLIES.**

Exodus 9: Fifth plague: **EGYPTIANS' BEASTS DIE** — Sixth plague: **BOILS UPON MAN AND UPON BEAST** — Seventh plague: **HAIL.**

Exodus 10: Eighth plague: **LOCUSTS** — Ninth plague: **DARKNESS.**

Exodus 11: Moses warns Pharaoh of the coming tenth plague: **DEATH OF THE EGYPTIANS' FIRSTBORN.**

Exodus 12: **The Lord instructs Moses and Aaron on the procedures of the first Passover observance, an observance to be kept annually** — The Israelites obey the Lord's command to sacrifice and eat an unblemished lamb and paint its blood outside their doors — That night, the Lord kills the Egyptians' firstborn, but not the firstborn of the Israelites — *"…at midnight the Lord smote all the firstborn in the land of Egypt, from the firstborn of Pharaoh that sat on his throne unto the firstborn of the captive that was in the dungeon; and all the firstborn of cattle"* (see 12:29) — **The Pharaoh allows the Israelites to depart from Egypt.**

Exodus 13: The Lord tells Moses to *"Sanctify unto me all the firstborn...both of man and beast: it is mine"* (see 13:2) — The Lord reviews instructions for the annual Passover observance — **God leads the Israelites in the wilderness** — *"And the Lord went before them by day in a pillar of a cloud, to lead them the way; and by night in a pillar of fire, to give them light; to go by day and night:"* (see 13:21).

Exodus 14: **The Israelites are afraid when they realize Pharaoh and his army are pursuing them** — *"And Moses said unto the people, Fear ye not, stand still, and see the salvation of the Lord, which he will shew to you to day: for the Egyptians whom ye have seen to day, ye shall see them again no more for ever. The Lord shall fight for you, and ye shall hold your peace"* (see 14:13-14) — **God parts the Red Sea** — *"And Moses stretched out his hand over the sea; and the Lord caused the sea to go back by a strong east wind all that night, and made the sea dry land, and the waters were divided. And the children of Israel went into the midst of the sea upon the dry ground: and the waters were a wall unto them on their right hand, and on their left"* (see 14:21-22) — The Israelites safely cross the Red Sea — When the Egyptians try to cross the sea where the waters are parted, Moses again stretches out his hand, and the waters cover the Pharaoh and all his army.

Exodus 15: *"Then sang Moses and the children of Israel this song unto the Lord,* and spake, saying, I will sing unto the Lord, for he hath triumphed gloriously: the horse and his rider hath he thrown into the sea. The Lord is my strength and song, and he is become my salvation: he is my God..."* (see 15:1-2) — This song continues through 15:21 — **The water of Marah is changed from bitter to sweet** when Moses obeys God by casting a tree into the water.

Exodus 16: **The Lord provides manna for the Israelites** — *"...Manna: and it was like coriander seed, white; and the taste of it was like wafers made with honey"* (see 16:31) — The Israelites complain, so the Lord also provides quail.

Exodus 17: **God provides water at the rock in Horeb — Joshua leads the Israelites in defeating Amalek in battle;** Aaron and Hur help hold up Moses' hands during the battle because when Moses' hands are raised, the Israelites are successful in fighting.

Exodus 18: **Jethro's visit** — Moses' father-in-law, Jethro, brings Moses' wife, Zipporah, and two sons, Gershom and Eliezer, to him — Jethro offers a sacrifice to God for all the good things God has done for Israel — Moses tries to be the judge for all the Israelites, but Jethro encourages Moses to choose many others to help in such a large task of ruling and judging the people.

Exodus 19: **At Mount Sinai,** the Lord causes thunder and lightning, trumpet sounds, a thick cloud, fire, and smoke — God calls Moses up into the mountain — The Israelites are warned that only Aaron and Moses are allowed on the mountain.

Exodus 20: *"And God spake all these words, saying, I am the Lord thy God, which have brought thee out of the land of Egypt, out of the house of bondage"* (see 20:1-2) — **"The Ten Commandments"** (see 20:3-17) **are listed on the following page:**

EXODUS 20:3:

THOU SHALT HAVE NO OTHER GODS BEFORE ME.

January 6-9 (Days 6-9), Memory Verses #12 to #26

Exodus 20:3-17 :

(The Ten Commandments)

I.

3. THOU SHALT HAVE NO OTHER GODS BEFORE ME.

II.

4. THOU SHALT NOT MAKE UNTO THEE ANY GRAVEN IMAGE,
OR ANY LIKENESS OF ANYTHING THAT IS IN HEAVEN ABOVE,
OR THAT IS IN THE EARTH BENEATH, OR THAT IS IN THE WATER UNDER THE EARTH:

5. THOU SHALT NOT BOW DOWN THYSELF TO THEM, NOR SERVE THEM:
FOR I THE LORD THY GOD AM A JEALOUS GOD,
VISITING THE INIQUITY OF THE FATHERS UPON THE CHILDREN
UNTO THE THIRD AND FOURTH GENERATION OF THEM THAT HATE ME;

6. AND SHEWING MERCY UNTO THOUSANDS OF THEM THAT LOVE ME,
AND KEEP MY COMMANDMENTS.

III.

7. THOU SHALT NOT TAKE THE NAME OF THE LORD THY GOD IN VAIN;
FOR THE LORD WILL NOT HOLD HIM GUILTLESS
THAT TAKETH HIS NAME IN VAIN.

IV.

8. REMEMBER THE SABBATH DAY, TO KEEP IT HOLY.

9. SIX DAYS SHALT THOU LABOUR, AND DO ALL THY WORK:

10. BUT THE SEVENTH DAY IS THE SABBATH OF THE LORD THY GOD:
IN IT THOU SHALT NOT DO ANY WORK, THOU, NOR THY SON,
NOR THY DAUGHTER, THY MANSERVANT, NOR THY MAIDSERVANT,
NOR THY CATTLE, NOR THY STRANGER THAT IS WITHIN THY GATES:

11. FOR IN SIX DAYS THE LORD MADE HEAVEN AND EARTH, THE SEA,
AND ALL THAT IN THEM IS, AND RESTED THE SEVENTH DAY:
WHEREFORE THE LORD BLESSED THE SABBATH DAY, AND HALLOWED IT.

V.

12. HONOUR THY FATHER AND THY MOTHER:
THAT THY DAYS MAY BE LONG UPON THE LAND
WHICH THE LORD THY GOD GIVETH THEE.

VI.

13. THOU SHALT NOT KILL.

VII.

14. THOU SHALT NOT COMMIT ADULTERY.

VIII.

15. THOU SHALT NOT STEAL.

IX.

16. THOU SHALT NOT BEAR FALSE WITNESS AGAINST THY NEIGHBOUR.

X.

17. THOU SHALT NOT COVET THY NEIGHBOUR'S HOUSE,
THOU SHALT NOT COVET THY NEIGHBOUR'S WIFE, NOR HIS MANSERVANT,
NOR HIS MAIDSERVANT, NOR HIS OX, NOR HIS ASS,
NOR ANY THING THAT IS THY NEIGHBOUR'S.

Exodus 21:   **Laws** about servants, and laws about causing injury to others.

Exodus 22-23:   **Laws** about stealing, damaging property, lying and cheating, sexual immorality, how to treat others, religious observances, and laws to observe when conquering others in battle.

Exodus 24:   Moses writes the words of the Lord and builds an altar and twelve stone pillars for the twelve tribes of Israel — Offerings are also made to the Lord, and Moses reads the book of the covenant — *"Then went up Moses, and Aaron, Nadab, and Abihu, and seventy elders of Israel: And they saw the God of Israel: and there was under his feet as it were a paved work of a sapphire stone, and as it were the body of heaven in his clearness"* (see 24:9-10) — *"And the Lord said unto Moses, Come up to me into the mount, and be there: and I will give thee tables of stone, and a law, and commandments which I have written; that thou mayest teach them"* (see 24:12) — *"...And Moses was in the mount forty days and forty nights"* (see 24:18).

Exodus 25:   **While on the mount, the Lord instructs Moses concerning the tabernacle** (see chapters 25-31) — These instructions include requirements for offerings made by the people and requirements for making the ark, the mercy seat, the table for the shewbread, and the candlestick.

Exodus 26: Instructions concerning constructing the tabernacle: ten curtains, boards, veils...

Exodus 27: ... the altar, the court, the oil for the lamp ...

Exodus 28: ... holy garments for the priests (Aaron and his sons).

Exodus 29:   Instructions for the priests — *"And I will dwell among the children of Israel, and will be their God"* (see 29:45).

Exodus 30: More instructions concerning the tabernacle: instructions concerning the altar for burning incense, how every man is to give a *"ransom for his soul unto the Lord"* (see 30:12), the brass laver, the oil of holy ointment, and the holy perfume made only for the Lord.

Exodus 31:   The Lord tells Moses which builders He has chosen; God says He has also given these builders the knowledge and wisdom they will need for building the tabernacle — The Sabbath is to be honored — *"Speak thou also unto the children of Israel, saying, Verily my sabbaths ye shall keep: for it is a sign between me and you throughout your generations; that ye may know that I am the Lord that doth sanctify you"* (see 31:13) — ***"And he gave unto Moses, when he had made an end of communing with him upon mount Sinai, two tablets of testimony, tables of stone, written with the finger of God"*** (see 31:18).

Exodus 32:   The people fear Moses will not return from Mount Sinai, so they have Aaron help them make a golden calf to worship — *"And the Lord said unto Moses, Go, get thee down; for thy people, which thou broughtest out of the land of Egypt, have corrupted themselves:"* (see 32:7) — Moses pleads to the Lord not to destroy the Israelites — *"And it came to pass, as soon as he came nigh unto the camp, that he saw the calf, and the dancing: and Moses' anger waxed hot, and he cast the tables out of his hands, and brake them beneath the mount"* (see 32:19) — Many are killed for their sin — Moses pleads for God to forgive the Israelites.

Exodus 33:   Moses has the tabernacle placed outside of the Israelite camp, and a cloud descends upon it as Moses enters; ***"And the Lord spake unto Moses face to face,*** *as a man speaketh unto his friend..."* (see 33:11) — Moses prays to God, *"...shew me now thy way, that I may know thee, that I may find grace in thy sight: and consider that this nation is thy people"* (see 33:13) — God promises:

Exodus 34: *"And he hewed two tables of stone like unto the first; and Moses rose up early in the morning, and went up unto mount Sinai, as the Lord had commanded him, and took in his hand the two tables of stone. And the Lord descended in the cloud, and stood with him there, and proclaimed the name of the Lord. And the Lord passed by before him, and proclaimed, The Lord, The Lord God, merciful and gracious, longsuffering, and abundant in goodness and truth,"* (see 34:4-6) — And the Lord says, *"... Behold, I make a covenant: before all thy people I will do marvels, such as have not been done in all the earth, nor in any nation: and all the people among which thou art shall see the work of the Lord: for it is a terrible (awesome, NIV) thing that I will do with thee"* (see 34:10) — *"And he was there with the Lord forty days and forty nights; he did neither eat bread, nor drink water. And he wrote upon the tables the words of the covenant, the ten commandments. And it came to pass, when Moses came down from mount Sinai with the two tablets of testimony in Moses' hand, when he came down from the mount, that Moses wist not (was not aware, NIV) that the skin of his face shone while he talked with him"* (see 34:28-29).

Exodus 35: **The Israelites bring offerings to the Lord,** more than enough for constructing the tabernacle.

Exodus 36: **The construction of the Tabernacle:** ten curtains, boards, veils…

Exodus 37: …the ark, the table, the candlestick, the altar of incense…

Exodus 38: …altar of burnt offering, brass laver, the court, review of the materials…

Exodus 39: …holy garments for Aaron — **Moses sees all the work and blesses the people.**

Exodus 40: **The tabernacle is finished** — *"Then a cloud covered the tent of the congregation, and **the glory of the Lord filled the tabernacle"*** (see 40:34) — *"For the cloud of the Lord was upon the tabernacle by day, and fire was on it by night, in the sight of all the house of Israel, throughout all their journeys"* (see 40:38).

EXODUS 20:8:

REMEMBER THE SABBATH DAY, TO KEEP IT HOLY.

LEVITICUS

Introduction: See the introduction to Genesis for notes on authorship.   Leviticus means "concerning the Levites." Leviticus was written as a manual of laws for the Israelites. It showed the Levite priests and the Levite tribe their duties and responsibilities in the tabernacle. It also instructed all of Israel how they were to use the tabernacle. Key words in Leviticus include priest, offerings, sacrifice, blood, and atonement. Leviticus has 27 chapters.

Key Contents and Key Memory Verses with Study Dates

Leviticus 1: Instructions for burnt offerings to the Lord.

Leviticus 2: Instructions for meat (grain, NIV) offerings.

Leviticus 3: Instructions for peace offerings.

Leviticus 4-5: Instructions for sin and trespass offerings.

Leviticus 6:   Continued instructions for sin and trespass offerings — Laws for burnt offerings, meat offerings, and sin offerings.

Leviticus 7: Laws concerning trespass offerings, peace offerings, and burnt offerings.

Leviticus 8: Moses gathers the congregation at the tabernacle and anoints the tabernacle, Aaron, and Aaron's sons — Moses offers both a sin offering and a burnt offering, sacrifices the ram of consecration, and offers a wave offering — Moses sanctifies Aaron, his sons, and their garments with oil and blood — Aaron and his sons must remain in the tabernacle for seven days.

Leviticus 9: *"And Aaron lifted up his hand toward the people, and blessed them, and came down from offering of the sin offering, and the burnt offering and peace offerings. And Moses and Aaron went into the tabernacle of the congregation, and came out, and blessed the people: and the glory of the Lord appeared unto all the people. And there came a fire out from before the Lord, and consumed upon the altar the burnt offering and the fat: which when all the people saw, they shouted, and fell on their faces"* (see 9:22-24).

Leviticus 10: Nadab and Abihu, sons of Aaron, are devoured by the fire of the Lord for disobeying the laws concerning the censer, fire, and incense — Laws for the priests.

Leviticus 11: Laws on what to eat and what not to eat (clean and unclean) — *"For I am the Lord your God: ye shall therefore sanctify yourselves, and ye shall be holy; for I am holy: ... For I am the Lord that bringeth you up out of the land of Egypt, to be your God: ye shall therefore be holy, for I am holy. This is the law of the beasts, and of the fowl, and of every living creature that moveth in the waters, and of every creature that creepeth upon the earth: To make a difference between the unclean and the clean, and between the beast that may be eaten and the beast that may not be eaten"* (see 11:44-47).

Leviticus 12: Laws concerning childbirth.

Leviticus 13: Laws concerning leprosy.

Leviticus 14: Laws concerning lepers and their day of cleansing.

Leviticus 15: Laws concerning discharges of the body.

Leviticus 16: Laws for offering annual atonement.

Leviticus 17: Laws about sacrifices.

Leviticus 18: Laws concerning sex.

Leviticus 19: Miscellaneous laws, many about how to treat others.

January 11 (Day 11), Memory Verse #28
Leviticus 19:18:

...THOU SHALT LOVE THY NEIGHBOUR AS THYSELF:
I AM THE LORD.

Leviticus 20: **Punishments for various sins including cursing parents, being a spiritualist, committing adultery, performing incest, and engaging in homosexual activities.**

January 11 (Day 11), Memory Verses #29 & #30
Leviticus 20:7-8:

7. SANCTIFY YOURSELVES THEREFORE, AND BE YE HOLY:
FOR I AM THE LORD YOUR GOD.

8. AND YE SHALL KEEP MY STATUTES, AND DO THEM:
I AM THE LORD WHICH SANCTIFY YOU.

Leviticus 21-22: **Laws concerning the conduct of priests and their offerings.**

Leviticus 23: **Laws concerning religious observances:** The Sabbath, Passover, Feast of Unleavened Bread, Feast of Firstfruits (meat offering or new grain offering, NIV), Feast of Weeks (Pentecost), Feast of Trumpets, Day of Atonement, and Feast of Tabernacles.

Leviticus 24: **Laws concerning the bread in the tabernacle and the oil to burn the lamps — The Israelites stone a man for blasphemy — Sins punishable by death —** See 24:19-20 concerning *"eye for eye;"* also, see Deuteronomy 19:21 and Matthew 5:38-42.

Leviticus 25: **Every seventh year is proclaimed a Sabbath of rest for the land and crops — Every fiftieth year sounds the trumpet of the jubilee** (see 25:8-11) when, among other laws, land is returned to original owners, slaves are set free, and there is neither sowing nor reaping.

Leviticus 26: **Various laws concerning sins.**

Leviticus 27: **Miscellaneous laws including laws on vows and tithes —** *"And all the tithe of the land, whether of the seed of the land, or of the fruit of the tree, is the Lord's: it is holy unto the Lord"* (see 27:30) — *"These are the commandments, which the Lord commanded Moses for the children of Israel in mount Sinai"* (see 27:34)**.**

LEVITICUS 19:18:

...THOU SHALT LOVE THY NEIGHBOUR AS THYSELF: I AM THE LORD.

NUMBERS

Introduction: The name for the book of Numbers is derived from the mention of census figures. Numbers centers around Israel's forty years of wandering in the desert, and God's continued love and mercy for the Israelites although they disobey God time after time. Authorship is traditionally attributed to Moses. The date of Moses' writings is thought to be between 1450-1400 B.C. or as late as the 1200's B.C., depending on the actual date of the Jews' departure from Egypt. See the introductions of Genesis and Exodus for additional authorship notes. Numbers has 36 chapters.

Key Contents and Key Memory Verses with Study Dates

Numbers 1: As directed by the Lord, a census is taken from the tribes of Israel of males 20 years and older and ready to go to war; the census number is 603,550 as recorded in 1:46 — The census is not taken in the Levite tribe since their duty is to be in charge of the tabernacle rather than be a part of the army.

Numbers 2: Moses assigns camping positions for each tribe around the tabernacle according to the Lord's instructions.

Numbers 3-4: The Levites have a special place of service in place of the Israelites' firstborn — *"And the Lord spake unto Moses, saying, And I, behold, I have taken the Levites from among the children of Israel instead of all the firstborn that openeth the matrix among the children of Israel: therefore the Levites shall be mine; Because all the firstborn are mine; for on the day that I smote all the firstborn in the land of Egypt I hallowed unto me all the firstborn in Israel, both man and beast: mine shall they be: I am the Lord"*(see 3:11-13 and Exodus 13:1-16).

Numbers 5: Laws concerning lepers and other unclean matters — Laws concerning confessing sins and repayment of a trespass — Laws on adultery.

Numbers 6: Requirements when taking the "Nazarite Vow" of service to the Lord — The Lord instructs the priests to bless the Israelites with the following prayer:

January 12 (Day 12), Memory Verses #31 to #33
Numbers 6:24-26:
(The Priest's Prayer of Blessing)

24. THE LORD BLESS THEE, AND KEEP THEE:

25. THE LORD MAKE HIS FACE SHINE UPON THEE,
AND BE GRACIOUS UNTO THEE:

26. THE LORD LIFT UP HIS COUNTENANCE UPON THEE,
AND GIVE THEE PEACE.

Numbers 7: Princes from the tribes bring offerings for the tabernacle.

Numbers 8: Cleansing of the Levites.

Numbers 9: Observance of the annual Passover — The Lord leads the Israelites with a cloud — *"And on the day that the tabernacle was reared up the cloud covered the tabernacle, namely, the tent of the testimony: and at even there was upon the tabernacle as it were the appearance of fire, until the morning. So it was always: the cloud covered it by day, and the appearance of fire by night. And when the cloud was taken up from the tabernacle, then after* *that the children of Israel journeyed: and in the place where the cloud abode, there the children of Israel pitched their tents"* (see 9:15-17).

Numbers 10: Two trumpets are made of silver to sound messages to the Israelites — The journey from Sinai begins — The Israelites carry the ark of the covenant in front of them as they travel with the cloud leading them — *"And it came to pass when the ark set forward, that Moses said, Rise up, Lord, and let thine enemies be scattered; and let them that hate thee flee before thee. And when it rested, he said, Return, O Lord, unto the many thousands of Israel"* (see 10:35-36).

Numbers 11: The people complain, and some are consumed by the fire of the Lord — **Manna is described:** *"And the manna was as coriander seed...and the taste of it was as the taste of fresh oil"* (see 11:7-8) — The people continue complaining about the manna they must eat for food — **Moses gathers 70 elders to the tabernacle** — *"And the Lord came down in a cloud, and spake unto him, and took of the spirit that was upon him, and gave it unto the seventy elders: and it came to pass, that when the spirit rested upon them, they prophesied, and did not cease"* (see 11:25) — **The Israelites will not cease complaining about the manna, so the Lord provides quail;** *"And there went forth a wind from the Lord, and brought quails from the sea, and let them fall by the camp..."* (see 11:31) — The Lord's anger due to the complaining is shown through a plague.

Numbers 12: Aaron and Miriam speak against Moses' authority, and the Lord causes Miriam to have leprosy — Aaron and Miriam repent of their doubting Moses and the Lord.

Numbers 13: Moses sends a man from each of the tribes to spy in Canaan — The spies return fearful and report that people of Canaan are men of giants — But Caleb, one of the spies, says, *"...Let us go up at once, and possess it; for we are well able to overcome it"* (see 13:30).

Numbers 14: The people are discouraged and plan to return to Egypt — Because of their disobedience, the Lord says, *"Doubtless ye shall not come into the land, concerning which I sware to make you dwell therein, save Caleb the son of Jephunneh, and Joshua the son of Nun"* (see 14:30) — But the next morning, some of the Israelites attempt to enter the promised land of Canaan without the Lord's leading and are struck down by the Amalekites and the Canaanites.

Numbers 15: Miscellaneous laws about offerings including an offering for unintentional sins — Laws concerning the breaking of the Sabbath — A man is stoned for gathering sticks on the Sabbath — Laws about garment fringes; the cord of blue on the fringe is to remind the Israelites to obey God's commandments *"...and be holy unto your God"* (see 15:40).

Numbers 16: Korah, Dathan, and Abiram lead others in a rebellion against the authority of Moses and Aaron — Moses' prediction comes true: the earth opens up and swallows many, and fire consumes 250 who were part of the rebellion — The people still rebel, and a plague kills 14,700 before Aaron can stop the plague by making an atonement for the people.

Numbers 17: The Lord tells Moses to have the children of Israel bring rods from the leaders of each tribe, and Moses places the rods in the tabernacle — The next day, **Aaron's rod from the Levite tribe blossoms and bears ripe almonds** — Moses keeps the rod to remind the people how they should respect the priest Aaron and stop their complaining and rebelling.

Numbers 18: The Levites are given instructions for various duties and offerings of the tabernacle.

Numbers 19:   **The Lord tells Aaron to have the people bring an unblemished red heifer to the priest Eleazar for a cleansing sacrifice.**

Numbers 20:   **In the desert of Zin, the people complain because of lack of water** — The Lord commands Moses and Aaron to speak to a rock to bring forth water — But they strike the rock twice with their rod instead of speaking to the rock; nevertheless, there is water —   God punishes them for not obeying His instruction by not allowing them to enter the promised land — Aaron dies on Mount Hor.

Numbers 21:   **The king of Arad captures some of the Israelites, but the Israelites destroy Arad's cities — The Israelites journey around Edom and complain of the route, speaking against God and Moses —   Because of the Israelites' complaining, the Lord sends fiery serpents, and many die** — The people repent, so the Lord tells Moses to make an image of a serpent — Moses makes a brass serpent and puts it on a pole; the people live when bitten by a serpent if they look at the brass serpent — **The Israelites defeat Sihon, king of the Amorites, and Og, king of Bashan.**

Numbers 22:   **Balak, the king of the Moabites, fears the Israelites and urges the prophet, Balaam, to curse the Israelites** — Balak sends princes of Moab to Balaam but *"...God said unto Balaam, Thou shalt not go with them; thou shalt not curse the people: for they are blessed"* (see 22:12) — Then Balak sends princes again, and Balaam disappoints the Lord by going with them this time — On the journey, Balaam's ass (donkey) turns three times from the angel of the Lord in its path — Balaam does not see the angel and strikes the ass each time; the ass speaks, and then Balaam sees the angel of the Lord — Balaam repents of his disobedience, and the Lord commands him to go with the princes and speak only what the Lord tells him — Balak takes Balaam to the *"high places of Baal"* (see 22:41).

Numbers 23-24:   Balaam has Balak build seven altars and give sacrifices —   Then to Balak's disappointment, **Balaam blesses Israel** — *"God is not a man, that he should lie; neither the son of man, that he should repent: hath he said, and shall he not do it? Or hath he spoken, and shall he not make it good? Behold, I have received commandment to bless: and he hath blessed; and I cannot reverse it"* (see 23:19-20) — Balak takes Balaam to Peor, and Balaam has Balak build seven more altars and give sacrifices — Balak is angry when Balaam still refuses to curse Israel — Balaam *"...saw the vision of the Almighty, falling into a trance, but having his eyes open:"* (see 24:4) — Balaam prophesies of future things including the fall of the Moabites.

Numbers 25:   **Many Israelites are slain for worshipping Baal-peor and for marrying the women of Moab.**

Numbers 26:   **The Lord tells Moses and the priest Eleazar to take another census** of the male Israelites who are 20 years old or older and able to go to war — The census figure is 601,730.

Numbers 27:   **Laws concerning inheritance — The Lord tells Moses to appoint Joshua as leader of the Israelites** so *"...that the congregation of the Lord be not as sheep which have no shepherd"* (see 27:17) — *"And Moses did as the Lord commanded him: and he took Joshua, and set him before Eleazar the priest, and before all the congregation: And he laid his hands upon him, and gave him a charge, as the Lord commanded by the hand of Moses"* (see 27:22-23).

Numbers 28–30:   **Instructions for offerings and various religious feasts and observances — Laws concerning vows.**

Numbers 31: The Israelites defeat the Midianites — The Israelites kill the Midianite men and take the women, children, and spoil back to their camp — Balaam is among those killed (see 31:8) — Moses also commands the killing of all the captive male children and all the captive females who are not virgins — The gold spoil is taken to the tabernacle.

Numbers 32: The tribes of Gad, Reuben, and half of the tribe of Manasseh settle on one side of the Jordan River, but they agree to help Israel conquer the other side of the Jordan River — Moses warns these tribes:

January 13 (Day 13), Memory Verse #34
Numbers 32:23:

...**AND** BE SURE YOUR SIN WILL FIND YOU OUT.

Numbers 33: The Israelites are reminded of their journey from Egypt to Moab — The Israelites are given instructions for conquering Canaan — *"And the Lord spake unto Moses in the plains of Moab by Jordan near Jericho, saying, Speak unto the children of Israel, and say unto them, When ye are passed over Jordan into the land of Canaan; Then ye shall drive out all the inhabitants of the land from before you, and destroy all their pictures, and destroy all their molten images, and quite pluck down all their high places: And ye shall dispossess the inhabitants of the land, and dwell therein: for I have given you the land to possess it. And ye shall divide the land by lot for an inheritance among your families:...But if ye will not drive out the inhabitants of the land from before you; then it shall come to pass, that those which ye let remain of them shall be pricks in your eyes, and thorns in your sides, and shall vex you in the land wherein ye dwell. Moreover it shall come to pass, that I shall do unto you, as I thought to do unto them"* (see 33:50-56).

Numbers 34: Moses instructs how the land of Canaan will be divided among the tribes.

Numbers 35: Forty-eight cities and their surrounding areas are set aside for the Levites — Six cities, three on each side of the Jordan, are set aside for manslayers who accidentally kill someone; these cities are called the **cities of refuge.**

Numbers 36: Laws of inheritance — Women must marry within their own tribe to receive an inheritance.

NUMBERS 6:24-26:

(The Priest's Prayer of Blessing)

24. THE LORD BLESS THEE, AND KEEP THEE:

25. THE LORD MAKE HIS FACE SHINE UPON THEE, AND BE GRACIOUS UNTO THEE:

26. THE LORD LIFT UP HIS COUNTENANCE UPON THEE, AND GIVE THEE PEACE.

DEUTERONOMY

Introduction: The title, Deuteronomy, is derived from a Greek phrase meaning "second or repeated law-giving." Authorship is traditionally attributed to Moses about 1410 B.C. or as late as the 1200's B.C. Of course, another author would have written of Moses' death in chapter 34. See the introductions to Genesis and Exodus for more notes on authorship. Moses continued to lead the Israelites in their journey in the wilderness and reminded them of their responsibilities as God's covenant people. He also gave many laws to the Israelites and urged the people to follow their new leader Joshua. Deuteronomy has 34 chapters.

Key Contents and Key Memory Verses with Study Dates

Deuteronomy 1: In chapters one through three, Moses reviews the Israelites' wanderings in the wilderness after leaving Egypt — His account includes: Israel at Sinai, Israel at Kadesh-barnea, fighting the Amorites without God's help, **...**

Deuteronomy 2:   ...wanderings from Kadesh to Moab, traveling through Seir (land which God had promised to Esau), traveling through Moab (land which God had given Lot), **...**

Deuteronomy 3:   ...the conquest of Bashan and their king Og, the conquest of Heshbon and their king Sihon, the land being divided among the tribes of Gad, Reuben and half of the tribe of Manasseh, and God letting Moses see the promised land across the Jordan River from Mount Pisgah although Moses was not allowed to enter the promised land.

Deuteronomy 4: Moses urges the Israelites to keep God's commandments and teach their children the Israelites' history — *"Behold, I have taught you statutes and judgments, even as the Lord my God commanded me, that ye should do so in the land whither ye go to possess it. Keep therefore and do them; for this is your wisdom and your understanding in the sight of the nations, which shall hear all these statutes, and say, Surely this great nation is a wise and understanding people. For what nation is there so great, who hath God so nigh unto them, as the Lord our God is in all things that we call upon him for?"* (see 4:5-7) — **Moses tells the Israelites to especially remember God's covenant and His giving them "The Ten Commandments" at Mount Sinai —** The Israelites are warned by Moses against repeating the error of making a graven image; they had made a golden calf at Mount Sinai — **But Moses prophesies that in many years the Israelites will again make graven images and turn from God —** *"And the Lord shall scatter you among the nations, and ye shall be left few in number among the heathen, whither the Lord shall lead you"* (see 4:27). *But if from thence thou shalt seek the Lord thy God, thou shalt find him, if thou seek him with all thy heart and with all thy soul"* (see 4:29) — **Moses tells the Israelites that they have been chosen by God and have seen great things so that they** *"...mightest know that the Lord he is God; there is none else beside them"* (see 4:35) — Also, Moses explains how God has promised the Israelites an inheritance of land from other nations — Moses proclaims to the Israelites**:**

January 13 (Day 13), Memory Verse #35
Deuteronomy 4:39:

KNOW THEREFORE THIS DAY, AND CONSIDER IT IN THINE HEART,
THAT THE LORD HE IS GOD IN HEAVEN ABOVE, AND UPON THE EARTH BENEATH:
THERE IS NONE ELSE.

— Moses mentions the cities of refuge.

Deuteronomy 5: "**The Ten Commandments**" (see 5:6-21) — Also, see Exodus 20:3-17 in this book which quotes "The Ten Commandments."

Deuteronomy 6: **Moses teaches the Israelites about loving God and keeping His commandments** — *"Now these are the commandments, the statutes, and the judgments, which the Lord your God commanded to teach you, that ye might do them in the land whither ye go to possess it: That thou mightest fear the Lord thy God, to keep all his statutes and his commandments, which I command thee, thou, and thy son, and thy son's son, all the days of thy life; and that thy days may be prolonged. Hear therefore, O Israel, and observe to do it; that it may be well with thee, and that ye may increase mightily, as the Lord God of thy fathers hath promised thee, in the land that floweth with milk and honey. Hear, O Israel: The Lord our God is one Lord:"* (see 6:1-4).

January 14 (Day 14), Memory Verse #36
Deuteronomy 6:5:

AND THOU SHALT LOVE THE LORD THY GOD WITH ALL THINE HEART,
AND WITH ALL THY SOUL, AND WITH ALL THY MIGHT.

— *"And these words, which I command thee this day, shall be in thine heart: And thou shalt teach them diligently unto thy children..."* (see 6:6-7) — *"Ye shall not tempt the Lord your God..."* (see 6:16).

Deuteronomy 7: **The Israelites are commanded to destroy the inhabitants and graven images of the lands they conquer** — *"Know therefore that the Lord thy God, he is God, the faithful God, which keepeth covenant and mercy with them that love him and keep his commandments to a thousand generations;"* (see 7:9).

Deuteronomy 8-11: **Moses tells the Israelites to continue loving and obeying God, and to remember their past history which is reviewed in these chapters** — *"...remember all the way which the Lord thy God led thee these forty years in the wilderness, to humble thee, and to prove thee, to know what was in thine heart, whether thou wouldest keep his commandments, or no. And he humbled thee, and suffered thee to hunger, and fed thee with manna, which thou knewest not, neither did thy fathers know; that he might make thee know that man doth not live by bread only, but by every word that proceedeth out of the mouth of the Lord doth man live"* (see 8:2-3).

January 14 (Day 14), Memory Verses #37 & #38
Deuteronomy 10:12-13:

12. AND NOW, ISRAEL, WHAT DOTH THE LORD THY GOD REQUIRE OF THEE,
BUT TO FEAR THE LORD THY GOD, TO WALK IN HIS WAYS,
AND TO LOVE HIM, AND TO SERVE THE LORD THY GOD
WITH ALL THY HEART AND WITH ALL THY SOUL,

13. TO KEEP THE COMMANDMENTS OF THE LORD, AND HIS STATUTES,
WHICH I COMMAND THEE THIS DAY FOR THY GOOD?

Deuteronomy 12: Laws pertaining to conquering and possessing nations.

Deuteronomy 13: **Laws concerning false prophets and others who try to make the Israelites worship other gods** — *"Ye shall walk after the Lord your God, and fear him, and keep his commandments, and obey his voice, and ye shall serve him, and cleave unto him"* (see 13:4) — *"...keep all his commandments which I command thee this day, to do that which is right in the eyes of the Lord thy God"* (see 13:18).

Deuteronomy 14: Laws concerning food — Laws concerning tithes.

Deuteronomy 15: Laws concerning the poor and the forgiving of debts within their own nation at the end of every seven years.

Deuteronomy 16: Laws concerning religious observances including the Passover, Feast of Unleavened Bread, Feast of Weeks, and Feast of Tabernacles — Laws concerning judges and officers.

Deuteronomy 17: Laws concerning judges, officers, and kings — *"When thou art come unto the land which the Lord thy God giveth thee, and shalt possess it, and shalt dwell therein, and shalt say, I will set a king over me, like as all the nations that are about me; Thou shalt in any wise set him king over thee, whom the Lord thy God shall choose: one from among thy brethren..."* (see 17:14-15).

Deuteronomy 18: Laws concerning Levites — Laws concerning witches and sorcery — Prediction of a Prophet — *"The Lord thy God will raise up unto thee a Prophet from the midst of thee, of thy brethren, like unto me; unto him ye shall hearken;"* (see 18:15) **— Advice to not fear false prophets.**

Deuteronomy 19: Laws concerning the cities of refuge — Law concerning *"thy neighbour's landmark"* (see 19:14) **— Laws concerning witnesses of those who have sinned —** *"And thine eye shall not pity; but life shall go for life, eye for eye, tooth for tooth, hand for hand, foot for foot"* (see 19:21) — In Matthew 5:38-42, Jesus shows how this law of Deuteronomy 19:21 has changed with the new covenant.

Deuteronomy 20: Laws concerning battles.

Deuteronomy 21: Laws concerning a slain man — Laws concerning marriage — Laws concerning rebellious sons.

Deuteronomy 22: Miscellaneous laws.

Deuteronomy 23:   Laws concerning the congregation of the Lord — Laws concerning usury.

Deuteronomy 24-25: Laws concerning divorce, marriage, stealing, and leprosy — Other miscellaneous laws.

Deuteronomy 26: Laws concerning the first fruits of the land.

Deuteronomy 27: Instructions for building stone monuments and an altar to God when the Israelites cross the Jordan — Instructions for writing the law in the stones — Instructions for cursing wrongdoing.

Deuteronomy 28: Exhortations that blessings will come to the Israelites if they obey God's commands, but curses will come if they disobey.

Deuteronomy 29-30: Moses tells the Israelites that God will now allow their generation to enter the promised land although they have not truly perceived how God has led them — *"The secret things belong unto the Lord our God: but those things which are revealed belong unto us and to our children for ever, that we may do all the words of this law"* (see 29:29)

— Moses again commands the Israelites to obey God in order to be blessed when it is time to possess the land on the other side of the Jordan River — Moses says, *"I call heaven and earth to record this day against you, that I have set before you life and death, blessing and cursing: therefore choose life, that both thou and thy seed may live: That thou mayest love the Lord thy God, and that thou mayest obey his voice, and that thou mayest cleave unto him: for he is thy life, and the length of thy days: that thou mayest dwell in the land which the Lord sware unto thy fathers, to Abraham, to Isaac, and to Jacob, to give them"* (see 30:19-20).

Deuteronomy 31: **Moses gives a final speech to the Israelites** — *"Be strong and of a good courage, fear not, nor be afraid of them: for the Lord thy God, he it is that doth go with thee; he will not fail thee, nor forsake thee"* (see 31:6) — **Moses takes Joshua to the tabernacle to lay hands on Joshua in preparation of his replacing Moses as Israel's leader** — At the tabernacle, the Lord tells Moses he will soon die — The Lord also explains how the Israelites will become rebellious against God after they cross the Jordan — **The Lord commands Moses to write a song** about the Israelites' rebellions so that it will serve as a reminder to them later — **The book of the law is placed in the side of the ark.**

Deuteronomy 32: **Moses speaks the words of the song** (see 32:1-43) **to the Israelites.**

January 15 (Day 15), Memory Verse #39
Deuteronomy 32:4:

HE IS THE ROCK, HIS WORK IS PERFECT; FOR ALL HIS WAYS ARE JUDGMENT: A GOD OF TRUTH AND WITHOUT INIQUITY, JUST AND RIGHT IS HE.

— **God tells Moses to go to Mount Nebo to die.**

Deuteronomy 33: **Moses blesses the tribes of Israel.**

January 15 (Day 15), Memory Verse #40
Deuteronomy 33:27:

THE ETERNAL GOD IS THY REFUGE, AND UNDERNEATH ARE THE EVERLASTING ARMS:

Deuteronomy 34: **Moses goes to Mount Nebo** — From the mountain, Moses sees the promised land across the Jordan River although God will not allow him to enter it — Moses dies on Mount Nebo at age 120 — *"And there arose not a prophet since in Israel like unto Moses, whom the Lord knew face to face, In all the signs and the wonders, which the Lord sent him to do in the land of Egypt to Pharaoh, and to all his servants, and to all his land, And in all that mighty hand, and in all the great terror which Moses shewed in the sight of all Israel"* (see 34:10-12).

DEUTERONOMY 6:5:

AND THOU SHALT LOVE THE LORD THY GOD WITH ALL THINE HEART, AND WITH ALL THY SOUL, AND WITH ALL THY MIGHT.

JOSHUA

Introduction: Joshua in Hebrew means "Yahweh is salvation."   This book describes the conquest and division of the promised land of Canaan with Joshua as the Israelites' leader. Authorship and date of writing are uncertain.   Traditionally, authorship is attributed to Joshua about 1400-1370 B.C. or as late as 1250 B.C.   Of course, another author would have written of Joshua's funeral.   Some believe Eleazar or Samuel may have helped write Joshua.   Others believe this book was written about 600 to 800 years after the events of Joshua by an unknown author (or authors).   Joshua has 24 chapters.

Key Contents and Key Memory Verses with Study Dates

Joshua 1:   God speaks to Joshua — *"Moses my servant is dead; now therefore arise, go over this Jordan, thou, and all this people, unto the land which I do give to them, even to the children of Israel"* (see 1:2) — *"This book of the law shall not depart out of thy mouth; but thou shalt meditate therein day and night, that thou mayest observe to do according to all that is written therein: for then thou shalt make thy way prosperous, and then thou shalt have good success"* (see 1:8) — **God continues speaking to Joshua:**

January 16 (Day 16), Memory Verse #41
Joshua 1:9:

HAVE NOT I COMMANDED THEE?
BE STRONG AND OF A GOOD COURAGE;
BE NOT AFRAID, NEITHER BE THOU DISMAYED;
FOR THE LORD THY GOD IS WITH THEE WHITHERSOEVER THOU GOEST.

— Joshua commands the officers of the Israelites to prepare the people — Joshua tells the officers, *"...for within three days ye shall pass over this Jordan, to go in to possess the land, which the Lord your God giveth you to possess it"* (see 1:11).

Joshua 2:   Joshua sends two spies to Jericho — The harlot Rahab lets the spies lodge with her — When the king of Jericho inquires about them, she hides them in flax stalks on the roof — The spies promise to spare her family when Israel attacks if a scarlet thread is tied in her window, the same window where she lowers them to safety to escape from Jericho.

Joshua 3:   The Israelites cross the Jordan River with the Levite priests carrying the ark of the covenant before them — *"And the Lord said unto Joshua, This day will I begin to magnify thee in the sight of all Israel, that they may know that, as I was with Moses, so I will be with thee"* (see 3:7) — When the feet of the priests carrying the ark enter the Jordan River, the waters are held back, and the priests stand on dry ground in the river bed until all the Israelites cross the Jordan on dry ground.

Joshua 4:   Joshua commands one man from each of the twelve tribes to take a stone out of the Jordan river bed as they cross and carry it to their next lodging site — Then they are to build a twelve stone memorial as a sign of their miraculous crossing of the Jordan River — *"...and these stones shall be for a memorial unto the children of Israel for ever"* (see 4:7) — *"And Joshua set up twelve stones in the midst of Jordan, in the place where the feet of the priests which bare the ark of the covenant stood: and they are there unto this day"* (see 4:9) — *"And it came to pass, when the priests that bare the ark of the covenant of the Lord were come up out of the midst of Jordan, and the soles of the priests' feet were lifted up unto the dry land, that the waters of Jordan returned unto their place, and flowed over all his banks, as they did before"* (see 4:18) — Joshua tells the Israelites, *"...When your children shall ask their fathers in time* *to come, saying, What mean these stones? Then ye shall let your children know, saying, Israel came over this Jordan on dry land"* (see 4:21-22) — *"That all the people of the earth might know the hand of the Lord, that it is mighty: that ye might fear the Lord your God for ever"* (see 4:24).

Joshua 5:   **The Lord commands Joshua to circumcise the Israelites** — The practice of circumcision had ceased in the wilderness, and now there existed a new generation — **The Israelites encamp at Gilgal and observe the Passover** — The manna ceases since *"...they did eat of the fruit of the land of Canaan that year"* (see 5:12) — **The captain of the Lord's host appears to Joshua** — *"...And Joshua fell on his face to the earth, and did worship, and said unto him, What saith my lord unto his servant? And the captain of the Lord's host said unto Joshua, Loose thy shoe from off thy foot; for the place whereon thou standest is holy. And Joshua did so"* (see 5:14-15).

Joshua 6:   **The Israelites conquer Jericho by obeying Joshua's instructions given to him by the Lord** — The Israelite men of war follow seven priests who are marching in front of the ark of the covenant and blowing trumpets made of ram horns — They circle the outside walls of Jericho once a day for six consecutive days — On the seventh day, they circle Jericho seven times, and *"...at the seventh time, when the priests blew with the trumpets, Joshua said unto the people, Shout; for the Lord hath given you the city"* (see 6:16) — When the people shout, *"...the wall fell down flat, so that the people went into the city, every man straight before him, and they took the city"* (see 6:20) — Rahab's family is spared as she was promised by the Israelite spies (see Joshua 2).

Joshua 7:   **Joshua sends approximately 3000 men to conquer Ai, but the people of Ai kill about 36 Israelites and cause the Israelites to flee** — The Lord tells Joshua they lost the battle because an Israelite had disobeyed the command of taking no spoil from Jericho — Achan and his family are stoned and then burned along with their possessions because Achan had taken from Jericho things which were banned.

Joshua 8:   **Joshua leads the Israelite army in a victorious battle against Ai** — The men of Ai chase the Israelites who pretend to be fleeing, but they are actually leading the men of Ai into an ambush — Ai is destroyed and burned — Joshua builds an altar to God at Mount Ebal and writes a copy of the law of Moses on its stones — Joshua also reads the book of the law of Moses to the Israelites.

Joshua 9:   **Men from the area of Gibeon disguise themselves in worn clothes and deceive the Israelite leaders, claiming they are from a distant land** — So the Israelite leaders, believing these men live faraway, make an oath not to destroy their cities — The men of Gibeon are made slaves because of their deception, and Joshua honors the promise of not destroying their cities; *"And Joshua made them that day hewers of wood and drawers of water for the congregation, and for the altar of the Lord..."* (see 9:27).

Joshua 10:   **Five kings of the Amorites decide to attack Gibeon since this city made peace with Israel — The people of Gibeon send for the Israelites' help, and the Israelites come immediately, helping defeat the Amorites** — Huge hailstones kill many of the Amorites, and *"Then spake Joshua to the Lord in the day when the Lord delivered up the Amorites before the children of Israel, and he said in the sight of Israel, Sun, stand thou still upon Gibeon; and thou, Moon, in the valley of Ajalon. **And the sun stood still, and the moon stayed, until the people had avenged themselves upon their enemies.** Is not this written in the book of Jasher? So the sun stood still in the midst of heaven, and hasted not to go down about a whole day"* (see 10:12-13) — The five Amorite kings hide in a cave at Makkedah — When the Israelites find the kings, they kill, hang, and then bury the kings in the cave — Israel conquers many more cities.

Joshua 11:   **Many of the Canaanite cities ban together to attack Israel, but Israel is victorious over them — Review of Israel's victories in Canaan** — *"So Joshua took the whole land, according to all that the Lord said unto Moses; and Joshua gave it for an inheritance unto Israel according to their divisions by their tribes. And the land rested from war"* (see 11:23).

Joshua 12: List of the kings and lands conquered by Israel in Canaan.

Joshua 13-21:   Division of the land of Canaan among the Israelite tribes — The cities of refuge are mentioned in Chapter 20.

Joshua 22:   Joshua speaks to the tribes of Reuben, Gad, and half-tribe of Manasseh — *"But take diligent heed to do the commandment and the law, which Moses the servant of the Lord charged you, to love the Lord your God, and to walk in all his ways, and to keep his commandments, and to cleave unto him, and to serve him with all your heart and with all your soul"* (see 22:5) — The Israelite tribes settle a dispute over the location of an altar which was built by the tribes of Reuben, Gad, and half-tribe of Manasseh.

Joshua 23:   Joshua speaks to all of Israel — *"Be ye therefore very courageous to keep and to do all that is written in the book of the law of Moses, that ye turn not aside therefrom to the right hand or to the left; That ye come not among these nations, these that remain among you; neither make mention of the name of their gods, nor cause to swear by them, neither serve them, nor bow yourselves unto them: But cleave unto the Lord your God, as ye have done unto this day"* (see 23:6-8).

Joshua 24: Joshua calls the Israelites to Shechem and reviews Israel's history (see 24:1-25).

January 17 (Day 17), Memory Verse #42
Joshua 24:15:

...CHOOSE YOU THIS DAY WHOM YE WILL SERVE; ...
BUT AS FOR ME AND MY HOUSE, WE WILL SERVE THE LORD.

— *"And Joshua wrote these words in the book of the law of God, and took a great stone, and set it up there under an oak, that was by the sanctuary of the Lord. And Joshua said unto all the people, Behold, this stone shall be a witness unto us; for it hath heard all the words of the Lord which he spake unto us: it shall be therefore a witness unto you, lest ye deny your God"* (see 24:26-27) — **Joshua dies at age 110.**

JOSHUA 24:15:

...CHOOSE YOU THIS DAY WHOM YE WILL SERVE; ... BUT AS FOR ME AND MY HOUSE, WE WILL SERVE THE LORD.

JUDGES

Introduction: Tradition attributes authorship of Judges to Samuel around 1050 B.C., but the author and date cannot be certain. Others believe Judges was written as late as the 700's B.C. After Joshua's death, the Hebrews tried to complete the occupation of the Canaanite land with judges ruling over them. The rule of judges proved to be chaotic. Time and time again the Israelites were disobedient to God, yet He was merciful toward them. Judges has 21 chapters.

List of judges who ruled the Israelites approximately 1380 to 1050 B.C:

OTHNIEL, EHUD, SHAMGAR, DEBORAH who was helped by BARAK, GIDEON, TOLA, JAIR, JEPHTHAH, IBZAN, ELON, ABDON, and SAMSON.

Key Contents and Key Memory Verses with Study Dates

Judges 1: After Joshua's death, the Israelites conquer more Canaanite cities but also leave many cities unconquered.

Judges 2: An angel of the Lord appears in Bochim near Gilgal — The angel is angry since the Hebrews are worshipping the Canaanite gods, Baal and Ashtaroth, and have not destroyed all the Canaanites — **The Lord gives judges to help rule Israel** — But during the time of judges, the Israelites will repeatedly repent of their sins and fall into sin again.

Judges 3: The king of Mesopotamia rules over the Israelites, and the Israelites cry to the Lord for help — The Lord has **OTHNIEL** rule as judge and deliver them from Chushan-rishathaim, king of Mesopotamia — *"And the land had rest forty years..."* (see 3:11) — But the Israelites are evil again, and they are overtaken by Eglon, the king of Moab, for eighteen years — Once again Israel cries to the Lord, and **EHUD** is made judge of Israel — Ehud rescues the Israelites by killing fat King Eglon with a dagger in a secret meeting with him — Ehud also leads Israel in defeating the Moabites in battle — *"...And the land had rest fourscore (eighty,* NIV) *years"* (see 3:30) — Israel's next judge, **SHAMGAR,** kills 600 Philistines with an ox goad.

Judges 4: The Israelites are evil again, and Jabin, king of Canaan, conquers them with Sisera as the captain of his army — Jabin rules the Israelites 20 years, and the Israelites cry again to the Lord — Prophetess **DEBORAH** summons **BARAK,** and according to the Lord's instructions, he gathers 10,000 men from the Zebulun and Naphtali tribes to go to Mount Tabor — At Mount Tabor, the Israelites defeat Sisera's army — Sisera escapes and hides in Jael's tent (Jael is the wife of Heber the Kenite), but Jael drives a nail through Sisera's head while he sleeps.

Judges 5: Deborah and Barak are Israel's new judges and sing a praise song describing Israel's victories — *"Praise ye the Lord for the avenging of Israel, when the people willingly offered themselves. Hear, O ye kings; give ear, O ye princes; I, even I, will sing unto the Lord; I will sing praise to the Lord God of Israel"* (see 5:2-3) — *"So let all thine enemies perish, O Lord: but let them that love him be as the sun when he goeth forth in his might. And the land rested forty years"* (see 5:31).

Judges 6: The Israelites are evil again, and the Midianites rule over them for seven years — Israel cries again to the Lord — An angel of the Lord appears to **GIDEON,** Israel's next judge, and calls him to deliver Israel from the Midianites — **Gideon, also known as Jerubbaal, asks for a sign,** so the angel of the Lord causes Gideon's food offering to burn when it is touched by the angel's staff — Gideon builds an altar to the Lord, and the Lord tells him to tear down his father's altar to Baal and replace it with an altar to God — When Gideon destroys Baal's altar, the men of the city are upset and want to kill Gideon — Joash, Gideon's father, says to *"...Let*

Baal plead against him, because he hath thrown down his altar" (see 6:32) — **Before Gideon goes to war for the Israelites, he asks the Lord for a sign showing he will conquer their enemy** — Gideon asks that a dry fleece of wool on the floor become wet with dew with the surrounding ground remaining dry — This happens as he requests, so he asks for one more sign — He asks that the fleece of wool the next night be dry and the surrounding ground wet — And God also provides this sign.

Judges 7: Gideon forms a small army — Before fighting the Midianites, Gideon sends away anyone afraid to give God the glory for a victory using a small army; his army decreases from 32,000 to 10,000 men — Then Gideon sends away anyone who does not lap water from their hands as he watches them drink; his army decreases from 10,000 to 300 men — The Lord reassures Gideon of victory by first allowing him to spy on the Midian camp with his servant Phurah; Gideon hears the Midianites tell of their dream showing Gideon's victory in battle against them — The Midianites flee when the 300 Israelites surround their camp and sound trumpets, break pitchers, and hold torches to appear as a very large army.

Judges 8: Gideon's small army pursues the fleeing Midianites, but some cities refuse to help them pursue the Midianites; therefore, Gideon returns after conquering the Midianites to punish those who would not help them — The people of Israel ask Gideon and his sons to rule over them, but Gideon replies, *"...I will not rule over you, neither shall my son rule over you:* **the Lord shall rule over you***"* (see 8:23) — There is peace for 40 years — But after Gideon dies, Israel turns evil again.

Judges 9: Abimelech requests of his kinsmen in Shechem to be their king — After they agree, he kills Gideon's sons, who are also his brothers — His brother Jotham hides and escapes death; there were 70 brothers — Jotham's speech, which includes a parable of trees searching for a king, warns Abimelech and the people of Shechem of punishment to come — The men of Shechem are led by Gaal and turn against Abimelech — Abimelech plans an ambush and defeats the men at Shechem — But at Thebez, *"...a certain woman cast a piece of a millstone upon Abimelech's head, and all to brake his skull"* (see 9:53) — Abimelech is still alive and does not want to be killed by a woman; he has one of his men thrust a sword through him to kill him — Jotham's prophecy comes true; both Abimelech and Shechem are punished, *"...and upon them came the curse of Jotham the son of Jerubbaal"* (see 9:57).

Judges 10: TOLA judges Israel 23 years — **JAIR** judges Israel for 22 years — Israel is evil again, worshipping many gods, so the Lord allows them to be ruled by the Philistines and the people of Ammon for 18 years — But Israel cries again to the Lord.

Judges 11: The people of Gilead first reject Jephthah's help since he is a son of a harlot, but then they send for him to fight Ammon — Jephthah agrees to lead them if they will make him their judge — **JEPHTHAH** vows to offer a burnt offering of the first thing out of his door when he returns home if the Lord will deliver Ammon into his hands — Jephthah returns victorious, but unfortunately, the first thing out of his door is his daughter, his only child — He honors his vow to the Lord.

Judges 12: Jephthah also defeats Ephraim and judges Israel six years — **IBZAN** judges Israel for seven years — **ELON** judges Israel for ten years — **ABDON** judges Israel for eight years.

Judges 13: Again Israel is evil, so they fall into the Philistine's hands for 40 years — **The angel of the Lord appears to Monoah's wife who is barren** and says, *"...For, lo, thou shalt conceive, and bear a son; and no razor shall come on his head: for the child shall be a Nazarite unto God from the womb: and he shall begin to deliver Israel out of the hands of the Philistines"*   (see 13:5) — The angel of the Lord appears again to Monoah and his wife — The angel of the Lord ascends in the smoke from the altar where Monoah has offered a meat offering — **Monoah's wife bears a son and names him Samson,** *"...and the child grew, and the Lord blessed him"* (see 13:24).

Judges 14:   Samson and his parents journey to Timnath because Samson has found a Philistine woman he wants to marry — At his seven day wedding feast, he presents a riddle with a prize to whoever can solve it; *"And he said unto them, Out of the eater came forth meat, and out of the strong came forth sweetness"* (see 14:14) — Samson's riddle came from his experience of wrestling a lion in which a bee swarm formed afterwards in its carcass — Samson's wife betrays him by giving the answer of the riddle — *"And the men of the city said unto him on the seventh day before the sun went down, What is sweeter then honey? And what is stronger than a lion?..."* (see 14:18) — Samson is angry and kills thirty men — Samson's wife is given to another.

Judges 15:   Samson is angry because his wife is given to his companion, so he sends 300 foxes with torches tied on their tails through Philistine corn fields — The Philistines then burn his wife and her father — This angers Samson again, so he slaughters many Philistines — Samson hides in a cave, but men of Judah discover his location and bind him to deliver him to the Philistines — Samson breaks the binding cords with his great strength and kills 1000 men with a jawbone of an ass — God supplies water for Samson — **SAMSON** is made judge of Israel for 20 years.

Judges 16:   Samson loves Delilah who tricks Samson into telling the secret of his strength — Samson lies and tells her three ways that will weaken his strength — After trying all three ways and failing, Delilah again begs Samson for his secret — Samson finally gives in and tells Delilah, *"...There hath not come a razor upon mine head; for I have been a Nazarite unto God from my mother's womb: if I be shaven, then my strength will go from me, and I shall become weak, and be like any other man"* (see 16:17) — Delilah betrays Samson and relays this information to the Philistines — **Delilah has Samson's hair cut while he sleeps, and *"...the Philistines took him, and put out his eyes, and brought him down to Gaza, and bound him with fetters of brass; and he did grind in the prison house"*** (see 16:21) — Samson's hair grows again and his strength returns — During a great celebration to the god Dagon, the Philistines bring Samson from prison and place him between the pillars of the house where approximately 3,000 have gathered — *"And Samson called unto the Lord, and said, O Lord God, remember me, I pray thee, and strengthen me, I pray thee, only this once, O God, that I may be at once avenged of the Philistines for my two eyes. And Samson took hold of the two middle pillars upon which the house stood, and on which it was borne up, of the one with his right hand, and of the other with his left. And Samson said, Let me die with the Philistines. And he bowed himself with all his might; and the house fell upon the lords, and upon all the people that were therein. So the dead which he slew at his death were more than they which he slew in his life"* (see 16:28-30).

Judges 17:   Although Micah has graven images in his house, he persuades a Levite priest to dwell with him.

Judges 18:   The Israelite Danites ask the Levite priest's advice on going into battle — The Israelites persuade the Levite priest to go with them and leave Micah, but they carry the graven images with them — The Danites conquer Laish and name it Dan, since they are from the Israelite tribe of Dan.

Judges 19:   A Levite's concubine is killed by evil men in Gibeah, who are also of the tribe of Benjamin — So the Levite cut her dead body into twelve pieces and *"...sent her into all the coasts of Israel"* (see 19:29).

Judges 20: The tribes of Israel gather to determine what should be done because of the horrible incident mentioned in chapter 19 — The Israelites go to Gibeah and ask only for those who killed the concubine — The Benjamites will not surrender the guilty men, so Israel goes to battle with the Benjamites — The Benjamites are winning the first two days of battle, but the tribes of Israel conquer the tribe of Benjamin on the third day.

Judges 21: The tribes of Israel mourn the separation of the tribe of Benjamin from Israel — The Israelites provide wives for the remnant of surviving Benjamite men by providing 400 virgins from the destroyed city of Jabesh-gilead, and by letting the Benjamites capture dancing women of Shiloh.

January 18 (Day 18), Memory Verse #43
Judges 21:25:

IN THOSE DAYS THERE WAS NO KING IN ISRAEL;
EVERY MAN DID THAT WHICH WAS RIGHT IN HIS OWN EYES.

JUDGES 8:23:

...I WILL NOT RULE OVER YOU,
NEITHER SHALL MY SON RULE OVER YOU:
THE LORD SHALL RULE OVER YOU.

RUTH

Introduction: The author and date of writing of Ruth are unknown. Many believe Samuel may have been the author. Between 950 to 700 B.C. or even later in the 500's or 400's B.C are suggested dates for the writing of Ruth. The story of Ruth is thought to have occurred during the judges' rule of Israel. Ruth is the story of a faithful Gentile who believed in God and faithfully cared for her widowed mother-in-law who was a Jew. Ruth's son, Obed, became the grandfather of King David, and, as shown in Matthew and Luke, David was an ancestor of Jesus. Ruth has four chapters.

Key Contents and Key Memory Verses with Study Dates

Ruth 1: Naomi's husband dies after moving from Judah to Moab because of a famine — Her two sons marry Orpah and Ruth, women of Moab, but then **both sons die** — Naomi returns to Judah but encourages her daughters-in-law to stay with their families in Moab — **Her daughter-in-law Ruth decides to return to Judah with Naomi and tells her:**

January 18 (Day 18), Memory Verse #44
Ruth 1:16:

...WHITHER THOU GOEST, I WILL GO; AND WHERE THOU LODGEST, I WILL LODGE; THY PEOPLE SHALL BE MY PEOPLE, AND THY GOD MY GOD:

Ruth 2: Ruth gleans in Boaz's field, and Boaz commends Ruth for taking care of her mother-in-law — Boaz tells Ruth, *"...The Lord recompense thy work, and a full reward be given thee of the Lord God of Israel, under whose wings thou art come to trust"* (see 2:12).

Ruth 3: Naomi tells Ruth to visit Boaz secretly by night so that Boaz may know of Ruth's interest in him.

Ruth 4: Boaz asks permission from Naomi's kinsman to marry Ruth and buy the land of Naomi's late husband and late sons to *"...raise up the name of the dead upon his inheritance, that the name of the dead be not cut off from among his brethren..."* (see 4:10) — The kinsman grants permission by the customary symbol of giving his shoe to Boaz (see 4:7-8) — Boaz and Ruth's son is Obed, Obed's son is Jesse, and Jesse's son is David; therefore, Ruth is David's great-grandmother.

RUTH 1:16:

...WHITHER THOU GOEST, I WILL GO; AND WHERE THOU LODGEST, I WILL LODGE; THY PEOPLE SHALL BE MY PEOPLE, AND THY GOD MY GOD:

I Samuel

Introduction: The author of I and II Samuel is unknown. Suggested authors include Samuel, Gad, Nathan, and Nathan's son Zabud.   The author may have combined the works of several written accounts. The approximate dates of events in I and II Samuel can be estimated between the beginning of Samuel's birth around 1100 B.C. and the end of David's kingship in about 970 B.C. I and II Samuel were originally one book until the writing of the Septuagint, the Greek translation of the Hebrew Bible written during the third to the first century B.C. I Samuel is primarily about the prophet Samuel and the beginning of the kingships of Israel, first with King Saul and then with King David. II Samuel tells of David's reign as king. The prophet Samuel anointed both Saul and David before their reigns as king. He urged the Israelites to remember that human kings should not take the place of the Lord God. Samuel also reminded the Israelites of their covenant relationship with God, their heavenly King. I Samuel has 31 chapters.

Key Contents and Key Memory Verses with Study Dates

<u>I Samuel 1</u>: **Elkanah's wife, Hannah, cannot bear children, so she prays for a son,** and *"... she vowed a vow, and said, O Lord of hosts, if thou wilt indeed look on the affliction of thine handmaid, and remember me, and not forget thine handmaid, but wilt give unto thine handmaid a man child, then I will give him unto the Lord all the days of his life, and there shall no razor come upon his head"* (see 1:11) — Her prayer is answered, and she has a son, Samuel — She allows the priest Eli to raise Samuel since she has dedicated her son to the Lord.

<u>I Samuel 2</u>: **Hannah's joyful prayer and praise** (see 2:1-10).

January 19 (Day 19), Memory Verse #45
<u>I Samuel 2:2</u>:

THERE IS NONE HOLY AS THE LORD: FOR THERE IS NONE BESIDE THEE:
NEITHER IS THERE ANY ROCK LIKE OUR GOD.

— **Samuel** *"...did minister unto the Lord before Eli the priest"* (see 2:11) — The Lord blesses Hannah with three more sons and two daughters — *"And the child Samuel grew on, and was in favour both with the Lord, and also with men"* (see 2:26) — **A man of God visits the priest Eli** and warns of the destruction of his family, for Eli's sons are sinful, and Eli does not restrain them — The man of God prophesies, *"...this shall be a sign unto thee, that shall come upon thy two sons, on Hophni and Phinehas; in one day they shall die both of them. And I will raise me up a faithful priest, that shall do according to that which is in mine heart and in my mind: and I will build him a sure house; and he shall walk before mine anointed for ever"* (see 2:34-35).

<u>I Samuel 3</u>: **The Lord calls Samuel at night,** and three times, thinking it is Eli calling him, Samuel rises from bed and goes to Eli — Eli realizes the Lord is calling Samuel and tells Samuel to answer the Lord — The Lord calls Samuel again and shows him in a vision how He will judge Eli's house — The next morning, Samuel reluctantly tells Eli of this vision.

<u>I Samuel 4</u>: **Israel fights the Philistines, but approximately 4,000 Israelites are slain —** Before fighting the Philistines again, the Israelites bring the ark of the covenant from Shiloh — Again the Israelites are defeated with about 30,000 footmen slain, and the Philistines take the ark — **Eli's sons, Hophni and Phinehas, are killed in the battle — When a messenger tells Eli all the news, he falls backwards off his chair, breaks his neck, and dies** — Eli was 98 years of age and had judged Israel for forty years — Phinehas' wife goes into labor when she hears the news; her newborn son is named Ichabod, but she dies in childbirth.

I Samuel 5: The Philistines place the ark in the house of their god Dagon, but twice they find Dagon fallen before the ark — Also, tumors plague the people of Ashdod, Gath, and Ekron when the ark is in their cities.

I Samuel 6: The Philistines send a trespass offering and return the ark to the Israelite city of Beth-shemite — Many Israelites in Beth-shemite are slain by the Lord because they look into the ark of the Lord — The men of Beth-shemite send messengers to ask the people of Kirjath-jearim to retrieve the ark.

I Samuel 7: The ark stays in the house of Abindab in Kirjath-jearim for twenty years — *"And Samuel spake unto all the house of Israel, saying, If ye do return unto the Lord with all your hearts, then put away the strange gods and Ashtaroth from among you, and prepare your hearts unto the Lord, and serve him only: and he will deliver you out of the hand of the Philistines"* (see 7:3) — **The Lord helps Israel defeat the Philistines** while Samuel offers a burnt offering, and all the lands that the Philistines had taken from Israel are restored to Israel — Samuel judges Israel the rest of his life, and there is peace with the Philistines and the Amorites.

I Samuel 8: Samuel appoints his sons as judges in Israel, but they are wicked — **The Israelites beg Samuel for a king** — *"And the Lord said unto Samuel, Hearken unto the voice of the people in all that they say unto thee: for they have not rejected thee, but they have rejected me, that I should not reign over them"* (see 8:7) — The Lord tells Samuel to inform the Israelites how life would be if ruled by a king, the king demanding most of their possessions — Even in hearing of the hardships caused by kings, the people still ask for a king — The Lord tells Samuel He will allow the Israelites to have a king.

I Samuel 9: Kish, a Benjamite, *"...had a son, whose name was Saul, a choice young man, and a goodly (an impressive young man without equal, NIV): and there was not among the children of Israel a goodlier person than he: from his shoulders and upward he was higher than any of the people"* (see 9:2) — **Kish sends his son, Saul, to hunt for his lost donkeys** — Saul goes to the prophet Samuel to receive help in finding the lost donkeys — The Lord tells Samuel of Saul's coming and instructs him to anoint Saul as the future king of Israel — Samuel has food prepared for Saul and his servant before their arrival.

I Samuel 10: When Saul leaves Samuel's home the next morning, *"Samuel took a vial of oil, and poured it upon his head, and kissed him, and said, Is it not because the Lord hath anointed thee to be captain over his inheritance?"* (see 10:1) — Samuel also tells Saul of things that will happen on his journey home; *"And it was so, that when he had turned his back to go from Samuel, God gave him another heart: and all those signs came to pass that day. And when they came thither to the hill, behold, a company of prophets met him; and the Spirit of God came upon him, and he prophesied among them"* (see 10:9-10) — **Samuel calls the Israelites together to show them their new king Saul** — *"...And all the people shouted, and said, God save the king"* (see 10:24) — Then everyone goes to their homes, and Saul goes to his home in Gibeah accompanied by *"...a band of men, whose hearts God had touched"* (see 10:26).

I Samuel 11: Nadash, the Ammonite, encamps around Jabesh-gilead — The men of Jabesh-gilead ask Nadash to make a covenant with them, but Nadash says, *"...On this condition will I make a covenant with you, that I may thrust out all your right eyes, and lay it for a reproach upon all Israel"* (see 11:2) — When Saul learns about Nadash, he cuts up a yoke of oxen and sends it throughout Israel with a message that anyone who does not fight for Jabesh-gilead will have their oxen mutilated — **Saul leads the Israelites in defeating the Ammonites — Then Samuel tells the Israelites to come to Gilgal** — *"And all the people went to Gilgal; and there* *they made Saul king before the Lord in Gilgal; and there they sacrificed sacrifices of peace offerings before the Lord; and there Saul and all the men of Israel rejoiced greatly"* (see 11:15).

I Samuel 12: Samuel's speech to the Israelites (see 12:1-25) — Samuel first reviews some of Israel's history and says, *"If ye will fear the Lord, and serve him, and obey his voice, and not rebel against the commandment of the Lord, then shall both ye and also the king that reigneth over you continue following the Lord your God:"* (see 12:14).

January 20 (Day 20), Memory Verse #46
I Samuel 12:24:

ONLY FEAR THE LORD, AND SERVE HIM IN TRUTH WITH ALL YOUR HEART;
FOR CONSIDER HOW GREAT THINGS HE HATH DONE FOR YOU.

I Samuel 13: Saul's son, Jonathan, defeats a garrison of Philistines in Geba — When the rest of the Philistines hear of this, they prepare for war with Israel — But Israel scatters for they fear the Philistines — Saul waits seven days in Gilgal for Samuel's arrival, but he grows impatient and offers a peace offering before Samuel arrives — **Samuel reprimands Saul since Saul disobeyed the command to wait for Samuel to make the offering** — *"And Samuel said to Saul, Thou hast done foolishly: thou hast not kept the commandment of the Lord thy God, which he commanded thee: for now would the Lord have established thy kingdom upon Israel for ever. But now thy kingdom shall not continue: the Lord hath sought him a man after his own heart, and the Lord hath commanded him to be captain over his people, because thou hast not kept that which the Lord commanded thee"* (see 13:13-14).

I Samuel 14: Jonathan and his armor-bearer secretly defeat a garrison of the Philistines, and when their success is known, they are joined by the other Israelites — *"So the Lord saved Israel that day: and the battle passed over unto Beth-aven"* (see 14:23) — The Israelites are successful in defeating the Philistines from Michmash to Aijalon, but they are weak because of Saul's command for no one to eat until the evening — Saul builds an altar to the Lord and asks if he should continue to conquer the Philistines, but the Lord does not answer him — Saul learns that Jonathan had violated the king's command by eating honey before the evening — Saul states Jonathan must die, but the people will not allow it — **Saul fights against the Philistines the rest of his days and also wins many battles with other nations.**

I Samuel 15: The Lord commands Saul to destroy all of Amalek, taking no spoil — But Saul disobeys God when he spares King Agag's life and takes spoil which includes sheep and oxen — Saul explains the sheep and oxen are for a sacrifice to God, but Samuel says:

January 20 (Day 20), Memory Verse #47
I Samuel 15:22:

...BEHOLD, TO OBEY IS BETTER THAN SACRIFICE,
AND TO HEARKEN THAN THE FAT OF RAMS.

— Samuel informs Saul that he will not remain king because of his disobedience — Samuel kills King Agag — *"And Samuel came no more to see Saul until the day of his death: nevertheless Samuel mourned for Saul: and the Lord repented that he had made Saul king over Israel"* (see 15:35).

I Samuel 16: The Lord tells Samuel to go to Jesse of Bethlehem to anoint the next king — Samuel takes a heifer to sacrifice in Bethlehem so Saul will not suspect his main mission of anointing a future king — Samuel instructs Jesse to call all his sons together; the Lord tells Samuel not to consider physical appearance when choosing the one to be anointed.

January 21-22 (Days 21-22), Memory Verse #48
I Samuel 16:7:

...**FOR** THE LORD SEETH NOT AS MAN SEETH;
FOR MAN LOOKETH ON THE OUTWARD APPEARANCE,
BUT THE LORD LOOKETH ON THE HEART.

— David, who had been tending the sheep, is chosen from his other brothers — *"Then Samuel took the horn of oil, and anointed him in the midst of his brethren: and the Spirit of the Lord came upon David from that day forward..."* (see 16:13) — **An evil spirit falls on Saul, and at his servant's suggestion, Saul sends for David to play the harp** — *"And it came to pass, when the evil spirit from God was upon Saul, that David took an harp, and played with his hand: so Saul was refreshed, and was well, and the evil spirit departed from him"* (see 16:23) — Saul loves David greatly and makes David his armor-bearer.

I Samuel 17: **The Philistines challenge Israel to have one of their men fight the Philistine, Goliath,** who is almost 10 feet tall; Goliath says, *"...choose you a man for you, and let him come down to me. If he be able to fight with me, and to kill me, then will we be your servants: but if I prevail against him, and kill him, then shall ye be our servants, and serve us"* (see 17:8-9) — David's older brothers are in Saul's army, but David is back in Bethlehem tending the sheep — After Goliath challenges the Israelites for 40 days, Jesse sends David to his brothers to check on their welfare and to take them food — **David offers to fight Goliath** — Saul supplies David with armor, but David removes the armor since he is more comfortable in his own clothes with just his sling as a weapon — *"Then said David to the Philistine; Thou comest to me with a sword, and with a spear, and with a shield: but I come to thee in the name of the Lord of hosts, the God of the armies of Israel, whom thou hast defied. This day will the Lord deliver thee into mine hand;..."* (see 17:45-46) — David runs toward Goliath and kills him by slinging a stone into his forehead — The Philistines flee from the Israelites.

I Samuel 18: **Saul envies David since the people were praising David** by saying, *"...Saul hath slain his thousands, and David his ten thousands"* (see 18:7) — Saul is afraid David will become king and tries to kill David with his javelin as David is playing his harp for him — Saul promises his daughter Merab to David as a wife, but Saul gives Merab to another to marry — Then Saul promises his daughter Michal to David if David can deliver 100 Philistine foreskins; Saul thinks David will be killed by the Philistines — David surprises Saul by collecting 200 Philistine foreskins; therefore, Saul gives Michal to David for his wife.

I Samuel 19: *"And Saul spoke to Jonathan his son, and to all his servants, that they should kill David"* (see 19:1), but Jonathan persuades Saul not to have David killed — Over time, Saul throws his javelin again at David as he plays for him — Michal helps David escape since she knows Saul has ordered messengers to kill David in the morning — She disguises an image in David's bed to resemble David asleep — David goes to the prophet Samuel in Ramah — Saul sends messengers three times to Ramah to capture David, but each time *"...the Spirit of God was upon the messengers of Saul, and they also prophesied"* (see 19:20) — Saul decides to go to Ramah himself, and the Spirit of God also falls on him causing him to prophesy.

I Samuel 20: **Saul misses David at the king's table** — David and Jonathan had agreed to tell Saul that David has gone to Bethlehem to perform sacrifices with his kin — Saul is angry and throws a javelin at Jonathan since he knows Jonathan has befriended David — As already agreed upon with David who is hiding in a field, Jonathan shoots arrows beyond David instead of in front of him as a warning that Saul wants to kill him — David flees from Saul.

I Samuel 21:   David visits the priest Ahimelech who gives him hallowed bread and also Goliath's sword — David continues to flee Saul by going to Achish, the king of Gath — Achish's servants recognize David and tell the king — **David pretends to be a madman before King Achish** to prevent Achish from recognizing him.

I Samuel 22:   David flees to the Cave of Adullam where his family and many others join him; he leaves his mother and father with the king of Moab for safety — Then the prophet Gad tells David to go to Judah — Saul has 85 priests killed since Ahimelech helped David and did not tell Saul of David's location — Saul also destroys the people and livestock of Nob, the city of the priests — Abiathar, Ahimelech's son, escapes and warns David.

I Samuel 23:   *"…the Lord said unto David, Go, and smite the Philistines, and save Keilah"* (see 23:2) — After defeating the Philistines at Keilah, David flees since Saul knows his location and plans to capture him — **Jonathan and David make a covenant before the Lord while David hides in the wilderness** — Saul pursues David in the wilderness, but turns from hunting David due to the Philistines' attack on the land.

I Samuel 24:   Saul once again hunts David in the wilderness — **Saul goes into a cave in the wilderness, and David sneaks into the cave and secretly cuts off the skirt of Saul's robe** — When Saul comes out of the cave, David calls to him, *"Behold, this day thine eyes have seen how that the Lord had delivered thee to day into mine hand in the cave: and some bade me kill thee: but mine eye spared thee; and I said, I will not put forth mine hand against my lord; for he is the Lord's anointed"* (see 24:10) — David shows Saul the skirt to prove he meant Saul no harm — Saul weeps and declares he truly knows David will be made king.

I Samuel 25:   Samuel dies — Nabal, a rich sheepshearer of evil doings, refuses to help David and his men who need food, although David's men had helped protect Nabal's sheep — David and his men decide to kill Nabal, but Nabal's wife, Abigail, offers them gifts of food and convinces them to spare Nabal and the sheep — Nabal dies soon afterward, and David marries Abigail — David also marries Ahinoam of Jezreel — Saul had given David's wife Michal to Phalti.

I Samuel 26:   Saul continues hunting David in the wilderness — **As Saul sleeps, David takes Saul's spear and water jug, but does not harm Saul** — David then stands on a hill near Saul's camp and calls to Saul and the people — *"Then said Saul, I have sinned: return, my son David: for I will no more do thee harm, because my soul was precious in thine eyes this day: behold, I have played the fool, and have erred exceedingly"* (see 26:21).   David answers, *"The Lord render to every man his righteousness and his faithfulness: for the Lord delivered thee into my hand to day, but I would not stretch forth mine hand against the Lord's anointed"* (see 26:23) — *"…So David went on his way, and Saul returned to his place"* (see 26:25).

I Samuel 27:   David lives with the Philistines at Gath where Achish is king — David goes throughout the land killing many people of non-Israelite tribes — He leads King Achish to believe it is the Israelite tribes he is destroying so that the king would not cause him trouble.

I Samuel 28:   King Achish asks David to help him and the Philistine army fight against Israel — Saul disguises himself and consults a woman fortune teller at Endor to see how the battle will go between the Israelites and the Philistines — The *"woman that hath a familiar spirit"* (see 28:7) calls Samuel from the dead to appear to them — **Samuel does appear and tells Saul bad news;** *"Moreover the Lord will also deliver Israel with thee into the hand of the Philistines: and to morrow shalt thou and thy sons be with me: the Lord also shall deliver the* *host (army, NIV) of Israel into the hand of the Philistines"* (see 28:19) — Saul is so distraught he cannot eat until finally his servants and the woman fortune teller persuade him to eat — The fortune teller cooks a calf and bread for him.

I Samuel 29: The princes of the Philistines persuade king Achish to send David and his Hebrew followers away since they fear David and his men will turn against the Philistines in battle.

I Samuel 30: When David and his men return to Ziklag, he learns the Amalekites have burned the city and have taken their wives, sons, and daughters captive — David and his men attack and defeat the Amalekites, retrieving all their families and the spoil taken by the Amalekites.

I Samuel 31: The Philistines defeat Israel — Three of Saul's sons, one being Jonathan, die in battle — Then Saul is shot by an archer — Saul asks his armor-bearer to kill him with his sword, but his armor-bearer is afraid to do so — *"...Therefore Saul took a sword, and fell upon it. And when his armourbearer saw that Saul was dead, he fell likewise upon his sword, and died with him"* (see 31:4-5) — The Philistines cut off Saul's head and fasten his body with his sons' bodies on the wall of Beth-shan — *"All the valiant men arose, and went all night, and took the body of Saul and the bodies of his sons from the wall of Beth-shan, and came to Jabesh, and burnt them there. And they took their bones, and buried them under a tree at Jabesh, and fasted seven days"* (see 31:12-13).

I SAMUEL 16:7:

...FOR THE LORD SEETH NOT AS MAN SEETH; FOR MAN LOOKETH ON THE OUTWARD APPEARANCE, BUT THE LORD LOOKETH ON THE HEART.

II Samuel

Introduction: See the introduction to I Samuel — II Samuel tells of David's reign as king of the Israelites. II Samuel has 24 chapters.

Key Contents and Key Memory Verses with Study Dates

II Samuel 1:   When David returns to Ziklag after his victory over the Amalekites, a messenger brings the news of the death of Saul and Jonathan — The Amalekite messenger says he found Saul still alive although Saul had fallen on a sword; the messenger also tells David he killed Saul since Saul asked to be killed — David and the people mourn for Saul and Jonathan, and David has this messenger killed since he killed Saul, the Lord's anointed — **David continues to mourn over the death of Saul and Jonathan** (see 1:17-27) — *"Saul and Jonathan were lovely and pleasant in their lives, and in their death they were not divided: they were swifter than eagles, they were stronger than lions"* (see 1:23).

II Samuel 2:   David, his men, and their families travel to Hebron where David is crowned king of Judah— But Abner, who was captain of Saul's army, makes Saul's son, Ishbosheth, king of the rest of Israel — Ishbosheth only reigns two years — This division of Israel creates a war between the tribes.

II Samuel 3:   Abner becomes angry at Ishbosheth and decides to serve David — David insists Abner must return Michal to him before Abner can form a league with David; Abner agrees and brings Michal to David — **Joab and Abishai murder Abner** since Abner had killed their brother in a previous battle — David mourns Abner's death.

II Samuel 4: The news of the death of Saul and his son Jonathan had caused the nurse of Jonathan's son, Mephibosheth, to flee with him; while fleeing, the nurse dropped Mephibosheth which caused his permanent lameness — **Baanah and Rechab behead Ishbosheth and bring the head to David,** thinking David would be glad, but David has them killed for this act — *"And David commanded his young men, and they slew them, and cut off their hands and their feet, and hanged them up over the pool in Hebron. But they took the head of Ishbosheth, and buried it in the sepulchre of Abner in Hebron"* (see 4:12).

II Samuel 5:   David is anointed king by the elders of all Israel — *"David was thirty years old when he began to reign, and he reigned forty years. In Hebron he reigned over Judah seven years and six months: and in Jerusalem he reigned thirty and three years over all Israel and Judah"* (see 5:4-5) — **David captures Jerusalem and calls it the city of David** — David wins many battles against the Philistines.

II Samuel 6:   David retrieves the ark from Abinadab's house — Uzzah is stricken dead for touching the ark; therefore, David leaves the ark in Obededom's house and waits until he sees Obededom's family blessed before bringing the ark to Jerusalem — **David brings the ark to Jerusalem** with much celebration along with burnt and peace offerings — Michal is angry at David's joyous behavior because he uncovers himself before the eyes of his servants' handmaids during the celebration.

II Samuel 7:   The Lord tells the prophet Nathan to inform David of God's covenant to establish David's kingdom and to build a house for God through David's seed (see 7:4-17) — **David praises God** — *"Wherefore, thou art great, O Lord God: for there is none like thee, neither is there any God beside thee; according to all that we have heard with our ears. And what one nation in the earth is like thy people, even like Israel, whom God went to redeem for a people to himself, and to make him a name..."* (see 7:22-23).

II Samuel 8:   David defeats the Philistines and the people of Moab, Zobah, Syria, and Edom.

II Samuel 9:   David requests to see Mephibosheth, Jonathan's lame son — David gives Mephibosheth status as one of his sons with servants and permission to eat at the king's table.

II Samuel 10:   David sends men to Ammon to show kindness to their king Hanun, but Hanun humiliates the messengers and hires the Syrians to fight Israel — Israel defeats the Syrians, and peace is made between Israel and Syria.

II Samuel 11:   Israel defeats Ammon —   While looking from his palace, David sees a beautiful woman bathing on a rooftop — He learns she is Bathseba, Uriah's wife, and David sends for her and commits adultery — When David learns Bathsheba is pregnant by him, he sends for Uriah out of Joab's army and encourages him to go to his wife — Uriah will not go to Bathsheba since his comrades in the army are not privileged as he is to be at home — David persuades Uriah to become drunk, but Uriah still refuses to go to Bathsheba — David resorts to sending a letter to Joab by Uriah — *"And he wrote in the letter, saying, Set ye Uriah in the forefront of the hottest battle, and retire ye from him, that he may be smitten, and die"* (see 11:15) — Bathsheba mourns for Uriah after receiving news of his death — After the mourning period, David takes Bathsheba for his wife, and she bears a son — *"...But the thing that David had done displeased the Lord"* (see 11:27).

II Samuel 12:   The prophet Nathan scorns David with a story of a poor man mistreated by a rich man — David is angered by the rich man, then Nathan tells him the rich man represents David — Nathan tells David of God's punishment to come because of David's evil deeds — Part of the punishment includes the **death of David's baby** — *"And Nathan departed unto his house. And the Lord struck the child that Uriah's wife bare unto David, and it was very sick"* (see 12:15) — The child dies after seven days of sickness — *"And David comforted Bathsheba his wife, and went in unto her, and lay with her:* **and she bare a son, and he called his name Solomon: and the Lord loved him"** (see 12:24) — **Joab sends for David to help the Israelite army conquer the city of Rabbah in Ammon** —   The Israelites make the people of Rabbah slaves.

II Samuel 13:   David's son, Amnon, pretends to be ill, calls for his sister Tamar to feed him, and then rapes Tamar — **Absalom flees after having his brother Amnon killed for raping their sister, Tamar** — Absalom stays in Geshur three years, and David greatly misses him.

II Samuel 14:   Through the story of a wise women, Joab persuades King David to allow Absalom's return to Jerusalem — *"But in all Israel there was none to be so much praised as Absalom for his beauty: from the sole of his foot even to the crown of his head there was no blemish in him. And when he polled (cut, NIV) his head, (for it was at every year's end that he polled it: because the hair was heavy on him, therefore he polled it) he weighed the hair of his head at two hundred shekels after the king's weight"* (see 14:25-26). — But David refuses to see Absalom — After two more years, Absalom requests of Joab to have David send for him — *"So Joab came to the king, and told him and when he had called for Absalom, he came to the king, and bowed himself on his face to the ground before the king: and the king kissed Absalom"* (see 14:33).

II Samuel 15:   Absalom persuades many Israelites, including David's counselor, Ahithophel, to follow him, for he plans to become king in place of his father David — David flees into the wilderness with his men and prays, *"...O Lord, I pray thee, turn the counsel of Ahithophel into foolishness"* (see 15:31).

II Samuel 16-17: Ahithophel counsels Absalom to go into David's concubines, and Absalom does as Ahithophel suggested — Next Ahithophel asks Absalom to let him overtake David that very night, but Hushai, who is secretly for David, counsels Absalom to wait and gather all of Israel before overtaking David — **Absalom takes Hushai's advice;** *"...For the Lord had appointed to defeat the good counsel of Ahithophel, to the intent that the Lord might bring evil upon Absalom"* (see 17:14) — Hushai sends Ahimaaz and Jonathan to inform David — Ahimaaz and Jonathan must hide in a woman's well on the way to warn David since Absalom's servants were searching for them — Ahithophel hangs himself because Absalom rejected his advice to immediately overtake David.

II Samuel 18: **During battle, Absalom's hair is caught in an oak tree** when his mule rides under the thick boughs, and Absalom is left hanging in the tree — Although David had commanded his army to deal gently with Absalom, Joab takes three darts and thrusts them into Absalom's heart — Messengers are sent to David with the news of Absalom's death, and David mourns — *"...O my son Absalom, my son, my son Absalom! Would God I had died for thee, O Absalom, my son, my son!"* (see 18:33).

II Samuel 19: **David crosses back across the Jordan to return to Jerusalem** — There is still unrest in the kingdom of Israel.

II Samuel 20: **Sheba, a Benjamite, leads an insurrection against David** — David commands Amasa to assemble an army in three days, but Amasa does not carry out the order in the allotted time — Therefore, David commands Abishai to lead an army against Sheba — Joab kills Amasa — David's army finds Sheba in the town of Abel, and they batter the wall of Abel — A wise woman meets with Joab, the captain of the army, and persuades him to stop the attack on the city in exchange for Sheba — *"Then the woman went unto all the people in her wisdom. And they cut off the head of Sheba the son of Bichri, and cast it out to Joab. And he blew a trumpet and they retired from the city, every man to his tent. And Joab returned to Jerusalem unto the king"* (see 20:22).

II Samuel 21: **There is a famine for three years;** the Lord tells David the famine is a result of Saul's sin toward the Gibeonites — David allows the Gibeonites to hang seven sons of Saul's descendants to avenge the Gibeonites — David gathers the bones of Saul and Jonathan and buries them in the sepulcher of Kish, Saul's father — The famine ceases — David has many victories in battles against the Philistines.

II Samuel 22: **David's song** (see 22:1-51) — *"And David spake unto the Lord the words of this song in the day that the Lord had delivered him out of the hand of all his enemies, and out of the hand of Saul. And he said, The Lord is my rock, and my fortress, and my deliverer; The God of my rock; in him will I trust; he is my shield, and the horn of my salvation, my high tower, and my refuge, my saviour; thou savest me from violence"* (see 22:1-3).

January 23 (Day 23), Memory Verse #49
II Samuel 22:29:

FOR THOU ART MY LAMP, O LORD:
AND THE LORD WILL LIGHTEN MY DARKNESS.

January 23 (Day 23), Memory Verse #50
II Samuel 22:31:

AS FOR GOD, HIS WAY IS PERFECT; THE WORD OF THE LORD IS TRIED:
HE IS A BUCKLER TO THEM THAT TRUST IN HIM.

January 23 (Day 23), Memory Verse #51
II Samuel 22:34:

HE MAKETH MY FEET LIKE HINDS' FEET: AND SETTETH ME UPON MY HIGH PLACES.

— *"Thou hast also given me the shield of thy salvation: and thy gentleness hath made me great. Thou hast enlarged my steps under me; so that my feet did not slip"* (see 22:36-37).

January 23 (Day 23), Memory Verse #52
II Samuel 22:47:

THE LORD LIVETH; AND BLESSED BE MY ROCK;
AND EXALTED BE THE GOD OF THE ROCK OF MY SALVATION.

— *"Therefore I will give thanks unto thee, O Lord, among the heathen, and I will sing praises unto thy name. He is the tower of salvation for his king: and sheweth mercy to his anointed, unto David, and to his seed for evermore"* (see 22:50-51).

II Samuel 23: David's last words (see 23:1-7).

January 24 (Day 24), Memory Verses #53 & #54
II Samuel 23:3-4:

3. ...HE THAT RULETH OVER MEN MUST BE JUST, RULING IN THE FEAR OF GOD.

4. AND HE SHALL BE AS THE LIGHT OF THE MORNING,
WHEN THE SUN RISETH, EVEN A MORNING WITHOUT CLOUDS;
AS THE TENDER GRASS SPRINGING OUT OF THE EARTH
BY CLEAR SHINING AFTER RAIN.

— **The names of David's mighty men** (see 23:8-39).

II Samuel 24: Against the will of the Lord, David has a census taken of Israel — The prophet Gad gives David three choices of punishment for taking the census; the three choices are seven years of famine (I Chronicles 21:12 says, "three years' famine"), fleeing the enemy for three months, or a plague in the land for three days — David chooses a plague in the land for three days — David repents when he sees the angel of the Lord killing the people, and he builds an altar unto the Lord — The plague ceases.

II SAMUEL 22:29:

FOR THOU ART MY LAMP, O LORD: AND THE LORD WILL LIGHTEN MY DARKNESS.

I KINGS

Introduction: Jewish tradition holds Jeremiah as the author of I and II Kings which were thought to be written sometime during the 500's B.C., but the authorship and date are really unknown. Originally one book, I and II Kings are the history of King Solomon and the kings of the divided kingdom of Israel. In the divided kingdom, the northern kingdom continued to be called Israel while the southern kingdom was called Judah. Sometimes the scripture refers to both kingdoms as Israel. The kingdom divided in 931 B.C. after King Solomon's rule. The northern kingdom of Israel consisted of 10 tribes. The southern kingdom of Judah consisted of the two remaining Israelite tribes, Judah and Benjamin. The events of I and II Kings began just before King David's death, approximately 965 B.C., and lasted till the Babylonian captivity of the southern kingdom of Judah in 586 B.C. The northern kingdom of Israel had fallen to Assyria in 722 B.C. During the division of the Israelite nation, 20 kings ruled the northern kingdom of Israel and 19 kings and one queen ruled the southern kingdom of Judah.   I Kings has 22 chapters.

Kings of Israel: JEROBOAM I, NADAB, BAASHA, ELAH, ZIMRI, OMRI, TIBNI, AHAB, AHAZIAH, JEHORAM also known as Joram, JEHU, JEHOAHAZ, JEHOASH, JEROBOAM II, ZECHARIAH, SHALLUM, MENAHEM, PEKAHIAH, PEKAH, and HOSHEA.

Kings and Queen of Judah: REHOBOAM, ABIJAH, ASA, JEHOSHAPHAT, JEHORAM also known as Joram, AHAZIAH, ATHALIAH (queen), JOASH, AMAZIAH , UZZIAH also known as Azariah, JOTHAM, AHAZ, HEZEKIAH, MANASSEH, AMON, JOSIAH, JEHOAHAZ, JEHOIAKIM also known as Eliakim, JEHOIACHIN, and ZEDEKIAH.

Eight of the kings of Judah were known as good kings: Asa, Jehoshaphat, Joash, Amaziah, Uzziah, Jotham, Hezekiah, and Josiah.

Note: The study of the kings of Israel and Judah can be confusing since each kingdom had a king by the name of Ahaziah, Jehoram, and Jehoahaz. And many of the names are similar such as Jeroboam and Rehoboam, Ahaziah and Amaziah, Jehoash and Joash, Ahab and Ahaz, and Jehoiakim and Jehoiachin. Also, some of the kings are known by two names.

Key Contents and Key Memory Verses with Study Dates

I Kings 1: David is very old, so a virgin named Abishag is brought to him to minister to him and keep him warm — **David's son, Adonijah, attempts becoming king** — Adonijah gathers all the king's sons, Joab who is the captain of the army, and the priest Abiathar to have a banquet and crown himself king; he does not invite his brother Solomon, Nathan the prophet, Zadok the priest, Benaiah, and David's mighty men — The prophet Nathan warns Bathsheba concerning Adonijah, and she tells David to make Solomon king — *"And David said, Call me Zadok the priest, and Nathan the prophet, and Benaiah the son of Jehoiada. And they came before the king. The king also said unto them, Take with you the servants of your lord, and cause Solomon my son to ride upon mine own mule, and bring him down to Gihon: And let Zadok the priest and Nathan the prophet anoint him there king over Israel: and blow ye with the trumpet, and say, God save king Solomon"* (see 1:32-34) — David's orders are carried out — When the people gather for Adonijah's feast, they hear the trumpets and **news of Solomon being crowned king** — After hearing this news, they disband, and Adonijah asks Solomon to spare his life — Solomon agrees to spare Adonijah as long as he is worthy and does not practice wickedness.

I Kings 2: Before his death, David gives Solomon advice (see 2:1-12).

January 25-27 (Days 25-27), Memory Verse #55
I Kings 2:3:

AND KEEP THE CHARGE OF THE LORD THY GOD,
TO WALK IN HIS WAYS, TO KEEP HIS STATUTES,
AND HIS COMMANDMENTS, AND HIS JUDGMENTS, AND HIS TESTIMONIES,
AS IT IS WRITTEN IN THE LAW OF MOSES,
THAT THOU MAYEST PROSPER IN ALL THAT THOU DOEST,
AND WHITHERSOEVER THOU TURNEST THYSELF:

— Solomon has Adonijah killed for plotting against him, and he has Abiathar banished as priest and exiled to Anathoth for siding with Adonijah — Solomon also commands Benaiah to kill Joab because Joab had murdered two captains of the host of David's army, Abner and Amasa — Benaiah takes Joab's place as captain of the army, and Zadok takes Abiathar's place as priest — Solomon also has Benaiah kill Shimei who had broken an oath with Solomon.

I Kings 3: Solomon takes Pharaoh's daughter — Solomon's Wisdom — Solomon goes to Gibeon to sacrifice to the Lord — *"In Gibeon the Lord appears to Solomon in a dream by night: and God said, Ask what I shall give thee"* (see 3:5) — **Solomon replies, "Give therefore thy servant an understanding heart to judge thy people,** that I may discern between good and bad: for who is able to judge this thy so great a people? And the speech pleased the Lord, that Solomon had asked this thing"* (see 3:9-10) — And the Lord tells Solomon, *"And I have also given thee that which thou hast not asked, both riches, and honour: so that there shall not be any among the kings like unto thee all thy days. And if thou wilt walk in my ways, to keep my statutes and my commandments, as thy father David did walk, then I will lengthen thy days. And Solomon awoke; and behold, it was a dream. And he came to Jerusalem, and stood before the ark of the covenant of the Lord, and offered up burnt offerings, and offered peace offerings, and made a feast to all his servants"* (see 3:13-15) — **Two harlots come to Solomon, both claiming they are the mother of a certain child —** *"And the king said, Bring me a sword. And they brought a sword before the king. And the king said, Divide the living child in two, and give half to the one, and half to the other. Then spake the woman whose the living child was unto the king, for her bowels yearned upon her son, and she said, O my lord, give her the living child, and in no wise slay it. But the other said, Let it be neither mine nor thine, but divide it. Then the king answered and said, Give her the living child, and in no wise slay it: she is the mother thereof. And all Israel heard of the judgment which the king had judged; and they feared the king: for they saw that the wisdom of God was in him, to do judgment"* (see 3:24-28).

I Kings 4: Lists of Solomon's princes, priests, officers, and things of his kingdom — *"And God gave Solomon wisdom and understanding exceeding much,** and largeness of heart, even as the sand that is on the sea shore"* (see 4:29) — *"...and his fame was in all nations round about. And he spake three thousand proverbs: and his songs were a thousand and five"* (see 4:31-32) — *"And there came of all people to hear the wisdom of Solomon, from all kings of the earth, which had heard of his wisdom"* (see 4:34).

I Kings 5: Solomon begins gathering timber and stones for building the temple — Hiram, the king of Tyre, provides cedar trees and fir trees for the temple — Solomon has thousands of workers gather the timber and hew the great stones for building the temple.

I Kings 6: Solomon completes the temple in 7 years — The magnificent temple is described.

I Kings 7: Solomon works on his home for 13 years — Solomon's home is described — The beautiful objects of brass and gold made for the temple are described — *"So was ended all which David his father had dedicated; even the silver, and the gold, and the vessels, did he put among the treasures of the house of the Lord"* (see 7:51).

I Kings 8:   The ark of the covenant is brought into the temple, and a cloud fills the house of the Lord *"...for the glory of the Lord had filled the house of the Lord"* (see 8:11) — *"And Solomon stood before the altar of the Lord in the presence of all the congregation of Israel, and spread forth his hands toward heaven: And he said, Lord God of Israel, there is no God like thee, in heaven above, or on earth beneath, who keepest covenant and mercy with thy servants that walk before thee with all their heart:"* (see 8:22-23) — **Solomon prays to God for Israel and gives a speech to the Israelites** — *"Blessed be the Lord, that hath given rest unto his people Israel, according to all that he promised: there hath not failed one word of all his good promise, which he promised by the hand of Moses his servant"* (see 8:56) — *"Let your heart therefore be perfect with the Lord our God, to walk in his statutes, and to keep his commandments, as at this day"* (see 8:61) — *"And Solomon offered a sacrifice of peace offerings, which he offered unto the Lord, two and twenty thousand oxen, and an hundred and twenty thousand sheep. So the Lord and all the children of Israel dedicated the house of the Lord"* (see 8:63) — There is feasting for seven days, and on the eighth day, the people *"...went unto their tents joyful and glad of heart for all the goodness that the Lord had done for David his servant, and for Israel his people"* (see 8:66).

I Kings 9:   God's covenant with Solomon — Solomon gives 20 cities to Hiram, the king of Tyre — Hiram is not pleased with the cities, yet he gives Solomon a gift of gold — Solomon's servants and officials of his kingdom are mentioned — Solomon's navy joins with Hiram's navy.

I Kings 10:   Hearing of Solomon's fame, the queen of Sheba visits Solomon, bringing gifts and testing him with hard questions — She is amazed and tells Solomon, *"Happy are thy men, happy are these thy servants, which stand continually before thee, and that hear thy wisdom. Blessed be the Lord thy God, which delighted in thee, to set thee on the throne of Israel: because the Lord loved Israel for ever, therefore made he thee king, to do judgment and justice"* (see 10:8-9) — **Solomon's riches are described.**

I Kings 11:   Solomon *"...had seven hundred wives, princesses, and three hundred concubines: and his wives turned away his heart. For it came to pass,* **when Solomon was old, that his wives turned away his heart after other gods:** *and his heart was not perfect with the Lord his God, as was the heart of David his father"* (see 11:3-4) — **Solomon's kingdom crumbles due to his breaking the covenant with God — The prophet Ahijah tears Jeroboam's garment into twelve pieces** and tells him, *"...Take thee ten pieces: for thus saith the Lord, the God of Israel, Behold, I will rend the kingdom out of the hand of Solomon, and will give ten tribes to thee: (But he shall have one tribe for my servant David's sake, and for Jerusalem's sake, the city which I have chosen out of all the tribes of Israel:)"* (see 11:31-32) — *"And the time that Solomon reigned in Jerusalem over all Israel was forty years.* **And Solomon slept with his fathers, and was buried in the city of David his father: and Rehoboam his son reigned in his stead"** (see 11:42-43).

I Kings 12:   Jeroboam and the congregation of Israel tell Rehoboam, *"Thy father made our yoke grievous: now therefore make thou the grievous service of thy father, and his heavy yoke which he put upon us, lighter, and we will serve you"* (see 12:4) — But Rehoboam takes the advice of the foolish young men over the advice of the wise older men who had served with Solomon, and proclaims his yoke upon the people will be even heavier than Solomon's yoke — Therefore, the kingdom splits — **JEROBOAM I (1st king of the northern kingdom of Israel)** is made king over the 10 northern tribes of Israel while **REHOBOAM (1st king of the southern kingdom of Judah)** is king over the southern tribes of Judah and Benjamin **(The northern kingdom is called Israel and the southern kingdom is called Judah for the remainder of I and II Kings)** — Jeroboam I makes two golden calves and builds altars to worship these idols in Bethel and Dan; *"And this thing became a sin:..."* (see 12:30) — He also chooses priests who are not Levites.

I Kings 13: A man of God prophesies of Josiah's birth and warns Jeroboam concerning the altar in Bethel — Jeroboam reaches out his hand and commands the man of God to be seized, but Jeroboam's hand is *"...dried up, so that he could not pull it in again to him"* (see 13:4) — The altar is rent and the ashes are poured out as the man of God had prophesied, and Jeroboam pleads for his hand to be restored, and it is so — The man of God would not stay with Jeroboam because God commanded him not to eat or drink water in Bethel — **An old prophet of Bethel tricks the man of God** into eating with him by saying an angel told him to feed the man of God — A lion kills the man of God as punishment for disobedience, and the old prophet proclaims that the man of God was truly sent by God.

I Kings 14: Jeroboam's son, Abijah, becomes very sick — **Jeroboam sends his wife in disguise to Shiloh to see the prophet Ahijah** — Ahijah tells her that her son will die when she returns, and the Lord will raise up another king over Israel because of Jeroboam's great sins — *"And the days which Jeroboam reigned were two and twenty years: and he slept with his fathers, and Nadab his son reigned in his stead"* (see 14:20) — Rehoboam rules 17 years in Jerusalem and also does evil, worshipping many gods — **Shishak, king of Egypt, steals all the treasures of the house of the Lord and of Solomon's house** — *"And there was war between Rehoboam and Jeroboam all their days. **And Rehoboam slept with his fathers,** and was buried with his fathers in the city of David..."* (see 14:30-31).

I Kings 15: Rehoboam's son, **ABIJAH (2nd king of Judah),** rules in Jerusalem three years, *"And he walked in all the sins of his father..."* (see 15:3) — Then Abijah's son, **ASA (3rd king of Judah),** rules in Jerusalem 41 years; *"...Asa's heart was perfect with the Lord all his days"* (see 15:14) — Asa removes the idols from the land — **NADAB (2nd king of Israel)** reigns over Israel for two years, but **BAASHA (3rd king of Israel)** kills Nadab and all of Jeroboam's family; then Baasha becomes king — Both Nadab and Baasha were evil in the sight of the Lord — *"And there was war between Asa and Baasha king of Israel all their days"* (see 15:32).

I Kings 16: The prophet Jehu predicts the destruction of Baasha's house — Baasha's son, **ELAH (4th king of Israel),** is made king of Israel when Baasha dies, but he reigns only two years — Elah's servant, **ZIMRI (5th king of Israel),** kills Elah while Elah is drunk — After becoming king, Zimri destroys the family of Baasha, thus fulfilling Jehu's prophecy — Then all of Israel hears of Zimri's conspiracy and makes **OMRI (6th king of Israel)** their king who reigns for 12 years — Zimri had only reigned seven days when Omri besieged Tirzah, the city where Zimri ruled — *"And it came to pass, when Zimri saw that the city was taken, that he went into the palace of the king's house, and burnt the king's house over him with fire, and died"* (see 16:18) — **TIBNI (7th king of Israel)** — *"Then were the people of Israel divided into two parts: half of the people followed Tibni the son of Ginath, to make him king; and half followed Omri. But the people that followed Omri prevailed against the people that followed Tibni the son of Ginath: so Tibni died, and Omri reigned"* (see 16:21-22) — *"But Omri wrought evil in the eyes of the Lord, and did worse than all that were before him"* (see 16:25) — Omri's wicked son, **AHAB (8th king of Israel),** reigns for 22 years over Israel with his evil wife, Jezebel, by his side — *"...Ahab did more to provoke the Lord God of Israel to anger than all the kings of Israel that were before him"* (see 16:33).

I Kings 17: The prophet Elijah warns Ahab of a coming drought — The Lord tells Elijah to go to the brook Cherith, and as the Lord had promised, there is water, and the ravens feed Elijah bread and flesh — The brook dries up, and the Lord tells Elijah to go to Zarephath where a widow will feed him   — When Elijah meets the widow, she tells him she has only a handful of meal and just a little oil — As instructed by God, Elijah causes the barrel of meal and the cruse of oil to continually be replenished until the end of the drought — The widow's son dies; Elijah cries to God, and her son rises from the dead.

I Kings 18: **Elijah has the prophet Obadiah tell Ahab he has come to see Ahab** (It was Obadiah who had hidden and fed 100 prophets in caves to prevent Jezebel from killing them) — Elijah meets with Ahab, and Ahab agrees to gather the people of Israel and the Baal prophets at Mount Carmel — Elijah asks all the people, *"How long halt ye between two opinions? If the Lord be God, follow him: but if Baal, then follow him..."* (see 18:21) — **Elijah challenges the 450 Baal prophets** by having them build an altar to Baal while he builds an altar to God; they agree that the sacrifice which is consumed by fire will show the true God — The Baal prophets build their altar and pray to Baal all day, even cutting their bodies with knives, but there is no response from their god — Elijah places twelve stones, representing the twelve tribes of Israel, on the altar he has built to God — Elijah has four barrels filled three times each with water and poured over the sacrifice and the wood on the altar — Elijah prays, *"...Lord God of Abraham, Isaac, and of Israel, let it be known this day that thou art God in Israel, and that I am thy servant, and that I have done all these things at thy word. Hear me, O Lord, hear me, that this people may know that thou art the Lord God, and that thou hast turned their heart back again. Then the fire of the Lord fell, and consumed the burnt sacrifice, and the wood, and the stones, and the dust, and licked up the water that was in the trench. And when all the people saw it, they fell on their faces:* **and they said, The Lord, he is the God; the Lord, he is the God**" (see 18:36-39) — Elijah has all the Baal prophets killed at the brook Kishon.

I Kings 19: **Jezebel determines to kill Elijah when she hears that Elijah has slain the Baal prophets** — Elijah wanders in the wilderness to hide from Jezebel and grows weary — The angel of the Lord feeds Elijah — God tells Elijah to stand upon Mount Horeb — At Mount Horeb, Elijah experiences a great wind, an earthquake, and fire, but he does not sense God; when there is a still small voice, he hears God's calling — **God tells Elijah to anoint Hazael to be king over Syria, Jehu to be king over Israel, and Elisha to be Israel's prophet after Elijah.**

I Kings 20: **The Lord is with Ahab as he defeats the Syrians who are led by Ben-hadad** — **A prophet appears to Ahab disguised as a wounded soldier,** but Ahab discerns he is a prophet — The prophet warns Ahab that he and his people must die because he made a covenant with Ben-hadad and let him live.

I Kings 21: **Naboth refuses to give Ahab his vineyard, so Jezebel has Naboth falsely accused of blaspheming both God and the king, and then she has him stoned** — Ahab possesses the vineyard, and Elijah appears to him in the vineyard with prophecies from the Lord: *"...In the place where dogs licked the blood of Naboth shall dogs lick thy blood, even thine"* (see 21:19); *"...The dogs shall eat Jezebel by the wall of Jezreel"* (see 21:23) — *"But there was none like unto Ahab, which did sell himself to work wickedness in the sight of the Lord, whom Jezebel his wife stirred up"* (see 21:25) — **Ahab repents of his sin** and humbles himself before the Lord; therefore, the Lord postpones for a while the evil that awaits Ahab's house.

I Kings 22: Ahab and **JEHOSHAPHAT (4th king of Judah)** join together to fight the Syrians — The prophet Micaiah warns that Ahab will be killed in battle — Ahab disguises himself to keep from being recognized as the king in battle, but he is slain in a chariot; then Elijah's prophecy comes true, *"...the dogs licked up the blood;..."* (see 22:38) — Jehoshaphat rules Judah 25 years, and he did *"...that which was right in the eyes of the Lord:..."* (see 22:43); when he dies he is buried in the city of David — His son, **JEHORAM (5th king of Judah),** becomes king — Ahab's son, **AHAZIAH (9th king of Israel),** reigns over Israel for two years, *"And he did evil in the sight of the Lord..."* (see 22:52).

II KINGS

Introduction: See I Kings' introduction. II Kings tells of the continued downfall and captivity of both the northern kingdom of Israel and the southern kingdom of Judah. II Kings has 25 chapters.

Key Contents and Key Memory Verses with Study Dates

II Kings 1: AHAZIAH (9th king of Israel) falls through a lattice in his upper chamber and is confined to bed — Elijah sends a message to Ahaziah, rebuking him for seeking advice from the god, Baal-zebub, rather than God concerning his recovery — Elijah is described as *"an hairy man, and girt with a girdle of leather about his loins"* (see 1:8) — Ahaziah sends a captain with his fifty men to Elijah, but fire from heaven consumes them — Ahaziah sends another captain with his fifty men, and once again Elijah calls the fires of heaven which consume them — The third time Ahaziah sends a captain of fifty men to Elijah, the captain begs for mercy, so Elijah goes with him to Ahaziah — Elijah prophesies that Ahaziah will not recover from his accident and will soon die; this prophecy comes to pass — **JEHORAM, also known as Joram (10th Israel king)**, becomes king since there are no sons of Ahaziah, his late brother.

II Kings 2: Elijah and Elisha journey via Bethel, Jericho, and Jordan to where Elijah would be taken to heaven — On the journey, many prophets tell Elisha how Elijah must depart that day — Elijah parts the Jordan waters by striking the water with his mantle; Elijah and Elisha cross the Jordan where the waters are parted — *"And it came to pass, as they still went on, and talked, that, behold, **there appeared a chariot of fire, and horses of fire, and parted them both asunder; and Elijah went up by a whirlwind into heaven**"* (see 2:11) — Elisha keeps Elijah's mantle and also parts the Jordan waters — Fifty men search for Elijah three days but cannot find the prophet — Elisha places salt in the water of Jericho, and the Lord heals the polluted waters — In Bethel, young people mock Elisha by saying, *"...Go up, thou bald head; go up, thou bald head. And he turned back, and looked on them, and cursed them in the name of the Lord. And there came forth two she bears out of the wood, and tare forty and two children (youths, NIV) of them"* (see 2:23-24).

II Kings 3: Israel's king, Jehoram (Joram), and Judah's King, Jehoshaphat, join to fight Moab, and they defeat Moab with Elisha's advice from God to dig many ditches — Seeing water in the ditches, the Moabites think it is blood, and they proceed to take spoil because they believe the battle has already been fought — But the men of Israel and Judah ambush the Moabites and cause them to flee — The king of Moab *"...took his eldest son that should have reigned in his stead, and offered him for a burnt offering upon the wall. And there was great indignation against Israel: and they departed from him, and returned to their own land"* (see 3:27).

II Kings 4: The son of a prophet dies, and his widow asks Elisha for help — Elisha tells the widow to gather as many vessels as possible from her neighbors, and miraculously the widow fills all the vessels by pouring what little oil she has into them — The oil is enough to pay her debts and to prevent her sons from serving as bondmen — **Elisha becomes friends with a Shunamite family and tells the wife she will have a son** — This prophecy comes true, but when the son is grown, he dies from a fall — The Shunamite mother sends for Elisha who raises her son from the dead — **Elisha purifies pottage and provides food during a famine at Gilgal.**

II Kings 5: Naaman, captain of the Syrian army, travels to see Elisha to be healed of leprosy — Naaman is angry when Elisha tells him to wash in the Jordan River seven times because he wanted Elisha to immediately call on God to heal him, and he preferred other rivers in which to wash — Naaman's servants tell him *"...My father, if the prophet had bid thee do some great thing, wouldest thou not have done it?..."* (see 5:13) — When Naaman obeys, he is healed — Elisha refuses to accept Naaman's gifts — Elisha's servant, Gehazi, follows Naaman to ask for the presents which Elisha refused and falsely says Elisha now wants the silver and garments — Elisha is angered by this, and Gehazi is striken with leprosy.

II Kings 6: **The sons of the prophets go to the Jordan to cut timber for making a larger dwelling — One of the workers loses his axe head when it slings into the Jordan River —** Elisha "...*said, Where fell it? And he shewed him the place. And he cut down a stick, and cast it in thither; and* **the iron did swim**" (see 6:6) — **The Syrians try to capture the Israelites,** but Elisha keeps the king of Israel informed as to the Syrians' locations — Therefore, the king of Syria sends his servants to find Elisha — Elisha prays, and the Lord causes one of the servants to see "*...the mountain was full of horses and chariots of fire round about Elisha*" (see 6:17) — Elisha prays again, and the servants become blind and are led to Samaria — The king of Israel feeds the servants and sends them back to Syria — **Ben-hadad, king of Syria, besieges Samaria** — Food is so scarce in Samaria that some eat their own children — The king of Israel becomes angry at Elisha and sends messengers to behead him; Elisha promises the Lord will cease the famine the next day, and he is not beheaded — One of the messengers mocks this prophecy.

II Kings 7: **Four lepers journey into the camp of the Syrians, but there is no one there —** "*For the Lord had made the host of the Syrians to hear a noise of chariots, and a noise of horses, even the noise of a great host: and they said one to another, Lo, the king of Israel hath hired against us the kings of the Hittites, and the kings of the Egyptians, to come upon us. Wherefore they arose and fled in the twilight, and left their tents, and their horses, and their asses, even the camp as it was, and fled for their life*" (see 7:6-7) — The lepers take spoil and decide to report their finding to the king of Israel — The king sends servants to the Syrian camp but fears the Syrians are plotting an ambush — When the servants return safely, the Israelites go to the Syrian tents and take spoil — Elisha's prediction that Samaria's famine would cease comes true, and the one who mocked his prophecy is trampled and killed at the city gate.

II Kings 8: **Elisha predicts a famine of seven years and tells the Shunamite woman to journey to another place —** She lives in the land of the Philistines, returning after the famine, and the king gives her land and house back to her — **Ben-hadad, the king of Syria, becomes ill** — He sends Hazael with presents to Elisha to ask if he will recover from his illness — Elisha sends Hazael back to Ben-hadad to inform him that he will recover, but Elisha knows Ben-hadad is going to die — Elisha also reveals to Hazael that he will be Syria's next king — "*So he departed from Elisha, and came to his master; who said to him, What said Elisha to thee? And he answered, He told me that thou shouldest surely recover. And it came to pass on the morrow, that he took a thick cloth, and dipped it in water, and spread it on his face, so that he died: and Hazael reigned in his stead*" (see 8:14 -15) — **JEHORAM, also known as JORAM (5th king of Judah),** follows Jehoshaphat as king and reigns for eight years in Jerusalem — Jehoram battles the Edomites — The son of Jehoram, **AHAZIAH (6th king of Judah),** becomes king and reigns only one year, "*And he walked in the way of the house of Ahab, and did evil in the sight of the Lord...*" (see 8:27).

II Kings 9: Elisha tells a prophet's child to take oil to Ramoth-gilead and anoint **JEHU (11th king of Israel)** as king of Israel — **Jehu kills Jehoram,** the tenth king of Israel, by shooting an arrow into him as they fight in chariots — Judah's king, Ahaziah, is also present in a chariot but flees — **Jehu has his men follow Ahaziah and kill him, also** — Ahaziah's servants take his body to Jerusalem to be buried "*...in his sepulchre with his fathers in the city of David*" (see 9:28) — **Jehu travels to Jezreel in search of Jezebel, and the eunuchs with Jezebel obey Jehu's command to cast her out of the window** — Then dogs eat Jezebel's flesh which fulfills Elijah's prophecy found in I Kings 21:23.

II Kings 10: **Jehu has Ahab's 70 sons beheaded and the rest of Ahab's family killed,** thus fulfilling Elijah's prophecy concerning the destruction of Ahab's house — Jehu calls an assembly of all Baal worshippers who do not suspect Jehu's real intention — Then Jehu has his men kill with swords all the Baal worshippers, making sure none of the servants of the Lord are present — And they burn the images of Baal and tear down the house of Baal — *"Thus Jehu destroyed Baal out of Israel"* (see 10:28), but does not *"...walk in the law of the Lord God of Israel with all his heart: for he departed not from the sins of Jeroboam which made Israel to sin"* (see 10:31) — Jehu reigns in Israel 28 years and is buried in Samaria — Jehu's son, Jehoahaz, becomes king.

II Kings 11: When Athaliah, Ahaziah's mother, learns of his death, she destroys all heirs of the throne except for Joash, Ahaziah's son — Ahaziah's sister, Jehosheba, hides Joash from Athaliah who does not realize one of Ahaziah's sons is still alive — **ATHALIAH (7th ruler of Judah)** becomes queen of Judah — The priest Jehoiada gathers the rulers and captains of Judah's army and shows them Joash, the king's son, who has been hidden for six years — They guard the temple and crown **JOASH, also known as Jehoash (8th ruler of Judah),** king at age seven — Athaliah comes to the temple when she hears the noise of the crowd and is surprised to learn Joash is alive — Athaliah is taken from the temple and is killed.

II Kings 12: **Joash (Jehoash) reigns 40 years in Judah** — *"And Jehoash did that which was right in the sight of the Lord all his days wherein Jehoiada the priest instructed him"* (see 12:2) — Jehoash allows the people to give according to their hearts for repairing the temple — Jehoash's servants kill him, and he is buried in the city of David — Jehoash's son, Amaziah, becomes king.

II Kings 13: **Reign of JEHOAHAZ (12th king of Israel)** — *"And he did that which was evil in the sight of the Lord..."* (see 13:2) — Israel is ruled by Syria most of Jehoahaz' reign — Jehoahaz is buried in Samaria, and his son **JEHOASH, also known as Joash (13th king of Israel),** reigns 16 years — Jehoash also *"...did that which was evil in the sight of the Lord;..."* (see 13:11) — Joash, king of Israel, fights against Amaziah, king of Judah — Joash visits sick Elisha just before his death — Elisha commands Joash to shoot an arrow and then strike the ground to determine whether Joash will defeat Syria — Elisha prophesies Joash will defeat Syria, but only three times, since Joash struck the ground only three times — After Elisha dies, a dead man cast into the sepulcher of Elisha is resurrected when his body touches the bones of Elisha.

II Kings 14: Joash's son, **AMAZIAH (9th ruler of Judah),** is king of Judah for 29 years and *"...did that which was right in the sight of the Lord..."* (see 14:3) — Amaziah is defeated by Jehoash, king of Israel, in battle — Jehoash *"...took all the gold and silver, and all the vessels that were found in the house of the Lord, and in the treasures of the king's house, and hostages, and returned to Samaria"* (see 14:14) — Jehoash dies and is buried in Samaria — Jehoash's son, **JEROBOAM II (14th king of Israel),** becomes king of Israel for 41 years — Amaziah lives 15 more years after Jehoash's death — The people of Jerusalem conspire against Amaziah; he flees to Lachish, but the people find and kill him — They return his body to Jerusalem for burial — Amaziah's son, **AZARIAH, also known as Uzziah (10th ruler of Judah),** becomes king of Judah for 52 years — Jeroboam II, king of Israel, *"...did that which was evil in the sight of the Lord..."* (see 14:24) — At Jeroboam II's death, his son, Zachariah, becomes king.

II Kings 15: Azariah (Uzziah) *"...did that which was right in the sight of the Lord, according to all that his father Amaziah had done"* (see 15:3) — The Lord causes Azariah to have leprosy (see II Chronicles 26:17-21), so he lives in a house to himself — Jotham, Azariah's son, judges the people of the land during Azariah's reign — Azariah is buried in Jerusalem, and **JOTHAM (11th ruler of Judah)** becomes king of Judah — Jeroboam II's son, **ZECHARIAH (15th king of Israel),** rules as king of Israel for six months; *"...he did that which was evil in the sight of the*

Lord..." (see 15:9) — *"And **SHALLUM**"* (**16th king of Israel**) *"the son of Jabesh conspired against him, and smote him before the people, and slew him, and reigned in his stead"* (see 15:10) for only one month — *"For **MENAHEM**"* (**17th king of Israel**) *"the son of Gadi went up from Tirzah, and came to Samaria, and smote Shallum the son of Jabesh in Samaria and slew him, and reigned in his stead"* (see 15:14) — Menahem reigns ten years in Samaria and *"...did that which was evil in the sight of the Lord:..."* (see 15:18) — Menahem gives Assyria money to keep the Assyrians from capturing Israel — After Menahem's death, his son, **PEKAHIAH (18th king of Israel),** reigns as Israel's king for two years, *"And he did that which was evil in the sight of the Lord:..."* (see 15:24) — *"But **PEKAH**"* (**19th king of Israel**) *"the son of Remaliah, a captain of his, conspired against him, and smote him in Samaria, in the palace of the king's house, with Argob and Arieh, and with him fifty men of the Gileadites: and he killed him, and reigned in his room"* (see 15:25) — After killing Pekahiah, Pekah reigns for 20 years and *"...did that which was evil in the sight of the Lord:..."* (see 15:28) — Assyria captures much of Israel's land during Pekah's reign — *"And **HOSHEA**"* (**20th king of Israel**) *"the son of Elah made a conspiracy against Pekah the son of Remaliah, and smote him, and slew him, and reigned in his stead..."* (see 15:30) — Jotham reigns as king of Judah for sixteen years and *"...did that which was right in the sight of the Lord:..."* (see 15:34) — *"In those days the Lord began to send against Judah Rezin the king of Syria, and Pekah the son of Remaliah"* (see 15:37) — Jotham dies and is buried in Jerusalem.

II Kings 16: Jotham's son, **AHAZ (12th ruler of Judah),** becomes king of Judah for 16 years, but *"...did not that which was right in the sight of the Lord his God..."* (see 16:2) — He sacrifices his own sons to heathen gods and changes the Lord's altars into heathen altars — Syria and Israel fight Judah but are unsuccessful — Ahaz receives help from Assyria in capturing Damascus and killing Syria's king, Rezin — When Ahaz dies, his son, Hezekiah, becomes king.

II Kings 17:   **Israel is defeated by Assyria** during Hoshea's nine year reign as king — Shalmaneser, the king of Assyria, allows Hoshea to remain king of his people as long as he remains a servant to Shalmaneser — When Shalmaneser learns Hoshea is plotting with Egypt against him, he puts Hoshea in prison — It was in Hoshea's ninth year as king, that Assyria *"...took Samaria, and carried Israel away into Assyria..."* (see 17:6) — Israel had broken God's covenant, and *"...the Lord removed Israel out of his sight, as he had said by all his servants and prophets, So was Israel carried away out of their own land to Assyria unto this day"* (see 17:23) — The Assyrians live in Samaria, but because of their worship of pagan gods, *"...the Lord sent lions among them, which slew some of them"* (see 17:25) — The Assyrians ask for an Israelite priest to teach them about God — A priest comes to teach them, but they try worshipping both God and their pagan gods — **God's covenant with the Israelites is reviewed:**

January 28 (Day 28), Memory Verses #56 to #58
II Kings 17:35-37:

35. WITH WHOM THE LORD HAD MADE A COVENANT, AND CHARGED THEM, SAYING,
YE SHALL NOT FEAR OTHER GODS, NOR BOW YOURSELVES TO THEM,
NOR SERVE THEM, NOR SACRIFICE TO THEM:

36. BUT THE LORD, WHO BROUGHT YOU UP OUT OF THE LAND OF EGYPT
WITH GREAT POWER AND A STRETCHED OUT ARM,
HIM SHALL YE FEAR, AND HIM SHALL YE WORSHIP,
AND TO HIM SHALL YE DO SACRIFICE.

37. AND THE STATUTES, AND THE ORDINANCES, AND THE LAW,
AND THE COMMANDMENT, WHICH HE WROTE FOR YOU,
YE SHALL OBSERVE TO DO FOR EVERMORE;

II Kings 18: Ahaz's son, **KING HEZEKIAH (13th ruler of Judah),** is king of Judah for 29 years — Hezekiah *"... trusted in the Lord God of Israel; so that after him was none like him among all the kings of Judah, nor any that were before him. For he clave to the Lord, and departed not from following him, but kept his commandments, which the lord commanded Moses. And the Lord was with him; and he prospered whithersoever he went forth: and he rebelled against the king of Assyria, and served him not"* (see 18:5-7) — King Sennacherib of Assyria defeats several cities in Judah and sends messengers to Jerusalem to persuade the people of Judah to be part of Assyria — The Assyrian messengers also tell the people of Judah that Hezekiah is wrong in saying that God will deliver Judah from Assyria.

II Kings 19: Hezekiah sends messengers to the prophet Isaiah for advice — The messengers return with a prophetic message from Isaiah saying not to fear the Assyrians since they will return to their own land and will fall by the sword — **Hezekiah prays for deliverance from Assyria's continued threats** — *"And it came to pass that night, that the angel of the Lord went out, and smote in the camp of the Assyrians an hundred four-score and five thousand (a hundred and eighty-five thousand men, NIV): and when they arose early in the morning, behold, they were all dead corpses. So Sennacherib king of Assyria departed, and went and returned, and dwelt at Ninevah. And it came to pass, as he was worshipping in the house of Nisroch his god, that Adrammelech and Sharezer his sons smote him with the sword: and they escaped into the land of Armenia. And Esar-haddon his son reigned in his stead"* (see 19:35-37).

II Kings 20: Hezekiah is near death, so Isaiah gives Hezekiah a message from the Lord to *"...Set thine house in order; for thou shalt die, and not live"* (see 20:1) — Hezekiah prays, *"I beseech thee, O Lord, remember now how I have walked before thee in truth and with a perfect heart, and have done that which is good in thy sight. And Hezekiah wept sore"* (see 20:3) — Then the Lord tells Isaiah to return to Hezekiah and say, *"...Thus saith the Lord, the God of David thy father, I have heard thy prayer, I have seen thy tears: behold, I will heal thee: on the third day thou shalt go up unto the house of the Lord. And I will add unto thy days fifteen years; and I will deliver thee and this city out of the hand of the king of Assyria; and I will defend this city for mine own sake, and for my servant David's sake. And Isaiah said, Take a lump of figs. And they took and laid it on the boil, and he recovered"* (see 20:5-7) — Hezekiah asks for a sign that Isaiah's prophecies are true; Isaiah cries to the Lord, and the shadow of the sun reverses ten degrees on Ahaz' sundial — During Hezekiah's sickness, the king of Babylon had sent letters and a present to him — Hezekiah foolishly shows the Babylonians all his treasures — Isaiah prophesies to Hezekiah that the days are coming when Babylon will conquer Judah and take all of Judah's treasures to Babylon — When Hezekiah dies, his son, Manasseh, becomes king.

II Kings 21: Hezekiah's son, **KING MANASSEH (14th ruler of Judah),** is king of Judah 55 years in Jerusalem — Manasseh again brings evil to Judah which includes graven images, Baal worship, wizards, and human sacrifices — Judah's destruction is foretold by the prophets — When Manasseh dies, his son, **AMON (15th ruler of Judah),** becomes king of Judah — Amon reigns for two years, and *"he did that which was evil in the sight of the Lord, as his father Manasseh did"* (see 21:20) — *"And the servants of Amon conspired against him, and slew the king in his own house"* (see 21:23) — Amon's son, Josiah, becomes king.

II Kings 22: Amon's son, **JOSIAH (16th ruler of Judah),** is only eight years old when he becomes king, and he rules Judah for 31 years — *"And he did that which was right in the sight of the Lord, and walked in all the way of David his father, and turned not aside to the right hand or to the left"* (see 22:2) — Josiah orders the restoring of the house of the Lord — Hilkiah, the high priest, finds the book of the law in the house of the Lord — Josiah tells the priests to inform him and all the people of Judah what the Lord says in the book of the law — The priests consult with Huldah, a prophetess, who tells them of Judah's coming destruction because of past sins — She sends a message from the Lord to Josiah saying, *"Because thine heart was tender, and thou hast humbled thyself before the Lord, when thou heardest what I spake against this place, and against the inhabitants thereof that they should become a desolation and a curse, and hast rent thy clothes, and wept before me; I also have heard thee, saith the Lord. Behold therefore, I will gather thee unto thy fathers, and thou shalt be gathered into thy grave in peace; and thine eyes shall not see evil which I will bring upon this place. And they brought the king word again"* (see 22:19-20).

II Kings 23: Josiah gathers all the people of Judah to the house of the Lord, *"...and he read in their ears all the words of the book of the covenant which was found in the house of the Lord.* *And the king stood by a pillar, and made a covenant before the Lord, to walk after the Lord, and to keep his commandments and his testimonies and his statutes with all their heart and all their soul, to perform the words of this covenant that were written in this book. And all the people stood to the covenant"* (see 23:2-3) — Among other reforms, Josiah destroys the vessels of Baal, stops human sacrifices, tears down pagan altars, burns the bones of false prophets, and kills pagan priests — He commands the people to reinstate the Passover celebration unto the Lord because the Passover had not been observed in strict accordance to the law since the days of the judges — Hezekiah had the people observe the Passover (see II Chronicles 30), but not strictly by the law — Josiah fights against Pharaoh-nechoh of Egypt, but the Pharaoh kills Josiah at Megiddo — Josiah's servants return his body to Jerusalem to be buried — Josiah's son, **JEHOAHAZ (17th ruler of Judah),** becomes king of Judah for only three months and *"...he did that which was evil in the sight of the Lord..."* (see 23:32) — Pharaoh-nechoh makes Eliakim, Jehoahaz's brother, king instead of Jehoahaz and takes Jehoahaz to Egypt — Jehoahaz dies in Egypt — Pharoah-nechoch changes Eliakim's name to Jehoiakim — **KING JEHOIAKIM, also known as Eliakim (18th ruler of Judah),** is king of Judah for eleven years, taxing the people greatly for Egypt, and *"...he did that which was evil in the sight of the Lord..."* (see 23:37).

II Kings 24: Babylon defeats Egypt — King Jehoiakim becomes a servant to Nebuchadnezzar, king of Babylon, for three years, but then Jehoiakim rebels — When Jehoiakim dies, his son, **JEHOIACHIN (19th ruler of Judah),** becomes king for only three months, and *"...he did that which was evil in the sight of the Lord..."* (see 24:9) — Nebuchadnezzar besieges Jerusalem and takes many from Jerusalem to Babylon; the captives include King Jehoiachin and Jehoiachin's mother, servants, princes, officers, craftsmen, and mighty men of war — Nebuchadnezzar appoints Jehoiachin's uncle, Mattaniah, as king and changes his name to **ZEDEKIAH (20th ruler of Judah)** — Zedekiah rules for eleven years in Jerusalem and *"...did that which was evil in the sight of the Lord..."* (see 24:19).

II Kings 25: Babylon besieges Jerusalem again, and because of famine, King Zedekiah and all the men of war flee the city — The Chaldees of Babylon capture King Zedekiah and bring him to Nebuchadnezzar — *"And they slew the sons of Zedekiah before his eyes, and put out the eyes of Zedekiah, and bound him with fetters of brass, and carried him to Babylon"* (see 25:7) — Babylon's captain of the guard, Nebuzar-adan, burns the house of the Lord, the king's house, and all the houses of Jerusalem — The Chaldees of Babylon break down the walls of Jerusalem — Nebuzar-adan leaves only the poor of the land to be vinedressers and husbandmen and carries away the remaining people of Jerusalem — Nebuchadnezzar leaves Gedaliah in Jerusalem as the ruler, but some of the men kill him — Many of the people in Jerusalem flee to Egypt — After Jehoiachin is held captive in Babylon for 37 years, the Babylonian king, Evil-merodach, releases him from prison and makes him a high ruler in Babylon.

I Chronicles

Introduction: I & II Chronicles are like a miniature Old Testament, reviewing and highlighting much of the Israelites' history. Emphasis is placed on Israel's covenant relationship with God. The author chose to omit some of the stories reflecting negative traits such as King David's adultery with Bathsheba. I Chronicles emphasizes the reign of David as king of Israel. II Chronicles reviews the reign of Solomon as king of Israel and the reigns of the ruling kings and queen of the southern kingdom of Judah after the nation of Israel divided in 931 B.C. The author and date of writing are unknown. Both books may have been written around 450-425 B.C. Jewish tradition points to Ezra as the author of I and II Chronicles, Ezra, and Nehemiah. Some scholars believe parts of I and II Chronicles point to later authors. In Hebrew, Chronicles means "the affairs of the days." Like I and II Samuel, and I and II Kings, I and II Chronicles were originally in one book until the writing of the Greek Septuagint. I Chronicles has 29 chapters.

Key Contents and Key Memory Verses with Study Dates

<u>I Chronicles 1</u>: **Descendants of Adam to Jacob.**

<u>I Chronicles 2</u>: **Descendants of Jacob (also called Israel) to David.**

<u>I Chronicles 3</u>: **Descendants of David.**

<u>I Chronicles 4</u>: **Descendants of the Israelite tribes:** JUDAH (Jabez is listed in the descendants of the tribe of Judah), SIMEON...

January 29 (Day 29), Memory Verses #59 & #60
<u>I Chronicles 4:9-10</u>:
(Prayer of Jabez)

9. AND JABEZ WAS MORE HONOURABLE THAN HIS BRETHREN: ...

10. AND JABEZ CALLED ON THE GOD OF ISRAEL,
SAYING, OH THAT THOU WOULDEST BLESS ME INDEED,
AND ENLARGE MY COAST,
AND THAT THINE HAND MIGHT BE WITH ME,
AND THAT THOU WOULDEST KEEP ME FROM EVIL,
THAT IT MAY NOT GRIEVE ME!
AND GOD GRANTED HIM THAT WHICH HE REQUESTED.

<u>I Chronicles 5</u>: ...REUBEN, GAD, MANASSEH...

<u>I Chronicles 6</u>: ...LEVI...

<u>I Chronicles 7</u>: ...ISSACHAR, BENJAMIN, NAPHTALI, MANASSEH, EPHRAIM, ASHER and...

<u>I Chronicles 8</u>: ...BENJAMIN.

<u>I Chronicles 9</u>: **Descendants of the Israelites who resettled Jerusalem after the Babylonian exile — Descendants of Saul's family.**

<u>I Chronicles 10</u>: **Death of Saul and his three sons** in battle with the Philistines (see key contents for I Samuel 31) — *"So Saul died for his transgression which he committed against the*

Lord, even against the word of the Lord, which he kept not, and also for asking counsel of one that had a familiar spirit, to enquire of it; And enquired not of the Lord: therefore he slew him, and turned the kingdom unto David the son of Jesse" (see 10:13-14) — Also, see key contents for I Samuel 28 concerning the *"one that had a familiar spirit."*

I Chronicles 11:   David is anointed king over Israel — David captures Jerusalem which becomes known as the city of David — David's chief mighty men of war are listed.

I Chronicles 12:   Continued list of David's mighty men of war — **There is a great celebration when David is made king.**

I Chronicles 13:   David journeys to Kirjath-jearim to bring the ark of God to Jerusalem — The Israelites celebrate as they bring the ark to Jerusalem; *"And David and all Israel played before God with all their might, and with singing, and with harps, and with psalteries, and with timbrels, and with cymbals, and with trumpets"* (see 13:8) —Uzza tries to steady the ark when the oxen stumble, but he is stricken dead for touching the ark — This incident causes David to fear the ark, so he leaves it at the house of Obed-edom three months — *"And the Lord blessed the house of Obed-edom, and all that he had"* (see 13:14).

I Chronicles 14:   Hiram, king of Tyre, gives David cedars and workmen to help build his house — David inquires of the Lord whether or not to fight the Philistines, and the Lord assures him of a victory — The Philistines flee David, and he burns their idols — The Lord instructs David to wait in the mulberry trees until the Lord tells him to attack again — David obeys and has more victories against the Philistines — *"And the fame of David went out into all lands; and the Lord brought the fear of him upon all nations"* (see 14:17).

I Chronicles 15:   David instructs the Levites to bring the ark to Jerusalem, and there is much celebration and an offering of *"seven bullocks and seven rams"* (see 15:26) — *"Thus all Israel brought up the ark of the covenant of the Lord with shouting, and with sound of the cornet, and with trumpets, and with cymbals, making a noise with psalteries and harps. And it came to pass, as the ark of the covenant of the Lord came to the city of David, that Michal the daughter of Saul looking out at a window saw king David dancing and playing: and she despised him in her heart"* (see 15:28-29).

I Chronicles 16:   *"Then on that day David delivered first this psalm to thank the Lord..."* (see 16:7) — Portions of David's psalm (see 16: 7-36) are listed below:

January 30-February 1 (Days 30-32), Memory Verses #61 to #69
I Chronicles 16:8-12, 23-25, 34:

8. GIVE THANKS UNTO THE LORD, CALL UPON HIS NAME,
MAKE KNOWN HIS DEEDS AMONG THE PEOPLE.

9. SING UNTO HIM, SING PSALMS UNTO HIM,
TALK YE OF ALL HIS WONDROUS WORKS.

10. GLORY YE IN HIS HOLY NAME:
LET THE HEART OF THEM REJOICE THAT SEEK THE LORD.

11. SEEK THE LORD AND HIS STRENGTH, SEEK HIS FACE CONTINUALLY.

12. REMEMBER HIS MARVELLOUS WORKS THAT HE HATH DONE,
HIS WONDERS, AND THE JUDGMENTS OF HIS MOUTH;

Continued on next page...

> **23.** SING UNTO THE LORD, ALL THE EARTH;
> SHEW FORTH FROM DAY TO DAY HIS SALVATION.
>
> **24.** DECLARE HIS GLORY AMONG THE HEATHEN;
> HIS MARVELLOUS WORKS AMONG THE NATIONS.
>
> **25.** FOR GREAT IS THE LORD, AND GREATLY TO BE PRAISED:
> HE ALSO IS TO BE FEARED ABOVE ALL GODS.
>
> **34.** O GIVE THANKS UNTO THE LORD FOR HE IS GOOD;
> FOR HIS MERCY ENDURETH FOR EVER.

I Chronicles 17: David desires to build a temple for the ark of the Lord — He asks the prophet Nathan to inquire of the Lord concerning building a temple — Nathan informs David of the Lord's answer: *"And it shall come to pass, when thy days be expired that thou must go to be with the fathers, that I will raise up thy seed after thee, which shall be of thy sons; and I will establish his kingdom. He shall build me an house, and I will establish his throne for ever"* (see 17:11-12).

I Chronicles 18-20: David's battles and victories.

I Chronicles 21: *"And Satan stood up against Israel, and provoked David to number Israel"* (see 21:1) — Joab warns David against numbering Israel since God does not need numbers to fulfill His will — David repents, and God tells the prophet Gad to give David three choices of a punishment: three years of famine, fleeing the enemy for three months, or pestilence in the land for three days — David chooses three days of pestilence — *"So the Lord sent pestilence upon Israel: and there fell of Israel seventy thousand men"* (see 21:14) — David sees the angel of the Lord, with a drawn sword, prepared to destroy Jerusalem, and David prays to God — God ceases the destruction and instructs David to build an altar for offering burnt and peace offerings.

I Chronicles 22: David organizes workmen and gathers the materials needed to build the temple including stones, iron, cedar trees, gold and silver — *"And David said, Solomon my son is young and tender, and the house that is to be builded for the Lord must be exceeding magnifical, of fame and of glory throughout all countries: I will therefore now make preparation for it. So David prepared abundantly before his death"* (see 22:5) — **"And David said to Solomon,** *My son, as for me, it was in my mind to build an house unto the name of the Lord my God: But the word of the Lord came to me, saying, Thou hast shed blood abundantly, and hast made great wars: thou shalt not build an house unto my name, because thou hast shed much blood upon the earth in my sight. Behold, a son shall be born to thee, who shall be a man of rest; and I will give him rest from all his enemies round about: for his name shall be Solomon, and I will give peace and quietness unto Israel in his days. He shall build an house for my name; and he shall be my son, and I will be his father; and I will establish the throne of his kingdom over Israel for ever"* (see 22:7-10) — **David commands the princes of Israel to help Solomon build the Lord's sanctuary and says:**

> **February 2 (Day 33), Memory Verse #70**
> **I Chronicles 22:19:**
>
> NOW SET YOUR HEART AND YOUR SOUL TO SEEK THE LORD YOUR GOD; ...

I Chronicles 23: *"So when David was old and full of days, he made Solomon his son king over Israel"* (see 23:1) — **David assigns duties for the princes, priests, and Levites.**

I Chronicles 24: The Levites are divided into 24 groups for service.

I Chronicles 25: David appoints musicians for the instruments (the harp, horn, cymbal, psalteries, etc.) — Many are taught the songs of the Lord.

I Chronicles 26: David assigns porters (gatekeepers, NIV) — David appoints those to watch over the treasure of the house of God — David assigns officers, judges, and "mighty men of valour" (see 26:29-32).

I Chronicles 27: David appoints twelve captains, each commanding 24,000 men, to serve the king; one captain and his group are to serve during one of the twelve months each year — **David appoints miscellaneous rulers:** rulers for the king's treasures, for the fields, for the vineyards, for the olive trees, for the herds, for the camels, for the flocks, and so forth — Counselors are also appointed — *"...and the general of the king's army was Joab"* (see 27:34).

I Chronicles 28: David assembles the Israelites and tells them how he had hoped to build the temple, but God has shown him that Solomon is the appointed one for this task — **David gives advice to the Israelites and Solomon** — *"Now therefore in the sight of all Israel the congregation of the Lord, and in the audience of our God, keep and seek for all the commandments of the Lord your God: that ye may possess this good land, and leave it for an inheritance for your children after you for ever. And thou, Solomon my son, know thou the God of thy father, and serve him with a perfect heart and with a willing mind: for the Lord searcheth all hearts, and understandeth all the imaginations of the thoughts: if thou seek him, he will be found of thee; but if thou forsake him, he will cast thee off for ever"* (see 28:8-9) — *"And David said to Solomon his son, Be strong and of good courage, and do it: fear not, nor be dismayed: for the Lord God, even my God, will be with thee; he will not fail thee, nor forsake thee, until thou hast finished all the work for the service of the house of the Lord"* (see 28:20).

I Chronicles 29: David and the Israelites offer gifts for the temple — *"Then the people rejoiced, for that they offered willingly, because with perfect heart they offered willingly to the Lord: and David the king also rejoiced with great joy"* (see 29:9) — **David prays a beautiful prayer** (see 29:10-19) — *"...Blessed be thou, Lord God of Israel our father, for ever and ever. Thine, O Lord, is the greatness, and the power, and the glory, and the victory, and the majesty: for all that is in the heaven and in the earth is thine; thine is the kingdom, O Lord, and thou art exalted as head above all"* (see 29:10-11) — *"I know also, my God, that thou triest the heart, and hast pleasure in uprightness..."* (see 29:17) — **The Israelites offer sacrifices to the Lord — David dies after reigning over Israel for forty years** — *"And he died in a good old age, full of days, riches, and honour: and Solomon his son reigned in his stead"* (see 29:28).

I CHRONICLES 28:9:

...FOR THE LORD SEARCHETH ALL HEARTS, AND UNDERSTANDETH ALL THE IMAGINATIONS OF THE THOUGHTS: IF THOU SEEK HIM, HE WILL BE FOUND OF THEE; ...

II CHRONICLES

Introduction: See the introduction to I Chronicles. II Chronicles is about King Solomon's reign in Israel, the ruling kings and queen of the southern kingdom of Judah (from Rehoboam in 931 B.C. through Zedekiah in 586 B.C.), and the Babylonian exile. See the introduction to I Kings for a list of the ruling kings and queen of Judah. II Chronicles ends with the decree of Cyrus of Persia in 538 B.C. which allowed the Jews to return to Jerusalem after Persia had conquered Babylon. II Chronicles has 36 chapters.

Key Contents and Key Memory Verses with Study Dates

II Chronicles 1: Solomon and the Israelites make offerings at Gibeon — *"In that night did God appear unto Solomon, and said unto him, Ask what I shall give thee"* (see 1:7) — **Solomon asks for wisdom to rule Israel,** and God also promises riches, wealth, and honor since Solomon only asked for wisdom (see key contents for I Kings 3) — **Solomon's riches are described.**

II Chronicles 2: *"And Solomon determined to build a house for the name of the Lord, and an house for his kingdom"* (see 2:1) — Solomon appoints workmen and their overseers, and receives help from Huram (called Hiram in I Kings), king of Tyre, who sends timber and craftsmen.

II Chronicles 3-4: The building and description of the beautiful and elaborate house of the Lord.

II Chronicles 5: When the temple is finished, Solomon assembles the Israelites to bring the ark of the Lord into the temple and make offerings during this great celebration — *"It came even to pass, as the trumpeters and singers were as one, to make one sound to be heard in praising and thanking the Lord; and when they lifted up their voice with the trumpets and cymbals and instruments of musick, and praised the Lord, saying, For he is good; for his mercy endureth for ever: that then the house was filled with a cloud, even the house of the Lord; So that the priests could not stand to minister by reason of the cloud: for the glory of the Lord had filled the house of God"* (see 5:13-14) — See key contents for I Kings 8.

II Chronicles 6: Solomon speaks to the people and then prays as he *"...kneeled down upon his knees before all the congregation of Israel, and spread forth his hands toward heaven, And said, O Lord God of Israel, there is no God like thee in the heaven, nor in the earth; which keepest covenant, and shewest mercy unto thy servants, that walk before thee with all their hearts:"* (see 6:13-14) — Solomon's prayer continues through verse 42.

II Chronicles 7: *"Now when Solomon had made an end praying, the fire came down from heaven, and consumed the burnt offering and the sacrifices; and the glory of the Lord filled the house.* And the priests could not enter into the house of the Lord, because the glory of the Lord had filled the Lord's house. And when all the children of Israel saw how the fire came down, and the glory of the Lord upon the house, they bowed themselves with their faces to the ground upon the pavement, and worshipped, and praised the Lord, saying, For he is good; for his mercy endureth for ever"* (see 7:1-3) — The people feast for seven days, and then after assembling on the eighth day, they go *"...away into their tents, glad and merry in heart for the goodness that the Lord had shewed unto David, and to Solomon, and to Israel his people"* (see 7:10) — **"And the Lord appeared to Solomon by night..."** (see 7:12), restating His covenant with the Israelites (see 7:14-22).

February 3 (Day 34), Memory Verse #71
II Chronicles 7:14:

IF MY PEOPLE, WHICH ARE CALLED BY MY NAME,
SHALL HUMBLE THEMSELVES, AND PRAY, AND SEEK MY FACE,
AND TURN FROM THEIR WICKED WAYS;
THEN WILL I HEAR FROM HEAVEN, AND WILL FORGIVE THEIR SIN,
AND WILL HEAL THEIR LAND.

II Chronicles 8: Solomon's cities — The people ruled by Solomon — Solomon's offerings — Solomon's assignments to the Levites — Solomon's ships given by Huram.

II Chronicles 9: The Queen of Sheba visits Solomon because she can hardly believe all the wonderful things she has heard about him — He exceeds all she has heard, and she gives him gifts — She tells Solomon, *"...thou exceedest the fame that I heard. Happy are thy men, and happy are these servants, which stand continually before thee, and hear thy wisdom. Blessed be the Lord thy God, which delighted in thee to set thee on his throne, to be king for the Lord thy God: because thy God loved Israel, to establish them for ever, therefore made he thee king over them, to do judgment and justice"* (see 9:6-8 and key contents for I Kings 10) — **Solomon's riches are described** — *"And Solomon reigned in Jerusalem over all Israel forty years. And Solomon slept with his fathers, and he was buried in the city of David his father: and Rehoboam his son reigned in his stead"* (see 9:30-31).

II Chronicles 10: REHOBOAM becomes the first king of Judah in the divided kingdom of Israel — *"...Jeroboam and all Israel came and spake to Rehoboam saying, Thy father made our yoke grievous: now therefore ease thou somewhat the grievous servitude of thy father, and his heavy yoke that he put upon us, and we will serve thee"* (see 10:3-4) — **But Rehoboam takes the foolish advice of the young men to increase the work load** rather than the wise advice of the older men to lighten the hardships of the people — *"And Israel rebelled against the house of David unto this day"* (see 10:19).

II Chronicles 11:   The man of God, Shemaiah, persuades Rehoboam not to fight the northern kingdom of Israel ruled by Jeroboam; *"Thus saith the Lord, Ye shall not go up, nor fight against your brethren:..."* (see 11:4) — Rehoboam builds many cities for defense — For three years, Rehoboam follows the commandments of God — The Levites move to the southern kingdom of Judah since Jeroboam, the king of Israel, removed their duties as priests — Rehoboam has many wives, concubines, and children.

II Chronicles 12: *"And it came to pass, when Rehoboam had established the kingdom, and had strengthened himself, he forsook the law of the Lord, and all Israel with him"* (see 12:1) — *"...Shishak king of Egypt came up against Jerusalem, because they had transgressed against the Lord"* (see 12:2) — *"Then came Shemaiah the prophet to Rehoboam, and to the princes of Judah, that were gathered together to Jerusalem because of Shishak, and said unto them, Thus saith the Lord, Ye have forsaken me, and therefore have I also left you in the hand of Shishak. Whereupon the princes of Israel and the king humbled themselves; and they said, The Lord is righteous. And when the Lord saw that they humbled themselves, the word of the Lord came to Shemaiah saying, They have humbled themselves; therefore I will not destroy them, but I will grant them some deliverance; and my wrath shall not be poured out upon Jerusalem by the hand of Shishak"* (see 12:5-7) — Shishak takes all the treasures of the house of the Lord and the king's house — Rehoboam reigns for 17 years but *"...did evil, because he prepared not his heart to seek the Lord"* (see 12:14) — *"...And there were wars between Rehoboam and Jeroboam continually. And Rehoboam slept with his fathers, and was buried in the city of David: and Abijah his son reigned in his stead"* (see 12:15-16).

II Chronicles 13: ABIJAH, the king of Judah, speaks from Mount Zemaraim to Jeroboam, king of Israel, and the people of Israel — **Abijah scolds Jeroboam for rebelling against Judah,** possessing idols, and casting out the Levite priests — Abijah tells the people of Israel, *"...God himself is with us for our captain, and his priests with sounding trumpets to cry alarm against you. O children of Israel, fight ye not against the Lord God of your fathers; for ye shall not prosper"* (see 13:12) — **Jeroboam and his men ambush Judah** — *"Then the men of Judah gave a shout: and as the men of Judah shouted, it came to pass, that God smote Jeroboam and all Israel before Abijah and Judah"* (see 13:15) — *"Thus the children of Israel were brought under at that time, and the children of Judah prevailed, because they relied upon the Lord God of their fathers"* (see 13:18).

II Chronicles 14: *"So Abijah slept with his fathers, and they buried him in the city of David: and* **ASA** *his son reigned in his stead. In his days the land was quiet ten years.* **And Asa did that which was good and right in the eyes of the Lord his God:** *For he took away the altars of the strange gods, and the high places, and brake down the images, and cut down the groves: And commanded Judah to seek the Lord God of their fathers, and to do the law and the commandment"* (see 14:1-4) — **Zerah, an Ethiopian, attacks Judah** — *"And Asa cried unto the Lord his God, and said, Lord, it is nothing with thee to help, whether with many, or with them that have no power: help us, O Lord our God; for we rest on thee, and in thy name we go against this multitude. O Lord, thou art our God; let not man prevail against thee. So the Lord smote the Ethiopians before Asa, and before Judah; and the Ethiopians fled"* (see 14:11-12).

II Chronicles 15: The prophet Azariah encourages Asa to continue following the Lord — Azariah calls the people of Judah together, and *"...they entered into a covenant to seek the Lord God of their fathers with all their heart and with all their soul;"* (see 15:12).

II Chronicles 16: *"In the six and thirtieth year of the reign of Asa, Baasha king of Israel came up against Judah, and built Ramah, to the intent that he might let none go out or come in to Asa king of Judah"* (see 16:1) — **Asa forms an alliance with Ben-ha-dad, king of Syria, who destroys many of Israel's cities and causes Baasha to cease the building of Ramah** — The prophet Hanani tells Asa that he has done wrong by relying on Syria rather than the Lord God to defeat Israel — Hanani proclaims to Asa:

February 4 (Day 35), Memory Verse #72
II Chronicles 16:9:

FOR THE EYES OF THE LORD RUN TO AND FRO THROUGHOUT THE WHOLE EARTH,
TO SHEW HIMSELF STRONG IN THE BEHALF OF THEM
WHOSE HEART IS PERFECT TOWARD HIM (fully committed to him, NIV)...

— Asa is angered by Hanani and throws him in prison — **"And Asa in the thirty and ninth year of his reign was diseased in his feet,** *until his disease was exceeding great: yet in his disease he sought not to the Lord, but to the physicians. And Asa slept with his fathers, and died in the one and fortieth year of his reign. And they buried him in his own sepulchres, which he had made for himself in the city of David..."* (see 16:12-14).

II Chronicles 17: Asa's son, **JEHOSHAPHAT,** becomes king — *"And the Lord was with Jehoshaphat, because he walked in the first ways of his father David, and sought not unto Baalim;"* (see 17:3) — **Jehoshaphat sends princes, Levites, and priests to teach in the cities of Judah** — *"And they taught in Judah, and had the book of the law of the Lord with them, and went about throughout all the cities of Judah, and taught the people. And the fear of the Lord fell upon all the kingdoms of the lands that were round about Judah, so that they made not war against Jehoshaphat"* (see 17:9-10).

II Chronicles 18: Jehoshaphat and Israel's King, Ahab, form an alliance to fight Ramoth-gilead of Syria — They consult the advice of prophets who agree the Israelites will defeat Ramoth-gilead, but the prophet Micaiah forewarns that Ahab will be killed in the battle — Ahab has Micaiah thrown in prison for prophesying his death — Ahab disguises himself so he would not be recognized as the king in battle, but *"...a certain man drew a bow at a venture, and smote the king of Israel between the joints of the harness: therefore he said to his chariot man, Turn thine hand, that thou mayest carry me out of the host; for I am wounded. And the battle increased that day: howbeit the king of Israel stayed himself up in his chariot against the Syrians until the even: and about the time of the sun going down he died"* (see 18:33-34).

II Chronicles 19: Jehu, the son of the prophet Hanani, scolds Jehoshaphat for having an alliance with Israel and says Israel is a nation of ungodly people who hate the Lord — **Jehoshaphat brings the people of Judah *"...back unto the Lord God of their fathers"*** (see 19:4) — He places judges throughout the land, and *"...said to the judges, Take heed what ye do: for ye judge not for man, but for the Lord, who is with you in the judgment"* (see 19:6) — Jehoshaphat also appoints *"...Levites, and of the priests, and of the chief of the fathers of Israel..."* (see 19:8) to judge Jerusalem — Jehoshaphat tells them, *"...Deal courageously, and the Lord shall be with the good"* (see 19:11).

II Chronicles 20: The people of Moab and Ammon join others to plan battle against the people of Judah and their king, Jehoshaphat — *"And Jehoshapaht feared, and set himself to seek the Lord, and proclaimed a fast throughout all Judah"* (see 20:3) — The Spirit of the Lord comes upon Jahaziel, and he says, *"...Hearken ye, all Judah, and ye inhabitants of Jerusalem, and thou king Jehoshaphat, Thus saith the Lord unto you, Be not afraid nor dismayed by reason of this great multitude; for the battle is not yours, but God's"* (see 20:15) — Jehoshaphat *"...appointed singers unto the Lord, and that should praise the beauty of holiness, as they went out before the army, and to say..."* (see 20:21)**:**

February 5-6 (Days 36-37), Memory Verse #73
II Chronicles 20:21:

...PRAISE THE LORD; FOR HIS MERCY ENDURETH FOR EVER.

— *"And when they began to sing and to praise, **the Lord set ambushments against the children of Ammon, Moab, and mount Seir, which were come against Judah; and they were smitten"*** (see 20:22) — The enemy fights among themselves and destroys each other — Judah takes spoil from the slain enemy and *"...they returned, every man of Judah and Jerusalem, and Jehoshaphat in the forefront of them, to go again to Jerusalem with joy; for the Lord had made them to rejoice over their enemies"* (see 20:27).

II Chronicles 21: *"Now Jehoshaphat slept with his fathers, and was buried with his fathers in the city of David. And **JEHORAM** his son reigned in his stead"* (see 21:1) for eight years — Jehoram kills his brothers, and *"...had the daughter of Ahab to wife: and he wrought that which was evil in the eyes of the Lord"* (see 21:6) — The Edomites join Libnah in fighting Judah; Judah wins the battle — Because of Jehoram's evil ways, Elijah sends written warnings**:** *"Behold, with a great plague will the Lord smite thy people, and thy children, and thy wives, and all thy goods: And thou shalt have great sickness by disease of thy bowels, until thy bowels fall out by reason of the sickness day by day"* (see 21:14-15) — The Philistines and Arabians invade Judah and carry away the treasures of the king's house — They also take captive Jehoram's wives and sons except for his youngest son, Jehoahaz, also known as Ahaziah — The prophecy by Elijah predicting Jehoram's sickness comes true, and Jehoram dies *"...without being desired. Howbeit they buried him in the city of David, but not in the sepulchres of the kings"* (see 21:20).

II Chronicles 22: Jehoram's youngest son, **AHAZIAH,** becomes king since the Arabians had killed all his older brothers, but Ahaziah only rules one year; *"He also walked in the ways of the house of Ahab: for his mother was his counselor to do wickedly"* (see 22:3) — Ahaziah forms an alliance with Jehoram, Ahab's son and king of Israel, to fight Hazael, king of Syria — After the battle with Syria, Ahaziah returns to Jezreel to heal from wounds — Ahaziah hears Jehoram is sick so he journeys to see him, but Ahaziah encounters Jehu who kills him along with his men and Jehoram — Ahaziah's mother, **ATHALIAH,** becomes the ruling queen and kills the royal offspring (her grandchildren); she is unaware that Jehoshabeath, sister of Ahaziah, has hidden Ahaziah's son, Joash, and his nurse in a bedchamber — Joash is hidden for six years.

II Chronicles 23: The priest, Jehoiada, leads the people in crowning **JOASH** king at the age of seven (see verse 24:1) and in killing Queen Athaliah — *"...they brought out the king's son, and put upon him the crown, and gave him the testimony, and made him king. And Jehoiada and his sons anointed him, and said, God save the king. Now when Athaliah heard the noise of the people running and praising the king, she came to the people into the house of the Lord: And she looked, and behold, the king stood at his pillar at the entering in, and the princes and the trumpets by the king: and all the people of the land rejoiced, and sounded with trumpets, also the singers with instruments of musick, and such as taught to sing praise. Than Athaliah rent her clothes, and said, Treason, Treason"* (see 23:11-13) — The people lead Athaliah out of the house of the Lord and kill her at the horse gate by the king's house — Also, the idols of Baal are destroyed, and Mattan, the priest of Baal, is killed.

II Chronicles 24: Joash *"...did that which was right in the sight of the Lord all the days of Jehoiada the priest"* (see 24:2) — **Joash gathers money and workmen to repair the temple** *"For the sons of Athaliah, that wicked woman, had broken up the house of God;..."* (see 24:7) — But after the priest Jehoiada dies, Judah again falls into idolatry — *"And the Spirit of God came upon Zechariah the son of Jehoiada the priest, which stood above the people, and said unto them, Thus saith God, Why transgress ye the commandments of the Lord, that ye cannot prosper? Because ye have forsaken the Lord, he hath also forsaken you. And they conspired against him, and stoned him with stones at the commandment of the king in the court of the house of the Lord"* (see 24:20-21) — The Syrian army destroys the princes of Judah and take spoil from them; the spoil is sent to the king of Damascus — Joash's servants conspire against him and kill him upon his bed; *"...they buried him in the city of David, but they buried him not in the sepulchres of the kings"* (see 24:25).

II Chronicles 25: Joash's son, **AMAZIAH,** becomes king and reigns for 29 years in Jerusalem; *"And he did that which was right in the sight of the Lord, but not with a perfect heart"* (see 25:2) — Amaziah kills the servants who killed his father, Joash — A man of God warns Amaziah not to let the army of Israel fight with the army of Judah; therefore, Amaziah orders those of Israel who have joined Judah's army to return to Israel — Judah wins the battle with Seir, the Edomites — But the men of Israel whom Amaziah sent away, go throughout many cities of Judah, killing and taking spoil — The Lord sends a prophet to Amaziah to express anger at Judah for taking and worshipping the gods of the Edomites — Joash, king of Israel, defeats Amaziah, king of Judah — Joash takes spoil from the house of God and the king's house, along with captives, back to Samaria — *"Now after the time that Amaziah did turn away from following the Lord they made a conspiracy against him in Jerusalem; and he fled to Lachish: but they sent to Lachish after him, and slew him there. And they brought him upon horses, and buried him with his fathers in the city of Judah"* (see 25:27-28).

II Chronicles 26: Amaziah's son, **UZZIAH, also known as Azariah,** becomes king at age 16 and rules 52 years; *"And he did that which was right in the sight of the Lord, according to all that his father Amaziah did"* (see 26:4) — Uzziah builds a strong army and has many victories — He also fortifies Jerusalem with towers, builds towers in the desert, and digs many wells for cattle and vineyards — *"But when he was strong, his heart was lifted up to his destruction: for he transgressed against the Lord his God, and went into the temple of the Lord to burn incense upon the altar of incense"* (see 26:16) — Uzziah's burning incense is a sin because only priests are allowed to burn the incense — Uzziah is stricken with leprosy in the temple, and *"...Uzziah the king was a leper unto the day of his death, and dwelt in a several house, being a leper; for he was cut off from the house of the Lord: and Jotham his son was over the king's house, judging the people of the land"* (see 26:21).

II Chronicles 27: Uzziah's son, **JOTHAM,** becomes king and reigns 16 years — *"And he did that which was right in the sight of the Lord, according to all that his father Uzziah did: howbeit he entered not into the temple of the Lord. And the people did yet corruptly"* (see 27:2) — During his reign, Jotham builds many structures for Judah which include cities, castles, and towers — Jotham defeats the Ammonites — *"So Jotham became mighty, because he prepared his ways before the Lord his God"* (see 27:6) — *"And Jotham slept with his fathers, and they buried him in the city of David: and Ahaz his son reigned in his stead"* (see 27:9).

II Chronicles 28: **AHAZ** *"...reigned sixteen years in Jerusalem: but he did not that which was right in the sight of the Lord, like David his father: For he walked in the ways of the kings of Israel, and made also molten images for Baalim"* (see 28:1-2) — Syria and Israel defeat Judah — Obed, a prophet of the Lord, warns Israel of God's anger since Israel fought and killed the people of Judah — Obed urges Israel to release the captives of Judah — So Israel releases the captives, first caring for their needs, and takes them to Jericho — King Ahaz asks help from Tilgath-pilneser, king of Assyria, because the Edomites and Philistines are attacking Judah — Assyria refuses to help — Ahaz *"...shut up the doors of the house of the Lord..."* (see 28:24) and worships the gods of Damascus — *"And Ahaz slept with his fathers, and they buried him in the city, even in Jerusalem: but they brought him not into the sepulchres of the kings of Israel: and Hezekiah his son reigned in his stead"* (see 28:27).

II Chronicles 29: Ahaz's son, **HEZEKIAH,** reigns for 29 years, and *"...he did that which was right in the sight of the Lord, according to all that David his father had done"* (see 29:2) — **Hezekiah reopens, repairs, and cleanses the house of the Lord** — The people of Judah gather to give offerings and make a covenant with the Lord God — *"So the service of the house of the Lord was set in order. And Hezekiah rejoiced, and all the people, that God had prepared the people: for the thing was done suddenly"* (see 29:35-36).

II Chronicles 30: **Hezekiah sends letters to all of Israel and Judah decreeing that all Israelites** *"...should come to keep the Passover unto the Lord God of Israel at Jerusalem: for they had not done it of a long time (in large numbers, NIV) in such sort as it was written"* (see 30:5) — *"And all the congregation of Judah, with the priests and the Levites, and all the congregation that came out of Israel, and the strangers that came out of the land of Israel, and that dwelt in Judah, rejoiced. So there was great joy in Jerusalem: for since the time of Solomon the son of David king of Israel there was not the like in Jerusalem. Then the priests the Levites arose and blessed the people: and their voice was heard, and their prayer came up to his holy dwelling place, even unto heaven"* (see 30:25-27).

II Chronicles 31: Idols are destroyed, and the people bring offerings and tithes to the temple — Hezekiah has chambers built to store the plentiful gifts brought by the people — **Hezekiah** *"...wrought that which was good and right and truth before the Lord his God. And in every* *work that he began in the service of the house of God, and in the law, and in the commandments, to seek his God, he did it with all his heart, and prospered"* (see 31:20-21).

II Chronicles 32: Sennacherib, king of Assyria, plans to attack Judah — Hezekiah prepares for battle and has the water supply shut off to prevent the enemy's use of the water — Hezekiah tells the people of Judah to rely on God to fight their battles — Sennacherib tells the people of Judah not to listen to Hezekiah and says no god of any nation can deliver them from Assyria — *"...Hezekiah the king, and the prophet Isaiah the son of Amoz, prayed and cried to heaven. And the Lord sent an angel, which cut off all the mighty men of valour, and the leaders and captains in the camp of the king of Assyria. So he returned with shame of face to his own land. And when he was come into the house of his god, they that came forth of his own bowels slew him there with the sword"* (see 32:20-21) — **Hezekiah is very sick, and the Lord gives him a sign** (see II Kings 20) — Hezekiah also repents of *"the pride of his heart"* (see 32:26) — *"And Hezekiah slept with his fathers, and they buried him in the chiefest of the sepulchres of the sons of David: and all Judah and the inhabitants of Jerusalem did him honour at his death. And Manasseh his son reigned in his stead"* (see 32:33).

II Chronicles 33: *"**MANASSEH** was twelve years old when he began to reign, and he reigned fifty and five years in Jerusalem: But did that which was evil in the sight of the Lord, like unto the abominations of the heathen, whom the Lord had cast out before the children of Israel"* (see 33:1) — *"And he set a carved image, the idol which he had made, in the house of God, of which God had said to David and to Solomon his son, In this house, and in Jerusalem, which I have chosen before all the tribes of Israel, will I put my name for ever:"* (see 33:7) — The Assyrians capture Manasseh and carry him to Babylon — Manasseh *"...humbled himself greatly before the God of his fathers, And prayed unto him: and he was intreated of him, and heard his supplication, and brought him again to Jerusalem into his kingdom. Then Manasseh knew that the Lord he was God"* (see 33:12-13) — Manasseh removes the idols he had placed in the house of the Lord, tears down altars to other gods, and *"...commanded Judah to serve the Lord God of Israel"* (see 33:16) — *"So Manasseh slept with his fathers, and they buried him in his own house: and **AMON** his son reigned in his stead"* (see 33:20) for two years in Jerusalem — Amon does evil, worshipping idols again, *"...and humbled not himself before the Lord, as Manasseh..."* (see 33:23) — Amon's servants kill him; then the people kill the servants who murdered Amon — *"...and the people of the land made Josiah his son king in his stead"* (see 33:25).

II Chronicles 34: JOSIAH is eight years old when he becomes king, and he reigns for 31 years — *"And he did that which was right in the sight of the Lord, and walked in the ways of David his father, and declined neither to the right hand, nor to the left"* (see 34:2) — Josiah cleanses the land of idol worship and orders a massive renovation of the temple of the Lord — *"...Hilkiah the priest found a book of the law of the Lord given by Moses"* (see 34:14) — Josiah sends men to inquire of Huldah, the prophetess, about the book of the law; Huldah sends back word to the king that Judah will be cursed for forsaking God, but not during Josiah's rule since he has humbled himself before God — *"And the king went up into the house of the Lord, and all the men of Judah, and all the inhabitants of Jerusalem, and the priests, and the Levites, and all the people, great and small: and he read in their ears all the words of the book of the covenant that was found in the house of the Lord. And the king stood in his place, and made a covenant before the Lord, to walk after the Lord, and to keep his commandments, and his testimonies, and his statutes, with all his heart, and with all his soul, to perform the words of the covenant which are written in this book"* (see 34:30-31).

II Chronicles 35: **Josiah decrees the observance of the Passover** for it had not been held in the proper manner, by the law, since the days of the prophet Samuel — Hezekiah had decreed the observance of the Passover in great numbers (see chapter 30), but the Passover was not observed properly, by the law — **Necho, the king of Egypt, comes to fight Charchemish** — Necho assures Josiah he is not there to fight him, but Josiah decides to fight Necho in disguise — Josiah is shot by archers and is carried by chariot to Jerusalem where he dies.

II Chronicles 36: Josiah's son, **JEHOAHAZ,** becomes king and reigns only three months — Necho, the king of Egypt, takes Jehoahaz to Egypt and makes Jehoahaz's brother, Eliakim, king over Judah (Necho changes Eliakim's name to **JEHOIAKIM**) — Jehoiakim reigns for eleven years and *"...did that which was evil in the sight of the Lord his God"* (see 36:5) — The Babylonian King, Nebuchadnezzar, captures Jerusalem, takes Jehoiakim to Babylon, and makes Jehoiakim's son, **JEHOIACHIN,** king — *"Jehoiachin was eight years old when he began to reign, and he reigned three months and ten days in Jerusalem: and he did that which was evil in the sight of the Lord"* (see 36:9) — Nebuchadnezzar has Jehoiachin taken to Babylon and makes Jehoiachin's uncle, **ZEDEKIAH,** king — Zedekiah reigns for eleven years and *"...he did that which was evil in the sight of the Lord his God, and humbled not himself before Jeremiah the prophet speaking from the mouth of the Lord"* (see 36:12) — God sends messengers to the people of Judah to warn them of their evil, but *"...they mocked the messengers of God, and despised his words, and misused his prophets, until the wrath of the Lord arose against his people, till there was no remedy. Therefore he brought upon them the king of the Chaldees, who slew their young men with the sword in the house of their sanctuary, and had no compassion upon young man or maiden, old man, or him that stooped for age: he gave them all into his hand. And all the vessels of the house of God, great and small, and the treasures of the house of the Lord, and the treasures of the king, and of his princes; all these he brought to Babylon. And they burnt the house of God, and brake down the wall of Jerusalem, and burnt all the palaces thereof with fire, and destroyed all the goodly vessels thereof. And them that had escaped from the sword carried he away to Babylon; where they were servants to him and his sons until the reign of he kingdom of Persia:"* (see 36:16-20) — The Babylonian exile lasts for 70 years until King Cyrus of Persia conquers Babylon and decrees the Jews can return to Jerusalem — ***"Thus saith Cyrus king of Persia, All the kingdoms of the earth hath the Lord God of heaven given me; and he hath charged me to build him an house in Jerusalem, which is in Judah. Who is there among you of all his people? The Lord his God be with him, and let him go up"*** (see 36:23).

II Chronicles 7:14:

If my people,
which are called by my name,
shall humble themselves,
and pray, and seek my face,
and turn from their wicked ways;
then will I hear from heaven,
and will forgive their sin,
and will heal their land.

EZRA

Introduction: Most scholars believe the same author who wrote I and II Chronicles wrote Ezra and Nehemiah as well. Jewish tradition points to Ezra as the author. See introduction to I Chronicles for more authorship notes. Like I and II Chronicles, Ezra and Nehemiah were combined in early Hebrew writings as one book. Chapters 1-6 describe both the return of the Jews from Babylonian captivity after Persia conquered Babylon in 539 B.C. and the completion of the new temple in 515 B.C. Cyrus's decree allowing the Jews to return to Jerusalem was in 538 B.C. Solomon's temple had been destroyed in 586 B.C. by Babylon. The first group of Jews, approximately 50,000, returned to Jerusalem in 536 B.C., led by the priest Joshua and the governor Zerubbabel. Many of the Jews decided to stay in Babylon. Ezra traveled to Jerusalem with approximately 6000 Jews in 458 B.C., and was followed by a group led by Nehemiah in 444 B.C. Chapters 7-10 describe Ezra helping the Israelites return to the Lord. Ezra has 10 chapters.

Key Contents and Key Memory Verses with Study Dates

Ezra 1: The decree of Cyrus — *"Now in the first year of Cyrus king of Persia, that the word of the Lord by the mouth of Jeremiah might be fulfilled, the Lord stirred up the spirit of Cyrus king of Persia, that he made a proclamation throughout all his kingdom, and put it also in writing saying, Thus saith Cyrus king of Persia, The Lord God of heaven hath given me all the kingdoms of the earth; and he hath charged me to build him an house at Jerusalem, which is in Judah. Who is there among you of all his people? his God be with him, and let him go up to Jerusalem, which is in Judah, and build the house of the Lord God of Israel, (he is the God,) which is in Jerusalem"* (see 1:1-3).

Ezra 2: List and number of people who had been carried into captivity by Nebuchadnezzar, king of Babylon, and now are returning to Jerusalem.

Ezra 3: Constructing the temple — The ancient men *"...wept with a loud voice; and many shouted aloud for joy"* (see 3:12).

Ezra 4: The adversaries of the Jews try to prevent the building of the temple.

Ezra 5: The building of the temple starts again after several years of delay.

Ezra 6: Darius decrees to uphold Cyrus' decree allowing the Jews to rebuild the temple — Darius also commands that those who tried to prevent the building of the temple, must pay money to the Jews — **Completion and dedication of the temple.**

Ezra 7: Ezra, a scribe and priest, returns to Jerusalem.

February 7 (Day 38), Memory Verse #74
Ezra 7:10:

FOR EZRA HAD PREPARED HIS HEART TO SEEK THE LAW OF THE LORD, AND TO DO IT, AND TO TEACH IN ISRAEL STATUTES AND JUDGMENTS.

— **King Artaxerxes becomes king of Persia after Darius' reign** — **King Artaxerxes' decree** gives treasures of gold and silver for the temple — *"Blessed be the Lord God of our fathers, which hath put such a thing as this in the king's heart, to beautify the house of the Lord which is in Jerusalem:"* (see 7:27).

Ezra 8-10: Chapter 8 tells of Ezra's journey to Jerusalem and God's protection (see 8:31) — This chapter also lists those who accompany Ezra — **In chapter 9, Ezra prays to God, confessing the sins of the Israelites** (see 9:5-15) — **Foreign wives are the topic of chapter 10.**

NEHEMIAH

Introduction: See the introduction to Ezra for authorship notes. Nehemiah was the cupbearer (the one who tasted the king's food and wine to insure it was not poisoned) for Artaxerxes I, king of Persia. King Artaxerxes allowed Nehemiah to oversee the building of Jerusalem's walls which took only 52 days, even through opposition. Nehemiah was also appointed governor of Judah by King Artaxerxes. Through Ezra's preaching came revival and renewal of Israel's covenant with God. Chapter 9 is a beautiful poem of Israel's history. Nehemiah has 13 chapters.

Key Contents and Key Memory Verses with Study Dates

Nehemiah 1: Jerusalem's condition troubles Nehemiah — Nehemiah's prayer.

Nehemiah 2: Nehemiah receives permission and support from King Artaxerxes to go to Jerusalem and help the people rebuild the Jerusalem walls.

Nehemiah 3: The building of the wall and the names of the workers.

Nehemiah 4: The Israelites continue building even with much opposition.

Nehemiah 5: Nehemiah helps the Israelites with their economic problems.

Nehemiah 6: The Jerusalem walls are finished in 52 days.

Nehemiah 7: Registration of the Israelites.

Nehemiah 8: Ezra, along with others, read the book of the law of Moses to the Israelites, and the people weep and praise God — The Israelites are reminded:

February 7 (Day 38), Memory Verse #75
Nehemiah 8:10:

...FOR THE JOY OF THE LORD IS YOUR STRENGTH.

— The people celebrate the Feast of Booths, a feast commanded by Moses.

Nehemiah 9: The Israelites confess their sin, read the law, and recount Israel's history (see 9:1-38).

February 7 (Day 38), Memory Verse #76
Nehemiah 9:17:

...BUT THOU ART A GOD READY TO PARDON, GRACIOUS AND MERCIFUL,
SLOW TO ANGER, AND OF GREAT KINDNESS, AND FORSOOKEST THEM NOT.

Nehemiah 10: The Israelites enter *"...into an oath to walk in God's law, which was given by Moses the servant of God, and to observe and do all the commandments of the Lord our Lord, and his judgments and his statutes"* (see 10:29).

Nehemiah 11: *"And the rulers of the people dwelt at Jerusalem: the rest of the people also cast lots, to bring one in ten to dwell in Jerusalem the holy city, and nine parts to dwell in other cities"* (see 11:1).

Nehemiah 12: Dedication of the walls of Jerusalem.

Nehemiah 13: Moses' laws are reinstated and enforced.

ESTHER

Introduction: The author is unknown, but Esther may have been written by a Jew in the 480's to 470's B.C. Others believe Esther may have been written as late as the 300's to late 100's B.C. Although God's name is never mentioned, the book of Esther shows God's protection of His people during the reign of the Persian king, Ahasuerus, also known by his Greek name, Xerxes I. The Jewish Feast of Purim originated during Ahasuerus' rule as king when Esther was queen. During this feast, the Jews celebrate the deliverance from persecution caused by Haman. Esther has 10 chapters.

Key Contents and Key Memory Verses with Study Dates

<u>**Esther 1**</u>: **King Ahasuerus** *"...which reigned from India even unto Ethiopia"* (see 1:1), **has a banquet, but Queen Vashti refuses to show her beauty at his request** — The king decides to take his princes' advice to select another queen.

<u>**Esther 2**</u>: **King Ahasuerus chooses Esther to be queen from the** *"fair young virgins"* (see 2:2) brought before the king — Esther's uncle, Mordecai, warns Esther that she should not tell the king she is a Jew — Mordecai tells Esther of the conspiracy by Bigthan and Teresh against the king, and Esther warns the king — Bigthan and Teresh are hanged.

<u>**Esther 3**</u>: **Haman is promoted** to a rank above the princes — He is angered when the Jew Mordecai will not bow down to him, and persuades the king to decree a day for destroying Jews.

<u>**Esther 4**</u>: **Mordecai sends a copy of the king's decree to Esther and urges that** *"...she should go in unto the king, to make supplication unto him, and to make request before him for her people"* (see 4:8) — Mordecai tells Esther:

February 8 (Day 39), Memory Verse #77
<u>**Esther 4:14:**</u>

...**AND** WHO KNOWETH WHETHER THOU ART COME
TO THE KINGDOM FOR SUCH A TIME AS THIS?

— Esther requests a fast for three days and nights by the Jews before she goes to the king.

<u>**Esther 5**</u>: **Esther appears before King Ahasuerus,** and he raises his golden scepter in approval — **Esther requests the king and Haman come to a banquet** which she has prepared for them that day — At the banquet, Esther requests their presence at another banquet the following day — **Haman makes gallows on which he plans to hang Mordecai.**

<u>**Esther 6**</u>: **Haman is surprised to learn the king plans to honor Mordecai rather than him.**

<u>**Esther 7**</u>: **Esther's second banquet** — **Haman's plot against Mordecai is revealed, and Haman is hanged on the same gallows he had prepared for Mordecai.**

<u>**Esther 8**</u>: **Mordecai is given Haman's position above the princes** — **The king decrees the Jews can defend themselves on the day which has been decreed for their destruction.**

<u>**Esther 9**</u>: **The Jews defeat their enemies and celebrate the days of Purim.**

<u>**Esther 10**</u>: *"For Mordecai the Jew was next unto king Ahasuerus, and great among the Jews, and accepted of the multitude of his brethren, seeking the wealth of his people, and speaking peace to all his seed"* (see 10:3).

JOB

Introduction: The author and date of writing of Job are uncertain. Some believe Job may have been written in the 500's B.C.   The story's setting probably takes place between 2000 to 1000 B.C. Job addresses the question of why God allows human suffering.   Job's three friends (Eliphaz, Bildad, and Zophar) wrongly blamed Job's suffering on his sins.   The theme of innocent suffering emphasizes faith in God in spite of and in the midst of undeserved suffering. Job has 42 chapters.

Key Contents and Key Memory Verses with Study Dates

Job 1: *"There was a man in the land of Uz, whose name was Job; and that man was perfect and upright, and one that feared God, and eschewed evil"* (see 1:1) — **God allows Satan to test Job by taking away his possessions including children and livestock** — Job remarks:

February 8 (Day 39), Memory Verse #78
Job 1:21:

... NAKED CAME I OUT OF MY MOTHER'S WOMB,
AND NAKED SHALL I RETURN THITHER:
THE LORD GAVE, AND THE LORD HATH TAKEN AWAY;
BLESSED BE THE NAME OF THE LORD.

— *"In all this Job sinned not, nor charged God foolishly"* (see Job 1:22).

Job 2: **Job remains upright throughout his calamity** — Next God allows Satan to test Job by taking his health, but not his life — Job's wife even tells Job, *"Dost thou still retain thine integrity? Curse God, and die"* (see 2:9).

Job 3: **Three of Job's friends (Eliphaz, Bildad, and Zophar) come to mourn with Job and comfort him** — Job curses the day he was born; *"Let the day perish wherein I was born, and the night in which it was said, There is a man child conceived"* (see 3:3).

Job 4-37: **Eliphaz, Bildad, and Zophar all give their opinions as to why these things have happened to Job; their main opinion is that Job has sinned** — **Elihu also expresses his opinion** and tells Job to accept his fate and not rebel against God — Each of these four men gives several speeches in chapters 4-37 — Eliphaz tells Job in his speech:

February 8 (Day 39), Memory Verse #79
Job 5:17:

BEHOLD, HAPPY IS THE MAN WHOM GOD CORRECTETH:
THEREFORE DESPISE NOT THOU THE CHASTENING OF THE ALMIGHTY:

— **Job defends his righteousness:**

February 8 (Day 39), Memory Verse #80
Job 6:25:

HOW FORCIBLE ARE RIGHT WORDS!...

— *"With the ancient is wisdom; and in length of days understanding"* (see 12:12).

February 9 (Day 40), Memory Verse #81
Job 19:25:

FOR I KNOW THAT MY REDEEMER LIVETH,
AND THAT HE SHALL STAND AT THE LATTER DAY UPON THE EARTH:

February 9 (Day 40), Memory Verse #82
Job 28:28:

AND UNTO MAN HE SAID, BEHOLD,
THE FEAR OF THE LORD, THAT IS WISDOM;
AND TO DEPART FROM EVIL IS UNDERSTANDING.

— *"Now Elihu saw that there was no answer in the mouth of these three men, then his wrath was kindled"* (see 32:5) — **Elihu speaks in chapters 32-37.**

February 9 (Day 40), Memory Verse #83
Job 37:14:

HEARKEN UNTO THIS, O JOB:
STAND STILL, AND CONSIDER THE WONDROUS WORKS OF GOD.

Job 38-39: Speaking out of a whirlwind, God asks Job many questions and shows Job his lack of knowledge when compared to God — *"Where wast thou when I laid the foundations of the earth? Declare, if thou has understanding. Who hath laid the measures thereof, if thou knowest? or who hath stretched the line (measuring line, NIV) upon it? Whereupon are the foundations thereof fastened? or who laid the corner stone thereof; When the morning stars sang together, and all the sons of God shouted for joy?* (see 38:4-7) — God continues to ask Job questions.

Job 40-41: Job does not know how to answer God — **God has shown Job that man should not question God's way** — God speaks again.

Job 42: Job repents of questioning God — *"I have heard of thee by the hearing of the ear: but now mine eye seeth thee"* (see 42:5) — The Lord commands Eliphaz, Bildad, and Zophar to make a sacrifice — *"...the Lord had spoken these words unto Job, the Lord said to Eliphaz the Temanite, My wrath is kindled against thee, and against thy two friends: for ye have not spoken of me the thing that is right, as my servant Job hath"* (see 42:7) — **"...also the Lord gave Job twice as much as he had before"** (see 42:10) — **"So Job died, being old and full of days"** (see 42:17).

JOB 37:14:

...STAND STILL,

AND CONSIDER

THE WONDROUS WORKS OF GOD.

PSALMS

Introduction: Psalms (a Greek word meaning a poem sung with musical accompaniment) is a collection of various songs, poems, acrostics, praises, laments, prayers, and reflections of the Jewish people by various authors. The Psalms were gathered over the course of several centuries beginning in the time of David and Solomon in the 900's B.C.   The Hebrews divided Psalms into five collections: Psalms 1-41, 42-72, 73-89, 90-106, and 107-150. It was assembled into 150 Psalms in about the third century B.C.   David's name is attached to 73 of the Psalms. Suggested authors for the other Psalms include Solomon, Moses, Asaph, sons of Korah, Heman and Ethan. There are 126 of Psalms' chapters which have a title. Various themes of the 150 Psalms include Israel's history, God's creation, the Messiah, praise, repentance, cries for Jerusalem, cries for help, wisdom for living, and requests for punishment of the wicked.. Many verses are similar in Psalms; therefore, in the following key contents and key verses, certain verses are not repeated when another alike verse has already been quoted. Psalms has 150 chapters.

Key Contents and Key Memory Verses with Study Dates

Psalms 1-150: Since individual Psalms many times contain more than one theme, it seems best to emphasize overall key verses rather than each Psalm when looking at Psalms "in a nutshell." You may enjoy reading from THE BIBLE one Psalm per day, choosing even more verses for study and memorization.

February 10 (Day 41), Memory Verses #84 & #85
Psalm 1:1-2:

1. BLESSED IS THE MAN THAT WALKETH NOT IN THE COUNSEL OF THE UNGODLY, NOR STANDETH IN THE WAY OF SINNERS, NOR SITTETH IN THE SEAT OF THE SCORNFUL.

2. BUT HIS DELIGHT IS IN THE LAW OF THE LORD, AND IN HIS LAW DOTH HE MEDITATE DAY AND NIGHT.

February 10 (Day 41), Memory Verse #86
Psalm 5:3:

MY VOICE SHALT THOU HEAR IN THE MORNING, O LORD; IN THE MORNING WILL I DIRECT MY PRAYER UNTO THEE, AND WILL LOOK UP.

— *"But let all those that put their trust in thee rejoice:* let them ever shout for joy, because thou defendest them: let them also that love thy name be joyful in thee. For thou, Lord, wilt bless the righteous; with favour wilt thou compass him as with a shield" (see 5:11-12).

— *"O Lord my God, in thee do I put my trust:* save me from all them that persecute me, and deliver me:" (see 7:1).

February 10 (Day 41), Memory Verse #87
Psalm 8:1:

O LORD OUR LORD, HOW EXCELLENT IS THY NAME IN ALL THE EARTH! ...

— *"When I consider thy heavens, the work of thy fingers, the moon and the stars, which thou hast ordained; What is man, that thou art mindful of him?* and the son of man, that thou visitest him? For thou hast made his a little lower than the angels, and hast crowned him with glory and honour. Thou madest him to have dominion over the works of thy hands; thou hast put all things under his feet: All sheep and oxen, yea, and the beasts of the field; The fowl of the air, *and the fish of the sea, and whatsoever passeth through the paths of the seas. O Lord our Lord, how excellent is thy name in all the earth!"* (see 8:3-9).

— **"I will praise thee, O Lord, with my whole heart;** *I will shew forth all thy marvelous works. I will be glad and rejoice in thee: I will sing praise to thy name, O thou most High"* (see 9:1-2) — *"But the Lord shall endure for ever: he hath prepared his throne for judgment.* **And he shall judge the world in righteousness,** *he shall minister judgment to the people in uprightness.* **The Lord also will be a refuge for the oppressed,** *a refuge in times of trouble. And they that know thy name will put their trust in thee: for thou, Lord, hast not forsaken them that seek thee. Sing praises to the Lord, which dwelleth in Zion: declare among the people his doings"* (see 9:7-11).

— *"For the righteous Lord loveth righteousness;* *his countenance doth behold the upright"* (see 11:7).

February 11 (Day 42), Memory Verses #88 & #89
Psalm 12:6-7:

6. THE WORDS OF THE LORD ARE PURE WORDS:
AS SILVER TRIED IN A FURNACE OF EARTH, PURIFIED SEVEN TIMES.

7. THOU SHALT KEEP THEM, O LORD,
THOU SHALT PRESERVE THEM FROM THIS GENERATION FOR EVER.

— **"But I have trusted in thy mercy; my heart shall rejoice in thy salvation.** *I will sing unto the Lord, because he hath dealt bountifully with me"* (see 13:5-6).

February 11 (Day 42), Memory Verse #90
Psalm 14:1:

THE FOOL HATH SAID IN HIS HEART, THERE IS NO GOD...

— **"Lord, who shall abide in thy tabernacle?** *Who shall dwell in thy holy hill? He that walketh uprightly, and worketh righteousness, and speaketh the truth in his heart. He that backbiteth not with his tongue, nor doeth evil to his neighbour, nor taketh up a reproach against his neighbour"* (see 15:1-3).

— **"Thou wilt shew me the path of life:** *in thy presence is fullness of joy; at thy right hand there are pleasures for evermore"* (see 16:11).

February 11 (Day 42), Memory Verse #91
Psalm 18:2:

THE LORD IS MY ROCK, AND MY FORTRESS, AND MY DELIVERER;
MY GOD, MY STRENGTH, IN WHOM I WILL TRUST;
MY BUCKLER, AND THE HORN OF MY SALVATION, AND MY HIGH TOWER.

February 12 (Day 43), Memory Verses #92 to #95
Psalm 18:30-33:

30. AS FOR GOD, HIS WAY IS PERFECT: THE WORD OF THE LORD IS TRIED:
HE IS A BUCKLER TO ALL THOSE THAT TRUST IN HIM.

31. FOR WHO IS GOD SAVE THE LORD? OR WHO IS A ROCK SAVE OUR GOD?

32. IT IS GOD THAT GIRDETH ME WITH STRENGTH, AND MAKETH MY WAY PERFECT.

33. HE MAKETH MY FEET LIKE HINDS' FEET, AND SETTETH ME UPON MY HIGH PLACES.

February 13 (Day 44), Memory Verse #96
Psalm 19:1:

THE HEAVENS DECLARE THE GLORY OF GOD;
AND THE FIRMAMENT SHEWETH HIS HANDIWORK.

February 13-14 (Days 44-45), Memory Verses #97 to #100
Psalm 19:7-10:

7. THE LAW OF THE LORD IS PERFECT,
CONVERTING THE SOUL:
THE TESTIMONY OF THE LORD IS SURE,
MAKING WISE THE SIMPLE.

8. THE STATUTES OF THE LORD ARE RIGHT,
REJOICING THE HEART:
THE COMMANDMENT OF THE LORD IS PURE,
ENLIGHTENING THE EYES.

9. THE FEAR OF THE LORD IS CLEAN,
ENDURING FOR EVER:
THE JUDGMENTS OF THE LORD ARE TRUE AND RIGHTEOUS ALTOGETHER.

10. MORE TO BE DESIRED ARE THEY THAN GOLD,
YEA, THAN MUCH FINE GOLD:
SWEETER ALSO THAN HONEY AND THE HONEYCOMB.

February 14 (Day 45), Memory Verse #101
Psalm 19:14:

LET THE WORDS OF MY MOUTH, AND THE MEDITATION OF MY HEART,
BE ACCEPTABLE IN THY SIGHT, O LORD, MY STRENGTH, AND MY REDEEMER.

February 14-15 (Days 45-46), Memory Verse #102 to #107
Psalm 22:1, 14-18:
(Verses seen as foretelling Jesus' crucifixion)

1. MY GOD, MY GOD, WHY HAST THOU FORSAKEN ME? ...

14. I AM POURED OUT LIKE WATER, AND ALL MY BONES ARE OUT OF JOINT:
MY HEART IS LIKE WAX; IT IS MELTED IN THE MIDST OF MY BOWELS.

15. MY STRENGTH IS DRIED UP LIKE A POTSHERD;
AND MY TONGUE CLEAVETH TO MY JAWS;
AND THOU HAST BROUGHT ME INTO THE DUST OF DEATH.

16. FOR DOGS HAVE COMPASSED ME:
THE ASSEMBLY OF THE WICKED HAVE ENCLOSED ME:
THEY PIERCED MY HANDS AND MY FEET.

17. I MAY TELL ALL MY BONES:
THEY LOOK AND STARE UPON ME.

18. THEY PART MY GARMENTS AMONG THEM,
AND CAST LOTS UPON MY VESTURE.

February 16-17 (Days 47-48), Memory Verses #108 to #113
Psalm 23:1-6:

1. THE LORD IS MY SHEPHERD; I SHALL NOT WANT.

2. HE MAKETH ME TO LIE DOWN IN GREEN PASTURES:
HE LEADETH ME BESIDE THE STILL WATERS.

3. HE RESTORETH MY SOUL:
HE LEADETH ME IN THE PATHS OF RIGHTEOUSNESS FOR HIS NAME'S SAKE.

4. YEA, THOUGH I WALK THROUGH THE VALLEY OF THE SHADOW OF DEATH,
I WILL FEAR NO EVIL: FOR THOU ART WITH ME;
THY ROD AND THY STAFF THEY COMFORT ME.

5. THOU PREPAREST A TABLE BEFORE ME IN THE PRESENCE OF MINE ENEMIES:
THOU ANOINTEST MY HEAD WITH OIL; MY CUP RUNNETH OVER.

6. SURELY GOODNESS AND MERCY SHALL FOLLOW ME ALL THE DAYS OF MY LIFE:
AND I WILL DWELL IN THE HOUSE OF THE LORD FOR EVER.

February 18 (Day 49), Memory Verse #114
Psalm 24:1:

THE EARTH IS THE LORD'S, AND THE FULNESS THEREOF;
THE WORLD, AND THEY THAT DWELL THEREIN.

February 18 (Day 49), Memory Verses #115 to #117
Psalm 25:6-8:

6. REMEMBER, O LORD, THY TENDER MERCIES AND THY LOVINGKINDNESSES;
FOR THEY HAVE BEEN EVER OF OLD.

7. REMEMBER NOT THE SINS OF MY YOUTH, NOR MY TRANSGRESSIONS:
ACCORDING TO THY MERCY REMEMBER THOU ME FOR THY GOODNESS' SAKE, O LORD.

8. GOOD AND UPRIGHT IS THE LORD:
THEREFORE WILL HE TEACH SINNERS IN THE WAY.

February 19 (Day 50), Memory Verse #118
Psalm 27:1:

THE LORD IS MY LIGHT AND MY SALVATION; WHOM SHALL I FEAR?
THE LORD IS THE STRENGTH OF MY LIFE; OF WHOM SHALL I BE AFRAID?

February 19 (Day 50), Memory Verse #119
Psalm 27:14:

WAIT ON THE LORD: BE OF GOOD COURAGE,
AND HE SHALL STRENGTHEN THINE HEART:
WAIT, I SAY, ON THE LORD.

February 19 (Day 50), Memory Verse #120
Psalm 28:7:

THE LORD IS MY STRENGTH AND MY SHIELD;
MY HEART TRUSTED IN HIM, AND I AM HELPED:
THEREFORE MY HEART GREATLY REJOICETH;
AND WITH MY SONG WILL I PRAISE HIM.

February 19 (Day 50), Memory Verse #121
Psalm 31:5:

INTO THINE HAND I COMMIT MY SPIRIT:...

February 20 (Day 51), Memory Verse #122
Psalm 31:24:

BE OF GOOD COURAGE, AND HE SHALL STRENGTHEN YOUR HEART,
ALL YE THAT HOPE IN THE LORD.

— *"Many sorrows shall be to the wicked: but he that trusteth in the Lord, mercy shall compass him about. Be glad in the Lord, and rejoice, ye righteous: and shout for joy, all ye that are upright in heart"* (see 32:10-11).

February 20 (Day 51), Memory Verse #123
Psalm 33:12:

BLESSED IS THE NATION WHOSE GOD IS THE LORD;...

February 20 (Day 51), Memory Verse #124
Psalm 35:9:

AND MY SOUL SHALL BE JOYFUL IN THE LORD:
IT SHALL REJOICE IN HIS SALVATION.

February 20 (Day 51), Memory Verse #125
Psalm 36:7:

HOW EXCELLENT IS THY LOVINGKINDNESS, O GOD!
THEREFORE THE CHILDREN OF MEN PUT THEIR TRUST
UNDER THE SHADOW OF THY WINGS.

— *"For with thee is the fountain of life: in thy light shall we see light"* (see 36:9).

February 21 (Day 52), Memory Verses #126 & #127
Psalm 37:4-5:

4. DELIGHT THYSELF ALSO IN THE LORD;
AND HE SHALL GIVE THEE THE DESIRES OF THINE HEART.

5. COMMIT THY WAY UNTO THE LORD; TRUST ALSO IN HIM;
AND HE SHALL BRING IT TO PASS.

February 21 (Day 52), Memory Verse #128
Psalm 37:7:

REST IN THE LORD, AND WAIT PATIENTLY FOR HIM: ...

February 22 (Day 53), Memory Verses #129 & #130
Psalm 37:23-24:

23. THE STEPS OF A GOOD MAN ARE ORDERED BY THE LORD:
AND HE DELIGHTETH IN HIS WAY.

24. THOUGH HE FALL, HE SHALL NOT BE UTTERLY CAST DOWN:
FOR THE LORD UPHOLDETH HIM WITH HIS HAND.

February 22 (Day 53), Memory Verse #131
Psalm 40:5:

MANY, O LORD MY GOD, ARE THY WONDERFUL WORKS WHICH THOU HAST DONE,
AND THY THOUGHTS WHICH ARE TO US-WARD:
THEY CANNOT BE RECKONED UP IN ORDER UNTO THEE:
(The things you planned for us no one can recount to you, NIV):
IF I WOULD DECLARE AND SPEAK OF THEM,
THEY ARE MORE THAN CAN BE NUMBERED.

— *"Let all those that seek thee rejoice and be glad in thee: let such as love thy salvation say continually, **The Lord be magnified"** (see 40:16).*

February 23 (Day 54), Memory Verse #132
Psalm 42:1:

AS THE HART PANTETH AFTER THE WATER BROOKS,
SO PANTETH MY SOUL AFTER THEE, O GOD.

February 23 (Day 54), Memory Verse #133
Psalm 44:21:

...HE KNOWETH THE SECRETS OF THE HEART.

February 23 (Day 54), Memory Verse #134
Psalm 46:1:

GOD IS OUR REFUGE AND STRENGTH, A VERY PRESENT HELP IN TROUBLE.

February 23 (Day 54), Memory Verse #135
Psalm 46:10:

BE STILL, AND KNOW THAT I AM GOD: ...

February 24 (Day 55), Memory Verse #136
Psalm 47:1:

O CLAP YOUR HANDS, ALL YE PEOPLE;
SHOUT UNTO GOD WITH THE VOICE OF TRIUMPH.

February 24 (Day 55), Memory Verses #137 & #138
Psalm 47:6-7:

6. SING PRAISES TO GOD, SING PRAISES:
SING PRAISES UNTO OUR KING, SING PRAISES.

7. FOR GOD IS THE KING OF ALL THE EARTH:
SING YE PRAISES WITH UNDERSTANDING.

— *"For this God is our God for ever and ever: he will be our guide even unto death"* (see 48:14).

February 24 (Day 55), Memory Verse #139
Psalm 49:17:

FOR WHEN HE DIETH HE SHALL CARRY NOTHING AWAY:
HIS GLORY (splendor, NIV) SHALL NOT DESCEND AFTER HIM.

February 25 (Day 56), Memory Verse #140
Psalm 51:7:

...WASH ME, AND I SHALL BE WHITER THAN SNOW.

February 25 (Day 56), Memory Verse #141
Psalm 51:10:

CREATE IN ME A CLEAN HEART, O GOD;
AND RENEW A RIGHT SPIRIT WITHIN ME.

February 25 (Day 56), Memory Verse #142
Psalm 51:12:

RESTORE UNTO ME THE JOY OF THY SALVATION; ...

February 25 (Day 56), Memory Verse #143
Psalm 53:1:

THE FOOL HATH SAID IN HIS HEART, THERE IS NO GOD...

February 26 (Day 57), Memory Verse #144
Psalm 55:22:

CAST THY BURDEN UPON THE LORD, AND HE SHALL SUSTAIN THEE:...

February 26 (Day 57), Memory Verse #145
Psalm 56:3:

WHAT TIME I AM AFRAID, I WILL TRUST IN THEE.

February 26 (Day 57), Memory Verse #146
Psalm 56:11:

IN GOD HAVE I PUT MY TRUST:
I WILL NOT BE AFRAID WHAT MAN CAN DO UNTO ME.

— *"Deliver me from mine enemies, O my God: defend me from them that rise up against me"* (see 59:1).

February 27 (Day 58), Memory Verses #147 to #150
Psalm 62:5-8:

5. MY SOUL, WAIT THOU ONLY UPON GOD;
FOR MY EXPECTATION IS FROM HIM.

6. HE ONLY IS MY ROCK AND MY SALVATION:
HE IS MY DEFENCE; I SHALL NOT BE MOVED.

7. IN GOD IS MY SALVATION AND MY GLORY:
THE ROCK OF MY STRENGTH, AND MY REFUGE, IS IN GOD.

8. TRUST IN HIM AT ALL TIMES;
YE PEOPLE, POUR OUT YOUR HEART BEFORE HIM:
GOD IS A REFUGE FOR US...

— *"Because thy lovingkindness is better than life, my lips shall praise thee. Thus will I bless thee while I live: I will lift up my hands in thy name"* (see 63:3-4).

— **Psalm 65:5-13 are beautiful verses of God's creation.**

February 28 (Day 59), Memory Verse #151
Psalm 67:1:

GOD BE MERCIFUL UNTO US, AND BLESS US;
AND CAUSE HIS FACE TO SHINE UPON US;

— *"Hear me, O Lord; for thy lovingkindness is good:* turn unto me according to the multitude of thy tender mercies" (see 69:16).

— **Psalm 78 recounts the history and rebellions of Israel.**

February 28 (Day 59), Memory Verse #152
Psalm 84:11:

FOR THE LORD GOD IS A SUN AND SHIELD:
THE LORD WILL GIVE GRACE AND GLORY:
NO GOOD THING WILL HE WITHHOLD FROM THEM THAT WALK UPRIGHTLY.

— *"O Lord of hosts, blessed is the man that trusteth in thee"* (see 84:12).

— *"Surely his salvation is nigh them that fear him;* that glory may dwell in our land. Mercy and truth are met together; righteousness and peace have kissed each other. Truth shall spring out of the earth; and righteousness shall look down from heaven" (see 85:9-11).

February 28 (Day 59), Memory Verse #153
Psalm 86:5:

FOR THOU, LORD, ART GOOD, AND READY TO FORGIVE;
AND PLENTEOUS IN MERCY UNTO ALL THEM THAT CALL UPON THEE.

February 28 (Day 59), Memory Verse #154
Psalm 86:11:

TEACH ME THY WAY, O LORD; I WILL WALK IN THY TRUTH:...

March 1 (Day 60), Memory Verse #155
Psalm 86:15:

BUT THOU, O LORD, ART A GOD FULL OF COMPASSION,
AND GRACIOUS, LONGSUFFERING, AND PLENTEOUS IN MERCY AND TRUTH.

— **Psalm 88 is considered the saddest lament of Psalms.**

— **Psalm 90 is titled "A Prayer of Moses the man of God."**

March 1 (Day 60), Memory Verse #156
Psalm 90:2:

BEFORE THE MOUNTAINS WERE BROUGHT FORTH,
OR EVER THOU HADST FORMED THE EARTH AND THE WORLD,
EVEN FROM EVERLASTING TO EVERLASTING, THOU ART GOD.

March 1 (Day 60), Memory Verse #157
Psalm 90:4:

FOR A THOUSAND YEARS IN THY SIGHT ARE BUT AS YESTERDAY WHEN IT IS PAST,
AND AS A WATCH IN THE NIGHT.

March 1 (Day 60), Memory Verse #158
Psalm 90:12:

SO TEACH US TO NUMBER OUR DAYS,
THAT WE MAY APPLY OUR HEARTS UNTO WISDOM.

March 2 (Day 61), Memory Verse #159
Psalm 91:2:

I WILL SAY OF THE LORD, HE IS MY REFUGE AND MY FORTRESS:
MY GOD; IN HIM WILL I TRUST.

March 2 (Day 61), Memory Verses #160 & #161
Psalm 92:1-2:

1. IT IS A GOOD THING TO GIVE THANKS UNTO THE LORD,
AND TO SING PRAISES UNTO THY NAME, O MOST HIGH:

2. TO SHEW FORTH THY LOVINGKINDNESS IN THE MORNING,
AND THY FAITHFULNESS EVERY NIGHT,

— *"O Lord, how great are thy works! and thy thoughts are very deep"* (see 92:5).

— *"The Lord on high is mightier than the noise of many waters, yea, than the mighty waves of the sea"* (see 93:4).

March 2 (Day 61), Memory Verse #162
Psalm 94:12:

BLESSED IS THE MAN WHOM THOU CHASTENEST (you discipline, NIV), O LORD,
AND TEACHEST HIM OUT OF THY LAW;

— *"O come, let us sing unto the Lord:* let us make a joyful noise to the rock of our salvation"* (see 95:1).

March 3 (Day 62), Memory Verses #163 & #164
Psalm 95:6-7:

6. O COME, LET US WORSHIP AND BOW DOWN:
LET US KNEEL BEFORE THE LORD OUR MAKER.

7. FOR HE IS OUR GOD;
AND WE ARE THE SHEEP OF HIS PASTURE,
AND THE SHEEP OF HIS HAND (the flock under his care, NIV) …

— **Psalm 96 calls people to sing, praise, worship, and rejoice unto the Lord.**

March 3-4 (Days 62-63), Memory Verses #165 to #169
Psalm 100: 1-5:

1. MAKE A JOYFUL NOISE UNTO THE LORD, ALL YE LANDS.

2. SERVE THE LORD WITH GLADNESS:
COME BEFORE HIS PRESENCE WITH SINGING.

3. KNOW YE THAT THE LORD HE IS GOD:
IT IS HE THAT HATH MADE US, AND NOT WE OURSELVES;
WE ARE HIS PEOPLE, AND THE SHEEP OF HIS PASTURE.

4. ENTER INTO HIS GATES WITH THANKSGIVING,
AND INTO HIS COURTS WITH PRAISE:
BE THANKFUL UNTO HIM, AND BLESS HIS NAME

5. FOR THE LORD IS GOOD; HIS MERCY IS EVERLASTING;
AND HIS TRUTH ENDURETH TO ALL GENERATIONS.

March 5 (Day 64), Memory Verse #170
Psalm 102:25:

OF OLD HAST THOU LAID THE FOUNDATION OF THE EARTH:
AND THE HEAVENS ARE THE WORK OF THY HANDS.

March 5 (Day 64), Memory Verses #171 & #172
Psalm 103:1-2:

1. BLESS THE LORD, O MY SOUL:
AND ALL THAT IS WITHIN ME, BLESS HIS HOLY NAME.

2. BLESS THE LORD, O MY SOUL, AND FORGET NOT ALL HIS BENEFITS:

— *"The Lord is merciful and gracious, slow to anger, and plenteous in mercy.* He will not always chide: neither will he keep his anger for ever... For as the heaven is high above the earth, so great is his mercy toward them that fear him" (see 103:8-9,11).

March 6 (Day 65), Memory Verse #173
Psalm 103:12:

AS FAR AS THE EAST IS FROM THE WEST,
SO FAR HATH HE REMOVED OUR TRANSGRESSIONS FROM US.

— **Psalm 104 praises God as the Creator.**

March 6 (Day 65), Memory Verses #174 & #175
Psalm 104:33-34:

33. I WILL SING UNTO THE LORD AS LONG AS I LIVE:
I WILL SING PRAISE TO MY GOD WHILE I HAVE MY BEING.

34. MY MEDITATION OF HIM SHALL BE SWEET:
I WILL BE GLAD IN THE LORD.

— *"O give thanks unto the Lord; call upon his name: make known his deeds among the people. Sing unto him: talk ye of all his wondrous works. Glory ye in his holy name: let the heart of them rejoice that seek the Lord. Seek the Lord, and his strength: seek his face evermore. Remember his marvelous works that he hath done; his wonders, and the judgments of his mouth;"* (see 105:1-5).

— **Psalms 105-107 tell of Israel's history** — *"And he brought forth his people with joy, and his chosen with gladness: And gave them the lands of the heathen: and they inherited the labour of the people; That they might observe his statutes, and keep his laws. Praise ye the Lord"* (see 105:43-45).

— ***"Give us help from trouble:*** *for vain is the help of man"* (see 108:12).

March 7 (Day 66), Memory Verse #176
Psalm 111:10:

THE FEAR OF THE LORD IS THE BEGINNING OF WISDOM:
A GOOD UNDERSTANDING HAVE ALL THEY THAT DO HIS COMMANDMENTS:
HIS PRAISE ENDURETH FOR EVER.

— **Psalm 113 is a beautiful praise psalm** — *"From the rising of the sun unto the going down of the same the Lord's name is to be praised"* (see 113:3).

March 7 (Day 66), Memory Verses #177 & #178
Psalm 117:1-2:

1. O PRAISE THE LORD, ALL YE NATIONS: PRAISE HIM, ALL YE PEOPLE.

2. FOR HIS MERCIFUL KINDNESS IS GREAT TOWARD US:
AND THE TRUTH OF THE LORD ENDURETH FOR EVER. PRAISE YE THE LORD.

March 8 (Day 67), Memory Verse #179
Psalm 118:8:

IT IS BETTER TO TRUST IN THE LORD THAN TO PUT CONFIDENCE IN MAN.

March 8 (Day 67), Memory Verse #180
Psalm 118:22:
(Jesus uses this cornerstone verse; see Matthew 21:42.)

THE STONE WHICH THE BUILDERS REFUSED
IS BECOME THE HEAD STONE OF THE CORNER.

March 8 (Day 67), Memory Verse #181
Psalm 118:24:

THIS IS THE DAY WHICH THE LORD HATH MADE; WE WILL REJOICE AND BE GLAD IN IT.

March 9 (Day 68), Memory Verse #182
Psalm 119:11:

THY WORD HAVE I HID IN MINE HEART, THAT I MIGHT NOT SIN AGAINST THEE.

— *"The earth, O Lord, is full of thy mercy;* ***teach me thy statutes"*** (see 119:64) — *"It is good for me that I have been afflicted; that I might learn thy statutes. The law of thy mouth is better unto me than thousands of gold and silver"* (see 119:71-72).

March 9 (Day 68), Memory Verse #183
Psalm 119: 80:

LET MY HEART BE SOUND IN THY STATUTES; THAT I BE NOT ASHAMED.

March 9 (Day 68), Memory Verse #184
Psalm 119: 103:

HOW SWEET ARE THY WORDS UNTO MY TASTE!
YEA, SWEETER THAN HONEY TO MY MOUTH!

March 10 (Day 69), Memory Verse #185
Psalm 119: 105:

THY WORD IS A LAMP UNTO MY FEET, AND A LIGHT UNTO MY PATH.

March 10 (Day 69), Memory Verse #186
Psalm 119: 127:

THEREFORE I LOVE THY COMMANDMENTS ABOVE GOLD; YEA, ABOVE FINE GOLD.

— **Psalms 120-134 are known as the Zion Psalms** since these Psalms were used by the Jews when traveling to Jerusalem and the temple on Mount Zion for various annual feasts including the Passover and Pentecost.

March 11-12 (Days 70-71), Memory Verses #187 to #194
Psalm 121:1-8:

1. I WILL LIFT UP MINE EYES UNTO THE HILLS, FROM WHENCE COMETH MY HELP.

2. MY HELP COMETH FROM THE LORD, WHICH MADE HEAVEN AND EARTH.

3. HE WILL NOT SUFFER THY FOOT TO BE MOVED:
HE THAT KEEPETH THEE WILL NOT SLUMBER.

4. BEHOLD, HE THAT KEEPETH ISRAEL SHALL NEITHER SLUMBER NOR SLEEP.

5. THE LORD IS THY KEEPER:
THE LORD IS THY SHADE UPON THY RIGHT HAND.

6. THE SUN SHALL NOT SMITE THEE BY DAY, NOR THE MOON BY NIGHT.

7. THE LORD SHALL PRESERVE THEE FROM ALL EVIL:
HE SHALL PRESERVE THY SOUL.

8. THE LORD SHALL PRESERVE THY GOING OUT AND THY COMING IN
FROM THIS TIME FORTH, AND EVEN FOR EVERMORE.

March 13 (Day 72), Memory Verse #195
Psalm 122:1:

I WAS GLAD WHEN THEY SAID UNTO ME,
LET US GO INTO THE HOUSE OF THE LORD.

March 13 (Day 72), Memory Verse #196
Psalm 130: 5:

I WAIT FOR THE LORD, MY SOUL DOTH WAIT,
AND IN HIS WORD DO I HOPE.

March 13 (Day 72), Memory Verse #197
Psalm 133:1:

BEHOLD, HOW GOOD AND HOW PLEASANT IT IS
FOR BRETHREN TO DWELL TOGETHER IN UNITY!

— *"Praise ye the Lord. Praise ye the name of the Lord; praise him, O ye servants of the Lord. Ye that stand in the house of the Lord, in the courts of the house of our God, Praise the Lord; for the Lord is good: sing praises unto his name; for it is pleasant"* (see 135:1-3).

March 14-15 (Days 73-74), Memory Verses #198 to #203
Psalm 136:1, 5-9:

1. O GIVE THANKS UNTO THE LORD; FOR HE IS GOOD:
   FOR HIS MERCY ENDURETH FOR EVER.

5. TO HIM THAT BY WISDOM MADE THE HEAVENS:
   FOR HIS MERCY ENDURETH FOR EVER.

6. TO HIM THAT STRETCHED OUT THE EARTH ABOVE THE WATERS:
   FOR HIS MERCY ENDURETH FOR EVER.

7. TO HIM THAT MADE GREAT LIGHTS:
   FOR HIS MERCY ENDURETH FOR EVER.

8. THE SUN TO RULE BY DAY:
   FOR HIS MERCY ENDURETH FOR EVER:

9. THE MOON AND STARS TO RULE BY NIGHT:
   FOR HIS MERCY ENDURETH FOR EVER.

March 16 (Day 75), Memory Verses #204 & #205
Psalm 139:9-10:

9. IF I TAKE THE WINGS OF THE MORNING,
   AND DWELL IN THE UTTERMOST PARTS OF THE SEA;

10. EVEN THERE SHALL THY HAND LEAD ME,
    AND THY RIGHT HAND SHALL HOLD ME.

March 16 (Day 75), Memory Verse #206
Psalm 139:14:

I WILL PRAISE THEE;
FOR I AM FEARFULLY AND WONDERFULLY MADE:
MARVELLOUS ARE THY WORKS;
AND THAT MY SOUL KNOWETH RIGHT (Full, NIV) WELL.

March 17 (Day 76) Memory Verses #207 & #208
Psalm 139:23-24:

23. SEARCH ME, O GOD, AND KNOW MY HEART:
    TRY ME, AND KNOW MY THOUGHTS:

24. AND SEE IF THERE BE ANY WICKED WAY IN ME,
    AND LEAD ME IN THE WAY EVERLASTING.

March 17 (Day 76), Memory Verse #209
Psalm 141:3:

SET A WATCH, O LORD, BEFORE MY MOUTH;
KEEP THE DOOR OF MY LIPS.

March 17 (Day 76), Memory Verse #210
Psalm 143:8:

CAUSE ME TO HEAR THY LOVINGKINDNESS IN THE MORNING;
FOR IN THEE DO I TRUST:
CAUSE ME TO KNOW THE WAY WHEREIN I SHOULD WALK;
FOR I LIFT UP MY SOUL UNTO THEE.

March 18 (Day 77), Memory Verse #211
Psalm 144:15:

...HAPPY IS THAT PEOPLE,
WHOSE GOD IS THE LORD.

March 18 (Day 77), Memory Verse #212
Psalm 145:3:

GREAT IS THE LORD,
AND GREATLY TO BE PRAISED;
AND HIS GREATNESS IS UNSEARCHABLE.

— *"The Lord is gracious, and full of compassion; slow to anger, and of great mercy. The Lord is good to all: and his tender mercies are over all his works"* (see 145:8-9). *"The Lord is nigh unto all them that call upon him, to all that call upon him in truth"* (see 145:18).

— *"Praise ye the Lord. Praise ye the Lord from the heavens: praise him in the heights"* (see 148:1).

March 18-19 (Days 77-78), Memory Verses #213 to #218
Psalm 150:1-6:

1. PRAISE YE THE LORD. PRAISE GOD IN HIS SANCTUARY:
PRAISE HIM IN THE FIRMAMENT OF HIS POWER.

2. PRAISE HIM FOR HIS MIGHTY ACTS:
PRAISE HIM ACCORDING TO HIS EXCELLENT GREATNESS.

3. PRAISE HIM WITH THE SOUND OF THE TRUMPET:
PRAISE HIM WITH THE PSALTERY AND HARP.

4. PRAISE HIM WITH THE TIMBREL AND DANCE:
PRAISE HIM WITH STRINGED INSTRUMENTS AND ORGANS.

5. PRAISE HIM UPON THE LOUD CYMBALS:
PRAISE HIM UPON THE HIGH SOUNDING CYMBALS.

6. LET EVERY THING THAT HATH BREATH PRAISE THE LORD.
PRAISE YE THE LORD.

PSALM 14:1 & 53:1:
THE FOOL HATH SAID IN HIS HEART, THERE IS NO GOD...

PSALM 19:1:
THE HEAVENS DECLARE THE GLORY OF GOD; AND THE FIRMAMENT SHEWETH HIS HANDIWORK.

PSALM 23:1:
THE LORD IS MY SHEPHERD; I SHALL NOT WANT.

PSALM 46:10:
BE STILL, AND KNOW THAT I AM GOD:...

PSALM 51:10:
CREATE IN ME A CLEAN HEART, O GOD; AND RENEW A RIGHT SPIRIT WITHIN ME.

PSALM 100: 1:
MAKE A JOYFUL NOISE UNTO THE LORD, ALL YE LANDS.

PSALM 144:15:
...HAPPY IS THAT PEOPLE, WHOSE GOD IS THE LORD.

PROVERBS

Introduction: This book is a collection of proverbs written by various authors about wisdom for living. Tradition and the book of Proverbs attribute authorship of most of the proverbs to Solomon during the 900's B.C. (see I Kings 4:29-32). Agur and Lemuel, teachers during King Hezekiah's rule in Jerusalem, are thought to have written the last two chapters. Proverbs has 31 chapters.

Key Contents and Key Memory Verses with Study Dates

Proverbs 1-31: Since Proverbs has such a varied mixture of wise sayings for living, it seems best to emphasize themes by key verses rather than chapters when looking at Proverbs "in a nutshell." You will also enjoy reading Proverbs from THE BIBLE and finding other verses for study.

— *"The proverbs of Solomon the son of David, king of Israel;* To know wisdom and instruction; to perceive the words of understanding; To receive the instruction of wisdom, justice, and judgment, and equity" (see 1:1-3).

March 20 (Day 79), Memory Verse #219
Proverbs 1:7:

THE FEAR OF THE LORD IS THE BEGINNING OF KNOWLEDGE:
BUT FOOLS DESPISE WISDOM AND INSTRUCTION.

March 20 (Day 79), Memory Verses #220 to #222
Proverbs 2:3-5:

3. YEA, IF THOU CRIEST AFTER KNOWLEDGE,
AND LIFTEST UP THY VOICE FOR UNDERSTANDING;

4. IF THOU SEEKEST HER AS SILVER, AND SEARCHEST FOR HER AS FOR HID TREASURES;

5. THEN SHALT THOU UNDERSTAND THE FEAR OF THE LORD,
AND FIND THE KNOWLEDGE OF GOD.

March 21-23 (Days 80-82), Memory Verses #223 to #231
Proverbs 3:1-9:

1. MY SON, FORGET NOT MY LAW; BUT LET THINE HEART KEEP MY COMMANDMENTS;

2. FOR LENGTH OF DAYS, AND LONG LIFE, AND PEACE, SHALL THEY ADD TO THEE.

3. LET NOT MERCY AND TRUTH FORSAKE THEE: BIND THEM ABOUT THY NECK;
WRITE THEM UPON THE TABLE OF THINE HEART:

4. SO SHALT THOU FIND FAVOUR AND GOOD UNDERSTANDING
IN THE SIGHT OF GOD AND MAN.

5. TRUST IN THE LORD WITH ALL THINE HEART;
AND LEAN NOT UNTO THINE OWN UNDERSTANDING.

6. IN ALL THY WAYS ACKNOWLEDGE HIM, AND HE SHALL DIRECT THY PATHS.

7. BE NOT WISE IN THINE OWN EYES: FEAR THE LORD, AND DEPART FROM EVIL.

8. IT SHALL BE HEALTH TO THY NAVEL, AND MARROW TO THY BONES.

9. HONOUR THE LORD WITH THY SUBSTANCE,
AND WITH THE FIRSTFRUITS OF ALL THINE INCREASE:

March 24 (Day 83), Memory Verses #232 & #233
Proverbs 3:11-12:

11. MY SON, DESPISE NOT THE CHASTENING OF THE LORD;
NEITHER BE WEARY OF HIS CORRECTION:

12. FOR WHOM THE LORD LOVETH HE CORRECTETH;
EVEN AS A FATHER THE SON IN WHOM HE DELIGHTETH.

— *"Hear ye children, the instruction of a father…"* (see 4:1).

March 25 (Day 84), Memory Verse #234
Proverbs 4:18:

BUT THE PATH OF THE JUST IS AS THE SHINING LIGHT,
THAT SHINETH MORE AND MORE UNTO THE PERFECT DAY.

March 25 (Day 84), Memory Verse #235
Proverbs 6:6:

GO TO THE ANT, THOU SLUGGARD;
CONSIDER HER WAYS, AND BE WISE:

— *"These six things doth the Lord hate: yea, seven are an abomination unto him: A proud look, a lying tongue, and hands that shed innocent blood, An heart that deviseth wicked imaginations, feet that be swift in running to mischief, A false witness that speaketh lies, and he that soweth discord among brethren"* (see 6:16-19).

March 26 (Day 85), Memory Verses #236 to #238
Proverbs 6:20-22:

20. MY SON, KEEP THY FATHER'S COMMANDMENT,
AND FORSAKE NOT THE LAW OF THY MOTHER:

21. BIND THEM CONTINUALLY UPON THINE HEART,
AND TIE THEM ABOUT THY NECK.

22. WHEN THOU GOEST, IT SHALL LEAD THEE;
WHEN THOU SLEEPEST, IT SHALL KEEP THEE;
AND WHEN THOU AWAKEST, IT SHALL TALK WITH THEE.

March 27 (Day 86), Memory Verse #239
Proverbs 9:10:

THE FEAR OF THE LORD IS THE BEGINNING OF WISDOM:
AND THE KNOWLEDGE OF THE HOLY IS UNDERSTANDING.

March 27 (Day 86), Memory Verse #240
Proverbs 10:1:

…A WISE SON MAKETH A GLAD FATHER:
BUT A FOOLISH SON IS THE HEAVINESS OF HIS MOTHER.

March 27 (Day 86), Memory Verse #241
Proverbs 10:12:

HATRED STIRRETH UP STRIFES: BUT LOVE COVERETH ALL SINS.

March 28 (Day 87), Memory Verse #242
Proverbs 11:30:

THE FRUIT OF THE RIGHTEOUS IS A TREE OF LIFE;
AND HE THAT WINNETH SOULS IS WISE.

March 28 (Day 87), Memory Verse #243
Proverbs 12:28:

IN THE WAY OF RIGHTEOUSNESS IS LIFE;
AND IN THE PATHWAY THEREOF THERE IS NO DEATH.

March 29 (Day 88), Memory Verse #244
Proverbs 14:21:

HE THAT DESPISETH HIS NEIGHBOUR SINNETH:
BUT HE THAT HATH MERCY ON THE POOR, HAPPY IS HE.

March 29 (Day 88), Memory Verse #245
Proverbs 14:30:

A SOUND HEART IS THE LIFE OF THE FLESH:
BUT ENVY THE ROTTENNESS OF THE BONES,

March 30 (Day 89), Memory Verse #246
Proverbs 15:1:

A SOFT ANSWER TURNETH AWAY WRATH: BUT GRIEVOUS WORDS STIR UP ANGER.

March 30 (Day 89), Memory Verse #247
Proverbs 15:6:

IN THE HOUSE OF THE RIGHTEOUS IS MUCH TREASURE:
BUT IN THE REVENUES OF THE WICKED IS TROUBLE.

March 30 (Day 89), Memory Verse #248
Proverbs 15:13:

A MERRY HEART MAKETH A CHEERFUL COUNTENANCE:
BUT BY SORROW OF THE HEART THE SPIRIT IS BROKEN.

March 31 (Day 90), Memory Verses #249 & #250
Proverbs 15:15-16:

15. ...HE THAT IS OF A MERRY HEART HATH A CONTINUAL FEAST.

16. BETTER IS LITTLE WITH THE FEAR OF THE LORD
THAN GREAT TREASURE AND TROUBLE THEREWITH.

March 31 (Day 90), Memory Verse #251
Proverbs 15:33:

THE FEAR OF THE LORD IS THE INSTRUCTION OF WISDOM;
AND BEFORE HONOUR IS HUMILITY.

April 1 (Day 91), Memory Verse #252
Proverbs 16:3:

COMMIT THY WORKS UNTO THE LORD, AND THY THOUGHTS SHALL BE ESTABLISHED.

April 1 (Day 91), Memory Verse #253
Proverbs 16:24:

PLEASANT WORDS ARE AS AN HONEYCOMB,
SWEET TO THE SOUL, AND HEALTH TO THE BONES.

April 1 (Day 91), Memory Verse #254
Proverbs 16:32:

HE THAT IS SLOW TO ANGER IS BETTER THAN THE MIGHTY;
AND HE THAT RULETH HIS SPIRIT THAN HE THAT TAKETH A CITY.

April 1 (Day 91), Memory Verse #255
Proverbs 17:3:

THE FINING POT IS FOR SILVER, AND THE FURNACE FOR GOLD:
BUT THE LORD TRIETH THE HEARTS.

April 2 (Day 92), Memory Verse #256
Proverbs 17:17:

A FRIEND LOVETH AT ALL TIMES,...

April 2 (Day 92), Memory Verse #257
Proverbs 17:22:

A MERRY HEART DOETH GOOD LIKE A MEDICINE:
BUT A BROKEN SPIRIT DRIETH THE BONES.

— *"The words of a man's mouth are as deep waters, and **the wellspring of wisdom as a flowing brook**"* (see 18:4).

April 2 (Day 92), Memory Verses #258 & #259
Proverbs 18:7-8:

7. A FOOL'S MOUTH IS HIS DESTRUCTION, AND HIS LIPS ARE THE SNARE OF HIS SOUL.

8. THE WORDS OF A TALEBEARER ARE AS WOUNDS,
AND THEY GO DOWN INTO THE INNERMOST PARTS OF THE BELLY.

April 3 (Day 93), Memory Verse #260
Proverbs 18:10:

THE NAME OF THE LORD IS A STRONG TOWER:
THE RIGHTEOUS RUNNETH INTO IT, AND IS SAFE.

April 3 (Day 93), Memory Verse #261
Proverbs 18:12:

BEFORE DESTRUCTION THE HEART OF MAN IS HAUGHTY,
AND BEFORE HONOUR IS HUMILITY.

April 3 (Day 93), Memory Verse #262
Proverbs 18:15:

THE HEART OF THE PRUDENT GETTETH KNOWLEDGE;
AND THE EAR OF THE WISE SEEKETH KNOWLEDGE.

April 4 (Day 94), Memory Verse #263
Proverbs 20:15:

THERE IS GOLD, AND A MULTITUDE OF RUBIES:
BUT THE LIPS OF KNOWLEDGE ARE A PRECIOUS JEWEL.

April 4 (Day 94), Memory Verse #264
Proverbs 21:2:

EVERY WAY OF A MAN IS RIGHT IN HIS OWN EYES:
BUT THE LORD PONDERETH THE HEARTS.

April 4 (Day 94), Memory Verse #265
Proverbs 22:1:

A GOOD NAME IS RATHER TO BE CHOSEN THAN GREAT RICHES,
AND LOVING FAVOUR RATHER THAN SILVER AND GOLD.

April 4 (Day 94), Memory Verse #266
Proverbs 22:6:

TRAIN UP A CHILD IN THE WAY HE SHOULD GO:
AND WHEN HE IS OLD, HE WILL NOT DEPART FROM IT.

April 5 (Day 95), Memory Verse #267
Proverbs 23:7:

FOR AS HE THINKETH IN HIS HEART, SO IS HE:...

April 5 (Day 95), Memory Verse #268
Proverbs 23:17:

LET NOT THINE HEART ENVY SINNERS:
BUT BE THOU IN THE FEAR OF THE LORD ALL THE DAY LONG.

April 5 (Day 95), Memory Verses #269 & #270
Proverbs 24:13-14:

13. MY SON, EAT THOU HONEY, BECAUSE IT IS GOOD;
AND THE HONEYCOMB, WHICH IS SWEET TO THY TASTE:

14. SO SHALL THE KNOWLEDGE OF WISDOM BE UNTO THY SOUL:
WHEN THOU HAST FOUND IT...

April 6 (Day 96), Memory Verse #271
Proverbs 25:11:

A WORD FITLY SPOKEN IS LIKE APPLES OF GOLD IN PICTURES OF SILVER.

April 6 (Day 96), Memory Verses #272 & #273
Proverbs 25:21-22:

21. IF THINE ENEMY BE HUNGRY, GIVE HIM BREAD TO EAT;
AND IF HE BE THIRSTY, GIVE HIM WATER TO DRINK:

22. FOR THOU SHALT HEAP COALS OF FIRE UPON HIS HEAD,
AND THE LORD SHALL REWARD THEE.

April 7 (Day 97), Memory Verse #274
Proverbs 27:2:

LET ANOTHER MAN PRAISE THEE, AND NOT THINE OWN MOUTH;
A STRANGER, AND NOT THINE OWN LIPS.

April 7 (Day 97), Memory Verse #275
Proverbs 29:23:

A MAN'S PRIDE SHALL BRING HIM LOW:
BUT HONOUR SHALL UPHOLD THE HUMBLE IN SPIRIT.

April 7 (Day 97), Memory Verses #276 & #277
Proverbs 29:25-26:

25. THE FEAR OF MAN BRINGETH A SNARE:
BUT WHOSO PUTTETH HIS TRUST IN THE LORD SHALL BE SAFE.

26. MANY SEEK THE RULER'S FAVOUR;
BUT EVERY MAN'S JUDGMENT COMETH FROM THE LORD.

April 8 (Day 98), Memory Verse #278
Proverbs 30:5:

EVERY WORD OF GOD IS PURE:
HE IS A SHIELD UNTO THEM THAT PUT THEIR TRUST IN HIM.

— **Proverbs 31 emphasizes the qualities of a virtuous woman** — *"The heart of her husband doth safely trust in her..."* (see 31:10) — She *"...worketh willingly with her hands"* (see 31:13) — *"She stretcheth out her hand to the poor; yea, she reacheth forth her hands to the needy"* (see 31:20) — *"Strength and honour are her clothing;... She openeth her mouth with wisdom; and in her tongue is the law of kindness"* (see 31:25-26) — *"Her children arise up, and call her blessed; her husband also, and he praiseth her"* (see 31:28).

April 8 (Day 98), Memory Verse #279
Proverbs 31:30:

FAVOUR (Charm, NIV) IS DECEITFUL, AND BEAUTY IS VAIN:
BUT A WOMAN THAT FEARETH THE LORD, SHE SHALL BE PRAISED.

PROVERBS 22:6:

TRAIN UP A CHILD IN THE WAY HE SHOULD GO: AND WHEN HE IS OLD, HE WILL NOT DEPART FROM IT.

ECCLESIASTES

Introduction: The title, Ecclesiastes, is derived from a Greek word meaning "teacher" or "preacher." The author is not mentioned. Tradition points to King Solomon as the author in the 900's B.C. Others believe someone not of royalty and living as late as the 300's B.C. was the author. Perhaps the author was recording Solomon's wisdom passed down through the centuries. The main conclusions from the author's searching for the meaning of life are as follows: life is to be enjoyed, life is a gift from God, and the wise man will be obedient to God. Ecclesiastes has 12 chapters.

Key Contents and Key Memory Verses with Study Dates

<u>**Ecclesiastes 1-2:**</u> **The author, who calls himself "the preacher," sees life, work, and the attainment of wealth as meaningless** — *"I the Preacher was king over Israel in Jerusalem. And I gave my heart to seek and search out by wisdom concerning all things that are done under heaven: this sore travail hath God given to the sons of man to be exercised therewith. I have seen all the works that are done under the sun; and, behold, all is vanity and vexation of spirit"* (see 1:12-14) — *"And I gave my heart to know wisdom, and to know madness and folly: I perceived that this also is vexation of spirit"* (see 1:17) — *"Then I looked on all the works that my hands had wrought, and on the labour that I had laboured to do: and, behold, all was vanity and vexation of spirit, and there was no profit under the sun"* (see 2:11) — The author states there *"...is nothing better for a man, than that he should eat and drink, and that he should make his soul enjoy good in his labour. This also I saw, that it was from the hand of God"* (see 2:24).

<u>**Ecclesiastes 3:**</u> **The author continues his search for wisdom and the meaning of life.**

April 9 (Day 99), Memory Verse #280
<u>**Ecclesiastes 3:1:**</u>

TO EVERYTHING THERE IS A SEASON,
AND A TIME TO EVERY PURPOSE UNDER THE HEAVEN: ...

— *"A time to be born, and a time to die; a time to plant, and a time to pluck up that which is planted; A time to kill, and a time to heal; a time to break down, and a time to build up; A time to weep, and a time to laugh; a time to mourn, and a time to dance; A time to cast away stones, and a time to gather stones together; a time to embrace, and a time to refrain from embracing; A time to get, and a time to lose; a time to keep, and a time to cast away; A time to rend, and a time to sew; a time to keep silence, and a time to speak; A time to love, and a time to hate; a time of war, and a time of peace"* (see 3:2-8) — ***"He hath made every thing beautiful in his time: ..."*** (see 3:11).

April 9 (Day 99), Memory Verse #281
<u>**Ecclesiastes 3:17:**</u>

I SAID IN MINE HEART, GOD SHALL JUDGE THE RIGHTEOUS AND THE WICKED:
FOR THERE IS A TIME THERE FOR EVERY PURPOSE AND FOR EVERY WORK.

<u>**Ecclesiastes 4:**</u>   **The author cannot see any purpose in the sufferings and hardships of humanity** — *"So I returned, and considered all the oppressions that are done under the sun: and behold the tears of such as were oppressed..."* (see 4:1).

Ecclesiastes 5: The author sees how striving for riches and not honoring God is foolish and vain — *"He that loveth silver shall not be satisfied with silver; nor he that loveth abundance with increase: this is all vanity"* (see 5:10).

April 10 (Day 100), Memory Verses #282 & #283
Ecclesiastes 5:18-19:

18. BEHOLD THAT WHICH I HAVE SEEN:
IT IS GOOD AND COMELY FOR ONE TO EAT AND DRINK,
AND TO ENJOY THE GOOD OF ALL HIS LABOUR THAT HE TAKETH UNDER THE SUN
ALL THE DAYS OF HIS LIFE, WHICH GOD GIVETH HIM:
FOR IT IS HIS PORTION.

19. EVERY MAN ALSO TO WHOM GOD HATH GIVEN RICHES AND WEALTH,
AND HATH GIVEN HIM POWER TO EAT THEREOF,
AND TO TAKE HIS PORTION, AND TO REJOICE IN HIS LABOUR;
THIS IS THE GIFT OF GOD.

Ecclesiastes 6: Striving for riches and honor is seen as foolishness.

Ecclesiastes 7-12:   These chapters emphasize wisdom as honoring God and keeping His commandments.

April 11 (Day 101), Memory Verse #284
Ecclesiastes 7:1:

A GOOD NAME IS BETTER THAN PRECIOUS OINTMENT; ...

April 11 (Day 101), Memory Verse #285
Ecclesiastes 7:20:

FOR THERE IS NOT A MAN UPON EARTH, THAT DOETH GOOD, AND SINNETH NOT.

April 11 (Day 101), Memory Verse #286
Ecclesiastes 9:10:

WHATSOEVER THY HAND FINDETH TO DO, DO IT WITH THY MIGHT;...

April 12 (Day 102), Memory Verse #287
Ecclesiastes 12:1:

REMEMBER NOW THY CREATOR IN THE DAYS OF THY YOUTH ...

April 12 (Day 102), Memory Verses #288 & #289
Ecclesiastes 12:13-14:

13. LET US HEAR THE CONCLUSION OF THE WHOLE MATTER:
FEAR GOD, AND KEEP HIS COMMANDMENTS:
FOR THIS IS THE WHOLE DUTY OF MAN.

14. FOR GOD SHALL BRING EVERY WORK INTO JUDGMENT, WITH EVERY SECRET THING,
WHETHER IT BE GOOD, OR WHETHER IT BE EVIL.

ECCLESIASTES 3:1:

TO EVERYTHING THERE IS A SEASON...

SONG OF SOLOMON

Introduction: Many believe Solomon wrote this book of love, courtship, and marriage in the 900's B.C. Others believe it may be the work of another or several authors. The story tells how the king falls in love, perhaps for the first time, with a Shulammite woman who tends her family's vineyard. The story also tells of their marriage. In the last chapter, the strong love of marriage is wonderfully described (see 8:6-7). The beauty of human sexuality is poetically expressed in this book. Sometimes the author's expression of love for his lover seems humorous today; for example, see 4:1-5. Song of Solomon has eight chapters.

Key Contents and Key Memory Verses with Study Dates

<u>Song of Solomon 1-8:</u> **The eight chapters of Song of Solomon are a discourse between the king, his lover, and their friends** — While having these conversations, the lovers meet at various occasions during courtship and marriage — This book begins with the words, *"The song of songs, which is Solomon's"* (see 1:1) — **The following are special verses expressing love:**

— *Let him kiss me with the kisses of his mouth: for thy love is better than wine"* (see 1: 2).

April 13 (Day 103), Memory Verse #290
<u>Song of Solomon 2:4:</u>

HE BROUGHT ME TO THE BANQUETING HOUSE,
HIS BANNER OVER ME IS LOVE.

April 13 (Day 103), Memory Verse #291
<u>Song of Solomon 2:16:</u>

MY BELOVED IS MINE, AND I AM HIS: ...

April 13 (Day 103), Memory Verses #292 & #293
<u>Song of Solomon 8:6-7:</u>

6. SET ME AS A SEAL UPON THINE HEART, AS A SEAL UPON THINE ARM:
FOR LOVE IS STRONG AS DEATH; JEALOUSY IS CRUEL AS THE GRAVE:
THE COALS THEREOF ARE COALS OF FIRE, WHICH HATH A MOST VEHEMENT FLAME.

7. MANY WATERS CANNOT QUENCH LOVE, NEITHER CAN THE FLOODS DROWN IT:
IF A MAN WOULD GIVE ALL THE SUBSTANCE OF HIS HOUSE FOR LOVE,
IT WOULD UTTERLY BE CONTEMNED (scorned, NIV).

SONG OF SOLOMON 2:16:

MY BELOVED IS MINE,

AND I AM HIS . . .

Isaiah

Introduction: Most scholars believe the first chapters of Isaiah were written by the prophet Isaiah to Judah between 739-680 B.C. Chapters 1-39 concern Isaiah's ministry and prophecies in Judah until the reign of King Hezekiah. Many scholars believe chapters 40-66 were written by another author, referred to as the "second Isaiah." Others believe a "third Isaiah" and additional authors contributed to this book. Isaiah predicted the judgment and fall of many nations including Israel and Judah. But he also predicted restoration for some of the nations. He prophesied how the Messiah would come to give all humanity salvation, and he spoke of "the last days." Isaiah's ministry as a prophet began in 739 B.C., the year of King Uzziah's death in Judah, and continued into King Manasseh's rule. The northern kingdom of Israel was captured by Assyria in 722 B.C. when Ahaz was king of the southern kingdom of Judah. Assyria also tried overtaking Judah but was prevented by God (see Isaiah 37:36-37 and II Kings 19:35-36). Ahaz's son, Hezekiah, instituted spiritual reform during his kingship in Judah; however, idols were reinstated when Hezekiah's son, Manasseh, ruled as king. Isaiah warned Judah of the coming Babylonian captivity. Tradition says Isaiah was martyred during Manasseh's reign by being sawed in two. Isaiah has 66 chapters.

Key Contents and Key Memory Verses with Study Dates

Isaiah 1:   *"The vision of Isaiah the son of Amoz, which he saw concerning Judah, and Jerusalem in the days of Uzziah, Jotham, Ahaz, and Hezekiah, kings of Judah"* (see 1:1) — **Isaiah proclaims, the people of Judah *"...have forsaken the Lord,** they have provoked the Holy One of Israel unto anger, they are gone away backward"* (see 1:4) — **The Lord gives Judah a chance to return to Him.**

April 14 (Day 104), Memory Verse #294
Isaiah 1:18:

COME NOW, AND LET US REASON TOGETHER, SAITH THE LORD:
THOUGH YOUR SINS BE AS SCARLET, THEY SHALL BE WHITE AS SNOW;
THOUGH THEY BE RED LIKE CRIMSON, THEY SHALL BE AS WOOL.

— **Isaiah prophesies Judah will be judged and restored** — *"Zion shall be redeemed with judgment, and her converts with righteousness"* (see 1:27).

Isaiah 2-4:   *"The word that Isaiah the son of Amoz saw concerning Judah and Jerusalem. **And it shall come to pass in the last days,** that the mountain of the Lord's house shall be established in the top of the mountains, and shall be exalted above the hills; and all nations shall flow unto it. And many people shall go and say, Come ye, and let us go up to the mountain of the Lord, to the house of the God of Jacob; and he will teach us of his ways, and we will walk in his paths: for out of Zion shall go forth the law, and the word of the Lord from Jerusalem"* (see 2:1-3). **Isaiah's vision continues:**

April 14 (Day 104), Memory Verse #295
Isaiah 2:4:

AND HE SHALL JUDGE AMONG THE NATIONS,
AND SHALL REBUKE MANY PEOPLE:
AND THEY SHALL BEAT THEIR SWORDS INTO PLOWSHARES,
AND THEIR SPEARS INTO PRUNINGHOOKS:
NATION SHALL NOT LIFT UP SWORD AGAINST NATION,
NEITHER SHALL THEY LEARN WAR ANY MORE.

— *"In that day a man shall cast his idols of silver, and his idols of gold, which they made each one for himself to worship, to the moles and to the bats;* To go into the clefts of the rocks, and into the tops of the ragged rocks, for fear of the Lord, and for the glory of his majesty, when he ariseth to shake terribly the earth" (see 2:20-21).

— *"Woe unto the wicked!* It shall be ill with him: for the reward of his hands shall be given him" (see 3:11).

— *"In that day shall the branch of the Lord be beautiful and glorious,* and the fruit of the earth shall be excellent and comely for them that are escaped of Israel. And it shall come to pass, that he that is left in Zion, and he that remaineth in Jerusalem, shall be called holy, even every one that is written among the living in Jerusalem: When the Lord shall have washed away the filth of the daughters of Zion, and shall have purged the blood of Jerusalem from the midst thereof by the spirit of judgment, and by the spirit of burning" (see 4:2-4).

Isaiah 5: Judah is compared to a vineyard which bears wild grapes rather than cultivated grapes; therefore, the vineyard is no longer tended and protected — *"For the vineyard of the Lord of hosts is the house of Israel, and the men of Judah his pleasant plant: and he looked for judgment, but behold oppression; for righteousness, but behold a cry"* (see 5:7) — The people of Judah are reprimanded for their sins with a series of verses beginning with *"Woe unto..."* — *"Woe unto them that call evil good..."* (see 5:20) — *"Therefore as the fire devoureth the stubble, and the flame consumeth the chaff, so their root shall be a rottenness, and their blossom shall go up as dust: because they have cast away the law of the Lord of hosts, and despised the word of the Holy One of Israel"* (see 5:24).

Isaiah 6: Isaiah sees in his vision *"the Lord sitting on a throne"* (see 6:1) — *"Then said I, Woe is me! For I am undone; because I am a man of unclean lips, and I dwell in the midst of a people of unclean lips: for mine eyes have seen the King, the Lord of hosts. Then flew one of the seraphims unto me, having a live coal in his hand, which he had taken with the tongs from off the altar: And he laid it upon my mouth, and said, Lo, this hath touched thy lips; and thine iniquity is taken away, and thy sin purged"* (see 6:5-7) **— Isaiah's call from the Lord:**

April 15 (Day 105), Memory Verse #296
Isaiah 6:8:

ALSO I HEARD THE VOICE OF THE LORD, SAYING,
WHOM SHALL I SEND, AND WHO WILL GO FOR US?
THEN SAID I, HERE AM I; SEND ME.

— *"And he said, Go, and tell this people, Hear ye indeed, but understand not; and see ye indeed, but perceive not"* (see 6:9).

Isaiah 7: Rezin, the king of Syria, and Pekah, the king of Israel, *"...went up toward Jerusalem to war against it, but could not prevail against it"* (see 7:1) — Ahaz is king of Judah at this time — The Lord tells Isaiah to assure Ahaz that Rezin and Pekah will not conquer Judah, and both Syria and Israel will soon fall — The Lord promises a sign:

April 15 (Day 105), Memory Verse #297
Isaiah 7:14:

THEREFORE THE LORD HIMSELF SHALL GIVE YOU A SIGN;
BEHOLD, A VIRGIN SHALL CONCEIVE, AND BEAR A SON,
AND SHALL CALL HIS NAME IMMANUEL.

— See Matthew 1:20-23 which shows the previous verse as referring to Jesus' birth.

Isaiah 8: The prophet Isaiah and his prophetess wife have a son, and the Lord names him Maher-shalal-hash-baz — The Lord tells Isaiah that before this son can speak, Assyria will have taken the riches of Damascus (Syria) and Samaria (Israel).

Isaiah 9: The coming of the Messiah — *"The people that walked in darkness have seen a great light: they that dwell in the land of the shadow of death, upon them hath the light shined"* (see 9:2).

April 16 (Day 106), Memory Verses #298 & #299
Isaiah 9:6-7:

6. FOR UNTO US A CHILD IS BORN, UNTO US A SON IS GIVEN:
AND THE GOVERNMENT SHALL BE UPON HIS SHOULDER:
AND HIS NAME SHALL BE CALLED WONDERFUL, COUNSELLOR,
THE MIGHTY GOD, THE EVERLASTING FATHER, THE PRINCE OF PEACE.

7. OF THE INCREASE OF HIS GOVERNMENT AND PEACE THERE SHALL BE NO END,
UPON THE THRONE OF DAVID, AND UPON HIS KINGDOM,
TO ORDER IT, AND TO ESTABLISH IT WITH JUDGMENT
AND WITH JUSTICE FROM HENCEFORTH EVEN FOR EVER.

— More prophecies — The northern kingdom of Israel will be judged and overtaken by its enemies.

Isaiah 10 : Jerusalem will be judged — The Lord says, *"Shall I not, as I have done unto Samaria and her idols, so do to Jerusalem and her idols?"* (see 10:11) **— Assyria will be punished for overthrowing Israel** — *"Wherefore it shall come to pass, that when the Lord hath performed his whole work upon mount Zion and on Jerusalem, I will punish the fruit of the stout heart of the king of Assyria, and the glory of his high looks"* (see 10:12) **— Promise of restoration** — *"The remnant shall return, even the remnant of Jacob, unto the mighty God"* (see 10:21).

Isaiah 11: The coming reign of the Messiah — *"And there shall come forth a rod out of the stem of Jesse, and a Branch shall grow out of his roots: And the spirit of the Lord shall rest upon him, the spirit of wisdom and understanding, the spirit of counsel and might, the spirit of knowledge and of the fear of the Lord;"* (see 11:1-2) — *"And righteousness shall be the girdle of his loins, and faithfulness the girdle of his reins"* (see 11:5).

April 16 (Day 106), Memory Verse #300
Isaiah 11:6:

THE WOLF ALSO SHALL DWELL WITH THE LAMB,
AND THE LEOPARD SHALL LIE DOWN WITH THE KID;
AND THE CALF AND THE YOUNG LION AND THE FATLING TOGETHER;
AND A LITTLE CHILD SHALL LEAD THEM.

— *"...for the earth shall be full of the knowledge of the Lord, as the waters cover the sea"* (see 11:9).

Isaiah 12: Isaiah praises God for the promise of Israel's restoration:

April 17 (Day 107), Memory Verses #301 to #304
Isaiah 12:2-5:

2. **BEHOLD,** GOD IS MY SALVATION; I WILL TRUST, AND NOT BE AFRAID:
FOR THE LORD JEHOVAH IS MY STRENGTH AND MY SONG;
HE ALSO IS BECOME MY SALVATION.

3. **THEREFORE** WITH JOY SHALL YE DRAW WATER
OUT OF THE WELLS OF SALVATION.

4. **AND** IN THAT DAY SHALL YE SAY, PRAISE THE LORD, CALL UPON HIS NAME,
DECLARE HIS DOINGS AMONG THE PEOPLE, MAKE MENTION THAT HIS NAME IS EXALTED.

5. **SING** UNTO THE LORD; FOR HE HATH DONE EXCELLENT THINGS:
THIS IS KNOWN IN ALL THE EARTH.

Isaiah 13: Punishment for Babylon and the world — *"Behold, the day of the Lord cometh, cruel both with wrath and fierce anger, to lay the land desolate: and he shall destroy the sinners thereof out of it. For the stars of heaven and the constellations thereof shall not give their light: the sun shall be darkened in his going forth, and the moon shall not cause her light to shine. And I will punish the world for their evil, and the wicked for their iniquity, and I will cause the arrogancy of the proud to cease, and will lay low the haughtiness of the terrible"* (see 13:9-11).

Isaiah 14: Punishment for Babylon — Punishment for Lucifer — *"How art thou fallen from heaven, O Lucifer, son of the morning! How art thou cut down to the ground, which didst weaken the nations! For thou hast said in thine heart, I will ascend into heaven, and I will exalt my throne above the stars of God: I will sit also upon the mount of the congregation, in the sides of the north: I will ascend above the heights of the clouds; I will be like the most High. Yet thou shalt be brought down to hell, to the sides of the pit"* (see 14:12-15) — **Punishment for Assyria.**

Isaiah 15-16: Punishment for Moab.

Isaiah 17: Punishment for Damascus (Syria) and Israel.

Isaiah 18: Punishment for Ethiopia.

Isaiah 19: Punishment for Egypt.

Isaiah 20: Punishment for Egypt and Ethiopia — God commands Isaiah to walk naked and barefoot — *"And the Lord said, Like as my servant Isaiah hath walked naked and barefoot three years for a sign and wonder upon Egypt and upon Ethiopia; So shall the king of Assyria lead away the Egyptians prisoners, and the Ethiopians captives, young and old, naked and barefoot, even with their buttocks uncovered, to the shame of Egypt"* (see 20:3-4).

Isaiah 21: Isaiah's fearful vision of the fall of Babylon, Dumah and Seir (lands of Edom), and Arabia.

Isaiah 22: Punishment for Judah.

Isaiah 23: Punishment for Tyre.

Isaiah 24-26: Prophecies of the future — *"Behold, the Lord maketh the earth empty, and maketh it waste, and turneth it upside down, and scattereth abroad the inhabitants thereof"* (see 24:1) — *"The earth is defiled under the inhabitants thereof; because they have transgressed the laws, changed the ordinance, broken the everlasting covenant. Therefore hath the curse devoured the earth, and they that dwell therein are desolate: therefore the inhabitants of* *the earth are burned, and few men left"* (see 24:5-6) — *"The earth shall reel to and fro like a drunkard, and shall be removed like a cottage; and the transgression thereof shall be heavy upon it; and it shall fall, and not rise again"* (see 24:20).

— *"O Lord, thou are my God; I will exalt thee, I will praise thy name; for thou hast done wonderful things; thy counsels of old are faithfulness and truth"* (see 25:1) — *"For thou hast been a strength to the poor, a strength to the needy in his distress, a refuge from the storm, a shadow from the heat..."* (see 25:4).

April 18 (Day 108), Memory Verse #305
Isaiah 25:8:

HE WILL SWALLOW UP DEATH IN VICTORY;
AND THE LORD GOD WILL WIPE AWAY TEARS FROM OFF ALL FACES;
AND THE REBUKE OF HIS PEOPLE SHALL HE TAKE AWAY FROM
OFF ALL THE EARTH: FOR THE LORD HATH SPOKEN IT.

April 18 (Day 108), Memory Verse #306
Isaiah 26:3:

THOU WILT KEEP HIM IN PERFECT PEACE, WHOSE MIND IS STAYED ON THEE:
BECAUSE HE TRUSTETH IN THEE.

— *"Trust ye in the Lord for ever: for in the Lord JEHOVAH is everlasting strength:"* (see 26:4).

Isaiah 27: **Promise of restoration** — *"...Israel shall blossom and bud, and fill the face of the world with fruit"* (see 27:6).

Isaiah 28: *"Woe to the crown of pride, to the drunkards of Ephraim, whose glorious beauty is a fading flower..."* (see 28:1), and woe to all of Israel.

Isaiah 29: *"Woe to Ariel"* (Jerusalem), *"to Ariel, the city where David dwelt!..."* (see 29:1).

Isaiah 30-31: **The Lord scolds Judah for turning to Egypt rather than Him when needing help against Assyria** — *"Woe to the rebellious children, saith the Lord, that take counsel, but not of me; and that cover with a covering, but not of my spirit, that they may add sin to sin:"* (see 30:1) — *"And therefore will the Lord wait, that he may be gracious unto you, and therefore will he be exalted, that he may have mercy upon you: for the Lord is a God of judgment: blessed are all they that wait for him"* (see 30:18) — *"For through the voice of the Lord shall the Assyrian be beaten down, which smote with a rod"* (see 30:31).

— *"Woe to them that go down to Egypt for help; and stay on horses, and trust in chariots, because they are many; and in horsemen, because they are very strong; but they look not unto the Holy One of Israel, neither seek the Lord!"* (see 31:1) — *"...Like as the lion and the young lion roaring on his prey, when a multitude of shepherds is called forth against him, he will not be afraid of their voice, nor abase himself for the noise of them: so shall the Lord of hosts come down to fight for mount Zion, and for the hill thereof"* (see 31:4).

Isaiah 32: *"Behold a king shall reign in righteousness..."* (see 32:1) — *"And the work of righteousness shall be peace; and the effect of righteousness quietness and assurance for ever. And my people shall dwell in a peaceable habitation, and in sure dwellings, and in quiet resting places;"* (see 32:17-18).

Isaiah 33: *"Woe to thee that spoilest, and thou wast not spoiled; and dealest treacherously, and they dealt not treacherously with thee!"* (see 33:1) — The previous verse may refer to Assyria's cruel attacks on other nations.

April 19 (Day 109), Memory Verses #307 & #308
Isaiah 33:15-16:

15. HE THAT WALKETH RIGHTEOUSLY, AND SPEAKETH UPRIGHTLY;
. HE THAT DESPISETH THE GAIN OF OPPRESSIONS,
THAT SHAKETH HIS HANDS FROM HOLDING OF BRIBES,
THAT STOPPETH HIS EARS FROM HEARING OF BLOOD,
AND SHUTTETH HIS EYES FROM SEEING EVIL;

16. HE SHALL DWELL ON HIGH:
HIS PLACE OF DEFENCE SHALL BE THE MUNITIONS OF ROCKS:
BREAD SHALL BE GIVEN HIM; HIS WATERS SHALL BE SURE.

— *"For the Lord is our judge, the Lord is our lawgiver, the Lord is our king; he will save us"* (see 33:22).

Isaiah 34: Judgment on nations — *"For the indignation of the Lord is upon all nations, and his fury is upon all their armies: he hath utterly destroyed them, he hath delivered them to the slaughter"* (see 34:2).

Isaiah 35: *"Say to them that are of a fearful heart, Be strong, fear not: behold, your God will come with vengeance, even God with a recompence; he will come and save you"* (see 35:4) — *"And an highway shall be there, and a way, and it shall be called The way of holiness; the unclean shall not pass over it;...but the redeemed shall walk there:"* (see 35:8-9).

Isaiah 36: Sennacherib, king of Assyria, sends Rabshakeh to Judah which is ruled by Hezekiah — Rabshakeh tries convincing the people of Judah to join Assyria — He scoffs at their belief that the Lord will deliver them from Assyria as King Hezekiah has promised.

Isaiah 37: Hezekiah's prayer (see 37:16-20) — *"Now therefore, O Lord our God, save us from his hand, that all the kingdoms of the earth may know that thou art the Lord, even thou only"* (see 37:20) — ***"Then the angel of the Lord went forth, and smote in the camp of the Assyrians a hundred and fourscore and five thousand (a hundred and eighty-five thousand men, NIV):*** *and when they arose early in the morning, behold, they were all dead corpses"* (see 37:36) — Sennacherib returns to Nineveh and is killed by two of his sons with a sword while he worships in the house of his god Nisroch — Their brother, Esar-haddon, becomes king of Assyria.

Isaiah 38: *"In those days was Hezekiah sick unto death. And Isaiah the prophet the son of Amoz came unto him, and said unto him, Thus saith the Lord, Set thine house in order: for thou shalt die, and not live"* (see 38:1) — **Hezekiah prays to God,** *"Remember now, O Lord, I beseech thee, how I have walked before thee in truth and with a perfect heart, and have done that which is good in thy sight. And Hezekiah wept sore"* (see 38:3) — Isaiah informs Hezekiah of the Lord's message: the Lord will add 15 years to Hezekiah's life, and Jerusalem will be saved from Assyria — Confirming this message, the Lord sends a sign of the sun's shadow moving backwards 10 degrees on Ahaz's sundial — Hezekiah praises God (also, see II Kings 20 concerning Hezekiah).

Isaiah 39: Hezekiah foolishly shows the men of Babylon his treasures — Isaiah warns, *"Behold, the days come that all that is in thine house and that which thy fathers have laid in store until this day, shall be carried to Babylon: nothing shall be left, saith the Lord"* (see 39:6).

Isaiah 40: **Chapters 40-66 offer comfort with prophecies of restoration** — *"Comfort ye, comfort ye my people, saith your God. Speak ye comfortably to Jerusalem, and cry unto her, that her warfare is accomplished, that her iniquity is pardoned: for she hath received of the Lord's hand double for all her sins"* (see 40:1-2) — Matthew 3:3 shows the following verse as referring to John the Baptist: *"The voice of him that crieth in the wilderness, Prepare ye the way of the Lord, make straight in the desert a highway for our God"* (see 40:3) — The Lord God *"...shall feed his flock like a shepherd: he shall gather the lambs with his arm, and carry them in his bosom, and shall gently lead those that are with young"* (see 40:11).

April 20 (Day 110), Memory Verse #309
Isaiah 40:8:

THE GRASS WITHERETH, THE FLOWER FADETH:
BUT THE WORD OF OUR GOD SHALL STAND FOR EVER.

April 20 (Day 110), Memory Verses #310 & #311
Isaiah 40:28-29:

28. HAST THOU NOT KNOWN? HAST THOU NOT HEARD?
THAT THE EVERLASTING GOD, THE LORD,
THE CREATOR OF THE ENDS OF THE EARTH,
FAINTETH NOT, NEITHER IS WEARY?
THERE IS NO SEARCHING OF HIS UNDERSTANDING.

29. HE GIVETH POWER TO THE FAINT;
AND TO THEM THAT HAVE NO MIGHT HE INCREASETH STRENGTH.

April 20 (Day 110), Memory Verse #312
Isaiah 40:31:

BUT THEY THAT WAIT UPON THE LORD SHALL RENEW THEIR STRENGTH;
THEY SHALL MOUNT UP WITH WINGS AS EAGLES;
THEY SHALL RUN, AND NOT BE WEARY;
AND THEY SHALL WALK, AND NOT FAINT.

Isaiah 41: **The Lord will help the Israelites.**

April 21 (Day 111), Memory Verse #313
Isaiah 41:4:

... I THE LORD, THE FIRST, AND WITH THE LAST; I AM HE.

— *"But thou, Israel, art my servant, Jacob whom I have chosen, the seed of Abraham my friend"* (see 41:8) — *"Fear thou not; for I am with thee: be not dismayed; for I am thy God"* (see 41:10).

Isaiah 42: See Matthew 12:18-20 which shows Isaiah 42:1-3 as referring to Jesus — **"Behold my servant** *whom I uphold; mine elect, in whom my soul delighteth; I have put my spirit upon him: he shall bring forth judgment to the Gentiles"* (see 42:1) — *"I the Lord have called thee in righteousness, and will hold thine hand, and will keep thee, and give thee for a covenant of the people, for a light of the Gentiles; To open the blind eyes, to bring out the prisoners from the prison, and them that sit in darkness out of the prison house"* (see 42:6-7) — *"...they shall be greatly ashamed, that trust in graven images, that say to the molten images, Ye are our gods"* (see 42:17).

Isaiah 43-44: God will punish and restore the Israelites — *"But thou hast not called upon me, O Jacob; but thou hast been weary of me, O Israel"* (see 43:22) — *"I, even I, am he that blotteth out thy transgressions for mine own sake, and will not remember thy sins" (see 43:25).*

April 21 (Day 111), Memory Verse #314
Isaiah 44:6:

... I AM THE FIRST, AND I AM THE LAST; AND BESIDE ME THERE IS NO GOD.

— **The foolishness of idols** — *"Remember these, O Jacob and Israel; for thou art my servant:* **I have formed thee; thou art my servant: O Israel, thou shalt not be forgotten of me:** (see 44:21) — *"Sing, O ye heavens; for the Lord hath done it: shout, ye lower parts of the earth: break forth into singing, ye mountains, O forest, and every tree therein: for the Lord hath redeemed Jacob, and glorified himself in Israel"* (see 44:23) — **Prophecy that God will use Cyrus, the king of Persia, for rebuilding His temple in Jerusalem** — The Lord *"... saith of Cyrus, He is my shepherd, and shall perform all my pleasure: even saying to Jerusalem, Thou shalt be built; and to the temple, Thy foundation shall be laid"* (see 44:28).

Isaiah 45: God will reward Cyrus with victories over other nations since Cyrus will help the Israelites.

April 21 (Day 111), Memory Verse #315
Isaiah 45:22:

LOOK UNTO ME, AND BE YE SAVED, ALL THE ENDS OF THE EARTH;
FOR I AM GOD, AND THERE IS NONE ELSE.

Isaiah 46-47: Babylon will be punished by Persia — Their enchantments, their sorceries (see 47:12), *"the astrologers, the stargazers, and the monthly prognosticators"* (see 47:13) will not be able to save them from being defeated by Persia.

Isaiah 48:   The Lord speaks to the Israelites — *"O that thou hadst hearkened to my commandments! Then had thy peace been as a river, and thy righteousness as the waves of the sea:"* (see 48:18) — **The Lord will deliver the Israelites from Babylon** — *"Go ye forth of Babylon, flee ye from the Chaldeans, with a voice of singing declare ye, tell this, utter it even to the end of the earth; say ye, The Lord hath redeemed his servant Jacob"* (see 48:20) — *"There is no peace, saith the Lord, unto the wicked"* (see 48:22).

Isaiah 49: Promise of future salvation — *"**Thou art my servant, O Israel, in whom I will be glorified**"* (see 49:3) — *"And he said, It is a light thing that thou shouldest be my servant to raise up the tribes of Jacob, and to restore the preserved of Israel:* **I will also give thee for a light to the Gentiles, that thou mayest be my salvation unto the end of the earth"** (see 49:6) — . *"Sing, O heavens; and be joyful, O earth; and break forth into singing, O mountains: for the Lord hath comforted his people, and will have mercy upon his afflicted"* (see 49:13).

April 22 (Day 112), Memory Verse #316
Isaiah 49:23:

...AND THOU SHALT KNOW THAT I AM THE LORD:
FOR THEY SHALL NOT BE ASHAMED THAT WAIT FOR ME.

Isaiah 50: *"Thus saith the Lord, Where is the bill of your mother's divorcement, whom I have put away? or which of my creditors is it to whom I have sold you?* **Behold, for your iniquities have ye sold yourselves,** *and for your transgressions is your mother put away"* (see 50:1) — *"**Who is among you that feareth the Lord, that obeyeth the voice of his servant,** that walketh in* *darkness, and hath no light? Let him trust in the name of the Lord, and stay upon his God"* (see 50:10).

Isaiah 51-52: *"Hearken to me, ye that follow after righteousness, ye that seek the Lord:* look unto the rock whence ye are hewn...Look unto Abraham your father, and unto Sarah that bare you: for I called him alone, and blessed him, and increased him. For the Lord shall comfort Zion..."* (see 51:1-3) — *"Lift up your eyes to the heavens, and look upon the earth beneath: for the heavens shall vanish away like smoke, and the earth shall wax old like a garment, and they that dwell therein shall die in like manner: but **my salvation shall be for ever,** and my righteousness shall not be abolished"* (see 51:6) — **The Lord tells the Israelites to remember how He has cared for them** — *"Thus saith thy Lord the Lord, and thy God that pleadeth the cause of his people, Behold, I have taken out of thine hand the cup of trembling, even the dregs of the cup of my fury; thou shalt no more drink it again: But I will put it into the hand of them that afflict thee;..."* (see 51:22-23).

April 22 (Day 112), Memory Verse #317
Isaiah 52:7:

HOW BEAUTIFUL UPON THE MOUNTAINS ARE THE FEET OF HIM
THAT BRINGETH GOOD TIDINGS, THAT PUBLISHETH PEACE;
THAT BRINGETH GOOD TIDINGS OF GOOD, THAT PUBLISHETH SALVATION;
THAT SAITH UNTO ZION, THY GOD REIGNETH!

Isaiah 53: The Lord's Servant and His suffering (see Isaiah 52:13-53:12).

April 23-24 (Days 113-114), Memory Verses #318 to #324
Isaiah 53:3-9:
(These verses are seen as referring to Jesus.)

3. HE IS DESPISED AND REJECTED OF MEN; A MAN OF SORROWS,
AND ACQUAINTED WITH GRIEF:
AND WE HID AS IT WERE OUR FACES FROM HIM;
HE WAS DESPISED, AND WE ESTEEMED HIM NOT.

4. SURELY HE HATH BORNE OUR GRIEFS, AND CARRIED OUR SORROWS:
YET WE DID ESTEEM HIM STRICKEN, SMITTEN OF GOD, AND AFFLICTED.

5. BUT HE WAS WOUNDED FOR OUR TRANSGRESSIONS,
HE WAS BRUISED FOR OUR INIQUITIES:
THE CHASTISEMENT OF OUR PEACE WAS UPON HIM;
AND WITH HIS STRIPES WE ARE HEALED.

6. ALL WE LIKE SHEEP HAVE GONE ASTRAY;
WE HAVE TURNED EVERY ONE TO HIS OWN WAY;
AND THE LORD HATH LAID ON HIM THE INIQUITY OF US ALL.

7. HE WAS OPPRESSED, AND HE WAS AFFLICTED, YET HE OPENED NOT HIS MOUTH:
HE IS BROUGHT AS A LAMB TO THE SLAUGHTER,
AND AS A SHEEP BEFORE HER SHEARERS IS DUMB, SO HE OPENETH NOT HIS MOUTH.

8. HE WAS TAKEN FROM PRISON AND FROM JUDGMENT:
AND WHO SHALL DECLARE HIS GENERATION?
FOR HE WAS CUT OFF OUT OF THE LAND OF THE LIVING:
FOR THE TRANSGRESSIONS OF MY PEOPLE WAS HE STRICKEN.

9. AND HE MADE HIS GRAVE WITH THE WICKED,
AND WITH THE RICH IN HIS DEATH; BECAUSE HE HAD DONE NO VIOLENCE,
NEITHER WAS ANY DECEIT IN HIS MOUTH.

Isaiah 54: *"...thy Maker is thine husband; the Lord of hosts is his name; and thy Redeemer the Holy One of Israel; The God of the whole earth shall he be called"* (see 54:5).

Isaiah 55: *"Incline your ear, and come unto me:* ***hear, and your soul shall live;*** *and I will make an everlasting covenant with you, even the sure mercies of David"* (see 55:3).

April 25 (Day 115), Memory Verse #325
Isaiah 55:6:

SEEK YE THE LORD WHILE HE MAY BE FOUND,
CALL YE UPON HIM WHILE HE IS NEAR:

April 25 (Day 115), Memory Verse #326
Isaiah 55:9:

FOR AS THE HEAVENS ARE HIGHER THAN THE EARTH,
SO ARE MY WAYS HIGHER THAN YOUR WAYS,
AND MY THOUGHTS THAN YOUR THOUGHTS.

— **Future peace;** *"For ye shall go out with joy, and be led forth with peace: the mountains and the hills shall break forth before you into singing, and all the trees of the field shall clap their hands. Instead of the thorn shall come up the fir tree, and instead of the briar shall come up the myrtle tree: and it shall be to the Lord for a name, for an everlasting sign that shall not be cut off"* (see 55:12-13).

Isaiah 56: Salvation is available to all people — *"...for mine house shall be called an house of prayer for all people. The Lord God, which gathereth the outcasts of Israel saith, Yet will I gather others to him, beside those that are gathered unto him"* (see 56:7-8).

Isaiah 57: Warning to the wicked — *"But the wicked are like the troubled sea, when it cannot rest, whose waters cast up mire and dirt. There is no peace, saith my God, to the wicked"* (see 57:20-21).

Isaiah 58: Helping the hungry and poor is more important than being concerned with fasting — Honor the Sabbath.

Isaiah 59: *"...your iniquities have separated between you and your God, and your sins have hid his face from you, that he will not hear"* (see 59:2) — *"So shall they fear the name of the Lord from the west, and his glory from the rising of the sun. When the enemy shall come in like a flood, the Spirit of the Lord shall lift up a standard against him. And the Redeemer shall come to Zion, and unto them that turn from transgression in Jacob, saith the Lord"* (see 59:19-20) — **The Lord covenants that His spirit and His words shall be with Israel forever.**

Isaiah 60: *"Arise, shine; for thy light is come, and the glory of the Lord is risen upon thee"* (see 60:1) — *"**And the Gentiles shall come to thy light,** and kings to the brightness of thy rising"* (see 60:3) — **Future prophecy:** *"Violence shall no more be heard in thy land, wasting nor destruction within thy borders; but thou shalt call thy walls Salvation, and thy gates Praise. The sun shall be no more thy light by day; neither for brightness shall the moon give light unto thee: but the Lord shall be unto thee an everlasting light, and thy God thy glory. Thy sun shall no more go down; neither shall thy moon withdraw itself: for the Lord shall be thine everlasting light..."* (see 60:18-20).

Isaiah 61: *"The Spirit of the Lord God is upon me; because the Lord anointed me to preach good tidings unto the meek; he hath sent me to bind up the brokenhearted, to proclaim liberty to the captives, and the opening of the prison to them that are bound"* (see 61:1) — See Luke 4:18 where Jesus shows He is the fulfillment of the previous verse.

April 26 (Day 116), Memory Verse #327
Isaiah 61:10:

I WILL GREATLY REJOICE IN THE LORD,
MY SOUL SHALL BE JOYFUL IN MY GOD;
FOR HE HATH CLOTHED ME WITH THE GARMENTS OF SALVATION,
HE HATH COVERED ME WITH THE ROBE OF RIGHTEOUSNESS...

— *"For as the earth bringeth forth the bud, and as the garden causeth the things that are sown in it to spring forth; so **the Lord God will cause righteousness and praise to spring forth before all the nations**"* (see 61:11).

Isaiah 62: The Lord proclaims concerning the Israelites, *"...they shall call them The holy people, The redeemed of the Lord: and thou shalt be called, Sought out, A city not forsaken"* (see 62:12).

Isaiah 63: **The wicked will be punished** — *"...thou, O Lord, art our father, our redeemer; thy name is from everlasting"* (see 63:16).

Isaiah 64: *"For since the beginning of the world men have not heard, nor perceived by the ear, neither hath the eye seen, O God, beside thee, what he hath prepared for him that waiteth for him"* (see 64:4).

April 26 (Day 116), Memory Verse #328
Isaiah 64:8:

BUT NOW, O LORD, THOU ART OUR FATHER;
WE ARE THE CLAY, AND THOU OUR POTTER;
AND WE ALL ARE THE WORK OF THY HAND.

Isaiah 65: *"And I will bring forth a seed out of Jacob, and out of Judah an inheritor of my mountains: and mine elect shall inherit it, and my servants shall dwell there"* (see 65:9) — *"For, behold, I create new heavens and a new earth: and the former shall not be remembered, nor come into mind. But be ye glad and rejoice for ever in that which I create: for, behold, I create Jerusalem a rejoicing, and her people a joy"* (see 65:17-18) — *"**The wolf and the lamb shall feed together...**They shall not hurt nor destroy in all my holy mountain, saith the Lord"* (see 65:25).

Isaiah 66: *"...it shall come, that I will gather all nations and tongues; and they shall come, and see my glory...and they shall declare my glory among the Gentiles"* (see 66:18-19) — *"For as the new heavens and the new earth, which I will make, shall remain before me, saith the Lord, so shall your seed and your name remain. And it shall come to pass, that from one new moon to another, and from one Sabbath to another, shall all flesh come to worship before me, saith the Lord. And they shall go forth, and look upon the carcases of the men that have transgressed against me: for their worm shall not die, neither shall their fire be quenched; and they shall be an abhorring unto all flesh"* (see 66:22-24).

Isaiah 40:31:

But they that wait

UPON THE LORD

SHALL RENEW THEIR STRENGTH;

THEY SHALL MOUNT UP

WITH WINGS AS EAGLES;

THEY SHALL RUN, AND NOT BE WEARY;

AND THEY SHALL WALK,

AND NOT FAINT.

JEREMIAH

Introduction: Jeremiah, a priest and prophet, is most likely the author of this book which was probably written between 627 to 585 B.C. Baruch helped in the writing of this book (see Jeremiah 36:4). Jeremiah is known as the "prophet of loneliness" or the "weeping prophet." The Lord commanded him not to marry. For 40 years (from the time of King Josiah until after the Babylonian's destruction of the temple and Jerusalem in 586 B.C.), he proclaimed God's judgment on Judah. Chapters 15, 16 and 20 show Jeremiah's struggles with such a lonely life and his sadness as he prophesies punishment for Judah. Fortunately, there is also prophecy of restoration. Jeremiah has 52 chapters.

Key Contents and Key Memory Verses with Study Dates

Jeremiah 1: Jeremiah's call: *"Then the word of the Lord came unto me, saying, Before I formed thee in the belly I knew thee; and before thou camest forth out of the womb I sanctified thee, and I ordained thee a prophet unto the nations"* (see 1:4-5) — Jeremiah says he cannot speak since he is a child, but the Lord says he will tell Jeremiah what to say — *"Then the Lord put forth his hand, and touched my mouth. And the Lord said unto me, Behold, I have put my words in thy mouth"* (see 1:9) — The Lord shows Jeremiah an almond tree branch and a *"seething pot"* (see 1:13) with its face toward the north; the pot symbolizes God's call to Jeremiah to speak to the people of the north concerning their wickedness.

Jeremiah 2: The Lord tells Jeremiah to speak these words to Jerusalem: *"Thine own wickedness shall correct thee, and thy back-slidings shall reprove thee: know therefore and see that it is an evil thing and bitter, that thou hast forsaken the Lord thy God, and that my fear is not in thee, saith the Lord God of hosts"* (see 2:19).

Jeremiah 3: Even in their unfaithfulness, the Lord is willing to take the people of Judah back — Judah is called a sister harlot of Israel who has not learned from Israel's mistakes and judgment — *"Go and proclaim these words toward the north, and say, Return, thou backsliding Israel, saith the Lord; and I will not cause mine anger to fall upon you: for I am merciful, saith the Lord, and I will not keep anger for ever"* (see 3:12).

Jeremiah 4: The Lord warns Judah of destruction from the north — *"O Jerusalem, wash thine heart from wickedness, that thou mayest be saved...* (see 4:14).

Jeremiah 5: The Lord challenges Jeremiah to find one righteous person in Jerusalem — *"Run ye to and fro through the streets of Jerusalem, and see now, and know, and seek in the broad places thereof, if ye can find a man, if there be any that executeth judgment, that seeketh the truth; and I will pardon it"* (see 5:1) — Jeremiah cannot find one righteous person among the poor or among the rulers (see 5:4-5) — **The Lord forewarns of coming judgment** — *"Lo, I will bring a nation upon you from far, O house of Israel, saith the Lord: it is a mighty nation, it is an ancient nation, a nation whose language thou knowest not, neither understandest what they say"* (see 5:15) — *"...Like as ye have forsaken me, and served strange gods in your land, so shall ye serve strangers in a land that is not yours"* (see 5:19).

Jeremiah 6: *"Hear, O earth: behold, I will bring evil upon this people, even the fruit of their thoughts, because they have not hearkened unto my words, nor to my law, but rejected it"* (see 6:19).

Jeremiah 7: Jeremiah is commanded by the Lord to stand in the gate of the Lord's house to call Judah to repentance — *"Thus saith the Lord of hosts, the God of Israel, Amend your ways and your doings, and I will cause you to dwell in this place"* (see 7:3) — *"Is this house,* *which is called by my name, become a den of robbers in your eyes?...*" (see 7:11); Jesus quotes the previous verse in Mark 11:17 and Luke 19:46 when He cleanses the temple — *"Since the day that your fathers came forth out of the land of Egypt unto this day I have even sent unto you all my servants the prophets, daily rising up early and sending them: Yet they hearkened not unto me, nor inclined their ear, but hardened their neck: they did worse than their fathers"* (see 7:25-26) — Judah's evil includes child sacrifices (see 7:31).

Jeremiah 8: *"Is there no balm in Gilead; is there no physician there? Why then is not the health of the daughter of my people recovered?"* (see 8:22).

Jeremiah 9: Jeremiah continues to warn of judgment, not only for Judah, but also for Egypt, Edom, Ammon, Moab, and *"...all that are in the utmost corners..."* (see 9:26).

April 27 (Day 117), Memory Verses #329 & #330
Jeremiah 9:23-24:

23. THUS SAITH THE LORD, LET NOT THE WISE GLORY IN HIS WISDOM,
NEITHER LET THE MIGHTY MAN GLORY IN HIS MIGHT,
LET NOT THE RICH MAN GLORY IN HIS RICHES:

24. BUT LET HIM THAT GLORIETH GLORY IN THIS,
THAT HE UNDERSTANDETH AND KNOWETH ME,
THAT I AM THE LORD WHICH EXERCISE LOVINGKINDNESS,
JUDGMENT, AND RIGHTEOUSNESS, IN THE EARTH:
FOR IN THESE THINGS I DELIGHT, SAITH THE LORD.

Jeremiah 10: Jeremiah speaks about the vanity of idols.

April 27 (Day 117), Memory Verse #331
Jeremiah 10:10:

BUT THE LORD IS THE TRUE GOD,
HE IS THE LIVING GOD, AND AN EVERLASTING KING...

— *"Thus shall ye say unto them, The gods that have not made the heavens and the earth, even they shall perish from the earth, and from under these heavens"* (see 10:11).

April 28 (Day 118), Memory Verses #332 & #333
Jeremiah 10:23-24:

23. O LORD, I KNOW THAT THE WAY OF MAN IS NOT IN HIMSELF
(that a man's life is not his own, NIV):
IT IS NOT IN MAN THAT WALKETH TO DIRECT HIS STEPS.

24. O LORD, CORRECT ME, BUT WITH JUDGMENT;
NOT IN THINE ANGER, LEST THOU BRING ME TO NOTHING.

Jeremiah 11: Jeremiah delivers the Lord's message to Judah — *"They are turned back to the iniquities of their forefathers, which refused to hear my words; and they went after other gods to serve them:* **the house of Israel and the house of Judah have broken my covenant which I made with their fathers**" (see 11:10).

Jeremiah 12: Jeremiah asks why the wicked and those that deal treacherously prosper (see 12:1) — *"Thus saith the Lord against all mine evil neighbours, that touch the inheritance which I have caused my people Israel to inherit; Behold, I will pluck them out of their land, and pluck out the house of Judah from among them"* (see 12:14) — **After punishing the wicked, God**

will have compassion on all people, giving them an opportunity to turn to Him; *"But if they will not obey, I will utterly pluck up and destroy that nation, saith the Lord"* (see 12:17).

Jeremiah 13: The Lord commands Jeremiah to wear a linen girdle on his loins, go to the Euphrates, and hide the girdle in a hole in a rock — Jeremiah does as the Lord commands — After many days, the Lord commands Jeremiah to retrieve the girdle, but the girdle is ruined — *"Then saith the Lord, After this manner will I mar the pride of Judah, and the great pride of Jerusalem. This evil people, which refuse to hear my words, which walk in the imagination of their heart, and walk after other gods, to serve them, and to worship them, shall even be as this girdle, which is good for nothing"* (see 13:9-10) — Like the girdle had been ruined over time, the Lord warns that the people of Judah will be marred in their coming destruction and captivity.

Jeremiah 14: The Lord tells Jeremiah of Judah's future drought — **Jeremiah pleads to the Lord not to forsake Judah, but the Lord tells Jeremiah to stop praying for Judah** — The Lord says, *"I will consume them by the sword, and by the famine, and by the pestilence"* (see 14:12) — The false prophets have promised peace, and no punishment by the sword or famine; therefore, the Lord says, *"...By sword and famine shall those prophets be consumed"* (see 14:15).

Jeremiah 15: Jeremiah sadly states, *"Woe is me, my mother, that thou hast borne me a man of strife and a man of contention to the whole earth! ..."* (see 15:10) — **The Lord still plans to punish Judah** — *"And I will make thee to pass with thine enemies into a land which thou knowest not: for a fire is kindled in mine anger, which shall burn upon you"* (see 15:14) — **Yet the Lord promises deliverance** — *"And I will deliver thee out of the hand of the wicked, and I will redeem thee out of the hand of the terrible"* (see 15:21).

Jeremiah 16: The Lord forbids Jeremiah to marry, to participate in funerals, or to attend celebrations; forbidding these things in Jeremiah's life shows the people the following warning: *"...thus saith the Lord of hosts, the God of Israel; Behold, I will cause to cease out of this place in your eyes, and in your days, the voice of mirth, and the voice of gladness, the voice of the bridegroom, and the voice of the bride"* (see 16:9) — **The Lord will punish the people of Judah to teach them a lesson** — *"Therefore, behold, I will this once cause them to know, I will cause them to know mine hand and my might; and they shall know that my name is The Lord"* (see 16:21).

Jeremiah 17: *"Thus saith the Lord; Cursed be the man that trusteth in man...and whose heart departeth from the Lord"* (see 17:5).

April 29 (Day 119), Memory Verses #334 to #337
Jeremiah 17:7-10:

7. **BLESSED** IS THE MAN THAT TRUSTETH IN THE LORD,
AND WHOSE HOPE THE LORD IS.

8. **FOR** HE SHALL BE AS A TREE PLANTED BY THE WATERS,
AND THAT SPREADETH OUT HER ROOTS BY THE RIVER,
AND SHALL NOT SEE WHEN HEAT COMETH, BUT HER LEAF SHALL BE GREEN;
AND SHALL NOT BE CAREFUL IN THE YEAR OF DROUGHT,
NEITHER SHALL CEASE FROM YIELDING FRUIT.

9. **THE** HEART IS DECEITFUL ABOVE ALL THINGS,
AND DESPERATELY WICKED: WHO CAN KNOW IT?

10. **I** THE LORD SEARCH THE HEART, I TRY THE REINS,
EVEN TO GIVE EVERY MAN ACCORDING TO HIS WAYS,
AND ACCORDING TO THE FRUIT OF HIS DOINGS.

— **Jeremiah tells the people of Judah that the Lord commands them to honor the Sabbath,** *"But they obeyed not..."* (see 17:23).

Jeremiah 18: The Lord commands Jeremiah to go to the potter's house — *"And the vessel that he made of clay was marred in the hand of the potter: so he made it again another vessel, as seemed good to the potter to make it. Then the word of the Lord came to me, saying, O house of Israel, cannot I do with you as this potter? saith the Lord. Behold, as the clay is in the potter's hand, so are ye in mine hand, O house of Israel"* (see 18:4-6) — **The Lord tells Jeremiah He can change His mind toward the nations, whether to bless or punish them, depending on their goodness or wickedness** — The Lord instructs Jeremiah to tell Judah, *"...return ye now every one from his evil way, and make your ways and your doings good"* (see 18:11) — But the people of Judah refuse to depart from evil, and the Lord warns of their future desolation and being scattered — **Jeremiah is angry at Judah and tells the Lord to "...*deal thus with them in the time of thine anger"* (see 18:23).

Jeremiah 19: The Lord tells Jeremiah to get a potter's earthen bottle and go to the valley of the son of Hinnom — When arriving in the valley, Jeremiah prophesies that the valley will be known as the valley of slaughter since God will cause Judah to fall by the sword in that place — The Lord then tells Jeremiah to break the bottle and say to the people of Judah, *"...Thus saith the Lord of hosts; Even so will I break this people and this city, as one breaketh a potter's vessel, that cannot be made whole again..."* (see 19:11).

Jeremiah 20: Pashur, chief governor in the house of the Lord, has Jeremiah beaten and put in stocks for prophesying Judah's desolation — Jeremiah warns Pashur that he will see his friends fall by the sword when Babylon defeats Judah and takes the people and the king's treasures into Babylonian captivity — Jeremiah decides to stop speaking of the Lord, but admits, *"... his word was in mine heart as a burning fire shut up in my bones..."* (see 20:9) — Jeremiah begins speaking the Lord's words again — Jeremiah curses the day he was born because of his misery and shame.

Jeremiah 21: King Zedekiah sends two messengers to Jeremiah to inquire how the battle will go between Babylon and Judah — Jeremiah tells the messengers that Babylon will defeat Judah, killing both man and beast — *"For I have set my face against this city of evil, and not for good, saith the Lord: it shall be given into the hand of the king of Babylon, and he shall burn it with fire"* (see 21:10).

Jeremiah 22: Jeremiah prophesies that Shallum (Jehoahaz), the son of Josiah, will never return to Judah — Another prophecy concerns Jehoiakim and foretells he will neither have mourners nor a decent burial at his death because of his wickedness — Prophecy concerning Coniah (Jehoiachin) foretells he will have no heirs to the throne, will be cast out of Judah, and will die in another country.

Jeremiah 23: Restoration predicted — *"And I will gather the remnant of my flock out of all countries whither I have driven them, and will bring them again to their folds; and they shall be fruitful and increase"* (see 23:3) — **The Messiah predicted** — *"Behold, the days come, saith the Lord, that I will raise unto David a righteous Branch, and a King shall reign and prosper, and shall execute judgment and justice in the earth. In his days Judah shall be saved, and Israel shall dwell safely: and this is his name whereby he shall be called, THE LORD OUR RIGHTEOUSNESS"* (see 23:5-6) — Jeremiah proclaims, *"Mine heart within me is broken because of the prophets* (see 23:9);*"* he compares their wickedness to the inhabitants of Sodom and Gomorrah — **The Lord says of the false prophets, *"...they speak a vision of their own heart, and not out of the mouth of the Lord"* (see 23:16) — *"Can any hide himself in secret* *places that I shall not see him? saith the Lord. Do not I fill heaven and earth? Saith the Lord"* (see 23:24).

Jeremiah 24:   The Lord shows Jeremiah a vision of two baskets filled with figs and set before the temple of the Lord after Nebuchadnezzar, king of Babylon, had taken Jeconiah to Babylon (The date when Jeconiah was taken to Babylon was around 597 B.C. before the final destruction of Jerusalem in 586 B.C.) — In the vision, one basket has good figs and one has evil figs — Those who will return to Judah after the Babylonian exile are the good figs; those who will not be allowed to return are the evil figs — Jeconiah (the son of the previous king, Jehoiakim), Zedekiah (the present king of Judah), and Zedekiah's princes are among those who will not allowed to return.

Jeremiah 25:   The Lord warns of His coming judgment on Judah and says Judah will be in Babylonian captivity for 70 years — After the 70 years, the Lord will punish Babylon and many other nations *"...according to their deeds, according to the works of their own hands"* (see 25:14)

Jeremiah 26:   In the beginning of Jehoiakim's reign, the Lord commands Jeremiah to speak in the court of the Lord's house to all the cities of Judah — Jeremiah asks the people to repent of their evil ways, but the people want to kill him — Jeremiah says, *"Therefore now amend your ways and your doings, and obey the voice of the Lord your God; and the Lord will repent him of the evil that he hath pronounced against you"* (see 26:13) — Elders of the land compare Jeremiah to the prophet Micah; they persuade the people to let Jeremiah live since they believe he is God's prophet.

Jeremiah 27:   The Lord tells Jeremiah to *"...Make thee bonds and yokes, and put them upon thy neck"* (see 27:2) — Then the Lord commands Jeremiah to send the yokes to the kings of Edom, Moab, Ammon, Tyrus, and Zidon; the yokes are to warn the kings that they should place their neck under the yoke of King Nebuchadnezzar or be punished by the Lord — Jeremiah warns Zedekiah, king of Judah, *"...Bring your necks under the yoke of the king of Babylon, and serve him and his people and live"* (see 27:12) — Jeremiah also warns that without this submission to Babylon, more vessels will be taken out of the Lord's house — Vessels had already been taken in 597 B.C. when Jeconiah had been taken captive to Babylon.

Jeremiah 28:   The false prophet Hananiah prophesies that the yoke of the king of Babylon will be broken within two years; he also prophesies that Jeconiah, the other captives, and the vessels of the Lord's house will be returned to Judah — Hananiah takes *"...the yoke from off the prophet Jeremiah's neck, and brake it"* (see 28:10) — *"And Hananiah spake in the presence of all the people, saying, Thus saith the Lord; Even so will I break the yoke of Nebuchadnezzar king of Babylon from the neck of all nations within the space of two full years. And the prophet Jeremiah went his way"* (see 28:11) — Jeremiah is sent by the Lord to Hananiah to tell him he will die for making the people believe a lie — *"So Hananiah the prophet died the same year..."* (see 28:17).

Jeremiah 29:   Jeremiah sends a letter to the captives in Babylon saying, *"Build ye houses, and dwell in them; and plant gardens, and eat the fruit of them; Take ye wives, and beget sons and daughters; and take wives for your sons, and give your daughters to husbands, that they may bear sons and daughters; that ye may be increased there, and not diminished. And seek the peace of the city whither I have caused you to be carried away captives, and pray unto the Lord for it: for in the peace thereof shall ye have peace"* (see 29:5-7) — Jeremiah writes of the captives' return to Judah in 70 years (see 29:10) — *"For I know the thoughts that I think toward you, saith the Lord, thoughts of peace, and not of evil, to give you an expected end. Then shall ye call upon me, and ye shall go and pray unto me, and I will hearken unto you"* (see 29:11-12) — The Lord also says:

April 30 (Day 120), Memory Verse #338
Jeremiah 29:13:

AND YE SHALL SEEK ME, AND FIND ME,
WHEN YE SHALL SEARCH FOR ME WITH ALL YOUR HEART.

— **Jeremiah warns the false prophet Shemaiah that the Lord will punish him and his seed.**

Jeremiah 30: *"Thus speaketh the Lord God of Israel, saying, Write thee all the words that I have spoken unto thee in a book"* (see 30:2) — **God promises Judah's restoration** — *"Therefore fear thou not, O my servant Jacob, saith the Lord; neither be dismayed, O Israel: for, lo, I will save thee from afar, and thy seed from the land of their captivity; and Jacob shall return, and shall be in rest, and be quiet, and none shall make him afraid"* (see 30:10).

Jeremiah 31: *"The Lord hath appeared of old unto me, saying, Yea, I have loved thee with an everlasting love: therefore with lovingkindness have I drawn thee. Again I will build thee..."* (see 31:3-4).

May 1 (Day 121), Memory Verses #339 to #342
Jeremiah 31:31-34:
(Old Testament passage foretelling the NEW COVENANT)

31. BEHOLD, THE DAYS COME, SAITH THE LORD,
THAT I WILL MAKE A NEW COVENANT WITH THE HOUSE OF ISRAEL,
AND WITH THE HOUSE OF JUDAH:

32. NOT ACCORDING TO THE COVENANT THAT I MADE WITH THEIR FATHERS
IN THE DAY THAT I TOOK THEM BY THE HAND
TO BRING THEM OUT OF THE LAND OF EGYPT;
WHICH MY COVENANT THEY BRAKE,
ALTHOUGH I WAS AN HUSBAND UNTO THEM, SAITH THE LORD:

33. BUT THIS SHALL BE THE COVENANT THAT I WILL MAKE
WITH THE HOUSE OF ISRAEL; AFTER THOSE DAYS, SAITH THE LORD,
I WILL PUT MY LAW IN THEIR INWARD PARTS, AND WRITE IT IN THEIR HEARTS;
AND WILL BE THEIR GOD, AND THEY SHALL BE MY PEOPLE.

34. AND THEY SHALL TEACH NO MORE EVERY MAN HIS NEIGHBOUR,
AND EVERY MAN HIS BROTHER, SAYING KNOW THE LORD:
FOR THEY SHALL ALL KNOW ME,
FROM THE LEAST OF THEM UNTO THE GREATEST OF THEM,
SAITH THE LORD: FOR I WILL FORGIVE THEIR INIQUITY,
AND I WILL REMEMBER THEIR SIN NO MORE.

Jeremiah 32: While in prison for prophesying that Babylon will capture Judah, Jeremiah buys a field from his uncle's son, Hanameel — His buying the land, which is part of Judah already taken by Babylon, shows Jeremiah's trust that Judah will be restored some day to God's people — The Lord assures Jeremiah of his right decision on buying the land — *"Behold, I am the Lord, the God of all flesh: is there any thing too hard for me?"* (see 32:27).

Jeremiah 33: While Jeremiah is still in prison, the Lord speaks through Jeremiah of His restoring Judah — The Lord says, *"...I will pardon all their iniquities...And it shall be to me a name of joy, a praise and an honour before all the nations of the earth, which shall hear all the good that I do unto them: and they shall fear and tremble for all the goodness and for all the prosperity that I procure unto it"* (see 33:8-9).

Jeremiah 34:   **The Lord tells Jeremiah to speak to Zedekiah, king of Judah, while Nebuchadnezzar and the Babylonian army are battling Judah** — Jeremiah prophesies Babylon will burn Jerusalem, and Zedekiah will be taken captive to Babylon; the prophecy also states Zedekiah will die in peace and not by the sword — Zedekiah hopes to please the Lord by having the people release their slaves of Hebrew blood, but the Lord is angered when the people make the slaves return after their release — The people had not been honoring the law of giving Hebrew slaves their freedom in the seventh year of slavery.

Jeremiah 35:   The Lord tells Jeremiah to bring the Rechabites to the house of the Lord and give them wine — The Rechabites visit Jeremiah but refuse the wine because they are faithful to their forefather Johadab's commands to drink no wine, build no houses, plant no vineyards, and dwell in tents — **The Lord uses the Rechabites to show Judah how they should have obeyed the Lord's commandments.**

Jeremiah 36:   The Lord tells Jeremiah to *"Take thee a roll of a book, and write therein all the words that I have spoken unto thee* against Israel, and against Judah, and against all the nations, from the day I spake unto thee, from the days of Josiah, even unto this day" (see 36:2) — Jeremiah dictates to Baruch who writes Jeremiah's words *"...upon a roll of a book"* (see 36:4) — Jeremiah has Baruch read the roll in the temple of the Lord — Baruch is summoned to read the roll to the princes of Judah, and the princes take the roll to the king — After hearing only three or four leaves of the roll, King Jehoiakim casts the roll into his fire on the hearth — The king sends for Jeremiah and Baruch, *"...but the Lord hid them"* (see 36:26) — The Lord commands Jeremiah to have the roll written again and to warn Jehoiakim that he will have no heirs to the throne, *"...and his dead body shall be cast out in the day to the heat, and in the night to the frost"* (see 36:30).

Jeremiah 37: King Zedekiah sends a messenger to Jeremiah to ask him to *"...Pray now unto the Lord our God for us"* (see 37:3) — *"Then came the word of the Lord unto the prophet Jeremiah saying, Thus saith the Lord, the God of Israel; Thus shall ye say to the king of Judah, that sent you unto me to enquire of me; Behold, Pharaoh's army, which is come forth to help you, shall return to Egypt into their own land. And the Chaldeans shall come again, and fight against this city, and take it, and burn it with fire"* (see 37:6-8) — Jeremiah is put in prison by false accusations from the people of Judah that he has joined the Chaldeans (Babylonians).

Jeremiah 38:   **The princes ask the king to have Jeremiah put to death for prophesying Judah's destruction** — *"Then Zedekiah the king said, Behold, he is in your hand: for the king is not he that can do any thing against you. Then took they Jeremiah, and cast him into the dungeon of Malchiah the son of Hammelech, that was in the court of the prison: and they let down Jeremiah with cords. And in the dungeon there was no water, but mire: so Jeremiah sunk in the mire"* (see 38:5-6) — Ebed-melech, an Ethiopian eunuch in the king's house, goes to the king to plead for Jeremiah; the king allows Ebed-melech to rescue Jeremiah out of the dungeon and to return Jeremiah to the court of the prison — Zedekiah asks Jeremiah to tell him the Lord's message — The Lord has Jeremiah tell the king to surrender to the Babylonians to prevent the destruction of Jerusalem and the peoples' death, but this message goes unheeded — *"So Jeremiah abode in the court of the prison until the day that Jerusalem was taken: ..."* (see 38:28).

Jeremiah 39:   Jerusalem is captured by Babylon; King Zedekiah and the men of war flee, but the Babylonians pursue them and capture them — Zedekiah is forced to watch his sons and the nobles of Judah killed; Zedekiah is then blinded, bound in chains, and carried to Babylon — King Nebuchadnezzar of Babylon makes sure Jeremiah is given good care, and Jeremiah tells Ebed-melech that his life will also be spared by the Babylonians.

Jeremiah 40: Nebuzar-adan, the captain of the Babylonian guard, frees Jeremiah of chains in Ramah — Jeremiah is given the choice to go to Babylon or stay in Judah; Jeremiah chooses to stay in Judah — The king of Babylon appoints Gedaliah as governor over the cities of Judah — Many Jews who are scattered in other nations return to Judah — Johanan warns Gedaliah that the king of the Ammonites plans to send Ishmael to kill Gedaliah — Gedaliah refuses to believe this news and will not let Johanan kill Ishmael.

Jeremiah 41: Ishmael and his ten men kill Gedaliah, the governor of the land, while eating bread with him in Mizpah; they also kill many Jews and Babylonians who had been present — Not knowing of Gedaliah's death, 80 men in mourning are tricked by Ishmael to come to Mizpah to visit Gedaliah — Then Ishmael kills all but ten of the 80 men, and he takes the surviving ten and others captive — Johanan rescues the captives from Ishmael, but Ishmael escapes — Johanan, along with the captains of the forces and the remnant recovered from Gedaliah, dwell in Chimham by Bethlehem and prepare to enter Egypt.

Jeremiah 42: Johanan, the captains of the forces, and those rescued from Ishmael come to Jeremiah to ask what God commands them to do — After ten days, Jeremiah replies with the Lord's message — *"The Lord hath said concerning you, O ye remnant of Judah; Go ye not into Egypt: know certainly that I have admonished you this day"* (see 42:19) — Jeremiah proclaims the Lord will take care of the remnant if they stay in Judah — But if the people go to Egypt, Jeremiah warns, *"Now therefore know certainly that ye shall die by the sword, by the famine, and by the pestilence, in the place whither ye desire to go and to sojourn"* (see 42:22).

Jeremiah 43: But the people claim that Jeremiah prophesies falsely, and they go to Egypt despite Jeremiah's warnings from the Lord — The Lord instructs Jeremiah to *"Take great stones in thine hand, and hide them in the clay in the brickkiln, which is at the entry of Pharaoh's house in Tahpanhes, in the sight of the men of Judah;"* (see 43:9) — This action prophesies that some day King Nebuchadnezzar will conquer that site and spread his royal pavilion over the stones — Nebuchadnezzar will also bring death, captivity, and much destruction to Egypt, including the burning of the Egyptian gods' houses.

Jeremiah 44: Jeremiah continues to warn of the Lord's punishment because of the peoples' disobedience and worshipping of other gods.

Jeremiah 45: Jeremiah tells Baruch the Lord will spare his life.

Jeremiah 46: Jeremiah prophesies that Egypt will be conquered by King Nebuchadnezzar of Babylon — *"Fear thou not, O Jacob my servant, saith the Lord: for I am with thee; for I will make a full end of all the nations whither I have driven thee: but I will not make a full end of thee, but correct thee in measure; yet will I not leave thee wholly unpunished"* (see 46:28).

Jeremiah 47: Jeremiah warns the Philistines of their destruction which will come from the north, the area of Babylon.

Jeremiah 48: Jeremiah prophesies of Moab's destruction — *"...Moab shall be destroyed from being a people, because he hath magnified himself against the Lord"* (see 48:42) — *"Yet will I bring again the captivity of Moab (Yet I will restore the fortunes of Moab, NIV) in the latter days, saith the Lord..."* (see 48:47).

Jeremiah 49: Jeremiah prophesies concerning the falls of Ammon, Edom, Damascus, Kedar and Hazor (nomadic people of the desert), and Elam — Ammon and Elam are given assurance of restoration.

Jeremiah 50-51: Jeremiah prophesies concerning the destruction of Babylon — *"Israel is a scattered sheep; the lions have driven him away: first the king of Assyria hath devoured him; and last this Nebuchadnezzar king of Babylon hath broken his bones. Therefore thus saith the Lord of hosts, the God of Israel; Behold, I will punish the king of Babylon and his land, as I have punished the king of Assyria. And I will bring Israel again to his habitation, and he shall feed on Carmel and Bachan, and his soul shall be satisfied upon mount Ephraim and Gilead"* (see 50:17-19) — *"**So Jeremiah wrote in a book all the evil that should come upon Babylon**...And Jeremiah said to Seraiah, When thou comest to Babylon, and shalt see, and shalt read all these words; Then shalt thou say, O Lord, thou hast spoken against this place, to cut it off, that none shall remain in it, neither man nor beast, but that it shall be desolate for ever. And it shall be, when thou hast made an end of reading this book, that thou shalt bind a stone to it, and cast it into the midst of Euphrates: And thou shalt say, Thus shall Babylon sink, and shall not rise from the evil that I will bring upon her: and they shall be weary. Thus far are the words of Jeremiah"* (see 51:60-64).

Jeremiah 52: During the reign of Zedekiah, Jerusalem is besieged approximately two years by Babylon until the city has no more food — Zedekiah and the men of war flee from Jerusalem at night, but they are pursued and captured by the Babylonians — The king of Babylon kills Zedekiah's sons and the princes of Judah before Zedekiah's eyes, and then Zedekiah is blinded, bound in chains, and thrown in prison in Babylon until his death — Nebuzar-adan, captain of the Babylonian guard, burns the Lord's house, the king's house, and all the houses of Jerusalem — He also carries the vessels of the Lord's house back to Babylon along with Jewish captives; many other Jews are slain — The king of Babylon releases Judah's previous king, Jehoiachin, from the Babylonian prison — Jehoiachin is also made a ruler and shares the king's food until his death.

JEREMIAH 17:7:

BLESSED IS THE MAN THAT TRUSTETH IN THE LORD, AND WHOSE HOPE THE LORD IS.

JEREMIAH 32:27:

BEHOLD, I AM THE LORD, THE GOD OF ALL FLESH: IS THERE ANY THING TOO HARD FOR ME?

LAMENTATIONS

Introduction: Tradition attributes authorship of Lamentations to Jeremiah. It is thought to have been written during the 500's B.C., after the fall of Jerusalem and the destruction of Solomon's temple by Babylon in 586 B.C. The prophet Jeremiah had repeatedly warned the Jews of coming destruction by Babylon and witnessed the fall of Jerusalem. The title, Lamentations, is derived from a Greek word meaning "to cry aloud." This book contains five mournful poems lamenting the destruction of Jerusalem and the temple, and the Babylonian exile of the people of Judah. Lamentations has five chapters.

Key Contents and Key Memory Verses with Study Dates

Lamentations 1-3: Chapter 1 expresses the mourning of Jerusalem's destruction — Chapter 2 shows how the Lord has judged Jerusalem — In chapter 3, the writer speaks of his trials, but shows how he regains hope through trusting God.

May 2 (Day 122), Memory Verses #343 & #344
Lamentations 3:22-23:

22. IT IS OF THE LORD'S MERCIES THAT WE ARE NOT CONSUMED, BECAUSE HIS COMPASSIONS FAIL NOT.

23. THEY ARE NEW EVERY MORNING: GREAT IS THY FAITHFULNESS.

May 2 (Day 122), Memory Verse #345
Lamentations 3:25:

THE LORD IS GOOD UNTO THEM THAT WAIT FOR HIM, TO THE SOUL THAT SEEKETH HIM.

May 3 (Day 123), Memory Verses #346 & #347
Lamentations 3:40-41:

40. LET US SEARCH AND TRY OUR WAYS, AND TURN AGAIN TO THE LORD.

41. LET US LIFT UP OUR HEART WITH OUR HANDS UNTO GOD IN THE HEAVENS.

— *"Thou drewest near in the day that I called upon thee:* thou saidst, Fear not. O Lord, thou hast pleaded the causes of my soul; thou hast redeemed my life. O Lord, thou hast seen my wrong: judge thou my cause" (see 3:57-59).

Lamentations 4-5: Chapter 4 shows how Jerusalem's destruction is a result Judah's sins; yet there is still hope — *"Rejoice and be glad..."* (see 4:21) — **In chapter 5, the Jews admit their sins** — *"The crown is fallen from our head: woe unto us, that we have sinned"* (see 5:16) — **The Jews pray to God:**

May 3 (Day 123), Memory Verse #348
Lamentations 5:19:

THOU, O LORD, REMAINEST FOR EVER; THY THRONE FROM GENERATION TO GENERATION.

— *"Turn thou us unto thee, O Lord, and we shall be turned; renew our days as of old"* (see 5:21).

EZEKIEL

Introduction: Most scholars believe Ezekiel is the author of this book. The suggested date of writing is sometime during 593 B.C. to 570 B.C. Ezekiel was both a priest and prophet, and he ministered to the exiled Jews in Babylon while Jeremiah ministered to Jews left in Jerusalem. Along with approximately 10,000 Jews and King Jehoiachin, Ezekiel had been taken captive to Babylon in 597 B.C. before the final fall of Jerusalem to Babylon in 586 B.C. Other Jews including Daniel, along with Judah's gold and silver, had already been taken to Babylon in 605 B.C. During the Babylonian exile, Ezekiel encouraged the Jews and gave them hope. While living in Babylon, Ezekiel experienced prophetic visions including visions that carried him back to Jerusalem. Ezekiel has 48 chapters.

Key Contents and Key Memory Verses with Study Dates

Ezekiel 1: Ezekiel sees visions from God — After being taken captive to Babylon, Ezekiel states, *"...as I was among the captives by the river of Chebar, that the heavens were opened, and I saw visions of God"* (see 1:1) — **Vision of four living creatures (cherubim),** each with four faces and four wings — The faces look like a man, a lion, an ox, and an eagle (see 1:4-14) — **Vision of wheels** (see 1:15-21) — **Vision of the firmament over the creatures and a throne above the firmament with a man upon it** (see 1:22-28) — *"...This was the appearance of the likeness of the glory of the Lord. And when I saw it, I fell upon my face, and I heard a voice of one that spake"* (see 1:28).

Ezekiel 2-3: The Lord calls Ezekiel — *"And he said unto me, Son of man, stand upon thy feet, and I will speak unto thee. And the spirit entered into me when he spake unto me, and set me upon my feet, that I heard him that spake unto me"* (see 2:1-2) — *"...open thy mouth, and eat that I give thee. And when I looked, behold, an hand was sent unto me; and, lo, a roll of a book was therein; And he spread it before me; and it was written within and without: and there was written therein lamentations, and mourning, and woe"* (see 2:8-10) — *"...eat this roll, and go speak unto the house of Israel. So I opened my mouth, and he caused me to eat that roll. And he said unto me, Son of man, cause thy belly to eat, and fill thy bowels with this roll that I give thee. Then did I eat it; and it was in my mouth as honey for sweetness"* (see 3:1-3) — *"And go, get thee to them of the captivity, unto the children of thy people, and speak unto them, and tell them, Thus saith the Lord God; whether they will hear, or whether they will forbear"* (see 3:11) — Ezekiel sits seven days with other captives by the river Chebar — On the seventh day, the word of the Lord comes to Ezekiel to let him know he is fully responsible for warning the people of their sins — The Lord tells Ezekiel to go to the plain; at the plain, he again sees God's glory just as he had seen at the river Chebar — Ezekiel falls on his face — The spirit enters Ezekiel, sets him on his feet, and says, *"...Go, shut thyself within thine house"* (see 3:24) — The Lord tells Ezekiel that he will only be able to speak when the Lord opens his mouth to speak to the people — *"...He that heareth, let him hear; and he that forbeareth, let him forbear: for they are a rebellious house"* (see 3:27).

Ezekiel 4: Ezekiel prophesies concerning Jerusalem's fall by taking a tile (brick), drawing an outline of Jerusalem on the tile, and then demonstrating the tile being besieged by an enemy fort and enemy camps — Ezekiel lies on his left side 390 days to represent Israel's sin and lies on his right side 40 days to represent Judah's sin — During the days of lying on his side, the Lord commands Ezekiel to drink only small amounts of water and eat bread made with dung; these actions illustrate the famine of food and water which Jerusalem will experience when besieged.

Ezekiel 5: The Lord tells Ezekiel to shave his head and beard, and then divide the hair; one third of the hair is to be burned in Jerusalem, a third is to be cut up with a knife, and another third is to be scattered in the wind — A few hairs are to be bound in Ezekiel's skirts and then cast into a fire to show *"...for thereof shall a fire come forth into the house of Israel"* (see 5:4) — **The Lord explains the three divisions of hair** — *"A third part of thee shall die with the pestilence, and with famine shall they be consumed in the midst of thee: and a third part shall fall by the sword round about thee; and I will scatter a third part into all the winds, and I will draw out a sword after them"* (see 5:12).

Ezekiel 6: The Lord speaks through Ezekiel; *"...Behold, I, even I, will bring a sword upon you...I will cast down your slain men before your idols"* (see 6:3-4) — *"...and ye shall know that I am the Lord. Yet will I leave a remnant, that ye may have some that shall escape the sword among the nations, when ye shall be scattered through the countries. And they that escape of you shall remember me among the nations whither they shall be carried captives..."* (see 6:7-9).

Ezekiel 7: All of Judah will be judged — *"...An end, the end is come upon the four corners of the land"* (see 7:2).

Ezekiel 8: *"...as I sat in mine house, and the elders of Judah sat before me, that the hand of the Lord God fell there upon me.* *Then I beheld, and lo a likeness as the appearance of fire: from the appearance of his loins even downward, fire; and from his loins even upward, as the appearance of brightness, as the colour of amber. And he put forth the form of an hand, and took me by a lock of mine head; and the spirit lifted me up between the earth and the heaven, and brought me in the visions of God to Jerusalem..."* (see 8:1-3) — **Ezekiel's visions from God show the sins of Jerusalem which include sun worship, idol worship, and the worship of other gods.**

Ezekiel 9: Visions from God show Ezekiel the slaughter of the people of Jerusalem; *"And, behold, six men came from the way of the higher gate, which lieth toward the north, and every man a slaughter weapon in his hand; and one man among them was clothed with linen, with a writer's inkhorn by his side: ..."* (see 9:2) — In this vision, those who repent of their sin have a mark placed on their foreheads by the man in linen; all without the mark are killed.

Ezekiel 10: Again in a vision, Ezekiel sees the four living creatures (cherubim) mentioned in the first chapter — As the vision continues, the man in linen is commanded to fill his hands with coals of fire found between the cherubim and scatter the coals over the city.

Ezekiel 11: Ezekiel sees a vision of princes giving wrong advice to the people; the princes are telling the people to continue building houses because there will be no destruction — Ezekiel asks the Lord, *"...Ah Lord God! wilt thou make a full end of the remnant of Israel?"* (see 11:13) — **Restoration promised** — *"...Thus saith the Lord God; ...although I have scattered them among the countries, yet will I be to them as a little sanctuary in the countries where they shall come...I will even gather you from the people, and assemble you out of the countries where ye have been scattered, and I will give you the land of Israel"* (see 11:16-17) — *"And I will give them one heart, and I will put a new spirit within you; and I will take the stony heart out of their flesh, and will give them an heart of flesh: That they may walk in my statutes, and keep mine ordinances, and do them: and they shall be my people, and I will be their God"* (see 11:19-20).

Ezekiel 12: Ezekiel's actions predict the coming captivity and King Zedekiah's fleeing the Babylonians; Ezekiel prophesies that Zedekiah will be captured and blinded — *"And I did* *so as I was commanded: I brought forth my stuff by day, as stuff for captivity, and in the even I digged through the wall with mine hand: I brought it forth in the twilight, and I bare it upon my shoulder in their sight"* (see 12:7) — Ezekiel covers his face while carrying the baggage — **Ezekiel's actions predict the coming famine and desolation of cities** — *"Moreover the word of the Lord came to me, saying, Son of man, eat thy bread with quaking, and drink thy water with trembling and with carefulness;"* (see 12:17-18) — Ezekiel proclaims the time of the visions' fulfillment is near.

Ezekiel 13: Ezekiel prophesies warnings to false prophets who foretell peace for Israel and give the people false hope — *"Thus saith the Lord God; Woe unto the foolish prophets, that follow their own spirit, and have seen nothing!"* (see 13:3).

Ezekiel 14: Ezekiel speaks to the elders of Israel and warns them of the idols in their hearts — Ezekiel tells the people that if Noah, Daniel, and Job were living in the land, even they could not save the Israelites from the coming judgment of the Lord — **A remnant of Israel is given promise of restoration** — *"Yet behold, therein shall be left a remnant that shall be brought forth, both sons and daughters: ...and ye shall be comforted concerning the evil that I have brought upon Jerusalem, even concerning all that I have brought upon it"* (see 14:22).

Ezekiel 15: Jerusalem is compared to a useless vine which is thrown into the fire.

Ezekiel 16: Israel is referred to as a harlot, *"...as a wife that committeth adultery, which taketh strangers instead of her husband"* (see 16:32) — Israel's sins include sacrificing their children (see 16:20) — **Again, restoration is promised** (see 16:60-63).

Ezekiel 17: The Lord has Ezekiel *"...speak a parable unto the house of Israel"* (see 17:2) — The parable tells of an eagle that crops off the top of the highest branch of a cedar and carries it to a city; then the eagle plants the seed of the land in very fertile soil by great waters — The seed grows into a healthy vine, producing much fruit — The vine spreads its branches toward another eagle to be nurtured; the vine withers and is plucked up by its roots, its fruit being destroyed — The parable prophesies that the prosperous Israelites will be "plucked up" and made captives by Babylon as punishment for their sins; their sins include disobeying God by becoming allies with Egypt (the second eagle in the parable) — The Lord will also plant a cedar branch which will flourish and bear much fruit.

May 4 (Day 124), Memory Verse #349
Ezekiel 17:24:

AND ALL THE TREES OF THE FIELD SHALL KNOW THAT
I THE LORD HAVE BROUGHT DOWN THE HIGH TREE,
HAVE EXALTED THE LOW TREE, HAVE DRIED UP THE GREEN TREE,
AND HAVE MADE THE DRY TREE TO FLOURISH:
I THE LORD HAVE SPOKEN AND HAVE DONE IT.

Ezekiel 18: *"The soul that sinneth, it shall die. The son shall not bear the iniquity of the father, neither shall the father bear the iniquity of the son: the righteousness of the righteous shall be upon him, and the wickedness of the wicked shall be upon him. But if the wicked will turn from all his sins that he hath committed, and keep all my statutes, and do that which is lawful and right, he shall surely live, he shall not die"* (see 18:20-21) — *"When a righteous man turneth away from his righteousness, and committeth iniquity, and dieth in them; for his iniquity that he hath done shall he die"* (see 18:26).

May 5 (Day 125), Memory Verses #350 to #352
Ezekiel 18:30-32:

30. THEREFORE I WILL JUDGE YOU, O HOUSE OF ISRAEL,
EVERY ONE ACCORDING TO HIS WAYS, SAITH THE LORD GOD.
REPENT, AND TURN YOURSELVES FROM ALL YOUR TRANSGRESSIONS;
SO INIQUITY SHALL NOT BE YOUR RUIN.

31. CAST AWAY FROM YOU ALL YOUR TRANSGRESSIONS,
WHEREBY YE HAVE TRANSGRESSED;
AND MAKE YOU A NEW HEART AND A NEW SPIRIT:
FOR WHY WILL YE DIE, O HOUSE OF ISRAEL?

32. FOR I HAVE NO PLEASURE IN THE DEATH OF HIM THAT DIETH,
SAITH THE LORD GOD: WHEREFORE TURN YOURSELVES, AND LIVE YE.

Ezekiel 19: Judah is compared to a lioness who sent out two cubs (see 19:1-9); the first cub is captured and taken to Egypt, the second cub is captured and taken to Babylon (the cubs most likely illustrate the kings Jehoahaz and Jehoiachin) — **Judah is compared to a healthy vine which is plucked up and cast down** (see 19:10-14); her fruit becomes dry, and her branches are broken, become withered, and are burned *"...so that she hath no strong rod to be a scepter to rule. This is a lamentation, and shall be for a lamentation"* (see 19:14).

Ezekiel 20: Elders of Israel come to Ezekiel, and he speaks God's message to them — Ezekiel reviews Israel's history and rebellious sins; the Lord states,*"...they had not executed my judgments, but had despised my statutes, and had polluted my sabbaths, and their eyes were after their fathers' idols"* (see 20:24) — **The Lord will restore Israel** — The Lord says, *"I will accept you with your sweet savour, when I bring you out from the people, and gather you out of the countries wherein ye have been scattered; and I will be sanctified in you before the heathen"* (see 20:41) — Ezekiel tells the parable of the Lord destroying the forest of the south by fire.

Ezekiel 21: The Lord's judgment: *"...I will cut off from thee the righteous and the wicked, therefore shall my sword go forth out of his sheath against all flesh from the south to the north:"* (see 21:4) — The king of Babylon will choose to attack Jerusalem instead of Ammon when this prophecy is fulfilled.

Ezekiel 22: Judah's sins are reviewed — Israel is compared to dross in a furnace (see 22:18-19) — *"As they gather silver, and brass, and iron, and lead, and tin, into the midst of the furnace, to blow the fire upon it, to melt it; so will I gather you in mine anger and in my fury, and I will leave you there, and melt you"* (see 22:20) — Ezekiel states the sins of the prophets, the priests, the princes, and the people of the land.

Ezekiel 23: Samaria (Israel) and Jerusalem (Judah) are compared to sister harlots, Aholah and Aholibah — Aholah defiles herself with the idols of the Assyrians and Aholibah defiles herself with the idols of both the Assyrians and the Babylonians — The Lord warns of punishment for Aholibah (Jerusalem) by attack from the very nations whose idols they worship; *"...ye shall bear the sins of your idols: and ye shall know that I am the Lord God"* (see 23:49).

Ezekiel 24: On the same day of the besieging of Jerusalem by Babylon, the Lord tells Ezekiel to speak a parable to Jerusalem — The parable says to boil choice pieces of meat, the thigh and shoulder, in a pot of water and burn the bones under the pot — *"Wherefore thus saith the Lord God; Woe to the bloody city, to the pot whose scum is therein, and whose scum is not gone out of it! ..."* (see 24:6) — Then the pot is to be set *"...empty upon the coals thereof, that* *the brass of it may be hot, and may burn, and that the filthiness of it may be molten in it, that the scum of it may be consumed"* (see 24:11) — **The Lord tells Ezekiel to command Israel not to openly mourn over Jerusalem's destruction, just as Ezekiel has not openly mourned over the death of his wife** — *"Also the word of the Lord came unto me saying, Son of man, behold, I take away from thee the desire of thine eyes with a stroke: yet neither shalt thou mourn nor weep, neither shall thy tears run down"* (see 24:15-16).

Ezekiel 25: Ezekiel prophesies punishment for Ammon, Moab, Edom and the Philistines.

Ezekiel 26: Ezekiel prophesies destruction for Tyrus (Tyre, NIV) by the Babylonians.

Ezekiel 27: Mourning for Tyrus — Tyrus' wealth is described.

Ezekiel 28: Prophecy of the death of the prince of Tyrus — *"...Thus saith the Lord; Because thine heart is lifted up, and thou hast said, I am a God, I sit in the seat of God..."* (see 28:2). *"Thou shalt die the deaths of the uncircumcised by the hand of strangers: for I have spoken it, saith the Lord God"* (see 28:10) — **Mourning for the King of Tyre's predicted destruction** — Some believe Ezekiel 28:11-19 is meant to compare the King of Tyre to Satan — Satan had once held a position of beauty and wisdom, but fell due to pride and iniquity — **Prophecy against Zidon (Sidon, NIV) — Restoration of Israel.**

Ezekiel 29-30: Prophecy against Egypt — *"Therefore thus saith the Lord God; Behold, I will give the land of Egypt unto Nebuchadnezzar king of Babylon; and he shall take her multitude, and take her spoil, and take her prey; and it shall be the wages for his army"* (see 29:19).

Ezekiel 31: The Lord has Ezekiel speak to the Pharaoh of Egypt — Egypt is compared to Assyria in greatness, but Assyria had fallen due to pride; *"...his heart is lifted up in his height;"* (see 31:10) — Ezekiel prophesies that Egypt, along with many other nations, will also fall.

Ezekiel 32: Continued prophecy of Egypt's fall — *"...the word of the Lord came unto me, saying, Son of Man, take up a lamentation for Pharaoh king of Egypt, and say unto him, Thou art like a young lion of the nations, and thou art as a whale in the seas: and thou camest forth with thy rivers, and troubledst the waters with thy feet, and fouledst their rivers. Thus saith the Lord God; I will therefore spread out my net over thee with a company of many people; and they shall bring thee up in my net. Then will I leave thee upon the land, I will cast thee forth upon the open field, and will cause all the fowls of the heaven to remain upon thee, and I will fill the beasts of the whole earth with thee"* (see 32:1-4).

Ezekiel 33: The Lord gives Ezekiel the responsibility of being a watchman for the house of Israel; *"So thou, O son of man, I have set thee a watchman unto the house of Israel; therefore thou shalt hear the word at my mouth, and warn them from me"* (see 33:7) — *"...As I live, saith the Lord God, I have no pleasure in the death of the wicked; but that the wicked turn from his way and live: turn ye, turn ye from your evil ways; ..."* (see 33:11) — *"When the righteous turneth from his righteousness, and committeth iniquity, he shall even die thereby. But if the wicked turn from his wickedness, and do that which is lawful and right, he shall live thereby. Yet ye say, The way of the Lord is not equal. O ye house of Israel, I will judge you every one after his ways"* (see 33:18-20) — **"...one that had escaped out of Jerusalem came unto me, saying, The city is smitten"** (see 33:21) — Ezekiel speaks of Israel's sins.

Ezekiel 34: *"And the word of the Lord came unto me, saying, Son of man, prophesy against the shepherds of Israel, prophesy, and say unto them, Thus saith the Lord God unto the shepherds;*

Woe be to the shepherds of Israel that do feed themselves? should not the shepherds feed the flocks?" (see 34:1-2) — ***"As a shepherd seeketh out his flock in the day that he is among his sheep that are scattered; so will I seek out my sheep,*** *and will deliver them out of all places where they have been scattered in the cloudy and dark day"* (see 34:12) — *"I will feed them in good pasture, and upon the high mountains of Israel shall their fold be: ..."* (see 34:14) — *"I will seek that which was lost..."* (see 34:16) — *"And I will set up one shepherd over them, and he shall feed them, even my servant David; he shall feed them, and he shall be their shepherd"* (see 34:23) — *"And I will make them and the places round about my hill a blessing; and I will cause the shower to come down in his season;* ***there will be showers of blessing"*** (see 34:26).

Ezekiel 35: Prophecies warning Mount Seir and all of Idumea (Edom, NIV) of their fall.

Ezekiel 36: Promise of restoration for Israel — *"For, behold, I am for you, and I will turn unto you, and ye shall be tilled and sown:"* (see 36:9) — *"Thus saith the Lord God; I do not this for your sakes, O house of Israel, but for mine holy name's sake, which ye have profaned among the heathen, whither ye went"* (see 36:22) — **Promise of a new covenant** — *"For I will take you from among the heathen, and gather you out of all countries, and will bring you into your own land. Then will I sprinkle clean water upon you, and ye shall be clean: from all your filthiness, and from all your idols, will I cleanse you. A new heart also will I give you, and a new spirit will I put within you: and I will take away the stony heart out of your flesh, and I will give you an heart of flesh. And I will put my spirit within you, and cause you to walk in my statutes, and ye shall keep my judgments, and do them. And ye shall dwell in the land that I gave to your fathers; and ye shall be my people, and I will be your God"* (see 36:24 -28).

Ezekiel 37: *"The hand of the Lord was upon me, and carried me out in the spirit of the Lord, and set me down in the midst of the valley which was full of bones...and lo, they were very dry.* *And he said unto me, Son of man, can these bones live? And I answered, O Lord God, thou knowest"* (see 37:1-3) — The Lord causes the bones to come to life, *"...an exceeding great army"* (see 37:10), complete with sinews, flesh, skin, and breath — *"Then he said unto me, Son of man, these bones are the whole house of Israel: behold, they say, Our bones are dried, and our hope is lost: we are cut off for our parts...Behold, O my people, I will open your graves, and cause you to come up out of your graves, and bring you into the land of Israel"* (see 37:11-12) — **The Lord tells Ezekiel to write on two sticks (on one he writes *"For Judah..."* and on the other he writes *"For Joseph...,"* see 37:16) to symbolize Israel will be made one nation, no longer divided into two kingdoms** — *"And David my servant shall be king over them; and they all shall have one shepherd:..."* (see 37:24) — *"Moreover I will make a covenant of peace with them; it shall be an everlasting covenant with them: ..."* (see 37:26).

Ezekiel 38-39: The Lord says, *"...when Gog shall come against the land of Israel,* *saith the Lord God, that my fury shall come up in my face. For in my jealousy and in the fire of my wrath have I spoken, Surely in that day there shall be a great shaking in the land of Israel;"* (see 38:18-19) — *"...every man's sword shall be against his brother"* (see 38:21) — *"...I will rain upon him, and upon his bands, and upon the many people that are with him, an overflowing rain, and great hailstones, fire, and brimstone. Thus will I magnify myself, and sanctify myself; and I will be known in the eyes of many nations, and they shall know that I am the Lord"* (see 38:22-23) — *"Neither will I hide my face any more from them: for I have poured out my spirit upon the house of Israel, saith the Lord God"* (see 39:29).

Ezekiel 40-43: God gives Ezekiel a vision (chapters 40-48) describing the new temple in great detail — In his vision *"...there was a man, whose appearance was like the appearance of brass, with a line of flax in his hand, and a measuring reed;..."* (see 40:3) —

"So the spirit took me up, and brought me into the inner court; and, behold, the glory of the Lord filled the house. And I heard him speaking unto me out of the house; and the man stood by me. And he said unto me, Son of man, the place of my throne, and the place of the soles of my feet, where I will dwell in the midst of the children of Israel for ever, and my holy name, shall the house of Israel no more defile, neither they, nor their kings, by their whoredom, nor by the carcases of their kings in their high places" (see 43:5-7).

Ezekiel 44: The priests and their duties for the new temple are described.

Ezekiel 45: Ezekiel's vision continues with specifications on setting aside holy land for the temple and land for the prince's portion — The prince's duties for giving offerings — The priest's duties in presenting offerings.

Ezekiel 46: Continued description of offerings.

Ezekiel 47: The river running through the land and the borders of the land are described.

Ezekiel 48: In the first of this chapter, **borders of the land are described for the tribes** of Dan, Asher, Naphtali, Manasseh, Ephraim, Reuben, and Judah; in the last of this chapter, borders are described for the tribes of Benjamin, Simeon, Issachar, Zebulun, and Gad — The land for the priests, Levites, and prince is described — *"...and the name of the city from that day shall be, The Lord is there"* (see 48:35).

EZEKIEL 18:30:

...REPENT, AND TURN YOURSELVES FROM ALL YOUR TRANSGRESSIONS; SO INIQUITY SHALL NOT BE YOUR RUIN.

DANIEL

Introduction: Tradition holds Daniel as the author of this book which is thought to have been written about 530 B.C. Some scholars believe this book was written much later by another author. Daniel was among the Jews taken captive to Babylon in 605 B.C. Other Jewish captives were taken to Babylon in 597 B.C., and the final capture of the Jews by Babylon was in 586 B.C. when Jerusalem was destroyed. The Jews were allowed to return to Jerusalem after Cyrus' decree in 538 B.C. Cyrus was king of Persia, the nation that conquered Babylon. The literature of Daniel is both historical (chapters 1-6) and apocalyptic (chapters 7-12). Two well-known stories are about the fiery furnace (chapter 3) and the lions' den (chapter 6). There are various interpretations of Daniel's apocalyptic writing as there are of other apocalyptic writings such as Revelation. In Daniel, one of the main reasons for various interpretations is due to the different viewpoints concerning the date of writing. Both the Hebrew and Babylonian names of Daniel and his three friends are listed in chapter one below. The Hebrew name is mentioned first. Daniel has 12 chapters.

Key Contents and Key Memory Verses with Study Dates

Daniel 1:   Daniel (Belteshazzar), Hananiah (Shadrach), Mishael (Meshach), and Azariah (Abednego) are among the selected choice men of Judah who are taken captive to Babylon —They are trained for King Nebuchadnezzar's service but refuse to eat the king's choice food — When they are tested, they are found stronger than the king's men.

Daniel 2: *"And in the second year of the reign of Nebuchadnezzar, Nebuchadnezzar dreamed dreams, wherewith his spirit was troubled, and his sleep brake from him"* (see 2:1) — **God gives Daniel the ability to reveal the content of King Nebuchadnezzar's dream and to interpret this dream of a gold, silver, bronze, iron, and clay statue** — Daniel explains how the different parts of the statue represent various kingdoms — The king's wise men had not been able to reveal the king's dream — Daniel praises God for making the dream known to him:

May 6 (Day 126), Memory Verse #353
Daniel 2:20:

DANIEL ANSWERED AND SAID, BLESSED BE THE NAME OF GOD FOR EVER AND EVER:
FOR WISDOM AND MIGHT ARE HIS:

May 6 (Day 126), Memory Verse #354
Daniel 2:22:

HE REVEALETH THE DEEP AND SECRET THINGS:
HE KNOWETH WHAT IS IN THE DARKNESS, AND THE LIGHT DWELLETH WITH HIM.

Daniel 3: Story of the fiery furnace — *"Nebuchadnezzar the king made an image of gold, whose height was threescore cubits, and the breadth thereof six cubits (...ninety feet high and nine feet wide..., NIV): he set it up in the plain of Dura, in the province of Babylon"* (see 3:1) — Because Shadrach, Meshach, and Abednego will not bow down to the king's image of gold, they are thrown into the fiery furnace — Only these three men are thrown in the furnace, but a fourth man is seen with them — Nebuchadnezzar says, *"...Lo, I see four men loose, walking in the midst of the fire, and they have no hurt; and the form of the fourth is like the Son of God"* (see 3:25) — God delivers Shadrach, Meshach, and Abednego safely out of the furnace — **Nebuchadnezzar decrees no one should speak against the God of these three men.**

Daniel 4: Daniel interprets Nebuchadnezzar's dream of a great tree — The dream foretells Nebuchadnezzar' temporary loss of his kingdom when he must live as a beast in the field until he acknowledges God's supremacy — Nebuchadnezzar does lose his kingdom until he honors God — *"And at the end of the days I Nebuchadnezzar lifted up mine eyes unto heaven, and mine understanding returned unto me, and I blessed the most High, and I praised and honored him that liveth for ever, whose dominion is an everlasting dominion, and his kingdom is from generation to generation;"* (see 4:34).

Daniel 5: Daniel interprets the miraculous handwriting on the wall during Belshazzar's feast — Belshazzar is one of Babylon's kings after Nebuchadnezzar — Belshazzar had turned from God and was using items which Nebuchadnezzar had stolen from the Jerusalem temple — The writing on the wall is a message to Belshazzar which says, *"...God hath numbered thy kingdom, and finished it"* (see 5:26) — *"In that night was Belshazzar the king of the Chaldeans slain"* (see 5:30) — *"And Darius the Median took the kingdom..."* (see 5:31).

Daniel 6: The new king Darius places Daniel in charge of the princes — Those jealous of Daniel trick the king and urge him to decree *"...that whosoever shall ask a petition of any God or man for thirty days, save of thee, O King, he shall be cast into the den of lions"* (see 6:7) — Daniel continues to pray openly, and the king is sad when **Daniel must be cast into the lion's den** — The next day, the king rushes to the den and is relieved when he hears Daniel saying, *"My God hath sent his angel, and hath shut the lions' mouths, that they have not hurt me..."* (see 6:22) — Then the king decrees, *"...That in every dominion of my kingdom men tremble and fear before the God of Daniel..."* (see 6:26) — The king has those who instigated the decree cast into the lion's den along with their families, and they are eaten by the lions.

Daniel 7-8: Daniel's visions of the future and their interpretations — His visions include images of four beasts, a ram, a goat, and a little horn — The interpretations speak of various nations.

Daniel 9: Daniel asks forgiveness for Israel, and Gabriel shows him future events — The vision of 70 sevens (weeks) is interpreted by some as 70 years.

Daniel 10-12: Daniel's vision of future things — *"And at that time shall Michael stand up, the great prince which standeth for the children of thy people: and there shall be a time of trouble, such as never was since there was a nation even to that same time: and at that time thy people shall be delivered, every one that shall be found written in the book. And many of them that sleep in the dust of the earth shall awake, some to everlasting life, and some to shame and everlasting contempt"* (see 12:1-2).

May 7 (Day 127), Memory Verse #355
Daniel 12:3:

AND THEY THAT BE WISE SHALL SHINE AS THE BRIGHTNESS OF THE FIRMAMENT; AND THEY THAT TURN MANY TO RIGHTEOUSNESS AS THE STARS FOR EVER AND EVER.

May 7 (Day 127), Memory Verse #356
Daniel 12:10:

MANY SHALL BE PURIFIED, AND MADE WHITE, AND TRIED; BUT THE WICKED SHALL DO WICKEDLY: AND NONE OF THE WICKED SHALL UNDERSTAND; BUT THE WISE SHALL UNDERSTAND.

DANIEL 2:20: ...BLESSED BE THE NAME OF GOD...

HOSEA

Introduction: It is unknown whether or not the prophet Hosea wrote this book although the book begins by saying, *"The word of the Lord that came unto Hosea..."* (see 1:1). Hosea's words may have been recorded by another author. Like Amos, Hosea prophesied to the northern kingdom of Israel in the 700's B.C., warning of coming judgment. Israel fell to the Assyrians in 722 B.C. The prophets saw how the religious leaders used religion to gain their own wealth and power. The leaders' sins included their lack of relying on God to lead the people, and their using religious position to obtain wealth and recognition. Without faithful leaders, the Israelites fell into immorality and worshipping false gods. Hosea compared unfaithful Israel to his unfaithful wife, Gomer. Hosea was willing to take back Gomer as God was willing to take back Israel if there were repentance. Hosea showed that he still loved Gomer, and God still loved Israel. Chapter 11 emphasizes God's love for Israel. Hosea has 14 chapters.

Key Contents and Key Memory Verses with Study Dates

Hosea 1-3: Israel is compared with Hosea's unfaithful wife known as a harlot — *"And the Lord said to Hosea, Go take unto thee a wife of whoredoms and children of whoredoms: for the land hath committed great whoredom, departing from the Lord"* (see 1:2) — **Israel will return to God —** *"Afterward shall the children of Israel return, and seek the Lord their God, and David their king; and shall fear the Lord and his goodness in the latter days"* (see 3:5).

Hosea 4-14: Prophecies of judgment for Israel's unfaithfulness and promises of restoration.

— God tells Israel, *"For I desired mercy, and not sacrifice; and the knowledge of God more than burnt offerings"* (see 6:6).

— *"When Israel was a child, then I loved him, and called my son out of Egypt"* (see 11:1).

May 8 (Day 128), Memory Verse #357
Hosea 12:6:

THEREFORE TURN THOU TO THY GOD:
KEEP MERCY AND JUDGMENT AND WAIT ON THY GOD CONTINUALLY.

May 8 (Day 128), Memory Verse #358
Hosea 13:4:

YET I AM THE LORD THY GOD FROM THE LAND OF EGYPT,
AND THOU SHALT KNOW NO GOD BUT ME:
FOR THERE IS NO SAVIOUR BESIDE ME.

— *"O Israel, return unto the Lord thy God; for thou hast fallen by thine iniquity"* (see 14:1) — *"I will heal their backsliding, I will love them freely: for mine anger is turned away from him"* (see 14:4).

May 8 (Day 128), Memory Verse #359
Hosea 14:9:

WHO IS WISE, AND HE SHALL UNDERSTAND THESE THINGS?
PRUDENT, AND HE SHALL KNOW THEM?
FOR THE WAYS OF THE LORD ARE RIGHT,
AND THE JUST SHALL WALK IN THEM:
BUT THE TRANSGRESSORS SHALL FALL THEREIN.

JOEL

Introduction: This book was probably written by the prophet Joel. Some suggest there were two authors. Suggested dates of writing are as early as the 800's B.C. and as late as the 300's B.C. Joel called the Israelites of Judah to repent of their sins and return to God. He proclaimed God's love for the Israelites and prophesied their restoration. Joel also spoke of the future day of the Lord. Joel has three chapters.

Key Contents and Key Memory Verses with Study Dates

Joel 1:   Locust invasion, drought, and fire cause great devastation — Joel foretells the day of the Lord which will also have great destruction.

Joel 2:   Joel prophesies future devastation and the day of the Lord — He calls the people of Judah to repent and return to God — *"Therefore also now, saith the Lord, turn ye even to me with all your heart, and with fasting, and with weeping, and with mourning:"* (see 2:12).

May 9 (Day 129), Memory Verse #360
Joel 2:13:

AND REND YOUR HEART, AND NOT YOUR GARMENTS,
AND TURN UNTO THE LORD YOUR GOD:
FOR HE IS GRACIOUS AND MERCIFUL, SLOW TO ANGER, AND OF GREAT KINDNESS,
AND REPENTETH HIM OF THE EVIL (he relents from sending calamity, NIV).

— Promise of restoration — *"And I will restore you to the years that the locust hath eaten...my great army which I sent among you. And ye shall eat in plenty, and be satisfied, and praise the name of the Lord your God, that hath dealt wondrously with you: ...And ye shall know that I am in the midst of Israel, and that I am the Lord your God, and none else..."* (see 2:25-27).

May 9 (Day 129), Memory Verse #361
Joel 2:21:

FEAR NOT, O LAND; BE GLAD AND REJOICE:
FOR THE LORD WILL DO GREAT THINGS.

May 9 (Day 129), Memory Verse #362
Joel 2:28:

AND IT SHALL COME TO PASS AFTERWARD,
THAT I WILL POUR OUT MY SPIRIT UPON ALL FLESH;
AND YOUR SONS AND YOUR DAUGHTERS SHALL PROPHESY,
YOUR OLD MEN SHALL DREAM DREAMS,
YOUR YOUNG MEN SHALL SEE VISIONS:

— *"And I will shew wonders in the heavens and in the earth,* *blood, and fire, and pillars of smoke. The sun shall be turned into darkness, and the moon into blood, before the great and the terrible day of the Lord come. And it shall come to pass, that whosoever shall call on the name of the Lord shall be delivered:..."* (see 2:30-32).

Joel 3:   Coming judgments and blessings for Israel — *"I will also gather all nations, and will bring them down into the valley of Jehoshaphat, and will plead with them there for my heritage Israel, whom they have scattered among the nations, and parted my land"* (see 3:2) — *"But Judah shall dwell for ever, and Jerusalem from generation to generation. For I will cleanse their blood that I have not cleansed: for the Lord dwelleth in Zion"* (see 3:20-21).

Amos

Introduction: See mention of Amos in the introduction to Hosea. Most scholars agree Amos was the author of this book which was probably written in the mid 700's B.C. before the northern kingdom of Israel was defeated by Assyria in 722 B.C. Amos was a sheep breeder of Tekoa near Jerusalem. He traveled to Bethel to preach during Jeroboam II's reign in Israel. Amaziah, the priest of Bethel, told Jeroboam II that Amos was conspiring against the king. Amaziah also told Amos to leave Bethel. Amos returned to Judah and wrote this book warning Israel of God's coming judgment. He also prophesied God would again have mercy on the disobedient Israelites. As in Jonah, Amos shows how God loves all people.   Amos has nine chapters.

Key Contents and Key Memory Verses with Study Dates

<u>Amos 1-2:</u> **Amos prophesies of God's coming punishment on Damascus, Gaza, Tyre, Ammon, Moab, Judah, and Israel.**

<u>Amos 3-6:</u> **More prophecy concerning Israel — The Lord does not approve of oppressing the needy —** *"Hear this word, ye kine of Bashan, that are in the mountain of Samaria, which oppress the poor, which crush the needy, which say to their masters, Bring, and let us drink"* (see 4:1) — **"...prepare to meet thy God, O Israel.** *For lo, he that formeth the mountains, and createth the wind, and declareth unto man what is his thought, that maketh the morning darkness, and treadeth upon the high places of the earth, The Lord, The God of hosts, is his name"* (see 4:12-13).

May 10 (Day 130), Memory Verse #363
<u>Amos 5:4:</u>

FOR THUS SAITH THE LORD UNTO THE HOUSE OF ISRAEL,
SEEK YE ME, AND YE SHALL LIVE:

— The Lord does not approve of the Israelites' feasts and sacrifices since their hearts were not right — The Lord says, *"I hate, I despise your feast days, and I will not smell in your solemn assemblies. Though ye offer me burnt offerings and your meat offerings, I will not accept them: neither will I regard the peace offerings of your fat beasts"* (see 5:21-23).

May 10 (Day 130), Memory Verse #364
<u>Amos 5:24:</u>

BUT LET JUDGMENT RUN DOWN AS WATERS, AND RIGHTEOUSNESS AS A MIGHTY STREAM.

<u>Amos 7-9:</u> **Amos' visions of Israel's coming devastation and restoration —** The visions include GRASSHOPPERS (locusts), FIRE, a PLUMB LINE, a BASKET OF SUMMER FRUIT, the LORD'S JUDGMENT, and ISRAEL'S FUTURE RESTORATION — Amos 7:8 states how the Lord symbolically uses a plumb line to measure the Israelites' spiritual condition — **Amos prophesies in Bethel concerning Israel —** *"Then Amaziah the priest of Bethel sent to Jeroboam king of Israel, saying, Amos hath conspired against thee in the midst of the house of Israel: the land is not able to bear all his words. For thus Amos saith, Jeroboam shall die by the sword, and Israel shall surely be led away captive out of their own land. Also Amaziah said unto Amos, O thou seer, go, flee thee away into the land of Judah, and there eat bread, and prophesy there: But prophesy not again any more at Bethel..."* (see 7:10-13) — **God promises Israel's restoration —** *"And I will plant them upon their land, and they shall no more be pulled up out of their land which I have given them, saith the Lord thy God"* (see 9:15).

Obadiah

Introduction: Most scholars consider the author of this book to be the prophet Obadiah. Obadiah was a common name, so it is unclear which Obadiah was the prophet. The book of Obadiah is thought to have been written in the mid 800's B.C. or in the 500's B.C., the date depending on which invasion of Jerusalem is meant by the author. Obadiah warned of Edom's coming judgment. The Edomites were descendants of Esau while the Israelites were descendants of Jacob, Esau's twin brother. Obadiah has only 21 verses.

Key Contents and Key Memory Verses with Study Dates

Obadiah verses 1-21: **Obadiah tells of Edom's future judgment because of her rejoicing over Jerusalem's fall** — *"The vision of Obadiah. Thus saith the Lord God concerning Edom..."* (see verse 1) — *"The pride of thine heart hath deceived thee, thou that dwelleth in the clefts of the rock, whose habitation is high; that saith in his heart, Who shall bring me down to the ground? Though thou exalt thyself as the eagle, and though thou set thy nest among the stars, thence will I bring thee down, saith the Lord"* (see verses 3-4) — *"For thy violence against thy brother Jacob shame shall cover thee, and thou shalt be cut off for ever"* (see verse 10).

May 11 (Day 131), Memory Verse #365
Obadiah verse 15:

FOR THE DAY OF THE LORD IS NEAR UPON ALL THE HEATHEN:
AS THOU HAST DONE, IT SHALL BE DONE UNTO THEE:
THY REWARD SHALL RETURN UPON THINE OWN HEAD.

Obadiah Verse 3:

The pride of thine heart hath deceived thee...

JONAH

Introduction: Although unknown, authorship is traditionally attributed to the Jewish prophet Jonah. This book may have been written in the 700's B.C. or after the fall of the Assyrian capital of Ninevah in 612 B.C.   Jonah is the great missionary book of the Old Testament.   Racial prejudice existed between the Assyrians and the Jews. God sent Jonah to Ninevah to call the Assyrians to repentance. Rebellious at first, Jonah finally obeyed God and understood God's love for all people, not just the Jews. Some believe Jonah is a parable or allegory, but Jesus refers to Jonah as an actual person (see Matthew 12:39-40 and Luke 11:29-32). Jonah has four chapters.

Key Contents and Key Memory Verses with Study Dates

Jonah 1: *"Now the word of the Lord came unto Jonah the son of Amittai, saying, Arise, go to Ninevah, that great city, and cry against it; for their wickedness is come up before me"* (see 1:1-2) — **But Jonah flees on a ship** bound for Tarshish — Jonah is blamed for a serious storm while at sea since he is running from God — He allows the ship's crew to toss him overboard — *"Now the Lord had prepared a great fish to swallow up Jonah. And Jonah was in the belly of the fish three days and three nights"* (see 1:17).

Jonah 2: *"Then Jonah prayed unto the Lord his God out of the fish's belly"* (see 2:1) — *"...yet hast thou brought up my life from corruption, O Lord my God. When my soul fainted within me I remembered the Lord: and my prayer came in unto thee, into thine holy temple. They that observe lying vanities (worthless idols, NIV) forsake their own mercy (forfeit the grace that could be theirs, NIV);"* (see 2:6-8).

May 12 (Day 132), Memory Verse #366
Jonah 2:9:

...SALVATION IS OF THE LORD.

— *"And the Lord spake unto the fish, and it vomited out Jonah upon the dry land"* (see 2:10).

Jonah 3: *"And the word of the Lord came unto Jonah the second time, saying, Arise, go unto Ninevah, that great city, and preach unto it the preaching that I bid thee. So Jonah arose, and went unto Ninevah..."* (see 3:1-3) — **The Ninevites ask God's forgiveness** and proclaim a fast.

Jonah 4: Jonah is angry at God's compassion for Israel's enemy, Ninevah — *"But it displeased Jonah exceedingly, and he was very angry. And he prayed unto the Lord, and said, I pray thee, O Lord, was not this my saying, when I was yet in my country? Therefore I fled before unto Tarshish: for I knew that thou art a gracious God, and merciful, slow to anger, and of great kindness, and repentest thee of the evil. Therefore now, O Lord, take, I beseech thee, my life from me; for it is better for me to die than to live"* (see 4:1-3) — **God teaches Jonah a lesson by using a gourd plant to illustrate compassion** — A gourd plant gives Jonah shade, but a worm causes the plant to die — Jonah is angered at the death of the plant — The Lord shows Jonah how he should have much more compassion for the many people of Ninevah than for a gourd plant.

JONAH 4:2:

...THOU ART A GRACIOUS GOD, AND MERCIFUL, SLOW TO ANGER, AND OF GREAT KINDNESS...

MICAH

Introduction: Micah was probably written about 700 B.C., most likely by the prophet Micah. Micah prophesied to the poor people of Judah during the kingships of Jotham, Ahaz, and Hezekiah. He encouraged justice for the poor and predicted the falls of Israel and Judah. He also predicted things of the "last days" (chapter 4) and the coming of the Messiah (chapter 5). Micah ends with a passage expressing God's great compassion; see Micah 7:18-20. Micah has seven chapters.

Key Contents and Key Memory Verses with Study Dates

<u>**Micah 1-3**</u>: **Prophecies of judgment for Samaria and Jerusalem — The judges, priests, and prophets are reprimanded for their mistreatment of the people and their seeking monetary rewards rather than God's guidance —** *"The heads thereof judge for reward, and the priests thereof teach for hire, and the prophets thereof divine for money: yet will they lean upon the Lord, and say, Is not the Lord among us? none evil can come upon us."* (see 3:11).

<u>**Micah 4**</u> : *"**But in the last days** it shall come to pass, that the mountain of the house of the Lord shall be established in the top of the mountains, and it shall be exalted above the hills; and people shall flow unto it"* (see 4:1).

May 13 (Day 133), Memory Verses #367 & #368
<u>**Micah 4:2-3:**</u>

2. **AND** MANY NATIONS SHALL COME, AND SAY,
COME, AND LET US GO UP TO THE MOUNTAIN OF THE LORD,
AND TO THE HOUSE OF THE GOD OF JACOB;
AND HE WILL TEACH US OF HIS WAYS, AND WE WILL WALK IN HIS PATHS:
FOR THE LAW SHALL GO FORTH OF ZION,
AND THE WORD OF THE LORD FROM JERUSALEM.

3. **AND** HE SHALL JUDGE AMONG MANY PEOPLE,
AND REBUKE STRONG NATIONS AFAR OFF;
AND THEY SHALL BEAT THEIR SWORDS INTO PLOWSHARES,
AND THEIR SPEARS INTO PRUNINGHOOKS:
NATION SHALL NOT LIFT UP A SWORD AGAINST NATION,
NEITHER SHALL THEY LEARN WAR ANY MORE.

<u>**Micah 5:**</u> **Micah prophesies of the coming ruler of Israel:**

May 14 (Day 134), Memory Verse #369
<u>**Micah 5:2:**</u>

BUT THOU, BETHLEHEM EPHRATAH,
THOUGH THOU BE LITTLE AMONG THE THOUSANDS OF JUDAH,
YET OUT OF THEE SHALL HE COME FORTH UNTO ME THAT IS TO BE RULER IN ISRAEL;
WHOSE GOINGS FORTH HAVE BEEN FROM OF OLD, FROM EVERLASTING.

— Matthew 2:6 and John 7:42 show the above verse as prophesying Jesus' birth in Bethlehem.

<u>**Micah 6:**</u> **The Lord speaks to the Israelites.**

May 14 (Day 134), Memory Verse #370
<u>Micah 6:8:</u>

HE HATH SHEWED THEE, O MAN, WHAT IS GOOD;
AND WHAT DOTH THE LORD REQUIRE OF THEE,
BUT TO DO JUSTLY, AND TO LOVE MERCY, AND TO WALK HUMBLY WITH THY GOD.

<u>Micah 7:</u> **God will have compassion on the Israelites again.**

May 15 (Day 135), Memory Verses #371 & #372
<u>Micah 7:7-8:</u>

7. THEREFORE I WILL LOOK UNTO THE LORD;
I WILL WAIT FOR THE GOD OF MY SALVATION:
MY GOD WILL HEAR ME.

8. REJOICE NOT AGAINST ME, O MINE ENEMY:
WHEN I FALL, I SHALL ARISE;
WHEN I SIT IN DARKNESS, THE LORD SHALL BE A LIGHT UNTO ME.

May 15 (Day 135), Memory Verse #373
<u>Micah 7:18:</u>

...HE RETAINETH NOT HIS ANGER FOR EVER, BECAUSE HE DELIGHTETH IN MERCY.

— *"He will turn again, he will have compassion upon us;* he will subdue our iniquities; and thou wilt cast all their sins into the depths of the sea. Thou wilt perform the truth to Jacob, and the mercy to Abraham, which thou hast sworn unto our fathers from the days of old" (see 7:19-20).

MICAH 6:8:

HE HATH SHEWED THEE, O MAN,
WHAT IS GOOD;
AND WHAT DOTH THE LORD
REQUIRE OF THEE,
BUT TO DO JUSTLY,
AND TO LOVE MERCY,
AND TO WALK HUMBLY
WITH THY GOD?

NAHUM

Introduction: Although not much is known about the prophet Nahum, he is considered the author of this book which was most likely written in the 600's B.C.   The people of Ninevah, the Assyrian capital, failed to continue heeding Jonah's message over the years, and they reverted to their evil ways. Nahum predicted Ninevah's fall which did occur in 612 B.C. In 722 B.C., the Assyrians had destroyed Samaria, the capital of the northern kingdom of Israel. In 701 B.C., the Assyrians had attempted to overtake Jerusalem, but they were unsuccessful. Nahum comforted the people of Judah who were fearful of the Assyrians, people known to torture their captives. Nahum has three chapters.

Key Contents and Key Memory Verses with Study Dates

Nahum 1: **The power of God and His judgment on Ninevah** — *"The Lord is slow to anger, and great in power, and will not at all acquit the wicked:"* (see 1:3).

May 16 (Day 136), Memory Verse #374
Nahum 1:7:

THE LORD IS GOOD,
A STRONG HOLD IN THE DAY OF TROUBLE;
AND HE KNOWETH THEM THAT TRUST IN HIM.

Nahum 2-3: **Ninevah's destruction is described** — *"Woe to the bloody city! it is all full of lies and robbery;..."* (see 3:1). *" Thy shepherds slumber, O king of Assyria: thy nobles shall dwell in the dust: thy people is scattered upon the mountains, and no man gathereth them. There is no healing of thy bruise; thy wound is grievous: all that hear the bruit of thee shall clap the hands over thee: for upon whom hath not thy wickedness passed continually?"* (see 3:18-19).

NAHUM 1:7:

THE LORD IS GOOD...

HABAKKUK

Introduction: Habakkuk was probably written by the prophet Habakkuk just a few years before the Babylonian exile of the southern kingdom of Judah in 586 B.C. Habakkuk warned of the coming exile. The Babylonians had already conquered the Assyrians. The Chaldeans mentioned in Habakkuk were part of the Babylonian Empire. Wicked Jehoiakim was king of Judah at this time. Habakkuk has three chapters.

Key Contents and Key Memory Verses with Study Dates

Habakkuk 1-3: Habakkuk asks God two main questions: 1) Why does God allow continued wickedness in Judah? God replies that He will punish Judah through the Chaldeans. 2) Why will God punish Judah with people (the Chaldeans of Babylon) more wicked than Judah? God replies that after He uses Babylon to punish Judah, then He will punish Babylon — **Habakkuk chooses to trust God.**

May 17 (Day 137), Memory Verse #375
Habakkuk 2:4:

...BUT THE JUST SHALL LIVE BY HIS FAITH.

May 17 (Day 137), Memory Verse #376
Habakkuk 2:20:

BUT THE LORD IS IN HIS HOLY TEMPLE:
LET ALL THE EARTH KEEP SILENCE BEFORE HIM.

May 17 (Day 137), Memory Verses #377 & #378
Habakkuk 3:18-19:

18. YET I WILL REJOICE IN THE LORD,
I WILL JOY IN THE GOD OF MY SALVATION.

19. THE LORD GOD IS MY STRENGTH,
AND HE WILL MAKE MY FEET LIKE HINDS' FEET,
AND HE WILL MAKE ME TO WALK UPON MINE HIGH PLACES...

HABAKKUK 2:4:

... THE JUST SHALL LIVE BY HIS FAITH.

ZEPHANIAH

Introduction: The prophet Zephaniah probably wrote this book between 650 and 600 B.C. Zephaniah helped prepare the southern kingdom of Judah for good King Josiah's reign which followed the evil reigns of the kings, Manasseh and Amon. Zephaniah prophesied about the coming Babylonian exile, God's judgment on Judah and many nations, and the day of the Lord (see 1:17-18 and 3:8). He also prophesied God's restoration of Judah and other nations. Zephaniah has three chapters.

Key Contents and Key Memory Verses with Study Dates

Zephaniah 1:   Prophecies of judgment on Judah and the *"...great day of the Lord..."* (see 1:14) — *"And I will bring distress upon men, that they shall walk like blind men, because they have sinned against the Lord: and their blood shall be poured out as dust, and their flesh as the dung. Neither their silver nor their gold shall be able to deliver them in the day of the Lord's wrath;..."* (see 1:17-18).

Zephaniah 2:   Zephaniah urges the people to repent and announces judgment on many nations.

May 18 (Day 138), Memory Verse #379
Zephaniah 2:3:

SEEK YE THE LORD, ALL YE MEEK OF THE EARTH,
WHICH HAVE WROUGHT HIS JUDGMENT:
SEEK RIGHTEOUSNESS, SEEK MEEKNESS:
IT MAY BE YE SHALL BE HID IN THE DAY OF THE LORD'S ANGER.

Zephaniah 3:   God's judgment on Judah and all the earth — *"...for all the earth shall be devoured with the fire of my jealousy"* (see 3:8) — **After judgment, God will restore many peoples** (see 3:9-10) **and the *"...remnant of Israel..."*** (see 3:13).

May 18 (Day 138), Memory Verse #380
Zephaniah 3:17:

THE LORD THY GOD IN THE MIDST OF THEE IS MIGHTY;
HE WILL SAVE, HE WILL REJOICE OVER THEE WITH JOY;
HE WILL REST IN HIS LOVE,
HE WILL JOY OVER THEE WITH SINGING.

— *"At that time will I bring you again, even in the time that I gather you: for **I will make you a name and a praise among all people of the earth**, when I turn back your captivity before your eyes, saith the Lord"* (see 3:20).

ZEPHANIAH 2:3:

SEEK YE THE LORD...

HAGGAI

Introduction: The prophet Haggai probably wrote this book about 520 B.C. The decree of the Persian king Cyrus, which allowed the Jews to return to Judah, was in 538 B.C. Approximately 50,000 Jews returned to Judah in 536 B.C. This was a small number compared to the approximate 2,000,000 Jews who were given permission to return. Haggai urged the people to continue rebuilding the temple in Jerusalem which they finally completed in 515 B.C. There had been a delay of 15 years between the first attempt to rebuild and the final rebuilding of the temple. Haggai's message prophesied how Judah would be blessed if they obeyed God. Haggai has two chapters.

Key Contents and Key Memory Verses with Study Dates

<u>Haggai 1-2:</u> **Haggai urges the Jews to rebuild the temple, and he also gives them words of encouragement** — *"Then came the word of the Lord by Haggai the prophet, saying, Is it time for you, O ye, to dwell in your ceiled houses, and this house lie waste? Now therefore thus saith the Lord of hosts; Consider your ways"* (see 1:3-5) — *"Go up to the mountain, and bring wood, and build the house; and I will take pleasure in it, and I will be glorified, saith the Lord"* (see 1:8) — ***"Then spake Haggai the Lord's messenger in the Lord's message unto the people, saying…"*** (see 1:13):

May 19 (Day 139), Memory Verse #381
<u>**Haggai 1:13:**</u>

…I AM WITH YOU, SAITH THE LORD.

— *"…be strong, all ye people of the land, saith the Lord, and work: for I am with you, saith the Lord of hosts: According to the word that I covenanted with you when ye came out of Egypt, so my spirit remaineth among you: fear ye not"* (see 2:4-5) — *"…I will fill this house with glory, saith the Lord of hosts"* (see 2:7) — *"The glory of the latter house shall be greater than of the former, saith the Lord of hosts: and in this place will I give peace, saith the Lord of hosts"* (see 2:9).

HAGGAI 1:13:

…I AM WITH YOU, SAITH THE LORD.

ZECHARIAH

Introduction: Zechariah, both a prophet and a priest, is thought to be the author of this book. Zechariah was probably written around 520 B.C. Some believe there was more than one author. More than 50,000 Jews had returned to Palestine after Cyrus' decree in 538 B.C. Both Zechariah and Haggai urged the people to rebuild and finish the temple which had been destroyed in 586 B.C. by Babylon. Zechariah contains many prophesies which include the coming of the Messiah. Zechariah has 14 chapters.

Key Contents and Key Memory Verses with Study Dates

Zechariah 1-6: **Visions of Zechariah promise restoration to the people of Judah, give encouragement to the people, and urge their return to the Lord** — These visions include: 1) horses and a horseman among the myrtle trees; 2) four horns and four carpenters; 3) a man with a measuring line; 4) Joshua, the high priest, having his filthy garments replaced with clean garments; 5) a gold candlestick, seven lamps, seven pipes, and two olive trees; 6) a flying roll (scroll, NIV); 7) a woman in the "ephah" (measuring basket, NIV); and 8) four chariots.

May 20 (Day 140), Memory Verse #382
Zechariah 1:3:

...TURN YE UNTO ME, SAITH THE LORD OF HOSTS,
AND I WILL TURN UNTO YOU, SAITH THE LORD OF HOSTS.

— *"...for, behold, I will bring forth my servant the BRANCH"* (see 3:8) — The crowning of Joshua, the son of the high priest Josedech (see 6:9-15); many interpret this passage as foretelling Jesus, the coming Messiah.

Zechariah 7: **The people are concerned with fasts, yet God is more concerned with their obedience to Him** — *"Thus speaketh the Lord of hosts, saying, Execute true judgment, and shew mercy and compassions every man to his brother: And oppress not the widow, nor the fatherless, the stranger, nor the poor; and let none of you imagine evil against his brother in your heart. But they refused to hearken, and pulled away the shoulder, and stopped their ears, that they should not hear. Yea, they made their hearts as an adamant stone..."* (see 7:9-12).

Zechariah 8: **Jerusalem's future** — *"Thus saith the Lord; I am returned unto Zion, and will dwell in the midst of Jerusalem: and Jerusalem shall be called a city of truth; and the mountain of the Lord of hosts the holy mountain"* (see 8:3) — *"These are the things that ye shall do; Speak ye every man the truth to his neighbour; execute the judgment of truth and peace in your gates: And let none of you imagine evil in your hearts against his neighbour; and love no false oath: for all these are things that I hate, saith the Lord"* (see 8:16-17).

Zechariah 9-14: **Future prophecies** (prophecies of the fall of nations, coming kings, the coming Messiah, the Lord's blessings and judgments, and the day of the Lord) — Some see Zechariah 9 as referring to the conquests of Alexander the Great in the 300's B.C. — Zechariah 11:12-13 is seen as prophesying Judas' betrayal of Jesus, 12:10 as Jesus being pierced on the cross, and 13:7 as Jesus being the shepherd — The following verse is seen as prophesying Jesus' entry into Jerusalem on Palm Sunday (see Matthew 21:5 and John 12:15):

May 20 (Day 140), Memory Verse #383
Zechariah 9:9:

REJOICE GREATLY, O DAUGHTER OF ZION; SHOUT, O DAUGHTER OF JERUSALEM:
BEHOLD, THY KING COMETH UNTO THEE: HE IS JUST, AND HAVING SALVATION;
LOWLY, AND RIDING UPON AN ASS, AND UPON A COLT THE FOAL OF AN ASS.

MALACHI

Introduction: The name of the author of this book may be Malachi, or the word Malachi, meaning "my messenger" in Hebrew, may explain this book was written by a prophet. Malachi was most likely written around 430 B.C. after Nehemiah's return to Jerusalem in 444 B.C. After returning to Jerusalem and rebuilding the temple (completed in 515 B.C.), the Jews had once again drifted from obeying God. Malachi urged the people to repent and return to trusting God. Malachi has four chapters.

Key Contents and Key Memory Verses with Study Dates

Malachi 1-2: God scolds the Israelites for their disobedience and turning from Him — *"A son honoureth his father, and a servant his master: If then I be a father , where is mine honour?... Ye offer polluted bread upon my altar;..."* (see 1:6-7) — Judah *"...hath married the daughter of a strange god"* (see 2:11) — *"...let none deal treacherously against the wife of thy youth"* (see 2:15) — *"Ye have wearied the Lord with your words. Yet ye say, Wherein have we wearied him? When ye say, Every one that doeth evil is good in the sight of the Lord, and he delighteth in them; or , Where is the God of judgment?"* (see 2:17).

Malachi 3: God urges the people to return to Him — In Matthew 11:10, Jesus refers to Malachi 3:1 as predicting the coming of John the Baptist and Himself: ***"Behold, I will send my messenger,*** *and he shall prepare the way before me: and the Lord, whom ye seek, shall suddenly come to his temple, even the messenger of the covenant, whom ye delight in: behold, he shall come, saith the Lord of hosts"*(see 3:1) — ***"Bring ye all the tithes into the storehouse..."*** (see 3:10).

May 21 (Day 141), Memory Verses #384 & #385
Malachi 3:6-7:

6. FOR I AM THE LORD, I CHANGE NOT;
THEREFORE, YE SONS OF JACOB ARE NOT CONSUMED.

7. EVEN FROM THE DAYS OF YOUR FATHERS YE ARE GONE AWAY
FROM MINE ORDINANCES, AND HAVE NOT KEPT THEM.
RETURN UNTO ME, AND I WILL RETURN UNTO YOU,
SAITH THE LORD OF HOSTS, ...

Malachi 4: The wicked will be punished — *"For, behold, the day cometh, that shall burn as an oven; and all the proud, yea, and all that do wickedly, shall be stubble: and the day that cometh shall burn them up, saith the Lord of hosts, that it shall leave them neither root nor branch"* (see 4:1).

May 21 (Day 141), Memory Verse #386
Malachi 4:2:

BUT UNTO YOU THAT FEAR MY NAME
SHALL THE SUN OF RIGHTEOUSNESS ARISE WITH HEALING IN HIS WINGS;
AND YE SHALL GO FORTH, AND GROW UP AS CALVES OF THE STALL.

MALACHI 3:6:

FOR I AM THE LORD, I CHANGE NOT; ...

THE NEW TESTAMENT KEY NOTES, MATTHEW TO REVELATION

Quoted Scripture is from The King James Version, KJV.
The New International Version, NIV, is quoted when clarifying some of the verses.

MATTHEW

Introduction: The first four books of the New Testament are known as the Gospels. The word gospel means "good news." Matthew, Mark, and Luke are called the synoptic Gospels since most of their content is similar in events, language, and sayings of Jesus. Matthew and Luke include most of Mark's content and add their own unique material. Matthew was written mainly to the Jews. Most scholars believe the apostle Matthew, a tax-collector surnamed Levi, was the author. Some believe another Jew was the author and named the book after Jesus' apostle. Various opinions date this book from the 50's to the 90's A.D. The main theme of Matthew is as follows: Jesus is the Messiah fulfilling Old Testament prophecy. Matthew has 28 chapters.

Key Contents and Key Memory Verses with Study Dates

<u>Note:</u> All key memory verses from the beginning of Matthew 4 to the end of the book are sayings of Jesus with the exception of Matthew 16:16.

<u>Matthew 1:</u> **Genealogy of Jesus beginning with Abraham** (see 1:1-17) — *"The book of the generation of Jesus Christ, the son of David, the son of Abraham"* (see 1:1) — **An angel appears to Joseph to let him know Mary's pregnancy is by the Holy Spirit** (see 1:18-25) — *"But while he thought on these things, behold, the angel of the Lord appeared unto him in a dream, saying, Joseph, thou son of David, fear not to take unto thee Mary thy wife: for that which is conceived in her is of the Holy Ghost. And she shall bring forth a son, and thou shalt call his name JESUS: for he shall save his people from their sins"* (see 1:20-21).

May 22 (Day 142), Memory Verses #387 & #388
<u>**Matthew 1:22-23:**</u>

22. NOW ALL THIS WAS DONE, THAT IT MIGHT BE FULFILLED
WHICH WAS SPOKEN OF THE LORD BY THE PROPHETS, SAYING,

23. BEHOLD, A VIRGIN SHALL BE WITH CHILD, AND SHALL BRING FORTH A SON,
AND THEY SHALL CALL HIS NAME EMMANUEL,
WHICH BEING INTERPRETED IS, GOD WITH US (also see Isaiah 7:14).

— Joseph *"...knew her not till she had brought forth her firstborn son: and he called his name JESUS"* (see 1:25).

<u>Matthew 2:</u> **Story of the Magi (wise men) and Herod's jealousy over Jesus' birth** (see 2:1-23) — *"Now when **Jesus was born in Bethlehem** of Judaea in the days of Herod the king, behold, there came wise men from the east to Jerusalem, Saying, Where is he that is born King of the Jews? For we have seen his star in the east, and are come to worship him"* (see 2:1-2) — *"And when they were come into the house, they saw the young child with Mary his mother, and fell down, and worshipped him: and when they had opened their treasures, they presented unto him gifts; gold, and frankincense, and myrrh. And being warned of God in a dream that they should not return to Herod, they departed into their own country another way"* (see 2:11-12) — *"And when they were departed, behold, **the angel of the Lord appeareth to Joseph in a***

dream, saying, Arise, and take the young child and his mother, and flee into Egypt, and be thou there until I bring word: for Herod will seek the young child to destroy him" (see 2:13) — *"Then Herod, when he saw that he was mocked of the wise men, was exceeding wroth, and sent forth, and slew all the children that were in Bethlehem, and in all the coasts thereof, from two years old and under, according to the time which he had diligently enquired of the wise men"* (see 2:16) — **When Herod dies, an angel tells Joseph to move his family to Israel — Joseph and his family settle in Nazareth in the area of Galilee.**

Matthew 3: The preaching of John the Baptist and Jesus' baptism (see 3:1-17) — *"In those days came John the Baptist, preaching in the wilderness of Judaea, And saying, Repent ye: for the kingdom of heaven is at hand. For this is he that was spoken of by the prophet Esaiah (Isaiah, NIV), saying, The voice of one crying in the wilderness, Prepare ye the way of the Lord, make his paths straight. And the same John had his raiment of camel's hair, and a leathern girdle about his loins; and his meat was locusts and wild honey"* (see 3:1-4) — John the Baptist's teachings include**:**

May 23 (Day 143), Memory Verse #389
Matthew 3:10:

...EVERY TREE WHICH BRINGETH NOT FORTH GOOD FRUIT IS HEWN DOWN,
AND CAST INTO THE FIRE.

— After baptizing Jesus, John the Baptist *"...saw the Spirit of God descending like a dove, and lighting upon him:"* (see 3:16).

May 23 (Day 143), Memory Verse #390
Matthew 3:17:

AND LO A VOICE FROM HEAVEN, SAYING,
THIS IS MY BELOVED SON, IN WHOM I AM WELL PLEASED.

Matthew 4: Jesus is tempted in the wilderness by the devil (see 4:1-11) — Jesus fasts forty days and nights and the devil says, *"...If thou be the Son of God, command that these stones be made bread"* (see 4:3) — Jesus says**:**

May 24 (Day 144), Memory Verse #391
Matthew 4:4:

...IT IS WRITTEN, MAN SHALL NOT LIVE BY BREAD ALONE,
BUT BY EVERY WORD THAT PROCEEDETH OUT OF THE MOUTH OF GOD.

— Next the devil tells Jesus to jump from a pinnacle of the temple since surely the angels will guarantee His safety; but Jesus answers**:**

May 24 (Day 144), Memory Verse #392
Matthew 4:7:

...IT IS WRITTEN AGAIN, THOU SHALT NOT TEMPT THE LORD THY GOD.

— Then the devil promises Jesus the glory of worldly kingdoms if He will worship the devil; Jesus says**:**

May 24 (Day 144), Memory Verse #393
Matthew 4:10:

...GET THEE HENCE, SATAN: FOR IT IS WRITTEN,
THOU SHALT WORSHIP THE LORD THY GOD, AND HIM ONLY SHALT THOU SERVE.

— **Jesus begins to preach and heal the sick** (see 4:12-25).

May 25 (Day 145), Memory Verse #394
Matthew 4:17:

...REPENT FOR THE KINGDOM OF HEAVEN IS AT HAND.

— **Jesus calls Peter, Andrew, James and John** (see 4:18-22).

May 25 (Day 145), Memory Verse #395
Matthew 4:19:

...FOLLOW ME, AND I WILL MAKE YOU FISHERS OF MEN.

Matthew 5-7: Jesus' "Sermon on the Mount" (see 5:1-7:29).

May 26-29 (Days 146-149), Memory Verses #396 to #407
Matthew 5:1-12:
(The Beatitudes)

1. AND SEEING THE MULTITUDES, HE WENT UP INTO THE MOUNTAIN: AND WHEN HE WAS SET, HIS DISCIPLES CAME UNTO HIM:

2. AND HE OPENED HIS MOUTH, AND TAUGHT THEM, SAYING,

3. BLESSED ARE THE POOR IN SPIRIT: FOR THEIRS IS THE KINGDOM OF HEAVEN.

4. BLESSED ARE THEY THAT MOURN: FOR THEY SHALL BE COMFORTED.

5. BLESSED ARE THE MEEK: FOR THEY SHALL INHERIT THE EARTH.

6. BLESSED ARE THEY WHICH DO HUNGER AND THIRST AFTER RIGHTEOUSNESS: FOR THEY SHALL BE FILLED.

7. BLESSED ARE THE MERCIFUL: FOR THEY SHALL OBTAIN MERCY.

8. BLESSED ARE THE PURE IN HEART: FOR THEY SHALL SEE GOD.

9. BLESSED ARE THE PEACEMAKERS: FOR THEY SHALL BE CALLED THE CHILDREN OF GOD.

10. BLESSED ARE THEY WHICH ARE PERSECUTED FOR RIGHTEOUSNESS' SAKE: FOR THEIRS IS THE KINGDOM OF HEAVEN.

11. BLESSED ARE YE, WHEN MEN SHALL REVILE YOU, AND PERSECUTE YOU, AND SHALL SAY ALL MANNER OF EVIL AGAINST YOU FALSELY, FOR MY SAKE.

12. REJOICE, AND BE EXCEEDING GLAD: FOR GREAT IS YOUR REWARD IN HEAVEN: FOR SO PERSECUTED THEY THE PROPHETS WHICH WERE BEFORE YOU.

May 30-31 (Days 150-151), Memory Verses #408 to #413
Matthew 5:13-18:

13. YE ARE THE SALT OF THE EARTH: BUT IF THE SALT HAVE LOST HIS SAVOUR, WHEREWITH SHALL IT BE SALTED? IT IS THENCEFORTH GOOD FOR NOTHING, BUT TO BE CAST OUT, AND TO BE TRODDEN UNDER FOOT OF MEN.

14. YE ARE THE LIGHT OF THE WORLD. A CITY THAT IS SET ON AN HILL CANNOT BE HID.

Continuation of Matthew 5:13-18:

15. NEITHER DO MEN LIGHT A CANDLE, AND PUT IT UNDER A BUSHEL,
BUT ON A CANDLESTICK;
AND IT GIVETH LIGHT UNTO ALL THAT ARE IN THE HOUSE.

16. LET YOUR LIGHT SO SHINE BEFORE MEN,
THAT THEY MAY SEE YOUR GOOD WORKS,
AND GLORIFY YOUR FATHER WHICH IS IN HEAVEN.

17. THINK NOT THAT I AM COME TO DESTROY THE LAW, OR THE PROPHETS:
I AM NOT COME TO DESTROY, BUT TO FULFIL.

18. FOR VERILY I SAY UNTO YOU, TILL HEAVEN AND EARTH PASS,
ONE JOT OR ONE TITTLE SHALL IN NO WISE PASS FROM THE LAW,
TILL ALL BE FULFILLED.

— **Jesus speaks on various topics including killing, adultery, divorce, oaths, love, giving, prayer, fasting, money, worry, and judging** (see 5:21-7:12).

June 1 (Day 152), Memory Verse #414
Matthew 5:39:

... WHOSOEVER SHALL SMITE THEE ON THY RIGHT CHEEK,
TURN TO HIM THE OTHER ALSO.

June 1 (Day 152), Memory Verse #415
Matthew 5:44:

...LOVE YOUR ENEMIES, BLESS THEM THAT CURSE YOU,
DO GOOD TO THEM THAT HATE YOU,
AND PRAY FOR THEM WHICH DESPITEFULLY USE YOU, AND PERSECUTE YOU;

June 2 (Day 153), Memory Verse #416
Matthew 5:48:

BE YE THEREFORE PERFECT,
EVEN AS YOUR FATHER WHICH IS IN HEAVEN IS PERFECT.

June 2 (Day 153), Memory Verses #417 & #418
Matthew 6:3-4:

3. BUT WHEN THOU DOEST ALMS,
LET NOT THY LEFT HAND KNOW WHAT THY RIGHT HAND DOETH:

4. THAT THINE ALMS MAY BE IN SECRET:
AND THY FATHER WHICH SEETH IN SECRET HIMSELF SHALL REWARD THEE OPENLY.

June 3 (Day 154), Memory Verse #419
Matthew 6:6:

BUT THOU, WHEN THOU PRAYEST,
ENTER INTO THY CLOSET, AND WHEN THOU HAST SHUT THY DOOR,
PRAY TO THY FATHER WHICH IS IN SECRET;
AND THY FATHER WHICH SEETH IN SECRET SHALL REWARD THEE OPENLY.

June 4 (Day 155), Memory Verses #420 to #424
Matthew 6:9-13:
(The Lord's Prayer)

9. AFTER THIS MANNER PRAY YE:
OUR FATHER WHICH ART IN HEAVEN, HALLOWED BE THY NAME.

10. THY KINGDOM COME. THY WILL BE DONE IN EARTH, AS IT IS IN HEAVEN.

11. GIVE US THIS DAY OUR DAILY BREAD.

12. AND FORGIVE US OUR DEBTS, AS WE FORGIVE OUR DEBTORS.

13. AND LEAD US NOT INTO TEMPTATION,
BUT DELIVER US FROM EVIL: FOR THINE IS THE KINGDOM,
AND THE POWER, AND THE GLORY, FOR EVER.   AMEN.

June 5 (Day 156), Memory Verses #425 & #426
Matthew 6:14-15:

14. FOR IF YE FORGIVE MEN THEIR TRESPASSES,
YOUR HEAVENLY FATHER WILL ALSO FORGIVE YOU:

15. BUT IF YE FORGIVE NOT MEN THEIR TRESPASSES,
NEITHER WILL YOUR FATHER FORGIVE YOUR TRESPASSES.

June 6 (Day 157), Memory Verses #427 & #428
Matthew 6:20-21:

20. BUT LAY UP FOR YOURSELVES TREASURES IN HEAVEN,
WHERE NEITHER MOTH NOR RUST DOTH CORRUPT,
AND WHERE THIEVES DO NOT BREAK THROUGH NOR STEAL:

21. FOR WHERE YOUR TREASURE IS, THERE WILL YOUR HEART BE ALSO.

June 7-8 (Days 158-159), Memory Verses #429 to #434
Matthew 6:24-29:

24. NO MAN CAN SERVE TWO MASTERS:
FOR EITHER HE WILL HATE THE ONE, AND LOVE THE OTHER;
OR ELSE HE WILL HOLD TO THE ONE, AND DESPISE THE OTHER.
YE CANNOT SERVE GOD AND MAMMON.

25. THEREFORE I SAY UNTO YOU, TAKE NO THOUGHT FOR YOUR LIFE,
WHAT YE SHALL EAT, OR WHAT YE SHALL DRINK;
NOR YET FOR YOUR BODY, WHAT YE SHALL PUT ON.
IS NOT THE LIFE MORE THAN MEAT, AND THE BODY THAN RAIMANT?

26. BEHOLD THE FOWLS OF THE AIR:
FOR THEY SOW NOT, NEITHER DO THEY REAP, NOR GATHER INTO BARNS;
YET YOUR HEAVENLY FATHER FEEDETH THEM.
ARE YE NOT MUCH BETTER THAN THEY?

27. WHICH OF YOU BY TAKING THOUGHT CAN ADD ONE CUBIT UNTO HIS STATURE?

28. AND WHY TAKE YE THOUGHT FOR RAIMENT?
CONSIDER THE LILIES OF THE FIELD, HOW THEY GROW;
THEY TOIL NOT, NEITHER DO THEY SPIN:

29. AND YET I SAY UNTO YOU,
THAT EVEN SOLOMON IN ALL HIS GLORY WAS NOT ARRAYED LIKE ONE OF THESE.

June 9 (Day 160), Memory Verses #435 & #436
<u>**Matthew 6: 33-34:**</u>

33. BUT SEEK YE FIRST THE KINGDOM OF GOD, AND HIS RIGHTEOUSNESS;
AND ALL THESE THINGS SHALL BE ADDED UNTO YOU.

34. TAKE THEREFORE NO THOUGHT FOR THE MORROW:
FOR THE MORROW SHALL TAKE THOUGHT FOR THE THINGS OF ITSELF.
SUFFICIENT UNTO THE DAY IS THE EVIL THEREOF.

June 10 (Day 161), Memory Verse #437
<u>**Matthew 7:1:**</u>

JUDGE NOT, THAT YE BE NOT JUDGED.

— *"For with what judgment ye judge, ye shall be judged:* and with what measure ye mete, it shall be measured to you again" (see 7:2).

June 10 (Day 161), Memory Verse #438
<u>**Matthew 7:5:**</u>

THOU HYPOCRITE, FIRST CAST OUT THE BEAM (plank, NIV) OUT OF THINE OWN EYE;
AND THEN SHALT THOU SEE CLEARLY
TO CAST OUT THE MOTE (speck, NIV) OUT OF THY BROTHER'S EYE.

June 11 (Day 162), Memory Verses #439 & #440
<u>**Matthew 7:7-8:**</u>

7. ASK, AND IT SHALL BE GIVEN YOU;
SEEK, AND YE SHALL FIND; KNOCK, AND IT SHALL BE OPENED UNTO YOU:

8. FOR EVERY ONE THAT ASKETH RECEIVETH; AND HE THAT SEEKETH FINDETH;
AND TO HIM THAT KNOCKETH IT SHALL BE OPENED.

June 11 (Day 162), Memory Verse #441
<u>**Matthew 7:12:**</u>
(The Golden Rule)

THEREFORE ALL THINGS WHATSOEVER YE WOULD THAT MEN SHOULD DO TO YOU,
DO YE EVEN SO TO THEM: FOR THIS IS THE LAW AND THE PROPHETS.

June 12 (Day 163), Memory Verse #442
<u>**Matthew 7:14**</u>

...STRAIT IS THE GATE, AND NARROW IS THE WAY,
WHICH LEADETH UNTO LIFE, AND FEW THERE BE THAT FIND IT.

— *"Beware of false prophets, which come to you in sheep's clothing, but inwardly they are ravening wolves"* (see 7:15) — Jesus tells the story of how the **wise man builds his house on the rock**, and the foolish man builds his house on the sand (see 7:24-27) — *"Therefore whosoever heareth these sayings of mine, and doeth them, I will liken him unto a wise man, which built his house upon a rock:"* (see 7:24) — *"...when Jesus had ended these sayings, the people were astonished at his doctrine. For he taught them as one having authority, and not as the scribes"* (see 7:28-29).

<u>Matthew 8:</u> **Jesus heals a leper** (see 8:1-4), **a centurion's servant** (see 8:5-13), **and Peter's mother-in-law who has been sick with fever** (see 8:14-17) — **Jesus calms the sea** (see 8:23-27) — **Jesus casts devils out of a man into a herd of swine** (see 8:28-34).

Matthew 9: Jesus heals a man *"...sick of the palsy (a paralytic, NIV)..."* (see 9:1-8) — **Jesus calls Matthew and dines with publicans (tax-collectors) and sinners** (see 9:9-13) — The Pharisees ask the disciples, *"...Why eateth your Master with publicans and sinners? But when Jesus heard that, he said unto them, They that be whole need not a physician, but they that are sick... for I am not come to call the righteous, but sinners to repentance"* (see 9:11-13) — **John the Baptist's disciples ask Jesus questions concerning fasting** (see 9:14-17) — **Jesus raises a certain ruler's (the ruler is called Jairus in Mark and Luke) daughter from the dead and heals a hemorrhaging lady** (see 9:18-26) — **Two blind men and a dumb man are healed** (see 9:27-34) — *"And Jesus went about all the cities and villages, teaching in their synagogues, and preaching the gospel of the kingdom, and healing every sickness and every disease among the people"* (see 9:35) — **Jesus teaches the disciples:**

June 12 (Day 163), Memory Verses #443 & #444
Matthew 9:37-38:

37. ...THE HARVEST TRULY IS PLENTEOUS, BUT THE LABOURERS ARE FEW;

38. PRAY YE THEREFORE THE LORD OF THE HARVEST,
THAT HE WILL SEND FORTH LABOURERS INTO HIS HARVEST.

Matthew 10: **Jesus sends out the twelve disciples (apostles) with instructions** (see 10:1-42) — *"The first, **Simon**, who is called Peter, and **Andrew** his brother; **James** the son of Zebedee, and **John** his brother; **Philip**, and **Bartholomew**; **Thomas**, and **Matthew** the publican; **James** the son of Alphaeus, and **Lebbaeus**"* (also called Judas, the brother of James, in Luke 6:16) *"whose surname was Thaddaeus; **Simon** the Canaanite, and **Judas Iscariot**, who also betrayed him"* (see 10:2-4) — *"Behold, I send you forth as sheep in the midst of wolves: be ye therefore wise as serpents, and harmless as doves"* (see 10:16).

June 13 (Day 164), Memory Verses #445 & #446
Matthew 10:32-33:

32. WHOSOEVER THEREFORE SHALL CONFESS ME BEFORE MEN,
HIM WILL I CONFESS BEFORE MY FATHER WHICH IS IN HEAVEN.

33. BUT WHOSOEVER SHALL DENY ME BEFORE MEN,
HIM WILL I ALSO DENY BEFORE MY FATHER WHICH IS IN HEAVEN.

June 13 (Day 164), Memory Verse #447
Matthew 10:39:

HE THAT FINDETH HIS LIFE SHALL LOSE IT:
AND HE THAT LOSETH HIS LIFE FOR MY SAKE SHALL FIND IT.

Matthew 11: **John the Baptist** who is in prison, sends his disciples to ask Jesus if He is the Christ — Jesus assures John's disciples He is the Christ (see 11:1-6) — **Jesus speaks to the multitudes** (see 11:7-30):

June 14 (Day 165), Memory Verses #448 to #450
Matthew 11:28-30:

28. COME UNTO ME, ALL YE THAT LABOUR AND ARE HEAVY LADEN,
AND I WILL GIVE YOU REST.

29. TAKE MY YOKE UPON YOU, AND LEARN OF ME;
FOR I AM MEEK AND LOWLY IN HEART:
AND YE SHALL FIND REST UNTO YOUR SOULS.

30. FOR MY YOKE IS EASY, AND MY BURDEN IS LIGHT.

Matthew 12:   Jesus and his disciples eat corn from the fields, and Jesus heals a man's withered hand on the Sabbath (see 12:1-14)**;** these actions anger the Pharisees, and Jesus says, *"For the Son of man is Lord even of the sabbath day"* (see 12:8) — **The Pharisees accuse Jesus of using Satan's power to cast out devils** (see 12:15-37 — Jesus says, *"...if Satan cast out Satan, he is divided against himself;..."* (see 12:26) — **The Pharisees ask Jesus for a miracle** (see 12:38-45); Jesus replies, *"...An evil and adulterous generation seeketh after a sign;..."* (see 12:39) — **When Jesus' mother and brethren come to see Him** (see 12:46-50), **He says:**

June 15 (Day 166), Memory Verse #451
Matthew 12:50:

FOR WHOSOEVER SHALL DO THE WILL OF MY FATHER WHICH IS IN HEAVEN,
THE SAME IS MY BROTHER, AND SISTER, AND MOTHER.

Matthew 13: Jesus teaches by the sea (see 13:1-53) — **Parable of the sower** (see 13:3-23).

June 15 (Day 166), Memory Verse #452
Matthew 13:12:

FOR WHOSOEVER HATH, TO HIM SHALL BE GIVEN,
AND HE SHALL HAVE MORE ABUNDANCE:
BUT WHOSOEVER HATH NOT, FROM HIM SHALL BE TAKEN AWAY EVEN THAT HE HATH.

— *"But he that received seed into the good ground is he that heareth the word, and understandeth it; which also beareth fruit, and bringeth forth, some an hundredfold, some sixty, some thirty"* (see 13:23) — **Jesus continues teaching the multitude with more parables:** wheat and tares (see 13:24-30, 34-43), mustard seed (see 13:31-32), leaven (see 13:33), hidden treasure (see 13:44), pearl of great price (see 13:45-46), dragnet (see 13:47-50), and the householder (see 13: 51-52) — **Jesus' hometown rejects Him** (see 13:53-58).

Matthew 14: Story of John the Baptist beheaded (see 14:1-13) — **A multitude, 5000 men plus women and children, is miraculously fed by Jesus from five loaves and two fish** (see 14:14-21) — Leftovers fill twelve baskets — **Jesus and Peter walk on water** (see 14:22-33); Peter becomes fearful and begins sinking, and Jesus stretches out His hand to Peter and says, *"O thou of little faith, wherefore didst thou doubt?"* (see 14:31)— **Jesus heals many** (see 14:34-36).

Matthew 15: The religious leaders are upset by the disciples eating bread without washing their hands — Jesus shows the Pharisees their sins which include not honoring their father and mother (see 15:1-20) — *"For out of the heart proceed evil thoughts, murders, adulteries, fornications, thefts, false witness, blasphemies: These are the things which defile a man: but to eat with unwashen hands defileth not a man"* (see 15:19-20) — **A Canaanite woman asks Jesus to cast a devil out of her daughter** (see 15:21-28) — Jesus tests the woman's faith by asking her why He should help a Gentile — The woman replies, *"...yet the dogs eat of the crumbs which fall from their masters' table"* (see 15:27) — Jesus casts out the devil from the daughter when He sees the mother's faith — **Jesus miraculously feeds the multitude, 4000 men plus women and children, from seven loaves and a few fish** (see 15:29-39).

Matthew 16:   Jesus warns (see 16:1-12) **of** *"...the leaven of the Pharisees and of the Sadducees"* (see 16:6) — **Jesus asks His disciples who they think He is** (see 16:13-20).

June 16 (Day 167), Memory Verse #453
Matthew 16:16:

AND SIMON PETER ANSWERED AND SAID,
THOU ART THE CHRIST, THE SON OF THE LIVING GOD.

— **Jesus talks of His death** (see 16:21-28) **and tells his disciples:**

June 17 (Day 168), Memory Verses #454 to #456
Matthew 16:24-26:

24. ...IF ANY MAN WILL COME AFTER ME,
LET HIM DENY HIMSELF, AND TAKE UP HIS CROSS, AND FOLLOW ME.

25. FOR WHOSOEVER WILL SAVE HIS LIFE SHALL LOSE IT:
AND WHOSOEVER WILL LOSE HIS LIFE FOR MY SAKE SHALL FIND IT.

26. FOR WHAT IS A MAN PROFITED, IF HE SHALL GAIN THE WHOLE WORLD,
AND LOSE HIS OWN SOUL? OR WHAT SHALL A MAN GIVE IN EXCHANGE FOR HIS SOUL?

Matthew 17:   Mount of Transfiguration (see 17:1-13) — Moses and Elijah appear to Jesus, James, and John — **Jesus heals a boy with seizures** (see 17:14-21) — Jesus tells the disciples:

June 18 (Day 169), Memory Verse #457
Matthew 17:20:

... IF YE HAVE FAITH AS A GRAIN OF MUSTARD SEED, YE SHALL SAY UNTO THIS MOUNTAIN,
REMOVE HENCE TO YONDER PLACE; AND IT SHALL REMOVE;
AND NOTHING SHALL BE IMPOSSIBLE UNTO YOU.

— **Jesus foretells His being betrayed, His death, and His resurrection** (see 17:22-23) — **Jesus pays taxes by having Simon fetch a coin from a fish's mouth** (see 17:24-27).

Matthew 18:   Jesus' disciples ask Jesus (see 18:1-6) *"...Who is the greatest in the kingdom of heaven?"* (see 18:1) — *"And Jesus called a little child unto him...And said..."* (see 18:2-3):

June 18 (Day 169), Memory Verses #458 & #459
Matthew 18:3-4:

3. ...EXCEPT YE BE CONVERTED, AND BECOME AS LITTLE CHILDREN,
YE SHALL NOT ENTER INTO THE KINGDOM OF HEAVEN.

4. WHOSOEVER THEREFORE SHALL HUMBLE HIMSELF AS THIS LITTLE CHILD,
THE SAME IS GREATEST IN THE KINGDOM OF HEAVEN.

— *"But whoso shall offend one of these little ones which believe in me* (But if anyone causes *one of these little ones who believe in me to sin,* NIV), *it were better for him that a millstone were hanged about his neck, and that he were drowned in the depth of the sea"* (see 18:6) — **Parable of one lost sheep** (see 18:7-14) — **How to handle trespasses among believers** (see 18:15-18) — **Lessons on prayer** (see 18:19-20) **and lessons on forgiveness** (see 18:21-35):

June 19 (Day 170), Memory Verses #460 to #463
Matthew 18:19-22:

19. AGAIN I SAY UNTO YOU, THAT IF TWO OF YOU SHALL AGREE ON EARTH
AS TOUCHING ANY THING THAT THEY SHALL ASK,
IT SHALL BE DONE FOR THEM OF MY FATHER WHICH IS IN HEAVEN.

20. FOR WHERE TWO OR THREE ARE GATHERED TOGETHER IN MY NAME,
THERE AM I IN THE MIDST OF THEM.

21. THEN CAME PETER TO HIM, AND SAID, LORD,
HOW OFT SHALL MY BROTHER SIN AGAINST ME, AND I FORGIVE HIM? TILL SEVEN TIMES?

22. JESUS SAITH UNTO HIM, I SAY NOT UNTO THEE,
UNTIL SEVEN TIMES: BUT UNTIL SEVENTY TIMES SEVEN.

— **Parable of a wicked servant who is forgiven but will not forgive others** (see 18:23-35).

Matthew 19: **Jesus speaks on marriage and divorce** (see 19:1-12) — **Children are brought to Jesus** (see 19:13-15), **and Jesus tells his disciples:**

June 20 (Day 171), Memory Verse #464
Matthew 19:14:

...SUFFER LITTLE CHILDREN AND FORBID THEM NOT, TO COME UNTO ME:
FOR OF SUCH IS THE KINGDOM OF HEAVEN.

— **A rich man is sad when Jesus asks him to sell his possessions** (see 19:16-26) — **Jesus teaches:**

June 20 (Day 171), Memory Verse #465
Matthew 19:26:

...WITH GOD ALL THINGS ARE POSSIBLE.

— **Peter asks Jesus what the disciples will receive for forsaking all and following Him** (see 19:27-30) — Jesus answers that those who follow him *"shall inherit everlasting life"* (see 19:29).

June 21 (Day 172), Memory Verse #466
Matthew 19:30:

BUT MANY THAT ARE FIRST SHALL BE LAST; AND THE LAST SHALL BE FIRST.

Matthew 20: **Parable of a landowner hiring laborers throughout the day** (see 20:1-16).

June 21 (Day 172), Memory Verse #467
Matthew 20:16:

SO THE LAST SHALL BE FIRST, AND THE FIRST LAST: FOR MANY BE CALLED, BUT FEW CHOSEN.

— **Jesus again speaks of His death** (see 20:17-19) — **A mother asks Jesus to allow her two sons, James and John, to sit at Jesus' right and left hands in His kingdom** (see 20:20-28) — Jesus explains to the disciples:

June 22 (Day 173), Memory Verses #468 & #469
Matthew 20:27-28:

27. AND WHOSOEVER WILL BE CHIEF AMONG YOU, LET HIM BE YOUR SERVANT:

28. EVEN AS THE SON OF MAN CAME NOT TO BE MINISTERED UNTO,
BUT TO MINISTER, AND TO GIVE HIS LIFE A RANSOM FOR MANY.

— **Jesus heals two blind men who are asking for mercy** (see 20:29-34).

Matthew 21: **Jesus' entry into Jerusalem on a colt** (see 21:1-11) — *"And a very great multitude spread their garments in the way; others cut down branches from the trees, and strawed them in the way. And the multitudes that went before, and that followed, cried, saying, Hosanna to the son of David: Blessed is he that cometh in the name of the Lord; Hosanna in the highest"* (see 21:8-9) — **Jesus cleanses the temple and heals in the temple** (see 21:12-17) — *"And Jesus went into the temple of God, and cast out all them that sold and bought in the temple, and overthrew the tables of the moneychangers, and the seats of them that sold doves, And said unto them, It is written, My house shall be called the house of prayer; but ye have made it a den of thieves"* (see 21:12-13) — **Cursing of a fig tree** (see 21:18-22).

> **June 22 (Day 173), Memory Verse #470**
> **Matthew 21:22:**
>
> AND ALL THINGS, WHATSOEVER YE SHALL ASK IN PRAYER, BELIEVING, YE SHALL RECEIVE.

— **The chief priests and elders question Jesus' authority** (see 21:23-27) — **Parable of an obedient son and a disobedient son** (see 21:28-32) — **Parable of a man with a vineyard** (see 21:33-46) — In the previous parable, Jesus shows how the religious leaders have rejected Him who is God's Son — *"Jesus saith unto them, Did ye never read in the scriptures, The stone which the builders rejected, the same is become the head of the corner:..."* (see 21:42).

Matthew 22: **Parable of a king changing the guest list of his son's wedding from only the elite to all who will come** (see 22:1-14).

> **June 23 (Day 174), Memory Verse #471**
> **Matthew 22:14:**
>
> FOR MANY ARE CALLED (invited, NIV), BUT FEW ARE CHOSEN.

— **Pharisees try to trick Jesus with the question of whether or not to pay taxes to Caesar** (see 22:15-22) — Jesus says:

> **June 23 (Day 174), Memory Verse #472**
> **Matthew 22:21:**
>
> ... RENDER UNTO CAESAR THE THINGS WHICH ARE CAESAR'S,
> AND UNTO GOD THE THINGS THAT ARE GOD'S.

— **Sadducees try to trick Jesus with a question concerning seven brothers at the resurrection who have all been married to the same woman** (see 22:23-33) — **A lawyer of the Pharisees asks what is the greatest commandment** (see 22:34-40), **and Jesus replies:**

> **June 24 (Day 175), Memory Verses #473 to #476**
> **Matthew 22:37-40:**
>
> 37. ...THOU SHALT LOVE THE LORD THY GOD WITH ALL THY HEART,
> AND WITH ALL THY SOUL, AND WITH ALL THY MIND.
>
> 38. THIS IS THE FIRST AND GREAT COMMANDMENT.
>
> 39. AND THE SECOND IS LIKE UNTO IT,
> THOU SHALT LOVE THY NEIGHBOUR AS THYSELF.
>
> 40. ON THESE TWO COMMANDMENTS HANG ALL THE LAW AND THE PROPHETS.

— **Jesus shows the Pharisees that Christ is the son of David (a descendant of David), and Christ was also called "Lord" by David** (see 22:41-46).

Matthew 23: **Jesus warns the multitude and His disciples of the scribes and Pharisees** (see 23:1-39) — *"Woe unto you scribes and Pharisees, hypocrites!..."* (see 23:13, 14, 15, 23, 25, 27, 29); *"But all their works they do to be seen of men:"* (see 23:5).

> **June 25 (Day 176), Memory Verse #477**
> **Matthew 23:11:**
>
> BUT HE THAT IS GREATEST AMONG YOU SHALL BE YOUR SERVANT.

Matthew 24: **Signs of the end times** (see 24:1-51) include destruction in Jerusalem, imposters of Christ, wars and rumors of wars, famines, pestilences, earthquakes, persecutions, betrayals, hatred, *"abomination of desolation"* in the temple, false prophets, darkened sun and moon, fallen stars, and the shaken heavens; *"For as the lightning cometh out of the east, and shineth even unto the west; so shall also the coming of the Son of man be"* (see 24:27) — *"...and they shall see the Son of man coming in the clouds of heaven with power and great glory. And he shall send his angels with a great sound of a trumpet, and they shall gather together his elect from the four winds, from one end of heaven to the other"* (see 24:30-31) — **Parable of the fig tree** (see 24:32-35).

June 25 (Day 176), Memory Verse #478
Matthew 24:35:

HEAVEN AND EARTH SHALL PASS AWAY, BUT MY WORDS SHALL NOT PASS AWAY.

June 26 (Day 177), Memory Verse #479
Matthew 24:40:

THEN SHALL TWO BE IN THE FIELD; THE ONE SHALL BE TAKEN, AND THE OTHER LEFT.

June 26 (Day 177), Memory Verse #480
Matthew 24:42:

WATCH THEREFORE: FOR YE KNOW NOT WHAT HOUR YOUR LORD DOTH COME.

— **The watchful house owner** (see 24:43-44) — **The faithful and wise servant** (see 24:45-51).

Matthew 25: Parable of ten virgins (see 25:1-13).

June 26 (Day 177), Memory Verse #481
Matthew 25:13:

WATCH THEREFORE, FOR YE KNOW NEITHER THE DAY NOR THE HOUR
WHEREIN THE SON OF MAN COMETH.

— **Parable of the talents** (see 25:14-30).

June 27 (Day 178), Memory Verse #482
Matthew 25:21:

...WELL DONE THY GOOD AND FAITHFUL SERVANT:
THOU HAST BEEN FAITHFUL OVER A FEW THINGS,
I WILL MAKE THEE RULER OVER MANY THINGS:...
ENTER THOU INTO THE JOY OF THY LORD.

June 27 (Day 178), Memory Verse #483
Matthew 25:29:

FOR UNTO EVERYONE THAT HATH SHALL BE GIVEN, AND HE SHALL HAVE ABUNDANCE:
BUT FROM HIM THAT HATH NOT SHALL BE TAKEN AWAY EVEN THAT WHICH HE HATH.

— **Separation of sheep and goats** (see 25:31-46) — *"When the Son of man shall come in his glory, and all the holy angels with him, then shall he sit upon the throne of his glory: And before him shall be gathered all nations: and he shall separate them one from another, as a shepherd divideth his sheep from the goats:"* (see 25:31-32) — ***"For I was hungred, and ye gave me meat: I was thirsty, and ye gave me drink: I was a stranger, and ye took me in: Naked, and ye clothed me: I was sick, and ye visited me: I was in prison, and ye came unto me.*** *Then shall the righteous answer him, saying, Lord, when saw we thee an hungred, and fed thee? or thirsty, and gave thee drink? When saw we thee a stranger, and took thee in? or naked, and* *clothed thee? Or when saw we thee sick, or in prison, and came unto thee? And the King shall answer and say unto them, Verily I say unto you...*" (see 25:35-40)**:**

June 28 (Day 179), Memory Verse #484
Matthew 25:40:

...INASMUCH AS YE HAVE DONE IT UNTO ONE OF THE LEAST OF THESE MY BRETHREN, YE HAVE DONE IT UNTO ME.

Matthew 26:   **The religious leaders conspire to kill Jesus** (see 26:1-5) — **A woman in Bethany anoints Jesus with precious ointment** (see 26:6-13) — Jesus says, *"For in that she hath poured this ointment on my body, she did it for my burial"* (see 26:12) — **The Passover and "The Lord's Supper"** (see 26:17-30) — *"And as they were eating, Jesus took bread, and blessed it, and brake it, and gave it to the disciples, and said, Take eat; this is my body. And he took the cup, and gave thanks, and gave it to them, saying, Drink ye all of it; For this is my blood of the new testament (covenant, NIV), which is shed for many for the remission of sins"* (see 26:26-28). — **Jesus tells Peter that he will three times deny knowing Him** (see 26:31-35) — **Prayer in the Garden of Gethsemane** (see 26:36-44).

June 28 (Day 179), Memory Verse #485
Matthew 26:39:

AND HE WENT A LITTLE FURTHER, AND FELL ON HIS FACE, AND PRAYED, SAYING, O MY FATHER, IF IT BE POSSIBLE, LET THIS CUP PASS FROM ME: NEVERTHELESS NOT AS I WILL, BUT AS THOU WILT.

June 28 (Day 179), Memory Verse #486
Matthew 26:41:

WATCH AND PRAY, THAT YE ENTER NOT INTO TEMPTATION: THE SPIRIT INDEED IS WILLING, BUT THE FLESH IS WEAK.

— **The betrayal by Judas Iscariot and Jesus' arrest** (see 26:45-56) — **Jesus before Caiaphas** (see 26:57-68) — **Peter denies Jesus three times** (see 26:69-75) — *"And Peter remembered the word of Jesus, which said unto him, Before the cock crow, thou shalt deny me thrice. And he went out, and wept bitterly"* (see 26:75).

Matthew 27:   **Judas repents and hangs himself** (see 27:1-10) — **Jesus before Pilate** (see 27:11-26) — Pilate's wife warns Pilate of her dream about Jesus (see 27:19) — The crowds plead to release Barabbas and crucify Jesus — *"When Pilate saw that he could prevail nothing, but that rather a tumult was made, he took water, and washed his hands before the multitude, saying, I am innocent of the blood of this just person: see ye to it"* (see 27:24) — **Crucifixion and burial** (see 27:27-66) — Soldiers mock Jesus and place a scarlet robe and crown of thorns on Him (see 27:27-31) — Simon of Cyrene helps Jesus carry the cross to Golgotha — *"Now from the sixth hour there was darkness over all the land unto the ninth hour. And about the ninth hour Jesus cried with a loud voice, saying, Eli, Eli, lama sabachthani? That is to say, My God, my God, why hast thou forsaken me?"* (see 27:45-46) — *"Jesus, when he had cried again with a loud voice, yielded up the ghost. And, behold, the veil of the temple was rent in twain from the top to the bottom; and the earth did quake, and the rocks rent; And the graves were opened; and many bodies of the saints which slept arose, And came out of the graves after his resurrection, and went into the holy city, and appeared unto many. Now when the centurion, and they that were with him, watching Jesus, saw the earthquake, and those things that were done, they feared greatly, saying, Truly this was the Son of God"* (see 27:50-54) — **Joseph of Arimathea receives permission from Pilate to take Jesus' body** — *"And when Joseph had taken the body, he* *wrapped it in a clean linen cloth, And laid it in his own new tomb, which he had hewn out in the rock: and he rolled a great stone to the door of the sepulchre, and departed"* (see 27:59-60) — **The chief priests and Pharisees persuade Pilate to place guards at the tomb to prevent Jesus' body from being stolen by His disciples.**

Matthew 28: Jesus' resurrection and appearances (see 28:1-20) — *"In the end of the sabbath, as it began to dawn toward the first day of the week, came Mary Magdalene and the other Mary to see the sepulchre. And, behold, there was a great earthquake: for the angel of the Lord descended from heaven, and came and rolled back the stone from the door, and sat upon it. His countenance was like lightning, and his raiment white as snow: And for fear of him the keepers did shake, and became as dead men. And the angel answered and said unto the women, Fear not ye: for I know that ye seek Jesus, which was crucified. He is not here: for he is risen, as he said..."* (see 28:1-6) — **The chief priests give money to the guards of Jesus' tomb and tell them to say,** *"...His disciples came by night, and stole him away while we slept"* (see 28:13) — **Jesus appears to His disciples in Galilee and says:**

June 29 (Day 180), Memory Verses #487 & #488
Matthew 28:19-20:
(The Great Commission)

19. GO YE THEREFORE, AND TEACH ALL NATIONS,
BAPTIZING THEM IN THE NAME OF THE FATHER,
AND OF THE SON, AND OF THE HOLY GHOST:

20. TEACHING THEM TO OBSERVE ALL THINGS
WHATSOEVER I HAVE COMMANDED YOU:
AND LO, I AM WITH YOU ALWAY,
EVEN UNTO THE END OF THE WORLD. AMEN.

MATTHEW 6:9-13: (THE LORD'S PRAYER)

9. AFTER THIS MANNER PRAY YE:
OUR FATHER WHICH ART IN HEAVEN,
HALLOWED BE THY NAME.
10. THY KINGDOM COME.
THY WILL BE DONE IN EARTH, AS IT IS IN HEAVEN.
11. GIVE US THIS DAY OUR DAILY BREAD.
12. AND FORGIVE US OUR DEBTS,
AS WE FORGIVE OUR DEBTORS.
13. AND LEAD US NOT INTO TEMPTATION,
BUT DELIVER US FROM EVIL:
FOR THINE IS THE KINGDOM, AND THE POWER,
AND THE GLORY, FOR EVER. AMEN.

MARK

Introduction: Most scholars believe John Mark is the author of Mark. John Mark accompanied Paul on part of his first missionary journey. The date of writing is thought to be between 50-65 A.D. John Mark wrote this book particularly to the Roman Gentiles and emphasized Jesus as a servant and minister. The book of Mark was most likely written in Rome where John Mark was taught by Peter about Jesus' life. Tradition says Peter was crucified upside down by Emperor Nero in 65 A.D. Mark has 16 chapters.

Key Contents and Key Memory Verses with Study Dates

<u>Note:</u> All key memory verses in Mark with the exception of Mark 9:24 are sayings of Jesus.

<u>**Mark 1:**</u> **John the Baptist** (see 1:1-8) — *"And John was clothed with camel's hair, and with a girdle of a skin about his loins; and he did eat locusts and wild honey; And preached, saying, There cometh one mightier than I after me, the latchet of whose shoes I am not worthy to stoop down and unloose. I indeed have baptized you with water: but he shall baptize you with the Holy Ghost"* (see 1:6-8) — **Jesus is baptized** (see 1:9-11) — The Spirit like a dove descends upon Jesus, and *"...there came a voice from heaven, saying, Thou art my beloved Son, in whom I am well pleased"* (see 1:11) — **Jesus is in the wilderness for 40 days** (see 1:12-13), *"...tempted of Satan; and was with the wild beasts; and the angels ministered unto him"* (see 1:13) — **John the Baptist is put in prison** (see 1:14) — **Simon, Andrew, James, and John are called as disciples** (see 1:15-20).

June 30 (Day 181), Memory Verse #489
<u>Mark 1:17:</u>

AND JESUS SAID UNTO THEM, COME YE AFTER ME,
AND I WILL MAKE YOU TO BECOME FISHERS OF MEN.

— **Jesus casts an unclean spirit out of a man in Capernaum** (see 1:21-28) — **Jesus heals many people including Simon's mother-in-law who has been sick with fever** (see 1:29-31) — **Jesus continues healing many and casts out devils** (see 1:32-39) — *"And in the morning, rising up a great while before day, he went out, and departed into a solitary place, and there prayed"* (see 1:35) — **Jesus heals a leper** (see 1:40-45).

<u>**Mark 2:**</u> **One sick of the palsy (a paralytic, NIV) is lowered through the roof to reach Jesus** (see 2:1-12) — Jesus tells the paralytic his sins are forgiven, and the scribes feel this is blasphemy — Jesus reveals He knows their thoughts and asks, *"Whether is it easier to say to the sick of the palsy, Thy sins be forgiven thee; or to say, Arise, and take up thy bed, and walk?"* (see 2:9) — Jesus heals the paralytic who takes up his bed and walks — Jesus wants the scribes to know He has power to forgive sins (see 2:10) — **Jesus calls Levi, a tax collector, to be His disciple** (see 2:13-14) — Scribes and Pharisees question Jesus' eating with publicans (tax-collectors, NIV) and sinners (see 2:15-17) — *"When Jesus heard it, he saith unto them, They that are whole have no need of the physician, but they that are sick: I came not to call the righteous, but the sinners to repentance"* (see 2:17) — **Pharisees and John's disciples ask questions on fasting** (see 2:18-22) — **Pharisees are upset by Jesus' disciples picking corn on the Sabbath** (see 2:23-28) — Jesus says:

June 30 (Day 181), Memory Verse #490
<u>Mark 2:27:</u>

...THE SABBATH WAS MADE FOR MAN, AND NOT MAN FOR THE SABBATH:

Mark 3: **Jesus heals a man with a withered hand on the Sabbath** (see 3:1-6) — The Pharisees will not answer Jesus when He asks, *"....Is it lawful to do good on the sabbath day, or to do evil? To save life, or to kill?"* (see 3:4) — **Jesus heals many** (see 3:7-12) — **Jesus ordains the twelve apostles** (see 3:13-19) — *"And he ordained twelve, that they should be with him, and that he might send them forth to preach, And to have power to heal sicknesses, and to cast out devils:"* (see 3:14-15) — **The twelve apostles are listed:** *"And **Simon** he surnamed Peter; And **James** the son of Zebedee, and **John** the brother of James; and he surnamed them Boanerges, which is, The Sons of thunder: And **Andrew**, and **Philip**, and **Bartholomew**, and **Matthew**, and **Thomas**, and **James** the son of Alpheus, and **Thaddaeus"** (also known as Judas the brother of James as listed in Luke 6:16), *"and **Simon** the Canaanite, And **Judas Iscariot**, which also betrayed him:..."* (see 3:16-19) — **Some accuse Jesus of being possessed by Satan** (see 3:20-30), but Jesus asks, *"...How can Satan cast out Satan?"* (see 3:23) — Jesus adds:

July 1 (Day 182), Memory Verse #491
Mark 3:25:

AND IF A HOUSE BE DIVIDED AGAINST ITSELF,
THAT HOUSE CANNOT STAND.

— **Jesus' mother and brethren come to visit Him** (see 3:31-35), **and He says:**

July 1 (Day 182), Memory Verse #492
Mark 3:35:

FOR WHOSOEVER SHALL DO THE WILL OF GOD,
THE SAME IS MY BROTHER, AND MY SISTER, AND MY MOTHER.

Mark 4: **Parable of the sower** (see 4:1-20) — *"And these are they which are sown on good ground; such as hear the word, and receive it, and bring forth fruit..."* (see 4:20) — **Illustration of the candle** (see 4:21-25).

July 2 (Day 183), Memory Verses #493 & #494
Mark 4:24-25:

24. AND HE SAID UNTO THEM, TAKE HEED WHAT YE HEAR:
WITH WHAT MEASURE YE METE, IT SHALL BE MEASURED TO YOU:
AND UNTO YOU THAT HEAR SHALL MORE BE GIVEN.

25. FOR HE THAT HATH, TO HIM SHALL BE GIVEN:
AND HE THAT HATH NOT, FROM HIM SHALL BE TAKEN EVEN THAT WHICH HE HATH.

— **The Kingdom of God is compared to a growing plant and a mustard seed** (see 4:26-34) — **Jesus and the disciples cross the Sea of Galilee in a boat, and a storm arises** (see 4:35-41) — Jesus *"...arose, and rebuked the wind, and said unto the sea, Peace, be still. And the wind ceased, and there was a great calm"* (see 4:39).

Mark 5: **Jesus casts devils named Legion out of a man into about 2000 swine** which then run into the sea (see 5:1-20) — Jesus tells Jairus, a ruler of the synagogue whose daughter has died, *"...Be not afraid, only believe"* (see 5:36) — **Jesus heals a hemorrhaging woman and raises Jairus' twelve-year-old daughter from the dead** (see 5:21-43).

Mark 6: **Jesus' hometown lacks faith in Him** (see 6:1-5) — **Jesus sends out the 12 disciples** (see 6:6-13) — *"And they went out, and preached that men should repent. And they cast out many devils, and anointed with oil many that were sick, and healed them"* (see 6:12-13) — **The story of John the Baptist beheaded** (see 6:14-29) — **Jesus miraculously feeds a multitude,**

5000 men plus women and children, with five loaves and two fish (see 6:30-44) — **Jesus walks on water** (see 6:45-52) — **Jesus heals many** (see 6:53-56).

Mark 7:   Jesus criticizes the Pharisees for their rules of clean and unclean and for not honoring their parents (see 7:1-23) — *Jesus says, "... That which cometh out of the man, that defileth the man. For from within, out of the heart of men, proceed evil thoughts, adulteries, fornications, murders, Thefts, covetousness, wickedness, deceit, lasciviousness, an evil eye, blasphemy, pride, foolishness: All these evil things come from within, and defile the man"* (see 7:20-23) — **Jesus casts a devil out of a young girl** (see 7:24-30) — **Jesus heals a deaf man with a speech impediment** (see 7:31-37).

Mark 8:   Jesus miraculously feeds a multitude, 4000 men plus women and children, with seven loaves of bread and a few fish (see 8:1-10) — **The Pharisees ask for a sign** (see 8:11-13) — **Jesus warns the disciples of the Pharisee's leaven** (see 8:14-21) — **A blind man is healed by Jesus** (see 8:22-26) — **Jesus asks his disciples, "...***Whom do men say that I am? And they answered, John the Baptist: but some say, Elias (Elijah, NIV); and others, One of the prophets. And he saith unto them, But whom say ye that I am? And Peter answereth and saith unto him, Thou art the Christ"* (see 8:27-29) — **Jesus talks about His death** (see 8:30-33) — *"And he began to teach them, that the Son of man must suffer many things, and be rejected of the elders, and of the chief priests, and scribes, and be killed, and after three days rise again"* (see 8:31) — **Jesus teaches concerning following Him** (see 8:34-9:1):

July 3-4 (Days 184-185), Memory Verses #495 to #499
Mark 8:34-38:

34. ...WHOSOEVER WILL COME AFTER ME,
LET HIM DENY HIMSELF, AND TAKE UP HIS CROSS, AND FOLLOW ME.

35. FOR WHOSOEVER WILL SAVE HIS LIFE SHALL LOSE IT;
BUT WHOSOEVER SHALL LOSE HIS LIFE FOR MY SAKE AND THE GOSPEL'S,
THE SAME SHALL SAVE IT.

36. FOR WHAT SHALL IT PROFIT A MAN,
IF HE SHALL GAIN THE WHOLE WORLD, AND LOSE HIS OWN SOUL?

37. OR WHAT SHALL A MAN GIVE IN EXCHANGE OF HIS SOUL?

38. WHOSOEVER THEREFORE SHALL BE ASHAMED OF ME
AND MY WORDS IN THIS ADULTEROUS AND SINFUL GENERATION;
OF HIM ALSO SHALL THE SON OF MAN BE ASHAMED,
WHEN HE COMETH IN THE GLORY OF HIS FATHER WITH THE HOLY ANGELS.

Mark 9:   Mount of Transfiguration (see 9:2-13) — *"...Jesus taketh with him Peter, and James, and John, and leadeth them up into an high mountain apart by themselves: and he was transfigured before them. And his raiment became shining, exceeding white as snow; ...And there appeared unto them Elias (Elijah, NIV) with Moses: and they were talking with Jesus"* (see 9:2-4) — **Jesus commands a deaf and dumb spirit to leave a boy after telling the boy's father the following** (see 9:14-29):

July 5 (Day 186), Memory Verses #500 & #501
Mark 9:23-24:

23. ...IF THOU CANST BELIEVE, ALL THINGS ARE POSSIBLE TO HIM THAT BELIEVETH.

24. AND STRAIGHTWAY THE FATHER OF THE CHILD CRIED OUT,
AND SAID WITH TEARS, LORD, I BELIEVE; HELP THOU MY UNBELIEF.

— **Jesus speaks about His death** (see 9:30-32) — **The disciples argue over who should be the greatest** (see 9:33-37).

July 6 (Day 187), Memory Verse #502
Mark 9:35:

...IF ANY MAN DESIRE TO BE FIRST, THE SAME SHALL BE LAST OF ALL, AND SERVANT OF ALL.

— **Jesus** *"took a child, and set him in the midst of them:* and when he had taken him in his arms, he said unto them" (see 9:36)**:**

July 6 (Day 187), Memory Verse #503
Mark 9:37:

WHOSOEVER SHALL RECEIVE ONE OF SUCH CHILDREN IN MY NAME, RECEIVETH ME: AND WHOSOEVER SHALL RECEIVE ME, RECEIVETH NOT ME, BUT HIM THAT SENT ME.

— **John asks Jesus what to do about those using Jesus' name to cast out devils** (see 9:38-41).

July 6 (Day 187), Memory Verse #504
Mark 9:40:

FOR HE THAT IS NOT AGAINST US IS ON OUR PART.

— **Jesus warns against offending others** (see 9:42-50).

July 7 (Day 188), Memory Verse #505
Mark 9:50:

...HAVE SALT IN YOURSELVES, AND HAVE PEACE ONE WITH ANOTHER.

Mark 10: **Jesus talks on divorce** (see 10:1-12) — **Jesus blesses the children** (see 10:13-16).

July 7 (Day 188), Memory Verse #506
Mark 10:15:

...WHOSOEVER SHALL NOT RECEIVE THE KINGDOM OF GOD AS A LITTLE CHILD, HE SHALL NOT ENTER THEREIN.

— **A rich man asks Jesus how to inherit eternal life** (see 10:17-31).

July 8 (Day 189), Memory Verse #507
Mark 10: 24:

...HOW HARD IS IT FOR THEM THAT TRUST IN RICHES TO ENTER INTO THE KINGDOM OF GOD!

July 8 (Day 189), Memory Verse #508
Mark 10: 27:

...FOR WITH GOD ALL THINGS ARE POSSIBLE.

July 8 (Day 189), Memory Verse #509
Mark 10:31:

BUT MANY THAT ARE FIRST SHALL BE LAST; AND THE LAST FIRST.

— **Jesus talks about His death and resurrection** (see 10:32-34) — **James and John ask to sit at Jesus' right and left hands in His glory** (see 10:35-45).

> **July 9 (Day 190), Memory Verses #510 to #512**
> **Mark 10:43-45:**
>
> 43. **BUT** SO SHALL IT NOT BE AMONG YOU:
> BUT WHOSOEVER WILL BE GREAT AMONG YOU, SHALL BE YOUR MINISTER:
>
> 44. **AND** WHOSOEVER OF YOU WILL BE THE CHIEFEST, SHALL BE SERVANT OF ALL.
>
> 45. **FOR** EVEN THE SON OF MAN CAME NOT TO BE MINISTERED UNTO,
> BUT TO MINISTER, AND TO GIVE HIS LIFE A RANSOM FOR MANY.

— Jesus heals blind Bartimaeus (see 10:46-52) — *"And Jesus said unto him, Go thy way; thy faith hath made thee whole. And immediately he received his sight, and followed Jesus in the way"* (see 10:52).

Mark 11: **On "Palm Sunday," Jesus rides a colt into Jerusalem** (see 11:1-11) — *"And they that went before, and they that followed, cried, saying, Hosanna; Blessed is he that cometh in the name of the Lord: Blessed be the kingdom of our father David, that cometh in the name of the Lord: Hosanna in the highest"* (see 11:9-10) — **Jesus curses the fig tree** (see 11:12-14, 20-21) — **Jesus cleanses the temple** (see 11:15-19) — *"And he taught, saying unto them, Is it not written, My house shall be called of all nations the house of prayer? But ye have made it a den of thieves"* (see 11:17) — **Jesus teaches to have faith that can move mountains** (see 11:22-24) — **Jesus also teaches to practice forgiveness** (see 11:25-26).

> **July 10 (Day 191), Memory Verse #513**
> **Mark 11:25:**
>
> **AND** WHEN YE STAND PRAYING, FORGIVE, IF YE HAVE OUGHT AGAINST ANY:
> THAT YOUR FATHER ALSO WHICH IS IN HEAVEN MAY FORGIVE YOU YOUR TRESPASSES.

— Religious leaders question Jesus' authority (see 11:27-33).

Mark 12: **Parable of the vineyard** (see 12:1-12) — **The religious leaders question Jesus concerning taxes** (see 12:13-17) — *"And Jesus answering said unto them, Render unto Caesar the things that are Caesar's, and to God the things that are God's. And they marvelled at him"* (see 12:17) — **The Sadducees question Jesus concerning seven brothers in the resurrection who have all been married to the same woman** (see 12:18-27) — **One of the scribes ask Jesus which is the greatest commandment** (see 12:28-34).

> **July 10 (Day 191), Memory Verses #514 to #516**
> **Mark 12:29-31:**
>
> 29. **AND** JESUS ANSWERED HIM, THE FIRST OF ALL COMMANDMENTS IS, HEAR, O ISRAEL:
> THE LORD OUR GOD IS ONE LORD:
>
> 30. **AND** THOU SHALT LOVE THE LORD THY GOD WITH ALL THY HEART,
> AND WITH ALL THY SOUL, AND WITH ALL THY MIND, AND WITH ALL THY STRENGTH:
> THIS IS THE FIRST COMMANDMENT.
>
> 31. **AND** THE SECOND IS LIKE, NAMELY THIS,
> THOU SHALT LOVE THY NEIGHBOUR AS THYSELF.
> THERE IS NONE OTHER COMMANDMENT GREATER THAN THESE.

— As Jesus is teaching in the temple, He is questioned about Christ being the son of David (see 12:35-37) — **Jesus teaches to beware of those who love recognition** (see 12:38-40) — **A widow gives all she owns (two mites) to the temple treasury** (see 12:41-44).

Mark 13: **Future events** (see 13:1-37) include imposters of Christ, false prophets, wars and rumors of wars, earthquakes, famines, the gospel published in all nations, the *"abomination of desolation"* (see 13:14), persecution of believers, family betrayals, the sun and moon darkened, and fallen stars — *"And then shall they see the Son of man coming in the clouds with great power and glory. And then shall he send his angels, and shall gather together his elect from the four winds, from the uttermost part of the earth to the uttermost part of heaven"* (see 13:26-27).

July 11 (Day 192), Memory Verse #517
Mark 13:31:

HEAVEN AND EARTH SHALL PASS AWAY: BUT MY WORDS SHALL NOT PASS AWAY.

— *"But of that day and that hour knoweth no man, no, not the angels which are in heaven, neither the Son, but the Father. **Take ye heed, watch, and pray: for ye know not when the time is"*** (see 13:32-33).

Mark 14: **A woman pours expensive and precious ointment on Jesus' head during the Passover** (see 14:1-9) — Jesus says, *"She hath done what she could: she is come aforehand to anoint my body to the burying. Verily I say unto you, Wheresoever this gospel shall be preached throughout the whole world, this also that she hath done shall be spoken of for a memorial of her"* (see 14:8-9) — **Judas Iscariot schemes with the chief priests to betray Jesus** (see 14:10-11) — **Passover meal, the first "Lord's Supper"** (see 14:12-25) — *"And as they did eat, Jesus took bread, and blessed, and brake it, and gave to them, and said, Take, eat: this is my body. And he took the cup, and when he had given thanks, he gave it to them: and they all drank of it. And he said unto them, This is my blood of the new testament (covenant, NIV), which is shed for many"* (see 14:22-24) — **Jesus tells Peter he will deny Him three times** (see 14:26-31) — **Garden of Gethsemane and Jesus' prayer** (see 14:32-42):

July 11 (Day 192), Memory Verses #518 & #519
Mark 14:35-36:

35. AND HE WENT FORWARD A LITTLE, AND FELL ON THE GROUND,
AND PRAYED THAT, IF IT WERE POSSIBLE, THE HOUR MIGHT PASS FROM HIM.

36. AND HE SAID, ABBA, FATHER, ALL THINGS ARE POSSIBLE UNTO THEE;
TAKE AWAY THIS CUP FROM ME:
NEVERTHELESS NOT WHAT I WILL, BUT WHAT THOU WILT.

— **Jesus is betrayed by Judas and arrested** (see 14:43-52) — **Jesus is taken to the palace of the High Priest** (see 14:53-65) — *"...Again the high priest asked him, and said unto him, Art thou the Christ, the Son of the Blessed? And Jesus said, I am: and ye shall see the Son of man sitting on the right hand of power, and coming in the clouds of heaven"* (see 14:61-62) — **Peter denies Jesus three times** (see 14:66-72).

Mark 15: **Jesus before Pilate** (see 15:1-15) — *"And so Pilate, willing to content the people, released Barabbas unto them, and delivered Jesus, when he had scourged him, to be crucified"* (see 15:15) — **Jesus' crucifixion and death** (see 15:16-41) — *"And at the ninth hour Jesus cried with a loud voice, saying, Eloi, Eloi, lama sabachthani? Which is, being interpreted, My God, my God, why hast thou forsaken me?"* (see 15:34) — *"And Jesus cried with a loud voice, and gave up the ghost. And the veil of the temple was rent in twain from the top to the bottom. And when the centurion, which stood over against him, saw that he so cried out, and gave up the ghost, he said, Truly this man was the Son of God"* (see 15:37-39) — **Jesus' burial** (see 15:42-47) — Joseph of Arimathea receives Pilate's permission to take Jesus' body; *"And he bought fine linen, and took him down, and wrapped him in the linen, and laid him in a sepulchre which was hewn out of a rock, and rolled a stone unto the door of the sepulchre"* (see 15:46).

Mark 16: **Jesus' resurrection** (see 16:1-8) — *"And when the Sabbath was past, Mary Magdalene, and Mary the mother of James, and Salome, had brought sweet spices, that they might come and anoint him"* (see 16:1) — *"And entering into the sepulchre, they saw a young man sitting on the right side, clothed in a long white garment; and they were affrighted. And he saith unto them, Be not affrighted: Ye seek Jesus of Nazareth, which was crucified: he is risen;..."* (see 16:5-6) — **Jesus' appearances after His resurrection** (see 16:9-18) — Jesus appears to the eleven disciples and says:

July 12 (Day 193), Memory Verses #520 & #521
Mark 16:15-16:

15. ...GO YE INTO ALL THE WORLD, AND PREACH THE GOSPEL TO EVERY CREATURE.

16. HE THAT BELIEVETH AND IS BAPTIZED SHALL BE SAVED;
BUT HE THAT BELIEVETH NOT SHALL BE DAMNED.

— **Jesus' ascension** — *"So then after the Lord had spoken unto them,* **he was received up into heaven,** *and sat on the right hand of God.* **And they went forth, and preached every where,** *the Lord working with them, and confirming the word with signs following. Amen"* (see 16:19-20).

MARK 12:29-31:

29. AND JESUS ANSWERED HIM,
THE FIRST OF ALL COMMANDMENTS IS,
HEAR, O ISRAEL;
THE LORD OUR GOD IS ONE LORD:
30. AND THOU SHALT LOVE THE LORD THY GOD
WITH ALL THY HEART,
AND WITH ALL THY SOUL,
AND WITH ALL THY MIND,
AND WITH ALL THY STRENGTH:
THIS IS THE FIRST COMMANDMENT.
31. AND THE SECOND IS LIKE, NAMELY THIS,
THOU SHALT LOVE THY NEIGHBOUR AS THYSELF.
THERE IS NONE OTHER COMMANDMENT
GREATER THAN THESE.

LUKE

Introduction: Most scholars agree that Luke, a Gentile physician, wrote the books of Luke and Acts. Luke ends with Jesus' ascension into heaven, and Acts begins with the ascension. Both books are addressed to Theophilus, but they are meant to be widely read. The book of Luke was probably written around 60 A.D., although some believe it was written as late as 80 A.D. Luke was not an eyewitness of Jesus but was a dedicated companion of Paul. The book of Luke emphasizes the humanity of Jesus. Luke has 24 chapters.

Key Contents and Key Memory Verses with Study Dates

<u>Note:</u> The key memory verses from Luke 4:4 to Luke 23:43 contain sayings of Jesus.

<u>Luke 1:</u> **Luke explains to Theophilus his reasons for writing this book** (see 1:1-4) — **Gabriel appears to the priest Zecharias (Zechariah, NIV)** (see 1:5-25) — *"But the angel said unto him, Fear not, Zacharias: for thy prayer is heard; and thy wife Elisabeth (Elizabeth, NIV) shall bear thee a son, and thou shalt call his name John"* (see 1:13) — **Gabriel causes Zechariah to be unable to speak until John is born** since Zechariah did not initially believe his message — **Gabriel appears to Mary** (see 1:26-56) — *"And the angel said unto her, Fear not, Mary: for thou hast found favour with God. And behold, thou shalt conceive in thy womb, and bring forth a son, and shalt call his name JESUS"* (see 1:30-31) — *"Then said Mary unto the angel, How shall this be, seeing I know not a man? And the angel answered and said unto her, The Holy Ghost shall come upon thee, and the power of the Highest shall over-shadow thee: therefore also that holy thing which shall be born of thee shall be called the Son of God. And, behold thy cousin Elisabeth, she hath also conceived a son in her old age: and this is the sixth month with her, who was called barren"* (see 1:34-36).

July 13 (Day 194), Memory Verse #522
<u>Luke 1:37:</u>

FOR WITH GOD NOTHING SHALL BE IMPOSSIBLE.

July 13 (Day 194), Memory Verses #523 to #525
<u>Luke 1:46-48:</u>

46. AND MARY SAID, MY SOUL DOTH MAGNIFY THE LORD,

47. AND MY SPIRIT HATH REJOICED IN GOD MY SAVIOUR.

48. FOR HE HATH REGARDED THE LOW ESTATE OF HIS HANDMAIDEN:
FOR, BEHOLD, FROM HENCEFORTH ALL GENERATIONS SHALL CALL ME BLESSED.

— **John the Baptist is born** (see 1:57-66) — **Zechariah is filled with the Holy Ghost and prophesies** (see 1:67-80):

July 14 (Day 195), Memory Verses #526 & #527
<u>Luke 1:76-77:</u>

76. AND THOU, CHILD, SHALT BE CALLED THE PROPHET OF THE HIGHEST:
FOR THOU SHALT GO BEFORE THE FACE OF THE LORD TO PREPARE HIS WAYS;

77. TO GIVE KNOWLEDGE OF SALVATION UNTO HIS PEOPLE
BY THE REMISSION OF THEIR SINS.

Luke 2: "The Christmas Story" (Jesus' birth in Bethlehem and the shepherds' visit).

July 15-July 22 (Days 196-203), Memory Verses #528 to #547
Luke 2:1-20:
(The Christmas Story)

1. AND IT CAME TO PASS IN THOSE DAYS,
THAT THERE WENT OUT A DECREE FROM CAESAR AUGUSTUS,
THAT ALL THE WORLD SHOULD BE TAXED.
2. (AND THIS TAXING WAS FIRST MADE WHEN CYRENIUS WAS GOVERNOR OF SYRIA.)
3. AND ALL WENT TO BE TAXED, EVERY ONE INTO HIS OWN CITY.
4. AND JOSEPH ALSO WENT UP FROM GALILEE, OUT OF THE CITY OF NAZARETH,
INTO JUDEA, UNTO THE CITY OF DAVID, WHICH IS CALLED BETHLEHEM;
(BECAUSE HE WAS OF THE HOUSE AND LINEAGE OF DAVID:)
5. TO BE TAXED WITH MARY HIS ESPOUSED WIFE, BEING GREAT WITH CHILD.
6. AND SO IT WAS, THAT, WHILE THEY WERE THERE,
THE DAYS WERE ACCOMPLISHED THAT SHE SHOULD BE DELIVERED.
7. AND SHE BROUGHT FORTH HER FIRSTBORN SON,
AND WRAPPED HIM IN SWADDLING CLOTHES, AND LAID HIM IN A MANGER;
BECAUSE THERE WAS NO ROOM FOR THEM IN THE INN.
8. AND THERE WERE IN THE SAME COUNTRY SHEPHERDS ABIDING IN THE FIELD,
KEEPING WATCH OVER THEIR FLOCK BY NIGHT.
9. AND, LO, THE ANGEL OF THE LORD CAME UPON THEM,
AND THE GLORY OF THE LORD SHONE ROUND ABOUT THEM:
AND THEY WERE SORE AFRAID.
10. AND THE ANGEL SAID UNTO THEM, FEAR NOT:
FOR, BEHOLD, I BRING YOU GOOD TIDINGS OF GREAT JOY,
WHICH SHALL BE TO ALL PEOPLE.
11. FOR UNTO YOU IS BORN THIS DAY IN THE CITY OF DAVID
A SAVIOUR, WHICH IS CHRIST THE LORD.
12. AND THIS SHALL BE A SIGN UNTO YOU;
YE SHALL FIND THE BABE WRAPPED IN SWADDLING CLOTHES,
LYING IN A MANGER.
13. AND SUDDENLY THERE WAS WITH THE ANGEL A MULTITUDE
OF THE HEAVENLY HOST PRAISING GOD, AND SAYING,
14. GLORY TO GOD IN THE HIGHEST,
AND ON EARTH PEACE, GOOD WILL TOWARD MEN.
15. AND IT CAME TO PASS,
AS THE ANGELS WERE GONE AWAY FROM THEM INTO HEAVEN,
THE SHEPHERDS SAID ONE TO ANOTHER,
LET US NOW GO EVEN UNTO BETHLEHEM,
AND SEE THIS THING WHICH IS COME TO PASS,
WHICH THE LORD HATH MADE KNOWN UNTO US.
16. AND THEY CAME WITH HASTE, AND FOUND MARY AND JOSEPH,
AND THE BABE LYING IN A MANGER.
17. AND WHEN THEY HAD SEEN IT, THEY MADE KNOWN ABROAD
THE SAYING WHICH WAS TOLD THEM CONCERNING THIS CHILD.
18. AND ALL THEY THAT HEARD IT WONDERED
AT THOSE THINGS WHICH WERE TOLD THEM BY THE SHEPHERDS.
19. BUT MARY KEPT ALL THESE THINGS, AND PONDERED THEM IN HER HEART.
20. AND THE SHEPHERDS RETURNED,
GLORIFYING AND PRAISING GOD FOR ALL THE THINGS THEY HAD HEARD AND SEEN,
AS IT WAS TOLD UNTO THEM.

— **Simeon and Anna see baby Jesus in the temple** (see 2:21-38) — After searching three days, **Jesus' parents find twelve-year-old Jesus in the temple having discussions with the doctors** (see 2:39-52) — *"And when they saw him they were amazed: and his mother said unto him, Son, why hast thou thus dealt with us? Behold, thy father and I have sought thee sorrowing. And he said unto them, How is it that ye sought me? wist ye not that I must be about my Father's business?"* (see 2:48-49).

July 23 (Day 204), Memory Verse #548
<u>Luke 2:52</u>:

AND JESUS INCREASED IN WISDOM AND STATURE,
AND IN FAVOUR WITH GOD AND MAN.

<u>**Luke 3**</u>:   **John the Baptist baptizes Jesus and is imprisoned by Herod** (see 3:1-22) — At Jesus' baptism the Holy Ghost descends upon Him.

July 23 (Day 204), Memory Verse #549
<u>Luke 3:22</u>:

AND THE HOLY GHOST DESCENDED IN A BODILY SHAPE LIKE A DOVE UPON HIM,
AND A VOICE CAME FROM HEAVEN, WHICH SAID,
THOU ART MY BELOVED SON; IN THEE I AM WELL PLEASED.

— **Jesus' genealogy, beginning with Jesus and going back to Adam** (see 3:23-38).

<u>**Luke 4**</u>:   **Jesus in the wilderness** (see 4:1-13) — *"And Jesus being full of the Holy Ghost returned from Jordan, and was led by the Spirit into the wilderness, Being forty days tempted of the devil. And in those days he did eat nothing: and when they were ended, he afterward hungered. And the devil said unto him, If thou be the Son of God, command this stone that it be made bread"* (see 4:1-3).

July 23 (Day 204), Memory Verse #550
<u>Luke 4:4</u>:

AND JESUS ANSWERED HIM SAYING, IT IS WRITTEN,
MAN SHALL NOT LIVE BY BREAD ALONE, BUT BY EVERY WORD OF GOD.

— *"And the devil said unto him, All this power will I give thee, and the glory of them: for that is delivered unto me; and to whomsoever I will I give it. If thou therefore wilt worship me, all shall be thine"* (see 4:6-7).

July 24 (Day 205), Memory Verse #551
<u>Luke 4:8</u>:

AND JESUS ANSWERED AND SAID UNTO HIM,
THOU SHALT WORSHIP THE LORD THY GOD, AND HIM ONLY SHALT THOU SERVE.

— *"And he brought him to Jerusalem, and set him on a pinnacle of the temple, and said unto him, If thou be the Son of God, cast thyself down from hence: For it is written, He shall give his angels charge over thee, to keep thee: And in their hands they shall bear thee up, lest at any time thou dash thy foot against a stone"* (see 4:9-11).

July 24 (Day 205), Memory Verse #552
<u>Luke 4:12</u>:

AND JESUS ANSWERING SAID UNTO HIM, IT IS SAID,
THOU SHALT NOT TEMPT THE LORD THY GOD.

— Jesus is rejected in His hometown, Nazareth (see 4:14-30) — Jesus shows how Isaiah 61:1 refers to Himself: *"The Spirit of the Lord is upon me, because he hath anointed me to preach the gospel to the poor; he hath sent me to heal the brokenhearted, to preach deliverance to the captives, and recovering of sight to the blind, to set at liberty them that are bruised"* (see 4:18) **— Jesus drives out a devil's spirit from a man** (see 4:31-37) **— Jesus heals Simon's mother-in-law who has been sick with fever, and he heals many others** (see 4:38-44).

Luke 5: Jesus preaches from Simon's boat and helps the fishermen miraculously catch fish (see 5:1-11) — The fishermen had not caught any fish all night; then Jesus told them to let down their nets, and *"...they inclosed a great multitude of fishes: and their net brake"* (see 5:6) — **Simon, James, and John follow Jesus — A leper is healed** (see 5:12-16) **— A man with palsy is let down through a housetop to Jesus and is healed** (see 5:17-26) **— Jesus calls Levi and dines with sinners and tax collectors** (see 5:27-32) — *"But their scribes and Pharisees murmured against his disciples, saying, Why do ye eat and drink with publicans and sinners? And Jesus answering said unto them, they that are whole need not a physician; but they that are sick. I came not to call the righteous, but sinners to repentance"* (see 5:30-32) — **The scribes and Pharisees question Jesus about fasting** (see 5:33-35) **— Parable of a new garment, old garment, new wine and old wine bottles** (see 5:36-39).

Luke 6: Jesus' disciples eat grain from the field on the Sabbath (see 6:1-5) **— Jesus heals a man's withered hand on the Sabbath and is scrutinized by the scribes and Pharisees** (see 6:6-11) — *"Then said Jesus unto them, I will ask you one thing; Is it lawful on the sabbath days to do good, or to do evil? To save life, or to destroy it?"* (see 6:9) — ***"And it came to pass in those days, that he went out into a mountain to pray,*** *and continued all night in prayer to God. And when it was day,* ***he called unto him his disciples: and of them he chose twelve,*** *whom also he named apostles;* ***Simon*** *(whom he also names Peter,) and* ***Andrew*** *his brother,* ***James*** *and* ***John***, ***Philip*** *and* ***Bartholomew***, ***Matthew*** *and* ***Thomas***, ***James*** *the son of Alpheus, and* ***Simon*** *called Zelotes, And* ***Judas*** *the brother of James, and* ***Judas Iscariot***, *which also was the traitor"* (see 6:12-16) — **Jesus' great sermon** in this chapter (see 6:17-49) is most likely the same occasion as Jesus' "Sermon on the Mount" recorded in Matthew 5-7.

July 25 (Day 206), Memory Verses #553 to #555
Luke 6:27-29:

27. ...LOVE YOUR ENEMIES, DO GOOD TO THEM WHICH HATE YOU,

28. BLESS THEM THAT CURSE YOU,
AND PRAY FOR THEM WHICH DESPITEFULLY USE YOU.

29. AND UNTO HIM THAT SMITETH THEE ON THE ONE CHEEK OFFER ALSO THE OTHER;
AND HIM THAT TAKETH AWAY THY CLOKE FORBID NOT TO TAKE THY COAT ALSO.

July 25 (Day 206), Memory Verse #556
Luke 6:31:
(The Golden Rule)

AND AS YE WOULD THAT MEN SHOULD DO TO YOU,
DO YE ALSO TO THEM LIKEWISE.

— *"For if ye love them which love you, what thank have ye? For sinners also love those that love them"* (see 6:32).

July 26 (Day 207), Memory Verses # 557 to #560
Luke 6:35-38:

35. BUT LOVE YE YOUR ENEMIES, AND DO GOOD, AND LEND,
HOPING FOR NOTHING AGAIN; AND YOUR REWARD SHALL BE GREAT,
AND YE SHALL BE THE CHILDREN OF THE HIGHEST:
FOR HE IS KIND UNTO THE UNTHANKFUL AND TO THE EVIL.

36. BE YE THEREFORE MERCIFUL, AS YOUR FATHER ALSO IS MERCIFUL.

37. JUDGE NOT, AND YE SHALL NOT BE JUDGED:
CONDEMN NOT, AND YE SHALL NOT BE CONDEMNED:
FORGIVE, AND YE SHALL BE FORGIVEN:

38. GIVE, AND IT SHALL BE GIVEN UNTO YOU; ...

July 27 (Day 208), Memory Verse #561
Luke 6:41:

AND WHY BEHOLDEST THOU THE MOTE (speck of sawdust, NIV)
THAT IS IN THY BROTHER'S EYE,
BUT PERCEIVETH NOT THE BEAM (plank, NIV) THAT IS IN THINE OWN EYE?

July 27 (Day 208), Memory Verse #562
Luke 6:45:

A GOOD MAN OUT OF THE GOOD TREASURE OF HIS HEART
BRINGETH FORTH THAT WHICH IS GOOD; ...

— Jesus tells the story of a wise man building on a rock foundation and a foolish man building on unstable earth (see 6:47-49).

Luke 7: **Jesus heals a centurion's slave** (see 7:1-10) — **Jesus raises a widow's son from the dead** (see 7:11-17) — **John the Baptist sends his disciples to ask Jesus if He is the Messiah predicted by the prophets** (see 7:18-23) — *"Art thou he that should come? Or look we for another?"* (see 7:20) — *"Then Jesus answering said unto them, Go your way, and tell John what things ye have seen and heard; how that the blind see, the lame walk, the lepers are cleansed, the deaf hear, the dead are raised, to the poor the gospel is preached"* (see 7:22) — **Jesus teaches the people about John the Baptist's ministry** (see 7:24-35) — **A woman who is known as a sinner anoints Jesus' feet with alabaster, and Jesus teaches Simon by using a story of a creditor and debtors** (see 7:36-50); *"And he said to the woman, Thy faith hath saved thee; go in peace"* (see 7:50).

Luke 8: **People minister to Jesus** (see 8:1-3) — **Parable of the sower** (see 8:4-15) — The sown seed *"...on the good ground are they which in an honest and good heart, having heard the word, keep it, and bring forth fruit with patience"* (see 8:15) — **Parable of a lighted candle which is put on a candlestick to be seen rather than hidden** (see 8:16-18) — *"For nothing is secret, that shall not be made manifest; neither any thing hid, that shall not be known and come abroad"* (see 8:17) — **Jesus' mother and brethren come to visit him** (see 8:19-21) — He says:

July 28 (Day 209), Memory Verse #563
Luke 8:21:

...MY MOTHER AND MY BRETHREN ARE THESE WHICH HEAR THE WORD OF GOD, AND DO IT.

— Jesus calms the sea (see 8:22-25) — **Jesus casts demons out of a man into swine** (see 8:26-39) — **A hemorrhaging woman is healed, and Jairus's daughter is resurrected** (see 8:40-56).

Luke 9: **Jesus sends out his twelve disciples** (see 9:1-6)*"...to preach the kingdom of God, and to heal the sick"* (see 9:2) — **Herod is perplexed as to who Jesus is** (see 9:7-9) — **Jesus miraculously feeds the multitude, 5000 men plus women and children** (see 9:10-17), with only *"...five loaves and two fishes..."* (see 9:13) — There are 12 baskets of leftover food — **Jesus asks the disciples, "...*But whom say ye that I am?*"** (see 9:18-27) — *"Peter answering said, The Christ of God"* (see 9:20) — Jesus tells them:

July 28 (Day 209), Memory Verse #564
Luke 9:23:

...IF ANY MAN WILL COME AFTER ME,
LET HIM DENY HIMSELF, AND TAKE UP HIS CROSS DAILY,
AND FOLLOW ME.

— **Mount of Transfiguration** (see 9:28-36) — *"And it came to pass about eight days after these sayings, he took Peter and John and James, and went up into a mountain to pray. And as he prayed, the fashion of his countenance was altered, and his raiment was white and glistering. And behold, there talked with him two men, which were Moses and Elias (Elijah, NIV)"* (see 9:28-30) — *"And there came a voice out of the cloud, saying, This is my beloved Son: hear him"* (see 9:35) — **Jesus honors a man's request to cast out a demon from his son** (see 9:37-45) — **Jesus** *"...took a child, and set him by him, And said unto them..."* (see 9:46-48):

July 29 (Day 210), Memory Verse #565
Luke 9:48:

...WHOSOEVER SHALL RECEIVE THIS CHILD IN MY NAME RECEIVETH ME:
AND WHOSOEVER SHALL RECEIVE ME RECEIVETH HIM THAT SENT ME:
FOR HE THAT IS LEAST AMONG YOU ALL, THE SAME SHALL BE GREAT.

The disciples do not allow a man to cast out devils in Jesus' name, but Jesus says, "...*he that is not against us is for us*" (see 9:50) — **Jesus is disappointed when the Samaritans reject Him** (see 9:51-56) — **Jesus explains the commitment of following Him** (see 9:57-62) — *"...No man, having put his hand to the plough, and looking back, is fit for the kingdom of God"* (see 9:62).

Luke 10: **Jesus sends out 70 more disciples** (see 10:1-24).

July 29 (Day 210), Memory Verse #566
Luke 10:2:

...THE HARVEST TRULY IS GREAT, BUT THE LABOURERS ARE FEW:
PRAY YE THEREFORE THE LORD OF THE HARVEST,
THAT HE WOULD SEND FORTH LABOURERS INTO HIS HARVEST.

— **A lawyer asks Jesus how to inherit eternal life** — *"And, behold, a certain lawyer stood up, and tempted him, saying Master, what shall I do to inherit eternal life? He said unto him, What is written in the law? How readest thou? And he answering said, Thou shalt love the Lord thy God with all thy heart, and with all thy soul, and with all thy strength, and with all thy mind; and thy neighbour as thyself. And he said unto him, Thou hast answered right: this do, and thou shalt live"* (see 10:25-28) — **Jesus proceeds to tell the parable of "The Good Samaritan" to this lawyer** (see 10:29-37) — *"Which now of these three, thinkest thou, was neighbour unto him that fell among the thieves? And he said, He that shewed mercy on him. Then said Jesus unto him, Go, and do thou likewise"* (see 10:36-37) — **Jesus visits in the home of Mary and Martha** (see 10:38-42).

Luke 11: "The Lord's Prayer" (see 11:1-4) — A longer version of "The Lord's Prayer" (Matthew 6:9-13) is quoted in this book — **Jesus teaches on prayer** (see 11:5-13):

July 30 (Day 211), Memory Verses #567 & #568
Luke 11:9-10:

9. ...ASK, AND IT SHALL BE GIVEN YOU;
SEEK, AND YE SHALL FIND;
KNOCK, AND IT SHALL BE OPENED UNTO YOU.

10. FOR EVERY ONE THAT ASKETH RECEIVETH;
AND HE THAT SEEKETH FINDETH;
AND TO HIM THAT KNOCKETH IT SHALL BE OPENED.

July 30 (Day 211), Memory Verse #569
Luke 11:13:

IF YE THEN, BEING EVIL, KNOW HOW TO GIVE GOOD GIFTS UNTO YOUR CHILDREN:
HOW MUCH MORE SHALL YOUR HEAVENLY FATHER
GIVE THE HOLY SPIRIT TO THEM THAT ASK HIM?

— **Jesus teaches those who doubt Him** (see 11:14-36) — People accuse Jesus by saying, *"...He casteth out devils through Beelzebub the chief of the devils"* (see 11:15) — Jesus warns that a demon will return to a clean body with more demons (see 11:24-26) — Jesus teaches that when your body is filled with light, it can be compared to a candle put on a candlestick for others to see (see 11:33-36) — **Jesus calls the scribes and Pharisees hypocrites** (see 11:37-54) — Jesus strongly speaks against the Pharisees and teachers of the law who are *"Laying wait for him, and seeking to catch something out of his mouth, that they might accuse him"* (see 11:54).

Luke 12: Jesus warns the disciples of hypocrisy (see 12:1-12) — *"...Beware ye of the leaven of the Pharisees, which is hypocrisy"* (see 12:1) — *"...Whoever shall confess me before men, him shall the Son of man also confess before the angels of God:"* (see 12:8).

July 31 (Day 212), Memory Verse #570
Luke 12:15:

...TAKE HEED, AND BEWARE OF COVETOUSNESS:
FOR A MAN'S LIFE CONSISTETH NOT IN THE ABUNDANCE
OF THE THINGS WHICH HE POSSESSETH.

— **Jesus continues to teach against covetousness** (see 12:13-15) — **Parable of the rich man** (see 12:16-21) — **Jesus uses illustrations of the raven, lilies, and grass to show how God provides for His flock** (see 12:22-34).

July 31 (Day 212), Memory Verse #571
Luke 12:31:

BUT RATHER SEEK YE THE KINGDOM OF GOD;
AND ALL THESE THINGS SHALL BE ADDED UNTO YOU.

July 31 (Day 212), Memory Verse #572
Luke 12:34:

FOR WHERE YOUR TREASURE IS, THERE WILL YOUR HEART BE ALSO.

— **Blessed are the faithful** (see 12:35-48) — *"Blessed are those servants, whom the lord when he cometh shall find watching:..."* (see 12:37).

August 1 (Day 213), Memory Verse #573
Luke 12:40:

BE YE THEREFORE READY ALSO:
FOR THE SON OF MAN COMETH AT AN HOUR WHEN YE THINK NOT.

—**Jesus scolds the people for not recognizing the presence of God's Kingdom** (see 12:49-59).

Luke 13: Jesus urges people to repent (see 13:1-5) — **Parable of a man with an unfruitful fig tree** (see 13:6-9) — **Jesus heals a lady** (see 13:10-17) who *"...was bowed together, and could in no wise lift up herself"* (see 13:11) — The ruler of the synagogue is critical of Jesus since He healed this lady on the Sabbath — **Jesus compares the Kingdom of God to a mustard seed and leaven** (see 13:18-21) — **Jesus teaches to live for Him** (see 13:22-30) — *"Strive to enter in at the strait gate: for many, I say unto you will seek to enter in, and shall not be able"* (see 13:24) — **Jesus mourns for Jerusalem** (see 13:31-35) — *"O Jerusalem, Jerusalem, which killest the prophets, and stonest them that are sent unto thee; how often would I have gathered thy children together, as a hen doth gather her brood under her wings, and ye would not! Behold, your house is left unto you desolate: and verily I say unto you, Ye shall not see me, until the time come when ye shall say, Blessed is he that cometh in the name of the Lord"* (see 13:34-35).

Luke 14: On the Sabbath, Jesus heals a man with dropsy (see 14:1-6) — Jesus asks the lawyers and the Pharisees, *"...Which of you shall have an ass or an ox fallen into a pit, and will not straightway pull him out on the sabbath day?"* (see 14:5) — **Parable of a man's seating location at a wedding** (see 14:7-11) — **Jesus teaches to invite the poor to a feast** (see 14:12-14) — **Parable of a man who makes a great supper** (see 14:15-24) — **Jesus teaches about the costs of discipleship** (see 14:25-35).

August 1 (Day 213), Memory Verse #574
Luke 14:27:

AND WHOSOEVER DOTH NOT BEAR HIS CROSS AND COME AFTER ME,
CANNOT BE MY DISCIPLE.

August 1 (Day 213), Memory Verse #575
Luke 14:33:

...WHOSOEVER HE BE OF YOU THAT FORSAKETH NOT ALL THAT HE HATH,
HE CANNOT BE MY DISCIPLE.

Luke 15: Parable of the lost sheep (see 15:1-7).

August 2 (Day 214), Memory Verse #576
Luke 15:7:

...JOY SHALL BE IN HEAVEN OVER ONE SINNER THAT REPENTETH,
MORE THAN OVER NINETY AND NINE JUST PERSONS, WHICH NEED NO REPENTANCE.

— **Parable of the lost coin** (see 15:8-10) — **Parable of the lost son**, also known as the parable of "The Prodigal Son" (see 15:11-32) — When the lost son returns home, he says, *"...Father, I have sinned against heaven, and in thy sight, and am no more worthy to be called thy son. But the father said to his servants, Bring forth the best robe, and put it on him; and put a ring on his hand, and shoes on his feet: And bring hither the fatted calf, and kill it; and let us eat, and be merry: For this my son was dead and is alive again; he was lost, and is found. And they began to be merry"* (see 15:21-24).

<u>Luke 16</u>: **Parable of the steward** (see 16:1-13).

August 2 (Day 214), Memory Verse #577
<u>Luke 16:10</u>:

HE THAT IS FAITHFUL IN THAT WHICH IS LEAST IS FAITHFUL ALSO IN MUCH: ...

August 2 (Day 214), Memory Verse #578
<u>Luke 16:13</u>:

NO SERVANT CAN SERVE TWO MASTERS:
FOR EITHER HE WILL HATE THE ONE, AND LOVE THE OTHER;
OR ELSE HE WILL HOLD TO THE ONE, AND DESPISE THE OTHER.
YE CANNOT SERVE GOD AND MAMMON (Money, NIV).

— **Jesus teaches the Pharisees that God knows their hearts; Jesus also mentions adultery** (see 16:14-18) — **Parable of the rich man and Lazarus** (see 16:19-31).

<u>Luke 17</u>: **Woe to the one who causes others to sin** (see 17:1-4) — *"...It were better for him that a millstone were hanged about his neck, and he be cast into the sea, than that he should offend one of these little ones"* (see 17:2) — **Jesus uses a mustard seed comparison to teach the apostles about faith.**

August 3 (Day 215), Memory Verse #579
<u>Luke 17:6</u>:

...IF YE HAD FAITH AS A GRAIN OF MUSTARD SEED,
YE MIGHT SAY UNTO THIS SYCAMINE TREE, BE THOU PLUCKED UP BY THE ROOT,
AND BE THOU PLANTED IN THE SEA; AND IT SHOULD OBEY YOU.

— **Jesus teaches about being a servant of Christ** (see 17:7-10) — **Ten lepers are healed, and only one expresses thanks** (see 17:11-19) — **Jesus teaches about the Kingdom of God and the coming of the Son of man** (see 17:20-37) — *"...the kingdom of God is within you"* (see 17:21).

August 3 (Day 215), Memory Verse #580
<u>Luke 17:33</u>:

WHOSOEVER SHALL SEEK TO SAVE HIS LIFE SHALL LOSE IT;
AND WHOSOEVER SHALL LOSE HIS LIFE SHALL PRESERVE IT.

— *"...the one shall be taken and the other shall be left"* (see 17:34).

<u>Luke 18</u>: **Parable of a widow and an unrighteous judge** (see 18:1-8) — *"...men ought always to pray, and not to faint;"* (see 18:1) — **Parable of the Pharisee's prayer compared to the tax collector's prayer** (see 18:9-14).

August 3 (Day 215), Memory Verse #581
<u>Luke 18:14</u>:

...FOR EVERY ONE THAT EXALTETH HIMSELF SHALL BE ABASED:
AND HE THAT HUMBLETH HIMSELF SHALL BE EXALTED.

— **Jesus tells the disciples to let the children come to Him** (see 18:15-17):

August 4 (Day 216), Memory Verses #582 & #583
Luke 18:16-17:

16. ...SUFFER LITTLE CHILDREN TO COME UNTO ME,
AND FORBID THEM NOT: FOR OF SUCH IS THE KINGDOM OF GOD.

17. VERILY I SAY UNTO YOU,
WHOSOEVER SHALL NOT RECEIVE THE KINGDOM OF GOD AS A LITTLE CHILD
SHALL IN NO WISE ENTER THEREIN.

— **A rich ruler asks Jesus how to inherit eternal life** (see 18:18-30).

August 5 (Day 217), Memory Verse #584
Luke 18:27:

...THE THINGS WHICH ARE IMPOSSIBLE WITH MEN ARE POSSIBLE WITH GOD.

— **Jesus speaks to the disciples concerning His death** (see 18:31-34) — **Jesus heals a blind man who begs for mercy** (see 18:35-43).

Luke 19: Story of Zaccheus (see 19:1-10).

August 5 (Day 217), Memory Verse #585
Luke 19:10:

FOR THE SON OF MAN IS COME TO SEEK AND TO SAVE THAT WHICH WAS LOST.

— **Parable of the nobleman who gives ten pounds (minas, NIV) of money to each of his slaves** (see 19:11-27).

August 5 (Day 217), Memory Verse #586
Luke 19:26:

...UNTO EVERYONE WHICH HATH SHALL BE GIVEN;
AND FROM HIM THAT HATH NOT,
EVEN THAT HE HATH SHALL BE TAKEN AWAY FROM HIM.

— **Jesus' entry into Jerusalem on a colt** (see 19:28-44) — *"...the whole multitude of the disciples began to rejoice and praise God with a loud voice for all the mighty works that they had seen; Saying, Blessed be the King that cometh in the name of the Lord: peace in heaven, and glory in the highest"* (see 19:37-38) — **Jesus casts sellers out of the temple** (see 19:45-48), *"Saying unto them, It is written, My house is the house of prayer: but ye have made it a den of thieves"* (see 19:46).

Luke 20: The religious leaders question Jesus' authority (see 20:1-8) — Jesus traps the chief priests, scribes, and elders by asking *"The baptism of John, was it from heaven, or by men?"* (see 20:4) — **Parable of the vineyard owner** (see 20:9-18) — Jesus says He is *"...The stone which the builders rejected, the same is become the head of the corner"* (see 20:17) — **Religious leaders try to trick Jesus with questions** (see 20:19-47): Should taxes be paid to Caesar? Whose wife will a woman be in the resurrection if she was married to seven brothers? How can Christ be David's son?

Luke 21: The poor widow's offering of two mites (see 21:1-4) — *"...Of a truth I say unto you, that this poor widow hath cast in more than they all: For all these have of their abundance cast in unto the offerings of God: but she of her penury (poverty, NIV) hath cast in all the living that she had"* (see 21:3-4) — **Future events** (see 21:5-38) **include the following:** the temple's destruction, imposters of Christ, wars, earthquakes, famines, pestilences, fearful sights, hatred, persecution, family and friends' betrayals, Jerusalem surrounded by armies, the ocean waves roaring, and signs in the sun, moon, and stars — *"And then shall they see the Son of man coming in a cloud with power and great glory"* (see 21:17) — **Parable of the fig tree and all trees** (see 21:29-31) — *"So likewise ye, when ye see these things come to pass, know ye that the kingdom of God is nigh at hand"* (see 21:31).

August 6 (Day 218), Memory Verse #587
Luke 21:33:

HEAVEN AND EARTH SHALL PASS AWAY: BUT MY WORDS SHALL NOT PASS AWAY.

— *"**Watch ye therefore, and pray always,** that ye may be accounted worthy to escape all these things that shall come to pass, and to stand before the Son of man"* (see 21:36).

Luke 22: Judas bargains with the religious leaders to betray Jesus (see 22:1-6) — **"The Lord's Supper" during the Passover** (see 22:7-38) — *"And he took bread, and gave thanks, and brake it, and gave unto them, saying , This is my body which is given for you: this do in remembrance of me. Likewise also the cup after supper, saying , This cup is the new testament (new covenant, NIV) in my blood, which is shed for you"* (see 22:19-20) — **Jesus tells Peter,** *"...the cock shall not crow this day, before that thou shalt thrice deny that thou knowest me"* (see 22:34) — **Prayer at the Mount of Olives** (see 22:39-46).

August 6 (Day 218), Memory Verse #588
Luke 22:42:

...FATHER, IF THOU BE WILLING, REMOVE THIS CUP FROM ME:
NEVERTHELESS NOT MY WILL, BUT THINE, BE DONE.

— **Jesus' arrest** (see 22:47-53) — Judas betrays Jesus, and during Jesus' arrest, *"... one of them smote the servant of the high priest, and cut off his right ear. And Jesus answered and said, Suffer ye thus far (No more of this, NIV). And he touched his ear, and healed him"* (see 22:50-51) — **Peter three times denies that he knows Jesus** (see 22:54-62) — *"And Peter went out, and wept bitterly"* (see 22:62) — **Jesus is mocked and beaten** (see 22:63-65) — **Jesus before the council of the elders, chief priests, and scribes** (see 22:66-71).

Luke 23: Jesus is taken before Pilate (see 23:1-5) — **Pilate sends Jesus to Herod** (see 23:6-12) — **Herod sends Jesus back to Pilate** (see 23:13-25) — Pilate desires to release Jesus, but the Jewish leaders want to release Barabbas and crucify Jesus — Pilate yields to their wishes — **Jesus' crucifixion** (see 23:26-49) — *"Then said Jesus, Father, forgive them; for they know not what they do. And they parted his raiment, and cast lots"* (see 23:34) — *"And a superscription also was written over him in letters of Greek, and Latin, and Hebrew, THIS IS THE KING OF THE JEWS"* (see 23:38) — **Two malefactors (criminals, NIV) are crucified with Christ** — One criminal mocks Jesus, but the other asks for Jesus to remember him:

August 7 (Day 219), Memory Verses # 589 & #590
Luke 23:42-43:

42. AND HE SAID UNTO JESUS, LORD,
REMEMBER ME WHEN THOU COMEST INTO THY KINGDOM.

43. AND JESUS SAID UNTO HIM, VERILY I SAY UNTO THEE,
TODAY SHALT THOU BE WITH ME IN PARADISE.

— **Jesus' death** — *"Father, into thy hands I commend my spirit: and having said thus, he gave up the ghost"* (see 23:46) — **Jesus' burial** (see 23:50-56) — Joseph of Arimathea takes the body of Jesus, wraps *"... it in linen, and laid it in a sepulchre that was hewn in stone, wherein never man before was laid"* (see 23:53).

Luke 24: Jesus' resurrection (see 24:1-12) — *"Now upon the first day of the week, very early in the morning, they came unto the sepulchre, bringing the spices which they had prepared, and certain others with them. And they found the stone rolled away from the sepulcher. And they entered in, and found not the body of the Lord Jesus. And it came to pass, as they were much perplexed thereabout, behold, two men stood by them in shining garments:"* (see 24:1-4).

August 8 (Day 220), Memory Verses #591 & #592
Luke 24:5-6:

5. ...THEY SAID UNTO THEM,
WHY SEEK YE THE LIVING AMONG THE DEAD?

6. HE IS NOT HERE, BUT IS RISEN: ...

— **Jesus appears to two men on the way to Emmaus** (see 24:13-35) — **Jesus appears to the disciples** (see 24:36-49) — *"Then opened he their understanding, that they might understand the scriptures, And said unto them, Thus it is written, and thus it behoved Christ to suffer, and to rise from the dead the third day: And that repentance and remission of sins should be preached in his name among all nations, beginning at Jerusalem. And ye are witnesses of these things"* (see 24:45-48) — **Jesus' ascension** (see 24:50-53) — *"And he led them out as far as to Bethany, and he lifted up his hands, and blessed them. And it came to pass, while he blessed them, he was parted from them, and carried up into heaven. And they worshipped him, and returned to Jerusalem with great joy: And were continually in the temple, praising and blessing God. Amen"* (see 24:50-53).

LUKE 1:37:

FOR WITH GOD NOTHING SHALL BE IMPOSSIBLE.

LUKE 6:27-28:

27. ...LOVE YOUR ENEMIES,
DO GOOD TO THEM WHICH HATE YOU,
28. BLESS THEM THAT CURSE YOU,
AND PRAY FOR THEM
WHICH DESPITEFULLY USE YOU.

JOHN

Introduction: It is widely accepted that John was written by the apostle John although some have suggested John the Elder. Others believe John the apostle and John the Elder are one in the same. The writer of John is also credited with the writing of the three epistles of John and the book of Revelation. Views on the date of writing vary from the 50's A.D. to around 90 A.D. John 20:31 states the main purpose for the writing of this book: *"But these"* (signs) *"are written, that ye might believe that Jesus is the Christ, the Son of God; and that believing ye might have life through his name."* There are many verses in John where Jesus states *"I am."* See 6:35 (*"...I am the bread of life..."*), 8:12 (*"...I am the light of the world..."*), 8:58 (*"...Before Abraham was, I am"*), 10:9 (*"I am the door..."*), 10:11 (*"I am the good shepherd..."*), 11:25 (*"...I am the resurrection..."*), 14:6 (*"...I am the way, the truth, and the life..."*), and 15:5 (*"I am the vine..."*). John has 21 chapters and is sometimes called "The Book of the Seven Signs" (seven miracles):

1) **Water is turned to wine — Chapter 2.**
2) **Nobleman's son is healed — Chapter 4.**
3) **Man by the Bethesda pool is healed — Chapter 5.**
4) **Multitude is fed — Chapter 6.**
5) **Jesus walks on water — Chapter 6.**
6) **A blind man is given sight — Chapter 9.**
7) **Lazarus is raised from the dead — Chapter 11.**

Key Contents and Key Memory Verses with Study Dates

Note: Beginning with John 2:19, the key memory verses are sayings of Jesus with the exceptions of John 3:30, 3:36, 20:31, and 21:25.

John 1: **"In the beginning was the Word"** (see 1:1-18).

August 9-10 (Days 221-222), Memory Verses #593 to #597
John 1:1-5:

1. IN THE BEGINNING WAS THE WORD,
AND THE WORD WAS WITH GOD, AND THE WORD WAS GOD.

2. THE SAME WAS IN THE BEGINNING WITH GOD.

3. ALL THINGS WERE MADE BY HIM;
AND WITHOUT HIM WAS NOT ANY THING MADE THAT WAS MADE.

4. IN HIM WAS LIFE; AND THE LIFE WAS THE LIGHT OF MEN.

5. AND THE LIGHT SHINETH IN DARKNESS;
AND THE DARKNESS COMPREHENDED IT NOT.

August 10 (Day 222), Memory Verse #598
John 1:10:

HE WAS IN THE WORLD, AND THE WORLD WAS MADE BY HIM,
AND THE WORLD KNEW HIM NOT.

August 11 (Day 223), Memory Verses #599 to #601
John 1:12-14:

12. **BUT** AS MANY AS RECEIVED HIM,
TO THEM GAVE HE POWER TO BECOME THE SONS OF GOD,
EVEN TO THEM THAT BELIEVE ON HIS NAME:

13. **WHICH** WERE BORN, NOT OF BLOOD, NOR OF THE WILL OF THE FLESH,
NOR OF THE WILL OF MAN, BUT OF GOD.

14. **AND** THE WORD WAS MADE FLESH, AND DWELT AMONG US,
(AND WE BEHELD HIS GLORY, THE GLORY AS OF THE ONLY BEGOTTEN OF THE FATHER,)
FULL OF GRACE AND TRUTH.

— *"For the law was given by Moses, but grace and truth came by Jesus Christ"* (see 1:17) —
John the Baptist speaks of Jesus and Jesus' baptism (see 1:19-34).

August 12 (Day 224), Memory Verse #602
John 1:29:

...**BEHOLD** THE LAMB OF GOD, WHICH TAKETH AWAY THE SIN OF THE WORLD.

— **John the Baptist** *"...bare record, saying, I saw the Spirit descending from heaven like a dove, and it abode upon him. And I knew him not: but he that sent me to baptize with water, the same said unto me, Upon whom thou shalt see the Spirit descending, and remaining on him, the same is he which baptizeth with the Holy Ghost. And I saw, and bare record that this is the Son of God"* (see 1:32-34) — **Jesus calls Andrew, Peter, Philip, and Nathanael** (see 1:35-51).

John 2: **Miracle of water turning to wine at the wedding in Cana** (see 2:1-11) — *"This beginning of miracles did Jesus in Cana of Galilee, and manifested forth his glory; and his disciples believed on him"* (see 2:11) — **Jesus cleanses the temple** (see 2:12-25) — Jesus says, *"...make not my Father's house an house of merchandise"* (see 2:16) — **Jesus foretells His resurrection:**

August 12 (Day 224), Memory Verse #603
John 2:19:

...**DESTROY** THIS TEMPLE, AND IN THREE DAYS I WILL RAISE IT UP.

John 3: **Nicodemus asks Jesus how to be born again** (see 3:1-21).

August 12 (Day 224), Memory Verse #604
John 3:3:

JESUS ANSWERED AND SAID UNTO HIM, VERILY, VERILY, I SAY UNTO THEE,
EXCEPT A MAN BE BORN AGAIN, HE CANNOT SEE THE KINGDOM OF GOD.

August 13 (Day 225), Memory Verses #605 to #607
John 3:16-18:

16. **FOR** GOD SO LOVED THE WORLD, THAT HE GAVE HIS ONLY BEGOTTEN SON,
THAT WHOSOEVER BELIEVETH IN HIM SHOULD NOT PERISH, BUT HAVE EVERLASTING LIFE.

17. **FOR** GOD SENT NOT HIS SON INTO THE WORLD TO CONDEMN THE WORLD,
BUT THAT THE WORLD THROUGH HIM MIGHT BE SAVED.

18. **HE** THAT BELIEVETH ON HIM IS NOT CONDEMNED:
BUT HE THAT BELIEVETH NOT IS CONDEMNED ALREADY,
BECAUSE HE HATH NOT BELIEVED IN THE NAME OF THE ONLY BEGOTTEN SON OF GOD.

— **John the Baptist testifies about Jesus** (see 3:22-36) — *"Ye yourselves bear me witness, that I said, I am not the Christ, but that I am sent before him"* (see 3:28).

August 13 (Day 225), Memory Verse #608
<u>John 3:30:</u>

HE MUST INCREASE, BUT I MUST DECREASE.

August 14 (Day 226), Memory Verse #609
<u>John 3:36:</u>

HE THAT BELIEVETH ON THE SON HATH EVERLASTING LIFE:
AND HE THAT BELIEVETH NOT THE SON SHALL NOT SEE LIFE;
BUT THE WRATH OF GOD ABIDETH ON HIM.

<u>John 4:</u> **Jesus tells a Samaritan woman how He can give her "living water"** (see 4:1-42) — Jesus says:

August 14 (Day 226), Memory Verse #610
<u>John 4:14:</u>

BUT WHOSOEVER DRINKETH OF THE WATER THAT I SHALL GIVE HIM
SHALL NEVER THIRST;
BUT THE WATER THAT I SHALL GIVE HIM SHALL BE IN HIM A WELL OF WATER
SPRINGING UP INTO EVERLASTING LIFE.

August 15 (Day 227), Memory Verses #611 to #612
<u>John 4:23-24:</u>

23. BUT THE HOUR COMETH, AND NOW IS,
WHEN THE TRUE WORSHIPPERS SHALL WORSHIP THE FATHER
IN SPIRIT AND IN TRUTH:
FOR THE FATHER SEEKETH SUCH TO WORSHIP HIM.

24. GOD IS A SPIRIT:
AND THEY THAT WORSHIP HIM MUST WORSHIP HIM IN SPIRIT AND IN TRUTH.

— **Jesus tells His disciples, "…I have meat to eat that ye know not of"** (see 4:32).

August 16 (Day 228), Memory Verses #613 to #615
<u>John 4:34-36:</u>

34. JESUS SAITH UNTO THEM,
MY MEAT IS TO DO THE WILL OF HIM THAT SENT ME, AND TO FINISH HIS WORK.

35. SAY NOT YE, THERE ARE YET FOUR MONTHS, AND THEN COMETH HARVEST?
BEHOLD, I SAY UNTO YOU, LIFT UP YOUR EYES,
AND LOOK ON THE FIELDS; FOR THEY ARE WHITE ALREADY TO HARVEST.

36. AND HE THAT REAPETH RECEIVETH WAGES,
AND GATHERETH FRUIT UNTO LIFE ETERNAL:
THAT BOTH HE THAT SOWETH AND HE THAT REAPETH MAY REJOICE TOGETHER.

— **Miracle of a nobleman's son being healed at Capernaum** (see 4:43-54) — *"Jesus saith unto him, Go thy way; thy son liveth. And the man believeth the word that Jesus had spoken unto him, and he went his way"* (see 4:50).

John 5: **Miracle of Jesus healing a man by the Bethesda pool** (see 5:1-18) — *"Jesus saith unto him, "Rise, take up thy bed, and walk. And immediately the man was made whole, and took up his bed, and walked: and on the same day was the sabbath"* (see 5:8-9) — **The Jews are angered at Jesus;** *"Therefore the Jews sought the more to kill him, because he not only had broken the sabbath, but said also that God was his Father, making himself equal with God"* (see 5:18) — **Jesus speaks to the angry Jews** (see 5:19-47).

August 17 (Day 229), Memory Verse #616
John 5:24:

VERILY, VERILY, I SAY UNTO YOU,
HE THAT HEARETH MY WORD, AND BELIEVETH ON HIM THAT SENT ME,
HATH EVERLASTING LIFE, AND SHALL NOT COME INTO CONDEMNATION;
BUT IS PASSED FROM DEATH UNTO LIFE.

John 6: **Miracle of feeding the multitude** (see 6:1-15) using *"...five barley loaves, and two small fishes..."* (see 6:9) — The number of men in the multitude is *"...about five thousand"* (see 6:10); this number does not include the women and children — **Miracle of Jesus walking on water** (see 6:16-21) — **Jesus teaches the people who find Him in Capernaum** (see 6:22-71):

August 17 (Day 229), Memory Verse #617
John 6:27:

LABOUR NOT FOR THE MEAT WHICH PERISHETH,
BUT FOR THAT MEAT WHICH ENDURETH UNTO EVERLASTING LIFE,
WHICH THE SON OF MAN SHALL GIVE UNTO YOU: FOR HIM HATH GOD THE FATHER SEALED.

August 18 (Day 230), Memory Verse #618
John 6:35:

AND JESUS SAID UNTO THEM, I AM THE BREAD OF LIFE;
HE THAT COMETH TO ME SHALL NEVER HUNGER;
AND HE THAT BELIEVETH ON ME SHALL NEVER THIRST.

August 18 (Day 230), Memory Verse #619
John 6:40:

AND THIS IS THE WILL OF HIM THAT SENT ME, THAT EVERY ONE WHICH SEETH THE SON,
AND BELIEVETH ON HIM, MAY HAVE EVERLASTING LIFE:
AND I WILL RAISE HIM UP AT THE LAST DAY.

August 19 (Day 231), Memory Verse #620
John 6:48:

I AM THAT BREAD OF LIFE.

August 19 (Day 231), Memory Verse #621
John 6:51:

I AM THE LIVING BREAD WHICH CAME DOWN FROM HEAVEN:
IF ANY MAN EAT OF THIS BREAD, HE SHALL LIVE FOR EVER:
AND THE BREAD THAT I WILL GIVE IS MY FLESH,
WHICH I WILL GIVE FOR THE LIFE OF THE WORLD.

August 19 (Day 231), Memory Verse #622
John 6:63:

IT IS THE SPIRIT THAT QUICKENETH; THE FLESH PROFITETH NOTHING:
THE WORDS THAT I SPEAK UNTO YOU, THEY ARE SPIRIT, AND THEY ARE LIFE.

— **Many disciples desert Jesus because they do not understand His teachings** — *"From that time many of his disciples went back, and walked no more with him. Then said Jesus unto the twelve, Will ye also go away? Then Simon Peter answered him, Lord, to whom shall we go? thou hast the words of eternal life. And we believe and are sure that thou art that Christ, the Son of the living God"* (see 6:66-69).

John 7:   **The Jewish leaders marvel at Jesus' knowledge as he speaks at the Feast of Tabernacles in Jerusalem** (see 7:1-53) — *"Then they sought to take him: but no man laid hands on him, because his hour was not yet come"* (see 7:30) — **Jesus continues teaching:**

August 20 (Day 232), Memory Verses #623 & #624
John 7:37-38:

37. ...IF ANY MAN THIRST, LET HIM COME UNTO ME, AND DRINK.

38. HE THAT BELIEVETH ON ME, AS THE SCRIPTURE HATH SAID,
OUT OF HIS BELLY SHALL FLOW RIVERS OF LIVING WATER.

John 8:   **The scribes and Pharisees bring to Jesus an adulterous woman** (see 8:1-11) — Jesus says:

August 20 (Day 232), Memory Verse #625
John 8:7:

...HE THAT IS WITHOUT SIN AMONG YOU, LET HIM FIRST CAST A STONE AT HER.

— **Jesus continues teaching** (see 8:12-59)**:**

August 21 (Day 233), Memory Verse #626
John 8:12:

...I AM THE LIGHT OF THE WORLD:
HE THAT FOLLOWETH ME SHALL NOT WALK IN DARKNESS,
BUT SHALL HAVE THE LIGHT OF LIFE.

August 21 (Day 233), Memory Verses #627 & #628
John 8:31-32:

31. ...IF YE CONTINUE IN MY WORD,
THEN ARE YE MY DISCIPLES INDEED;

32. AND YE SHALL KNOW THE TRUTH,
AND THE TRUTH SHALL MAKE YOU FREE.

August 22 (Day 234), Memory Verse #629
John 8:51:

VERILY, VERILY, I SAY UNTO YOU,
IF A MAN KEEP MY SAYING, HE SHALL NEVER SEE DEATH.

August 22 (Day 234), Memory Verse #630
John 8:58:

JESUS SAID UNTO THEM, VERILY, VERILY, I SAY UNTO YOU,
BEFORE ABRAHAM WAS, I AM.

— *"**Then took they up stones to cast at him:** but Jesus hid himself, and went out of the temple, going through the midst of them, and so passed by"* (see 8:59).

John 9: **Jesus heals a man, blind from birth, and teaches the people** (see 9:1-41) — *"Jesus answered, Neither hath this man sinned, nor his parents: but that the works of God should be made manifest in him. I must work the works of him that sent me...I am the light of the world. When he had thus spoken, he spat on the ground, and made clay of the spittle, and he anointed the eyes of the blind man with the clay, And said unto him, Go, wash in the pool of Siloam (which is by interpretation, Sent.) He went his way therefore, and washed, and came seeing"* (see 9:3-7).

August 23 (Day 235), Memory Verse #631
John 9:39:

...FOR JUDGMENT I AM COME INTO THE WORLD,
THAT THEY WHICH SEE NOT MIGHT SEE;
AND THAT THEY WHICH SEE MIGHT BE MADE BLIND.

John 10: **Jesus continues His teaching** (see 10:1-42) — *"Then Jesus said unto them again, Verily, verily, I say unto you, **I AM the door of the sheep"** (see 10:7).*

August 23 (Day 235), Memory Verses #632 to #634
John 10:9-11:

9. I AM THE DOOR: BY ME IF ANY MAN ENTER IN,
HE SHALL BE SAVED, AND SHALL GO IN AND OUT, AND FIND PASTURE.

10. THE THIEF COMETH NOT, BUT FOR TO STEAL, AND TO KILL, AND TO DESTROY:
I AM COME THAT THEY MIGHT HAVE LIFE,
AND THAT THEY MIGHT HAVE IT MORE ABUNDANTLY.

11. I AM THE GOOD SHEPHERD:
THE GOOD SHEPHERD GIVETH HIS LIFE FOR THE SHEEP.

August 24 (Day 236), Memory Verses #635 & #636
John 10:14-15:

14. I AM THE GOOD SHEPHERD,
AND KNOW MY SHEEP, AND AM KNOWN OF MINE.

15. AS THE FATHER KNOWETH ME, EVEN SO KNOW I THE FATHER:
AND I LAY DOWN MY LIFE FOR THE SHEEP.

— *"And it was at Jerusalem the feast of the dedication, and it was winter. And Jesus walked in the temple in Solomon's porch. **Then came the Jews round about him, and said unto him, How long dost thou make us to doubt? If thou be the Christ, tell us plainly.** Jesus answered them, I told you, and ye believed not: the works that I do in my Father's name, they bear witness of me"* (see 10:22-25).

August 25 (Day 237), Memory Verses #637 & #638
John 10:27-28:

27. MY SHEEP HEAR MY VOICE, AND I KNOW THEM, AND THEY FOLLOW ME:

28. AND I GIVE UNTO THEM ETERNAL LIFE; AND THEY SHALL NEVER PERISH,
NEITHER SHALL ANY MAN PLUCK THEM OUT OF MY HAND.

August 25 (Day 237), Memory Verse #639
John 10:30:

I AND MY FATHER ARE ONE.

— **Again the Jews** *"...sought again to take him: but he escaped out of their hand, And went away again beyond Jordan into the place where John at first baptized; and there he abode"* (see 10:39-40).

John 11: Miracle of Jesus raising Lazarus from the dead (see 11:1-57) — Jesus ministers to Mary and Martha because of their brother Lazarus' death — Jesus tells Martha**:**

August 26 (Day 238), Memory Verses #640 & #641
John 11:25-26:

25. **...I AM** THE RESURRECTION, AND THE LIFE:
HE THAT BELIEVETH IN ME, THOUGH HE WERE DEAD, YET SHALL HE LIVE:

26. **AND** WHOSOEVER LIVETH AND BELIEVETH IN ME SHALL NEVER DIE.
BELIEVEST THOU THIS?

Martha proclaims, *"...Yea, Lord: I believe that thou art the Christ, the Son of God, which should come into the world"* (see 11:27) — *"Jesus wept"* (see 11:35) — Jesus commands, *"Lazarus, come forth"* (see 11:43), and Lazarus arises from the dead — **The religious leaders are distraught since so many are believing in Jesus, and they conspire to kill Jesus — Caiaphas is unaware that his words are prophecy:** *"And one of them, named Caiaphas, being the high priest that same year, said unto them, Ye know nothing at all, Nor consider that it is expedient for us, that one man should die for the people, and that the whole nation perish not. And this spake he not of himself: but being high priest that year, he prophesied that Jesus should die for that nation; And not for that nation only, but that also he should gather together in one the children of God scattered abroad. Then from that day forth they took counsel together for to put him to death"* (see 11:49-53).

John 12: Mary anoints Jesus' feet (see 12:1-11) — *"Then took Mary a pound of ointment of spikenard, very costly, and anointed the feet of Jesus, and wiped his feet with her hair: and the house was filled with the odour of the ointment"* (see 12:3) — **Jesus' entry into Jerusalem on a colt** (see 12:12-19) — *"On the next day much people that were come to the feast, when they heard that Jesus was coming to Jerusalem, Took branches of palm trees, and went forth to meet him and cried, Hosanna: Blessed is the King of Israel that cometh in the name of the Lord"* (see 12:12-13) — **Jesus again teaches the people** (see 12:20-50).

August 27 (Day 239), Memory Verse #642
John 12:25:

HE THAT LOVETH HIS LIFE SHALL LOSE IT;
AND HE THAT HATETH HIS LIFE IN THIS WORLD SHALL KEEP IT UNTO LIFE ETERNAL.

August 27 (Day 239), Memory Verse #643
John 12:46:

I **AM** COME A LIGHT INTO THE WORLD,
THAT WHOSOEVER BELIEVETH ON ME SHOULD NOT ABIDE IN DARKNESS.

John 13: Jesus washes the apostles' feet after supper (see 13:1-20) — *"Now before the feast of the Passover, when Jesus knew that his hour was come that he should depart out of this world unto the Father, having loved his own which were in the world, he loved them to the end"* (see 13:1).

August 28 (Day 240), Memory Verses #644 & #645
John 13:14-15:

14. **IF** I THEN, YOUR LORD AND MASTER, HAVE WASHED YOUR FEET;
YE ALSO OUGHT TO WASH ONE ANOTHER'S FEET.

15. **FOR** I HAVE GIVEN YOU AN EXAMPLE, THAT YE SHOULD DO AS I HAVE DONE TO YOU.

— **Jesus predicts Judas will betray Him** (see 13:21-30) — *"...he was troubled in spirit, and testified, and said, Verily, verily, I say unto you, that one of you shall betray me"* (see 13:21) — **Jesus tells the disciples His time to be glorified is at hand** (see 13:31-38).

August 29 (Day 241), Memory Verses #646 & #647
John 13:34-35:

34. **A** NEW COMMANDMENT I GIVE UNTO YOU,
THAT YE LOVE ONE ANOTHER; AS I HAVE LOVED YOU,
THAT YE ALSO LOVE ONE ANOTHER.

35. **BY** THIS SHALL ALL MEN KNOW THAT YE ARE MY DISCIPLES,
IF YE HAVE LOVE ONE TO ANOTHER.

— *"Peter said unto him, Lord, why cannot I follow thee now? I will lay down my life for thy sake. Jesus answered him, Wilt thou lay down thy life for my sake? Verily, verily, I say unto thee, **The cock shall not crow, till thou hast denied me thrice"*** (see 13:37-38).

John 14: Jesus teaches about heaven, the Father, the Comforter (Holy Spirit), and Himself (see 14:1-31).

August 30 (Day 242), Memory Verses #648 to #650
John 14:1-3:

1. **LET** NOT YOUR HEART BE TROUBLED:
YE BELIEVE IN GOD, BELIEVE ALSO IN ME.

2. **IN** MY FATHER'S HOUSE ARE MANY MANSIONS:
IF IT WERE NOT SO, I WOULD HAVE TOLD YOU.
I GO TO PREPARE A PLACE FOR YOU.

3. **AND** IF I GO AND PREPARE A PLACE FOR YOU,
I WILL COME AGAIN, AND RECEIVE YOU UNTO MYSELF;
THAT WHERE I AM, THERE YE MAY BE ALSO.

August 31 (Day 243), Memory Verse #651
John 14:6:

...**I AM** THE WAY, THE TRUTH, AND THE LIFE;
NO MAN COMETH UNTO THE FATHER, BUT BY ME.

August 31 (Day 243), Memory Verses #652 to #654
John 14:13-15:

13. **AND** WHATSOEVER YE SHALL ASK IN MY NAME,
THAT WILL I DO, THAT THE FATHER MAY BE GLORIFIED IN THE SON.

14. **IF** YE SHALL ASK ANY THING IN MY NAME, I WILL DO IT.

15. **IF** YE LOVE ME, KEEP MY COMMANDMENTS.

— *"And **I will pray the Father, and he shall give you another Comforter**, that he may abide with you for ever; Even the Spirit of truth; whom the world cannot receive, because it seeth him* *not, neither knoweth him: but ye know him; for he dwelleth with you, and shall be in you. I will not leave you comfortless: I will come to you"* (see 14:16-18).

September 1 (Day 244), Memory Verse #655
John 14:21:

HE THAT HATH MY COMMANDMENTS, AND KEEPETH THEM,
HE IT IS THAT LOVETH ME:
AND HE THAT LOVETH ME SHALL BE LOVED OF MY FATHER,
AND I WILL LOVE HIM, AND WILL MANIFEST MYSELF TO HIM.

September 2 (Day 245), Memory Verses #656 & #657
John 14:26-27:

26. BUT THE COMFORTER, WHICH IS THE HOLY GHOST,
WHOM THE FATHER WILL SEND IN MY NAME,
HE SHALL TEACH YOU ALL THINGS, AND BRING ALL THINGS TO YOUR REMEMBRANCE,
WHATSOEVER I HAVE SAID UNTO YOU.

27. PEACE I LEAVE WITH YOU, MY PEACE I GIVE UNTO YOU:
NOT AS THE WORLD GIVETH, GIVE I UNTO YOU.
LET NOT YOUR HEART BE TROUBLED, NEITHER LET IT BE AFRAID.

John 15: **Jesus is the true vine** (see 15:1-8) — *"I am the true vine, and my Father is the husbandman"* (see 15:1).

September 3 (Day 246), Memory Verse #658
John 15:5:

I AM THE VINE, YE ARE THE BRANCHES:
HE THAT ABIDETH IN ME, AND I IN HIM, THE SAME BRINGETH FORTH MUCH FRUIT:
FOR WITHOUT ME YE CAN DO NOTHING.

— **Jesus teaches to keep the Father's commandments and abide in His love** (see 15:9-17).

September 3 (Day 246), Memory Verses #659 & #660
John 15:12-13:

12. THIS IS MY COMMANDMENT,
THAT YE LOVE ONE ANOTHER AS I HAVE LOVED YOU.

13. GREATER LOVE HATH NO MAN THAN THIS,
THAT A MAN LAY DOWN HIS LIFE FOR HIS FRIENDS.

— *"These things I command you, that ye love one another"* (see 15:17) — **Jesus speaks concerning the world's hatred for Him and His followers** (see 15:18-27).

John 16: **Jesus speaks concerning His going to the Father and the coming of the Holy Spirit** (see 16:1-33) — *"It is expedient for you that I go away: for if I go not away, the Comforter will not come unto you; but if I depart, I will send him unto you"* (see 16:7).

September 4 (Day 247), Memory Verse #661
John 16:33:

...IN THE WORLD YE SHALL HAVE TRIBULATION:
BUT BE OF GOOD CHEER; I HAVE OVERCOME THE WORLD.

John 17: **Jesus prays for Himself, His disciples, and all believers, not only believers during Jesus' time, but all future believers as well** (see 17:1-26) — *"Father, the hour is come; glorify thy Son, that thy Son may glorify thee: As thou hast given him power over all flesh, that he should give eternal life to as many as thou hast given him. And this is life eternal, that they might know thee the only true God, and Jesus Christ, whom thou hast sent"* (see 17:1-3) — **Jesus' prayer continues:**

September 4 (Day 247), Memory Verse #662
John 17:5:

AND NOW, O FATHER, GLORIFY THOU ME,
WITH THINE OWN SELF WITH THE GLORY
WHICH I HAD WITH THEE BEFORE THE WORLD WAS.

September 4 (Day 247), Memory Verse #663
John 17:11:

AND NOW I AM NO MORE IN THE WORLD,
BUT THESE ARE IN THE WORLD, AND I COME TO THEE.
HOLY FATHER, KEEP THROUGH THINE OWN NAME THOSE WHOM THOU HAST GIVEN ME,
THAT THEY MAY BE ONE, AS WE ARE.

— *"And now come I to thee; and these things I speak in the world, that they might have my joy fulfilled in themselves"* (see 17:13) — *"I pray not that thou shouldest take them out of the world, but that thou shouldest keep them from the evil"* (see 17:15) — *"Sanctify them through thy truth, thy word is truth"* (see 17:17).

September 5 (Day 248), Memory Verses #664 & #665
John 17:20-21:

20. NEITHER PRAY I FOR THESE ALONE,
BUT FOR THEM ALSO WHICH SHALL BELIEVE ON ME THROUGH THEIR WORD;

21. THAT THEY ALL MAY BE ONE; AS THOU, FATHER, ART IN ME, AND I IN THEE,
THAT THEY ALSO MAY BE ONE IN US:
THAT THE WORLD MAY BELIEVE THAT THOU HAST SENT ME.

— *"And I have declared unto them thy name, and will declare it: that the love wherewith thou hast loved me may be in them, and I in them"* (see 17:26).

John 18: **Judas betrays Jesus** (see 18:1-9) — **Simon Peter cuts off the ear of Malchus, the high priest's servant** (see 18:10-11) — **Jesus is brought before Annas, the father-in-law of Caiaphas** (see 18:12-23) — *"Then the band and the captain and officers of the Jews took Jesus, and bound him"* (see 18:12) — **Jesus is taken to Caiaphas, the high priest, and Peter denies Jesus** (see 18:24-27) — **Jesus is taken before Pilate at the Roman judgment hall** (see 18:28-40) — Pilate says, *"...ye have a custom, that I should release unto you one at the Passover: will ye therefore that I release unto you the King of the Jews? Then cried they all again, saying, Not this man, but Barabbas. Now Barabbas was a robber"* (see 18:39-40).

John 19: **Jesus is beaten, mocked, questioned by Pilate, and then crucified** (see 19:1-37) — *"Then Pilate therefore took Jesus, and scourged him. And the soldiers platted a crown of thorns, and put it on his head, and they put on him a purple robe, And said, Hail, King of the Jews! And they smote him with their hands"* (see 19:1-3) — *"Then delivered he him therefore unto them to be crucified. And they took Jesus, and led him away. And he bearing his cross went forth into a place called the place of a skull, which is called in the Hebrew **Golgotha: Where they crucified***

him, and two other with him, on either side one, and Jesus in the midst. And Pilate wrote a title, and put it on the cross. And the writing was, JESUS OF NAZARETH THE KING OF THE JEWS" (see 19:16-19) — **Joseph of Arimathea and Nicodemus take Jesus' body to a new sepulcher for burial** (see 19:38-42).

John 20: Jesus' resurrection and appearances (see 20:1-31) — Mary Magdalene finds the stone rolled away from the sepulcher and the tomb empty — She runs to tell Peter and the other disciples who also come to the empty tomb — Two angels and Jesus appear to Mary Magdalene — Jesus appears to the disciples when Thomas is absent — Thomas says he will have to see and touch Jesus' wounds to believe He is risen — Jesus appears to Thomas and the other disciples.

September 5 (Day 248), Memory Verse #666
John 20:29:

JESUS SAITH UNTO HIM, THOMAS,
BECAUSE THOU HAST SEEN ME, THOU HAST BELIEVED:
BLESSED ARE THEY THAT HAVE NOT SEEN, AND YET HAVE BELIEVED.

September 6 (Day 249), Memory Verse #667
John 20:31:

BUT THESE (SIGNS, see John 20:30) ARE WRITTEN,
THAT YE MIGHT BELIEVE THAT JESUS IS THE CHRIST, THE SON OF GOD;
AND THAT BELIEVING YE MIGHT HAVE LIFE THROUGH HIS NAME.

John 21: Jesus appears to the disciples while they fish (see 21:1-14) — **Jesus asks Simon Peter if he loves Him, and Jesus says to follow Him** (see 21:15-25).

September 6 (Day 249), Memory Verse #668
John 21:16:

HE SAITH TO HIM AGAIN THE SECOND TIME, SIMON, SON OF JONAS, LOVEST THOU ME?
HE SAITH UNTO HIM, YEA, LORD: THOU KNOWEST THAT I LOVE THEE.
HE SAITH UNTO HIM, FEED MY SHEEP.

September 6 (Day 249), Memory Verse #669
John 21:25:

AND THERE ARE ALSO MANY OTHER THINGS WHICH JESUS DID, THE WHICH,
IF THEY SHOULD BE WRITTEN EVERY ONE,
I SUPPOSE THAT EVEN THE WORLD ITSELF COULD NOT CONTAIN
THE BOOKS THAT SHOULD BE WRITTEN. AMEN.

JOHN 3:16:

FOR GOD SO LOVED THE WORLD, THAT HE GAVE HIS ONLY BEGOTTEN SON, THAT WHOSOEVER BELIEVETH IN HIM SHOULD NOT PERISH, BUT HAVE EVERLASTING LIFE.

ᴀCTS

Introduction: Most scholars believe Acts was written by Luke, a Gentile physician and companion of Paul. Acts is a continuation of the book of Luke (see Luke's introduction). Luke ends with Jesus' ascension into heaven. Acts begins with the ascension and shows the gospel message spreading. Many support the 60's A.D. opinion as the date of writing for Acts since historical events soon afterward, including the destruction of Jerusalem in 70 A.D., are not mentioned. Others believe Acts was written in the 80's A.D. Acts includes the coming of the Holy Spirit, the persecution of believers, Saul's conversion, the three missionary journeys of Paul, the beginnings of the church, and guidelines for the church. Saul, a Jew, began using his Roman name, Paul, when he started preaching to the Gentiles (see 13:9). Acts emphasizes salvation for both the Jews and the Gentiles (all people). Paul may have had a fourth missionary journey to Spain, but Acts does not mention it (see Romans 15:24-26). Acts has 28 chapters.

Key Contents and Key Memory Verses with Study Dates

Acts 1:   Jesus' last 40 days on earth before His ascension (see 1:1-11) — Jesus tells the apostles, *"John truly baptized with water; but ye shall be baptized with the Holy Ghost..."* (see 1:5) — Jesus also says:

September 7 (Day 250), Memory Verse #670
Acts 1:8:

Bᴜᴛ ʏᴇ sʜᴀʟʟ ʀᴇᴄᴇɪᴠᴇ ᴘᴏᴡᴇʀ,
ᴀFᴛᴇʀ ᴛʜᴀᴛ ᴛʜᴇ ʜᴏʟʏ ɢʜᴏsᴛ ɪs ᴄᴏᴍᴇ ᴜᴘᴏɴ ʏᴏᴜ:
ᴀɴᴅ ʏᴇ sʜᴀʟʟ ʙᴇ ᴡɪᴛɴᴇssᴇs ᴜɴᴛᴏ ᴍᴇ ʙᴏᴛʜ ɪɴ ᴊᴇʀᴜsᴀʟᴇᴍ, ᴀɴᴅ ɪɴ ᴀʟʟ ᴊᴜᴅᴀᴇᴀ,
ᴀɴᴅ ɪɴ sᴀᴍᴀʀɪᴀ, ᴀɴᴅ ᴜɴᴛᴏ ᴛʜᴇ ᴜᴛᴛᴇʀᴍᴏsᴛ ᴘᴀʀᴛ ᴏF ᴛʜᴇ ᴇᴀʀᴛʜ.

— **Jesus** *"...was taken up; and a cloud received him out of their sight. And while they looked stedfastly toward heaven as he went up, behold, two men stood by them in white apparel;"* (see 1:9-10), and said *"...this same Jesus, which is taken up from you into heaven, shall so come in like manner as ye have seen him go into heaven"* (see 1:11) — **Matthias is chosen to take the place of the apostle Judas** (see 1:12-26).

Acts 2:   Pentecost (Feast of Weeks) and the coming of the Holy Spirit (see 2:1-13) — *"And suddenly there came a sound from heaven as of a rushing mighty wind, and it filled all the house where they were sitting. And there appeared unto them cloven tongues like as of fire, and it sat upon each of them. And they were filled with the Holy Ghost, and began to speak with other tongues, as the Spirit gave them utterance. And there were dwelling at Jerusalem Jews, devout men, out of every nation under heaven: Now when this was noised abroad, the multitude came together, and were confounded, because that every man heard them speak in his own language"* (see 2:2-6) — **Peter speaks to the crowd in Jerusalem** (see 2:14-41) — Peter quotes the Old Testament prophet Joel in Acts 2:16-21 when speaking about the last days (see Joel 2:28-32).

September 7 (Day 250), Memory Verse #671
Acts 2:21:

...ᴡʜᴏsᴏᴇᴠᴇʀ sʜᴀʟʟ ᴄᴀʟʟ ᴏɴ ᴛʜᴇ ɴᴀᴍᴇ ᴏF ᴛʜᴇ ʟᴏʀᴅ sʜᴀʟʟ ʙᴇ sᴀᴠᴇᴅ.

September 7 (Day 250), Memory Verse #672
Acts 2:24:

ᴡʜᴏᴍ ɢᴏᴅ ʜᴀᴛʜ ʀᴀɪsᴇᴅ ᴜᴘ, ʜᴀᴠɪɴɢ ʟᴏᴏsᴇᴅ ᴛʜᴇ ᴘᴀɪɴs ᴏF ᴅᴇᴀᴛʜ:
ʙᴇᴄᴀᴜsᴇ ɪᴛ ᴡᴀs ɴᴏᴛ ᴘᴏssɪʙʟᴇ ᴛʜᴀᴛ ʜᴇ sʜᴏᴜʟᴅ ʙᴇ ʜᴏʟᴅᴇɴ ᴏF ɪᴛ.

> **September 8 (Day 251), Memory Verse #673**
> **Acts 2:38:**
>
> **THEN** PETER SAID UNTO THEM, REPENT, AND BE BAPTIZED
> EVERY ONE OF YOU IN THE NAME OF JESUS CHRIST FOR THE REMISSION OF SINS,
> AND YE SHALL RECEIVE THE GIFT OF THE HOLY GHOST.

— **Believers sell their possessions and give to the needy** (see 2:42-47) — *"...And the Lord added to the church daily such as should be saved"* (see 2:47).

Acts 3: **A crippled man is healed** (see 3:1-10) after Peter tells him, *"...Silver and gold have I none; but such as I have give I thee: In the name of Jesus Christ of Nazareth rise up and walk"* (see 3:6) — **Peter again speaks to the crowd at the temple in Jerusalem** (see 3:11-26).

Acts 4: **Peter and John are put in jail overnight,** but the religious leaders are afraid to keep them in jail since the crowds know of the crippled man's miraculously healing (see 4:1-22) — Peter tells the religious leaders:

> **September 8 (Day 251), Memory Verse #674**
> **Acts 4:12:**
>
> **NEITHER** IS THERE SALVATION IN ANY OTHER:
> FOR THERE IS NONE OTHER NAME UNDER HEAVEN GIVEN AMONG MEN,
> WHEREBY WE MUST BE SAVED.

— **After being released from jail, Peter and John pray with the believers** (see 4:23-31) — *"And when they had prayed, the place was shaken where they were assembled together; and they were all filled with the Holy Ghost, and they spake the word of God with boldness"* (see 4:31) — **Believers share their property** (see 4:32-37) with each other and *"...had all things common"* (see 4:32).

Acts 5: **Ananias and Sapphira die after lying about their giving** (see 5:1-11) — **Many are healed in Jerusalem through the apostles** (see 5:12-16) — **The Jewish religious leaders have the apostles put in jail again** (see 5:17-42), but *"...the angel of the Lord by night opened the prison doors, and brought them forth..."* (see 5:19), telling them to speak in the temple — The apostles are brought before the Jewish council and high priest — The apostle Peter and the other apostles proclaim the following verse:

> **September 9 (Day 252), Memory Verse #675**
> **Acts 5:29:**
>
> ...**WE** OUGHT TO OBEY GOD RATHER THAN MEN.

— **Gamaliel offers his wise advice to the council:** *"...if this counsel or this work be of men, it will come to nought: But if it be of God, ye cannot overthrow it; lest haply ye be found even to fight against God"* (see 5:38-39) — **The Jewish council has the apostles beaten and released** with instructions that *"...they should not speak in the name of Jesus..."* (see 5:40).

> **September 9 (Day 252), Memory Verse #676**
> **Acts 5:41:**
>
> **AND** THEY DEPARTED FROM THE PRESENCE OF THE COUNCIL,
> REJOICING THAT THEY WERE COUNTED WORTHY TO SUFFER SHAME FOR HIS NAME.

— *"And daily in the temple, and in every house, they ceased not to teach and preach Jesus Christ"* (see 5:42).

Acts 6: **Seven men are chosen to help in serving** (see 6:1-7); this allows the 12 apostles to devote themselves to *"...prayer, and to the ministry of the word"* (see 6:4) — **Stephen, one of the seven, is falsely accused of blasphemy** (see 6:8-15) by the religious leaders and is brought before the Jewish council — Stephen's face appears like *"the face of an angel"* (see 6:15).

Acts 7: **Stephen delivers a sermon before the Jewish council and high priest** (see 7:1-53) — The sermon includes Israel's history "in a nutshell" — Stephen angers the Jews by saying, *"Ye stiffnecked and uncircumcised in heart and ears, ye do always resist the Holy Ghost: as your fathers did, so do ye"* (see 7:51) — **The Jews stone Stephen to death** (see 7:54-60) — *While they were stoning him, Stephen prayed, 'Lord Jesus, receive my spirit,'* (see 7:59, NIV) — *And he kneeled down and cried with a loud voice, Lord, lay not this sin to their charge. And when he had said this, he fell asleep"* (see 7:60).

Acts 8: **Saul is known for consenting to Stephen's death and persecuting the Christians** (see 8:1-3) — **While Philip, Peter, and John preach in Samaria, a sorcerer by the name of Simon believes and is baptized, but he does not truly understand God's gift of salvation** (see 8:4-25) — Peter tells Simon, *"...thou hast thought that the gift of God may be purchased with money ...thy heart is not right in the sight of God. Repent therefore of this thy wickedness, and pray God, if perhaps the thought of thine heart may be forgiven thee"* (see 8:20-22) — **Philip explains Christ to an Ethiopian eunuch who believes and is baptized** (see 8:26-40).

Acts 9: **Saul has a dramatic spiritual conversion; the Lord speaks to Saul while he is traveling to Damascus to persecute the Christians** (see 9:1-18) — *"And as he journeyed, he came near Damascus: and suddenly there shined round about him a light from heaven: And he fell to the earth, and heard a voice saying unto him, Saul, Saul, why persecutest thou me?"* (see 9:3-4) — Saul temporarily loses his sight — **The Lord sends Ananias to Saul**, and *"...immediately there fell from his eyes as it had been scales: and he received sight forthwith, and arose, and was baptized"* (see 9:18) — **Saul begins preaching** (see 9:19-31) — He preaches about Christ in Damascus, and the Jews conspire to kill him — The disciples help Saul escape — *"Then the disciples took him by night, and let him down by the wall in a basket"* (see 9:25) — Saul preaches in Jerusalem, but the disciples send him to Tarsus because some in Jerusalem want to kill Saul — **Peter ministers in Lydda and Joppa** (see 9:32-43) — In Lydda, Peter finds Aeneas, who has been in *"...bed eight years, and was sick of the palsy. And Peter said unto him, Aeneas, Jesus Christ maketh thee whole: arise, and make thy bed. And he arose immediately"* (see 9:33-34) — In Joppa, one of the disciples named Tabitha dies — Peter prays and says, *"...Tabitha, arise. And she opened her eyes: and when she saw Peter, she sat up"* (see 9:40).

Acts 10: **Peter and Cornelius** (see 10:1-48) — In a vision, God tells Cornelius of Caesarea to go to Peter in Joppa — God also gives Peter a vision concerning clean and unclean — When Cornelius arrives, Peter explains, *"God hath shewed me that I should not call any man common or unclean"* (see 10:28).

September 10 (Day 253), Memory Verses #677 & #678
Acts 10:34-35:

34. THEN PETER OPENED HIS MOUTH, AND SAID,
OF A TRUTH I PERCEIVE THAT GOD IS NO RESPECTER OF PERSONS
(God does not show favoritism, NIV):

35. BUT IN EVERY NATION HE THAT FEARETH HIM,
AND WORKETH RIGHTEOUSNESS, IS ACCEPTED WITH HIM.

— Peter preaches about Jesus to Cornelius' friends and kinsmen (see 10:24-48).

September 10 (Day 253), Memory Verse #679
Acts 10:43:

TO HIM GIVE ALL THE PROPHETS WITNESS,
THAT THROUGH HIS NAME WHOSOEVER BELIEVETH IN HIM
SHALL RECEIVE REMISSION (forgiveness, NIV) OF SINS.

Acts 11: The apostles and brethren debate as to whether Gentiles can receive the Word of God without being circumcised (see 11:1-18) — Peter speaks of his vision when he heard a voice from heaven saying, *"...What God hath cleansed, that call not thou common (Do not call anything impure that God has made clean, NIV)"* (see 11:9) — Peter tells how the Gentile Cornelius received the Holy Spirit — Then those listening remark, *"...Then hath God also to the Gentiles granted repentance unto life"* (see 11:18) — **The church at Antioch grows in number** (see 11:19-30) — *"...And the disciples were called Christians first in Antioch"* (see 11:26).

Acts 12: Herod kills the apostle James (see 12:1-2) — **Herod also has Peter imprisoned, and an angel leads Peter out of prison** (see 12:1-19) — Herod is stricken dead (see 12:20-23) by *"the angel of the Lord"* (see 12:23) and is eaten by worms — **Saul, Barnabas, and John Mark travel to Jerusalem** (see 12:24-25) — *"...the word of God grew and multiplied"* (see 12:24).

PAUL'S FIRST MISSIONARY JOURNEY, about 2 years in length (see 13:1 to 14:28)

Acts 13: Saul begins using his Roman (Gentile) name, Paul — Paul, Barnabas, and John Mark journey to the island of Cyprus (see 12:25-13:13) — Sergius Paulus, who is the deputy of the country, *"...called for Barnabas and Saul, and desired to hear the word of God"* (see 13:7) — Elymas, a sorcerer, tries to prevent Saul and Barnabas meeting with Sergius Paulas; therefore, Elymas is blinded when Paul calls on God's power, and Sergius Paulas becomes a believer — John Mark returns to Jerusalem —**In Pisidian Antioch, Paul preaches** (see 13:14-52) **to mostly Jews at first** — His message includes a summary of Israel's history (see 13:16-42) — Paul preaches next to mostly Gentiles at their request and says, *"...so hath the Lord commanded us, saying, I have set thee to be a light of the Gentiles; that thou shouldest be for salvation unto the ends of the earth"* (see 13:47 which quotes from Isaiah 49:6) — After more preaching, Paul and Barnabas wipe the dust off their feet as they are driven out of this city.

Acts 14: Paul and Barnabas go to Iconium (see 14:1-6), and*"...they went both together into the synagogue of the Jews, and so spake, that a great multitude both of the Jews and also of the Greeks believed. But the unbelieving Jews stirred up the Gentiles, and made their minds evil affected against the brethren"*(see 14:1-2) — The people try to stone Paul and Barnabas in Iconium, so they flee to Lystra — **In Lystra** (see 14:7-20)**, a lame man is healed;** people think Barnabas is the god Jupiter (Zeus, NIV) and Paul is the god Mercurious (Hermes, NIV) — Also in Lystra, **Paul is stoned and left for dead** — *"...as the disciples stood round about him, he rose up, and came into the city: and the next day he departed with Barnabas to Derbe"* (see 14:20) — **After visiting several more cities, Paul and Barnabas return to Antioch and stay for a long time** (see 14:21-28).

Acts 15: The elders and apostles meet in Jerusalem and decide the Gentiles do not have to be circumcised or keep all the strict laws to become Christians (see 15:1-35) — Judas, Silas, Paul, and Barnabas deliver a letter to Antioch concerning this decision.

PAUL'S SECOND MISSIONARY JOURNEY, about ~~12~~ 4 years in length (see 15:36 to 18:22)

— **Paul and Barnabas disagree about John Mark accompanying them on the second missionary journey, so Barnabas and John Mark depart for Cyprus while Paul and Silas depart for Syria and Cilicia** (see 15:36-41) — Judas returns to Jerusalem.

Acts 16: **Timotheus (Timothy, NIV) joins Paul and Silas in Lystra, and they preach in many cities** (see 16:1-5) — *"And so were the churches established in the faith, and increased in number daily"* (see 16:5) — **Paul, Silas, and Timothy journey to Macedonia** (see 16:6-40) — In Troas *"... a vision appeared to Paul in the night; There stood a man of Macedonia, and prayed him, saying, Come over into Macedonia, and help us"* (see 16:9) — **Lydia, a seller of purple, is converted in Philippi, a city of Macedonia** — **Paul commands a evil spirit to leave a soothsaying (fortune-telling) slave girl** — **Paul and Silas are thrown in prison in Philippi** — *"And at midnight Paul and Silas prayed, and sang praises unto God: and the prisoners heard them. And suddenly there was a great earthquake, so that the foundations of the prison were shaken: and immediately all the doors were opened, and every one's bands were loosed"* (see 16:25-26) — **The Philippian jailer asks, "...Sirs, what must I do to be saved?"** (see 16:30).

September 11 (Day 254), Memory Verse #680
Act 16:31:

AND THEY SAID, BELIEVE ON THE LORD JESUS CHRIST,
AND THOU SHALT BE SAVED, AND THY HOUSE.

— **The Philippian jailer brings them to his home** and *"...rejoiced, believing God with all his house"* (see 16:34) — They return to jail and are released the next day.

Acts 17: **Journey to Thessalonica, Berea, and Athens** (see 17:1-34) — In Thessalonica, the people are angered at Jason for welcoming Paul and Silas and claiming Jesus is King — Paul and Silas flee to Berea at night — Paul journeys ahead to Athens and preaches there; some believe his message and others mock him (see 17:22-34). Paul proclaims:

September 11 (Day 254), Memory Verse #681
Acts 17:28:

FOR IN HIM WE LIVE, AND MOVE, AND HAVE OUR BEING; ...

Acts 18: Paul spends 18 months in Corinth (see 18:1-17), staying with Aquila and Priscilla — Silas and Timothy arrive later — Many Jews reject Paul's teachings — Titius Justus and Crispus believe in God — Gallio, proconsul of Achaia, refuses to judge Paul on the Jews' accusations — The Jews then beat Sosthenes, the chief ruler of the synagogue — **After visiting a few more cities, Paul returns to Antioch and ends his second missionary journey** (see 18:18-22).

PAUL'S THIRD MISSIONARY JOURNEY, about 5 years in length (see 18:23 to 21:26)

— **Paul travels throughout Galatia and Phrygia** (see 18:23-28) — Paul has Aquila and Priscilla stay in Ephesus and teach the people; Aquilla and Priscilla teach Apollos who becomes a great leader for the Christians in Achaia.

Act 19: Paul teaches about the Holy Ghost in Ephesus (see 19:1-41) — Seven sons of Sceva and others try to use the names of Paul and Jesus to cast out evil spirits but are attacked by a man with an evil spirit — **Also in Ephesus, Magic books worth 50,000 silver pieces are burned** — The silversmith Demetrius joins with other craftsmen in causing an uproar against Paul's teachings; they fear their business will suffer since they are the craftsmen for the idols to the goddess Diana (Artemis, NIV).

Acts 20: Paul and his disciples travel to many cities (see 20:1-38) — While Paul is preaching **in Troas, Eutychus falls asleep and drops from a three-story window to his death** (see 20:7-12) — Eutychus is raised from the dead after Paul embraces him — **In Miletus, Paul speaks to the church elders from Ephesus** (see 20:17-38); Paul gives his testimony concerning his desire to finish God's plan for his life, and *"...to testify the gospel of the grace of God"* (see 20:24).

...REMEMBER THE WORDS OF THE LORD JESUS, HOW HE SAID,
IT IS MORE BLESSED TO GIVE THAN TO RECEIVE.

Acts 21: Journey to Caesarea (see 21:1-14) — Paul is warned by Agabus at Caesarea that he will be arrested in Jerusalem — **Paul travels to the church in Jerusalem and discusses Gentile Christians** (see 21:15-26); some have accused Paul of forsaking Moses' law since he teaches Gentiles do not need to be circumcised to be Christians — **The Jews seize Paul in Jerusalem, and the Roman soldiers rescue him** (see 21:27-40).

Acts 22: Paul speaks to the crowd in Jerusalem (see 22:1-29) and includes his testimony — The Roman chief captain scourges Paul — When a centurion learns Paul is a Roman citizen, he is frightened since it is illegal to beat a Roman citizen — The centurion informs the chief captain.

Acts 23: Paul is brought before Ananias, the high priest, and the chief priests and their council (see 22:30-23:10) — A dispute arises between the Pharisees and Sadducees — The Roman chief captain rescues Paul from the Jews again — *"And the night following the Lord stood by him, and said, Be of good cheer, Paul: for as thou hast testified of me in Jerusalem, so must thou bear witness also at Rome"* (see 23:11) — Forty Jews vow to fast until they kill Paul — Paul's nephew warns Paul and the chief captain — **Paul is taken to Caesarea to Felix the governor** (see 23:11-35), **escorted by 200 soldiers, 70 horsemen, and 200 spearmen.**

Acts 24: Paul defends himself (see 24:1-27) **before Governor Felix, the Jews, and the Jew's** spokesman, Tertullus — Paul is kept two years in a centurion's custody — Then Porcius Festus becomes governor.

Acts 25: Paul defends himself before Festus (see 25:1-27); Paul appeals his case to Caesar.

Acts 26: Paul gives his defense and testimony before King Agrippa (see 26:1-32) — King Agrippa considers becoming a Christian.

Acts 27: Paul's shipwreck while traveling toward Rome (see 27:1-44) — Paul warns of a shipwreck, but the crew continues to sail — When the shipwreck is imminent, Paul assures the crew that no lives will be lost.

Acts 28: After being shipwrecked on the island of Melita (see 27:1-10), Paul is bitten by a deadly snake — Paul miraculously has no physical effects from the bite — Publius is the governor of the island — Through Paul, Publius' father and others are healed in Melita (Malta, NIV) — **Journey to Rome** (see 27:11-16) — After finally arriving in Rome, Paul is under house arrest and is allowed to preach to the people (see 28:17-31).

ACTS 20:35: ...REMEMBER THE WORDS OF THE LORD JESUS, HOW HE SAID, IT IS MORE BLESSED TO GIVE THAN TO RECEIVE.

ROMANS

Introduction: The books of Romans to Jude are epistles (letters). Scholars agree Paul is the author of Romans. He was probably in Corinth around 57 A.D. on his third missionary journey when he wrote this letter to the church in Rome. Paul most likely dictated this letter to his secretary Tertius (see 16:22). Phoebe, a Christian woman, is thought to have delivered the letter to Rome (see 16:1-2). Paul had planned to visit Rome as he mentioned in this letter, but he was arrested in Jerusalem where he was delivering an offering gathered from the churches to give to the poor (see 15:24-26). Ironically, Paul did visit Rome, but as a Roman prisoner. The book of Romans emphasizes that the gospel is for both Jews and Gentiles (for all people) since salvation comes by faith alone, not by legalistic keeping of the Jewish law. Key words in Romans include justified, righteous, redemption, and atonement. Romans has 16 chapters.

Key Contents and Key Memory Verses with Study Dates

Romans 1: Paul's greeting includes a summary of the gospel message (see 1:1-6).

September 12 (Day 255), Memory Verse #683
Romans 1:1:

PAUL, A SERVANT OF JESUS CHRIST...

"...called to be an apostle, separated unto the gospel of God, (Which he had promised afore by his prophets in the holy scriptures,) Concerning his Son Jesus Christ our Lord, which was made of the seed of David according to the flesh; And declared to be the Son of God with power, according to the spirit of holiness, by the resurrection from the dead: By whom we have received grace and apostleship, for obedience to the faith among all nations, for his name: Among whom are ye also the called of Jesus Christ:" (see 1:1-6) — **Paul shows his thankfulness for the Romans, talks of plans to visit Rome, and expresses his desire to preach the gospel to the Romans** (see 1:7-17).

September 13 (Day 256), Memory Verses #684 & #685
Romans 1:16-17:

16. FOR I AM NOT ASHAMED OF THE GOSPEL OF CHRIST:
FOR IT IS THE POWER OF GOD UNTO SALVATION TO EVERY ONE THAT BELIEVETH; ...

17. ...THE JUST SHALL LIVE BY FAITH.

— **Humanity sees God through creation and should worship the Creator rather than the creation** (see 1:18-25) — *"For the invisible things of him from the creation of the world are clearly seen, being understood by the things that are made, even his eternal power and Godhead; so that they are without excuse:"* (see 1:20) — **Many sins often thought of as pleasurable by humanity are listed** (see 1:26-32).

Romans 2: God who *"...will render to everyone according to his deeds"* (see 2:6), is **humanity's judge; people should not judge one another** (see 2:1-16) — **God's goodness and fairness will lead one to repentance.**

September 13 (Day 256), Memory Verse #686
Romans 2:4:

...NOT KNOWING THE GOODNESS OF GOD LEADETH THEE TO REPENTANCE?

September 13 (Day 256), Memory Verse #687
Romans 2:11:

FOR THERE IS NO RESPECT (favoritism, NIV) OF PERSONS WITH GOD.

— **Those who do not know the law have their conscience which bears witness "...of the law written in their hearts..."** (see 2:15) — **The true Jew** (see 2:17-29) — *"But he is a Jew, which is one inwardly; and* **circumcision is that of the heart, in the spirit, and not in the letter;** *whose praise is not of men, but of God"* (see 2:29).

Romans 3:   All people can receive God's grace (free gift of salvation) by faith; the law makes each person aware of their sins and need for repentance (see 3:1-31) — **All have sinned and need to ask God's forgiveness.**

September 14 (Day 257), Memory Verse #688
Romans 3:10:

AS IT IS WRITTEN, THERE IS NONE RIGHTEOUS, NO, NOT ONE:

— *"...for by the law is the knowledge of sin"* (see 3:20).

September 14 (Day 257), Memory Verse #689
Romans 3:23:

FOR ALL HAVE SINNED, AND COME SHORT OF THE GLORY OF GOD;

— *"Being justified freely by his grace through the redemption that is in Christ Jesus: Whom God hath set forth to be a propitiation for the remission of sins that are past, through the forbearance of God (...a sacrifice of atonement through faith in his blood...NIV); To declare, I say, at this time his righteousness: that he might be just, and the justifier of him which believeth in Jesus"* (see 3:24-26).

Romans 4:   Even Abraham was justified by his faith (see 4:1-25) — *"For if Abraham were justified by works, he hath whereof to glory; but not before God. For what saith the scripture? Abraham believed God, and it was counted unto him for righteousness"* (see 4:2-3) — *"For the promise, that he should be the heir of the world, was not to Abraham, or to his seed, through the law, but through the righteousness of faith"* (see 4:13) — *"He staggered not at the promise of God through unbelief; but was strong in faith, giving glory to God; And being fully persuaded that, what he had promised, he was able also to perform. And therefore it was imputed to him for righteousness.* **Now it was not written for his sake alone, that it was imputed to him; But for us also, to whom it shall be imputed, if we believe on him that raised up Jesus our Lord from the dead; Who was delivered for our offences, and was raised again for our justification"** (see 4:20-25).

Romans 5:   Believers are justified by their faith (see 5:1-11).

September 14 (Day 257), Memory Verse #690
Romans 5:1:

THEREFORE BEING JUSTIFIED BY FAITH,
WE HAVE PEACE WITH GOD THOUGH OUR LORD JESUS CHRIST:

— *"...we glory in tribulations also: knowing that* **tribulation worketh patience; And patience, experience; and experience, hope:"** (see 5:3-4).

September 14 (Day 257), Memory Verse #691
Romans 5:8:

BUT GOD COMMENDETH HIS LOVE TOWARD US, IN THAT,
WHILE WE WERE YET SINNERS, CHRIST DIED FOR US.

— **Sin entered the world with the sin of one man, Adam, and the gift of righteousness entered the world by one, Jesus Christ** (see 5:12-21).

Romans 6:   Sin and sinful desires no longer rule believers' lives when they live in God's grace rather than under the requirements of the law (see 6:1-23).

September 15 (Day 258), Memory Verses #692 & #693
Romans 6:3-4:

3. KNOW YE NOT, THAT SO MANY OF US AS WERE
BAPTIZED INTO JESUS CHRIST WERE BAPTIZED INTO HIS DEATH?

4. THEREFORE WE ARE BURIED WITH HIM BY BAPTISM INTO DEATH:
THAT LIKE AS CHRIST WAS RAISED UP FROM THE DEAD BY THE GLORY
OF THE FATHER, EVEN SO WE ALSO SHOULD WALK IN NEWNESS OF LIFE.

— *"What then? Shall we sin, because we are not under the law, but under grace? God forbid"* (see 6:15).

September 15 (Day 258), Memory Verse #694
Romans 6:23:

FOR THE WAGES OF SIN IS DEATH;
BUT THE GIFT OF GOD IS ETERNAL LIFE THROUGH JESUS CHRIST OUR LORD.

Romans 7:   Paul explains the correct view of the law (see 7:1-25) — *"Wherefore, my brethren, ye also are become dead to the law by the body of Christ; that ye should be married to another, even to him who is raised from the dead, that we should bring forth fruit unto God"* (see 7:4) — **Paul shows how believers, including himself, are not exempt from struggles with the law and the sinful desires of the flesh** — *"But I see another law in my members, warring against the law of my mind, and bringing me into captivity to the law of sin which is in my members. O wretched man that I am! who shall deliver me from the body of this death? I thank God through Jesus Christ our Lord. So then with the mind I myself serve the law of God; but with the flesh the law of sin"* (see 7:23-25).

Romans 8: Walking in the spirit is compared to walking in the flesh (see 8:1-39).

September 16 (Day 259), Memory Verse #695
Romans 8:1:

THERE IS THEREFORE NOW NO COMDEMNATION
TO THEM WHICH ARE IN CHRIST JESUS,
WHO WALK NOT AFTER THE FLESH, BUT AFTER THE SPIRIT.

September 16 (Day 259), Memory Verse #696
Romans 8:3:

FOR WHAT THE LAW COULD NOT DO, IN THAT IT WAS WEAK THROUGH THE FLESH,
GOD SENDING HIS OWN SON IN THE LIKENESS OF SINFUL FLESH,
AND FOR SIN, CONDEMNED SIN IN THE FLESH:

September 16 (Day 259), Memory Verse #697
Romans 8:6:

FOR TO BE CARNALLY MINDED IS DEATH;
BUT TO BE SPIRITUALLY MINDED IS LIFE AND PEACE.

September 17 (Day 260), Memory Verses #698 to #700
Romans 8:15-17:

15. ...BUT YE HAVE RECEIVED THE SPIRIT
OF ADOPTION, WHEREBY WE CRY, ABBA, FATHER.

16. THE SPIRIT ITSELF BEARETH WITNESS WITH OUR SPIRIT,
THAT WE ARE THE CHILDREN OF GOD:

17. AND IF CHILDREN, THEN HEIRS; HEIRS OF GOD,
AND JOINT-HEIRS WITH CHRIST; ...

— *"For we are saved by hope: but hope that is seen is not hope: for what a man seeth, why doth he yet hope for? But if we hope for that we see not, then do we **with patience wait** for it. Likewise the Spirit also helpeth our infirmities: for we know not what we should pray for as we ought: but **the Spirit itself maketh intercession for us** with groanings which cannot be uttered (with groans that words cannot express, NIV)"* (see 8:24-26).

September 18 (Day 261), Memory Verse #701
Romans 8:28:

AND WE KNOW THAT ALL THINGS WORK TOGETHER FOR GOOD
TO THEM THAT LOVE GOD,
TO THEM WHO ARE THE CALLED ACCORDING TO HIS PURPOSE.

September 18 (Day 261), Memory Verse #702
Romans 8:31:

...IF GOD BE FOR US, WHO CAN BE AGAINST US?

September 19 (Day 262), Memory Verses #703 & #704
Romans 8:38-39:

38. FOR I AM PERSUADED, THAT NEITHER DEATH,
NOR LIFE, NOR ANGELS, NOR PRINCIPALITIES, NOR POWERS,
NOR THINGS PRESENT, NOR THINGS TO COME,

39. NOR HEIGHT, NOR DEPTH, NOR ANY OTHER CREATURE,
SHALL BE ABLE TO SEPARATE US FROM THE LOVE OF GOD,
WHICH IS IN CHRIST JESUS OUR LORD.

Romans 9-11: God chose the Israelites, the seed of Abraham, as His people — But Paul sadly states that the Jews turned from God many times throughout history because of their unbelief — **Paul shows that God provides His grace to all people, Jews and Gentiles, when they believe by faith** (see 9:1-11:36) — *"Brethren, my heart's desire and prayer to God for Israel is, that they might be saved"* (see 10:1).

September 20 (Day 263), Memory Verse #705
Romans 10:9:

THAT IF THOU SHALT CONFESS WITH THY MOUTH THE LORD JESUS,
AND SHALT BELIEVE IN THINE HEART THAT GOD HATH RAISED HIM FROM THE DEAD,
THOU SHALT BE SAVED.

— *"For there is no difference between the Jew and the Greek: for **the same Lord over all is rich unto all that call upon him**"* (see 10:12).

September 20 (Day 263), Memory Verse #706
Romans 10:13:

FOR WHOSOEVER SHALL CALL UPON THE NAME OF THE LORD SHALL BE SAVED.

— *"How then shall they call upon the name of him in whom they have not believed? and how shall they believe in him of whom they have not heard? And how shall they hear without a preacher? And how shall they preach, except they be sent? as it is written, **How beautiful are the feet of them that preach the gospel** of peace, and bring glad tidings of good things!"* (see 10:14-15).

September 20 (Day 263), Memory Verse #707
Romans 10:17:

SO THEN FAITH COMETH BY HEARING, AND HEARING BY THE WORD OF GOD.

September 21 (Day 264), Memory Verses #708 to #711
Romans 11:33-36:

33. O THE DEPTH OF THE RICHES BOTH OF THE WISDOM AND KNOWLEDGE OF GOD!
HOW UNSEARCHABLE ARE HIS JUDGMENTS, AND HIS WAYS PAST FINDING OUT!

34. FOR WHO HATH KNOWN THE MIND OF THE LORD?
OR WHO HATH BEEN HIS COUNSELLOR?

35. OR WHO HATH FIRST GIVEN TO HIM,
AND IT SHALL BE RECOMPENSED UNTO HIM AGAIN?

36. FOR OF HIM, AND THROUGH HIM, AND TO HIM, ARE ALL THINGS:
TO WHOM BE GLORY FOR EVER. AMEN.

Romans 12-15: Living the Christian life (see 12:1-15:33).

September 22 (Day 265), Memory Verses #712 & #713
Romans 12:1-2:

1. I BESEECH YOU THEREFORE, BRETHREN,
BY THE MERCIES OF GOD, THAT YE PRESENT YOUR BODIES
A LIVING SACRIFICE, HOLY, ACCEPTABLE UNTO GOD,
WHICH IS YOUR REASONABLE SERVICE.

2. AND BE NOT CONFORMED TO THIS WORLD:
BUT BE YE TRANSFORMED BY THE RENEWING OF YOUR MIND,
THAT YE MAY PROVE WHAT IS THAT GOOD,
AND ACCEPTABLE, AND PERFECT, WILL OF GOD.

September 23 (Day 266), Memory Verse #714
Romans 12:5:

SO WE, BEING MANY, ARE ONE BODY IN CHRIST,
AND EVERY ONE MEMBERS ONE OF ANOTHER.

September 23 (Day 266), Memory Verse #715
Romans 12:10:

BE KINDLY AFFECTIONED ONE TO ANOTHER WITH BROTHERLY LOVE;…

September 23 (Day 266), Memory Verses #716 & #717
Romans 12:14-15:

14. BLESS THEM WHICH PERSECUTE YOU: BLESS, AND CURSE NOT.

15. REJOICE WITH THEM THAT DO REJOICE, AND WEEP WITH THEM THAT WEEP.

September 24 (Day 267), Memory Verse #718
Romans 12:18:

IF IT BE POSSIBLE, AS MUCH AS LIETH IN YOU, LIVE PEACEABLY WITH ALL MEN.

September 24 (Day 267), Memory Verses #719 & #720
Romans 12:20-21:

20. THEREFORE IF THINE ENEMY HUNGER, FEED HIM;
IF HE THIRST, GIVE HIM DRINK:
FOR IN SO DOING THOU SHALT HEAP COALS OF FIRE ON HIS HEAD.

21. BE NOT OVERCOME OF EVIL, BUT OVERCOME EVIL WITH GOOD.

September 25 (Day 268), Memory Verses #721 to #723
Romans 13:8-10:

8. OWE NO MAN ANY THING, BUT TO LOVE ONE ANOTHER:
FOR HE THAT LOVETH ANOTHER HATH FULFILLED THE LAW.

9. FOR THIS, THOU SHALT NOT COMMIT ADULTERY,
THOU SHALT NOT KILL, THOU SHALT NOT STEAL,
THOU SHALT NOT BEAR FALSE WITNESS, THOU SHALT NOT COVET;
AND IF THERE BE ANY OTHER COMMANDMENT,
IT IS BRIEFLY COMPREHENDED IN THIS SAYING, NAMELY,
THOU SHALT LOVE THY NEIGHBOUR AS THYSELF.

10. LOVE WORKETH NO ILL TO HIS NEIGHBOUR:
THEREFORE LOVE IS THE FULFILLING OF THE LAW.

— *"But put ye on the Lord Jesus Christ, and make not provision for the flesh, to fulfil the lusts thereof"* (see 13:14).

September 26 (Day 269), Memory Verses #724 & #725
Romans 14:12-13:

12. SO THEN EVERY ONE OF US SHALL GIVE ACCOUNT OF HIMSELF TO GOD.

13. LET US NOT THEREFORE JUDGE ONE ANOTHER ANY MORE:
BUT JUDGE THIS RATHER,
THAT NO MAN PUT A STUMBLINGBLOCK
OR AN OCCASION TO FALL IN HIS BROTHER'S WAY.

— **Paul speaks of his plans** — *"Whensoever I take my journey into Spain, I will come to you: for I trust to see you in my journey, and to be brought on my way thitherward by you, if first I be somewhat filled with your company. But now I go unto Jerusalem to minister unto the saints. For it hath pleased them of Macedonia and Achaia to make a certain contribution for the poor saints which are at Jerusalem"* (see 15:24-26).

Romans 16: Paul's greetings to fellow Christians and closing remarks (see 16:1-27).

ROMANS 6:23:

FOR THE WAGES OF SIN IS DEATH;
BUT THE GIFT OF GOD
IS ETERNAL LIFE
THROUGH JESUS CHRIST OUR LORD.

ROMANS 10:9:

THAT IF THOU SHALT CONFESS
WITH THY MOUTH THE LORD JESUS,
AND SHALT BELIEVE
IN THINE HEART
THAT GOD HATH RAISED HIM
FROM THE DEAD,
THOU SHALT BE SAVED.

I Corinthians

Introduction: Scholars agree Paul is the author of I Corinthians.   It was written from Ephesus about 54 A.D. to the church at Corinth. Paul had lived in Corinth 18 months during his second missionary journey and worked there with Aquila and Priscilla. The city of Corinth was known for its immoral lifestyle. The Corinthian church asked Paul many questions concerning Christian behavior. In response, Paul gave instructions on sexual behavior, marriage, lawsuits with fellow Christians, and church practices. He was concerned about the divisions in the church and urged the church to labor together. His instructions to the church included teachings about the Lord's Supper, the resurrection, spiritual gifts, and the offerings to the poor. I Corinthians is well-known for "The Love Chapter," I Corinthians 13. I Corinthians has 16 chapters.

Key Contents and Key Memory Verses with Study Dates

I Corinthians 1: Paul's greetings to the church at Corinth (see 1:1-3) **— Paul shows his thankfulness for the Corinthians** (see 1:4-9) **and discusses the divisions in the church** (see 1:10-31) — *"Now I beseech you, brethren, by the name of our Lord Jesus Christ, that ye all speak the same thing, and that there be no divisions among you; but that ye **be perfectly joined together in the same mind** and in the same judgment"* (see 1:10).

September 27 (Day 270), Memory Verse #727
I Corinthians 1:18:

FOR THE PREACHING OF THE CROSS IS TO THEM THAT PERISH FOOLISHNESS;
BUT UNTO US WHICH ARE SAVED IT IS THE POWER OF GOD.

September 27 (Day 270), Memory Verse #728
I Corinthians 1:27:

BUT GOD HATH CHOSEN THE FOOLISH THINGS OF THE WORLD TO CONFOUND THE WISE;
AND GOD HATH CHOSEN THE WEAK THINGS OF THE WORLD
TO CONFOUND THE THINGS WHICH ARE MIGHTY.

September 27 (Day 270), Memory Verse #729
I Corinthians 1:31:

...HE THAT GLORIETH (boasts, NIV), LET HIM GLORY (boast, NIV) IN THE LORD.
(Also see II CORINTHIANS 10:17)

I Corinthians 2: Paul explains that God's spirit, not the spirit of the world, gives wisdom to the believer (see 2:1-16).

September 28 (Day 271), Memory Verses #730 & #731
I Corinthians 2:9-10:

9. BUT AS IT IS WRITTEN, EYE HATH NOT SEEN, NOR EAR HEARD,
NEITHER HAVE ENTERED INTO THE HEART OF MAN,
THE THINGS WHICH GOD HATH PREPARED FOR THEM THAT LOVE HIM.

10. BUT GOD HATH REVEALED THEM UNTO US BY HIS SPIRIT:
FOR THE SPIRIT SEARCHETH ALL THINGS, YEA THE DEEP THINGS OF GOD.

I Corinthians 3: Paul compares the Corinthians to spiritual babies and encourages them to be united, laboring together for God (see 3:1-23).

— *"For we are labourers together with God: ye are God's husbandry, ye are God's building. According to the grace of God which is given unto me, as a wise masterbuilder, I have laid the foundation, and another buildeth thereon;   But let every man take heed how he buildeth thereupon"* (see 3:9-10).

September 29 (Day 272), Memory Verse #732
I Corinthians 3:16:

KNOW YE NOT THAT YE ARE THE TEMPLE OF GOD,
AND THAT THE SPIRIT OF GOD DWELLETH IN YOU?

I Corinthians 4:   Paul gives fatherly admonitions and calls the Corinthians his "beloved sons" (see 4:1-21) — *"Let a man so account of us, as of the ministers of Christ, and stewards of the mysteries of God"* (see 4:1).

September 29 (Day 272), Memory Verse #733
I Corinthians 4:2:

MOREOVER IT IS REQUIRED IN STEWARDS, THAT A MAN BE FOUND FAITHFUL.

September 29 (Day 272), Memory Verse #734
I Corinthians 4:4:

FOR I KNOW NOTHING BY MYSELF; YET AM I NOT HEREBY JUSTIFIED:
BUT HE THAT JUDGETH ME IS THE LORD.

I Corinthians 5:   Paul discusses the problem of fornication among the Corinthians and how to deal with this situation (see 5:1-13) — *"But now I have written unto you **not to keep company, if** any man that is called a brother be a fornicator, or covetous, or an idolater, or a railer, or a drunkard, or an extortioner; ..."* (see 5:11).

I Corinthians 6:   Paul urges the believers to settle disputes within themselves rather than go to the legal authorities (see 6:1-8) — **Paul warns that the unrighteous will not inherit the Kingdom of God; he also speaks on being washed, sanctified and justified by the name of Jesus Christ and the Spirit of God** (see 6:9-20).

September 30 (Day 273), Memory Verse #735
I Corinthians 6:15:

KNOW YE NOT THAT YOUR BODIES ARE THE MEMBERS OF CHRIST? ...

September 30 (Day 273), Memory Verse #736
I Corinthians 6:17:

BUT HE THAT IS JOINED UNTO THE LORD IS ONE SPIRIT.

October 1 (Day 274), Memory Verses #737 & #738
I Corinthians 6:19-20:

19. WHAT? KNOW YE NOT THAT YOUR BODY IS THE TEMPLE OF THE HOLY GHOST
WHICH IS IN YOU, WHICH YE HAVE OF GOD, AND YE ARE NOT YOUR OWN?

20. FOR YE ARE BOUGHT WITH A PRICE:
THEREFORE GLORIFY GOD IN YOUR BODY, AND IN YOUR SPIRIT, WHICH ARE GOD'S.

I Corinthians 7: Paul speaks on marriage and divorce (see 7:1-40) — *"Nevertheless, to **avoid fornication**, let every man have his own wife, and let every woman have her own husband"* (see 7:2).

I Corinthians 8: Paul discusses the question of eating food offered to idols and the broader question concerning one's actions being a stumbling block to another (see 8:1-13).

October 1 (Day 274), Memory Verse #739
I Corinthians 8:1:

...KNOWLEDGE PUFFETH UP, BUT CHARITY (love, NIV) EDIFIETH.

— *"But take heed lest by any means this liberty of yours become a stumblingblock to them that are weak"* (see 8:9).

I Corinthians 9: Paul defends his apostleship and the gospel message (see 9:1-27) — *"For though I preach the gospel, I have nothing to glory of; for necessity is laid upon me; yea, **woe is unto me, if I preach not the gospel!**"* (see 9:16).

I Corinthians 10: Paul shows how to avoid sin by relying upon God (see 10:1-33).

October 2 (Day 275), Memory Verse #740
I Corinthians 10:13:

THERE HATH NO TEMPTATION TAKEN YOU BUT SUCH AS IS COMMON TO MAN:
BUT GOD IS FAITHFUL,
WHO WILL NOT SUFFER YOU TO BE TEMPTED ABOVE THAT YE ARE ABLE;
BUT WILL WITH THE TEMPTATION ALSO MAKE A WAY TO ESCAPE,
THAT YE MAY BE ABLE TO BEAR IT.

— *"Wherefore, my dearly beloved, **flee from idolatry**"* (see 10:14).

October 3 (Day 276), Memory Verse #741
I Corinthians 10:24:

LET NO MAN SEEK HIS OWN, BUT EVERY MAN ANOTHER'S WEALTH.

October 3 (Day 276), Memory Verse #742
I Corinthians 10:31:

WHETHER THEREFORE YE EAT, OR DRINK, OR WHATSOEVER YE DO,
DO ALL TO THE GLORY OF GOD.

I Corinthians 11: Paul discusses the covering of a woman's head during prayer or prophesying (see 11:1-16) — **Explanation of "The Lord's Supper"** (see 11:17-34).

I Corinthians 12: Spiritual gifts are discussed (see 12:1-31).

October 3 (Day 276), Memory Verse #743
I Corinthians 12:4:

NOW THERE ARE DIVERSITIES OF GIFTS, BUT THE SAME SPIRIT.

— *"For as the body is one, and hath many members, and all the members of that one body, being many, are one body: so also is Christ. **For by one Spirit are we all baptized into one body**, whether we be Jews or Gentiles, whether we be bond or free; and have been all made to drink into one Spirit"* (see 12:12-13) — *"And whether one member suffer, **all the members suffer** with it; or one member be honoured, **all the members rejoice** with it"* (see 12:26).

I Corinthians 13: Chapter 13 is well-known as "The Love Chapter" (see 13:1-13).

October 4-7 (Days 277-280), Memory Verses #744 to #756
I Corinthians 13:1-13:
(The Love Chapter)

1. **THOUGH** I SPEAK WITH THE TONGUES OF MEN AND OF ANGELS,
AND HAVE NOT CHARITY (love, NIV),
I AM BECOME AS SOUNDING BRASS, OR A TINKLING CYMBAL.

2. **AND** THOUGH I HAVE THE GIFT OF PROPHECY,
AND UNDERSTAND ALL MYSTERIES, AND ALL KNOWLEDGE;
AND THOUGH I HAVE ALL FAITH, SO THAT I COULD REMOVE MOUNTAINS,
AND HAVE NOT CHARITY, I AM NOTHING.

3. **AND** THOUGH I BESTOW ALL MY GOODS TO FEED THE POOR,
AND THOUGH I GIVE MY BODY TO BE BURNED,
AND HAVE NOT CHARITY, IT PROFITETH ME NOTHING.

4. **CHARITY** SUFFERETH LONG, AND IS KIND; CHARITY ENVIETH NOT;
CHARITY VAUNTETH NOT ITSELF, IS NOT PUFFED UP,

5. **DOTH** NOT BEHAVE ITSELF UNSEEMLY, SEEKETH NOT HER OWN,
IS NOT EASILY PROVOKED, THINKETH NO EVIL;

6. **REJOICETH** NOT IN INIQUITY, BUT REJOICETH IN THE TRUTH;

7. **BEARETH** ALL THINGS, BELIEVETH ALL THINGS,
HOPETH ALL THINGS, ENDURETH ALL THINGS.

8. **CHARITY** NEVER FAILETH:
BUT WHETHER THERE BE PROPHECIES, THEY SHALL FAIL;
WHETHER THERE BE TONGUES, THEY SHALL CEASE;
WHETHER THERE BE KNOWLEDGE, IT SHALL VANISH AWAY.

9. **FOR** WE KNOW IN PART, AND WE PROPHESY IN PART.

10. **BUT** WHEN THAT WHICH IS PERFECT IS COME,
THEN THAT WHICH IS IN PART SHALL BE DONE AWAY.

11. **WHEN** I WAS A CHILD, I SPAKE AS A CHILD,
I UNDERSTOOD AS A CHILD, I THOUGHT AS A CHILD:
BUT WHEN I BECAME A MAN, I PUT AWAY CHILDISH THINGS.

12. **FOR** NOW WE SEE THROUGH A GLASS, DARKLY;
BUT THEN FACE TO FACE: NOW I KNOW IN PART;
BUT THEN SHALL I KNOW EVEN AS ALSO I AM KNOWN.

13. **NOW** ABIDETH FAITH, HOPE, CHARITY, THESE THREE;
BUT THE GREATEST OF THESE IS CHARITY (love, NIV).

I Corinthians 14: Instructions concerning speaking in tongues (see 14:1-40) — *"If any man speak in an unknown tongue, let it be by two, or at the most by three, and that by course; and let one interpret"* (see 14:27).

October 8 (Day 281), Memory Verse #757
I Corinthians 14:33:

FOR GOD IS NOT THE AUTHOR OF CONFUSION,
BUT OF PEACE, AS IN ALL CHURCHES OF THE SAINTS.

I Corinthians 15: Paul discusses Christ's resurrection and triumph over death (see 1:1-58).

October 8 (Day 281), Memory Verses #758 & #759
I Corinthians 15:3-4:

3. FOR I DELIVERED TO YOU FIRST OF ALL THAT WHICH I ALSO RECEIVED,
HOW THAT CHRIST DIED FOR OUR SINS ACCORDING TO THE SCRIPTURES;

4. AND THAT HE WAS BURIED AND THAT HE ROSE AGAIN THE THIRD DAY
ACCORDING TO THE SCRIPTURES;

— *"And that he was seen of Cephas, then of the twelve: After that, he was seen of above five hundred brethren at once; of whom the greater part remain unto this present, but some are fallen asleep. After that, he was seen of James; then of all the apostles. And **last of all he was seen of me** also, as of one born out of due time. For I am the least of the apostles, that am not meet to be called an apostle, because I persecuted the church of God"* (see 15:5-9) — **"Now if Christ be preached that he rose from the dead, how say some among you that there is no resurrection of the dead?"** (see 15:12).

October 9 (Day 282), Memory Verse #760
I Corinthians 15:33:

BE NOT DECEIVED:
EVIL COMMUNICATIONS (company, NIV) CORRUPT GOOD MANNERS (character, NIV).

— *"Behold, I shew you a mystery; We shall not all sleep, but we shall all be changed, In a moment, in a twinkling of an eye, at the last trump: for the trumpet shall sound, and the dead shall be raised incorruptible, and **we shall be changed.** For this corruptible must put on incorruption, and this mortal must put on immortality"* (see 15:51-53).

October 9 & 10 (Days 282-283), Memory Verses #761 to #765
I Corinthians 15:54-58:

54. SO WHEN THIS CORRUPTIBLE SHALL HAVE PUT ON THE INCORRUPTION,
AND THIS MORTAL SHALL HAVE PUT ON IMMORTALITY,
THEN SHALL BE BROUGHT TO PASS THE SAYING THAT IS WRITTEN,
DEATH IS SWALLOWED UP IN VICTORY.

55. O DEATH, WHERE IS THY STING? O GRAVE, WHERE IS THY VICTORY?

56. THE STING OF DEATH IS SIN; AND THE STRENGTH OF SIN IS THE LAW.

57. BUT THANKS BE TO GOD,
WHICH GIVETH US THE VICTORY THROUGH OUR LORD JESUS CHRIST.

58. THEREFORE, MY BELOVED BRETHREN, BE YE STEDFAST, UNMOVEABLE,
ALWAYS ABOUNDING IN THE WORK OF THE LORD,
FORASMUCH AS YE KNOW THAT YOUR LABOUR IS NOT IN VAIN IN THE LORD.

I Corinthians 16: Paul tells the Corinthians to remember their monetary collections for the believers in Jerusalem (see 16:1-4) — **He also tells the Corinthians he plans to visit them** (see 16:5-9) — **Paul's closing statements** (see 16:10-24).

I Corinthians 13:13:

Now abideth
faith,
hope,
charity,
these three;
but the greatest of these
is charity (love, niv).

I Corinthians 10:31:

Whether therefore ye eat,
or drink,
or whatsoever ye do,
do all to the glory of god.

II Corinthians

Introduction: Scholars agree Paul is the author of II Corinthians. This book was most likely written around 55 A.D. from Macedonia to the church at Corinth. Paul visited the Corinthian church between the writing of I Corinthians and II Corinthians. He was sad to find the church was still having many of the same problems he mentioned in I Corinthians. Paul then wrote a letter known as "the sorrowful letter" (see 2:4) to the church. This letter has been lost, but some believe chapters 10-13 of II Corinthians are part of this sorrowful letter. In II Corinthians, Paul also defended his apostleship and claimed his accusers were false teachers. Even with the problems in the church, Paul expressed joy that the church was finally accepting his teachings as was reported to him by Titus. II Corinthians has 13 chapters.

Key Contents and Key Memory Verses with Study Dates

II Corinthians 1-2: Paul's opening greetings to the church at Corinth (see 1:1-2) — **Paul praises God and thanks the Corinthians for prayers** (see 1:3-11).

October 11 (Day 284), Memory Verses #766 & #767
II Corinthians 1:3-4:

3. BLESSED BE GOD, EVEN THE FATHER OF OUR LORD JESUS CHRIST,
THE FATHER OF MERCIES, AND THE GOD OF ALL COMFORT;

4. WHO COMFORTETH US IN ALL OUR TRIBULATION,
THAT WE MAY BE ABLE TO COMFORT THEM WHICH ARE IN ANY TROUBLE,
BY THE COMFORT WHEREWITH WE OURSELVES ARE COMFORTED OF GOD.

— **Paul writes how his plans to revisit Corinth have changed, but he insists his words spoken by God's wisdom can be trusted** (see 1:12-2:4) — **Paul speaks about forgiving a certain man who has already been punished** (see 2:5-11) — **Paul is disturbed by Titus' absence in Troas** (see 2:12-13) — **Spreading the gospel message is like spreading a sweet fragrance** (see 2:14-17) — *"For we are unto God a sweet savour of Christ..."* (see 2:15).

II Corinthians 3: God's Spirit, not the keeping of the law, provides life and liberty (see 3:1-18) — *"...where the Spirit of the Lord is, there is liberty"* (see 3:17).

October 11 (Day 284), Memory Verse #768
II Corinthians 3:18:

BUT WE ALL, WITH OPEN FACE, BEHOLDING AS IN A GLASS THE GLORY OF THE LORD,
ARE CHANGED INTO THE SAME IMAGE FROM GLORY TO GLORY,
EVEN AS BY THE SPIRIT OF THE LORD.

II Corinthians 4: Paul reflects on his ministry (see 4:1-18) — *"**For God who commanded the light to shine out of darkness, hath shined in our hearts,** to give the light of the knowledge of the glory of God in the face of Jesus Christ"* (see 4:6) — *"While we look not at the things which are seen, but at the things which are not seen: for the things which are seen are temporal; but **the things which are not seen are eternal**"* (see 4:18).

II Corinthians 5: A believer's body is God's house (see 5:1-21) — **A believer's earthly body will perish, but the believer's spiritual body will live, appearing before the judgment seat of Christ** — *"For we know that if our earthly house of this tabernacle were dissolved, **we have a building of God, an house not made with hands, eternal in the heavens**"* (see 5:1).

> **October 12 (Day 285), Memory Verse #769**
> **II Corinthians 5:7:**
>
> (FOR WE WALK BY FAITH, NOT BY SIGHT:)

— *"For we must all appear before the judgment seat of Christ; that every one may receive the things done in his body, according to that he hath done, whether it be good or bad"* (see 5:10).

> **October 12 (Day 285), Memory Verse #770**
> **II Corinthians 5:15:**
>
> AND THAT HE DIED FOR ALL,
> THAT THEY WHICH LIVE SHOULD NOT HENCEFORTH LIVE UNTO THEMSELVES,
> BUT UNTO HIM WHICH DIED FOR THEM, AND ROSE AGAIN.

> **October 13 (Day 286), Memory Verse #771**
> **II Corinthians 5:17:**
>
> THEREFORE IF ANY MAN BE IN CHRIST, HE IS A NEW CREATURE:
> OLD THINGS ARE PASSED AWAY; BEHOLD, ALL THINGS ARE BECOME NEW.

— *"Now then we are ambassadors for Christ…"* (see 5:20).

> **October 13 (Day 286), Memory Verse #772**
> **II Corinthians 5:21:**
>
> FOR HE HATH MADE HIM TO BE SIN FOR US, WHO KNEW NO SIN;
> THAT WE MIGHT BE MADE THE RIGHTEOUSNESS OF GOD IN HIM.

II Corinthians 6: Instructions for living the spiritual life (see 6:1-7:1).

> **October 13 (Day 286), Memory Verse #773**
> **II Corinthians 6:2:**
>
> …BEHOLD, NOW IS THE DAY OF SALVATION.

— *"Be ye not unequally yoked with unbelievers: for what fellowship hath righteousness with unrighteousness? and what communion hath light with darkness?"* (see 6:14).

II Corinthians 7: Paul gives assurance his intentions and words are true (see 7:2-16) — *"For godly sorrow worketh repentance to salvation not to be repented of (Godly sorrow brings repentance that leads to salvation and leaves no regrets, NIV): but the sorrow of the world worketh death"* (see 7:10).

II Corinthians 8-9: Paul teaches about Christ's giving and the believer's responsibility in giving (see 8:1-9:15) — *"For we know the grace of our Lord Jesus Christ, that, though he was rich, yet for your sakes he became poor, that **ye through his poverty might be rich**"* (see 8:9) — *"But this I say, He which soweth sparingly shall reap also sparingly; and **he which soweth bountifully shall reap also bountifully**"* (see 9:6).

> **October 14 (Day 287), Memory Verses #774 & #775**
> **II Corinthians 9:7-8:**
>
> 7. EVERY MAN ACCORDING AS HE PURPOSETH IN HIS HEART, SO LET HIM GIVE;
> NOT GRUDGINGLY, OR OF NECESSITY: FOR GOD LOVETH A CHEERFUL GIVER.
>
> 8. AND GOD IS ABLE TO MAKE ALL GRACE ABOUND TOWARD YOU;
> THAT YE, ALWAYS HAVING ALL SUFFICIENCY IN ALL THINGS,
> MAY ABOUND TO EVERY GOOD WORK:

II Corinthians 10-11: Paul defends his ministry (see 10:1-11:15).

October 14 (Day 287), Memory Verse #776
II Corinthians 10:17:

BUT HE THAT GLORIETH, LET HIM GLORY IN THE LORD.

— Paul lists hardships he has experienced (see 11:16-33); he has been beaten many times, stoned, shipwrecked three times, etc.

II Corinthians 12-13: Paul remarks concerning an experience of being "caught up into paradise" and hearing "unspeakable words" (see 12:1-10).

October 14 (Day 287), Memory Verse #777
II Corinthians 12:10:

THEREFORE I TAKE PLEASURE IN INFIRMITIES,
IN REPROACHES, IN NECESSITIES, IN PERSECUTIONS, IN DISTRESSES
FOR CHRIST'S SAKE: FOR WHEN I AM WEAK, THEN AM I STRONG.

— Paul explains how he does not want to burden the church at Corinth (see 12:11-18) — **Paul urges the Corinthians to examine themselves, repent of their sins, and live in faith** (see 12:19-13:10) — *"For though he was crucified through weakness, yet he liveth by the power of God. For we also are weak in him, but **we shall live with him by the power of God** toward you"* (see 13:4) — **Paul's closing statements** (see 13:11-14).

II CORINTHIANS 5:17:

THEREFORE IF ANY MAN

BE IN CHRIST,

HE IS A NEW CREATURE:

OLD THINGS ARE PASSED AWAY;

BEHOLD,

ALL THINGS ARE BECOME NEW.

GALATIANS

Introduction: Scholars widely agree that Paul is the author of Galatians. He probably wrote Galatians during the late 40's or early 50's A.D. to the churches of North or South Galatia. These were churches he had visited on his first missionary journey. Paul wrote about justification by faith and warned against religious legalism. Paul also defended his apostleship. Galatians is well-known for its passage on the fruit of the Spirit (see 5:22-23). Galatians has six chapters.

Key Contents and Key Memory Verses with Study Dates

Galatians 1-2: **Paul's opening statements** (see 1:1-10) — **Paul defends his apostleship** (see 1:11-2:21).

October 15 (Day 288), Memory Verse #778
Galatians 2:16:

...WE HAVE BELIEVED IN JESUS CHRIST,
THAT WE MIGHT BE JUSTIFIED BY THE FAITH OF CHRIST,
AND NOT BY THE WORKS OF THE LAW:
FOR BY THE WORKS OF THE LAW SHALL NO FLESH BE JUSTIFIED.

— *"I am crucified with Christ: nevertheless I live; yet not I, but Christ liveth in me: and the life which I now live in the flesh I live by the faith of the Son of God, who loved me, and gave himself for me"* (see 2:20)

Galatians 3: **Humanity is justified by faith** (see 3:1-29) — *"Even as Abraham believed God, and it was accounted to him for righteousness. Know ye therefore that they which are of faith, the same are the children of Abraham"* (see 3:6-7).

October 15 (Day 288), Memory Verse #779
Galatians 3:8:

AND THE SCRIPTURE, FORESEEING THAT GOD
WOULD JUSTIFY THE HEATHEN THROUGH FAITH,
PREACHED BEFORE THE GOSPEL UNTO ABRAHAM, SAYING,
IN THEE SHALL ALL NATIONS BE BLESSED.   (see Genesis 12:3)

October 15 (Day 288), Memory Verse #780
Galatians 3:11:

BUT THAT NO MAN IS JUSTIFIED BY THE LAW IN THE SIGHT OF GOD, IT IS EVIDENT:
FOR, THE JUST SHALL LIVE BY FAITH.

— *"Wherefore the law was our schoolmaster to bring us unto Christ, that we might be justified by faith. But after that faith is come, we are no longer under a schoolmaster.* ***For ye are all the children of God by faith in Christ Jesus.*** *For as many of you as have been baptized into Christ have put on Christ"* (see 3:24 -27).

October 16 (Day 289), Memory Verses #781 & #782
Galatians 3:28-29:

28. THERE IS NEITHER JEW NOR GREEK,
THERE IS NEITHER BOND NOR FREE,THERE IS NEITHER MALE NOR FEMALE:
FOR YE ARE ALL ONE IN CHRIST JESUS.

29. AND IF YE BE CHRIST'S, THEN ARE YE ABRAHAM'S SEED,
AND HEIRS ACCORDING TO THE PROMISE.

Galatians 4: There is bondage under the law; there is freedom in Christ — *"But when the fulness of the time was come, God sent forth his Son, made of a woman, made under the law, To redeem them that were under the law, that we might receive the adoption of sons. And because ye are sons, God hath sent forth the Spirit of his Son into your hearts, crying, Abba, Father.* **Wherefore thou art no more a servant, but a son; and if a son, then an heir of God through Christ***" (see 4:4-7)* — **Paul tries to understand why the Galatians are sometimes supportive of him but seem as an enemy at other times** (see 4:12-20) — **Paul speaks concerning the difference between living under the bondage of the law and living free from the bondage of the law;** he compares Isaac, born of a free woman, and Ishmael, born of a bondwoman (see 4:21-31).

Galatians 5: Paul speaks on faith, love, and walking in the spirit (see 5:1-26) — *"For in Jesus Christ neither circumcision availeth any thing, nor uncircumcision;* **but faith which worketh by love***" (see 5:6).*

October 17 (Day 290), Memory Verses #783 & #784
Galatians 5:13-14:

13. ...BUT BY LOVE SERVE ONE ANOTHER.

14. FOR ALL THE LAW IS FULFILLED IN ONE WORD, EVEN IN THIS;
THOU SHALT LOVE THY NEIGHBOUR AS THYSELF.

October 18 (Day 291), Memory Verse #785
Galatians 5:16:

THIS I SAY THEN, WALK IN THE SPIRIT,
AND YE SHALL NOT FULFIL THE LUST OF THE FLESH.

— *"Now the works of the flesh are manifest, which are these;* Adultery, fornication, uncleanness, lasciviousness, Idolatry, witchcraft, hatred, variance, emulations, wrath, strife, seditions, heresies, Envyings, murders, drunkenness, revellings, and such like: of the which I tell you before, as I have also told you in times past, that they which do such things shall not inherit the kingdom of God" (see 5:19-21).*

October 18 (Day 291), Memory Verses #786 & #787
Galatians 5:22-23:
(Fruit of the Spirit)

22. BUT THE FRUIT OF THE SPIRIT IS LOVE, JOY,
PEACE, LONGSUFFERING, GENTLENESS, GOODNESS, FAITH,

23. MEEKNESS, TEMPERANCE: AGAINST SUCH THERE IS NO LAW.

October 19 (Day 292), Memory Verse #788
Galatians 5:25:

IF WE LIVE IN THE SPIRIT, LET US ALSO WALK IN THE SPIRIT.

Galatians 6: Paul gives various exhortations (see 6:1-18) — **Paul teaches to bear one another's burdens** (see 6:1-5) — *"Brethren, if a man be overtaken in a fault, ye which are spiritual,* **restore such an one in the spirit of meekness;** *considering thyself, lest thou also be tempted" (see 6:1).*

October 19 (Day 292), Memory Verse #789
Galatians 6:2:

BEAR YE ONE ANOTHER'S BURDENS, AND SO FULFIL THE LAW OF CHRIST.

October 19 (Day 292), Memory Verse #790
<u>Galatians 6:7:</u>

BE NOT DECEIVED; GOD IS NOT MOCKED:
FOR WHATSOEVER A MAN SOWETH, THAT SHALL HE ALSO REAP.

— **People will reap what they sow** (see 6:6-10) — *"For he that soweth to his flesh shall of the flesh reap corruption; but he that soweth to the Spirit shall of the Spirit reap life everlasting"* (see 6:8).

October 20 (Day 293), Memory Verses #791 & #792
<u>Galatians 6:9-10:</u>

9. AND LET US NOT BE WEARY IN WELL DOING:
FOR IN DUE SEASON WE SHALL REAP, IF WE FAINT NOT.

10. AS WE HAVE OPPORTUNITY, LET US DO GOOD UNTO ALL MEN,
ESPECIALLY UNTO THEM WHO ARE OF THE HOUSEHOLD OF FAITH.

— **Paul's closing statements** (see 6:11-18) — *"But God forbid that I should glory, save (except, NIV) in the cross of our Lord Jesus Christ..."* (see 6:14).

GALATIANS 5:22-23:

22. BUT THE FRUIT OF THE SPIRIT IS

LOVE,

JOY,

PEACE,

LONGSUFFERING,

GENTLENESS,

GOODNESS,

FAITH,

23. MEEKNESS,

TEMPERANCE:

AGAINST SUCH THERE IS NO LAW.

Ephesians

Introduction: The books of Ephesians, Philippians, Colossians, and Philemon are known as "The Prison Letters" since it is thought all four were written by Paul while imprisoned in Rome. Most scholars believe Paul authored Ephesians about 60 A.D. This letter was written to the church at Ephesus, and perhaps was meant for other churches as well. One of the main themes of the letter is that the church is God's body with Christ as the head (see 4:14-16). Paul also wrote concerning relationships between husbands and wives, parents and children, and masters and slaves (see 5:21-6:9). Ephesians has six chapters.

Key Contents and Key Memory Verses with Study Dates

<u>Ephesians 1:</u> **Paul's greetings** (see 1:1-2) — **Believers have an inheritance through Jesus Christ** (see 1:3-23).

October 21 (Day 294), Memory Verses #793 & #794
<u>Ephesians 1:4-5:</u>

4. **ACCORDING** AS HE HATH CHOSEN US IN HIM
BEFORE THE FOUNDATION OF THE WORLD,
THAT WE SHOULD BE HOLY AND WITHOUT BLAME BEFORE HIM IN LOVE:

5. **HAVING** PREDESTINATED US UNTO THE ADOPTION
OF CHILDREN BY JESUS CHRIST TO HIMSELF,
ACCORDING TO THE GOOD PLEASURE OF HIS WILL,

October 22 (Day 295), Memory Verses #795 & #796
<u>Ephesians 1:22-23:</u>

22. **AND** HATH PUT ALL THINGS UNDER HIS FEET,
AND GAVE HIM TO BE THE HEAD OVER ALL THINGS TO THE CHURCH,

23. **WHICH** IS HIS BODY,
THE FULNESS OF HIM THAT FILLETH ALL IN ALL.

<u>Ephesians 2:</u> **Believers are saved by grace** (see 2:1-10).

October 23 (Day 296), Memory Verses #797 & #798
<u>Ephesians 2:4-5:</u>

4. **BUT** GOD, WHO IS RICH IN MERCY,
FOR HIS GREAT LOVE WHEREWITH HE LOVED US,

5. **EVEN** WHEN WE WERE DEAD IN SINS, HATH QUICKENED US
TOGETHER WITH CHRIST, (BY GRACE YE ARE SAVED;)

October 24 (Day 297), Memory Verse #799 & #800
<u>Ephesians 2:8-9:</u>

8. **FOR** BY GRACE ARE YE SAVED THROUGH FAITH;
AND THAT NOT OF YOURSELVES: IT IS THE GIFT OF GOD:

9. **NOT** OF WORKS, LEST ANY MAN SHOULD BOAST.

— **Believers are one body through Jesus Christ** (see 2:11-22).

October 24 (Day 297), Memory Verse #801
Ephesians 2:22:

IN WHOM YE ALSO ARE BUILDED TOGETHER FOR
AN HABITATION OF GOD THROUGH THE SPIRIT.

Ephesians 3:   All believers are fellow heirs of Christ (see 3:1-21) — *"That the Gentiles should be fellowheirs, and of the same body, and partakers of the promise in Christ by the gospel:"* (see 3:6) — *"That Christ may dwell in your hearts by faith; that ye, being rooted and grounded in love, May be able to comprehend with all saints what is the breadth, and length, and depth, and height (may have power, together with all the saints, to grasp how wide and long and high and deep is the love of Christ, NIV);"* (see 3:17-18).

October 25 (Day 298), Memory Verses #802 to #804
Ephesians 3:19-21:

19. AND TO KNOW THE LOVE OF CHRIST, WHICH PASSETH KNOWLEDGE,
THAT YE MAY BE FILLED WITH ALL THE FULNESS OF GOD.

20. NOW UNTO HIM THAT IS ABLE TO DO EXCEEDING ABUNDANTLY
ABOVE ALL THAT WE ASK OR THINK,
ACCORDING TO THE POWER THAT WORKETH IN US,

21. UNTO HIM BE GLORY IN THE CHURCH BY CHRIST JESUS
THROUGHOUT ALL AGES, WORLD WITHOUT END. AMEN.

Ephesians 4: Believers are united in one body (see 4:1-6).

October 26 (Day 299), Memory Verses #805 to #807
Ephesians 4:4-6:

4. THERE IS ONE BODY, AND ONE SPIRIT,
EVEN AS YE ARE CALLED IN ONE HOPE OF YOUR CALLING;

5. ONE LORD, ONE FAITH, ONE BAPTISM,

6. ONE GOD AND FATHER OF ALL,
WHO IS ABOVE ALL, AND THROUGH ALL, AND IN YOU ALL.

— God gives each believer a different gift which creates unity in the whole body (see 4:7-16) — *"That we henceforth be no more children, tossed to and fro, and carried about with every wind of doctrine, by the sleight of men, and cunning craftiness, whereby they lie in wait to deceive; But speaking the truth in love, may grow up into him in all things, which is the head, even Christ: From whom the whole body fitly joined together and compacted by that which every joint supplieth, according to the effectual working in the measure of every part, maketh increase of the body unto the edifying of itself in love"* (see 4:14-16) — **Believers should put away sin and be renewed through Christ** (see 4:17-32).

October 27 (Day 300), Memory Verse #808
Ephesians 4:26:

...LET NOT THE SUN GO DOWN UPON YOUR WRATH:

October 27 (Day 300), Memory Verse #809
Ephesians 4:32:

AND BE YE KIND ONE TO ANOTHER, TENDERHEARTED, FORGIVING ONE ANOTHER,
EVEN AS GOD FOR CHRIST'S SAKE HATH FORGIVEN YOU.

Ephesians 5-6: **Chapter 5 and chapter 6 speak on relationships** between God and humanity, husbands and wives, parents and children, and masters and slaves (see 5:1-6:9).

October 27 (Day 300), Memory Verse #810
Ephesians 5:2:

AND WALK IN LOVE, AS CHRIST ALSO HATH LOVED US,
AND HATH GIVEN HIMSELF FOR US AN OFFERING AND A SACRIFICE
TO GOD FOR A SWEETSMELLING SAVOUR.

— *"For ye were sometimes darkness, but now are ye light in the Lord:* **walk as children of light:** (see 5:8) — *"And be not drunk with wine, wherein is excess; but* **be filled with the Spirit;** *Speaking to yourselves in psalms and hymns and spiritual songs, singing and making melody in your heart to the Lord; Giving thanks always for all things unto God and the Father in the name of our Lord Jesus Christ;"* (see 5:18-20).

October 28 (Day 301), Memory Verses #811 & #812
Ephesians 5:21-22:

21. SUBMITTING YOURSELVES ONE TO ANOTHER
IN THE FEAR OF GOD (out of reverence for Christ, NIV).

22. WIVES, SUBMIT YOURSELVES UNTO YOUR OWN HUSBANDS, AS UNTO THE LORD.

October 28 (Day 301), Memory Verse #813
Ephesians 5:25:

HUSBANDS, LOVE YOUR WIVES,
EVEN AS CHRIST ALSO LOVED THE CHURCH, AND GAVE HIMSELF FOR IT;

October 28 (Day 301), Memory Verse #814
Ephesians 5:31:

FOR THIS CAUSE SHALL A MAN LEAVE HIS FATHER AND MOTHER,
AND SHALL BE JOINED UNTO HIS WIFE, AND THEY TWO SHALL BE ONE FLESH.

October 29 (Day 302), Memory Verses #815 to #818
Ephesians 6:1-4:

1. CHILDREN, OBEY YOUR PARENTS IN THE LORD: FOR THIS IS RIGHT.

2. HONOUR THY FATHER AND MOTHER;
(WHICH IS THE FIRST COMMANDMENT WITH PROMISE;)

3. THAT IT MAY BE WELL WITH THEE,
AND THOU MAYEST LIVE LONG ON THE EARTH.

4. AND, YE FATHERS, PROVOKE NOT YOUR CHILDREN TO WRATH:
BUT BRING THEM UP IN THE NURTURE AND ADMONITION OF THE LORD.

— **Believers should put on the whole armor of God** (see 6:10-20).

October 30 (Day 303), Memory Verses #819 to #821
Ephesians 6:10-12:

10. **FINALLY,** MY BRETHREN, BE STRONG IN THE LORD,
AND IN THE POWER OF HIS MIGHT.

11. **PUT** ON THE WHOLE ARMOUR OF GOD,
THAT WE MAY BE ABLE TO STAND AGAINST THE WILES OF THE DEVIL.

12. **FOR** WE WRESTLE NOT AGAINST FLESH AND BLOOD,
BUT AGAINST THE PRINCIPALITIES, AGAINST POWERS,
AGAINST THE RULERS OF THE DARKNESS OF THIS WORLD,
AGAINST SPIRITUAL WICKEDNESS IN HIGH PLACES.

— *"Stand therefore, having your loins girt about with **truth,** and having on the breastplate of **righteousness;** And your feet shod with the preparation of the gospel of **peace;** Above all, taking the shield of **faith,** wherewith ye shall be able to quench all the fiery darts of the wicked. And take the helmet of **salvation,** and the sword of **the Spirit,** which is **the word of God:"** (see 6:14-17).

October 31 (Day 304), Memory Verse #822
Ephesians 6:18:
PRAYING ALWAYS WITH ALL PRAYER AND SUPPLICATION IN THE SPIRIT, ...

— **Closing statements** (see 6:21-24).

EPHESIANS 2:8-9:

8. **FOR BY GRACE ARE YE SAVED THROUGH FAITH; AND NOT OF YOURSELVES: IT IS THE GIFT OF GOD:**

9. **NOT OF WORKS, LEST ANY MAN SHOULD BOAST.**

PHILIPPIANS

Introduction: Philippians is a thank-you letter by Paul, most likely written between the late 50's and early 60's A.D. while Paul was imprisoned in Rome. He thanked the church in Philippi for sending Epaphroditus to help in his ministry. Paul had visited Philippi, a city in Macedonia, during his second missionary journey. In this letter, Paul warned the church against Judaizers (Jewish religious legalists) and also encouraged them in living the Christian life (see 2:5-11 about the attitude of Christ). The book of Philippians shows how Christians can be joyful in all situations knowing God is ever present with them. Philippians has four chapters.

Key Contents and Key Memory Verses with Study Dates

<u>Philippians 1</u>: **Paul's gives greetings and expresses thankfulness for the Philippians** (see 1:1-11).

November 1 (Day 305), Memory Verse #823
<u>Philippians 1:3</u>:

I THANK MY GOD UPON EVERY REMEMBRANCE OF YOU.

— Paul testifies concerning his desire to magnify Christ whether it be in life, in suffering, or in death (see 1:12-30).

November 1 (Day 305), Memory Verse #824
<u>Philippians 1:21</u>:

FOR TO ME TO LIVE IS CHRIST, AND TO DIE IS GAIN.

<u>Philippians 2</u>: **Paul encourages believers to live in humility with Christ as their example** (see 2:1-18).

November 2-3 (Days 306-307), Memory Verses #825 to #831
<u>Philippians 2:5-11</u>:

5. LET THIS MIND BE IN YOU, WHICH WAS ALSO IN CHRIST JESUS:

6. WHO, BEING IN THE FORM OF GOD,
THOUGHT IT NOT ROBBERY TO BE EQUAL WITH GOD:

7. BUT MADE HIMSELF OF NO REPUTATION,
AND TOOK UPON HIM THE FORM OF A SERVANT,
AND WAS MADE IN THE LIKENESS OF MEN:

8. AND BEING FOUND IN FASHION AS A MAN,
HE HUMBLED HIMSELF, AND BECAME OBEDIENT UNTO DEATH,
EVEN THE DEATH OF THE CROSS.

9. WHEREFORE GOD ALSO HATH HIGHLY EXALTED HIM,
AND GIVEN HIM A NAME WHICH IS ABOVE EVERY NAME:

10. THAT AT THE NAME OF JESUS EVERY KNEE SHOULD BOW,
OF THINGS IN HEAVEN, AND THINGS IN EARTH, AND THINGS UNDER THE EARTH;

11. AND THAT EVERY TONGUE SHOULD CONFESS THAT
JESUS CHRIST IS LORD, TO THE GLORY OF GOD THE FATHER.

— Paul tells of his plans to send Epaphroditus, who had been very ill, back to the Philippians, and he thanks them for Epaphroditus' help in his ministry (see 2:19-30).

Philippians 3: Paul warns the Philippians of evil workers (see 3:1-3) — Paul testifies how the things he once thought were important are now like dung compared to the knowledge of Christ Jesus (see 3:4-21).

November 4 (Day 308), Memory Verse #832
Philippians 3:8:

YEA DOUBTLESS, AND I COUNT ALL THINGS BUT LOSS
FOR THE EXCELLENCY OF THE KNOWLEDGE OF CHRIST JESUS MY LORD:
FOR WHOM I HAVE SUFFERED THE LOSS OF ALL THINGS,
AND DO COUNT THEM BUT DUNG, THAT I MAY WIN CHRIST.

November 4 (Day 308), Memory Verse #833
Philippians 3:14:

I PRESS TOWARD THE MARK FOR THE PRIZE OF THE HIGH CALLING OF GOD IN CHRIST JESUS.

Philippians 4: Paul encourages the Philippians to live in peace and be prayerful in all things (see 4:1-20).

November 4 (Day 308), Memory Verse #834
Philippians 4:4:

REJOICE IN THE LORD ALWAY: AND AGAIN I SAY, REJOICE.

November 5 (Day 309), Memory Verses #835 to #837
Philippians 4:6-8:

6. BE CAREFUL FOR NOTHING;
BUT IN EVERY THING BY PRAYER AND SUPPLICATION WITH THANKSGIVING
LET YOUR REQUESTS BE MADE KNOWN UNTO GOD.

7. AND THE PEACE OF GOD WHICH PASSETH ALL UNDERSTANDING,
SHALL KEEP YOUR HEARTS AND MINDS THROUGH CHRIST JESUS.

8. FINALLY, BRETHREN, WHATSOEVER THINGS ARE TRUE,
WHATSOEVER THINGS ARE HONEST, WHATSOEVER THINGS ARE JUST,
WHATSOEVER THINGS ARE PURE, WHATSOEVER THINGS ARE LOVELY,
WHATSOEVER THINGS ARE OF GOOD REPORT;
IF THERE BE ANY VIRTUE, AND IF THERE BE ANY PRAISE,
THINK ON THESE THINGS.

November 6 (Day 310), Memory Verse #838
Philippians 4:11:

...FOR I HAVE LEARNED, IN WHATSOEVER STATE I AM, THEREWITH TO BE CONTENT.

November 6 (Day 310), Memory Verse #839
Philippians 4:13:

I CAN DO ALL THINGS THROUGH CHRIST WHICH STRENGTHENETH ME.

November 6 (Day 310), Memory Verse #840
Philippians 4:19:

BUT MY GOD SHALL SUPPLY ALL YOUR NEED
ACCORDING TO HIS RICHES IN GLORY BY CHRIST JESUS

— **Paul's closing statements** (see 4:21-23).

PHILIPPIANS 4:6:

Be careful for nothing;
but in every thing by prayer
and supplication
with thanksgiving
let your requests
be made known unto God.

PHILIPPIANS 4:13:

I can do all things
through Christ
which strengtheneth me.

COLOSSIANS

Introduction: Most scholars believe Paul wrote Colossians. The suggested date of writing is around 60 A.D. while Paul was imprisoned in Rome. Epaphras preached the gospel in his hometown Colossae after becoming a Christian through Paul's influence in Ephesus. There were many false teachings (see 2:8-9) in Colossae, and Epaphras visited Paul in his imprisonment to ask for advice. Paul wrote this letter to the city of Colossae to address the false teachings. Colossians has four chapters.

Key Contents and Key Memory Verses with Study Dates

Colossians 1: Paul's greetings (see 1:1-2) — **Paul expresses his gratitude for the Colossians and their faith in Christ Jesus** (see 1:3-14) — **Paul writes a beautiful passage about Christ** (see 1:15-23) — *"Who is the image of the invisible God, the firstborn of every creature: For by him were all things created, that are in heaven, and that are in earth, visible and invisible, whether they be thrones, or dominions, or principalities, or powers: **all things were created by him, and for him:"** (see 1:15-16).

November 7 (Day 311), Memory Verse #841
Colossians 1:17:

AND HE IS BEFORE ALL THINGS, AND BY HIM ALL THINGS CONSIST.

— *"And he is the head of the body, the church: who is the beginning, the firstborn from the dead; that in all things he might have the preeminence. For it pleased the Father that in him should all fulness dwell; And, having made peace through the blood of his cross, by him to reconcile all things unto himself; by him, I say, whether they be things in earth, or things in heaven"* (see 1:18-20) — **Paul speaks concerning his ministry** (see 1:24-29).

Colossians 2: In Christ are "hid all the treasures of wisdom and knowledge" (see 2:1-10) — *"As ye have therefore received Christ Jesus the Lord, **so walk ye in him:"** (see 2:6).

November 7 (Day 311), Memory Verses #842 & #843
Colossians 2:8-9:

8. BEWARE LEST ANY MAN SPOIL YOU THROUGH PHILOSOPHY AND VAIN DECEIT, AFTER THE TRADITION OF MEN, AFTER THE RUDIMENTS OF THE WORLD, AND NOT AFTER CHRIST.

9. FOR IN HIM DWELLETH ALL THE FULNESS OF THE GODHEAD BODILY.

— **The way to Christ cannot be through the keeping of the law, the worship of angels, or denying the body** (see 2:11-23) — *"And you, being dead in your sins and the uncircumcision of your flesh (sinful nature, NIV), hath he quickened together with him, having forgiven you all trespasses"* (see 2:13).

Colossians 3: Put off sin and put on love through Christ (see 3:1-17).

November 7 (Day 311), Memory Verse #844
Colossians 3:2:

SET YOUR AFFECTION ON THINGS ABOVE, NOT ON THINGS ON THE EARTH.

— *"But now ye also put off all these; anger, wrath, malice, blasphemy, filthy communication out of your mouth. Lie not one to another, seeing that **ye have put off the old man with his deeds; And have put on the new man,** which is renewed in knowledge after the image of him that created him"* (see 3:8-10).

November 8-9 (Days 312-313), Memory Verses #845 to #850
<u>**Colossians 3:12-17:**</u>

12. PUT ON THEREFORE, AS THE ELECT OF GOD, HOLY AND BELOVED,
BOWELS OF MERCIES, KINDNESS, HUMBLENESS OF MIND, MEEKNESS, LONGSUFFERING;

13. FORBEARING ONE ANOTHER, AND FORGIVING ONE ANOTHER,
IF ANY MAN HAVE A QUARREL AGAINST ANY:
EVEN AS CHRIST FORGAVE YOU, SO ALSO DO YE.

14. AND ABOVE ALL THESE THINGS PUT ON CHARITY (love, NIV),
WHICH IS THE BOND OF PERFECTNESS.

15. AND LET THE PEACE OF GOD RULE IN YOUR HEARTS,
TO THE WHICH ALSO YE ARE CALLED IN ONE BODY;
AND BE YE THANKFUL.

16. LET THE WORD OF CHRIST DWELL IN YOU RICHLY IN ALL WISDOM;
TEACHING AND ADMONISHING ONE ANOTHER
IN PSALMS AND HYMNS AND SPIRITUAL SONGS,
SINGING WITH GRACE IN YOUR HEARTS TO THE LORD.

17. AND WHATSOEVER YE DO IN WORD OR DEED,
DO ALL IN THE NAME OF THE LORD JESUS,
GIVING THANKS TO GOD AND THE FATHER BY HIM.

— **Paul speaks on relationships** (see 3:18-4:1) between husbands and wives, parents and children, and masters and slaves. Also see chapters 5-6 of Ephesians concerning relationships — *"And whatsoever ye do, do it heartily, as to the Lord, and not unto men"* (see 3:23).

<u>**Colossians 4:**</u> **Paul urges the Colossians to continue in prayer and to walk in wisdom** (see 4:2-6) — *"Let your speech be always with grace, seasoned with salt, that ye may know how ye ought to answer every man"* (see 4:6) — **Paul's closing statements** (see 4:7-18).

<u>COLOSSIANS 1:17:</u>

AND HE IS BEFORE ALL THINGS, AND BY HIM ALL THINGS CONSIST.

<u>COLOSSIANS 3:2:</u>

SET YOUR AFFECTION ON THINGS ABOVE, NOT ON THINGS ON THE EARTH.

I THESSALONIANS

Introduction: Scholars agree Paul is the author of I Thessalonians, and most scholars believe Paul authored II Thessalonians. These books were probably written in the early 50's A.D. from Corinth to the church at Thessalonica. Thessalonica was the capital of Macedonia. On Paul's second missionary journey, he had fled Thessalonica with Silas because a group of Jews had organized a mob against them. Paul then sent Timothy to visit Thessalonica and report back about the Thessalonians. After hearing Timothy's report, Paul wrote I Thessalonians to encourage new converts, defend his ministry, answer questions about the fate of Christians who die before Christ's return (see 4:13-18), and give instructions for Christian living. Both I and II Thessalonians speak much about Christ's second coming. I Thessalonians has five chapters.

Key Contents and Key Memory Verses with Study Dates

I Thessalonians 1: Paul's greetings (see 1:1) — **Paul praises the Thessalonians for serving God and turning from idols** (see 1:2-10) — *"Remembering without ceasing your work of faith, and labour of love, and patience of hope in our Lord Jesus Christ..."* (see 1:3) — *"For our gospel came not unto you in word only, but also in power, and in the Holy Ghost..."* (see 1:5).

I Thessalonians 2: Paul defends his ministry (see 2:1-12) — *"But as we were allowed of God to be put in trust with the gospel, even so we speak; not as pleasing men, but God, which trieth our hearts"* (see 2:4) — *"Ye are witnesses, and God also, how holily and justly and unblameably we beheld ourselves among you that believe. As ye know how we exhorted and comforted and charged every one of you, as a father doth his children. That ye would walk worthy of God, who hath called you unto his kingdom and glory"* (see 2:10-12) — **Paul again praises the Thessalonians for their faith even through suffering** (see 2:13-20).

I Thessalonians 3: Paul writes how he sent Timothy to encourage the Thessalonians in their faith and spiritual growth (see 3:1-13) — *"But now when Timotheus (Timothy, NIV) came from you unto us, and brought us good tidings of your faith and charity, and that ye have good remembrance of us always, desiring greatly to see us, as we also to see you: Therefore, brethren, we were comforted over you in all our affliction and distress by your faith:"*(see 3:6-7).

I Thessalonians 4-5: Paul writes about Christian living (see 4:1-12) — *"...ye should abstain from fornication:"* (see 4:3) — *"For God hath not called us unto uncleanness, but unto holiness"* (see 4:7) — *"...love one another"* (see 4:9) — *"...work with your own hands..."* (see 4:11) — **Paul writes about the day of the Lord** (see 4:13-5:11).

November 10 (Day 314), Memory Verses #851 to #852
I Thessalonians 4:16-17:

16. FOR THE LORD HIMSELF SHALL DESCEND FROM HEAVEN WITH A SHOUT,
WITH THE VOICE OF THE ARCHANGEL, AND WITH THE TRUMP OF GOD:
AND THE DEAD IN CHRIST SHALL RISE FIRST:

17. THEN WE WHICH ARE ALIVE AND REMAIN SHALL BE CAUGHT UP
TOGETHER WITH THEM IN THE CLOUDS, TO MEET THE LORD IN THE AIR:
AND SO SHALL WE EVER BE WITH THE LORD.

November 10 (Day 314), Memory Verse #853
I Thessalonians 5:2:

FOR YOURSELVES, KNOW PERFECTLY
THAT THE DAY OF THE LORD SO COMETH AS A THIEF IN THE NIGHT.

November 11 (Day 315), Memory Verse #854
I Thessalonians 5:8:

BUT LET US, WHO ARE OF THE DAY, BE SOBER,
PUTTING ON THE BREASTPLATE OF FAITH AND LOVE;
AND FOR AN HELMET, THE HOPE OF SALVATION.

— **Paul gives more instructions on living the Christian life** (see 5:12-24).

November 11-12 (Days 315-316), Memory Verses #855 to #860
I Thessalonians 5:13-18:

13. ...AND BE AT PEACE AMONG YOURSELVES.

14. ...BE PATIENT TOWARD ALL MEN.

15. SEE THAT NONE RENDER EVIL FOR EVIL UNTO ANY MAN;
BUT EVER FOLLOW THAT WHICH IS GOOD,
BOTH AMONG YOURSELVES, AND TO ALL MEN.

16. REJOICE EVERMORE.

17. PRAY WITHOUT CEASING.

18. IN EVERYTHING GIVE THANKS:
FOR THIS IS THE WILL OF GOD IN CHRIST JESUS CONCERNING YOU.

November 13 (Day 317), Memory Verse #861
I Thessalonians 5:22:

ABSTAIN FROM ALL APPEARANCE OF EVIL.

— **Paul's closing statements** (see 5:25-28).

I THESSALONIANS 5:16-18:

16. REJOICE EVERMORE.

17. PRAY WITHOUT CEASING.

18. IN EVERYTHING GIVE THANKS:
FOR THIS IS THE WILL OF GOD
IN CHRIST JESUS CONCERNING YOU.

II Thessalonians

Introduction: See the introduction to I Thessalonians. Most scholars believe Paul wrote II Thessalonians within a year after writing I Thessalonians. He continued to encourage the converts, and wrote about evil and the "son of perdition" (see 2:3-9) in the end times. Many of the Thessalonians had quit working because they believed the time for Christ's return was near. Paul urged them to keep working and not be idle since the time of the Lord's return is known by no one. II Thessalonians has three chapters.

Key Contents and Key Memory Verses with Study Dates

II Thessalonians 1: Paul's greetings (see 1:1-2) — **Paul gives thanks for the Thessalonians and encourages them to persevere through persecutions** (see 1:3-12).

II Thessalonians 2: Paul speaks of Christ's coming and gives warnings concerning the "son of perdition" (see 2:1-17) — *"Let no man deceive you by any means: for that day shall not come except there come a falling away first, and that man of sin be revealed, the son of perdition; Who opposeth and exalteth himself above all that is called God, or that is worshipped; so that he as God sitteth in the temple of God, shewing himself that he is God (proclaiming himself to be God, NIV)"* (see 2:3-4) — *"Now our Lord Jesus Christ himself, and God, even our Father, which hath loved us, and hath given us everlasting consolation and good hope through grace,* **Comfort your hearts, and stablish you in every good word and work"** (see 2:16-17).

II Thessalonians 3: Instructions for Christian living and encouragement for the Thessalonians to keep working faithfully until the Lord comes (see 3:1-15) — *"And the Lord direct your hearts into the love of God, and into the patient waiting for Christ"* (see 3:5) — *"For even when we were with you, this we commanded you, that* **if any would not work, neither should he eat"** (see 3:10).

November 13 (Day 317), Memory Verse #862
II Thessalonians 3:13:

BUT YE BRETHREN, BE NOT WEARY IN WELL DOING.

— Paul's closing statements (see 3:16-18) — *"Now the Lord of peace himself give you peace always by all means. The Lord be with you all"* (see 3:16).

II Thessalonians 3:13:

... BE NOT WEARY IN WELL DOING.

I TIMOTHY

Introduction: I and II Timothy and Titus are known as "The Pastoral Letters" since pastoral advice for the churches is given to Timothy and Titus. Timothy had been with Paul and Silas on Paul's second missionary journey (see Acts 16). Tradition points to Paul as the author of these three letters, but many scholars believe they were written by another author in the 100's A.D. The suggested traditional date for the writing of I Timothy is about 63-65 A.D. when Paul was in Macedonia, most likely between imprisonments. At this time, Titus was in Crete, and Timothy was in Ephesus. This letter includes warnings of false teachings (chapter 1), teachings on prayer and instructions for women (chapter 2), qualifications for bishops and deacons (chapter 3), discussion of latter times (chapter 4), directions for treatment of family members and the elderly (chapter 5), and warnings about the love of money (chapter 6). I Timothy has six chapters.

Key Contents and Key Memory Verses with Study Dates

I Timothy 1: **Paul's greetings** (see 1:1-2) — **Warnings against false teachings** (see 1:3-11).

November 14 (Day 318), Memory Verse #863
I Timothy 1:5:

NOW THE END (goal, NIV) OF THE COMMANDMENT IS CHARITY (love, NIV)
OUT OF A PURE HEART,
AND OF A GOOD CONSCIENCE, AND OF FAITH UNFEIGNED (sincere faith, NIV):

— **Once "chief" of sinners, Paul praises God for choosing him to minister** (see 1:12-17) — **Encouragement for Timothy** (see 1:18-20).

I Timothy 2: **Teachings concerning prayers** (see 2:1-8) **and women's behavior in the church** (see 2:9-15) — *"I exhort therefore, that, first of all, supplications, prayers, intercessions, and giving of thanks, be made for all men; For kings, and for all that are in authority; that we may lead a quiet and peaceable life in all godliness and honesty"* (see 2:1-2).

November 14 (Day 318), Memory Verses #864 & #865
I Timothy 2:5-6:

5. FOR THERE IS ONE GOD, AND ONE MEDIATOR BETWEEN GOD AND MEN,
THE MAN CHRIST JESUS;

6. WHO GAVE HIMSELF A RANSOM FOR ALL, TO BE TESTIFIED IN DUE TIME.

I Timothy 3: **Requirements for bishops** (see 3:1-7) **and deacons** (see 3:8-16).

November 14 (Day 318), Memory Verse #866
I Timothy 3:16:

AND WITHOUT CONTROVERSY GREAT IS THE MYSTERY OF GODLINESS:
GOD WAS MANIFEST IN THE FLESH, JUSTIFIED IN THE SPIRIT,
SEEN OF ANGELS, PREACHED UNTO THE GENTILES,
BELIEVED ON IN THE WORLD, RECEIVED UP INTO GLORY.

I Timothy 4: **Warnings that some will depart from the faith in latter times** (see 4:1-16).

November 15 (Day 319), Memory Verse #867
I Timothy 4:12:

LET NO MAN DESPISE THY YOUTH; BUT BE THOU AN EXAMPLE OF THE BELIEVERS,
IN WORD, IN CONVERSATION, IN CHARITY, IN SPIRIT, IN FAITH, IN PURITY.

I Timothy 5: Teachings about the treatment of widows and the elderly (see 5:1-25) — *"Rebuke not an elder, but intreat him as a father; and the younger men as brethren; The elder women as mothers; the younger as sisters, with all purity. Honour widows that are widows indeed"* (see 5:1-3).

November 15 (Day 319), Memory Verse #868
I Timothy 5:8:

BUT IF ANY PROVIDE NOT FOR HIS OWN (relatives, NIV),
AND SPECIALLY FOR THOSE OF HIS OWN HOUSE (immediate family, NIV),
HE HATH DENIED THE FAITH, AND IS WORSE THAN AN INFIDEL (unbeliever, NIV).

November 15 (Day 319), Memory Verses #869 & #870
I Timothy 6:6-7:

6. BUT GODLINESS WITH CONTENTMENT IS GREAT GAIN.

7. FOR WE BROUGHT NOTHING INTO THIS WORLD,
AND IT IS CERTAIN WE CAN CARRY NOTHING OUT.

I Timothy 6: Relationships between masters and slaves (see 6:1-2) — **False teachings** (see 6:3-5) — **The values of godliness and dangers of money** (see 6:6-19) — **Paul's closing statements** (see 6:20-21).

November 16 (Day 320), Memory Verses #871 to #873
I Timothy 6:10-12:

10. FOR THE LOVE OF MONEY IS THE ROOT OF ALL EVIL:
WHICH WHILE SOME COVETED AFTER, THEY HAVE ERRED FROM THE FAITH,
AND PIERCED THEMSELVES THROUGH WITH MANY SORROWS.

11. BUT THOU, O MAN OF GOD, FLEE THESE THINGS;
AND FOLLOW AFTER RIGHTEOUSNESS,
GODLINESS, FAITH, LOVE, PATIENCE, AND MEEKNESS.

12. FIGHT THE GOOD FIGHT OF FAITH, LAY HOLD ON ETERNAL LIFE,
WHEREUNTO THOU ART ALSO CALLED,
AND HAST PROFESSED A GOOD PROFESSION BEFORE MANY WITNESSES.

November 17 (Day 321), Memory Verses #874 & #875
I Timothy 6:17-18:

17. CHARGE THEM THAT ARE RICH IN THIS WORLD, THAT THEY NOT BE HIGH-MINDED,
NOR TRUST IN UNCERTAIN RICHES, BUT IN THE LIVING GOD,
WHO GIVETH US RICHLY ALL THINGS TO ENJOY;

18. THAT THEY DO GOOD, THAT THEY BE RICH IN GOOD WORKS,
READY TO DISTRIBUTE, WILLING TO COMMUNICATE;

I TIMOTHY 6:10: FOR THE LOVE OF MONEY IS THE ROOT OF ALL EVIL: ...

II TIMOTHY

Introduction: See I Timothy's introduction. The traditional date for the writing of II Timothy is about 66 A.D. Paul addressed the letter to Timothy who was most likely in Ephesus. Paul was imprisoned for his last and second time in Rome, just before he was beheaded. It is believed the emperor Nero burned Rome in 64 A.D. and blamed the Christians. Perhaps this is why Paul was imprisoned again. Paul encouraged Timothy to be a "good soldier of Jesus Christ" (see 2:3) and asked Timothy to visit him (see 4:9). II Timothy has four chapters.

Key Contents and Key Memory Verses with Study Dates

II Timothy 1: Paul's greetings (see 1:1-2) — **Paul is thankful for Timothy** (see 1:3-7) — **He encourages Timothy to spread the gospel even through suffering; Paul mentions the suffering he has endured** (see 1:8-18).

November 18 (Day 322), Memory Verses #876 & #877
II Timothy 1:7-8:

7. FOR GOD HATH NOT GIVEN US THE SPIRIT OF FEAR;
BUT OF POWER, AND OF LOVE, AND OF A SOUND MIND.

8. BE NOT THOU THEREFORE ASHAMED OF THE TESTIMONY OF OUR LORD...

— *"Who hath saved us, and called us with an holy calling, not according to our works, but according to his own purpose and grace, **which was given us in Christ Jesus before the world began,** But is now made manifest by the appearing of our Saviour Jesus Christ who hath abolished death, and hath brought life and immortality to light through the gospel:"*(see 1:9-10).

November 18 (Day 322), Memory Verse #878
II Timothy 1:12:

...FOR I KNOW WHOM I HAVE BELIEVED, AND AM PERSUADED THAT HE IS ABLE TO KEEP
THAT WHICH I HAVE COMMITTED UNTO HIM AGAINST THAT DAY.

II Timothy 2: Paul describes how to be "strong in the grace that is in Christ Jesus" (see 2:1-26) — *"Thou therefore endure hardness, as a good soldier of Jesus Christ"* (see 2:3).

November 18 (Day 322), Memory Verse #879
II Timothy 2:15:

STUDY TO SHEW THYSELF APPROVED UNTO GOD,
A WORKMAN THAT NEEDETH NOT TO BE ASHAMED,
RIGHTLY DIVIDING THE WORD OF TRUTH.

II Timothy 3: Paul warns of trying times in the end days (see 3:1-9) **and gives instructions on how to remain faithful even through tribulations** (see 3:10-17).

November 19 (Day 323), Memory Verses #880 to #882
II Timothy 3:15-17:

15. AND THAT FROM A CHILD THOU HAST KNOWN THE HOLY SCRIPTURES,
WHICH ARE ABLE TO MAKE THEE WISE UNTO SALVATION
THROUGH FAITH WHICH IS IN CHRIST JESUS.

16. ALL SCRIPTURE IS GIVEN BY INSPIRATION OF GOD, AND IS PROFITABLE FOR DOCTRINE,
FOR REPROOF, FOR CORRECTION, FOR INSTRUCTION IN RIGHTEOUSNESS:

17. THAT THE MAN OF GOD MAY BE PERFECT,
THROUGHLY FURNISHED UNTO ALL GOOD WORKS.

II Timothy 4: **Paul encourages Timothy to preach sound doctrine and remain faithful** (see 4:1-8).

November 20 (Day 324), Memory Verse #883
II Timothy 4:7:

I HAVE FOUGHT A GOOD FIGHT,
I HAVE FINISHED MY COURSE,
I HAVE KEPT THE FAITH:

— *"Henceforth there is laid up for me a crown of righteousness, which the Lord, the righteous judge, shall give me at that day: and not to me only, but unto all them also that love his appearing"* (see 4:8) — **Paul's closing statements** (see 4:9-22).

II TIMOTHY 3:16:

ALL SCRIPTURE IS GIVEN BY INSPIRATION OF GOD, AND IS PROFITABLE FOR DOCTRINE, FOR REPROOF, FOR CORRECTION, FOR INSTRUCTION IN RIGHTEOUSNESS:

TITUS

Introduction: Traditionally, it is thought Paul wrote Titus after his first release from a Roman prison in the early 60's A.D.   Many scholars believe a later author other than Paul was the writer. This letter is addressed to Titus, a Gentile Christian who worked with Paul in Ephesus, Crete, Nicopolis, and Dalmatia.   Titus is not mentioned in Acts, but is found in Galatians and II Corinthians. Paul had left Titus in Crete to help with the converts. Zenas and Apollas may have been the deliverers of this letter to Titus. The book of Titus gives the qualifications of a bishop in the church, warns of false teachers, and places emphasis on faith and doing good. Two important Christian doctrine passages are Titus 2:11-14 and Titus 3:4-7.   Titus has three chapters.

Key Contents and Key Memory Verses with Study Dates

<u>Titus 1:</u> **In the greeting of the letter** (see 1:1-4), **the following verse is found:**

November 21 (Day 325), Memory Verse #884
<u>Titus 1:2:</u>

IN HOPE OF ETERNAL LIFE, WHICH GOD THAT CANNOT LIE,
PROMISED BEFORE THE WORLD BEGAN;

Duties of the bishop of a church (see 1:5-9) — *"For a bishop must be blameless, as the steward of God; not selfwilled, not soon angry, not given to wine, no striker, not given to filthy lucre; But a lover of hospitality, a lover of good men, sober, just, holy, temperate; Holding fast the faithful word as he hath been taught, that he may be able by sound doctrine both to exhort and to convince the gainsayers"* (see 1:7-9) — **Vain and deceiving teachers** (see 1:10-16).

<u>Titus 2:</u> **Duties of church members** (see 2:1-15).

November 22 (Day 326), Memory Verses #885 to #888
<u>Titus 2:11-14:</u>

11. FOR THE GRACE OF GOD THAT BRINGETH SALVATION HATH APPEARED TO ALL MEN,

12. TEACHING US THAT, DENYING UNGODLINESS AND WORLDLY LUSTS,
WE SHOULD LIVE SOBERLY, RIGHTEOUSLY, AND GODLY,
IN THIS PRESENT WORLD;

13. LOOKING FOR THAT BLESSED HOPE,
AND THE GLORIOUS APPEARING OF THE GREAT GOD
AND OUR SAVIOUR JESUS CHRIST;

14. WHO GAVE HIMSELF FOR US, THAT HE MIGHT REDEEM US FROM ALL INIQUITY,
AND PURIFY UNTO HIMSELF A PECULIAR PEOPLE (a people that are his very own, NIV),
ZEALOUS IN GOOD WORKS.

<u>Titus 3:</u> **How believers should act toward others and handle deceitful teachers** (see 3:1-11).

November 23 (Day 327), Memory Verses #889 to #892
<u>**Titus 3:4-7:**</u>

4. ...THE KINDNESS AND LOVE OF GOD OUR SAVIOUR TOWARD MAN APPEARED,

5. NOT BY WORKS OF RIGHTEOUSNESS WHICH WE HAVE DONE,
BUT ACCORDING TO HIS MERCY HE SAVED US,
BY THE WASHING OF REGENERATION,
AND RENEWING OF THE HOLY GHOST;

6. WHICH HE SHED ON US ABUNDANTLY THROUGH JESUS CHRIST OUR SAVIOUR;

7. THAT BEING JUSTIFIED BY HIS GRACE,
WE SHOULD BE MADE HEIRS ACCORDING TO THE HOPE OF ETERNAL LIFE.

— **Closing statements** (see 3:12-15).

TITUS 3:5:

NOT BY WORKS OF RIGHTEOUSNESS WHICH WE HAVE DONE, BUT ACCORDING TO HIS MERCY HE SAVED US...

PHILEMON

Introduction: Scholars agree Paul is the author of Philemon. He probably wrote Philemon about 61 A.D. while imprisoned in Rome. Paul wrote this letter to Philemon, a Christian in Colossae, and also greeted other believers. Philemon's slave, Onesimus, had stolen from Philemon, run away, and then met Paul. Onesimus became a Christian through Paul's influence, and wanted to return and receive forgiveness from his owner. Onesimus could be punished by death, but Paul urged Philemon to forgive his slave and take him back. Although the fate of Onesimus is uncertain, a letter by the Christian teacher Ignatius years later is addressed to a bishop of Ephesus named Onesimus. Perhaps this was the same Onesimus mentioned in Philemon. Philemon has only 25 verses.

Key Contents and Key Memory Verses with Study Dates

<u>**Philemon verses 1-25:**</u> **Paul's greetings** (see verses 1-3) — **Paul urges Philemon to receive Onesimus** (see verses 4-21) not *"... now as a servant, but above a servant, a brother beloved, specially to me, but how much more unto thee, both in the flesh, and in the Lord? If thou count me therefore a partner, receive him as myself "* (see verses 16-17).

November 24 (Day 328), Memory Verses #893 & #894
<u>**Philemon verses 4-5:**</u>

4. I THANK MY GOD,
MAKING MENTION OF THEE ALWAYS IN MY PRAYERS.

5. HEARING OF THY LOVE AND FAITH,
WHICH THOU HAST TOWARD THE LORD JESUS,
AND TOWARD ALL SAINTS;

— **Paul's closing remarks** (see verses 22-25).

PHILEMON VERSE 4:

I THANK MY GOD, MAKING MENTION OF THEE ALWAYS IN MY PRAYERS.

HEBREWS

Introduction: The author of Hebrews is unknown. This epistle was most likely written to Jewish Christians before the destruction of Jerusalem and the temple in 70 A.D. Suggested authors include Paul, Barnabas, Silas, Aquila and Priscilla, Apollos, Epaphras, and Clement of Rome. Hebrews shows the superiority of Christ to other leaders, prophets, priests and even angels. This letter encourages Christians to persevere through persecutions and emphasizes that Christ is the believer's High Priest, mediator, and way to eternal inheritance (see Hebrews 7:22-27 and 9:11-15). Many Old Testament verses are quoted in Hebrews. Hebrews has 13 chapters.

Key Contents and Key Memory Verses with Study Dates

Hebrews 1: Christ reigns at God's right hand and is superior to the angels (see 1:1-14).

November 25 (Day 329), Memory Verses #895 to #897
Hebrews 1:1-3:

1. **GOD,** WHO AT SUNDRY TIMES AND IN DIVERS MANNERS
(at many times and in various ways, NIV),
SPAKE IN TIME PAST UNTO THE FATHERS BY THE PROPHETS.

2. **HATH** IN THESE LAST DAYS SPOKEN UNTO US BY HIS SON,
WHOM HE HATH APPOINTED HEIR OF ALL THINGS,
BY WHOM ALSO HE MADE THE WORLDS;

3. **WHO** BEING THE BRIGHTNESS OF HIS GLORY,
AND THE EXPRESS IMAGE OF HIS PERSON,
AND UPHOLDING ALL THINGS BY THE WORD OF HIS POWER,
WHEN HE HAD BY HIMSELF PURGED OUR SINS,
SAT DOWN ON THE RIGHT HAND OF THE MAJESTY ON HIGH;

— *"Being made so much better than the angels, as he hath by inheritance obtained a more excellent name than they"* (see 1:4) — *"But to which of the angels said he at any time, Sit on my right hand, until I make thine enemies thy footstool? Are they not all **ministering spirits**, sent forth to minister for them who shall be heirs of salvation?"* (see 1:13-14).

Hebrews 2: Christ is the believer's merciful and faithful High Priest (see 2:1-18) — *"Forasmuch then as the children are partakers of flesh and blood, he also himself likewise took part of the same; that **through death he might destroy him that had the power of death, that is, the devil;**"* (see 2:14) — *"Wherefore in all things it behoved him to be made like unto his brethren, that he might be a merciful and faithful high priest in things pertaining to God, **to make reconciliation for the sins of the people.** For in that he himself hath suffered being tempted, he is able to succour (help, NIV) them that are tempted"* (see 2:17-18).

Hebrews 3-4: Christ is superior to Moses and all humanity (see 3:1-6); *"For every house is builded by some man; but he that built all things is God"* (see 3:4) — Believers are the house of Christ (see 3:6) — **Beware of unbelief** (see 3:7-4:16).

> **November 25 (Day 329), Memory Verse #898**
> **Hebrews 4:12:**
>
> FOR THE WORD OF GOD IS QUICK, AND POWERFUL,
> AND SHARPER THAN ANY TWOEDGED SWORD,
> PIERCING EVEN TO THE DIVIDING ASUNDER OF SOUL AND SPIRIT,
> AND OF THE JOINTS AND MARROW,
> AND IS A DISCERNER OF THE THOUGHTS AND INTENTS OF THE HEART.

Hebrews 5-10: **Christ is superior to earthly high priests** (see 5:1-10:39).

> **November 26 (Day 330), Memory Verses #899 to #901**
> **Hebrews 4:14-16:**
>
> 14. SEEING THEN THAT WE HAVE A GREAT HIGH PRIEST,
> THAT IS PASSED INTO THE HEAVENS, JESUS THE SON OF GOD,
> LET US HOLD FAST OUR PROFESSION.
>
> 15. FOR WE HAVE NOT AN HIGH PRIEST WHICH CANNOT
> BE TOUCHED WITH THE FEELINGS OF OUR INFIRMITIES;
> BUT WAS IN ALL POINTS TEMPTED LIKE AS WE ARE, YET WITHOUT SIN.
>
> 16. LET US THEREFORE COME BOLDLY UNTO THE THRONE OF GRACE
> THAT WE MAY OBTAIN MERCY,
> AND FIND GRACE TO HELP IN TIME OF NEED.

— *"For such an high priest became us (meets our needs, NIV), who is holy, harmless, undefiled, separate from sinners, and made higher than the heavens; Who needeth not daily, as those high priests, to offer up sacrifice, first for his own sins, and then for the people's: for this he did once, when he offered up himself"* (see 7:26-27).

— *"For this is the covenant that I will make with the house of Israel after those days, saith the Lord; I will put my laws into their mind, and write them in their hearts: and I will be to them a God, and they shall be to me a people: ...for all shall know me, from the least to the greatest. For I will be merciful to their unrighteousness, and their sins and their iniquities will I remember no more. In that he saith, A new covenant, he hath made the first old..."* (see 8:10-13).

— *"Neither by the blood of goats and calves, but by his own blood he entered in once into the holy place, having obtained eternal redemption for us. For if the blood of bulls and of goats, and the ashes of an heifer sprinkling the unclean, sanctifieth to the purifying of the flesh: How much more shall the blood of Christ, who through the eternal Spirit offered himself without spot to God, purge your conscience from dead works to serve the living God?"* (see 9:12-14).

> **November 27 (Day 331), Memory Verse #902**
> **Hebrews 9:27:**
>
> AND AS IT IS APPOINTED UNTO MEN ONCE TO DIE,
> BUT AFTER THIS THE JUDGMENT:

November 27 (Day 331), Memory Verses #903 to #905
Hebrews 10:23-25:

23. LET US HOLD FAST THE PROFESSION OF OUR FAITH
WITHOUT WAVERING; (FOR HE IS FAITHFUL THAT PROMISED;)

24. AND LET US CONSIDER ONE ANOTHER TO PROVOKE
UNTO LOVE AND TO GOOD WORKS:

25. NOT FORSAKING THE ASSEMBLING OF OURSELVES TOGETHER,
AS THE MANNER OF SOME IS; BUT EXHORTING ONE ANOTHER:
AND SO MUCH THE MORE AS YE SEE THE DAY APPROACHING.

November 28 (Day 332), Memory Verse #906
Hebrews 10:38:

NOW THE JUST SHALL LIVE BY FAITH: …

Hebrews 11: **This chapter** (see 11:1-30) **is known as "The Faith Chapter" and lists the following heroes of the faith:** ABEL, ENOCH, NOAH, ABRAHAM, ISAAC, JACOB, JOSEPH, MOSES' PARENTS, MOSES, RAHAB, GIDEON, BARAK, SAMSON, JEPHTHAE (Jephthah, NIV), DAVID, SAMUEL, THE PROPHETS, AND OTHERS.

November 28 (Day 332), Memory Verse #907
Hebrews 11:1:

NOW FAITH IS THE SUBSTANCE OF THINGS HOPED FOR,
THE EVIDENCE OF THINGS NOT SEEN.

November 28 (Day 332), Memory Verse #908
Hebrews 11:6:

BUT WITHOUT FAITH IT IS IMPOSSIBLE TO PLEASE HIM;
FOR HE THAT COMETH TO GOD MUST BELIEVE THAT HE IS,
AND THAT HE IS A REWARDER OF THEM THAT DILIGENTLY SEEK HIM.

Hebrews 12: **Believers are encouraged to persevere through tribulations** (see 12:1-3), **accept God's discipline** (see 12:4-11), **and honor and follow God** (see 12:12-29).

November 29 (Day 333), Memory Verses #909 & #910
Hebrews 12:1-2:

1. WHEREFORE SEEING WE ALSO ARE COMPASSED ABOUT
WITH SO GREAT A CLOUD OF WITNESSES,
LET US LAY ASIDE EVERY WEIGHT, AND THE SIN WHICH DOTH SO EASILY BESET US,
AND LET US RUN WITH PATIENCE THE RACE THAT IS SET BEFORE US.

2. LOOKING UNTO JESUS THE AUTHOR AND FINISHER OF OUR FAITH;
WHO FOR THE JOY THAT WAS SET BEFORE HIM ENDURED THE CROSS,
DESPISING THE SHAME,
AND IS SET DOWN AT THE RIGHT HAND OF THE THRONE OF GOD.

November 29 (Day 333), Memory Verse #911
Hebrews 12:6:

FOR WHOM THE LORD LOVETH HE CHASTENETH,
AND SCOURGETH EVERY SON WHOM HE RECEIVETH.

Hebrews 13: **Guidelines for the Christian life** (see 13:1-19).

November 30 (Day 334), Memory Verses #912 & #913
Hebrews 13:1-2:

1. LET BROTHERLY LOVE CONTINUE.

2. BE NOT FORGETFUL TO ENTERTAIN STRANGERS:
FOR THEREBY SOME HAVE ENTERTAINED ANGELS UNAWARES.

November 30 (Day 334), Memory Verse #914
Hebrews 13:8:

JESUS CHRIST THE SAME YESTERDAY, AND TO DAY, AND FOR EVER.

— **Closing verses** (see 13:20-25) — *"Now the God of peace, that brought again from the dead our Lord Jesus, that great shepherd of the sheep, through the blood of the everlasting covenant, Make you perfect in every good work to do his will, working in you that which is well-pleasing in his sight, through Jesus Christ; to whom be glory for ever and ever. Amen"* (see 13:20-21).

HEBREWS 13:8:

JESUS CHRIST THE SAME

YESTERDAY,
AND TO DAY,
AND FOR EVER.

JAMES

Introduction: Most scholars attribute authorship of this letter to James, Jesus' oldest half brother. This James was thrown down from the temple wall and stoned by the Jewish religious leaders in 62 A.D.   Some suggest the author is James, the son of Zebedee and brother of John. This James was killed by Herod Agrippa (see Acts 12:1-2). James wrote to Jewish Christians, *"to the twelve tribes which are scattered abroad"* (see James 1:1). Most likely this letter was written in the 40's A.D. James contains instructions on Christian living and emphasizes faith will produce works. James refers to many verses from the Old Testament and Jesus' "Sermon on the Mount.'' James has five chapters.

Key Contents and Key Memory Verses with Study Dates

James 1:   Greetings from James (see 1:1) — **James writes about temptation** (see 1:2-15), **good and perfect gifts from God** (see 1:16-18), **and being doers of the word** (see 1:19-27) — *"My brethren, count it all joy when ye fall into divers temptations; Knowing this, that the* **trying of your faith worketh patience"** (1:2-3).

December 1 (Day 335), Memory Verse #915
James 1:5:

IF ANY OF YOU LACK WISDOM, LET HIM ASK OF GOD,
THAT GIVETH TO ALL MEN LIBERALLY, AND UPBRAIDETH NOT;
AND IT SHALL BE GIVEN HIM.

December 1 (Day 335), Memory Verses #916 & #917
James 1:12-13:

12. BLESSED IS THE MAN THAT ENDURETH TEMPTATION:
FOR WHEN HE IS TRIED, HE SHALL RECEIVE THE CROWN OF LIFE,
WHICH THE LORD HATH PROMISED TO THEM THAT LOVE HIM.

13. LET NO MAN SAY WHEN HE IS TEMPTED, I AM TEMPTED OF GOD:
FOR GOD CANNOT BE TEMPTED WITH EVIL, NEITHER TEMPTETH HE ANY MAN:

— *"But every man is tempted, when he is drawn away of his own lust, and enticed. Then when lust hath conceived, it bringeth forth sin: and* **sin, when it is finished, bringeth forth death"** (1:14-15).

December 2 (Day 336), Memory Verse #918
James 1:17:

EVERY GOOD GIFT AND EVERY PERFECT GIFT IS FROM ABOVE,
AND COMETH DOWN FROM THE FATHER OF LIGHTS,
WITH WHOM IS NO VARIABLENESS, NEITHER SHADOW OF TURNING.

— **"Wherefore, my beloved brethren, let every man be swift to hear, slow to speak, slow to wrath:** *For the wrath of man worketh not the righteousness of God"* (1:19-20).

December 2 (Day 336), Memory Verse #919
James 1:22:

BUT BE YE DOERS OF THE WORD, AND NOT HEARERS ONLY,
DECEIVING YOUR OWN SELVES.

December 2 (Day 336), Memory Verse #920
James 1:26:

IF ANY MAN AMONG YOU SEEM TO BE RELIGIOUS,
AND BRIDLETH NOT HIS TONGUE, BUT DECEIVETH HIS OWN HEART,
THIS MAN'S RELIGION IS IN VAIN.

— *"Pure religion and undefiled before God and the Father is this, To visit the fatherless and widows in their affliction, and to keep himself unspotted from the world"* (see 1:27).

James 2: James speaks on loving one's neighbor (see 2:1-13) — James emphasizes that faith without works is dead (see 2:14-26).

December 3 (Day 337), Memory Verse #921
James 2:8:

IF YE FULFIL THE ROYAL LAW ACCORDING TO THE SCRIPTURE,
THOU SHALT LOVE THY NEIGHBOUR AS THYSELF, YE DO WELL:

December 3 (Day 337), Memory Verse #922
James 2:17:

EVEN SO FAITH, IF IT HATH NOT WORKS, IS DEAD, BEING ALONE.

— *"Thou believest that there is one God; thou doest well: the devils also believe, and tremble"* (see 2:19).

December 3 (Day 337), Memory Verse #923
James 2:26:

FOR AS THE BODY WITHOUT THE SPIRIT IS DEAD, SO FAITH WITHOUT WORKS IS DEAD ALSO.

James 3: James shows the importance of controlling one's words and tongue (see 3:1-18).

December 4 (Day 338), Memory Verses #924 & #925
James 3:17-18:

17. BUT THE WISDOM THAT IS FROM ABOVE IS FIRST PURE,
THEN PEACEABLE, GENTLE, AND EASY TO BE ENTREATED,
FULL OF MERCY AND GOOD FRUITS, WITHOUT PARTIALITY, AND WITHOUT HYPOCRISY.

18. AND THE FRUIT OF RIGHTEOUSNESS IS SOWN IN PEACE
OF THEM THAT MAKE PEACE.

James 4: James condemns sin and shows how to resist the devil (see 4:1-17).

December 4 (Day 338), Memory Verses #926 & #927
James 4:7-8:

7. SUBMIT YOURSELVES THEREFORE TO GOD.
RESIST THE DEVIL, AND HE WILL FLEE FROM YOU.

8. DRAW NIGH TO GOD, AND HE WILL DRAW NIGH TO YOU...

December 5 (Day 339), Memory Verse #928
James 4:11:

SPEAK NOT EVIL ONE OF ANOTHER, BRETHREN...

December 5 (Day 339), Memory Verse #929
James 4:17:

THEREFORE TO HIM THAT KNOWETH TO DO GOOD,
AND DOETH IT NOT, TO HIM IT IS SIN.

James 5: James writes about the danger of riches (see 5:1-6), being patient and free from grudges (see 5:7-12), prayer (see 5:13-18), and rescuing those who err from the truth (see 5:19-20).

December 6 (Day 340), Memory Verse #930
James 5:12:

BUT ABOVE ALL THINGS, MY BRETHREN,
SWEAR NOT, NEITHER BY HEAVEN, NEITHER BY EARTH,
NEITHER BY ANY OTHER OATH:
BUT LET YOUR YEA BE YEA; AND YOUR NAY BE NAY; LEST YE FALL IN CONDEMNATION.

December 6 (Day 340), Memory Verse #931
James 5:16:

CONFESS YOUR FAULTS ONE TO ANOTHER,
AND PRAY ONE FOR ANOTHER, THAT YE MAY BE HEALED.
THE EFFECTUAL FERVENT PRAYER OF A RIGHTEOUS MAN AVAILETH MUCH.

— *"Brethren, if any of you do err from the truth, and one convert him; Let him know, that he which converteth the sinner from the error of his way shall **save a soul from death**, and shall hide a multitude of sins"* (see 5:19-20).

JAMES 2:8:

IF YE FULFIL THE ROYAL LAW ACCORDING TO THE SCRIPTURE, THOU SHALT LOVE THY NEIGHBOUR AS THYSELF, YE DO WELL:

I PETER

Introduction: Tradition and most scholars hold the apostle Peter as the author of I Peter. This letter was probably written in the early 60's A.D. before the Roman emperor Nero's persecution of the Christians in 64 A.D.   I Peter was written from "*Babylon*" (see 5:13), often used to refer to Rome, to the scattered Christians of various places (see 1:1). God's grace, Christian duties, and Christian suffering are emphasized in this letter. I Peter has five chapters.

Key Contents and Key Memory Verses with Study Dates

I Peter 1-2:   Peter's greetings (see 1:1-2) — **Peter writes concerning God's "abundant mercy"** (see 1:3-9)**; the ministry of the prophets** (see 1:10-12); **how believers are to be holy, honor God, and love others** (see 1:13-25); **and Christian growth** (see 2:1-10).

December 7 (Day 341), Memory Verse #932
I Peter 1:15:

BUT AS HE WHICH HATH CALLED YOU IS HOLY,
SO BE YE HOLY IN ALL MANNER OF CONVERSATION; (so be holy in all you do, NIV);

— **The Father,** "*...without respect of persons judgeth according to every man's work...*" (see 1:17) — **You are redeemed** "*...with the precious blood of Christ, as of a lamb without blemish and without spot: Who verily was foreordained before the foundation of the world, but was manifest in these last times for you. Who by him do believe in God, that raised him up from the dead, and gave him glory; that your faith and hope might be in God*" (see 1:19-21).

December 7 (Day 341), Memory Verse #933
I Peter 1:22:

...SEE THAT YE LOVE ONE ANOTHER WITH A PURE HEART FERVENTLY:

December 8 (Day 342), Memory Verses #934 & #935
I Peter 1:24-25:

24. ...THE GRASS WITHERETH, AND THE FLOWER THEREOF FALLETH AWAY:

25. BUT THE WORD OF THE LORD ENDURETH FOREVER...

December 8 (Day 342), Memory Verse #936
I Peter 2:2:

AS NEWBORN BABES, DESIRE THE SINCERE MILK OF THE WORD,
THAT YE MAY GROW THEREBY:

— **Peter writes about relationships between rulers and the people** (see 2:11-17), **and between masters and servants** (see 2:18-25).

December 9 (Day 343), Memory Verses #937 & #938
I Peter 2:24-25:

24. WHO HIS OWN SELF BARE OUR SINS IN HIS OWN BODY ON THE TREE,
THAT WE, BEING DEAD TO SINS, SHOULD LIVE UNTO RIGHTEOUSNESS:
BY WHOSE STRIPES YE WERE HEALED.

25. FOR YE WERE AS SHEEP GOING ASTRAY;
BUT ARE NOW RETURNED UNTO THE SHEPHERD AND BISHOP OF YOUR SOULS.

I Peter 3-5: Peter writes about relationships between husbands and wives (see 3:1-7), **relationships with others** (see 3:8-12), **Christian suffering** (see 3:13-4:19), **and servant-hood** (see 5:1-11).

December 9 (Day 343), Memory Verse #939
I Peter 3:8:

FINALLY, BE YE ALL OF ONE MIND,
HAVING COMPASSION ONE OF ANOTHER, LOVE AS BRETHREN,
BE PITIFUL (be compassionate and humble, NIV), BE COURTEOUS:

— *"For he that will love life, and see good days, let him refrain his tongue from evil, and his lips that they speak no guile:"* (see 3:10).

December 10 (Day 344), Memory Verse #940
I Peter 3:12:

FOR THE EYES OF THE LORD ARE OVER THE RIGHTEOUS,
AND HIS EARS ARE OPEN UNTO THEIR PRAYERS:
BUT THE FACE OF THE LORD IS AGAINST THEM THAT DO EVIL.

— *"And who is he that will harm you, if ye be followers of that which is good? **But and if ye suffer for righteousness' sake, happy are ye:** and be not afraid of their terror, neither be troubled;"* (see 3:13-14).

December 10 (Day 344), Memory Verse #941
I Peter 3:15:

BUT SANCTIFY THE LORD GOD IN YOUR HEARTS:
AND BE READY ALWAYS TO GIVE AN ANSWER TO EVERY MAN THAT ASKETH YOU
A REASON OF THE HOPE THAT IS IN YOU WITH MEEKNESS AND FEAR:

December 11 (Day 345), Memory Verse #942
I Peter 3:18:

FOR CHRIST ALSO HATH ONCE SUFFERED FOR SINS,
THE JUST FOR THE UNJUST, THAT HE MIGHT BRING US TO GOD,
BEING PUT TO DEATH IN THE FLESH, BUT QUICKENED BY THE SPIRIT:

December 11 (Day 345), Memory Verses #943 & #944
I Peter 4:8-9:

8. AND ABOVE ALL THINGS HAVE FERVENT CHARITY AMONG
YOURSELVES: FOR CHARITY SHALL COVER THE MULTITUDE OF SINS.

9. USE HOSPITALITY ONE TO ANOTHER WITHOUT GRUDGING.

December 12 (Day 346), Memory Verse #945
I Peter 5:5:

...GOD RESISTETH THE PROUD, AND GIVETH GRACE TO THE HUMBLE.

December 12 (Day 346), Memory Verse #946
I Peter 5:7:

CASTING ALL YOUR CARE UPON HIM; FOR HE CARETH FOR YOU.

— **Closing Statements** (see 5:12-14).

II Peter

Introduction: Traditionally, the apostle Peter is thought to have authored II Peter between 65-67 A.D. This letter was most likely written from Rome. Nero's rule ended in 68 A.D., and Peter is thought to have been martyred the previous year in 67 A.D. Many scholars believe someone else authored II Peter in the 80's A.D., customarily using another's name as the author (Peter in this instance). II Peter has three chapters.

Key Contents and Key Memory Verses with Study Dates

II Peter 1-3: Peter emphasizes **Christian growth** (chapter 1), **false teachers** (chapter 2), **and Christ's return** (chapter 3) — *"Accordingly as his divine power hath given unto us all things that pertain unto life and godliness, through the knowledge of him that hath called us to glory and virtue:"* (see 1:3) — *"...no prophecy of the scripture is of any private interpretation. For the prophecy came not in old time by the will of man:* but **holy men of God spake as they were moved by the Holy Ghost"** (see 1:21).

December 13-14 (Days 347-348), Memory Verses #947 to #951
II Peter 1:5-9:

5. AND BESIDE THIS, GIVING ALL DILIGENCE,
ADD TO YOUR FAITH VIRTUE; AND TO VIRTUE KNOWLEDGE,

6. AND TO KNOWLEDGE TEMPERANCE;
AND TO TEMPERANCE PATIENCE; AND TO PATIENCE GODLINESS;

7. AND TO GODLINESS BROTHERLY KINDNESS;
AND TO BROTHERLY KINDNESS CHARITY.

8. FOR IF THESE THINGS BE IN YOU, AND ABOUND,
THEY MAKE YOU THAT YE SHALL NEITHER BE BARREN
NOR UNFRUITFUL IN THE KNOWLEDGE OF OUR LORD JESUS CHRIST.

9. BUT HE THAT LACKETH THESE THINGS IS BLIND, AND CANNOT SEE AFAR OFF,
AND HATH FORGOTTEN THAT HE WAS PURGED FROM HIS OLD SINS.

— *"**Knowing this first, that there shall come in the last days scoffers**, walking after their own lusts, And saying, Where is the promise of his coming? for since the fathers fell asleep, all things continue as they were from the beginning of the creation"* (see 3:3-4).

December 14 (Day 348), Memory Verse #952
II Peter 3:8:

BUT BELOVED, BE NOT IGNORANT OF THIS ONE THING,
THAT ONE DAY IS WITH THE LORD AS A THOUSAND YEARS,
AND A THOUSAND YEARS AS ONE DAY.

— *"The Lord is not slack concerning his promise, as some men count slackness; but is longsuffering to us-ward,* **not willing that any should perish, but that all should come to repentance. But the day of the Lord will come as a thief in the night;..."** (see 3:9-10) — *"...we, according to his promise, look for new heavens and a new earth..."* (see 3:13) — *"...be diligent that ye may be found of him in peace, without spot, and blameless"* (see 3:14).

II Peter 3:8: ...One day is with the Lord as a thousand years, and a thousand years as one day.

I John

Introduction: Most scholars believe I John was written by John the apostle from Ephesus during 85-95 A.D.   I John was written for Christians in various places, perhaps all over Asia Minor.   God's love and Christian behavior are emphasized in this letter.   Much is also written against false teachers (most likely the Gnostics). I John has five chapters.

Key Contents and Key Memory Verses with Study Dates

I John 1-3: John's greeting (see 1:1-4) — **In these three chapters, John shows how believers should walk in the light and love each other** (see 1:5-3:24) — **"...God is light, and in him is no darkness at all.** *If we say that we have fellowship with him, and walk in darkness, we lie, and do not the truth:"* (see 1:5-6).

December 15 (Day 349), Memory Verse #953
I John 1:7:

BUT IF WE WALK IN THE LIGHT, AS HE IS IN THE LIGHT,
WE HAVE FELLOWSHIP ONE WITH ANOTHER,
AND THE BLOOD OF JESUS CHRIST HIS SON CLEANSETH US FROM ALL SIN.

December 15 (Day 349), Memory Verse #954
I John 1:9:

IF WE CONFESS OUR SINS, HE IS FAITHFUL AND JUST TO FORGIVE US OUR SINS,
AND TO CLEANSE US FROM ALL UNRIGHTEOUSNESS.

December 16 (Day 350), Memory Verses #955 to #957
I John 2:1-3:

1. MY LITTLE CHILDREN, THESE THINGS WRITE I UNTO YOU, THAT YE SIN NOT.
AND IF ANY MAN SIN, WE HAVE AN ADVOCATE WITH THE FATHER,
JESUS CHRIST THE RIGHTEOUS:

2. AND HE IS THE PROPITIATION FOR OUR SINS:
AND NOT OURS ONLY, BUT ALSO FOR THE SINS OF THE WHOLE WORLD.

3. AND HEREBY WE DO KNOW THAT WE KNOW HIM,
IF WE KEEP HIS COMMANDMENTS.

December 17 (Day 351), Memory Verse #958
I John 2:6:

HE THAT SAITH HE ABIDETH IN HIM OUGHT HIMSELF ALSO SO TO WALK,
EVEN AS HE WALKED.

December 17 (Day 351), Memory Verse #959
I John 2:9:

HE THAT SAITH HE IS IN THE LIGHT, AND HATETH HIS BROTHER,
IS IN DARKNESS EVEN UNTIL NOW.

December 17 (Day 351), Memory Verse #960
I John 2:15:

LOVE NOT THE WORLD, NEITHER THE THINGS THAT ARE IN THE WORLD.
IF ANY MAN LOVE THE WORLD, THE LOVE OF THE FATHER IS NOT IN HIM.

December 18 (Day 352), Memory Verse #961
I John 2:17:

AND THE WORLD PASSETH AWAY, AND THE LUST THEREOF:
BUT HE THAT DOETH THE WILL OF GOD ABIDETH FOR EVER.

— *"But the anointing which ye have received of him abideth in you, and ye need not that any man teach you: but as the same anointing teacheth you of all things, and is truth,* and is no lie, and even as it hath taught you, ye shall abide in him" (see 2:27).

December 18 (Day 352), Memory Verse #962
I John 3:1:

BEHOLD, WHAT MANNER OF LOVE THE FATHER HATH BESTOWED UPON US,
THAT WE SHOULD BE CALLED THE SONS OF GOD:
THEREFORE THE WORLD KNOWETH US NOT, BECAUSE IT KNEW HIM NOT.

December 19 (Day 353), Memory Verses #963 to #965
I John 3:16-18:

16. HEREBY PERCEIVE WE THE LOVE OF GOD,
BECAUSE HE LAID DOWN HIS LIFE FOR US:
AND WE OUGHT TO LAY DOWN OUR LIVES FOR THE BRETHREN.

17. BUT WHOSO HATH THIS WORLD'S GOOD,
AND SEETH HIS BROTHER HAVE NEED,
AND SHUTTETH UP HIS BOWELS OF COMPASSION FROM HIM,
HOW DWELLETH THE LOVE OF GOD IN HIM?

18. MY LITTLE CHILDREN, LET US NOT LOVE IN WORD,
NEITHER IN TONGUE; BUT IN DEED AND IN TRUTH.

December 20 (Day 354), Memory Verses #966 & #967
I John 3:23-24:

23. AND THIS IS HIS COMMANDMENT,
THAT WE SHOULD BELIEVE ON THE NAME OF HIS SON JESUS CHRIST,
AND LOVE ONE ANOTHER, AS HE GAVE US COMMANDMENT.

24. AND HE THAT KEEPETH HIS COMMANDMENTS DWELLETH IN HIM,
AND HE IN HIM. AND HEREBY WE KNOW THAT HE ABIDETH IN US,
BY THE SPIRIT WHICH HE HATH GIVEN US.

— *"Beloved, believe not every spirit, but try the spirits whether they are of God: because many false prophets are gone out into the world. Hereby know ye the Spirit of God: Every spirit that confesseth that Jesus Christ is come in the flesh is of God:"* (see 4:1-2).

John 4-5: **John warns against false prophets** (see 4:1-6), **speaks on love** (see 4:7-5:3), **emphasizes overcoming the world by believing Jesus is the Son of God** (see 5:4-13, 18-21), **and speaks on prayer** (see 5:14-17).

December 20 (Day 354), Memory Verse #968
I John 4:4:

YE ARE OF GOD, LITTLE CHILDREN, AND HAVE OVERCOME THEM:
BECAUSE GREATER IS HE THAT IS IN YOU, THAN HE THAT IS IN THE WORLD.

December 21-22 (Days 355-356), Memory Verses #969 to #974
I John 4:7-12:

7. BELOVED, LET US LOVE ONE ANOTHER: FOR LOVE IS OF GOD;
AND EVERY ONE THAT LOVETH IS BORN OF GOD, AND KNOWETH GOD.

8. HE THAT LOVETH NOT KNOWETH NOT GOD; FOR GOD IS LOVE.

9. IN THIS WAS MANIFESTED THE LOVE OF GOD TOWARD US,
BECAUSE THAT GOD SENT HIS ONLY BEGOTTEN SON INTO THE WORLD,
THAT WE MIGHT LIVE THROUGH HIM.

10. HEREIN IS LOVE, NOT THAT WE LOVED GOD, BUT THAT HE LOVED US,
AND SENT HIS SON TO BE THE PROPITIATION FOR OUR SINS.

11. BELOVED, IF GOD SO LOVED US, WE OUGHT ALSO TO LOVE ONE ANOTHER.

12. NO MAN HATH SEEN GOD AT ANY TIME.
IF WE LOVE ONE ANOTHER, GOD DWELLETH IN US, AND HIS LOVE IS PERFECTED IN US.

December 23 (Day 357), Memory Verse #975
I John 4:15:

WHOSOEVER SHALL CONFESS THAT JESUS IS THE SON OF GOD,
GOD DWELLETH IN HIM, AND HE IN GOD.

December 23 (Day 357), Memory Verses #976 to #977
I John 4:18-19:

18. THERE IS NO FEAR IN LOVE; BUT PERFECT LOVE CASTETH OUT FEAR:
BECAUSE FEAR HATH TORMENT. HE THAT FEARETH IS NOT MADE PERFECT IN LOVE.

19. WE LOVE HIM, BECAUSE HE FIRST LOVED US.

— *"And this commandment have we from him, That he who loveth God love his brother also"* (see 4:21) — *"For there are three that bear record in heaven, **the Father, the Word, and the Holy Ghost: and these three are one**"* (see 5:7) — *"He that believeth on the Son of God hath the witness in himself: he that believeth not God hath made him a liar; because he believeth not the record that God gave of his Son. **And this is the record, that God hath given to us eternal life, and this life is in his Son**"* (see 5:10-11).

December 24 (Day 358), Memory Verse #978
I John 5:12:

HE THAT HATH THE SON HATH LIFE;
AND HE THAT HATH NOT THE SON OF GOD HATH NOT LIFE.

— *"These things have I written unto you that believe on the name of the Son of God; that ye may know that ye have eternal life, and that ye may believe on the name of the Son of God"* (see 5:13).

December 24 (Day 358), Memory Verses #979 & #980
I John 5:14-15:

14. AND THIS IS THE CONFIDENCE THAT WE HAVE IN HIM, THAT,
IF WE ASK ANY THING ACCORDING TO HIS WILL, HE HEARETH US:

15. AND IF WE KNOW THAT HE HEAR US, WHATSOEVER WE ASK,
WE KNOW THAT WE HAVE THE PETITIONS THAT WE DESIRED OF HIM.

II John

Introduction: Most scholars believe I, II, and III John were written by John the apostle from Ephesus during 85-95 A.D. II John is written to a lady and her children. The lady may be symbolic of a church. This letter emphasizes the commandment of loving one another. II John has only 13 verses.

Key Contents and Key Memory Verses with Study Dates

II John verses 1-13: Both II and III John have brief greetings and closing statements — John states, *"I rejoiced greatly that I found of thy children walking in truth, as we have received a commandment from the Father"* (see verse 4).

December 25 (Day 359), Memory Verses #981 & #982
On Christmas Day, you may also want to read Matthew 2 and Luke 2.
II John verses 5-6:

5. ...LOVE ONE ANOTHER.

6. AND THIS IS LOVE, THAT WE WALK AFTER HIS COMMANDMENTS...

— John warns against showing hospitality to traveling false teachers (see verses 7-11).

II John verse 5:   ...Love one another.

III John

Introduction: III John was most likely written by John the apostle from Ephesus during 85-95 A.D. John addressed the letter to Gaius and wrote about the treatment of traveling teachers. Demetrius, one of the teachers, was most likely the deliverer of this letter. III John has 14 verses.

Key Contents and Key Memory Verses with Study Dates

III John verses 1-14: John writes about the treatment of traveling teachers — Diotrephes is mistreating traveling teachers sent by John; therefore, John reprimands Diotrephes and praises Gaius for his hospitality to the teachers — John opens with these words, *"The elder unto the well-beloved Gaius, whom I love in the truth"* (see verse 1).

December 25 (Day 359), Memory Verse #983
III John verse 2:

BELOVED, I WISH ABOVE ALL THINGS THAT THOU MAYEST PROSPER
AND BE IN HEALTH, EVEN AS THY SOUL PROSPERETH.

— *"For I rejoiced greatly, when the brethren came and testified of the truth that is in thee, even as thou walkest in the truth. I have no greater joy than to hear that my children walk in truth"* (see verses 3-4).

December 25 (Day 359), Memory Verse #984
III John verse 11:

BELOVED, FOLLOW NOT THAT WHICH IS EVIL, BUT THAT WHICH IS GOOD...

JUDE

Introduction: Most scholars attribute authorship of Jude to Jude, the brother of James and half brother of Jesus. It is thought Jude's intention was to write to all Christians. In the first verse, Jude states that his letter is *"...to them that are sanctified by God the Father, and preserved in Jesus Christ, and called."* Jude's main emphasis is warnings against false teachers (most likely early Gnostics). Most believe Jude was written sometime during 65-80 A.D. Some believe Jude was written much earlier, which would make it one of the first New Testament books. Jude is a small book of only 25 verses.

Key Contents and Key Memory Verses with Study Dates

Jude verses 1-25: Jude's greeting (see verses 1-4) — *"Beloved, when I gave all diligence to write unto you of the common salvation, it was needful for me to write unto you, and exhort you that ye should earnestly contend for the faith which was once delivered unto the saints. For there are certain men crept in unawares, who were before of old ordained to this condemnation, ungodly men, turning the grace of our God into lasciviousness, and denying the only Lord God, and our Lord Jesus Christ"* (see verses 3-4) — **Jude warns against false teachers and gives encouragement to the believers** (see verses 5-23).

December 26 (Day 360), Memory Verses #985 to #987
Jude verses 21-23:

21. **KEEP** YOURSELVES IN THE LOVE OF GOD,
LOOKING FOR THE MERCY OF OUR LORD JESUS CHRIST UNTO ETERNAL LIFE
(to bring you to eternal life, NIV).

22. **AND** OF SOME HAVE COMPASSION, MAKING A DIFFERENCE
(be merciful to those that doubt, NIV):

23. **AND** OTHERS SAVE WITH FEAR, PULLING THEM OUT OF THE FIRE;
HATING EVEN THE GARMENT SPOTTED BY THE FLESH.

— Closing statements (see verses 24-25).

December 27 (Day 361), Memory Verses #988 & #989
Jude verses 24-25:

24. **NOW** UNTO HIM THAT IS ABLE TO KEEP YOU FROM FALLING,
AND TO PRESENT YOU FAULTLESS BEFORE THE PRESENCE OF HIS GLORY
WITH EXCEEDING JOY,

25. **TO** THE ONLY WISE GOD OUR SAVIOUR, BE GLORY AND MAJESTY,
DOMINION AND POWER, BOTH NOW AND EVER. AMEN

JUDE VERSE 21:

KEEP YOURSELVES IN THE LOVE OF GOD...

REVELATION

Introduction: Tradition attributes authorship of Revelation to John the apostle, although some scholars believe it to be written by John the Elder (Presbyter) or another John. Most scholars date the writing of Revelation around 95 A.D., although some believe it to be written 10 to 30 years earlier. John wrote about his vision while on the island of Patmos, an island for prisoners located in the Aegean Sea. It is thought the Roman emperor Domitian had sent John the apostle into exile since he was a leader of the Christians. Revelation is symbolic apocalyptic literature. There are various interpretations as to the meaning of its symbols. Some believe most of the events predicted in Revelation have already happened, while others believe most of these predictions will happen in the future. And some believe Revelation uses imagery to show the battle between good and evil. Revelation uses numbers symbolically, especially the numbers 7, 12 and 24. The number seven is used often since it represents wholeness and completeness. There are seven churches, seven seals, seven trumpets, seven vials, etc. During the first century A.D., there was much Christian persecution by the Roman government. John encouraged believers to be strong and unwavering in their faith throughout tribulations. Revelation has 22 chapters.

Key Contents and Key Memory Verses with Study Dates

<u>Revelation 1</u>: John sends greetings *"...to the seven churches which are in Asia: ..."* (1:4).

December 28 (Day 362), Memory Verse #990
<u>Revelation 1:8</u>:

I AM ALPHA AND OMEGA, THE BEGINNING AND THE ENDING, SAITH THE LORD,
WHICH IS, AND WHICH WAS, AND WHICH IS TO COME, THE ALMIGHTY.

— **John writes of his vision** (his vision continues throughout Revelation) and says he was *"...in the isle that is called Patmos, for the word of God, and for the testimony of Jesus Christ"* (see 1:9) — The Lord tells John to *"Write the things which thou hast seen, and the things which are, and the things which shall be hereafter;"* (see 1:19).

<u>Revelation 2-3</u>:   **Messages to the churches of EPHESUS, SMYRNA, PERGAMOS, THYATIRA, SARDIS, PHILADELPHIA, and LAODICEA** — The Lord says:

December 28 (Day 362), Memory Verses #991 & #992
<u>Revelation 3:19-20</u>:

19. AS MANY AS I LOVE, I REBUKE AND CHASTEN:
BE ZEALOUS THEREFORE, AND REPENT.

20. BEHOLD, I STAND AT THE DOOR, AND KNOCK:
IF ANY MAN HEAR MY VOICE, AND OPEN THE DOOR,
I WILL COME IN TO HIM, AND WILL SUP WITH HIM, AND HE WITH ME.

<u>Revelation 4</u>: **John's vision continues** — *"...a throne was set in heaven, and one sat on the throne...there was a rainbow round about the throne, in sight like unto an emerald"* (see 4:2-3) — Round about the throne included 24 elders with *"...crowns of gold"* (see 4:4), *"...seven lamps of fire burning before the throne, which are the seven Spirits of God"* (see 4:5), and four beasts.

<u>Revelation 5</u>: **John sees** *"...in the right hand of him that sat on the throne a book** written within and on the backside, sealed with seven seals"* (see 5:1) — The angels, beasts, and elders around the throne exclaim, *"**Worthy is the Lamb** that was slain to receive power, and riches, and wisdom, and strength, and honour, and glory, and blessing"* (see 5:12).

Revelation 6: As the Lamb opens six seals, John sees the following:
1) a man on a WHITE HORSE going *"...forth conquering..."* (see 6:2);
2) another on a RED HORSE taking *"...peace from the earth,..."* (see 6:4);
3) one on a BLACK HORSE representing the scarcity of food;
4) a PALE HORSE, *"...and his name that sat on him was Death, and Hell followed with him..."* (see 6:8);
5) *"...the souls of them that were slain for the word of God..."* (see 6:9); and...
6) *"...a great earthquake; and the sun became black as sackcloth of hair, and the moon became as blood;"* (see 6:12) — *"And the stars of heaven fell unto earth..."* (see 6:13) — *"...and every mountain and island were moved out of their places"* (see 6:14).

Revelation 7: Angels seal 144,000 from the 12 tribes of Israel — A multitude of people from all nations gather and are clothed in white robes; they had washed their robes, making *"...them white in the blood of the Lamb."* (see 7:14) — *"...and God shall wash away all tears from their eyes."* (see 7:17).

Revelation 8-9: The seventh seal is opened — Seven trumpets are given to seven angels and six trumpets are sounded — Various destructions accompany the sounding of each trumpet — The seventh trumpet is sounded in Chapter 11.

Revelation 10: John sees an angel with a little book — A voice from heaven tells John to eat the book — John says, *"...it was in my mouth sweet as honey: and as I had eaten it, my belly was bitter."* (see 10:10).

Revelation 11: Two witnesses are killed by the beast from the bottomless pit — After three and one-half days, *"...the spirit of life from God entered into them..."* (see 11:11), and *"...they ascended up to heaven in a cloud;..."* (see 11:12) — **The seventh trumpet is sounded.**

Revelation 12: War on earth and in heaven — A woman gives birth to a child *"...who was to rule all nations with a rod of iron: and her child was caught up unto God, and to his throne."* (see 12:5) — *"And there was war in heaven: Michael and his angels fought against the dragon; and the dragon fought and his angels."* (see 12:7) — *"And the great dragon was cast out, that old serpent, called the Devil, and Satan, which deceiveth the whole world: he was cast out into the earth, and his angels were cast out with him."* (see 12:9) — The dragon makes war with the woman and *"...with the remnant of her seed, which keep the commandments of God, and have the testimony of Jesus Christ."* (see 12:17).

Revelation 13: The dragon gives the beast power *"...and great authority."* (see 13:2) — The beast is healed of a *"...deadly wound..."* (see 13:3) — Another beast causes all *"...to receive a mark in their right hand, or in their foreheads:"* (see 13:16) — The number of the beast is 666, *"...Six hundred threescore and six."* (see 13:18).

Revelation 14: *"And I looked, and, lo, a Lamb stood on the mount Sion (Zion, NIV), and with him an hundred forty and four thousand, having his Father's name written in their foreheads"* (see 14:1) — **John hears proclamations by a voice from heaven and also angels — An angel warns that *"...If any man worship the beast and his image..."*** (see 14: 9), then the *"...same shall drink of the wine of the wrath of God,...."* (see 14:10) — The saints *"...keep the commandments of God, and the faith of Jesus."* (see 14:12).

Revelation 15: John sees *"...seven angels having the seven last plagues; for in them is filled up the wrath of God."* (see 15:1)

Revelation 16: Seven angels pour out the seven vials of plagues.

Revelation 17: One of the angels shows John a woman on a beast with seven heads and ten horns — On the woman's forehead is written a name**:** *"... MYSTERY, BABYLON THE GREAT, THE MOTHER OF HARLOTS AND ABOMINATIONS OF THE EARTH."* (see 17:5) — The angel interprets this part of the vision.

Revelation 18: Judgment on Babylon.

Revelation 19: Heaven praises God — *"...Alleluia: for the Lord God omnipotent reigneth."* (see 19:6) — The rider of a white horse is called *"...Faithful and True,..."* (see 19:11), *"...The Word of God."* (see 19:13), and *"...KING OF KINGS, AND LORD OF LORDS."* (see 19:16) — **The beast and false prophet are *"...cast alive into a lake of fire*** *burning with brimstone."* (see 19:20).

Revelation 20: Satan is bound and cast into the bottomless pit for a thousand years, *"...and after that he must be loosed a little season."* (see 20:3) — **Then *"...the devil that deceived them was cast into the lake of fire*** *and brimstone, where the beast and the false prophet are, and shall be tormented day and night for ever and ever."* (see 20:10) — *"And I saw the dead, small and great, stand before God; and the books were opened: and another book was opened, which is the book of life: and the dead were judged out of those things which were written in the books, according to their works"* (see 20:12).

December 29 (Day 363), Memory Verse #993
Revelation 20:15:

AND WHOSOEVER WAS NOT FOUND WRITTEN IN THE BOOK OF LIFE
WAS CAST INTO THE LAKE OF FIRE.

Revelation 21: New heaven and new earth.

December 29 (Day 363), Memory Verse #994
Revelation 21:1:

AND I SAW A NEW HEAVEN AND A NEW EARTH: ...

December 30 (Day 364), Memory Verse #995
Revelation 21:4:

AND GOD SHALL WIPE AWAY ALL TEARS FROM THEIR EYES;
AND THERE SHALL BE NO MORE DEATH, NEITHER SORROW, NOR CRYING,
NEITHER SHALL THERE BE ANY MORE PAIN:
FOR THE FORMER THINGS ARE PASSED AWAY.

— Jerusalem is called *"...the bride, the Lamb's wife"* (see 21:9) — **The new Jerusalem is described —** *"And the twelve gates were twelve pearls; every several gate was of one pearl: and the street of the city was pure gold, as it were transparent glass"* (see 21:21).

December 30 (Day 364), Memory Verses #996 & #997
Revelation 21:22-23:

22. AND I SAW NO TEMPLE THEREIN:
FOR THE LORD GOD ALMIGHTY AND THE LAMB ARE THE TEMPLE OF IT.

23. AND THE CITY HAD NO NEED OF THE SUN, NEITHER OF THE MOON, TO SHINE IN IT:
FOR THE GLORY OF GOD DID LIGHTEN IT, AND THE LAMB IS THE LIGHT THEREOF.

— Those who can enter the new Jerusalem are *"...they which are written in the Lamb's book of life"* (see 21:27).

Revelation 22: *"...a pure river of water of life, clear as crystal, proceeding out of the throne of God and of the Lamb."* (see 22:1).

December 31 (Day 365), Memory Verses #998 & #999
Revelation 22:13-14:

13. I AM ALPHA AND OMEGA,
THE BEGINNING AND THE END, THE FIRST AND THE LAST.

14. BLESSED ARE THEY THAT DO HIS COMMANDMENTS,
THAT THEY MAY HAVE RIGHT TO THE TREE OF LIFE,
AND MAY ENTER IN THROUGH THE GATES INTO THE CITY.

— *"I Jesus have sent mine angel to testify unto you these things in the churches. I am the root and the offspring of David, and the bright and morning star"* (see 22:16).

December 31 (Day 365), Memory Verse #1000
Revelation 22:17:

...AND WHOSOEVER WILL, LET HIM TAKE THE WATER OF LIFE FREELY.

— *"And if any man shall take away the words of the book of this prophecy,* God shall take away his part out of the book of life, and out of the holy city, and from the things which are written in this book" (see 22:19).

THE GRACE OF OUR

LORD JESUS CHRIST

BE WITH YOU ALL. AMEN.

REVELATION 22:21

1000 Key Memory Verses with Study Dates

BIBLE IN A NUTSHELL
KEY SCRIPTURE, GENESIS TO REVELATION,
TO HIDE IN YOUR HEART AND LIGHT YOUR PATH

Quoted Scripture is from The King James Version, KJV.
The New International Version, NIV, is quoted when clarifying some of the verses.

These key memory verses are the same ones found previously in the key notes. They are listed separately here to allow your reviewing only the memory verses. Realistically, it would be difficult to memorize one to four memory verses per day for a full year. It is recommended you mark one or just a few verses per week to memorize and simply review the others. Each time you read through these verses, you may want to mark more verses for memorization.   Of course, you can choose not to memorize scripture at this time, and just enjoy reading and studying through the verses.

GENESIS

January 1 (Day 1), Memory Verse # 1
Genesis 1:1:

IN THE BEGINNING, GOD CREATED THE HEAVENS AND THE EARTH.

January 1 (Day 1), Memory Verses #2 & #3
Genesis 1:27-28:

27. SO GOD CREATED MAN IN HIS OWN IMAGE,
IN THE IMAGE OF GOD CREATED HE HIM;
MALE AND FEMALE CREATED HE THEM.

28. AND GOD BLESSED THEM, AND GOD SAID UNTO THEM,
BE FRUITFUL, AND MULTIPLY, AND REPLENISH THE EARTH, AND SUBDUE IT:
AND HAVE DOMINION OVER THE FISH OF THE SEA, AND THE FOWL OF THE AIR,
AND OVER EVERY LIVING THING THAT MOVETH UPON THE EARTH.

January 1 (Day 1), Memory Verse #4
Genesis 2:3:

AND GOD BLESSED THE SEVENTH DAY, AND SANCTIFIED IT:
BECAUSE THAT IN IT HE HAD RESTED FROM ALL HIS WORK
WHICH GOD CREATED AND MADE.

January 2 (Day 2), Memory Verse #5
Genesis 2:24:

THEREFORE SHALL A MAN LEAVE HIS FATHER AND MOTHER,
AND CLEAVE UNTO HIS WIFE;
AND THEY SHALL BE ONE FLESH.

January 2 (Day 2), Memory Verses #6 to #8
<u>Genesis 12:1-3:</u>
(God's Call of Abram)

1. **NOW** THE LORD HAD SAID UNTO ABRAM,
GET THEE OUT OF THY COUNTRY,
AND FROM THY KINDRED, AND FROM THY FATHER'S HOUSE,
UNTO A LAND THAT I WILL SHEW THEE:

2. **AND** I WILL MAKE OF THEE A GREAT NATION,
AND I WILL BLESS THEE, AND MAKE THY NAME GREAT;
AND THOU SHALT BE A BLESSING:

3. **AND** I WILL BLESS THEM THAT BLESS THEE,
AND CURSE THEM THAT CURSETH THEE:
AND IN THEE SHALL ALL FAMILIES OF THE EARTH BE BLESSED.

January 3 (Day 3), Memory Verse #9
<u>Genesis 18:14:</u>

IS ANYTHING TOO HARD FOR THE LORD?...

January 4 (Day 4), Memory Verse #10
<u>Genesis 31:49:</u>

...**THE** LORD WATCH BETWEEN ME AND THEE,
WHEN WE ARE ABSENT ONE FROM ANOTHER.

EXODUS

January 5 (Day 5), Memory Verse #11
<u>Exodus 3:14:</u>

AND GOD SAID UNTO MOSES, **I AM THAT I AM**:
AND HE SAID,
THUS SHALT THOU SAY UNTO THE CHILDREN OF ISRAEL,
I AM HATH SENT ME UNTO YOU.

January 6-9 (Days 6-9), Memory Verses #12 to #26
<u>Exodus 20:3-17:</u>
(The Ten Commandments)
SEE FOLLOWING PAGE:

January 6-9 (Days 6-9), Memory Verses #12 to #26
<u>Exodus 20:3-17:</u>
(The Ten Commandments)
I.

3. THOU SHALT HAVE NO OTHER GODS BEFORE ME.
II.

4. THOU SHALT NOT MAKE UNTO THEE ANY GRAVEN IMAGE,
OR ANY LIKENESS OF ANYTHING THAT IS IN HEAVEN ABOVE,
OR THAT IS IN THE EARTH BENEATH, OR THAT IS IN THE WATER UNDER THE EARTH:

5. THOU SHALT NOT BOW DOWN THYSELF TO THEM, NOR SERVE THEM:
FOR I THE LORD THY GOD AM A JEALOUS GOD,
VISITING THE INIQUITY OF THE FATHERS UPON THE CHILDREN
UNTO THE THIRD AND FOURTH GENERATION OF THEM THAT HATE ME;

6. AND SHEWING MERCY UNTO THOUSANDS OF THEM THAT LOVE ME,
AND KEEP MY COMMANDMENTS.
III.

7. THOU SHALT NOT TAKE THE NAME OF THE LORD THY GOD IN VAIN;
FOR THE LORD WILL NOT HOLD HIM GUILTLESS THAT TAKETH HIS NAME IN VAIN.
IV.

8. REMEMBER THE SABBATH DAY, TO KEEP IT HOLY.

9. SIX DAYS SHALT THOU LABOUR, AND DO ALL THY WORK:

10. BUT THE SEVENTH DAY IS THE SABBATH OF THE LORD THY GOD:
IN IT THOU SHALT NOT DO ANY WORK, THOU, NOR THY SON,
NOR THY DAUGHTER, THY MANSERVANT, NOR THY MAIDSERVANT,
NOR THY CATTLE, NOR THY STRANGER THAT IS WITHIN THY GATES:

11. FOR IN SIX DAYS THE LORD MADE HEAVEN AND EARTH, THE SEA,
AND ALL THAT IN THEM IS, AND RESTED THE SEVENTH DAY:
WHEREFORE THE LORD BLESSED THE SABBATH DAY, AND HALLOWED IT.
V.

12. HONOUR THY FATHER AND THY MOTHER:
THAT THY DAYS MAY BE LONG UPON THE LAND
WHICH THE LORD THY GOD GIVETH THEE.
VI.

13. THOU SHALT NOT KILL.
VII.

14. THOU SHALT NOT COMMIT ADULTERY.
VIII.

15. THOU SHALT NOT STEAL.
IX.

16. THOU SHALT NOT BEAR FALSE WITNESS AGAINST THY NEIGHBOUR.
X.

17. THOU SHALT NOT COVET THY NEIGHBOUR'S HOUSE,
THOU SHALT NOT COVET THY NEIGHBOUR'S WIFE, NOR HIS MANSERVANT,
NOR HIS MAIDSERVANT, NOR HIS OX, NOR HIS ASS,
NOR ANY THING THAT IS THY NEIGHBOUR'S.

January 10 (Day 10), Memory Verse #27
Exodus 33:14

... MY PRESENCE SHALL GO WITH THEE, AND I WILL GIVE THEE REST.

LEVITICUS

January 11 (Day 11), Memory Verse #28
Leviticus 19:18:

...THOU SHALT LOVE THY NEIGHBOUR AS THYSELF:
I AM THE LORD.

January 11 (Day 11), Memory Verses #29 & #30
Leviticus 20:7-8:

7. SANCTIFY YOURSELVES THEREFORE, AND BE YE HOLY:
FOR I AM THE LORD YOUR GOD.

8. AND YE SHALL KEEP MY STATUTES, AND DO THEM:
I AM THE LORD WHICH SANCTIFY YOU.

NUMBERS

January 12 (Day 12), Memory Verses #31 to #33
Numbers 6:24-26:
(The Priest's Prayer of Blessing)

24. THE LORD BLESS THEE, AND KEEP THEE:

25. THE LORD MAKE HIS FACE SHINE UPON THEE,
AND BE GRACIOUS UNTO THEE:

26. THE LORD LIFT UP HIS COUNTENANCE UPON THEE,
AND GIVE THEE PEACE.

January 13 (Day 13), Memory Verse #34
Numbers 32:23:

...AND BE SURE YOUR SIN WILL FIND YOU OUT.

DEUTERONOMY

January 13 (Day 13), Memory Verse #35
Deuteronomy 4:39:

KNOW THEREFORE THIS DAY, AND CONSIDER IT IN THINE HEART,
THAT THE LORD HE IS GOD IN HEAVEN ABOVE, AND UPON THE EARTH BENEATH:
THERE IS NONE ELSE.

January 14 (Day 14), Memory Verse #36
Deuteronomy 6:5:

AND THOU SHALT LOVE THE LORD THY GOD WITH ALL THINE HEART,
AND WITH ALL THY SOUL, AND WITH ALL THY MIGHT.

January 14 (Day 14), Memory Verses #37 & #38
Deuteronomy 10:12-13:

12. AND NOW, ISRAEL, WHAT DOTH THE LORD THY GOD REQUIRE OF THEE,
BUT TO FEAR THE LORD THY GOD, TO WALK IN HIS WAYS,
AND TO LOVE HIM, AND TO SERVE THE LORD THY GOD
WITH ALL THY HEART AND WITH ALL THY SOUL,

13. TO KEEP THE COMMANDMENTS OF THE LORD, AND HIS STATUTES,
WHICH I COMMAND THEE THIS DAY FOR THY GOOD?

January 15 (Day 15), Memory Verse #39
Deuteronomy 32:4:

HE IS THE ROCK, HIS WORK IS PERFECT; FOR ALL HIS WAYS ARE JUDGMENT:
A GOD OF TRUTH AND WITHOUT INIQUITY, JUST AND RIGHT IS HE.

January 15 (Day 15), Memory Verse #40
Deuteronomy 33:27:

THE ETERNAL GOD IS THY REFUGE,
AND UNDERNEATH ARE THE EVERLASTING ARMS:

JOSHUA

January 16 (Day 16), Memory Verse #41
Joshua 1:9:

HAVE NOT I COMMANDED THEE?
BE STRONG AND OF A GOOD COURAGE;
BE NOT AFRAID, NEITHER BE THOU DISMAYED;
FOR THE LORD THY GOD IS WITH THEE WHITHERSOEVER THOU GOEST.

January 17 (Day 17), Memory Verse #42
Joshua 24:15:

...CHOOSE YOU THIS DAY WHOM YE WILL SERVE;
...BUT AS FOR ME AND MY HOUSE, WE WILL SERVE THE LORD.

JUDGES

January 18 (Day 18), Memory Verse #43
Judges 21:25:

IN THOSE DAYS THERE WAS NO KING IN ISRAEL;
EVERY MAN DID THAT WHICH WAS RIGHT IN HIS OWN EYES.

Ruth

January 18 (Day 18), Memory Verse #44
Ruth 1:16:

...WHITHER THOU GOEST, I WILL GO; AND WHERE THOU LODGEST, I WILL LODGE;
THY PEOPLE SHALL BE MY PEOPLE, AND THY GOD MY GOD:

I Samuel

January 19 (Day 19), Memory Verse #45
I Samuel 2:2:

THERE IS NONE HOLY AS THE LORD: FOR THERE IS NONE BESIDE THEE:
NEITHER IS THERE ANY ROCK LIKE OUR GOD.

January 20 (Day 20), Memory Verse #46
I Samuel 12:24:

ONLY FEAR THE LORD, AND SERVE HIM IN TRUTH WITH ALL YOUR HEART;
FOR CONSIDER HOW GREAT THINGS HE HATH DONE FOR YOU.

January 20 (Day 20), Memory Verse #47
I Samuel 15:22:

...BEHOLD, TO OBEY IS BETTER THAN SACRIFICE,
AND TO HEARKEN THAN THE FAT OF RAMS.

January 21-22 (Days 21-22), Memory Verse #48
I Samuel 16:7:

...FOR THE LORD SEETH NOT AS MAN SEETH;
FOR MAN LOOKETH ON THE OUTWARD APPEARANCE,
BUT THE LORD LOOKETH ON THE HEART.

II Samuel

January 23 (Day 23), Memory Verse #49
II Samuel 22:29:

FOR THOU ART MY LAMP, O LORD:
AND THE LORD WILL LIGHTEN MY DARKNESS.

January 23 (Day 23), Memory Verse #50
II Samuel 22:31:

AS FOR GOD, HIS WAY IS PERFECT; THE WORD OF THE LORD IS TRIED:
HE IS A BUCKLER TO THEM THAT TRUST IN HIM.

January 23 (Day 23), Memory Verse #51
II Samuel 22:34:

HE MAKETH MY FEET LIKE HINDS' FEET: AND SETTETH ME UPON MY HIGH PLACES.

January 23 (Day 23), Memory Verse #52
II Samuel 22:47:

THE LORD LIVETH; AND BLESSED BE MY ROCK;
AND EXALTED BE THE GOD OF THE ROCK OF MY SALVATION.

January 24 (Day 24), Memory Verses #53 & #54
II Samuel 23:3-4:

3. ...HE THAT RULETH OVER MEN MUST BE JUST, RULING IN THE FEAR OF GOD.

4. AND HE SHALL BE AS THE LIGHT OF THE MORNING,
WHEN THE SUN RISETH, EVEN A MORNING WITHOUT CLOUDS;
AS THE TENDER GRASS SPRINGING OUT OF THE EARTH
BY CLEAR SHINING AFTER RAIN.

I KINGS

January 25-27 (Day 25-27), Memory Verse #55
I Kings 2:3:

AND KEEP THE CHARGE OF THE LORD THY GOD,
TO WALK IN HIS WAYS, TO KEEP HIS STATUTES,
AND HIS COMMANDMENTS, AND HIS JUDGMENTS, AND HIS TESTIMONIES,
AS IT IS WRITTEN IN THE LAW OF MOSES,
THAT THOU MAYEST PROSPER IN ALL THAT THOU DOEST,
AND WHITHERSOEVER THOU TURNEST THYSELF:

II KINGS

January 28 (Day 28), Memory Verses #56 to #58
II Kings 17:35-37:

35. WITH WHOM THE LORD HAD MADE A COVENANT, AND CHARGED THEM, SAYING,
YE SHALL NOT FEAR OTHER GODS, NOR BOW YOURSELVES TO THEM,
NOR SERVE THEM, NOR SACRIFICE TO THEM:

36. BUT THE LORD, WHO BROUGHT YOU UP OUT OF THE LAND OF EGYPT
WITH GREAT POWER AND A STRETCHED OUT ARM,
HIM SHALL YE FEAR, AND HIM SHALL YE WORSHIP,
AND TO HIM SHALL YE DO SACRIFICE.

37. AND THE STATUTES, AND THE ORDINANCES, AND THE LAW,
AND THE COMMANDMENT, WHICH HE WROTE FOR YOU,
YE SHALL OBSERVE TO DO FOR EVERMORE;

I Chronicles

January 29 (Day 29), Memory Verses #59 & #60
I Chronicles 4:9-10:
(Prayer of Jabez)

9. **AND** JABEZ WAS MORE HONOURABLE THAN HIS BRETHREN: ...

10. **AND** JABEZ CALLED ON THE GOD OF ISRAEL,
SAYING, OH THAT THOU WOULDEST BLESS ME INDEED,
AND ENLARGE MY COAST,
AND THAT THINE HAND MIGHT BE WITH ME,
AND THAT THOU WOULDEST KEEP ME FROM EVIL,
THAT IT MAY NOT GRIEVE ME!
AND GOD GRANTED HIM THAT WHICH HE REQUESTED.

January 30-February 1 (Days 30-32), Memory Verses #61 to #69
I Chronicles 16:8-12, 23-25, 34:

8. **GIVE** THANKS UNTO THE LORD, CALL UPON HIS NAME,
MAKE KNOWN HIS DEEDS AMONG THE PEOPLE.

9. **SING** UNTO HIM, SING PSALMS UNTO HIM,
TALK YE OF ALL HIS WONDROUS WORKS.

10. **GLORY** YE IN HIS HOLY NAME:
LET THE HEART OF THEM REJOICE THAT SEEK THE LORD.

11. **SEEK** THE LORD AND HIS STRENGTH, SEEK HIS FACE CONTINUALLY.

12. **REMEMBER** HIS MARVELLOUS WORKS THAT HE HATH DONE,
HIS WONDERS, AND THE JUDGMENTS OF HIS MOUTH;

23. **SING** UNTO THE LORD, ALL THE EARTH;
SHEW FORTH FROM DAY TO DAY HIS SALVATION.

24. **DECLARE** HIS GLORY AMONG THE HEATHEN;
HIS MARVELLOUS WORKS AMONG THE NATIONS.

25. **FOR** GREAT IS THE LORD, AND GREATLY TO BE PRAISED:
HE ALSO IS TO BE FEARED ABOVE ALL GODS.

34. **O** GIVE THANKS UNTO THE LORD FOR HE IS GOOD;
FOR HIS MERCY ENDURETH FOR EVER.

February 2 (Day 33), Memory Verse #70
I Chronicles 22:19:

NOW SET YOUR HEART AND YOUR SOUL
TO SEEK THE LORD YOUR GOD; ...

II CHRONICLES

February 3 (Day 34), Memory Verse #71
II Chronicles 7:14:

IF MY PEOPLE, WHICH ARE CALLED BY MY NAME,
SHALL HUMBLE THEMSELVES, AND PRAY, AND SEEK MY FACE,
AND TURN FROM THEIR WICKED WAYS;
THEN WILL I HEAR FROM HEAVEN, AND WILL FORGIVE THEIR SIN,
AND WILL HEAL THEIR LAND.

February 4 (Day 35), Memory Verse #72
II Chronicles 16:9:

FOR THE EYES OF THE LORD RUN TO AND FRO THROUGHOUT THE WHOLE EARTH,
TO SHEW HIMSELF STRONG IN THE BEHALF OF THEM
WHOSE HEART IS PERFECT TOWARD HIM (fully committed to him, NIV)...

February 5-6 (Days 36-37), Memory Verse #73
II Chronicles 20:21:

...PRAISE THE LORD; FOR HIS MERCY ENDURETH FOR EVER.

EZRA

February 7 (Day 38), Memory Verse #74
Ezra 7:10:

FOR EZRA HAD PREPARED HIS HEART
TO SEEK THE LAW OF THE LORD, AND TO DO IT,
AND TO TEACH IN ISRAEL STATUTES AND JUDGMENTS.

NEHEMIAH

February 7 (Day 38), Memory Verse #75
Nehemiah 8:10:

...FOR THE JOY OF THE LORD IS YOUR STRENGTH.

February 7 (Day 38), Memory Verse #76
Nehemiah 9:17:

...BUT THOU ART A GOD READY TO PARDON,
GRACIOUS AND MERCIFUL, SLOW TO ANGER,
AND OF GREAT KINDNESS, AND FORSOOKEST THEM NOT.

ESTHER

February 8 (Day 39), Memory Verse #77
Esther 4:14:

...AND WHO KNOWETH WHETHER THOU ART COME
TO THE KINGDOM FOR SUCH A TIME AS THIS?

JOB

February 8 (Day 39), Memory Verse #78
Job 1:21:

... NAKED CAME I OUT OF MY MOTHER'S WOMB,
AND NAKED SHALL I RETURN THITHER:
THE LORD GAVE, AND THE LORD HATH TAKEN AWAY;
BLESSED BE THE NAME OF THE LORD.

February 8 (Day 39), Memory Verse #79
Job 5:17:

BEHOLD, HAPPY IS THE MAN WHOM GOD CORRECTETH:
THEREFORE DESPISE NOT THOU THE CHASTENING OF THE ALMIGHTY:

February 8 (Day 39), Memory Verse #80
Job 6:25:

HOW FORCIBLE ARE RIGHT WORDS!...

February 9 (Day 40), Memory Verse #81
Job 19:25:

FOR I KNOW THAT MY REDEEMER LIVETH,
AND THAT HE SHALL STAND AT THE LATTER DAY UPON THE EARTH:

February 9 (Day 40), Memory Verse #82
Job 28:28:

AND UNTO MAN HE SAID, BEHOLD,
THE FEAR OF THE LORD, THAT IS WISDOM;
AND TO DEPART FROM EVIL IS UNDERSTANDING.

February 9 (Day 40), Memory Verse #83
Job 37:14:

HEARKEN UNTO THIS, O JOB:
STAND STILL, AND CONSIDER THE WONDROUS WORKS OF GOD.

Psalms

February 10 (Day 41), Memory Verses #84 & #85
<u>Psalm 1:1-2:</u>

1. BLESSED IS THE MAN THAT WALKETH NOT IN THE COUNSEL OF THE UNGODLY,
NOR STANDETH IN THE WAY OF SINNERS,
NOR SITTETH IN THE SEAT OF THE SCORNFUL.

2. BUT HIS DELIGHT IS IN THE LAW OF THE LORD,
AND IN HIS LAW DOTH HE MEDITATE DAY AND NIGHT.

February 10 (Day 41), Memory Verse #86
<u>Psalm 5:3:</u>

MY VOICE SHALT THOU HEAR IN THE MORNING, O LORD;
IN THE MORNING WILL I DIRECT MY PRAYER UNTO THEE, AND WILL LOOK UP.

February 10 (Day 41), Memory Verse #87
<u>Psalm 8:1:</u>

O LORD OUR LORD, HOW EXCELLENT IS THY NAME IN ALL THE EARTH!

February 11 (Day 42), Memory Verses #88 & #89
<u>Psalm 12:6-7:</u>

6. THE WORDS OF THE LORD ARE PURE WORDS:
AS SILVER TRIED IN A FURNACE OF EARTH, PURIFIED SEVEN TIMES.

7. THOU SHALT KEEP THEM, O LORD,
THOU SHALT PRESERVE THEM FROM THIS GENERATION FOR EVER.

February 11 (Day 42), Memory Verse #90
<u>Psalm 14:1:</u>

THE FOOL HATH SAID IN HIS HEART, THERE IS NO GOD…

February 11 (Day 42), Memory Verse #91
<u>Psalm 18:2:</u>

THE LORD IS MY ROCK, AND MY FORTRESS, AND MY DELIVERER;
MY GOD, MY STRENGTH, IN WHOM I WILL TRUST;
MY BUCKLER, AND THE HORN OF MY SALVATION, AND MY HIGH TOWER.

February 12 (Day 43), Memory Verses #92 to #95
<u>Psalm 18:30-33:</u>

30. AS FOR GOD, HIS WAY IS PERFECT: THE WORD OF THE LORD IS TRIED:
HE IS A BUCKLER TO ALL THOSE THAT TRUST IN HIM.

31. FOR WHO IS GOD SAVE THE LORD? OR WHO IS A ROCK SAVE OUR GOD?

32. IT IS GOD THAT GIRDETH ME WITH STRENGTH, AND MAKETH MY WAY PERFECT.

33. HE MAKETH MY FEET LIKE HINDS' FEET, AND SETTETH ME UPON MY HIGH PLACES.

February 13 (Day 44), Memory Verse #96
Psalm 19:1:

THE HEAVENS DECLARE THE GLORY OF GOD;
AND THE FIRMAMENT SHEWETH HIS HANDIWORK.

February 13-14 (Days 44-45), Memory Verses #97 to #100
Psalm 19:7-10:

7. THE LAW OF THE LORD IS PERFECT, CONVERTING THE SOUL:
THE TESTIMONY OF THE LORD IS SURE, MAKING WISE THE SIMPLE.

8. THE STATUTES OF THE LORD ARE RIGHT, REJOICING THE HEART:
THE COMMANDMENT OF THE LORD IS PURE, ENLIGHTENING THE EYES.

9. THE FEAR OF THE LORD IS CLEAN, ENDURING FOR EVER:
THE JUDGMENTS OF THE LORD ARE TRUE AND RIGHTEOUS ALTOGETHER.

10. MORE TO BE DESIRED ARE THEY THAN GOLD, YEA, THAN MUCH FINE GOLD:
SWEETER ALSO THAN HONEY AND THE HONEYCOMB.

February 14 (Day 45), Memory Verse #101
Psalm 19:14:

LET THE WORDS OF MY MOUTH,
AND THE MEDITATION OF MY HEART,
BE ACCEPTABLE IN THY SIGHT,
O LORD, MY STRENGTH, AND MY REDEEMER.

February 14-15 (Days 45-46), Memory Verses #102 to #107
Psalm 22:1, 14-18:
(Verses seen as foretelling Jesus' crucifixion; also see 31:5)

1. MY GOD, MY GOD, WHY HAST THOU FORSAKEN ME? ...

14. I AM POURED OUT LIKE WATER,
AND ALL MY BONES ARE OUT OF JOINT:
MY HEART IS LIKE WAX;
IT IS MELTED IN THE MIDST OF MY BOWELS.

15. MY STRENGTH IS DRIED UP LIKE A POTSHERD;
AND MY TONGUE CLEAVETH TO MY JAWS;
AND THOU HAST BROUGHT ME INTO THE DUST OF DEATH.

16. FOR DOGS HAVE COMPASSED ME:
THE ASSEMBLY OF THE WICKED HAVE ENCLOSED ME:
THEY PIERCED MY HANDS AND MY FEET.

17. I MAY TELL ALL MY BONES:
THEY LOOK AND STARE UPON ME.

18. THEY PART MY GARMENTS AMONG THEM,
AND CAST LOTS UPON MY VESTURE.

February 16-17 (Days 47-48), Memory Verses #108 to #113
<u>Psalm 23:1-6:</u>

1. THE LORD IS MY SHEPHERD; I SHALL NOT WANT.

2. HE MAKETH ME TO LIE DOWN IN GREEN PASTURES:
HE LEADETH ME BESIDE THE STILL WATERS.

3. HE RESTORETH MY SOUL:
HE LEADETH ME IN THE PATHS OF RIGHTEOUSNESS FOR HIS NAME'S SAKE.

4. YEA, THOUGH I WALK THROUGH THE VALLEY OF THE SHADOW OF DEATH,
I WILL FEAR NO EVIL: FOR THOU ART WITH ME;
THY ROD AND THY STAFF THEY COMFORT ME.

5. THOU PREPAREST A TABLE BEFORE ME IN THE PRESENCE OF MINE ENEMIES:
THOU ANOINTEST MY HEAD WITH OIL; MY CUP RUNNETH OVER.

6. SURELY GOODNESS AND MERCY SHALL FOLLOW ME ALL THE DAYS OF MY LIFE:
AND I WILL DWELL IN THE HOUSE OF THE LORD FOR EVER.

February 18 (Day 49), Memory Verse #114
<u>Psalm 24:1:</u>

THE EARTH IS THE LORD'S, AND THE FULNESS THEREOF;
THE WORLD, AND THEY THAT DWELL THEREIN.

February 18 (Day 49), Memory Verses #115 to #117
<u>Psalm 25:6-8:</u>

6. REMEMBER, O LORD, THY TENDER MERCIES AND THY LOVINGKINDNESSES;
FOR THEY HAVE BEEN EVER OF OLD.

7. REMEMBER NOT THE SINS OF MY YOUTH, NOR MY TRANSGRESSIONS:
ACCORDING TO THY MERCY REMEMBER THOU ME FOR THY GOODNESS' SAKE, O LORD.

8. GOOD AND UPRIGHT IS THE LORD:
THEREFORE WILL HE TEACH SINNERS IN THE WAY.

February 19 (Day 50), Memory Verse #118
<u>Psalm 27:1:</u>

THE LORD IS MY LIGHT AND MY SALVATION; WHOM SHALL I FEAR?
THE LORD IS THE STRENGTH OF MY LIFE; OF WHOM SHALL I BE AFRAID?

February 19 (Day 50), Memory Verse #119
<u>Psalm 27:14:</u>

WAIT ON THE LORD: BE OF GOOD COURAGE,
AND HE SHALL STRENGTHEN THINE HEART:
WAIT, I SAY, ON THE LORD.

February 19 (Day 50), Memory Verse #120
<u>Psalm 28:7:</u>

THE LORD IS MY STRENGTH AND MY SHIELD;
MY HEART TRUSTED IN HIM, AND I AM HELPED:
THEREFORE MY HEART GREATLY REJOICETH;
AND WITH MY SONG WILL I PRAISE HIM.

February 19 (Day 50), Memory Verse #121
Psalm 31:5:

INTO THINE HAND I COMMIT MY SPIRIT:...

February 20 (Day 51), Memory Verse #122
Psalm 31:24:

BE OF GOOD COURAGE, AND HE SHALL STRENGTHEN YOUR HEART,
ALL YE THAT HOPE IN THE LORD.

February 20 (Day 51), Memory Verse #123
Psalm 33:12:

BLESSED IS THE NATION WHOSE GOD IS THE LORD;...

February 20 (Day 51), Memory Verse #124
Psalm 35:9:

AND MY SOUL SHALL BE JOYFUL IN THE LORD:
IT SHALL REJOICE IN HIS SALVATION.

February 20 (Day 51), Memory Verse #125
Psalm 36:7:

HOW EXCELLENT IS THY LOVINGKINDNESS, O GOD!
THEREFORE THE CHILDREN OF MEN PUT THEIR TRUST
UNDER THE SHADOW OF THY WINGS.

February 21 (Day 52), Memory Verses #126 & #127
Psalm 37:4-5:

4. DELIGHT THYSELF ALSO IN THE LORD;
AND HE SHALL GIVE THEE THE DESIRES OF THINE HEART.

5. COMMIT THY WAY UNTO THE LORD; TRUST ALSO IN HIM;
AND HE SHALL BRING IT TO PASS.

February 21 (Day 52), Memory Verse #128
Psalm 37:7:

REST IN THE LORD, AND WAIT PATIENTLY FOR HIM: ...

February 22 (Day 53), Memory Verses #129 & #130
Psalm 37:23-24:

23. THE STEPS OF A GOOD MAN ARE ORDERED BY THE LORD:
AND HE DELIGHTETH IN HIS WAY.

24. THOUGH HE FALL, HE SHALL NOT BE UTTERLY CAST DOWN:
FOR THE LORD UPHOLDETH HIM WITH HIS HAND.

February 22 (Day 53), Memory Verse #131
Psalm 40:5:

MANY, O LORD MY GOD, ARE THY WONDERFUL WORKS WHICH THOU HAST DONE,
AND THY THOUGHTS WHICH ARE TO US-WARD:
THEY CANNOT BE RECKONED UP IN ORDER UNTO THEE:
(The things you planned for us no one can recount to you, NIV);
IF I WOULD DECLARE AND SPEAK OF THEM,
THEY ARE MORE THAN CAN BE NUMBERED.

February 23 (Day 54), Memory Verse #132
Psalm 42:1:

AS THE HART PANTETH AFTER THE WATER BROOKS,
SO PANTETH MY SOUL AFTER THEE, O GOD.

February 23 (Day 54), Memory Verse #133
Psalm 44:21:

...HE (God) KNOWETH THE SECRETS OF THE HEART.

February 23 (Day 54), Memory Verse #134
Psalm 46:1:

GOD IS OUR REFUGE AND STRENGTH, A VERY PRESENT HELP IN TROUBLE.

February 23 (Day 54), Memory Verse #135
Psalm 46:10:

BE STILL, AND KNOW THAT I AM GOD: ...

February 24 (Day 55), Memory Verse #136
Psalm 47:1:

O CLAP YOUR HANDS, ALL YE PEOPLE;
SHOUT UNTO GOD WITH THE VOICE OF TRIUMPH.

February 24 (Day 55), Memory Verses #137 & #138
Psalm 47:6-7:

6. SING PRAISES TO GOD, SING PRAISES:
SING PRAISES UNTO OUR KING, SING PRAISES.

7. FOR GOD IS THE KING OF ALL THE EARTH:
SING YE PRAISES WITH UNDERSTANDING.

February 24 (Day 55), Memory Verse #139
Psalm 49:17:

FOR WHEN HE DIETH HE SHALL CARRY NOTHING AWAY:
HIS GLORY (splendor, NIV) SHALL NOT DESCEND AFTER HIM.

February 25 (Day 56), Memory Verse #140
Psalm 51:7:

...WASH ME, AND I SHALL BE WHITER THAN SNOW.

February 25 (Day 56), Memory Verse #141
Psalm 51:10:

CREATE IN ME A CLEAN HEART, O GOD;
AND RENEW A RIGHT SPIRIT WITHIN ME.

February 25 (Day 56), Memory Verse #142
Psalm 51:12:

RESTORE UNTO ME THE JOY OF THY SALVATION; ...

February 25 (Day 56), Memory Verse #143
Psalm 53:1:

THE FOOL HATH SAID IN HIS HEART, THERE IS NO GOD...

February 26 (Day 57), Memory Verse #144
Psalm 55:22:

CAST THY BURDEN UPON THE LORD, AND HE SHALL SUSTAIN THEE:...

February 26 (Day 57), Memory Verse #145
Psalm 56:3:

WHAT TIME I AM AFRAID, I WILL TRUST IN THEE.

February 26 (Day 57), Memory Verse #146
Psalm 56:11:

IN GOD HAVE I PUT MY TRUST:
I WILL NOT BE AFRAID WHAT MAN CAN DO UNTO ME.

February 27 (Day 58), Memory Verses #147 to #150
Psalm 62:5-8:

5. MY SOUL, WAIT THOU ONLY UPON GOD;
FOR MY EXPECTATION IS FROM HIM.

6. HE ONLY IS MY ROCK AND MY SALVATION:
HE IS MY DEFENCE; I SHALL NOT BE MOVED.

7. IN GOD IS MY SALVATION AND MY GLORY:
THE ROCK OF MY STRENGTH, AND MY REFUGE, IS IN GOD.

8. TRUST IN HIM AT ALL TIMES;
YE PEOPLE, POUR OUT YOUR HEART BEFORE HIM:
GOD IS A REFUGE FOR US...

February 28 (Day 59), Memory Verse #151
Psalm 67:1:

GOD BE MERCIFUL UNTO US, AND BLESS US;
AND CAUSE HIS FACE TO SHINE UPON US;

February 28 (Day 59), Memory Verse #152
Psalm 84:11:

FOR THE LORD GOD IS A SUN AND SHIELD: THE LORD WILL GIVE GRACE AND GLORY:
NO GOOD THING WILL HE WITHHOLD FROM THEM THAT WALK UPRIGHTLY.

February 28 (Day 59), Memory Verse #153
Psalm 86:5:

FOR THOU, LORD, ART GOOD, AND READY TO FORGIVE;
AND PLENTEOUS IN MERCY UNTO ALL THEM THAT CALL UPON THEE.

February 28 (Day 59), Memory Verse #154
Psalm 86:11:

TEACH ME THY WAY, O LORD; I WILL WALK IN THY TRUTH:...

March 1 (Day 60), Memory Verse #155
Psalm 86:15:

BUT THOU, O LORD, ART A GOD FULL OF COMPASSION,
AND GRACIOUS, LONGSUFFERING, AND PLENTEOUS IN MERCY AND TRUTH.

March 1 (Day 60), Memory Verse #156
Psalm 90:2:

BEFORE THE MOUNTAINS WERE BROUGHT FORTH,
OR EVER THOU HADST FORMED THE EARTH AND THE WORLD,
EVEN FROM EVERLASTING TO EVERLASTING, THOU ART GOD.

March 1 (Day 60), Memory Verse #157
Psalm 90:4:

FOR A THOUSAND YEARS IN THY SIGHT ARE BUT AS YESTERDAY WHEN IT IS PAST,
AND AS A WATCH IN THE NIGHT.

March 1 (Day 60), Memory Verse #158
Psalm 90:12:

SO TEACH US TO NUMBER OUR DAYS,
THAT WE MAY APPLY OUR HEARTS UNTO WISDOM.

March 2 (Day 61), Memory Verse #159
Psalm 91:2:

I WILL SAY OF THE LORD, HE IS MY REFUGE AND MY FORTRESS:
MY GOD; IN HIM WILL I TRUST.

March 2 (Day 61), Memory Verses #160 & #161
Psalm 92:1-2:

1. IT IS A GOOD THING TO GIVE THANKS UNTO THE LORD,
AND TO SING PRAISES UNTO THY NAME, O MOST HIGH:

2. TO SHEW FORTH THY LOVINGKINDNESS IN THE MORNING,
AND THY FAITHFULNESS EVERY NIGHT,

March 2 (Day 61), Memory Verse #162
Psalm 94:12:

BLESSED IS THE MAN WHOM THOU CHASTENEST (you discipline, NIV), O LORD,
AND TEACHEST HIM OUT OF THY LAW;

March 3 (Day 62), Memory Verses #163 & #164
Psalm 95:6-7:

6. O COME, LET US WORSHIP AND BOW DOWN:
LET US KNEEL BEFORE THE LORD OUR MAKER.

7. FOR HE IS OUR GOD;
AND WE ARE THE SHEEP OF HIS PASTURE,
AND THE SHEEP OF HIS HAND (the flock under his care, NIV) …

March 3-4 (Days 62-63), Memory Verses #165 to #169
<u>**Psalm 100: 1-5:**</u>

1. MAKE A JOYFUL NOISE UNTO THE LORD, ALL YE LANDS.

2. SERVE THE LORD WITH GLADNESS:
COME BEFORE HIS PRESENCE WITH SINGING.

3. KNOW YE THAT THE LORD HE IS GOD:
IT IS HE THAT HATH MADE US, AND NOT WE OURSELVES;
WE ARE HIS PEOPLE, AND THE SHEEP OF HIS PASTURE.

4. ENTER INTO HIS GATES WITH THANKSGIVING,
AND INTO HIS COURTS WITH PRAISE:
BE THANKFUL UNTO HIM, AND BLESS HIS NAME

5. FOR THE LORD IS GOOD; HIS MERCY IS EVERLASTING;
AND HIS TRUTH ENDURETH TO ALL GENERATIONS.

March 5 (Day 64), Memory Verse #170
<u>**Psalm 102:25:**</u>

OF OLD HAST THOU LAID THE FOUNDATION OF THE EARTH:
AND THE HEAVENS ARE THE WORK OF THY HANDS.

March 5 (Day 64), Memory Verses #171 & #172
<u>**Psalm 103:1-2:**</u>

1. BLESS THE LORD, O MY SOUL:
AND ALL THAT IS WITHIN ME, BLESS HIS HOLY NAME.

2. BLESS THE LORD, O MY SOUL, AND FORGET NOT ALL HIS BENEFITS:

March 6 (Day 65), Memory Verse #173
<u>**Psalm 103:12:**</u>

AS FAR AS THE EAST IS FROM THE WEST,
SO FAR HATH HE REMOVED OUR TRANSGRESSIONS FROM US.

March 6 (Day 65), Memory Verses #174 & #175
<u>**Psalm 104:33-34:**</u>

33. I WILL SING UNTO THE LORD AS LONG AS I LIVE:
I WILL SING PRAISE TO MY GOD WHILE I HAVE MY BEING.

34. MY MEDITATION OF HIM SHALL BE SWEET:
I WILL BE GLAD IN THE LORD.

March 7 (Day 66), Memory Verse #176
<u>**Psalm 111:10:**</u>

THE FEAR OF THE LORD IS THE BEGINNING OF WISDOM:
A GOOD UNDERSTANDING HAVE ALL THEY THAT DO HIS COMMANDMENTS:
HIS PRAISE ENDURETH FOR EVER.

March 7 (Day 66), Memory Verses #177 & #178
<u>**Psalm 117:1-2:**</u>

1. O PRAISE THE LORD, ALL YE NATIONS: PRAISE HIM, ALL YE PEOPLE.

2. FOR HIS MERCIFUL KINDNESS IS GREAT TOWARD US:
AND THE TRUTH OF THE LORD ENDURETH FOR EVER.
PRAISE YE THE LORD.

March 8 (Day 67), Memory Verse #179
Psalm 118:8:

IT IS BETTER TO TRUST IN THE LORD
THAN TO PUT CONFIDENCE IN MAN.

March 8 (Day 67), Memory Verse #180
Psalm 118:22:
(Jesus uses this cornerstone verse; see Matthew 21:42.)

THE STONE WHICH THE BUILDERS REFUSED
IS BECOME THE HEAD STONE OF THE CORNER.

March 8 (Day 67), Memory Verse #181
Psalm 118:24:

THIS IS THE DAY WHICH THE LORD HATH MADE;
WE WILL REJOICE AND BE GLAD IN IT.

March 9 (Day 68), Memory Verse #182
Psalm 119:11:

THY WORD HAVE I HID IN MINE HEART,
THAT I MIGHT NOT SIN AGAINST THEE.

March 9 (Day 68), Memory Verse #183
Psalm 119: 80:

LET MY HEART BE SOUND IN THY STATUTES;
THAT I BE NOT ASHAMED.

March 9 (Day 68), Memory Verse #184
Psalm 119: 103:

HOW SWEET ARE THY WORDS UNTO MY TASTE!
YEA, SWEETER THAN HONEY TO MY MOUTH!

March 10 (Day 69), Memory Verse #185
Psalm 119: 105:

THY WORD IS A LAMP UNTO MY FEET,
AND A LIGHT UNTO MY PATH.

March 10 (Day 69), Memory Verse #186
Psalm 119: 127:

THEREFORE I LOVE THY COMMANDMENTS ABOVE GOLD;
YEA, ABOVE FINE GOLD.

March 11-12 (Days 70-71), Memory Verses #187 to #194
Psalm 121:1-8:

1. I WILL LIFT UP MINE EYES UNTO THE HILLS, FROM WHENCE COMETH MY HELP.

2. MY HELP COMETH FROM THE LORD, WHICH MADE HEAVEN AND EARTH.

3. HE WILL NOT SUFFER THY FOOT TO BE MOVED:
HE THAT KEEPETH THEE WILL NOT SLUMBER.

4. BEHOLD, HE THAT KEEPETH ISRAEL SHALL NEITHER SLUMBER NOR SLEEP.

5. THE LORD IS THY KEEPER:
THE LORD IS THY SHADE UPON THY RIGHT HAND.

6. THE SUN SHALL NOT SMITE THEE BY DAY, NOR THE MOON BY NIGHT.

7. THE LORD SHALL PRESERVE THEE FROM ALL EVIL:
HE SHALL PRESERVE THY SOUL.

8. THE LORD SHALL PRESERVE THY GOING OUT AND THY COMING IN
FROM THIS TIME FORTH, AND EVEN FOR EVERMORE.

March 13 (Day 72), Memory Verse #195
Psalm 122:1:

I WAS GLAD WHEN THEY SAID UNTO ME,
LET US GO INTO THE HOUSE OF THE LORD.

March 13 (Day 72), Memory Verse #196
Psalm 130: 5:

I WAIT FOR THE LORD, MY SOUL DOTH WAIT,
AND IN HIS WORD DO I HOPE.

March 13 (Day 72), Memory Verse #197
Psalm 133:1:

BEHOLD, HOW GOOD AND HOW PLEASANT IT IS
FOR BRETHREN TO DWELL TOGETHER IN UNITY!

March 14-15 (Days 73-74), Memory Verses #198 to #203
Psalm 136:1, 5-9:

1. O GIVE THANKS UNTO THE LORD; FOR HE IS GOOD:
FOR HIS MERCY ENDURETH FOR EVER.

5. TO HIM THAT BY WISDOM MADE THE HEAVENS:
FOR HIS MERCY ENDURETH FOR EVER.

6. TO HIM THAT STRETCHED OUT THE EARTH ABOVE THE WATERS:
FOR HIS MERCY ENDURETH FOR EVER.

7. TO HIM THAT MADE GREAT LIGHTS:
FOR HIS MERCY ENDURETH FOR EVER.

8. THE SUN TO RULE BY DAY:
FOR HIS MERCY ENDURETH FOR EVER:

9. THE MOON AND STARS TO RULE BY NIGHT:
FOR HIS MERCY ENDURETH FOR EVER.

March 16 (Day 75), Memory Verses #204 & #205
Psalm 139:9-10:

9. IF I TAKE THE WINGS OF THE MORNING,
AND DWELL IN THE UTTERMOST PARTS OF THE SEA;

10. EVEN THERE SHALL THY HAND LEAD ME,
AND THY RIGHT HAND SHALL HOLD ME.

March 16 (Day 75), Memory Verse #206
Psalm 139:14:

I WILL PRAISE THEE;
FOR I AM FEARFULLY AND WONDERFULLY MADE:
MARVELLOUS ARE THY WORKS;
AND THAT MY SOUL KNOWETH RIGHT (Full, NIV) WELL.

March 17 (Day 76), Memory Verses #207 & #208
Psalm 139:23-24:

23. SEARCH ME, O GOD, AND KNOW MY HEART:
TRY ME, AND KNOW MY THOUGHTS:

24. AND SEE IF THERE BE ANY WICKED WAY IN ME,
AND LEAD ME IN THE WAY EVERLASTING.

March 17 (Day 76), Memory Verse #209
Psalm 141:3:

SET A WATCH, O LORD, BEFORE MY MOUTH;
KEEP THE DOOR OF MY LIPS.

March 17 (Day 76), Memory Verse #210
Psalm 143:8:

CAUSE ME TO HEAR THY LOVINGKINDNESS IN THE MORNING;
FOR IN THEE DO I TRUST:
CAUSE ME TO KNOW THE WAY WHEREIN I SHOULD WALK;
FOR I LIFT UP MY SOUL UNTO THEE.

March 18 (Day 77), Memory Verse #211
Psalm 144:15:

...HAPPY IS THAT PEOPLE,
WHOSE GOD IS THE LORD.

March 18 (Day 77), Memory Verse #212
Psalm 145:3:

GREAT IS THE LORD, AND GREATLY TO BE PRAISED;
AND HIS GREATNESS IS UNSEARCHABLE.

March 18-19 (Days 77-78), Memory Verses #213 to #218
<u>**Psalm 150:1-6:**</u>

1. PRAISE YE THE LORD.
PRAISE GOD IN HIS SANCTUARY:
PRAISE HIM IN THE FIRMAMENT OF HIS POWER.

2. PRAISE HIM FOR HIS MIGHTY ACTS:
PRAISE HIM ACCORDING TO HIS EXCELLENT GREATNESS.

3. PRAISE HIM WITH THE SOUND OF THE TRUMPET:
PRAISE HIM WITH THE PSALTERY AND HARP.

4. PRAISE HIM WITH THE TIMBREL AND DANCE:
PRAISE HIM WITH STRINGED INSTRUMENTS AND ORGANS.

5. PRAISE HIM UPON THE LOUD CYMBALS:
PRAISE HIM UPON THE HIGH SOUNDING CYMBALS.

6. LET EVERY THING THAT HATH BREATH PRAISE THE LORD.
PRAISE YE THE LORD.

PROVERBS

March 20 (Day 79), Memory Verse #219
<u>**Proverbs 1:7:**</u>

THE FEAR OF THE LORD IS THE BEGINNING OF KNOWLEDGE:
BUT FOOLS DESPISE WISDOM AND INSTRUCTION.

March 20 (Day 79), Memory Verses #220 to #222
<u>**Proverbs 2:3-5:**</u>

3. YEA, IF THOU CRIEST AFTER KNOWLEDGE,
AND LIFTEST UP THY VOICE FOR UNDERSTANDING;

4. IF THOU SEEKEST HER AS SILVER,
AND SEARCHEST FOR HER AS FOR HID TREASURES;

5. THEN SHALT THOU UNDERSTAND THE FEAR OF THE LORD,
AND FIND THE KNOWLEDGE OF GOD.

March 21-23 (Days 80-82), Memory Verses #223 to #231
Proverbs 3:1-9:

1. MY SON, FORGET NOT MY LAW;
BUT LET THINE HEART KEEP MY COMMANDMENTS;

2. FOR LENGTH OF DAYS, AND LONG LIFE, AND PEACE, SHALL THEY ADD TO THEE.

3. LET NOT MERCY AND TRUTH FORSAKE THEE: BIND THEM ABOUT THY NECK;
WRITE THEM UPON THE TABLE OF THINE HEART:

4. SO SHALT THOU FIND FAVOUR AND GOOD UNDERSTANDING
IN THE SIGHT OF GOD AND MAN.

5. TRUST IN THE LORD WITH ALL THINE HEART;
AND LEAN NOT UNTO THINE OWN UNDERSTANDING.

6. IN ALL THY WAYS ACKNOWLEDGE HIM, AND HE SHALL DIRECT THY PATHS.

7. BE NOT WISE IN THINE OWN EYES: FEAR THE LORD, AND DEPART FROM EVIL.

8. IT SHALL BE HEALTH TO THY NAVEL, AND MARROW TO THY BONES.

9. HONOUR THE LORD WITH THY SUBSTANCE,
AND WITH THE FIRSTFRUITS OF ALL THINE INCREASE:

March 24 (Day 83), Memory Verses #232 & #233
Proverbs 3:11-12:

11. MY SON, DESPISE NOT THE CHASTENING OF THE LORD;
NEITHER BE WEARY OF HIS CORRECTION:

12. FOR WHOM THE LORD LOVETH HE CORRECTETH;
EVEN AS A FATHER THE SON IN WHOM HE DELIGHTETH.

March 25 (Day 84), Memory Verse #234
Proverbs 4:18:

BUT THE PATH OF THE JUST IS AS THE SHINING LIGHT,
THAT SHINETH MORE AND MORE UNTO THE PERFECT DAY.

March 25 (Day 84), Memory Verse #235
Proverbs 6:6:

GO TO THE ANT, THOU SLUGGARD;
CONSIDER HER WAYS, AND BE WISE:

March 26 (Day 85), Memory Verses #236 to #238
Proverbs 6:20-22:

20. MY SON, KEEP THY FATHER'S COMMANDMENT,
AND FORSAKE NOT THE LAW OF THY MOTHER:

21. BIND THEM CONTINUALLY UPON THINE HEART,
AND TIE THEM ABOUT THY NECK.

22. WHEN THOU GOEST, IT SHALL LEAD THEE;
WHEN THOU SLEEPEST, IT SHALL KEEP THEE;
AND WHEN THOU AWAKEST, IT SHALL TALK WITH THEE.

March 27 (Day 86), Memory Verse #239
Proverbs 9:10:

THE FEAR OF THE LORD IS THE BEGINNING OF WISDOM:
AND THE KNOWLEDGE OF THE HOLY IS UNDERSTANDING.

March 27 (Day 86), Memory Verse #240
Proverbs 10:1:

A WISE SON MAKETH A GLAD FATHER:
BUT A FOOLISH SON IS THE HEAVINESS OF HIS MOTHER.

March 27 (Day 86), Memory Verse #241
Proverbs 10:12:

HATRED STIRRETH UP STRIFES: BUT LOVE COVERETH ALL SINS.

March 28 (Day 87), Memory Verse #242
Proverbs 11:30:

THE FRUIT OF THE RIGHTEOUS IS A TREE OF LIFE;
AND HE THAT WINNETH SOULS IS WISE.

March 28 (Day 87), Memory Verse #243
Proverbs 12:28:

IN THE WAY OF RIGHTEOUSNESS IS LIFE;
AND IN THE PATHWAY THEREOF THERE IS NO DEATH.

March 29 (Day 88), Memory Verse #244
Proverbs 14:21:

HE THAT DESPISETH HIS NEIGHBOUR SINNETH:
BUT HE THAT HATH MERCY ON THE POOR, HAPPY IS HE.

March 29 (Day 88), Memory Verse #245
Proverbs 14:30:

A SOUND HEART IS THE LIFE OF THE FLESH:
BUT ENVY THE ROTTENNESS OF THE BONES,

March 30 (Day 89), Memory Verse #246
Proverbs 15:1:

A SOFT ANSWER TURNETH AWAY WRATH:
BUT GRIEVOUS WORDS STIR UP ANGER.

March 30 (Day 89), Memory Verse #247
Proverbs 15:6:

IN THE HOUSE OF THE RIGHTEOUS IS MUCH TREASURE:
BUT IN THE REVENUES OF THE WICKED IS TROUBLE.

March 30 (Day 89), Memory Verse #248
Proverbs 15:13:

A MERRY HEART MAKETH A CHEERFUL COUNTENANCE:
BUT BY SORROW OF THE HEART THE SPIRIT IS BROKEN.

March 31 (Day 90), Memory Verses #249 & #250
Proverbs 15:15-16:

15. ...HE THAT IS OF A MERRY HEART HATH A CONTINUAL FEAST.

16. BETTER IS LITTLE WITH THE FEAR OF THE LORD
THAN GREAT TREASURE AND TROUBLE THEREWITH.

March 31 (Day 90), Memory Verse #251
Proverbs 15:33:

THE FEAR OF THE LORD IS THE INSTRUCTION OF WISDOM;
AND BEFORE HONOUR IS HUMILITY.

April 1 (Day 91), Memory Verse #252
Proverbs 16:3:

COMMIT THY WORKS UNTO THE LORD,
AND THY THOUGHTS SHALL BE ESTABLISHED.

April 1 (Day 91), Memory Verse #253
Proverbs 16:24:

PLEASANT WORDS ARE AS AN HONEYCOMB,
SWEET TO THE SOUL, AND HEALTH TO THE BONES.

April 1 (Day 91), Memory Verse #254
Proverbs 16:32:

HE THAT IS SLOW TO ANGER IS BETTER THAN THE MIGHTY;
AND HE THAT RULETH HIS SPIRIT THAN HE THAT TAKETH A CITY.

April 1 (Day 91), Memory Verse #255
Proverbs 17:3:

THE FINING POT IS FOR SILVER, AND THE FURNACE FOR GOLD:
BUT THE LORD TRIETH THE HEARTS.

April 2 (Day 92), Memory Verse #256
Proverbs 17:17:

A FRIEND LOVETH AT ALL TIMES,...

April 2 (Day 92), Memory Verse #257
Proverbs 17:22:

A MERRY HEART DOETH GOOD LIKE A MEDICINE:
BUT A BROKEN SPIRIT DRIETH THE BONES.

April 2 (Day 92), Memory Verses #258 & #259
Proverbs 18:7-8:

7. A FOOL'S MOUTH IS HIS DESTRUCTION,
AND HIS LIPS ARE THE SNARE OF HIS SOUL.

8. THE WORDS OF A TALEBEARER ARE AS WOUNDS,
AND THEY GO DOWN INTO THE INNERMOST PARTS OF THE BELLY.

April 3 (Day 93), Memory Verse #260
Proverbs 18:10:

THE NAME OF THE LORD IS A STRONG TOWER:
THE RIGHTEOUS RUNNETH INTO IT, AND IS SAFE.

April 3 (Day 93), Memory Verse #261
Proverbs 18:15:

THE HEART OF THE PRUDENT GETTETH KNOWLEDGE;
AND THE EAR OF THE WISE SEEKETH KNOWLEDGE.

April 3 (Day 93), Memory Verse #262
Proverbs 18:12:

BEFORE DESTRUCTION THE HEART OF MAN IS HAUGHTY,
AND BEFORE HONOUR IS HUMILITY.

April 4 (Day 94), Memory Verse #263
Proverbs 20:15:

THERE IS GOLD, AND A MULTITUDE OF RUBIES:
BUT THE LIPS OF KNOWLEDGE ARE A PRECIOUS JEWEL.

April 4 (Day 94), Memory Verse #264
Proverbs 21:2:

EVERY WAY OF A MAN IS RIGHT IN HIS OWN EYES:
BUT THE LORD PONDERETH THE HEARTS.

April 4 (Day 94), Memory Verse #265
Proverbs 22:1:

A GOOD NAME IS RATHER TO BE CHOSEN THAN GREAT RICHES,
AND LOVING FAVOUR RATHER THAN SILVER AND GOLD.

April 4 (Day 94), Memory Verse #266
Proverbs 22:6:

TRAIN UP A CHILD IN THE WAY HE SHOULD GO:
AND WHEN HE IS OLD, HE WILL NOT DEPART FROM IT.

April 5 (Day 95), Memory Verse #267
Proverbs 23:7:

FOR AS HE THINKETH IN HIS HEART, SO IS HE:...

April 5 (Day 95), Memory Verse #268
Proverbs 23:17:

LET NOT THINE HEART ENVY SINNERS:
BUT BE THOU IN THE FEAR OF THE LORD ALL THE DAY LONG.

April 5 (Day 95), Memory Verses #269 & #270
Proverbs 24:13-14:

13. MY SON, EAT THOU HONEY, BECAUSE IT IS GOOD;
AND THE HONEYCOMB, WHICH IS SWEET TO THY TASTE:

14. SO SHALL THE KNOWLEDGE OF WISDOM BE UNTO THY SOUL:
WHEN THOU HAST FOUND IT.

April 6 (Day 96), Memory Verse #271
Proverbs 25:11:

A WORD FITLY SPOKEN IS LIKE APPLES OF GOLD IN PICTURES OF SILVER.

April 6 (Day 96), Memory Verses #272 & #273
Proverbs 25:21-22:

21. IF THINE ENEMY BE HUNGRY, GIVE HIM BREAD TO EAT;
AND IF HE BE THIRSTY, GIVE HIM WATER TO DRINK:

22. FOR THOU SHALT HEAP COALS OF FIRE UPON HIS HEAD,
AND THE LORD SHALL REWARD THEE.

April 7 (Day 97), Memory Verse #274
Proverbs 27:2:

LET ANOTHER MAN PRAISE THEE, AND NOT THINE OWN MOUTH;
A STRANGER, AND NOT THINE OWN LIPS.

April 7 (Day 97), Memory Verse #275
Proverbs 29:23:

A MAN'S PRIDE SHALL BRING HIM LOW:
BUT HONOUR SHALL UPHOLD THE HUMBLE IN SPIRIT.

April 7 (Day 97), Memory Verses #276 & #277
Proverbs 29:25-26:

25. THE FEAR OF MAN BRINGETH A SNARE:
BUT WHOSO PUTTETH HIS TRUST IN THE LORD SHALL BE SAFE.

26. MANY SEEK THE RULER'S FAVOUR;
BUT EVERY MAN'S JUDGMENT COMETH FROM THE LORD.

April 8 (Day 98), Memory Verse #278
Proverbs 30:5:

EVERY WORD OF GOD IS PURE:
HE IS A SHIELD UNTO THEM THAT PUT THEIR TRUST IN HIM.

April 8 (Day 98), Memory Verse #279
Proverbs 31:30:

FAVOUR (Charm, NIV) IS DECEITFUL,
AND BEAUTY IS VAIN:
BUT A WOMAN THAT FEARETH THE LORD,
SHE SHALL BE PRAISED.

ECCLESIASTES

April 9 (Day 99), Memory Verse #280
Ecclesiastes 3:1:

TO EVERYTHING THERE IS A SEASON,
AND A TIME TO EVERY PURPOSE UNDER THE HEAVEN: ...

April 9 (Day 99), Memory Verse #281
Ecclesiastes 3:17:

I SAID IN MINE HEART, GOD SHALL JUDGE THE RIGHTEOUS AND THE WICKED:
FOR THERE IS A TIME THERE FOR EVERY PURPOSE AND FOR EVERY WORK.

April 10 (Day 100), Memory Verses #282 & #283
Ecclesiastes 5:18-19:

18. BEHOLD THAT WHICH I HAVE SEEN:
IT IS GOOD AND COMELY FOR ONE TO EAT AND DRINK,
AND TO ENJOY THE GOOD OF ALL HIS LABOUR THAT HE TAKETH UNDER THE SUN
ALL THE DAYS OF HIS LIFE, WHICH GOD GIVETH HIM: FOR IT IS HIS PORTION.

19. EVERY MAN ALSO TO WHOM GOD HATH GIVEN RICHES AND WEALTH,
AND HATH GIVEN HIM POWER TO EAT THEREOF,
AND TO TAKE HIS PORTION, AND TO REJOICE IN HIS LABOUR;
THIS IS THE GIFT OF GOD.

April 11 (Day 101), Memory Verse #284
Ecclesiastes 7:1:

A GOOD NAME IS BETTER THAN PRECIOUS OINTMENT; ...

April 11 (Day 101), Memory Verse #285
Ecclesiastes 7:20:

FOR THERE IS NOT A MAN UPON EARTH, THAT DOETH GOOD, AND SINNETH NOT.

April 11 (Day 101), Memory Verse #286
Ecclesiastes 9:10:

WHATSOEVER THY HAND FINDETH TO DO, DO IT WITH THY MIGHT; ...

April 12 (Day 102), Memory Verse #287
Ecclesiastes 12:1:

REMEMBER NOW THY CREATOR IN THE DAYS OF THY YOUTH ...

April 12 (Day 102), Memory Verses #288 & #289
Ecclesiastes 12:13-14:

13. LET US HEAR THE CONCLUSION OF THE WHOLE MATTER:
FEAR GOD, AND KEEP HIS COMMANDMENTS:
FOR THIS IS THE WHOLE DUTY OF MAN.

14. FOR GOD SHALL BRING EVERY WORK INTO JUDGMENT, WITH EVERY SECRET THING,
WHETHER IT BE GOOD, OR WHETHER IT BE EVIL.

SONG OF SOLOMON

April 13 (Day 103), Memory Verse #290
Song of Solomon 2:4:

HE BROUGHT ME TO THE BANQUETING HOUSE,
HIS BANNER OVER ME IS LOVE.

April 13 (Day 103), Memory Verse #291
Song of Solomon 2:16:

MY BELOVED IS MINE, AND I AM HIS: ...

April 13 (Day 103), Memory Verses #292 & #293
Song of Solomon 8:6-7:

6. SET ME AS A SEAL UPON THINE HEART, AS A SEAL UPON THINE ARM:
FOR LOVE IS STRONG AS DEATH; JEALOUSY IS CRUEL AS THE GRAVE:
THE COALS THEREOF ARE COALS OF FIRE, WHICH HATH A MOST VEHEMENT FLAME.

7. MANY WATERS CANNOT QUENCH LOVE, NEITHER CAN THE FLOODS DROWN IT:
IF A MAN WOULD GIVE ALL THE SUBSTANCE OF HIS HOUSE FOR LOVE,
IT WOULD UTTERLY BE CONTEMNED (scorned, NIV).

ISAIAH

April 14 (Day 104), Memory Verse #294
Isaiah 1:18:

COME NOW, AND LET US REASON TOGETHER, SAITH THE LORD:
THOUGH YOUR SINS BE AS SCARLET, THEY SHALL BE WHITE AS SNOW;
THOUGH THEY BE RED LIKE CRIMSON, THEY SHALL BE AS WOOL.

April 14 (Day 104), Memory Verse #295
Isaiah 2:4:

AND HE SHALL JUDGE AMONG THE NATIONS,
AND SHALL REBUKE MANY PEOPLE:
AND THEY SHALL BEAT THEIR SWORDS INTO PLOWSHARES,
AND THEIR SPEARS INTO PRUNINGHOOKS:
NATION SHALL NOT LIFT UP SWORD AGAINST NATION,
NEITHER SHALL THEY LEARN WAR ANY MORE.

April 15 (Day 105), Memory Verse #296
Isaiah 6:8:

ALSO I HEARD THE VOICE OF THE LORD, SAYING,
WHOM SHALL I SEND, AND WHO WILL GO FOR US?
THEN SAID I, HERE AM I; SEND ME.

April 15 (Day 105), Memory Verse #297
Isaiah 7:14:

THEREFORE THE LORD HIMSELF SHALL GIVE YOU A SIGN;
BEHOLD, A VIRGIN SHALL CONCEIVE, AND BEAR A SON,
AND SHALL CALL HIS NAME IMMANUEL.

April 16 (Day 106), Memory Verses #298 & #299
Isaiah 9:6-7:

6. FOR UNTO US A CHILD IS BORN, UNTO US A SON IS GIVEN:
AND THE GOVERNMENT SHALL BE UPON HIS SHOULDER:
AND HIS NAME SHALL BE CALLED WONDERFUL, COUNSELLOR,
THE MIGHTY GOD, THE EVERLASTING FATHER, THE PRINCE OF PEACE.

7. OF THE INCREASE OF HIS GOVERNMENT AND PEACE THERE SHALL BE NO END,
UPON THE THRONE OF DAVID, AND UPON HIS KINGDOM,
TO ORDER IT, AND TO ESTABLISH IT WITH JUDGMENT
AND WITH JUSTICE FROM HENCEFORTH EVEN FOR EVER.

April 16 (Day 106), Memory Verse #300
Isaiah 11:6:

THE WOLF ALSO SHALL DWELL WITH THE LAMB,
AND THE LEOPARD SHALL LIE DOWN WITH THE KID;
AND THE CALF AND THE YOUNG LION AND THE FATLING TOGETHER;
AND A LITTLE CHILD SHALL LEAD THEM.

April 17 (Day 107), Memory Verses #301 to #304
Isaiah 12:2-5:

2. BEHOLD, GOD IS MY SALVATION; I WILL TRUST, AND NOT BE AFRAID:
FOR THE LORD JEHOVAH IS MY STRENGTH AND MY SONG;
HE ALSO IS BECOME MY SALVATION.

3. THEREFORE WITH JOY SHALL YE DRAW WATER
OUT OF THE WELLS OF SALVATION.

4. AND IN THAT DAY SHALL YE SAY, PRAISE THE LORD, CALL UPON HIS NAME,
DECLARE HIS DOINGS AMONG THE PEOPLE, MAKE MENTION THAT HIS NAME IS EXALTED.

5. SING UNTO THE LORD; FOR HE HATH DONE EXCELLENT THINGS:
THIS IS KNOWN IN ALL THE EARTH.

April 18 (Day 108), Memory Verse #305
Isaiah 25:8:

HE WILL SWALLOW UP DEATH IN VICTORY;
AND THE LORD GOD WILL WIPE AWAY TEARS FROM OFF ALL FACES;
AND THE REBUKE OF HIS PEOPLE SHALL HE TAKE AWAY FROM
OFF ALL THE EARTH: FOR THE LORD HATH SPOKEN IT.

April 18 (Day 108), Memory Verse #306
Isaiah 26:3:

THOU WILT KEEP HIM IN PERFECT PEACE, WHOSE MIND IS STAYED ON THEE:
BECAUSE HE TRUSTETH IN THEE.

April 19 (Day 109), Memory Verses #307 & #308
Isaiah 33:15-16:

15. HE THAT WALKETH RIGHTEOUSLY, AND SPEAKETH UPRIGHTLY;
HE THAT DESPISETH THE GAIN OF OPPRESSIONS,
THAT SHAKETH HIS HANDS FROM HOLDING OF BRIBES,
THAT STOPPETH HIS EARS FROM HEARING OF BLOOD,
AND SHUTTETH HIS EYES FROM SEEING EVIL;

16. HE SHALL DWELL ON HIGH:
HIS PLACE OF DEFENCE SHALL BE THE MUNITIONS OF ROCKS:
BREAD SHALL BE GIVEN HIM; HIS WATERS SHALL BE SURE.

April 20 (Day 110), Memory Verse #309
Isaiah 40:8:

THE GRASS WITHERETH, THE FLOWER FADETH:
BUT THE WORD OF OUR GOD SHALL STAND FOR EVER.

April 20 (Day 110), Memory Verses #310 & #311
Isaiah 40:28-29:

28. HAST THOU NOT KNOWN? HAST THOU NOT HEARD?
THAT THE EVERLASTING GOD, THE LORD,
THE CREATOR OF THE ENDS OF THE EARTH,
FAINTETH NOT, NEITHER IS WEARY?
THERE IS NO SEARCHING OF HIS UNDERSTANDING.

29. HE GIVETH POWER TO THE FAINT;
AND TO THEM THAT HAVE NO MIGHT HE INCREASETH STRENGTH.

April 20 (Day 110), Memory Verse #312
Isaiah 40:31:

BUT THEY THAT WAIT UPON THE LORD SHALL RENEW THEIR STRENGTH;
THEY SHALL MOUNT UP WITH WINGS AS EAGLES;
THEY SHALL RUN, AND NOT BE WEARY;
AND THEY SHALL WALK, AND NOT FAINT.

April 21 (Day 111), Memory Verse #313
Isaiah 41:4:

...I THE LORD, THE FIRST, AND WITH THE LAST; I AM HE.

April 21 (Day 111), Memory Verse #314
Isaiah 44:6:

...I AM THE FIRST, AND I AM THE LAST; AND BESIDE ME THERE IS NO GOD.

April 21 (Day 111), Memory Verse #315
Isaiah 45:22:

LOOK UNTO ME, AND BE YE SAVED, ALL THE ENDS OF THE EARTH;
FOR I AM GOD, AND THERE IS NONE ELSE.

April 22 (Day 112), Memory Verse #316
Isaiah 49:23:

...AND THOU SHALT KNOW THAT I AM THE LORD:
FOR THEY SHALL NOT BE ASHAMED THAT WAIT FOR ME.

April 22 (Day 112), Memory Verse #317
Isaiah 52:7:

HOW BEAUTIFUL UPON THE MOUNTAINS ARE THE FEET OF HIM
THAT BRINGETH GOOD TIDINGS, THAT PUBLISHETH PEACE;
THAT BRINGETH GOOD TIDINGS OF GOOD, THAT PUBLISHETH SALVATION;
THAT SAITH UNTO ZION, THY GOD REIGNETH!

April 23-24 (Days 113-114), Memory Verses #318 to #324
Isaiah 53:3-9:
(These verses are seen as referring to Jesus.)

3. HE IS DESPISED AND REJECTED OF MEN; A MAN OF SORROWS,
AND ACQUAINTED WITH GRIEF:
AND WE HID AS IT WERE OUR FACES FROM HIM;
HE WAS DESPISED, AND WE ESTEEMED HIM NOT.

4. SURELY HE HATH BORNE OUR GRIEFS, AND CARRIED OUR SORROWS:
YET WE DID ESTEEM HIM STRICKEN, SMITTEN OF GOD, AND AFFLICTED.

5. BUT HE WAS WOUNDED FOR OUR TRANSGRESSIONS,
HE WAS BRUISED FOR OUR INIQUITIES:
THE CHASTISEMENT OF OUR PEACE WAS UPON HIM;
AND WITH HIS STRIPES WE ARE HEALED.

6. ALL WE LIKE SHEEP HAVE GONE ASTRAY;
WE HAVE TURNED EVERY ONE TO HIS OWN WAY;
AND THE LORD HATH LAID ON HIM THE INIQUITY OF US ALL.

7. HE WAS OPPRESSED, AND HE WAS AFFLICTED,
YET HE OPENED NOT HIS MOUTH:
HE IS BROUGHT AS A LAMB TO THE SLAUGHTER,
AND AS A SHEEP BEFORE HER SHEARERS IS DUMB,
SO HE OPENETH NOT HIS MOUTH.

8. HE WAS TAKEN FROM PRISON AND FROM JUDGMENT:
AND WHO SHALL DECLARE HIS GENERATION?
FOR HE WAS CUT OFF OUT OF THE LAND OF THE LIVING:
FOR THE TRANSGRESSIONS OF MY PEOPLE WAS HE STRICKEN.

9. AND HE MADE HIS GRAVE WITH THE WICKED,
AND WITH THE RICH IN HIS DEATH;
BECAUSE HE HAD DONE NO VIOLENCE,
NEITHER WAS ANY DECEIT IN HIS MOUTH.

April 25 (Day 115), Memory Verse #325
Isaiah 55:6:

SEEK YE THE LORD WHILE HE MAY BE FOUND,
CALL YE UPON HIM WHILE HE IS NEAR:

April 25 (Day 115), Memory Verse #326
Isaiah 55:9:

FOR AS THE HEAVENS ARE HIGHER THAN THE EARTH,
SO ARE MY WAYS HIGHER THAN YOUR WAYS,
AND MY THOUGHTS THAN YOUR THOUGHTS.

April 26 (Day 116), Memory Verse #327
Isaiah 61:10:

I WILL GREATLY REJOICE IN THE LORD,
MY SOUL SHALL BE JOYFUL IN MY GOD;
FOR HE HATH CLOTHED ME WITH THE GARMENTS OF SALVATION,
HE HATH COVERED ME WITH THE ROBE OF RIGHTEOUSNESS...

April 26 (Day 116), Memory Verse #328
Isaiah 64:8:

BUT NOW, O LORD, THOU ART OUR FATHER;
WE ARE THE CLAY, AND THOU OUR POTTER;
AND WE ALL ARE THE WORK OF THY HAND.

JEREMIAH

April 27 (Day 117), Memory Verses #329 & #330
Jeremiah 9:23-24:

23. THUS SAITH THE LORD,
LET NOT THE WISE GLORY IN HIS WISDOM,
NEITHER LET THE MIGHTY MAN GLORY IN HIS MIGHT,
LET NOT THE RICH MAN GLORY IN HIS RICHES:

24. BUT LET HIM THAT GLORIETH GLORY IN THIS,
THAT HE UNDERSTANDETH AND KNOWETH ME,
THAT I AM THE LORD WHICH EXERCISE LOVINGKINDNESS,
JUDGMENT, AND RIGHTEOUSNESS, IN THE EARTH:
FOR IN THESE THINGS I DELIGHT, SAITH THE LORD.

April 27 (Day 117), Memory Verse #331
Jeremiah 10:10:

BUT THE LORD IS THE TRUE GOD,
HE IS THE LIVING GOD, AND AN EVERLASTING KING...

April 28 (Day 118), Memory Verses #332 & #333
Jeremiah 10:23-24:

23. O LORD, I KNOW THAT THE WAY OF MAN IS NOT IN HIMSELF:
IT IS NOT IN MAN THAT WALKETH TO DIRECT HIS STEPS.

24. O LORD, CORRECT ME, BUT WITH JUDGMENT;
NOT IN THINE ANGER, LEST THOU BRING ME TO NOTHING.

April 29 (Day 119), Memory Verses #334 to #337
Jeremiah 17:7-10:

7. BLESSED IS THE MAN THAT TRUSTETH IN THE LORD,
AND WHOSE HOPE THE LORD IS.

8. FOR HE SHALL BE AS A TREE PLANTED BY THE WATERS,
AND THAT SPREADETH OUT HER ROOTS BY THE RIVER,
AND SHALL NOT SEE WHEN HEAT COMETH,
BUT HER LEAF SHALL BE GREEN;
AND SHALL NOT BE CAREFUL IN THE YEAR OF DROUGHT,
NEITHER SHALL CEASE FROM YIELDING FRUIT.

9. THE HEART IS DECEITFUL ABOVE ALL THINGS,
AND DESPERATELY WICKED: WHO CAN KNOW IT?

10. I THE LORD SEARCH THE HEART, I TRY THE REINS,
EVEN TO GIVE EVERY MAN ACCORDING TO HIS WAYS,
AND ACCORDING TO THE FRUIT OF HIS DOINGS.

April 30 (Day 120), Memory Verse #338
Jeremiah 29:13:

AND YE SHALL SEEK ME, AND FIND ME,
WHEN YE SHALL SEARCH FOR ME WITH ALL YOUR HEART.

May 1 (Day 121), Memory Verses #339 to #342
Jeremiah 31:31-34:
(Old Testament passage foretelling the NEW COVENANT)

31. BEHOLD, THE DAYS COME, SAITH THE LORD,
THAT I WILL MAKE A NEW COVENANT WITH THE HOUSE OF ISRAEL,
AND WITH THE HOUSE OF JUDAH:

32. NOT ACCORDING TO THE COVENANT THAT I MADE WITH THEIR FATHERS
IN THE DAY THAT I TOOK THEM BY THE HAND
TO BRING THEM OUT OF THE LAND OF EGYPT;
WHICH MY COVENANT THEY BRAKE,
ALTHOUGH I WAS AN HUSBAND UNTO THEM, SAITH THE LORD:

33. BUT THIS SHALL BE THE COVENANT THAT I WILL MAKE
WITH THE HOUSE OF ISRAEL; AFTER THOSE DAYS, SAITH THE LORD,
I WILL PUT MY LAW IN THEIR INWARD PARTS,
AND WRITE IT IN THEIR HEARTS;
AND WILL BE THEIR GOD,
AND THEY SHALL BE MY PEOPLE.

34. AND THEY SHALL TEACH NO MORE EVERY MAN HIS NEIGHBOUR,
AND EVERY MAN HIS BROTHER,
SAYING KNOW THE LORD:
FOR THEY SHALL ALL KNOW ME,
FROM THE LEAST OF THEM UNTO THE GREATEST OF THEM,
SAITH THE LORD:
FOR I WILL FORGIVE THEIR INIQUITY,
AND I WILL REMEMBER THEIR SIN NO MORE.

LAMENTATIONS

May 2 (Day 122), Memory Verses #343 & #344
Lamentations 3:22-23:

22. IT IS OF THE LORD'S MERCIES THAT WE ARE NOT CONSUMED,
BECAUSE HIS COMPASSIONS FAIL NOT.

23. THEY ARE NEW EVERY MORNING: GREAT IS THY FAITHFULNESS.

May 2 (Day 122), Memory Verse #345
Lamentations 3:25:

THE LORD IS GOOD UNTO THEM THAT WAIT FOR HIM, TO THE SOUL THAT SEEKETH HIM.

May 3 (Day 123), Memory Verses #346 & #347
Lamentations 3:40-41:

40. LET US SEARCH AND TRY OUR WAYS, AND TURN AGAIN TO THE LORD.

41. LET US LIFT UP OUR HEART WITH OUR HANDS UNTO GOD IN THE HEAVENS.

May 3 (Day 123), Memory Verse #348
Lamentations 5:19:

THOU, O LORD, REMAINEST FOR EVER;
THY THRONE FROM GENERATION TO GENERATION.

EZEKIEL

May 4 (Day 124), Memory Verse #349
Ezekiel 17:24:

AND ALL THE TREES OF THE FIELD SHALL KNOW THAT
I THE LORD HAVE BROUGHT DOWN THE HIGH TREE,
HAVE EXALTED THE LOW TREE, HAVE DRIED UP THE GREEN TREE,
AND HAVE MADE THE DRY TREE TO FLOURISH:
I THE LORD HAVE SPOKEN AND HAVE DONE IT.

May 5 (Day 125), Memory Verses #350 to #352
Ezekiel 18:30-32:

30. THEREFORE I WILL JUDGE YOU, O HOUSE OF ISRAEL,
EVERY ONE ACCORDING TO HIS WAYS, SAITH THE LORD GOD.
REPENT, AND TURN YOURSELVES FROM ALL YOUR TRANSGRESSIONS;
SO INIQUITY SHALL NOT BE YOUR RUIN.

31. CAST AWAY FROM YOU ALL YOUR TRANSGRESSIONS,
WHEREBY YE HAVE TRANSGRESSED;
AND MAKE YOU A NEW HEART AND A NEW SPIRIT:
FOR WHY WILL YE DIE, O HOUSE OF ISRAEL?

32. FOR I HAVE NO PLEASURE IN THE DEATH OF HIM THAT DIETH,
SAITH THE LORD GOD: WHEREFORE TURN YOURSELVES, AND LIVE YE.

DANIEL

May 6 (Day 126), Memory Verse #353
Daniel 2:20:

DANIEL ANSWERED AND SAID,
BLESSED BE THE NAME OF GOD FOR EVER AND EVER:
FOR WISDOM AND MIGHT ARE HIS:

May 6 (Day 126), Memory Verse #354
Daniel 2:22:

HE REVEALETH THE DEEP AND SECRET THINGS:
HE KNOWETH WHAT IS IN THE DARKNESS, AND THE LIGHT DWELLETH WITH HIM.

May 7 (Day 127), Memory Verse #355
Daniel 12:3:

AND THEY THAT BE WISE SHALL SHINE AS THE BRIGHTNESS OF THE FIRMAMENT;
AND THEY THAT TURN MANY TO RIGHTEOUSNESS AS THE STARS FOR EVER AND EVER.

May 7 (Day 127), Memory Verse #356
Daniel 12:10:

MANY SHALL BE PURIFIED, AND MADE WHITE, AND TRIED;
BUT THE WICKED SHALL DO WICKEDLY:
AND NONE OF THE WICKED SHALL UNDERSTAND; BUT THE WISE SHALL UNDERSTAND.

HOSEA

May 8 (Day 128), Memory Verse #357
Hosea 12:6:

THEREFORE TURN THOU TO THY GOD:
KEEP MERCY AND JUDGMENT AND WAIT ON THY GOD CONTINUALLY.

May 8 (Day 128), Memory Verse #358
Hosea 13:4:

YET I AM THE LORD THY GOD FROM THE LAND OF EGYPT,
AND THOU SHALT KNOW NO GOD BUT ME:
FOR THERE IS NO SAVIOUR BESIDE ME.

May 8 (Day 128), Memory Verse #359
Hosea 14:,9:

WHO IS WISE, AND HE SHALL UNDERSTAND THESE THINGS?
PRUDENT, AND HE SHALL KNOW THEM?
FOR THE WAYS OF THE LORD ARE RIGHT,
AND THE JUST SHALL WALK IN THEM:
BUT THE TRANSGRESSORS SHALL FALL THEREIN.

JOEL

May 9 (Day 129), Memory Verse #360
Joel 2:13:

AND REND YOUR HEART, AND NOT YOUR GARMENTS,
AND TURN UNTO THE LORD YOUR GOD:
FOR HE IS GRACIOUS AND MERCIFUL, SLOW TO ANGER,
AND OF GREAT KINDNESS, AND REPENTETH HIM OF THE EVIL.

May 9 (Day 129), Memory Verse #361
Joel 2:21:

FEAR NOT, O LAND; BE GLAD AND REJOICE:
FOR THE LORD WILL DO GREAT THINGS.

May 9 (Day 129), Memory Verse #362
Joel 2:28:

AND IT SHALL COME TO PASS AFTERWARD,
THAT I WILL POUR OUT MY SPIRIT UPON ALL FLESH;
AND YOUR SONS AND YOUR DAUGHTERS SHALL PROPHESY,
YOUR OLD MEN SHALL DREAM DREAMS,
YOUR YOUNG MEN SHALL SEE VISIONS:

AMOS

May 10 (Day 130), Memory Verse #363
Amos 5:4:

FOR THUS SAITH THE LORD UNTO THE HOUSE OF ISRAEL,
SEEK YE ME, AND YE SHALL LIVE:

May 10 (Day 130), Memory Verse #364
Amos 5:24:

BUT LET JUDGMENT RUN DOWN AS WATERS,
AND RIGHTEOUSNESS AS A MIGHTY STREAM.

OBADIAH

May 11 (Day 131), Memory Verse #365
Obadiah verse 15:

FOR THE DAY OF THE LORD IS NEAR UPON ALL THE HEATHEN:
AS THOU HAST DONE, IT SHALL BE DONE UNTO THEE:
THY REWARD SHALL RETURN UPON THINE OWN HEAD.

JONAH

May 12 (Day 132), Memory Verse #366
Jonah 2:9:

...SALVATION IS OF THE LORD.

MICAH

May 13 (Day 133), Memory Verses #367 & #368
Micah 4:2-3:

2. AND MANY NATIONS SHALL COME, AND SAY,
COME, AND LET US GO UP TO THE MOUNTAIN OF THE LORD,
AND TO THE HOUSE OF THE GOD OF JACOB;
AND HE WILL TEACH US OF HIS WAYS, AND WE WILL WALK IN HIS PATHS:
FOR THE LAW SHALL GO FORTH OF ZION,
AND THE WORD OF THE LORD FROM JERUSALEM.

3. AND HE SHALL JUDGE AMONG MANY PEOPLE,
AND REBUKE STRONG NATIONS AFAR OFF;
AND THEY SHALL BEAT THEIR SWORDS INTO PLOWSHARES,
AND THEIR SPEARS INTO PRUNINGHOOKS:
NATION SHALL NOT LIFT UP A SWORD AGAINST NATION,
NEITHER SHALL THEY LEARN WAR ANY MORE.

May 14 (Day 134), Memory Verse #369
Micah 5:2:

BUT THOU, BETHLEHEM EPHRATAH,
THOUGH THOU BE LITTLE AMONG THE THOUSANDS OF JUDAH,
YET OUT OF THEE SHALL HE COME FORTH UNTO ME THAT IS TO BE RULER IN ISRAEL;
WHOSE GOINGS FORTH HAVE BEEN FROM OF OLD, FROM EVERLASTING.

May 14 (Day 134), Memory Verse #370
Micah 6:8:

HE HATH SHEWED THEE, O MAN, WHAT IS GOOD;
AND WHAT DOTH THE LORD REQUIRE OF THEE,
BUT TO DO JUSTLY, AND TO LOVE MERCY, AND TO WALK HUMBLY WITH THY GOD?

May 15 (Day 135), Memory Verses #371 & #372
Micah 7:7-8:

7. THEREFORE I WILL LOOK UNTO THE LORD;
I WILL WAIT FOR THE GOD OF MY SALVATION: MY GOD WILL HEAR ME.

8. REJOICE NOT AGAINST ME, O MINE ENEMY: WHEN I FALL, I SHALL ARISE;
WHEN I SIT IN DARKNESS, THE LORD SHALL BE A LIGHT UNTO ME.

May 15 (Day 135), Memory Verse #373
Micah 7:18:

...HE RETAINETH NOT HIS ANGER FOR EVER,
BECAUSE HE DELIGHTETH IN MERCY.

Nahum

May 16 (Day 136), Memory Verse #374
Nahum 1:7:

THE LORD IS GOOD,
A STRONG HOLD IN THE DAY OF TROUBLE;
AND HE KNOWETH THEM THAT TRUST IN HIM.

Habakkuk

May 17 (Day 137), Memory Verse #375
Habakkuk 2:4:

...BUT THE JUST SHALL LIVE BY HIS FAITH.

May 17 (Day 137), Memory Verse #376
Habakkuk 2:20:

BUT THE LORD IS IN HIS HOLY TEMPLE:
LET ALL THE EARTH KEEP SILENCE BEFORE HIM.

May 17 (Day 137), Memory Verses #377 & #378
Habakkuk 3:18-19:

18. YET I WILL REJOICE IN THE LORD,
I WILL JOY IN THE GOD OF MY SALVATION.

19. THE LORD GOD IS MY STRENGTH,
AND HE WILL MAKE MY FEET LIKE HINDS' FEET,
AND HE WILL MAKE ME TO WALK UPON MINE HIGH PLACES...

Zephaniah

May 18 (Day 138), Memory Verse #379
Zephaniah 2:3:

SEEK YE THE LORD, ALL YE MEEK OF THE EARTH,
WHICH HAVE WROUGHT HIS JUDGMENT:
SEEK RIGHTEOUSNESS, SEEK MEEKNESS:
IT MAY BE YE SHALL BE HID IN THE DAY OF THE LORD'S ANGER.

May 18 (Day 138), Memory Verse #380
Zephaniah 3:17:

THE LORD THY GOD IN THE MIDST OF THEE IS MIGHTY;
HE WILL SAVE, HE WILL REJOICE OVER THEE WITH JOY;
HE WILL REST IN HIS LOVE,
HE WILL JOY OVER THEE WITH SINGING.

HAGGAI

May 19 (Day 139), Memory Verse #381
<u>Haggai 1:13:</u>

...I AM WITH YOU, SAITH THE LORD.

ZECHARIAH

May 20 (Day 140), Memory Verse #382
<u>Zechariah 1:3:</u>

...TURN YE UNTO ME, SAITH THE LORD OF HOSTS,
AND I WILL TURN UNTO YOU, SAITH THE LORD OF HOSTS.

May 20 (Day 140), Memory Verse #383
<u>Zechariah 9:9:</u>

REJOICE GREATLY, O DAUGHTER OF ZION; SHOUT, O DAUGHTER OF JERUSALEM:
BEHOLD, THY KING COMETH UNTO THEE: HE IS JUST, AND HAVING SALVATION;
LOWLY, AND RIDING UPON AN ASS, AND UPON A COLT THE FOAL OF AN ASS.

MALACHI

May 21 (Day 141), Memory Verses #384 & #385
<u>Malachi 3:6-7:</u>

6. FOR I AM THE LORD, I CHANGE NOT;
THEREFORE, YE SONS OF JACOB ARE NOT CONSUMED.

7. EVEN FROM THE DAYS OF YOUR FATHERS YE ARE GONE AWAY
FROM MINE ORDINANCES, AND HAVE NOT KEPT THEM.
RETURN UNTO ME, AND I WILL RETURN UNTO YOU,
SAITH THE LORD OF HOSTS, ...

May 21 (Day 141), Memory Verse #386
<u>Malachi 4:2:</u>

BUT UNTO YOU THAT FEAR MY NAME
SHALL THE SUN OF RIGHTEOUSNESS ARISE WITH HEALING IN HIS WINGS;
AND YE SHALL GO FORTH, AND GROW UP AS CALVES OF THE STALL.

MATTHEW

May 22 (Day 142), Memory Verses #387 & #388
<u>Matthew 1:22-23:</u>

22. NOW ALL THIS WAS DONE, THAT IT MIGHT BE FULFILLED
WHICH WAS SPOKEN OF THE LORD BY THE PROPHETS, SAYING,

23. BEHOLD, A VIRGIN SHALL BE WITH CHILD, AND SHALL BRING FORTH A SON,
AND THEY SHALL CALL HIS NAME EMMANUEL,
WHICH BEING INTERPRETED IS, GOD WITH US.

May 23 (Day 143), Memory Verse #389
<u>Matthew 3:10:</u>

...EVERY TREE WHICH BRINGETH NOT FORTH GOOD FRUIT IS HEWN DOWN,
AND CAST INTO THE FIRE.

May 23 (Day 143), Memory Verse #390
<u>Matthew 3:17:</u>

AND LO A VOICE FROM HEAVEN, SAYING,
THIS IS MY BELOVED SON, IN WHOM I AM WELL PLEASED.

May 24 (Day 144), Memory Verse #391
<u>Matthew 4:4:</u>

...IT IS WRITTEN, MAN SHALL NOT LIVE BY BREAD ALONE,
BUT BY EVERY WORD THAT PROCEEDETH OUT OF THE MOUTH OF GOD.

May 24 (Day 144), Memory Verse #392
<u>Matthew 4:7:</u>

...IT IS WRITTEN AGAIN, THOU SHALT NOT TEMPT THE LORD THY GOD.

May 24 (Day 144), Memory Verse #393
<u>Matthew 4:10:</u>

...GET THEE HENCE, SATAN: FOR IT IS WRITTEN,
THOU SHALT WORSHIP THE LORD THY GOD, AND HIM ONLY SHALT THOU SERVE.

May 25 (Day 145), Memory Verse #394
<u>Matthew 4:17:</u>

...REPENT FOR THE KINGDOM OF HEAVEN IS AT HAND.

May 25 (Day 145), Memory Verse #395
<u>Matthew 4:19:</u>

...FOLLOW ME, AND I WILL MAKE YOU FISHERS OF MEN.

Matthew 5-7: JESUS' SERMON ON THE MOUNT

May 26-29 (Days 146-149), Memory Verses #396 to #407
Matthew 5:1-12:
(The Beatitudes)

1. **AND** SEEING THE MULTITUDES, HE WENT UP INTO THE MOUNTAIN:
AND WHEN HE WAS SET, HIS DISCIPLES CAME UNTO HIM:

2. **AND** HE OPENED HIS MOUTH, AND TAUGHT THEM, SAYING,

3. **BLESSED** ARE THE POOR IN SPIRIT: FOR THEIRS IS THE KINGDOM OF HEAVEN.

4. **BLESSED** ARE THEY THAT MOURN: FOR THEY SHALL BE COMFORTED.

5. **BLESSED** ARE THE MEEK: FOR THEY SHALL INHERIT THE EARTH.

6. **BLESSED** ARE THEY WHICH DO HUNGER AND THIRST AFTER RIGHTEOUSNESS:
FOR THEY SHALL BE FILLED.

7. **BLESSED** ARE THE MERCIFUL: FOR THEY SHALL OBTAIN MERCY.

8. **BLESSED** ARE THE PURE IN HEART: FOR THEY SHALL SEE GOD.

9. **BLESSED** ARE THE PEACEMAKERS:
FOR THEY SHALL BE CALLED THE CHILDREN OF GOD.

10. **BLESSED** ARE THEY WHICH ARE PERSECUTED FOR RIGHTEOUSNESS' SAKE:
FOR THEIRS IS THE KINGDOM OF HEAVEN.

11. **BLESSED** ARE YE, WHEN MEN SHALL REVILE YOU, AND PERSECUTE YOU,
AND SHALL SAY ALL MANNER OF EVIL AGAINST YOU FALSELY, FOR MY SAKE.

12. **REJOICE,** AND BE EXCEEDING GLAD:
FOR GREAT IS YOUR REWARD IN HEAVEN:
FOR SO PERSECUTED THEY THE PROPHETS WHICH WERE BEFORE YOU.

May 30-31 (Days 150-151), Memory Verses #408 to #413
Matthew 5:13-18:

13. **YE** ARE THE SALT OF THE EARTH:
BUT IF THE SALT HAVE LOST HIS SAVOUR, WHEREWITH SHALL IT BE SALTED?
IT IS THENCEFORTH GOOD FOR NOTHING, BUT TO BE CAST OUT,
AND TO BE TRODDEN UNDER FOOT OF MEN.

14. **YE** ARE THE LIGHT OF THE WORLD.
A CITY THAT IS SET ON AN HILL CANNOT BE HID.

15. **NEITHER** DO MEN LIGHT A CANDLE, AND PUT IT UNDER A BUSHEL,
BUT ON A CANDLESTICK;
AND IT GIVETH LIGHT UNTO ALL THAT ARE IN THE HOUSE.

16. **LET** YOUR LIGHT SO SHINE BEFORE MEN,
THAT THEY MAY SEE YOUR GOOD WORKS,
AND GLORIFY YOUR FATHER WHICH IS IN HEAVEN.

17. **THINK** NOT THAT I AM COME TO DESTROY THE LAW, OR THE PROPHETS:
I AM NOT COME TO DESTROY, BUT TO FULFIL.

18. **FOR** VERILY I SAY UNTO YOU, TILL HEAVEN AND EARTH PASS,
ONE JOT OR ONE TITTLE SHALL IN NO WISE PASS FROM THE LAW,
TILL ALL BE FULFILLED.

June 1 (Day 152), Memory Verse #414
Matthew 5:39:

... WHOSOEVER SHALL SMITE THEE ON THY RIGHT CHEEK,
TURN TO HIM THE OTHER ALSO.

June 1 (Day 152), Memory Verse #415
Matthew 5:44:

... LOVE YOUR ENEMIES, BLESS THEM THAT CURSE YOU,
DO GOOD TO THEM THAT HATE YOU,
AND PRAY FOR THEM WHICH DESPITEFULLY USE YOU, AND PERSECUTE YOU;

June 2 (Day 153), Memory Verse #416
Matthew 5:48:

BE YE THEREFORE PERFECT,
EVEN AS YOUR FATHER WHICH IS IN HEAVEN IS PERFECT.

June 2 (Day 153), Memory Verses #417 & #418
Matthew 6:3-4:

3. BUT WHEN THOU DOEST ALMS,
LET NOT THY LEFT HAND KNOW WHAT THY RIGHT HAND DOETH:

4. THAT THINE ALMS MAY BE IN SECRET:
AND THY FATHER WHICH SEETH IN SECRET HIMSELF SHALL REWARD THEE OPENLY.

June 3 (Day 154), Memory Verse #419
Matthew 6:6:

BUT THOU, WHEN THOU PRAYEST,
ENTER INTO THY CLOSET, AND WHEN THOU HAST SHUT THY DOOR,
PRAY TO THY FATHER WHICH IS IN SECRET;
AND THY FATHER WHICH SEETH IN SECRET SHALL REWARD THEE OPENLY.

June 4 (Day 155), Memory Verses #420 to #424
Matthew 6:9-13:
(The Lord's Prayer)

9. AFTER THIS MANNER PRAY YE:
OUR FATHER WHICH ART IN HEAVEN, HALLOWED BE THY NAME.

10. THY KINGDOM COME. THY WILL BE DONE IN EARTH, AS IT IS IN HEAVEN.

11. GIVE US THIS DAY OUR DAILY BREAD.

12. AND FORGIVE US OUR DEBTS, AS WE FORGIVE OUR DEBTORS.

13. AND LEAD US NOT INTO TEMPTATION,
BUT DELIVER US FROM EVIL: FOR THINE IS THE KINGDOM,
AND THE POWER, AND THE GLORY, FOR EVER.   AMEN.

June 5 (Day 156), Memory Verses #425 & #426
Matthew 6:14-15:

14. FOR IF YE FORGIVE MEN THEIR TRESPASSES,
YOUR HEAVENLY FATHER WILL ALSO FORGIVE YOU:

15. BUT IF YE FORGIVE NOT MEN THEIR TRESPASSES,
NEITHER WILL YOUR FATHER FORGIVE YOUR TRESPASSES.

June 6 (Day 157), Memory Verses #427 & #428
Matthew 6:20-21:

20. **BUT** LAY UP FOR YOURSELVES TREASURES IN HEAVEN,
WHERE NEITHER MOTH NOR RUST DOTH CORRUPT,
AND WHERE THIEVES DO NOT BREAK THROUGH NOR STEAL:

21. **FOR** WHERE YOUR TREASURE IS, THERE WILL YOUR HEART BE ALSO.

June 7-8 (Days 158-159), Memory Verses #429 to #434
Matthew 6:24-29:

24. **NO** MAN CAN SERVE TWO MASTERS:
FOR EITHER HE WILL HATE THE ONE, AND LOVE THE OTHER;
OR ELSE HE WILL HOLD TO THE ONE, AND DESPISE THE OTHER.
YE CANNOT SERVE GOD AND MAMMON.

25. **THEREFORE** I SAY UNTO YOU, TAKE NO THOUGHT FOR YOUR LIFE,
WHAT YE SHALL EAT, OR WHAT YE SHALL DRINK;
NOR YET FOR YOUR BODY, WHAT YE SHALL PUT ON.
IS NOT THE LIFE MORE THAN MEAT, AND THE BODY THAN RAIMANT?

26. **BEHOLD** THE FOWLS OF THE AIR:
FOR THEY SOW NOT, NEITHER DO THEY REAP, NOR GATHER INTO BARNS;
YET YOUR HEAVENLY FATHER FEEDETH THEM.
ARE YE NOT MUCH BETTER THAN THEY?

27. **WHICH** OF YOU BY TAKING THOUGHT CAN ADD ONE CUBIT UNTO HIS STATURE?

28. **AND** WHY TAKE YE THOUGHT FOR RAIMENT?
CONSIDER THE LILIES OF THE FIELD, HOW THEY GROW;
THEY TOIL NOT, NEITHER DO THEY SPIN:

29. **AND** YET I SAY UNTO YOU,
THAT EVEN SOLOMON IN ALL HIS GLORY WAS NOT ARRAYED LIKE ONE OF THESE.

June 9 (Day 160), Memory Verses #435 & #436
Matthew 6: 33-34:

33. **BUT** SEEK YE FIRST THE KINGDOM OF GOD, AND HIS RIGHTEOUSNESS;
AND ALL THESE THINGS SHALL BE ADDED UNTO YOU.

34. **TAKE** THEREFORE NO THOUGHT FOR THE MORROW:
FOR THE MORROW SHALL TAKE THOUGHT FOR THE THINGS OF ITSELF.
SUFFICIENT UNTO THE DAY IS THE EVIL THEREOF.

June 10 (Day 161), Memory Verse #437
Matthew 7:1:

JUDGE NOT, THAT YE BE NOT JUDGED.

June 10 (Day 161), Memory Verse #438
Matthew 7:5:

THOU HYPOCRITE, FIRST CAST OUT THE BEAM (plank, NIV) OUT OF THINE OWN EYE;
AND THEN SHALT THOU SEE CLEARLY
TO CAST OUT THE MOTE (speck, NIV) OUT OF THY BROTHER'S EYE.

June 11 (Day 162), Memory Verses #439 & #440
Matthew 7:7-8:

7. ASK, AND IT SHALL BE GIVEN YOU;
SEEK, AND YE SHALL FIND; KNOCK, AND IT SHALL BE OPENED UNTO YOU:

8. FOR EVERY ONE THAT ASKETH RECEIVETH; AND HE THAT SEEKETH FINDETH;
AND TO HIM THAT KNOCKETH IT SHALL BE OPENED.

June 11 (Day 162), Memory Verse #441
Matthew 7:12:
(The Golden Rule)

THEREFORE ALL THINGS WHATSOEVER YE WOULD THAT MEN SHOULD DO TO YOU,
DO YE EVEN SO TO THEM: FOR THIS IS THE LAW AND THE PROPHETS.

June 12 (Day 163), Memory Verse #442
Matthew 7:14

...STRAIT IS THE GATE, AND NARROW IS THE WAY,
WHICH LEADETH UNTO LIFE, AND FEW THERE BE THAT FIND IT.

June 12 (Day 163), Memory Verses #443 & #444
Matthew 9:37-38:

37. ...THE HARVEST TRULY IS PLENTEOUS, BUT THE LABOURERS ARE FEW;

38. PRAY YE THEREFORE THE LORD OF THE HARVEST,
THAT HE WILL SEND FORTH LABOURERS INTO HIS HARVEST.

June 13 (Day 164), Memory Verses #445 & #446
Matthew 10:32-33:

32. WHOSOEVER THEREFORE SHALL CONFESS ME BEFORE MEN,
HIM WILL I CONFESS BEFORE MY FATHER WHICH IS IN HEAVEN.

33. BUT WHOSOEVER SHALL DENY ME BEFORE MEN,
HIM WILL I ALSO DENY BEFORE MY FATHER WHICH IS IN HEAVEN.

June 13 (Day 164), Memory Verse #447
Matthew 10:39:

HE THAT FINDETH HIS LIFE SHALL LOSE IT:
AND HE THAT LOSETH HIS LIFE FOR MY SAKE SHALL FIND IT.

June 14 (Day 165), Memory Verses #448 to #450
Matthew 11:28-30:

28. COME UNTO ME, ALL YE THAT LABOUR AND ARE HEAVY LADEN,
AND I WILL GIVE YOU REST.

29. TAKE MY YOKE UPON YOU, AND LEARN OF ME;
FOR I AM MEEK AND LOWLY IN HEART:
AND YE SHALL FIND REST UNTO YOUR SOULS.

30. FOR MY YOKE IS EASY, AND MY BURDEN IS LIGHT.

June 15 (Day 166), Memory Verse #451
Matthew 12:50:

FOR WHOSOEVER SHALL DO THE WILL OF MY FATHER WHICH IS IN HEAVEN,
THE SAME IS MY BROTHER, AND SISTER, AND MOTHER.

June 15 (Day 166), Memory Verse #452
Matthew 13:12:

FOR WHOSOEVER HATH, TO HIM SHALL BE GIVEN,
AND HE SHALL HAVE MORE ABUNDANCE:
BUT WHOSOEVER HATH NOT,
FROM HIM SHALL BE TAKEN AWAY EVEN THAT HE HATH.

June 16 (Day 167), Memory Verse #453
Matthew 16:16:

AND SIMON PETER ANSWERED AND SAID,
THOU ART THE CHRIST, THE SON OF THE LIVING GOD.

June 17 (Day 168), Memory Verses #454 to #456
Matthew 16:24-26:

24. ...IF ANY MAN WILL COME AFTER ME,
LET HIM DENY HIMSELF, AND TAKE UP HIS CROSS, AND FOLLOW ME.

25. FOR WHOSOEVER WILL SAVE HIS LIFE SHALL LOSE IT:
AND WHOSOEVER WILL LOSE HIS LIFE FOR MY SAKE SHALL FIND IT.

26. FOR WHAT IS A MAN PROFITED, IF HE SHALL GAIN THE WHOLE WORLD,
AND LOSE HIS OWN SOUL?
OR WHAT SHALL A MAN GIVE IN EXCHANGE FOR HIS SOUL?

June 18 (Day 169), Memory Verse #457
Matthew 17:20:

... IF YE HAVE FAITH AS A GRAIN OF MUSTARD SEED,
YE SHALL SAY UNTO THIS MOUNTAIN,
REMOVE HENCE TO YONDER PLACE; AND IT SHALL REMOVE;
AND NOTHING SHALL BE IMPOSSIBLE UNTO YOU.

June 18 (Day 169), Memory Verses #458 & #459
Matthew 18:3-4:

3. ...EXCEPT YE BE CONVERTED, AND BECOME AS LITTLE CHILDREN,
YE SHALL NOT ENTER INTO THE KINGDOM OF HEAVEN.

4. WHOSOEVER THEREFORE SHALL HUMBLE HIMSELF AS THIS LITTLE CHILD,
THE SAME IS GREATEST IN THE KINGDOM OF HEAVEN.

June 19 (Day 170), Memory Verses #460 to #463
Matthew 18:19-22:

19. AGAIN I SAY UNTO YOU, THAT IF TWO OF YOU SHALL AGREE ON EARTH
AS TOUCHING ANY THING THAT THEY SHALL ASK,
IT SHALL BE DONE FOR THEM OF MY FATHER WHICH IS IN HEAVEN.

20. FOR WHERE TWO OR THREE ARE GATHERED TOGETHER IN MY NAME,
THERE AM I IN THE MIDST OF THEM.

21. THEN CAME PETER TO HIM, AND SAID,
LORD, HOW OFT SHALL MY BROTHER SIN AGAINST ME,
AND I FORGIVE HIM? TILL SEVEN TIMES?

22. JESUS SAITH UNTO HIM, I SAY NOT UNTO THEE,
UNTIL SEVEN TIMES: BUT UNTIL SEVENTY TIMES SEVEN.

June 20 (Day 171), Memory Verse #464
Matthew 19:14:

...SUFFER LITTLE CHILDREN AND FORBID THEM NOT, TO COME UNTO ME:
FOR OF SUCH IS THE KINGDOM OF HEAVEN.

June 20 (Day 171), Memory Verse #465
Matthew 19:26:

...WITH GOD ALL THINGS ARE POSSIBLE.

June 21 (Day 172), Memory Verse #466
Matthew 19:30:

BUT MANY THAT ARE FIRST SHALL BE LAST; AND THE LAST SHALL BE FIRST.

June 21 (Day 172), Memory Verse #467
Matthew 20:16:

SO THE LAST SHALL BE FIRST, AND THE FIRST LAST:
FOR MANY BE CALLED, BUT FEW CHOSEN.

June 22 (Day 173), Memory Verses #468 & #469
Matthew 20:27-28:

27. AND WHOSOEVER WILL BE CHIEF AMONG YOU, LET HIM BE YOUR SERVANT:

28. EVEN AS THE SON OF MAN CAME NOT TO BE MINISTERED UNTO,
BUT TO MINISTER, AND TO GIVE HIS LIFE A RANSOM FOR MANY.

June 22 (Day 173), Memory Verse #470
Matthew 21:22:

AND ALL THINGS, WHATSOEVER YE SHALL ASK IN PRAYER,
BELIEVING, YE SHALL RECEIVE.

June 23 (Day 174), Memory Verse #471
Matthew 22:14:

FOR MANY ARE CALLED (invited, NIV), BUT FEW ARE CHOSEN.

June 23 (Day 174), Memory Verse #472
Matthew 22:21:

...RENDER UNTO CAESAR THE THINGS WHICH ARE CAESAR'S,
AND UNTO GOD THE THINGS THAT ARE GOD'S.

June 24 (Day 175), Memory Verses #473 to #476
Matthew 22:37-40:

37. ...THOU SHALT LOVE THE LORD THY GOD WITH ALL THY HEART,
AND WITH ALL THY SOUL, AND WITH ALL THY MIND.

38. THIS IS THE FIRST AND GREAT COMMANDMENT.

39. AND THE SECOND IS LIKE UNTO IT,
THOU SHALT LOVE THY NEIGHBOUR AS THYSELF.

40. ON THESE TWO COMMANDMENTS HANG ALL THE LAW AND THE PROPHETS.

June 25 (Day 176), Memory Verse #477
Matthew 23:11:

BUT HE THAT IS GREATEST AMONG YOU SHALL BE YOUR SERVANT.

June 25 (Day 176), Memory Verse #478
Matthew 24:35:

HEAVEN AND EARTH SHALL PASS AWAY,
BUT MY WORDS SHALL NOT PASS AWAY.

June 26 (Day 177), Memory Verse #479
Matthew 24:40:

THEN SHALL TWO BE IN THE FIELD;
THE ONE SHALL BE TAKEN, AND THE OTHER LEFT.

June 26 (Day 177), Memory Verse #480
Matthew 24:42:

WATCH THEREFORE: FOR YE KNOW NOT WHAT HOUR YOUR LORD DOTH COME.

June 26 (Day 177), Memory Verse #481
Matthew 25:13:

WATCH THEREFORE, FOR YE KNOW NEITHER THE DAY NOR THE HOUR
WHEREIN THE SON OF MAN COMETH.

June 27 (Day 178), Memory Verse #482
Matthew 25:21:

...WELL DONE THY GOOD AND FAITHFUL SERVANT:
THOU HAST BEEN FAITHFUL OVER A FEW THINGS,
I WILL MAKE THEE RULER OVER MANY THINGS: ...
ENTER THOU INTO THE JOY OF THY LORD.

June 27 (Day 178), Memory Verse #483
Matthew 25:29:

FOR UNTO EVERYONE THAT HATH SHALL BE GIVEN, AND HE SHALL HAVE ABUNDANCE:
BUT FROM HIM THAT HATH NOT SHALL BE TAKEN AWAY EVEN THAT WHICH HE HATH.

June 28 (Day 179), Memory Verse #484
Matthew 25:40:

...INASMUCH AS YE HAVE DONE IT UNTO ONE OF THE LEAST OF THESE MY BRETHREN,
YE HAVE DONE IT UNTO ME.

June 28 (Day 179), Memory Verse #485
Matthew 26:39:

AND HE WENT A LITTLE FURTHER, AND FELL ON HIS FACE, AND PRAYED, SAYING,
O MY FATHER, IF IT BE POSSIBLE, LET THIS CUP PASS FROM ME:
NEVERTHELESS NOT AS I WILL, BUT AS THOU WILT.

June 28 (Day 179), Memory Verse #486
Matthew 26:41:

WATCH AND PRAY, THAT YE ENTER NOT INTO TEMPTATION:
THE SPIRIT INDEED IS WILLING, BUT THE FLESH IS WEAK.

June 29 (Day 180), Memory Verses #487 & #488
Matthew 28:19-20:
(The Great Commission)

19. GO YE THEREFORE, AND TEACH ALL NATIONS,
BAPTIZING THEM IN THE NAME OF THE FATHER,
AND OF THE SON, AND OF THE HOLY GHOST:

20. TEACHING THEM TO OBSERVE ALL THINGS
WHATSOEVER I HAVE COMMANDETH YOU:
AND LO, I AM WITH YOU ALWAY,
EVEN UNTO THE END OF THE WORLD.   AMEN.

MARK

June 30 (Day 181), Memory Verse #489
Mark 1:17:

AND JESUS SAID UNTO THEM, COME YE AFTER ME,
AND I WILL MAKE YOU TO BECOME FISHERS OF MEN.

June 30 (Day 181), Memory Verse #490
Mark 2:27:

...THE SABBATH WAS MADE FOR MAN,
AND NOT MAN FOR THE SABBATH:

July 1 (Day 182), Memory Verse #491
Mark 3:25:

AND IF A HOUSE BE DIVIDED AGAINST ITSELF,
THAT HOUSE CANNOT STAND.

July 1 (Day 182), Memory Verse #492
Mark 3:35:

FOR WHOSOEVER SHALL DO THE WILL OF GOD,
THE SAME IS MY BROTHER, AND MY SISTER, AND MY MOTHER.

July 2 (Day 183), Memory Verses #493 & #494
Mark 4:24-25:

24. AND HE SAID UNTO THEM, TAKE HEED WHAT YE HEAR:
WITH WHAT MEASURE YE METE, IT SHALL BE MEASURED TO YOU:
AND UNTO YOU THAT HEAR SHALL MORE BE GIVEN.

25. FOR HE THAT HATH, TO HIM SHALL BE GIVEN:
AND HE THAT HATH NOT, FROM HIM SHALL BE TAKEN EVEN THAT WHICH HE HATH.

July 3-4 (Days 184-185), Memory Verses #495 to #499
Mark 8:34-38:

34. ...WHOSOEVER WILL COME AFTER ME,
LET HIM DENY HIMSELF, AND TAKE UP HIS CROSS, AND FOLLOW ME.

35. FOR WHOSOEVER WILL SAVE HIS LIFE SHALL LOSE IT;
BUT WHOSOEVER SHALL LOSE HIS LIFE FOR MY SAKE AND THE GOSPEL'S,
THE SAME SHALL SAVE IT.

36. FOR WHAT SHALL IT PROFIT A MAN,
IF HE SHALL GAIN THE WHOLE WORLD, AND LOSE HIS OWN SOUL?

37. OR WHAT SHALL A MAN GIVE IN EXCHANGE OF HIS SOUL?

38. WHOSOEVER THEREFORE SHALL BE ASHAMED OF ME
AND MY WORDS IN THIS ADULTEROUS AND SINFUL GENERATION;
OF HIM ALSO SHALL THE SON OF MAN BE ASHAMED,
WHEN HE COMETH IN THE GLORY OF HIS FATHER WITH THE HOLY ANGELS.

July 5 (Day 186), Memory Verses #500 & #501
Mark 9:23-24:

23. ...IF THOU CANST BELIEVE, ALL THINGS ARE POSSIBLE TO HIM THAT BELIEVETH.

24. AND STRAIGHTWAY THE FATHER OF THE CHILD CRIED OUT,
AND SAID WITH TEARS, LORD, I BELIEVE; HELP THOU MY UNBELIEF.

July 6 (Day 187), Memory Verse #502
Mark 9:35:

...IF ANY MAN DESIRE TO BE FIRST,
THE SAME SHALL BE LAST OF ALL, AND SERVANT OF ALL.

July 6 (Day 187), Memory Verse #503
Mark 9:37:

WHOSOEVER SHALL RECEIVE ONE OF SUCH CHILDREN IN MY NAME, RECEIVETH ME:
AND WHOSOEVER SHALL RECEIVE ME, RECEIVETH NOT ME,
BUT HIM THAT SENT ME.

July 6 (Day 187), Memory Verse #504
Mark 9:40:

FOR HE THAT IS NOT AGAINST US IS ON OUR PART.

July 7 (Day 188), Memory Verse #505
Mark 9:50:

...HAVE SALT IN YOURSELVES, AND HAVE PEACE ONE WITH ANOTHER.

July 7 (Day 188), Memory Verse #506
Mark 10:15:

...WHOSOEVER SHALL NOT RECEIVE THE KINGDOM OF GOD AS A LITTLE CHILD,
HE SHALL NOT ENTER THEREIN.

July 8 (Day 189), Memory Verse #507
Mark 10: 24:

...HOW HARD IS IT FOR THEM THAT TRUST IN RICHES
TO ENTER INTO THE KINGDOM OF GOD!

July 8 (Day 189), Memory Verse #508
Mark 10: 27:

...FOR WITH GOD ALL THINGS ARE POSSIBLE.

July 8 (Day 189), Memory Verse #509
Mark 10:31:

BUT MANY THAT ARE FIRST SHALL BE LAST; AND THE LAST FIRST.

July 9 (Day 190), Memory Verses #510 to #512
Mark 10:43-45:

43. BUT SO SHALL IT NOT BE AMONG YOU:
BUT WHOSOEVER WILL BE GREAT AMONG YOU, SHALL BE YOUR MINISTER:

44. AND WHOSOEVER OF YOU WILL BE THE CHIEFEST, SHALL BE SERVANT OF ALL.

45. FOR EVEN THE SON OF MAN CAME NOT TO BE MINISTERED UNTO,
BUT TO MINISTER, AND TO GIVE HIS LIFE A RANSOM FOR MANY.

July 10 (Day 191), Memory Verse #513
Mark 11:25:

AND WHEN YE STAND PRAYING, FORGIVE, IF YE HAVE OUGHT AGAINST ANY:
THAT YOUR FATHER ALSO WHICH IS IN HEAVEN MAY FORGIVE YOU YOUR TRESPASSES.

July 10 (Day 191), Memory Verses #514 to #516
Mark 12:29-31:

29. AND JESUS ANSWERED HIM, THE FIRST OF ALL COMMANDMENTS IS,
HEAR, O ISRAEL; THE LORD OUR GOD IS ONE LORD:

30. AND THOU SHALT LOVE THE LORD THY GOD WITH ALL THY HEART,
AND WITH ALL THY SOUL, AND WITH ALL THY MIND, AND WITH ALL THY STRENGTH:
THIS IS THE FIRST COMMANDMENT.

31. AND THE SECOND IS LIKE, NAMELY THIS,
THOU SHALT LOVE THY NEIGHBOUR AS THYSELF.
THERE IS NONE OTHER COMMANDMENT GREATER THAN THESE.

July 11 (Day 192), Memory Verse #517
Mark 13:31:

HEAVEN AND EARTH SHALL PASS AWAY: BUT MY WORDS SHALL NOT PASS AWAY.

July 11 (Day 192), Memory Verses #518 & #519
Mark 14:35-36:

35. AND HE WENT FORWARD A LITTLE, AND FELL ON THE GROUND,
AND PRAYED THAT, IF IT WERE POSSIBLE, THE HOUR MIGHT PASS FROM HIM.

36. AND HE SAID, ABBA, FATHER, ALL THINGS ARE POSSIBLE UNTO THEE;
TAKE AWAY THIS CUP FROM ME:
NEVERTHELESS NOT WHAT I WILL, BUT WHAT THOU WILT.

July 12 (Day 193), Memory Verses #520 & #521
Mark 16:15-16:

15. ...GO YE INTO ALL THE WORLD, AND PREACH THE GOSPEL TO EVERY CREATURE.

16. HE THAT BELIEVETH AND IS BAPTIZED SHALL BE SAVED;
BUT HE THAT BELIEVETH NOT SHALL BE DAMNED.

LUKE

July 13 (Day 194), Memory Verse #522
Luke 1:37:

FOR WITH GOD NOTHING SHALL BE IMPOSSIBLE.

July 13 (Day 194), Memory Verses #523 to #525
Luke 1:46-48:

46. AND MARY SAID, MY SOUL DOTH MAGNIFY THE LORD,

47. AND MY SPIRIT HATH REJOICED IN GOD MY SAVIOUR.

48. FOR HE HATH REGARDED THE LOW ESTATE OF HIS HANDMAIDEN:
FOR, BEHOLD, FROM HENCEFORTH ALL GENERATIONS SHALL CALL ME BLESSED.

July 14 (Day 195), Memory Verses #526 & #527
Luke 1:76-77:

76. AND THOU, CHILD, SHALT BE CALLED THE PROPHET OF THE HIGHEST:
FOR THOU SHALT GO BEFORE THE FACE OF THE LORD TO PREPARE HIS WAYS;

77. TO GIVE KNOWLEDGE OF SALVATION UNTO HIS PEOPLE
BY THE REMISSION OF THEIR SINS.

July 15-July 22 (Days 196-203), Memory Verses #528 to #547
Luke 2:1-20:
(The Christmas Story)

SEE THE FOLLOWING PAGE:

July 15-July 22 (Days 196-203), Memory Verses #528 to #547
<u>Luke 2:1-20:</u>
(The Christmas Story)

1. AND IT CAME TO PASS IN THOSE DAYS,
THAT THERE WENT OUT A DECREE FROM CAESAR AUGUSTUS,
THAT ALL THE WORLD SHOULD BE TAXED.

2. (**AND** THIS TAXING WAS FIRST MADE WHEN CYRENIUS WAS GOVERNOR OF SYRIA.)

3. AND ALL WENT TO BE TAXED, EVERY ONE INTO HIS OWN CITY.

4. AND JOSEPH ALSO WENT UP FROM GALILEE, OUT OF THE CITY OF NAZARETH,
INTO JUDEA, UNTO THE CITY OF DAVID, WHICH IS CALLED BETHLEHEM;
(BECAUSE HE WAS OF THE HOUSE AND LINEAGE OF DAVID:)

5. TO BE TAXED WITH MARY HIS ESPOUSED WIFE, BEING GREAT WITH CHILD.

6. AND SO IT WAS, THAT, WHILE THEY WERE THERE,
THE DAYS WERE ACCOMPLISHED THAT SHE SHOULD BE DELIVERED.

7. AND SHE BROUGHT FORTH HER FIRSTBORN SON,
AND WRAPPED HIM IN SWADDLING CLOTHES, AND LAID HIM IN A MANGER;
BECAUSE THERE WAS NO ROOM FOR THEM IN THE INN.

8. AND THERE WERE IN THE SAME COUNTRY SHEPHERDS ABIDING IN THE FIELD,
KEEPING WATCH OVER THEIR FLOCK BY NIGHT.

9. AND, LO, THE ANGEL OF THE LORD CAME UPON THEM,
AND THE GLORY OF THE LORD SHONE ROUND ABOUT THEM:
AND THEY WERE SORE AFRAID.

10. AND THE ANGEL SAID UNTO THEM, FEAR NOT:
FOR, BEHOLD, I BRING YOU GOOD TIDINGS OF GREAT JOY,
WHICH SHALL BE TO ALL PEOPLE.

11. FOR UNTO YOU IS BORN THIS DAY IN THE CITY OF DAVID
A SAVIOUR, WHICH IS CHRIST THE LORD.

12. AND THIS SHALL BE A SIGN UNTO YOU;
YE SHALL FIND THE BABE WRAPPED IN SWADDLING CLOTHES,
LYING IN A MANGER.

13. AND SUDDENLY THERE WAS WITH THE ANGEL A MULTITUDE
OF THE HEAVENLY HOST PRAISING GOD, AND SAYING,

14. GLORY TO GOD IN THE HIGHEST,
AND ON EARTH PEACE, GOOD WILL TOWARD MEN.

15. AND IT CAME TO PASS,
AS THE ANGELS WERE GONE AWAY FROM THEM INTO HEAVEN,
THE SHEPHERDS SAID ONE TO ANOTHER,
LET US NOW GO EVEN UNTO BETHLEHEM,
AND SEE THIS THING WHICH IS COME TO PASS,
WHICH THE LORD HATH MADE KNOWN UNTO US.

16. AND THEY CAME WITH HASTE, AND FOUND MARY AND JOSEPH,
AND THE BABE LYING IN A MANGER.

17. AND WHEN THEY HAD SEEN IT, THEY MADE KNOWN ABROAD
THE SAYING WHICH WAS TOLD THEM CONCERNING THIS CHILD.

18. AND ALL THEY THAT HEARD IT WONDERED
AT THOSE THINGS WHICH WERE TOLD THEM BY THE SHEPHERDS.

19. BUT MARY KEPT ALL THESE THINGS, AND PONDERED THEM IN HER HEART.

20. AND THE SHEPHERDS RETURNED,
GLORIFYING AND PRAISING GOD FOR ALL THE THINGS THEY HAD HEARD AND SEEN,
AS IT WAS TOLD UNTO THEM.

July 23 (Day 204), Memory Verse #548
<u>Luke 2:52</u>:

AND JESUS INCREASED IN WISDOM AND STATURE,
AND IN FAVOUR WITH GOD AND MAN.

July 23 (Day 204), Memory Verse #549
<u>Luke 3:22</u>:

...**AND** THE HOLY GHOST DESCENDED IN A BODILY SHAPE LIKE A DOVE UPON HIM,
AND A VOICE CAME FROM HEAVEN, WHICH SAID,
THOU ART MY BELOVED SON; IN THEE I AM WELL PLEASED.

July 23 (Day 204), Memory Verse #550
<u>Luke 4:4</u>:

AND JESUS ANSWERED HIM SAYING, IT IS WRITTEN,
MAN SHALL NOT LIVE BY BREAD ALONE,
BUT BY EVERY WORD OF GOD.

July 24 (Day 205), Memory Verse #551
<u>Luke 4:8</u>:

AND JESUS ANSWERED AND SAID UNTO HIM,
THOU SHALT WORSHIP THE LORD THY GOD,
AND HIM ONLY SHALT THOU SERVE.

July 24 (Day 205), Memory Verse #552
<u>Luke 4:12</u>:

AND JESUS ANSWERING SAID UNTO HIM, IT IS SAID,
THOU SHALT NOT TEMPT THE LORD THY GOD.

July 25 (Day 206), Memory Verses #553 to #555
<u>Luke 6:27-29</u>:

27. ...**LOVE** YOUR ENEMIES, DO GOOD TO THEM WHICH HATE YOU,

28. **BLESS** THEM THAT CURSE YOU,
AND PRAY FOR THEM WHICH DESPITEFULLY USE YOU.

29. **AND** UNTO HIM THAT SMITETH THEE ON THE ONE CHEEK OFFER ALSO THE OTHER;
AND HIM THAT TAKETH AWAY THY CLOKE FORBID NOT TO TAKE THY COAT ALSO.

July 25 (Day 206), Memory Verse #556
<u>Luke 6:31</u>:
(The Golden Rule)

AND AS YE WOULD THAT MEN SHOULD DO TO YOU,
DO YE ALSO TO THEM LIKEWISE.

July 26 (Day 207), Memory Verses # 557 to #560
<u>**Luke 6:35-38:**</u>

35. BUT LOVE YE YOUR ENEMIES,
AND DO GOOD, AND LEND, HOPING FOR NOTHING AGAIN;
AND YOUR REWARD SHALL BE GREAT,
AND YE SHALL BE THE CHILDREN OF THE HIGHEST:
FOR HE IS KIND UNTO THE UNTHANKFUL AND TO THE EVIL.

36. BE YE THEREFORE MERCIFUL,
AS YOUR FATHER ALSO IS MERCIFUL.

37. JUDGE NOT, AND YE SHALL NOT BE JUDGED:
CONDEMN NOT, AND YE SHALL NOT BE CONDEMNED:
FORGIVE, AND YE SHALL BE FORGIVEN:

38. GIVE, AND IT SHALL BE GIVEN UNTO YOU; ...

July 27 (Day 208), Memory Verse #561
<u>**Luke 6:41:**</u>

AND WHY BEHOLDEST THOU THE MOTE (speck of sawdust, NIV)
THAT IS IN THY BROTHER'S EYE,
BUT PERCEIVETH NOT THE BEAM (plank, NIV) THAT IS IN THINE OWN EYE?

July 27 (Day 208), Memory Verse #562
<u>**Luke 6:45:**</u>

A GOOD MAN OUT OF THE GOOD TREASURE OF HIS HEART
BRINGETH FORTH THAT WHICH IS GOOD; ...

July 28 (Day 209), Memory Verse #563
<u>**Luke 8:21:**</u>

...MY MOTHER AND MY BRETHREN ARE THESE WHICH HEAR THE WORD OF GOD,
AND DO IT.

July 28 (Day 209), Memory Verse #564
<u>**Luke 9:23:**</u>

...IF ANY MAN WILL COME AFTER ME,
LET HIM DENY HIMSELF,
AND TAKE UP HIS CROSS DAILY,
AND FOLLOW ME.

July 29 (Day 210), Memory Verse #565
<u>**Luke 9:48:**</u>

...WHOSOEVER SHALL RECEIVE THIS CHILD IN MY NAME RECEIVETH ME:
AND WHOSOEVER SHALL RECEIVE ME RECEIVETH HIM THAT SENT ME:
FOR HE THAT IS LEAST AMONG YOU ALL,
THE SAME SHALL BE GREAT.

July 29 (Day 210), Memory Verse #566
<u>**Luke 10:2:**</u>

...THE HARVEST TRULY IS GREAT, BUT THE LABOURERS ARE FEW:
PRAY YE THEREFORE THE LORD OF THE HARVEST,
THAT HE WOULD SEND FORTH LABOURERS INTO HIS HARVEST.

July 30 (Day 211), Memory Verses #567 & #568
Luke 11:9-10:

9. ...ASK, AND IT SHALL BE GIVEN YOU;
SEEK, AND YE SHALL FIND;
KNOCK, AND IT SHALL BE OPENED UNTO YOU.

10. FOR EVERY ONE THAT ASKETH RECEIVETH;
AND HE THAT SEEKETH FINDETH;
AND TO HIM THAT KNOCKETH IT SHALL BE OPENED.

July 30 (Day 211), Memory Verse #569
Luke 11:13:

IF YE THEN, BEING EVIL, KNOW HOW TO GIVE GOOD GIFTS UNTO YOUR CHILDREN:
HOW MUCH MORE SHALL YOUR HEAVENLY FATHER
GIVE THE HOLY SPIRIT TO THEM THAT ASK HIM?

July 31 (Day 212), Memory Verse #570
Luke 12:15:

...TAKE HEED, AND BEWARE OF COVETOUSNESS:
FOR A MAN'S LIFE CONSISTETH NOT IN THE ABUNDANCE
OF THE THINGS WHICH HE POSSESSETH.

July 31 (Day 212), Memory Verse #571
Luke 12:31:

BUT RATHER SEEK YE THE KINGDOM OF GOD;
AND ALL THESE THINGS SHALL BE ADDED UNTO YOU.

July 31 (Day 212), Memory Verse #572
Luke 12:34:

FOR WHERE YOUR TREASURE IS, THERE WILL YOUR HEART BE ALSO.

August 1 (Day 213), Memory Verse #573
Luke 12:40:

BE YE THEREFORE READY ALSO:
FOR THE SON OF MAN COMETH AT AN HOUR WHEN YE THINK NOT.

August 1 (Day 213), Memory Verse #574
Luke 14:27:

AND WHOSOEVER DOTH NOT BEAR HIS CROSS AND COME AFTER ME,
CANNOT BE MY DISCIPLE.

August 1 (Day 213), Memory Verse #575
Luke 14:33:

...WHOSOEVER HE BE OF YOU THAT FORSAKETH NOT ALL THAT HE HATH,
HE CANNOT BE MY DISCIPLE.

August 2 (Day 214), Memory Verse #576
Luke 15:7:

...JOY SHALL BE IN HEAVEN OVER ONE SINNER THAT REPENTETH,
MORE THAN OVER NINETY AND NINE JUST PERSONS, WHICH NEED NO REPENTANCE.

August 2 (Day 214), Memory Verse #577
<u>Luke 16:10:</u>

HE THAT IS FAITHFUL IN THAT WHICH IS LEAST IS FAITHFUL ALSO IN MUCH: ...

August 2 (Day 214), Memory Verse #578
<u>Luke 16:13:</u>

NO SERVANT CAN SERVE TWO MASTERS:
FOR EITHER HE WILL HATE THE ONE, AND LOVE THE OTHER;
OR ELSE HE WILL HOLD TO THE ONE, AND DESPISE THE OTHER.
YE CANNOT SERVE GOD AND MAMMON (Money, NIV).

August 3 (Day 215), Memory Verse #579
<u>Luke 17:6:</u>

...IF YE HAD FAITH AS A GRAIN OF MUSTARD SEED,
YE MIGHT SAY UNTO THIS SYCAMINE TREE, BE THOU PLUCKED UP BY THE ROOT,
AND BE THOU PLANTED IN THE SEA; AND IT SHOULD OBEY YOU.

August 3 (Day 215), Memory Verse #580
<u>Luke 17:33:</u>

WHOSOEVER SHALL SEEK TO SAVE HIS LIFE SHALL LOSE IT;
AND WHOSOEVER SHALL LOSE HIS LIFE SHALL PRESERVE IT.

August 3 (Day 215), Memory Verse #581
<u>Luke 18:14:</u>

...FOR EVERY ONE THAT EXALTETH HIMSELF SHALL BE ABASED:
AND HE THAT HUMBLETH HIMSELF SHALL BE EXALTED.

August 4 (Day 216), Memory Verses #582 & #583
<u>Luke 18:16-17:</u>

16. ...SUFFER LITTLE CHILDREN TO COME UNTO ME,
AND FORBID THEM NOT: FOR OF SUCH IS THE KINGDOM OF GOD.

17. VERILY I SAY UNTO YOU,
WHOSOEVER SHALL NOT RECEIVE THE KINGDOM OF GOD AS A LITTLE CHILD
SHALL IN NO WISE ENTER THEREIN.

August 5 (Day 217), Memory Verse #584
<u>Luke 18:27:</u>

...THE THINGS WHICH ARE IMPOSSIBLE WITH MEN ARE POSSIBLE WITH GOD.

August 5 (Day 217), Memory Verse #585
<u>Luke 19:10:</u>

FOR THE SON OF MAN IS COME TO SEEK AND TO SAVE THAT WHICH WAS LOST.

August 5 (Day 217), Memory Verse #586
<u>Luke 19:26:</u>

...UNTO EVERYONE WHICH HATH SHALL BE GIVEN;
AND FROM HIM THAT HATH NOT,
EVEN THAT HE HATH SHALL BE TAKEN AWAY FROM HIM.

August 6 (Day 218), Memory Verse #587
Luke 21:33:

HEAVEN AND EARTH SHALL PASS AWAY:
BUT MY WORDS SHALL NOT PASS AWAY.

August 6 (Day 218), Memory Verse #588
Luke 22:42:

...FATHER, IF THOU BE WILLING, REMOVE THIS CUP FROM ME:
NEVERTHELESS NOT MY WILL, BUT THINE, BE DONE.

August 7 (Day 219), Memory Verses # 589 & #590
Luke 23:42-43:

42. AND HE SAID UNTO JESUS, LORD,
REMEMBER ME WHEN THOU COMEST INTO THY KINGDOM.

43. AND JESUS SAID UNTO HIM, VERILY I SAY UNTO THEE,
TODAY SHALT THOU BE WITH ME IN PARADISE.

August 8 (Day 220), Memory Verses #591 & #592
Luke 24:5-6:

5. ...THEY SAID UNTO THEM,
WHY SEEK YE THE LIVING AMONG THE DEAD?

6. HE IS NOT HERE, BUT IS RISEN: ...

JOHN

August 9-10 (Days 221-222), Memory Verses #593 to #597
John 1:1-5:

1. IN THE BEGINNING WAS THE WORD,
AND THE WORD WAS WITH GOD, AND THE WORD WAS GOD.

2. THE SAME WAS IN THE BEGINNING WITH GOD.

3. ALL THINGS WERE MADE BY HIM;
AND WITHOUT HIM WAS NOT ANY THING MADE THAT WAS MADE.

4. IN HIM WAS LIFE; AND THE LIFE WAS THE LIGHT OF MEN.

5. AND THE LIGHT SHINETH IN DARKNESS;
AND THE DARKNESS COMPREHENDED IT NOT.

August 10 (Day 222), Memory Verse #598
John 1:10:

HE WAS IN THE WORLD, AND THE WORLD WAS MADE BY HIM,
AND THE WORLD KNEW HIM NOT.

August 11 (Day 223), Memory Verses #599 to #601
John 1:12-14:

12. BUT AS MANY AS RECEIVED HIM,
TO THEM GAVE HE POWER TO BECOME THE SONS OF GOD,
EVEN TO THEM THAT BELIEVE ON HIS NAME:

13. WHICH WERE BORN, NOT OF BLOOD, NOR OF THE WILL OF THE FLESH,
NOR OF THE WILL OF MAN, BUT OF GOD.

14. AND THE WORD WAS MADE FLESH, AND DWELT AMONG US,
(AND WE BEHELD HIS GLORY, THE GLORY AS OF THE ONLY BEGOTTEN OF THE FATHER,)
FULL OF GRACE AND TRUTH.

August 12 (Day 224), Memory Verse #602
John 1:29:

...BEHOLD THE LAMB OF GOD, WHICH TAKETH AWAY THE SIN OF THE WORLD.

August 12 (Day 224), Memory Verse #603
John 2:19:

...DESTROY THIS TEMPLE, AND IN THREE DAYS I WILL RAISE IT UP.

August 12 (Day 224), Memory Verse #604
John 3:3:

JESUS ANSWERED AND SAID UNTO HIM,
VERILY, VERILY, I SAY UNTO THEE,
EXCEPT A MAN BE BORN AGAIN,
HE CANNOT SEE THE KINGDOM OF GOD.

August 13 (Day 225), Memory Verses #605 to #607
John 3:16-18:

16. FOR GOD SO LOVED THE WORLD, THAT HE GAVE HIS ONLY BEGOTTEN SON,
THAT WHOSOEVER BELIEVETH IN HIM SHOULD NOT PERISH,
BUT HAVE EVERLASTING LIFE.

17. FOR GOD SENT NOT HIS SON INTO THE WORLD TO CONDEMN THE WORLD,
BUT THAT THE WORLD THROUGH HIM MIGHT BE SAVED.

18. HE THAT BELIEVETH ON HIM IS NOT CONDEMNED:
BUT HE THAT BELIEVETH NOT IS CONDEMNED ALREADY,
BECAUSE HE HATH NOT BELIEVED IN THE NAME OF THE ONLY BEGOTTEN SON OF GOD.

August 13 (Day 225), Memory Verse #608
John 3:30:

HE MUST INCREASE, BUT I MUST DECREASE.

August 14 (Day 226), Memory Verse #609
John 3:36:

HE THAT BELIEVETH ON THE SON HATH EVERLASTING LIFE:
AND HE THAT BELIEVETH NOT THE SON SHALL NOT SEE LIFE;
BUT THE WRATH OF GOD ABIDETH ON HIM.

August 14 (Day 226), Memory Verse #610
John 4:14:

BUT WHOSOEVER DRINKETH OF THE WATER THAT I SHALL GIVE HIM
SHALL NEVER THIRST;
BUT THE WATER THAT I SHALL GIVE HIM SHALL BE IN HIM A WELL OF WATER
SPRINGING UP INTO EVERLASTING LIFE.

August 15 (Day 227), Memory Verses #611 & #612
John 4:23-24:

23. BUT THE HOUR COMETH, AND NOW IS,
WHEN THE TRUE WORSHIPPERS SHALL WORSHIP THE FATHER IN SPIRIT
AND IN TRUTH:
FOR THE FATHER SEEKETH SUCH TO WORSHIP HIM.

24. GOD IS A SPIRIT:
AND THEY THAT WORSHIP HIM MUST WORSHIP HIM IN SPIRIT AND IN TRUTH.

August 16 (Day 228), Memory Verses #613 to #615
John 4:34-36:

34. JESUS SAITH UNTO THEM,
MY MEAT IS TO DO THE WILL OF HIM THAT SENT ME, AND TO FINISH HIS WORK.

35. SAY NOT YE, THERE ARE YET FOUR MONTHS, AND THEN COMETH HARVEST?
BEHOLD, I SAY UNTO YOU, LIFT UP YOUR EYES,
AND LOOK ON THE FIELDS; FOR THEY ARE WHITE ALREADY TO HARVEST.

36. AND HE THAT REAPETH RECEIVETH WAGES,
AND GATHERETH FRUIT UNTO LIFE ETERNAL:
THAT BOTH HE THAT SOWETH AND HE THAT REAPETH MAY REJOICE TOGETHER.

August 17 (Day 229), Memory Verse #616
John 5:24:

VERILY, VERILY, I SAY UNTO YOU,
HE THAT HEARETH MY WORD, AND BELIEVETH ON HIM THAT SENT ME,
HATH EVERLASTING LIFE, AND SHALL NOT COME INTO CONDEMNATION;
BUT IS PASSED FROM DEATH UNTO LIFE.

August 17 (Day 229), Memory Verse #617
John 6:27:

LABOUR NOT FOR THE MEAT WHICH PERISHETH,
BUT FOR THAT MEAT WHICH ENDURETH UNTO EVERLASTING LIFE,
WHICH THE SON OF MAN SHALL GIVE UNTO YOU:
FOR HIM HATH GOD THE FATHER SEALED.

August 18 (Day 230), Memory Verse #618
John 6:35:

AND JESUS SAID UNTO THEM, I AM THE BREAD OF LIFE;
HE THAT COMETH TO ME SHALL NEVER HUNGER;
AND HE THAT BELIEVETH ON ME SHALL NEVER THIRST.

August 18 (Day 230), Memory Verse #619
John 6:40:

AND THIS IS THE WILL OF HIM THAT SENT ME,
THAT EVERY ONE WHICH SEETH THE SON,
AND BELIEVETH ON HIM, MAY HAVE EVERLASTING LIFE:
AND I WILL RAISE HIM UP AT THE LAST DAY.

August 19 (Day 231), Memory Verse #620
John 6:48:

I AM THAT BREAD OF LIFE.

August 19 (Day 231), Memory Verse #621
John 6:51:

I AM THE LIVING BREAD WHICH CAME DOWN FROM HEAVEN:
IF ANY MAN EAT OF THIS BREAD, HE SHALL LIVE FOR EVER:
AND THE BREAD THAT I WILL GIVE IS MY FLESH,
WHICH I WILL GIVE FOR THE LIFE OF THE WORLD.

August 19 (Day 231), Memory Verse #622
John 6:63:

IT IS THE SPIRIT THAT QUICKENETH; THE FLESH PROFITETH NOTHING:
THE WORDS THAT I SPEAK UNTO YOU, THEY ARE SPIRIT, AND THEY ARE LIFE.

August 20 (Day 232), Memory Verses #623 & #624
John 7:37-38:

37. ...IF ANY MAN THIRST, LET HIM COME UNTO ME, AND DRINK.

38. HE THAT BELIEVETH ON ME, AS THE SCRIPTURE HATH SAID,
OUT OF HIS BELLY SHALL FLOW RIVERS OF LIVING WATER.

August 20 (Day 232), Memory Verse #625
John 8:7:

...HE THAT IS WITHOUT SIN AMONG YOU, LET HIM FIRST CAST A STONE AT HER.

August 21 (Day 233), Memory Verse #626
John 8:12:

...I AM THE LIGHT OF THE WORLD:
HE THAT FOLLOWETH ME SHALL NOT WALK IN DARKNESS,
BUT SHALL HAVE THE LIGHT OF LIFE.

August 21 (Day 233), Memory Verses #627 & #628
John 8:31-32:

31. ...IF YE CONTINUE IN MY WORD, THEN ARE YE MY DISCIPLES INDEED;

32. AND YE SHALL KNOW THE TRUTH, AND THE TRUTH SHALL MAKE YOU FREE.

August 22 (Day 234), Memory Verse #629
John 8:51:

VERILY, VERILY, I SAY UNTO YOU,
IF A MAN KEEP MY SAYING, HE SHALL NEVER SEE DEATH.

August 22 (Day 234), Memory Verse #630
John 8:58:

JESUS SAID UNTO THEM, VERILY, VERILY, I SAY UNTO YOU,
BEFORE ABRAHAM WAS, I AM.

August 23 (Day 235), Memory Verse #631
John 9:39:

...FOR JUDGMENT I AM COME INTO THE WORLD,
THAT THEY WHICH SEE NOT MIGHT SEE;
AND THAT THEY WHICH SEE MIGHT BE MADE BLIND.

August 23 (Day 235), Memory Verses #632 to #634
John 10:9-11:

9. I AM THE DOOR: BY ME IF ANY MAN ENTER IN,
HE SHALL BE SAVED, AND SHALL GO IN AND OUT, AND FIND PASTURE.

10. THE THIEF COMETH NOT, BUT FOR TO STEAL, AND TO KILL, AND TO DESTROY:
I AM COME THAT THEY MIGHT HAVE LIFE,
AND THAT THEY MIGHT HAVE IT MORE ABUNDANTLY.

11. I AM THE GOOD SHEPHERD:
THE GOOD SHEPHERD GIVETH HIS LIFE FOR THE SHEEP.

August 24 (Day 236), Memory Verses #635 & #636
John 10:14-15:

14. I AM THE GOOD SHEPHERD,
AND KNOW MY SHEEP, AND AM KNOWN OF MINE.

15. AS THE FATHER KNOWETH ME, EVEN SO KNOW I THE FATHER:
AND I LAY DOWN MY LIFE FOR THE SHEEP.

August 25 (Day 237), Memory Verses #637 & #638
John 10:27-28:

27. MY SHEEP HEAR MY VOICE, AND I KNOW THEM, AND THEY FOLLOW ME:

28. AND I GIVE UNTO THEM ETERNAL LIFE; AND THEY SHALL NEVER PERISH,
NEITHER SHALL ANY MAN PLUCK THEM OUT OF MY HAND.

August 25 (Day 237), Memory Verse #639
John 10:30:

I AND MY FATHER ARE ONE.

August 26 (Day 238), Memory Verses #640& #641
John 11:25-26:

25. ...I AM THE RESURRECTION, AND THE LIFE:
HE THAT BELIEVETH IN ME, THOUGH HE WERE DEAD,YET SHALL HE LIVE:

26. AND WHOSOEVER LIVETH AND BELIEVETH IN ME SHALL NEVER DIE.
BELIEVEST THOU THIS?

August 27 (Day 239), Memory Verse #642
John 12:25:

HE THAT LOVETH HIS LIFE SHALL LOSE IT;
AND HE THAT HATETH HIS LIFE IN THIS WORLD SHALL KEEP IT UNTO LIFE ETERNAL.

August 27 (Day 239), Memory Verse #643
John 12:46:

I AM COME A LIGHT INTO THE WORLD,
THAT WHOSOEVER BELIEVETH ON ME SHOULD NOT ABIDE IN DARKNESS.

August 28 (Day 240), Memory Verses #644 & #645
John 13:14-15:

14. IF I THEN, YOUR LORD AND MASTER, HAVE WASHED YOUR FEET;
YE ALSO OUGHT TO WASH ONE ANOTHER'S FEET.

15. FOR I HAVE GIVEN YOU AN EXAMPLE,
THAT YE SHOULD DO AS I HAVE DONE TO YOU.

August 29 (Day 241), Memory Verses #646 & #647
John 13:34-35:

34. A NEW COMMANDMENT I GIVE UNTO YOU,
THAT YE LOVE ONE ANOTHER; AS I HAVE LOVED YOU,
THAT YE ALSO LOVE ONE ANOTHER.

35. BY THIS SHALL ALL MEN KNOW THAT YE ARE MY DISCIPLES,
IF YE HAVE LOVE ONE TO ANOTHER.

August 30 (Day 242), Memory Verses #648 to #650
John 14:1-3:

1. LET NOT YOUR HEART BE TROUBLED:
YE BELIEVE IN GOD, BELIEVE ALSO IN ME.

2. IN MY FATHER'S HOUSE ARE MANY MANSIONS:
IF IT WERE NOT SO, I WOULD HAVE TOLD YOU.
I GO TO PREPARE A PLACE FOR YOU.

3. AND IF I GO AND PREPARE A PLACE FOR YOU,
I WILL COME AGAIN, AND RECEIVE YOU UNTO MYSELF;
THAT WHERE I AM, THERE YE MAY BE ALSO.

August 31 (Day 243), Memory Verse #651
John 14:6:

...I AM THE WAY, THE TRUTH, AND THE LIFE;
NO MAN COMETH UNTO THE FATHER, BUT BY ME.

August 31 (Day 243), Memory Verses #652 to #654
John 14:13-15:

13. AND WHATSOEVER YE SHALL ASK IN MY NAME,
THAT WILL I DO, THAT THE FATHER MAY BE GLORIFIED IN THE SON.

14. IF YE SHALL ASK ANY THING IN MY NAME, I WILL DO IT.

15. IF YE LOVE ME, KEEP MY COMMANDMENTS.

September 1 (Day 244), Memory Verse #655
John 14:21:

HE THAT HATH MY COMMANDMENTS, AND KEEPETH THEM,
HE IT IS THAT LOVETH ME:
AND HE THAT LOVETH ME SHALL BE LOVED OF MY FATHER,
AND I WILL LOVE HIM, AND WILL MANIFEST MYSELF TO HIM.

September 2 (Day 245), Memory Verses #656 & #657
John 14:26-27:

26. BUT THE COMFORTER, WHICH IS THE HOLY GHOST,
WHOM THE FATHER WILL SEND IN MY NAME,
HE SHALL TEACH YOU ALL THINGS,
AND BRING ALL THINGS TO YOUR REMEMBRANCE,
WHATSOEVER I HAVE SAID UNTO YOU.

27. PEACE I LEAVE WITH YOU, MY PEACE I GIVE UNTO YOU:
NOT AS THE WORLD GIVETH, GIVE I UNTO YOU.
LET NOT YOUR HEART BE TROUBLED, NEITHER LET IT BE AFRAID.

September 3 (Day 246), Memory Verse #658
John 15:5:

I AM THE VINE, YE ARE THE BRANCHES:
HE THAT ABIDETH IN ME, AND I IN HIM, THE SAME BRINGETH FORTH MUCH FRUIT:
FOR WITHOUT ME YE CAN DO NOTHING.

September 3 (Day 246), Memory Verses #659 & #660
John 15:12-13:

12. THIS IS MY COMMANDMENT,
THAT YE LOVE ONE ANOTHER AS I HAVE LOVED YOU.

13. GREATER LOVE HATH NO MAN THAN THIS,
THAT A MAN LAY DOWN HIS LIFE FOR HIS FRIENDS.

September 4 (Day 247), Memory Verse #661
John 16:33:

...IN THE WORLD YE SHALL HAVE TRIBULATION:
BUT BE OF GOOD CHEER;
I HAVE OVERCOME THE WORLD.

September 4 (Day 247), Memory Verse #662
John 17:5:

AND NOW, O FATHER, GLORIFY THOU ME, WITH THINE OWN SELF WITH THE GLORY
WHICH I HAD WITH THEE BEFORE THE WORLD WAS.

September 4 (Day 247), Memory Verse #663
John 17:11:

AND NOW I AM NO MORE IN THE WORLD,
BUT THESE ARE IN THE WORLD, AND I COME TO THEE.
HOLY FATHER, KEEP THROUGH THINE OWN NAME THOSE WHOM THOU HAST GIVEN ME,
THAT THEY MAY BE ONE, AS WE ARE.

September 5 (Day 248), Memory Verses #664 & #665
John 17:20-21:

20. NEITHER PRAY I FOR THESE ALONE,
BUT FOR THEM ALSO WHICH SHALL BELIEVE ON ME THROUGH THEIR WORD;

21. THAT THEY ALL MAY BE ONE;
AS THOU, FATHER, ART IN ME, AND I IN THEE,
THAT THEY ALSO MAY BE ONE IN US:
THAT THE WORLD MAY BELIEVE THAT THOU HAST SENT ME.

September 5 (Day 248), Memory Verse #666
John 20:29:

JESUS SAITH UNTO HIM, THOMAS,
BECAUSE THOU HAST SEEN ME, THOU HAST BELIEVED:
BLESSED ARE THEY THAT HAVE NOT SEEN,
AND YET HAVE BELIEVED.

September 6 (Day 249), Memory Verse #667
John 20:31:

BUT THESE (Signs, see John 20:30) ARE WRITTEN,
THAT YE MIGHT BELIEVE THAT JESUS IS THE CHRIST, THE SON OF GOD:
AND THAT BELIEVING YE MIGHT HAVE LIFE THROUGH HIS NAME.

September 6 (Day 249), Memory Verse #668
John 21:16:

HE SAITH TO HIM AGAIN THE SECOND TIME,
SIMON, SON OF JONAS, LOVEST THOU ME?
HE SAITH UNTO HIM, YEA, LORD: THOU KNOWEST THAT I LOVE THEE.
HE SAITH UNTO HIM, FEED MY SHEEP.

September 6 (Day 249), Memory Verse #669
John 21:25:

AND THERE ARE ALSO MANY OTHER THINGS WHICH JESUS DID, THE WHICH,
IF THEY SHOULD BE WRITTEN EVERY ONE,
I SUPPOSE THAT EVEN THE WORLD ITSELF COULD NOT CONTAIN
THE BOOKS THAT SHOULD BE WRITTEN.
AMEN.

ACTS

September 7 (Day 250), Memory Verse #670
Acts 1:8:

BUT YE SHALL RECEIVE POWER, AFTER THAT THE HOLY GHOST IS COME UPON YOU:
AND YE SHALL BE WITNESSES UNTO ME BOTH IN JERUSALEM,
AND IN ALL JUDAEA, AND IN SAMARIA,
AND UNTO THE UTTERMOST PART OF THE EARTH.

September 7 (Day 250), Memory Verse #671
Acts 2:21:

...WHOSOEVER SHALL CALL ON THE NAME OF THE LORD SHALL BE SAVED.

September 7 (Day 250), Memory Verse #672
Acts 2:24:

WHOM GOD HATH RAISED UP, HAVING LOOSED THE PAINS OF DEATH:
BECAUSE IT WAS NOT POSSIBLE THAT HE SHOULD BE HOLDEN OF IT.

September 8 (Day 251), Memory Verse #673
Acts 2:38:

THEN PETER SAID UNTO THEM, REPENT,
AND BE BAPTIZED EVERY ONE OF YOU IN THE NAME OF JESUS CHRIST
FOR THE REMISSION OF SINS,
AND YE SHALL RECEIVE THE GIFT OF THE HOLY GHOST.

September 8 (Day 251), Memory Verse #674
Acts 4:12:

NEITHER IS THERE SALVATION IN ANY OTHER:
FOR THERE IS NONE OTHER NAME UNDER HEAVEN GIVEN AMONG MEN,
WHEREBY WE MUST BE SAVED.

September 9 (Day 252), Memory Verse #675
Acts 5:29:

...WE OUGHT TO OBEY GOD RATHER THAN MEN.

September 9 (Day 252), Memory Verse #676
Acts 5:41:

AND THEY DEPARTED FROM THE PRESENCE OF THE COUNCIL,
REJOICING THAT THEY WERE COUNTED WORTHY TO SUFFER SHAME FOR HIS NAME.

September 10 (Day 253), Memory Verses #677& #678
Acts 10:34-35:

34. THEN PETER OPENED HIS MOUTH, AND SAID,
OF A TRUTH I PERCEIVE THAT GOD IS NO RESPECTER OF PERSONS
(God does not show favoritism, NIV):

35. BUT IN EVERY NATION HE THAT FEARETH HIM,
AND WORKETH RIGHTEOUSNESS, IS ACCEPTED WITH HIM.

September 10 (Day 253), Memory Verse #679
<u>Acts 10:43:</u>

TO HIM GIVE ALL THE PROPHETS WITNESS,
THAT THROUGH HIS NAME WHOSOEVER BELIEVETH IN HIM
SHALL RECEIVE REMISSION (forgiveness, NIV) OF SINS.

September 11 (Day 254), Memory Verse #680
<u>Act 16:31:</u>

AND THEY SAID, BELIEVE ON THE LORD JESUS CHRIST,
AND THOU SHALT BE SAVED, AND THY HOUSE.

September 11 (Day 254), Memory Verse #681
<u>Acts 17:28:</u>

FOR IN HIM WE LIVE, AND MOVE, AND HAVE OUR BEING; ...

September 12 (Day 255), Memory Verse #682
<u>Acts 20:35:</u>

...REMEMBER THE WORDS OF THE LORD JESUS, HOW HE SAID,
IT IS MORE BLESSED TO GIVE THAN TO RECEIVE.

ROMANS

September 12 (Day 255), Memory Verse #683
<u>Romans 1:1:</u>

PAUL, A SERVANT OF JESUS CHRIST...

September 13 (Day 256), Memory Verses #684 & #685
<u>Romans 1:16-17:</u>

16. FOR I AM NOT ASHAMED OF THE GOSPEL OF CHRIST:
FOR IT IS THE POWER OF GOD UNTO SALVATION TO EVERY ONE THAT BELIEVETH; ...

17. ...THE JUST SHALL LIVE BY FAITH.

September 13 (Day 256), Memory Verse #686
<u>Romans 2:4:</u>

...NOT KNOWING THE GOODNESS OF GOD LEADETH THEE TO REPENTANCE?

September 13 (Day 256), Memory Verse #687
<u>Romans 2:11:</u>

FOR THERE IS NO RESPECT (favoritism, NIV) OF PERSONS WITH GOD.

September 14 (Day 257), Memory Verse #688
<u>Romans 3:10:</u>

AS IT IS WRITTEN, THERE IS NONE RIGHTEOUS, NO, NOT ONE:

September 14 (Day 257), Memory Verse #689
<u>Romans 3:23:</u>

FOR ALL HAVE SINNED, AND COME SHORT OF THE GLORY OF GOD;

September 14 (Day 257), Memory Verse #690
Romans 5:1:

THEREFORE BEING JUSTIFIED BY FAITH,
WE HAVE PEACE WITH GOD THOUGH OUR LORD JESUS CHRIST:

September 14 (Day 257), Memory Verse #691
Romans 5:8:

BUT GOD COMMENDETH HIS LOVE TOWARD US, IN THAT,
WHILE WE WERE YET SINNERS, CHRIST DIED FOR US.

September 15 (Day 258), Memory Verses #692 & #693
Romans 6:3-4:

3. KNOW YE NOT, THAT SO MANY OF US AS WERE
BAPTIZED INTO JESUS CHRIST WERE BAPTIZED INTO HIS DEATH?

4. THEREFORE WE ARE BURIED WITH HIM BY BAPTISM INTO DEATH:
THAT LIKE AS CHRIST WAS RAISED UP FROM THE DEAD BY THE GLORY OF THE
FATHER, EVEN SO WE ALSO SHOULD WALK IN NEWNESS OF LIFE.

September 15 (Day 258), Memory Verse #694
Romans 6:23:

FOR THE WAGES OF SIN IS DEATH;
BUT THE GIFT OF GOD IS ETERNAL LIFE THROUGH JESUS CHRIST OUR LORD.

September 16 (Day 259), Memory Verse #695
Romans 8:1:

THERE IS THEREFORE NOW NO COMDEMNATION
TO THEM WHICH ARE IN CHRIST JESUS,
WHO WALK NOT AFTER THE FLESH, BUT AFTER THE SPIRIT.

September 16 (Day 259), Memory Verse #696
Romans 8:3:

FOR WHAT THE LAW COULD NOT DO, IN THAT IT WAS WEAK THROUGH THE FLESH,
GOD SENDING HIS OWN SON IN THE LIKENESS OF SINFUL FLESH,
AND FOR SIN, CONDEMNED SIN IN THE FLESH:

September 16 (Day 259), Memory Verse #697
Romans 8:6:

FOR TO BE CARNALLY MINDED IS DEATH;
BUT TO BE SPIRITUALLY MINDED IS LIFE AND PEACE.

September 17 (Day 260), Memory Verses #698 to #700
Romans 8:15-17:

15. ...BUT YE HAVE RECEIVED THE SPIRIT
OF ADOPTION, WHEREBY WE CRY, ABBA, FATHER.

16. THE SPIRIT ITSELF BEARETH WITNESS WITH OUR SPIRIT,
THAT WE ARE THE CHILDREN OF GOD:

17. AND IF CHILDREN, THEN HEIRS; HEIRS OF GOD,
AND JOINT-HEIRS WITH CHRIST; ...

September 18 (Day 261), Memory Verse #701
Romans 8:28:

AND WE KNOW THAT ALL THINGS WORK TOGETHER FOR GOOD
TO THEM THAT LOVE GOD,
TO THEM WHO ARE THE CALLED ACCORDING TO HIS PURPOSE.

September 18 (Day 261), Memory Verse #702
Romans 8:31:

...IF GOD BE FOR US, WHO CAN BE AGAINST US?

September 19 (Day 262), Memory Verses #703 & #704
Romans 8:38-39:

38. FOR I AM PERSUADED, THAT NEITHER DEATH,
NOR LIFE, NOR ANGELS, NOR PRINCIPALITIES, NOR POWERS,
NOR THINGS PRESENT, NOR THINGS TO COME,

39. NOR HEIGHT, NOR DEPTH, NOR ANY OTHER CREATURE,
SHALL BE ABLE TO SEPARATE US FROM THE LOVE OF GOD,
WHICH IS IN CHRIST JESUS OUR LORD.

September 20 (Day 263), Memory Verse #705
Romans 10:9:

THAT IF THOU SHALT CONFESS WITH THY MOUTH THE LORD JESUS,
AND SHALT BELIEVE IN THINE HEART THAT GOD HATH RAISED HIM FROM THE DEAD,
THOU SHALT BE SAVED.

September 20 (Day 263), Memory Verse #706
Romans 10:13:

FOR WHOSOEVER SHALL CALL UPON THE NAME OF THE LORD SHALL BE SAVED.

September 20 (Day 263), Memory Verse #707
Romans 10:17:

SO THEN FAITH COMETH BY HEARING,
AND HEARING BY THE WORD OF GOD.

September 21 (Day 264), Memory Verses #708 to #711
Romans 11:33-36:

33. O THE DEPTH OF THE RICHES BOTH OF THE WISDOM AND KNOWLEDGE OF GOD!
HOW UNSEARCHABLE ARE HIS JUDGMENTS,
AND HIS WAYS PAST FINDING OUT!

34. FOR WHO HATH KNOWN THE MIND OF THE LORD?
OR WHO HATH BEEN HIS COUNSELLOR?

35. OR WHO HATH FIRST GIVEN TO HIM,
AND IT SHALL BE RECOMPENSED UNTO HIM AGAIN?

36. FOR OF HIM, AND THROUGH HIM,
AND TO HIM, ARE ALL THINGS:
TO WHOM BE GLORY FOR EVER.
AMEN.

September 22 (Day 265), Memory Verses #712 & #713
<u>Romans 12:1-2</u>:

1. I BESEECH YOU THEREFORE, BRETHREN,
BY THE MERCIES OF GOD, THAT YE PRESENT YOUR BODIES
A LIVING SACRIFICE, HOLY, ACCEPTABLE UNTO GOD,
WHICH IS YOUR REASONABLE SERVICE.

2. AND BE NOT CONFORMED TO THIS WORLD:
BUT BE YE TRANSFORMED BY THE RENEWING OF YOUR MIND,
THAT YE MAY PROVE WHAT IS THAT GOOD,
AND ACCEPTABLE, AND PERFECT, WILL OF GOD.

September 23 (Day 266), Memory Verse #714
<u>Romans 12:5</u>:

SO WE, BEING MANY, ARE ONE BODY IN CHRIST,
AND EVERY ONE MEMBERS ONE OF ANOTHER.

September 23 (Day 266), Memory Verse #715
<u>Romans 12:10</u>:

BE KINDLY AFFECTIONED ONE TO ANOTHER WITH BROTHERLY LOVE;...

September 23 (Day 266), Memory Verses #716 & #717
<u>Romans 12:14-15</u>:

14. BLESS THEM WHICH PERSECUTE YOU: BLESS, AND CURSE NOT.

15. REJOICE WITH THEM THAT DO REJOICE, AND WEEP WITH THEM THAT WEEP.

September 24 (Day 267), Memory Verse #718
<u>Romans 12:18</u>:

IF IT BE POSSIBLE, AS MUCH AS LIETH IN YOU, LIVE PEACEABLY WITH ALL MEN.

September 24 (Day 267), Memory Verses #719 & #720
<u>Romans 12:20-21</u>:

20. THEREFORE IF THINE ENEMY HUNGER, FEED HIM;
IF HE THIRST, GIVE HIM DRINK:
FOR IN SO DOING THOU SHALT HEAP COALS OF FIRE ON HIS HEAD.

21. BE NOT OVERCOME OF EVIL, BUT OVERCOME EVIL WITH GOOD.

September 25 (Day 268), Memory Verses #721 to #723
<u>Romans 13:8-10</u>:

8. OWE NO MAN ANY THING, BUT TO LOVE ONE ANOTHER:
FOR HE THAT LOVETH ANOTHER HATH FULFILLED THE LAW.

9. FOR THIS, THOU SHALT NOT COMMIT ADULTERY,
THOU SHALT NOT KILL, THOU SHALT NOT STEAL,
THOU SHALT NOT BEAR FALSE WITNESS,
THOU SHALT NOT COVET;
AND IF THERE BE ANY OTHER COMMANDMENT,
IT IS BRIEFLY COMPREHENDED IN THIS SAYING, NAMELY,
THOU SHALT LOVE THY NEIGHBOUR AS THYSELF.

10. LOVE WORKETH NO ILL TO HIS NEIGHBOUR:
THEREFORE LOVE IS THE FULFILLING OF THE LAW.

September 26 (Day 269), Memory Verses #724 & #725
<u>**Romans 14:12-13:**</u>

12. SO THEN EVERY ONE OF US SHALL GIVE ACCOUNT OF HIMSELF TO GOD.

13. LET US NOT THEREFORE JUDGE ONE ANOTHER ANY MORE:
BUT JUDGE THIS RATHER,
THAT NO MAN PUT A STUMBLINGBLOCK
OR AN OCCASION TO FALL IN HIS BROTHER'S WAY.

September 26 (Day 269), Memory Verse #726
<u>**Romans 15:1:**</u>

WE THEN THAT ARE STRONG OUGHT TO BEAR THE INFIRMITIES OF THE WEAK,
AND NOT TO PLEASE OURSELVES.

I CORINTHIANS

September 27 (Day 270), Memory Verse #727
<u>**I Corinthians 1:18:**</u>

FOR THE PREACHING OF THE CROSS IS TO THEM THAT PERISH FOOLISHNESS;
BUT UNTO US WHICH ARE SAVED IT IS THE POWER OF GOD.

September 27 (Day 270), Memory Verse #728
<u>**I Corinthians 1:27:**</u>

BUT GOD HATH CHOSEN THE FOOLISH THINGS OF THE WORLD TO CONFOUND THE WISE;
AND GOD HATH CHOSEN THE WEAK THINGS OF THE WORLD
TO CONFOUND THE THINGS WHICH ARE MIGHTY.

September 27 (Day 270), Memory Verse #729
<u>**I Corinthians 1:31:**</u>

...HE THAT GLORIETH (boasts, NIV), LET HIM GLORY (boast, NIV) IN THE LORD.
(Also see II CORINTHIANS 10:17)

September 28 (Day 271), Memory Verses #730 & #731
<u>**I Corinthians 2:9-10:**</u>

9. BUT AS IT IS WRITTEN, EYE HATH NOT SEEN, NOR EAR HEARD,
NEITHER HAVE ENTERED INTO THE HEART OF MAN,
THE THINGS WHICH GOD HATH PREPARED FOR THEM THAT LOVE HIM.

10. BUT GOD HATH REVEALED THEM UNTO US BY HIS SPIRIT:
FOR THE SPIRIT SEARCHETH ALL THINGS,
YEA THE DEEP THINGS OF GOD.

September 29 (Day 272), Memory Verse #732
<u>**I Corinthians 3:16:**</u>

KNOW YE NOT THAT YE ARE THE TEMPLE OF GOD,
AND THAT THE SPIRIT OF GOD DWELLETH IN YOU?

September 29 (Day 272), Memory Verse #733
I Corinthians 4:2:

MOREOVER IT IS REQUIRED IN STEWARDS, THAT A MAN BE FOUND FAITHFUL.

September 29 (Day 272), Memory Verse #734
I Corinthians 4:4:

FOR I KNOW NOTHING BY MYSELF; YET AM I NOT HEREBY JUSTIFIED:
BUT HE THAT JUDGETH ME IS THE LORD.

September 30 (Day 273), Memory Verse #735
I Corinthians 6:15:

KNOW YE NOT THAT YOUR BODIES ARE THE MEMBERS OF CHRIST? ...

September 30 (Day 273), Memory Verse #736
I Corinthians 6:17:

BUT HE THAT IS JOINED UNTO THE LORD IS ONE SPIRIT.

October 1 (Day 274), Memory Verses #737 & #738
I Corinthians 6:19-20:

19. WHAT? KNOW YE NOT THAT YOUR BODY IS THE TEMPLE OF THE HOLY GHOST
WHICH IS IN YOU, WHICH YE HAVE OF GOD, AND YE ARE NOT YOUR OWN?

20. FOR YE ARE BOUGHT WITH A PRICE:
THEREFORE GLORIFY GOD IN YOUR BODY, AND IN YOUR SPIRIT, WHICH ARE GOD'S.

October 1 (Day 274), Memory Verse #739
I Corinthians 8:1:

...KNOWLEDGE PUFFETH UP, BUT CHARITY (love, NIV) EDIFIETH.

October 2 (Day 275), Memory Verse #740
I Corinthians 10:13:

THERE HATH NO TEMPTATION TAKEN YOU BUT SUCH AS IS COMMON TO MAN:
BUT GOD IS FAITHFUL,
WHO WILL NOT SUFFER YOU TO BE TEMPTED ABOVE THAT YE ARE ABLE;
BUT WILL WITH THE TEMPTATION ALSO MAKE A WAY TO ESCAPE,
THAT YE MAY BE ABLE TO BEAR IT.

October 3 (Day 276), Memory Verse #741
I Corinthians 10:24:

LET NO MAN SEEK HIS OWN, BUT EVERY MAN ANOTHER'S WEALTH.

October 3 (Day 276), Memory Verse #742
I Corinthians 10:31:

WHETHER THEREFORE YE EAT, OR DRINK, OR WHATSOEVER YE DO,
DO ALL TO THE GLORY OF GOD.

October 3 (Day 276), Memory Verse #743
I Corinthians 12:4:

NOW THERE ARE DIVERSITIES OF GIFTS, BUT THE SAME SPIRIT.

October 4-7 (Day 277-280), Memory Verses #744 to #756
I Corinthians 13:1-13:
(The Love Chapter)

1. THOUGH I SPEAK WITH THE TONGUES OF MEN AND OF ANGELS,
AND HAVE NOT CHARITY (love, NIV),
I AM BECOME AS SOUNDING BRASS, OR A TINKLING CYMBAL.

2. AND THOUGH I HAVE THE GIFT OF PROPHECY,
AND UNDERSTAND ALL MYSTERIES, AND ALL KNOWLEDGE;
AND THOUGH I HAVE ALL FAITH, SO THAT I COULD REMOVE MOUNTAINS,
AND HAVE NOT CHARITY, I AM NOTHING.

3. AND THOUGH I BESTOW ALL MY GOODS TO FEED THE POOR,
AND THOUGH I GIVE MY BODY TO BE BURNED,
AND HAVE NOT CHARITY, IT PROFITETH ME NOTHING.

4. CHARITY SUFFERETH LONG, AND IS KIND; CHARITY ENVIETH NOT;
CHARITY VAUNTETH NOT ITSELF, IS NOT PUFFED UP,

5. DOTH NOT BEHAVE ITSELF UNSEEMLY, SEEKETH NOT HER OWN,
IS NOT EASILY PROVOKED, THINKETH NO EVIL;

6. REJOICETH NOT IN INIQUITY, BUT REJOICETH IN THE TRUTH;

7. BEARETH ALL THINGS, BELIEVETH ALL THINGS,
HOPETH ALL THINGS, ENDURETH ALL THINGS.

8. CHARITY NEVER FAILETH:
BUT WHETHER THERE BE PROPHECIES, THEY SHALL FAIL;
WHETHER THERE BE TONGUES, THEY SHALL CEASE;
WHETHER THERE BE KNOWLEDGE, IT SHALL VANISH AWAY.

9. FOR WE KNOW IN PART, AND WE PROPHESY IN PART.

10. BUT WHEN THAT WHICH IS PERFECT IS COME,
THEN THAT WHICH IS IN PART SHALL BE DONE AWAY.

11. WHEN I WAS A CHILD, I SPAKE AS A CHILD,
I UNDERSTOOD AS A CHILD, I THOUGHT AS A CHILD:
BUT WHEN I BECAME A MAN, I PUT AWAY CHILDISH THINGS.

12. FOR NOW WE SEE THROUGH A GLASS, DARKLY;
BUT THEN FACE TO FACE: NOW I KNOW IN PART;
BUT THEN SHALL I KNOW EVEN AS ALSO I AM KNOWN.

13. NOW ABIDETH FAITH, HOPE, CHARITY, THESE THREE;
BUT THE GREATEST OF THESE IS CHARITY (love, NIV).

October 8 (Day 281), Memory Verse #757
I Corinthians 14:33:

FOR GOD IS NOT THE AUTHOR OF CONFUSION,
BUT OF PEACE, AS IN ALL CHURCHES OF THE SAINTS.

October 8 (Day 281), Memory Verses #758 & #759
I Corinthians 15:3-4:

3. FOR I DELIVERED TO YOU FIRST OF ALL THAT WHICH I ALSO RECEIVED,
HOW THAT CHRIST DIED FOR OUR SINS ACCORDING TO THE SCRIPTURES;

4. AND THAT HE WAS BURIED AND THAT HE ROSE AGAIN THE THIRD DAY
ACCORDING TO THE SCRIPTURES;

October 9 (Day 282), Memory Verse #760
I Corinthians 15:33:

BE NOT DECEIVED:
EVIL COMMUNICATIONS (company, NIV) CORRUPT GOOD MANNERS (character, NIV).

October 9-10 (Days 282-283), Memory Verses #761 to #765
I Corinthians 15:54-58:

54. SO WHEN THIS CORRUPTIBLE SHALL HAVE PUT ON THE INCORRUPTION,
AND THIS MORTAL SHALL HAVE PUT ON IMMORTALITY,
THEN SHALL BE BROUGHT TO PASS THE SAYING THAT IS WRITTEN,
DEATH IS SWALLOWED UP IN VICTORY.

55. O DEATH, WHERE IS THY STING? O GRAVE, WHERE IS THY VICTORY?

56. THE STING OF DEATH IS SIN; AND THE STRENGTH OF SIN IS THE LAW.

57. BUT THANKS BE TO GOD,
WHICH GIVETH US THE VICTORY THROUGH OUR LORD JESUS CHRIST.

58. THEREFORE, MY BELOVED BRETHREN, BE YE STEDFAST, UNMOVEABLE,
ALWAYS ABOUNDING IN THE WORK OF THE LORD,
FORASMUCH AS YE KNOW THAT YOUR LABOUR IS NOT IN VAIN IN THE LORD.

II CORINTHIANS

October 11 (Day 284), Memory Verses #766 & #767
II Corinthians 1:3-4:

3. BLESSED BE GOD, EVEN THE FATHER OF OUR LORD JESUS CHRIST,
THE FATHER OF MERCIES, AND THE GOD OF ALL COMFORT;

4. WHO COMFORTETH US IN ALL OUR TRIBULATION,
THAT WE MAY BE ABLE TO COMFORT THEM WHICH ARE IN ANY TROUBLE,
BY THE COMFORT WHEREWITH WE OURSELVES ARE COMFORTED OF GOD.

October 11 (Day 284), Memory Verse #768
II Corinthians 3:18:

BUT WE ALL, WITH OPEN FACE, BEHOLDING AS IN A GLASS THE GLORY OF THE LORD,
ARE CHANGED INTO THE SAME IMAGE FROM GLORY TO GLORY,
EVEN AS BY THE SPIRIT OF THE LORD.

October 12 (Day 285), Memory Verse #769
II Corinthians 5:7:

(FOR WE WALK BY FAITH, NOT BY SIGHT:)

October 12 (Day 285), Memory Verse #770
II Corinthians 5:15:

AND THAT HE DIED FOR ALL,
THAT THEY WHICH LIVE SHOULD NOT HENCEFORTH LIVE UNTO THEMSELVES,
BUT UNTO HIM WHICH DIED FOR THEM, AND ROSE AGAIN.

October 13 (Day 286), Memory Verse #771
II Corinthians 5:17:

THEREFORE IF ANY MAN BE IN CHRIST, HE IS A NEW CREATURE:
OLD THINGS ARE PASSED AWAY; BEHOLD, ALL THINGS ARE BECOME NEW.

October 13 (Day 286), Memory Verse #772
II Corinthians 5:21:

FOR HE HATH MADE HIM TO BE SIN FOR US, WHO KNEW NO SIN;
THAT WE MIGHT BE MADE THE RIGHTEOUSNESS OF GOD IN HIM.

October 13 (Day 286), Memory Verse #773
II Corinthians 6:2:

...BEHOLD, NOW IS THE DAY OF SALVATION.

October 14 (Day 287), Memory Verses #774 & #775
II Corinthians 9:7-8:

7. EVERY MAN ACCORDING AS HE PURPOSETH IN HIS HEART, SO LET HIM GIVE;
NOT GRUDGINGLY, OR OF NECESSITY: FOR GOD LOVETH A CHEERFUL GIVER.

8. AND GOD IS ABLE TO MAKE ALL GRACE ABOUND TOWARD YOU;
THAT YE, ALWAYS HAVING ALL SUFFICIENCY IN ALL THINGS,
MAY ABOUND TO EVERY GOOD WORK:

October 14 (Day 287), Memory Verse #776
II Corinthians 10:17:

BUT HE THAT GLORIETH, LET HIM GLORY IN THE LORD.

October 14 (Day 287), Memory Verse #777
II Corinthians 12:10:

THEREFORE I TAKE PLEASURE IN INFIRMITIES,
IN REPROACHES, IN NECESSITIES, IN PERSECUTIONS, IN DISTRESSES
FOR CHRIST'S SAKE: FOR WHEN I AM WEAK, THEN AM I STRONG.

GALATIANS

October 15 (Day 288), Memory Verse #778
Galatians 2:16:

...WE HAVE BELIEVED IN JESUS CHRIST,
THAT WE MIGHT BE JUSTIFIED BY THE FAITH OF CHRIST,
AND NOT BY THE WORKS OF THE LAW:
FOR BY THE WORKS OF THE LAW SHALL NO FLESH BE JUSTIFIED.

October 15 (Day 288), Memory Verse #779
Galatians 3:11:

BUT THAT NO MAN IS JUSTIFIED BY THE LAW IN THE SIGHT OF GOD, IT IS EVIDENT:
FOR, THE JUST SHALL LIVE BY FAITH.

October 15 (Day 288), Memory Verse #780
Galatians 3:8:

AND THE SCRIPTURE, FORESEEING THAT GOD
WOULD JUSTIFY THE HEATHEN THROUGH FAITH,
PREACHED BEFORE THE GOSPEL UNTO ABRAHAM, SAYING,
IN THEE SHALL ALL NATIONS BE BLESSED.

October 16 (Day 289), Memory Verses #781 & #782
Galatians 3:28-29:

28. THERE IS NEITHER JEW NOR GREEK,
THERE IS NEITHER BOND NOR FREE,
THERE IS NEITHER MALE NOR FEMALE:
FOR YE ARE ALL ONE IN CHRIST JESUS.

29. AND IF YE BE CHRIST'S, THEN ARE YE ABRAHAM'S SEED,
AND HEIRS ACCORDING TO THE PROMISE.

October 17 (Day 290), Memory Verses #783 & #784
Galatians 5:13-14:

13. ...BUT BY LOVE SERVE ONE ANOTHER.

14. FOR ALL THE LAW IS FULFILLED IN ONE WORD, EVEN IN THIS;
THOU SHALT LOVE THY NEIGHBOUR AS THYSELF.

October 18 (Day 291), Memory Verse #785
Galatians 5:16:

THIS I SAY THEN, WALK IN THE SPIRIT,
AND YE SHALL NOT FULFIL THE LUST OF THE FLESH.

October 18 (Day 291), Memory Verses #786 & #787
Galatians 5:22-23:
(Fruits of the Spirit)

22. BUT THE FRUIT OF THE SPIRIT IS LOVE, JOY, PEACE,
LONGSUFFERING, GENTLENESS, GOODNESS, FAITH,

23. MEEKNESS, TEMPERANCE: AGAINST SUCH THERE IS NO LAW.

October 19 (Day 292), Memory Verse #788
Galatians 5:25:

IF WE LIVE IN THE SPIRIT,
LET US ALSO WALK IN THE SPIRIT.

October 19 (Day 292), Memory Verse #789
Galatians 6:2:

BEAR YE ONE ANOTHER'S BURDENS,
AND SO FULFIL THE LAW OF CHRIST.

October 19 (Day 292), Memory Verse #790
Galatians 6:7:

BE NOT DECEIVED; GOD IS NOT MOCKED:
FOR WHATSOEVER A MAN SOWETH, THAT SHALL HE ALSO REAP.

October 20 (Day 293), Memory Verses #791 & #792
<u>Galatians 6:9-10:</u>

9. AND LET US NOT BE WEARY IN WELL DOING:
FOR IN DUE SEASON WE SHALL REAP,
IF WE FAINT NOT.

10. AS WE HAVE OPPORTUNITY,
LET US DO GOOD UNTO ALL MEN,
ESPECIALLY UNTO THEM WHO ARE OF THE HOUSEHOLD OF FAITH.

EPHESIANS

October 21 (Day 294), Memory Verses #793 & #794
<u>Ephesians 1:4-5:</u>

4. ACCORDING AS HE HATH CHOSEN US IN HIM
BEFORE THE FOUNDATION OF THE WORLD,
THAT WE SHOULD BE HOLY AND WITHOUT BLAME BEFORE HIM IN LOVE:

5. HAVING PREDESTINATED US UNTO THE ADOPTION
OF CHILDREN BY JESUS CHRIST TO HIMSELF,
ACCORDING TO THE GOOD PLEASURE OF HIS WILL,

October 22 (Day 295), Memory Verses #795 & #796
<u>Ephesians 1:22-23:</u>

22. AND HATH PUT ALL THINGS UNDER HIS FEET,
AND GAVE HIM TO BE THE HEAD OVER ALL THINGS TO THE CHURCH,

23. WHICH IS HIS BODY,
THE FULNESS OF HIM THAT FILLETH ALL IN ALL.

October 23 (Day 296), Memory Verses #797 & #798
<u>Ephesians 2:4-5:</u>

4. BUT GOD, WHO IS RICH IN MERCY,
FOR HIS GREAT LOVE WHEREWITH HE LOVED US,

5. EVEN WHEN WE WERE DEAD IN SINS, HATH QUICKENED US
TOGETHER WITH CHRIST, (BY GRACE YE ARE SAVED;)

October 24 (Day 297), Memory Verses #799 & #800
<u>Ephesians 2:8-9:</u>

8. FOR BY GRACE ARE YE SAVED THROUGH FAITH;
AND THAT NOT OF YOURSELVES: IT IS THE GIFT OF GOD:

9. NOT OF WORKS, LEST ANY MAN SHOULD BOAST.

October 24 (Day 297), Memory Verse #801
<u>Ephesians 2:22:</u>

IN WHOM YE ALSO ARE BUILDED TOGETHER FOR
AN HABITATION OF GOD THROUGH THE SPIRIT.

October 25 (Day 298), Memory Verses #802 to #804
Ephesians 3:19-21:

19. **AND** TO KNOW THE LOVE OF CHRIST, WHICH PASSETH KNOWLEDGE,
THAT YE MAY BE FILLED WITH ALL THE FULNESS OF GOD.

20. **NOW** UNTO HIM THAT IS ABLE TO DO EXCEEDING ABUNDANTLY
ABOVE ALL THAT WE ASK OR THINK,
ACCORDING TO THE POWER THAT WORKETH IN US,

21. **UNTO** HIM BE GLORY IN THE CHURCH BY CHRIST JESUS
THROUGHOUT ALL AGES, WORLD WITHOUT END.
AMEN.

October 26 (Day 299), Memory Verses #805 to #807
Ephesians 4:4-6:

4. **THERE** IS ONE BODY, AND ONE SPIRIT,
EVEN AS YE ARE CALLED IN ONE HOPE OF YOUR CALLING;

5. **ONE** LORD, ONE FAITH, ONE BAPTISM,

6. **ONE** GOD AND FATHER OF ALL,
WHO IS ABOVE ALL, AND THROUGH ALL, AND IN YOU ALL.

October 27 (Day 300), Memory Verse #808
Ephesians 4:26:

...**LET** NOT THE SUN GO DOWN UPON YOUR WRATH:

October 27 (Day 300), Memory Verse #809
Ephesians 4:32:

AND BE YE KIND ONE TO ANOTHER,
TENDERHEARTED, FORGIVING ONE ANOTHER,
EVEN AS GOD FOR CHRIST'S SAKE HATH FORGIVEN YOU.

October 27 (Day 300), Memory Verse #810
Ephesians 5:2:

AND WALK IN LOVE, AS CHRIST ALSO HATH LOVED US,
AND HATH GIVEN HIMSELF FOR US AN OFFERING AND A SACRIFICE
TO GOD FOR A SWEET-SMELLING SAVOUR.

October 28 (Day 301), Memory Verses #811 & #812
Ephesians 5:21-22:

21. **SUBMITTING** YOURSELVES ONE TO ANOTHER
IN THE FEAR OF GOD (out of reverence for Christ, NIV).

22. **WIVES,** SUBMIT YOURSELVES UNTO YOUR OWN HUSBANDS,
AS UNTO THE LORD.

October 28 (Day 301), Memory Verse #813
Ephesians 5:25:

HUSBANDS, LOVE YOUR WIVES,
EVEN AS CHRIST ALSO LOVED THE CHURCH,
AND GAVE HIMSELF FOR IT;

October 28 (Day 301), Memory Verse #814
Ephesians 5:31:

FOR THIS CAUSE SHALL A MAN LEAVE HIS FATHER AND MOTHER,
AND SHALL BE JOINED UNTO HIS WIFE,
AND THEY TWO SHALL BE ONE FLESH.

October 29 (Day 302), Memory Verses #815 to #818
Ephesians 6:1-4:

1. CHILDREN, OBEY YOUR PARENTS IN THE LORD: FOR THIS IS RIGHT.

2. HONOUR THY FATHER AND MOTHER;
(WHICH IS THE FIRST COMMANDMENT WITH PROMISE;)

3. THAT IT MAY BE WELL WITH THEE,
AND THOU MAYEST LIVE LONG ON THE EARTH.

4. AND, YE FATHERS, PROVOKE NOT YOUR CHILDREN TO WRATH:
BUT BRING THEM UP IN THE NURTURE AND ADMONITION OF THE LORD.

October 30 (Day 303), Memory Verses #819 to #821
Ephesians 6:10-12:

10. FINALLY, MY BRETHREN, BE STRONG IN THE LORD,
AND IN THE POWER OF HIS MIGHT.

11. PUT ON THE WHOLE ARMOUR OF GOD,
THAT WE MAY BE ABLE TO STAND AGAINST THE WILES OF THE DEVIL.

12. FOR WE WRESTLE NOT AGAINST FLESH AND BLOOD,
BUT AGAINST THE PRINCIPALITIES, AGAINST POWERS,
AGAINST THE RULERS OF THE DARKNESS OF THIS WORLD,
AGAINST SPIRITUAL WICKEDNESS IN HIGH PLACES.

October 31 (Day 304), Memory Verse #822
Ephesians 6:18:

PRAYING ALWAYS WITH ALL PRAYER
AND SUPPLICATION IN THE SPIRIT... .

PHILIPPIANS

November 1 (Day 305), Memory Verse #823
Philippians 1:3:

I THANK MY GOD UPON EVERY REMEMBRANCE OF YOU.

November 1 (Day 305), Memory Verse #824
Philippians 1:21:

FOR TO ME TO LIVE IS CHRIST, AND TO DIE IS GAIN.

November 2-3 (Days 306-307), Memory Verses #825 to #831
Philippians 2:5-11:

5. LET THIS MIND BE IN YOU, WHICH WAS ALSO IN CHRIST JESUS:

6. WHO, BEING IN THE FORM OF GOD,
THOUGHT IT NOT ROBBERY TO BE EQUAL WITH GOD:

7. BUT MADE HIMSELF OF NO REPUTATION,
AND TOOK UPON HIM THE FORM OF A SERVANT,
AND WAS MADE IN THE LIKENESS OF MEN:

8. AND BEING FOUND IN FASHION AS A MAN,
HE HUMBLED HIMSELF, AND BECAME OBEDIENT UNTO DEATH,
EVEN THE DEATH OF THE CROSS.

9. WHEREFORE GOD ALSO HATH HIGHLY EXALTED HIM,
AND GIVEN HIM A NAME WHICH IS ABOVE EVERY NAME:

10. THAT AT THE NAME OF JESUS EVERY KNEE SHOULD BOW,
OF THINGS IN HEAVEN, AND THINGS IN EARTH, AND THINGS UNDER THE EARTH;

11. AND THAT EVERY TONGUE SHOULD CONFESS THAT
JESUS CHRIST IS LORD, TO THE GLORY OF GOD THE FATHER.

November 4 (Day 308), Memory Verse #832
Philippians 3:8:

YEA DOUBTLESS, AND I COUNT ALL THINGS BUT LOSS
FOR THE EXCELLENCY OF THE KNOWLEDGE OF CHRIST JESUS MY LORD:
FOR WHOM I HAVE SUFFERED THE LOSS OF ALL THINGS,
AND DO COUNT THEM BUT DUNG, THAT I MAY WIN CHRIST.

November 4 (Day 308), Memory Verse #833
Philippians 3:14:

I PRESS TOWARD THE MARK FOR THE PRIZE
OF THE HIGH CALLING OF GOD IN CHRIST JESUS

November 4 (Day 308), Memory Verse #834
Philippians 4:4:

REJOICE IN THE LORD ALWAY: AND AGAIN I SAY, REJOICE.

November 5 (Day 309), Memory Verses #835 to #837
Philippians 4:6-8:

6. BE CAREFUL FOR NOTHING;
BUT IN EVERY THING BY PRAYER AND SUPPLICATION WITH THANKSGIVING
LET YOUR REQUESTS BE MADE KNOWN UNTO GOD.

7. AND THE PEACE OF GOD WHICH PASSETH ALL UNDERSTANDING,
SHALL KEEP YOUR HEARTS AND MINDS THROUGH CHRIST JESUS.

8. FINALLY, BRETHREN, WHATSOEVER THINGS ARE TRUE,
WHATSOEVER THINGS ARE HONEST, WHATSOEVER THINGS ARE JUST,
WHATSOEVER THINGS ARE PURE, WHATSOEVER THINGS ARE LOVELY,
WHATSOEVER THINGS ARE OF GOOD REPORT;
IF THERE BE ANY VIRTUE, AND IF THERE BE ANY PRAISE,
THINK ON THESE THINGS.

November 6 (Day 310), Memory Verse #838
Philippians 4:11:

...FOR I HAVE LEARNED, IN WHATSOEVER STATE I AM, THEREWITH TO BE CONTENT.

November 6 (Day 310), Memory Verse #839
Philippians 4:13:

I CAN DO ALL THINGS THROUGH CHRIST WHICH STRENGTHENETH ME.

November 6 (Day 310), Memory Verse #840
Philippians 4:19:

BUT MY GOD SHALL SUPPLY ALL YOUR NEED
ACCORDING TO HIS RICHES IN GLORY BY CHRIST JESUS.

COLOSSIANS

November 7 (Day 311), Memory Verse #841
Colossians 1:17:

AND HE IS BEFORE ALL THINGS, AND BY HIM ALL THINGS CONSIST.

November 7 (Day 311), Memory Verses #842 & #843
Colossians 2:8-9:

8. BEWARE LEST ANY MAN SPOIL YOU THROUGH PHILOSOPHY AND VAIN DECEIT,
AFTER THE TRADITION OF MEN, AFTER THE RUDIMENTS OF THE WORLD,
AND NOT AFTER CHRIST.

9. FOR IN HIM DWELLETH ALL THE FULNESS OF THE GODHEAD BODILY.

November 7 (Day 311), Memory Verse #844
Colossians 3:2:

SET YOUR AFFECTION ON THINGS ABOVE,
NOT ON THINGS ON THE EARTH.

November 8-9 (Days 312-313), Memory Verses #845 to #850
Colossians 3:12-17:

12. PUT ON THEREFORE, AS THE ELECT OF GOD, HOLY AND BELOVED,
BOWELS OF MERCIES, KINDNESS, HUMBLENESS OF MIND, MEEKNESS, LONGSUFFERING;

13. FORBEARING ONE ANOTHER, AND FORGIVING ONE ANOTHER,
IF ANY MAN HAVE A QUARREL AGAINST ANY:
EVEN AS CHRIST FORGAVE YOU, SO ALSO DO YE.

14. AND ABOVE ALL THESE THINGS PUT ON CHARITY (love, NIV),
WHICH IS THE BOND OF PERFECTNESS.

15. AND LET THE PEACE OF GOD RULE IN YOUR HEARTS,
TO THE WHICH ALSO YE ARE CALLED IN ONE BODY;
AND BE YE THANKFUL.

16. LET THE WORD OF CHRIST DWELL IN YOU RICHLY IN ALL WISDOM;
TEACHING AND ADMONISHING ONE ANOTHER
IN PSALMS AND HYMNS AND SPIRITUAL SONGS,
SINGING WITH GRACE IN YOUR HEARTS TO THE LORD.

17. AND WHATSOEVER YE DO IN WORD OR DEED,
DO ALL IN THE NAME OF THE LORD JESUS,
GIVING THANKS TO GOD AND THE FATHER BY HIM.

I THESSALONIANS

November 10 (Day 314), Memory Verses #851 & #852
I Thessalonians 4:16-17:

16. FOR THE LORD HIMSELF SHALL DESCEND FROM HEAVEN WITH A SHOUT,
WITH THE VOICE OF THE ARCHANGEL, AND WITH THE TRUMP OF GOD:
AND THE DEAD IN CHRIST SHALL RISE FIRST:

17. THEN WE WHICH ARE ALIVE AND REMAIN SHALL BE CAUGHT UP
TOGETHER WITH THEM IN THE CLOUDS,
TO MEET THE LORD IN THE AIR:
AND SO SHALL WE EVER BE WITH THE LORD.

November 10 (Day 314), Memory Verse #853
I Thessalonians 5:2:

FOR YOURSELVES, KNOW PERFECTLY
THAT THE DAY OF THE LORD SO COMETH AS A THIEF IN THE NIGHT.

November 11 (Day 315), Memory Verse #854
I Thessalonians 5:8:

BUT LET US, WHO ARE OF THE DAY, BE SOBER,
PUTTING ON THE BREASTPLATE OF FAITH AND LOVE;
AND FOR AN HELMET, THE HOPE OF SALVATION.

November 11-12 (Days 315-316), Memory Verses #855 to #860
I Thessalonians 5:13-18:

13. ...AND BE AT PEACE AMONG YOURSELVES.

14. ...BE PATIENT TOWARD ALL MEN.

15. SEE THAT NONE RENDER EVIL FOR EVIL UNTO ANY MAN;
BUT EVER FOLLOW THAT WHICH IS GOOD,
BOTH AMONG YOURSELVES, AND TO ALL MEN.

16. REJOICE EVERMORE.

17. PRAY WITHOUT CEASING.

18. IN EVERYTHING GIVE THANKS:
FOR THIS IS THE WILL OF GOD IN CHRIST JESUS CONCERNING YOU.

November 13 (Day 317), Memory Verse #861
I Thessalonians 5:22:

ABSTAIN FROM ALL APPEARANCE OF EVIL.

II THESSALONIANS

November 13 (Day 317), Memory Verse #862
II Thessalonians 3:13:

BUT YE BRETHREN, BE NOT WEARY IN WELL DOING.

I TIMOTHY

November 14 (Day 318), Memory Verse #863
I Timothy 1:5:

NOW THE END (goal, NIV) OF THE COMMANDMENT IS CHARITY (love, NIV)
OUT OF A PURE HEART,
AND OF A GOOD CONSCIENCE, AND OF FAITH UNFEIGNED (sincere faith, NIV):

November 14 (Day 318), Memory Verses #864 & #865
I Timothy 2:5-6:

5. FOR THERE IS ONE GOD, AND ONE MEDIATOR BETWEEN GOD AND MEN,
THE MAN CHRIST JESUS;

6. WHO GAVE HIMSELF A RANSOM FOR ALL, TO BE TESTIFIED IN DUE TIME.

November 14 (Day 318), Memory Verse #866
I Timothy 3:16:

AND WITHOUT CONTROVERSY GREAT IS THE MYSTERY OF GODLINESS:
GOD WAS MANIFEST IN THE FLESH, JUSTIFIED IN THE SPIRIT,
SEEN OF ANGELS, PREACHED UNTO THE GENTILES,
BELIEVED ON IN THE WORLD, RECEIVED UP INTO GLORY.

November 15 (Day 319), Memory Verse #867
I Timothy 4:12:

LET NO MAN DESPISE THY YOUTH; BUT BE THOU AN EXAMPLE OF THE BELIEVERS,
IN WORD, IN CONVERSATION, IN CHARITY, IN SPIRIT, IN FAITH, IN PURITY.

November 15 (Day 319), Memory Verse #868
I Timothy 5:8:

BUT IF ANY PROVIDE NOT FOR HIS OWN (relatives, NIV),
AND SPECIALLY FOR THOSE OF HIS OWN HOUSE (immediate family, NIV),
HE HATH DENIED THE FAITH, AND IS WORSE THAN AN INFIDEL (unbeliever, NIV).

November 15 (Day 319), Memory Verses #869 & #870
I Timothy 6:6-7:

6. BUT GODLINESS WITH CONTENTMENT IS GREAT GAIN.

7. FOR WE BROUGHT NOTHING INTO THIS WORLD,
AND IT IS CERTAIN WE CAN CARRY NOTHING OUT.

November 16 (Day 320), Memory Verses #871 to #873
I Timothy 6:10-12:

10. FOR THE LOVE OF MONEY IS THE ROOT OF ALL EVIL:
WHICH WHILE SOME COVETED AFTER, THEY HAVE ERRED FROM THE FAITH,
AND PIERCED THEMSELVES THROUGH WITH MANY SORROWS.

11. BUT THOU, O MAN OF GOD, FLEE THESE THINGS;
AND FOLLOW AFTER RIGHTEOUSNESS,
GODLINESS, FAITH, LOVE, PATIENCE, AND MEEKNESS.

12. FIGHT THE GOOD FIGHT OF FAITH, LAY HOLD ON ETERNAL LIFE,
WHEREUNTO THOU ART ALSO CALLED,
AND HAST PROFESSED A GOOD PROFESSION BEFORE MANY WITNESSES.

November 17 (Day 321), Memory Verses #874 & #875
I Timothy 6:17-18:

17. CHARGE THEM THAT ARE RICH IN THIS WORLD, THAT THEY NOT BE HIGH-MINDED,
NOR TRUST IN UNCERTAIN RICHES, BUT IN THE LIVING GOD,
WHO GIVETH US RICHLY ALL THINGS TO ENJOY;

18. THAT THEY DO GOOD, THAT THEY BE RICH IN GOOD WORKS,
READY TO DISTRIBUTE, WILLING TO COMMUNICATE;

II Timothy

November 18 (Day 322), Memory Verses #876 & #877
II Timothy 1:7-8:

7. FOR GOD HATH NOT GIVEN US THE SPIRIT OF FEAR;
BUT OF POWER, AND OF LOVE, AND OF A SOUND MIND.

8. BE NOT THOU THEREFORE ASHAMED OF THE TESTIMONY OF OUR LORD...

November 18 (Day 322), Memory Verse #878
II Timothy 1:12:

...FOR I KNOW WHOM I HAVE BELIEVED,
AND AM PERSUADED THAT HE IS ABLE TO KEEP
THAT WHICH I HAVE COMMITTED UNTO HIM AGAINST THAT DAY.

November 18 (Day 322), Memory Verse #879
II Timothy 2:15:

STUDY TO SHEW THYSELF APPROVED UNTO GOD,
A WORKMAN THAT NEEDETH NOT TO BE ASHAMED,
RIGHTLY DIVIDING THE WORD OF TRUTH.

November 19 (Day 323), Memory Verses #880 to #882
II Timothy 3:15-17:

15. AND THAT FROM A CHILD THOU HAST KNOWN THE HOLY SCRIPTURES,
WHICH ARE ABLE TO MAKE THEE WISE UNTO SALVATION
THROUGH FAITH WHICH IS IN CHRIST JESUS.

16. ALL SCRIPTURE IS GIVEN BY INSPIRATION OF GOD,
AND IS PROFITABLE FOR DOCTRINE, FOR REPROOF, FOR CORRECTION,
FOR INSTRUCTION IN RIGHTEOUSNESS:

17. THAT THE MAN OF GOD MAY BE PERFECT,
THROUGHLY FURNISHED UNTO ALL GOOD WORKS.

November 20 (Day 324), Memory Verse #883
II Timothy 4:7:

I HAVE FOUGHT A GOOD FIGHT,
I HAVE FINISHED MY COURSE, I HAVE KEPT THE FAITH:

Titus

November 21 (Day 325), Memory Verse #884
Titus 1:2:

IN HOPE OF ETERNAL LIFE, WHICH GOD THAT CANNOT LIE,
PROMISED BEFORE THE WORLD BEGAN;

November 22 (Day 326), Memory Verses #885 to #888
Titus 2:11-14:

11. FOR THE GRACE OF GOD THAT BRINGETH SALVATION
HATH APPEARED TO ALL MEN,

12. TEACHING US THAT, DENYING UNGODLINESS AND WORLDLY LUSTS,
WE SHOULD LIVE SOBERLY, RIGHTEOUSLY, AND GODLY, IN THIS PRESENT WORLD;

13. LOOKING FOR THAT BLESSED HOPE,
AND THE GLORIOUS APPEARING OF THE GREAT GOD
AND OUR SAVIOUR JESUS CHRIST;

14. WHO GAVE HIMSELF FOR US, THAT HE MIGHT REDEEM US FROM ALL INIQUITY,
AND PURIFY UNTO HIMSELF A PECULIAR PEOPLE (a people that are his very own, NIV),
ZEALOUS IN GOOD WORKS.

November 23 (Day 327), Memory Verses #889 to #892
Titus 3:4-7:

4. ...THE KINDNESS AND LOVE OF GOD OUR SAVIOUR TOWARD MAN APPEARED,

5. NOT BY WORKS OF RIGHTEOUSNESS WHICH WE HAVE DONE,
BUT ACCORDING TO HIS MERCY HE SAVED US,
BY THE WASHING OF REGENERATION, AND RENEWING OF THE HOLY GHOST;

6. WHICH HE SHED ON US ABUNDANTLY THROUGH JESUS CHRIST OUR SAVIOUR;

7. THAT BEING JUSTIFIED BY HIS GRACE,
WE SHOULD BE MADE HEIRS ACCORDING TO THE HOPE OF ETERNAL LIFE.

Philemon

November 24 (Day 328), Memory Verses #893 & #894
Philemon verses 4-5:

4. I THANK MY GOD,
MAKING MENTION OF THEE ALWAYS IN MY PRAYERS.

5. HEARING OF THY LOVE AND FAITH,
WHICH THOU HAST TOWARD THE LORD JESUS, AND TOWARD ALL SAINTS;

Hebrews

November 25 (Day 329), Memory Verses #895 to #897
Hebrews 1:1-3:

1. **GOD,** WHO AT SUNDRY TIMES AND IN DIVERS MANNERS
(at many times and in various ways, NIV),
SPAKE IN TIME PAST UNTO THE FATHERS BY THE PROPHETS.

2. **HATH** IN THESE LAST DAYS SPOKEN UNTO US BY HIS SON,
WHOM HE HATH APPOINTED HEIR OF ALL THINGS,
BY WHOM ALSO HE MADE THE WORLDS;

3. **WHO** BEING THE BRIGHTNESS OF HIS GLORY,
AND THE EXPRESS IMAGE OF HIS PERSON,
AND UPHOLDING ALL THINGS BY THE WORD OF HIS POWER,
WHEN HE HAD BY HIMSELF PURGED OUR SINS,
SAT DOWN ON THE RIGHT HAND OF THE MAJESTY ON HIGH;

November 25 (Day 329), Memory Verse #898
Hebrews 4:12:

FOR THE WORD OF GOD IS QUICK, AND POWERFUL,
AND SHARPER THAN ANY TWOEDGED SWORD,
PIERCING EVEN TO THE DIVIDING ASUNDER OF SOUL AND SPIRIT,
AND OF THE JOINTS AND MARROW,
AND IS A DISCERNER OF THE THOUGHTS AND INTENTS OF THE HEART.

November 26 (Day 330), Memory Verses #899 to #901
Hebrews 4:14-16:

14. **SEEING** THEN THAT WE HAVE A GREAT HIGH PRIEST,
THAT IS PASSED INTO THE HEAVENS, JESUS THE SON OF GOD,
LET US HOLD FAST OUR PROFESSION.

15. **FOR** WE HAVE NOT AN HIGH PRIEST WHICH CANNOT
BE TOUCHED WITH THE FEELINGS OF OUR INFIRMITIES;
BUT WAS IN ALL POINTS TEMPTED LIKE AS WE ARE,
YET WITHOUT SIN.

16. **LET** US THEREFORE COME BOLDLY UNTO THE THRONE OF GRACE
THAT WE MAY OBTAIN MERCY,
AND FIND GRACE TO HELP IN TIME OF NEED.

November 27 (Day 331), Memory Verse #902
Hebrews 9:27:

AND AS IT IS APPOINTED UNTO MEN ONCE TO DIE,
BUT AFTER THIS THE JUDGMENT:

November 27 (Day 331), Memory Verses #903 to #905
Hebrews 10:23-25:

23. LET US HOLD FAST THE PROFESSION OF OUR FAITH
WITHOUT WAVERING; (FOR HE IS FAITHFUL THAT PROMISED;)

24. AND LET US CONSIDER ONE ANOTHER TO PROVOKE
UNTO LOVE AND TO GOOD WORKS:

25. NOT FORSAKING THE ASSEMBLING OF OURSELVES TOGETHER,
AS THE MANNER OF SOME IS; BUT EXHORTING ONE ANOTHER:
AND SO MUCH THE MORE AS YE SEE THE DAY APPROACHING.

November 28 (Day 332), Memory Verse #906
Hebrews 10:38:

NOW THE JUST SHALL LIVE BY FAITH: …

November 28 (Day 332), Memory Verse #907
Hebrews 11:1:

NOW FAITH IS THE SUBSTANCE OF THINGS HOPED FOR,
THE EVIDENCE OF THINGS NOT SEEN.

November 28 (Day 332), Memory Verse #908
Hebrews 11:6:

BUT WITHOUT FAITH IT IS IMPOSSIBLE TO PLEASE HIM;
FOR HE THAT COMETH TO GOD MUST BELIEVE THAT HE IS,
AND THAT HE IS A REWARDER OF THEM THAT DILIGENTLY SEEK HIM.

November 29 (Day 333), Memory Verses #909 & #910
Hebrews 12:1-2:

1. WHEREFORE SEEING WE ALSO ARE COMPASSED ABOUT
WITH SO GREAT A CLOUD OF WITNESSES,
LET US LAY ASIDE EVERY WEIGHT, AND THE SIN WHICH DOTH SO EASILY BESET US,
AND LET US RUN WITH PATIENCE THE RACE THAT IS SET BEFORE US.

2. LOOKING UNTO JESUS THE AUTHOR AND FINISHER OF OUR FAITH;
WHO FOR THE JOY THAT WAS SET BEFORE HIM ENDURED THE CROSS,
DESPISING THE SHAME,
AND IS SET DOWN AT THE RIGHT HAND OF THE THRONE OF GOD.

November 29 (Day 333), Memory Verse #911
Hebrews 12:6:

FOR WHOM THE LORD LOVETH HE CHASTENETH,
AND SCOURGETH EVERY SON WHOM HE RECEIVETH.

November 30 (Day 334), Memory Verses #912 & #913
Hebrews 13:1-2:

1. LET BROTHERLY LOVE CONTINUE.

2. BE NOT FORGETFUL TO ENTERTAIN STRANGERS:
FOR THEREBY SOME HAVE ENTERTAINED ANGELS UNAWARES.

November 30 (Day 334), Memory Verse #914
Hebrews 13:8:

JESUS CHRIST THE SAME YESTERDAY, AND TO DAY, AND FOR EVER.

JAMES

December 1 (Day 335), Memory Verse #915
James 1:5:

IF ANY OF YOU LACK WISDOM, LET HIM ASK OF GOD,
THAT GIVETH TO ALL MEN LIBERALLY, AND UPBRAIDETH NOT;
AND IT SHALL BE GIVEN HIM.

December 1 (Day 335), Memory Verses #916 & #917
James 1:12-13:

12. BLESSED IS THE MAN THAT ENDURETH TEMPTATION:
FOR WHEN HE IS TRIED, HE SHALL RECEIVE THE CROWN OF LIFE,
WHICH THE LORD HATH PROMISED TO THEM THAT LOVE HIM.

13. LET NO MAN SAY WHEN HE IS TEMPTED, I AM TEMPTED OF GOD:
FOR GOD CANNOT BE TEMPTED WITH EVIL, NEITHER TEMPTETH HE ANY MAN:

December 2 (Day 336), Memory Verse #918
James 1:17:

EVERY GOOD GIFT AND EVERY PERFECT GIFT IS FROM ABOVE,
AND COMETH DOWN FROM THE FATHER OF LIGHTS,
WITH WHOM IS NO VARIABLENESS, NEITHER SHADOW OF TURNING.

December 2 (Day 336), Memory Verse #919
James 1:22:

BUT BE YE DOERS OF THE WORD, AND NOT HEARERS ONLY,
DECEIVING YOUR OWN SELVES.

December 2 (Day 336), Memory Verse #920
James 1:26:

IF ANY MAN AMONG YOU SEEM TO BE RELIGIOUS,
AND BRIDLETH NOT HIS TONGUE, BUT DECEIVETH HIS OWN HEART,
THIS MAN'S RELIGION IS IN VAIN.

December 3 (Day 337), Memory Verse #921
James 2:8:

IF YE FULFIL THE ROYAL LAW ACCORDING TO THE SCRIPTURE,
THOU SHALT LOVE THY NEIGHBOUR AS THYSELF, YE DO WELL:

December 3 (Day 337), Memory Verse #922
James 2:17:

EVEN SO FAITH, IF IT HATH NOT WORKS, IS DEAD, BEING ALONE.

December 3 (Day 337), Memory Verse #923
James 2:26:

FOR AS THE BODY WITHOUT THE SPIRIT IS DEAD,
SO FAITH WITHOUT WORKS IS DEAD ALSO.

December 4 (Day 338), Memory Verses #924 & #925
James 3:17-18:

17. BUT THE WISDOM THAT IS FROM ABOVE IS FIRST PURE,
THEN PEACEABLE, GENTLE, AND EASY TO BE ENTREATED,
FULL OF MERCY AND GOOD FRUITS, WITHOUT PARTIALITY, AND WITHOUT HYPOCRISY.
18. AND THE FRUIT OF RIGHTEOUSNESS IS SOWN IN PEACE
OF THEM THAT MAKE PEACE.

December 4 (Day 338), Memory Verses #926 & #927
James 4:7-8:

7. SUBMIT YOURSELVES THEREFORE TO GOD.
RESIST THE DEVIL, AND HE WILL FLEE FROM YOU.
8. DRAW NIGH TO GOD, AND HE WILL DRAW NIGH TO YOU…

December 5 (Day 339), Memory Verse #928
James 4:11:

SPEAK NOT EVIL ONE OF ANOTHER, BRETHREN…

December 5 (Day 339), Memory Verse #929
James 4:17:

THEREFORE TO HIM THAT KNOWETH TO DO GOOD,
AND DOETH IT NOT, TO HIM IT IS SIN.

December 6 (Day 340), Memory Verse #930
James 5:12:

BUT ABOVE ALL THINGS, MY BRETHREN,
SWEAR NOT, NEITHER BY HEAVEN, NEITHER BY EARTH,
NEITHER BY ANY OTHER OATH:
BUT LET YOUR YEA BE YEA; AND YOUR NAY BE NAY;
LEST YE FALL IN CONDEMNATION.

December 6 (Day 340), Memory Verse #931
James 5:16:

CONFESS YOUR FAULTS ONE TO ANOTHER,
AND PRAY ONE FOR ANOTHER, THAT YE MAY BE HEALED.
THE EFFECTUAL FERVENT PRAYER OF A RIGHTEOUS MAN AVAILETH MUCH.

I Peter

December 7 (Day 341), Memory Verse #932
I Peter 1:15:

BUT AS HE WHICH HATH CALLED YOU IS HOLY,
SO BE YE HOLY IN ALL MANNER OF CONVERSATION; (so be holy in all you do, NIV);

December 7 (Day 341), Memory Verse #933
I Peter 1:22:

...SEE THAT YE LOVE ONE ANOTHER WITH A PURE HEART FERVENTLY:

December 8 (Day 342), Memory Verses #934 & #935
I Peter 1:24-25:

24. ...THE GRASS WITHERETH, AND THE FLOWER THEREOF FALLETH AWAY:

25. BUT THE WORD OF THE LORD ENDURETH FOREVER...

December 8 (Day 342), Memory Verse #936
I Peter 2:2:

AS NEWBORN BABES, DESIRE THE SINCERE MILK OF THE WORD,
THAT YE MAY GROW THEREBY:

December 9 (Day 343), Memory Verses #937 & #938
I Peter 2:24-25:

24. WHO HIS OWN SELF BARE OUR SINS IN HIS OWN BODY ON THE TREE,
THAT WE, BEING DEAD TO SINS, SHOULD LIVE UNTO RIGHTEOUSNESS:
BY WHOSE STRIPES YE WERE HEALED.

25. FOR YE WERE AS SHEEP GOING ASTRAY;
BUT ARE NOW RETURNED UNTO THE SHEPHERD AND BISHOP OF YOUR SOULS.

December 9 (Day 343), Memory Verse #939
I Peter 3:8:

FINALLY, BE YE ALL OF ONE MIND,
HAVING COMPASSION ONE OF ANOTHER, LOVE AS BRETHREN,
BE PITIFUL (be compassionate and humble, NIV), BE COURTEOUS:

December 10 (Day 344), Memory Verse #940
I Peter 3:12:

FOR THE EYES OF THE LORD ARE OVER THE RIGHTEOUS,
AND HIS EARS ARE OPEN UNTO THEIR PRAYERS:
BUT THE FACE OF THE LORD IS AGAINST THEM THAT DO EVIL.

December 10 (Day 344), Memory Verse #941
I Peter 3:15:

BUT SANCTIFY THE LORD GOD IN YOUR HEARTS:
AND BE READY ALWAYS TO GIVE AN ANSWER TO EVERY MAN
THAT ASKETH YOU A REASON OF THE HOPE THAT IS IN YOU
WITH MEEKNESS AND FEAR:

December 11 (Day 345), Memory Verse #942
I Peter 3:18:

FOR CHRIST ALSO HATH ONCE SUFFERED FOR SINS,
THE JUST FOR THE UNJUST, THAT HE MIGHT BRING US TO GOD,
BEING PUT TO DEATH IN THE FLESH, BUT QUICKENED BY THE SPIRIT:

December 11 (Day 345), Memory Verses #943 & #944
I Peter 4:8-9:

8. AND ABOVE ALL THINGS HAVE FERVENT CHARITY AMONG
YOURSELVES: FOR CHARITY SHALL COVER THE MULTITUDE OF SINS.

9. USE HOSPITALITY ONE TO ANOTHER WITHOUT GRUDGING.

December 12 (Day 346), Memory Verse #945
I Peter 5:5:

...GOD RESISTETH THE PROUD, AND GIVETH GRACE TO THE HUMBLE.

December 12 (Day 346), Memory Verse #946
I Peter 5:7:

CASTING ALL YOUR CARE UPON HIM; FOR HE CARETH FOR YOU.

II PETER

December 13-14 (Days 347-348), Memory Verses #947 to #951
II Peter 1:5-9:

5. AND BESIDE THIS, GIVING ALL DILIGENCE,
ADD TO YOUR FAITH VIRTUE; AND TO VIRTUE KNOWLEDGE,

6. AND TO KNOWLEDGE TEMPERANCE;
AND TO TEMPERANCE PATIENCE; AND TO PATIENCE GODLINESS;

7. AND TO GODLINESS BROTHERLY KINDNESS;
AND TO BROTHERLY KINDNESS CHARITY.

8. FOR IF THESE THINGS BE IN YOU, AND ABOUND,
THEY MAKE YOU THAT YE SHALL NEITHER BE BARREN
NOR UNFRUITFUL IN THE KNOWLEDGE OF OUR LORD JESUS CHRIST.

9. BUT HE THAT LACKETH THESE THINGS IS BLIND, AND CANNOT SEE AFAR OFF,
AND HATH FORGOTTEN THAT HE WAS PURGED FROM HIS OLD SINS.

December 14 (Day 348), Memory Verse #952
II Peter 3:8:

BUT BELOVED, BE NOT IGNORANT OF THIS ONE THING,
THAT ONE DAY IS WITH THE LORD AS A THOUSAND YEARS,
AND A THOUSAND YEARS AS ONE DAY.

I John

December 15 (Day 349), Memory Verse #953
I John 1:7:

BUT IF WE WALK IN THE LIGHT, AS HE IS IN THE LIGHT,
WE HAVE FELLOWSHIP ONE WITH ANOTHER,
AND THE BLOOD OF JESUS CHRIST HIS SON CLEANSETH US FROM ALL SIN.

December 15 (Day 349), Memory Verse #954
I John 1:9:

IF WE CONFESS OUR SINS, HE IS FAITHFUL AND JUST TO FORGIVE US OUR SINS,
AND TO CLEANSE US FROM ALL UNRIGHTEOUSNESS.

December 16 (Day 350), Memory Verses #955 to #957
I John 2:1-3:

1. MY LITTLE CHILDREN, THESE THINGS WRITE I UNTO YOU, THAT YE SIN NOT.
AND IF ANY MAN SIN, WE HAVE AN ADVOCATE WITH THE FATHER,
JESUS CHRIST THE RIGHTEOUS:

2. AND HE IS THE PROPITIATION FOR OUR SINS:
AND NOT OURS ONLY, BUT ALSO FOR THE SINS OF THE WHOLE WORLD.

3. AND HEREBY WE DO KNOW THAT WE KNOW HIM, IF WE KEEP HIS COMMANDMENTS.

December 17 (Day 351), Memory Verse #958
I John 2:6:

HE THAT SAITH HE ABIDETH IN HIM OUGHT HIMSELF ALSO SO TO WALK,
EVEN AS HE WALKED.

December 17 (Day 351), Memory Verse #959
I John 2:9:

HE THAT SAITH HE IS IN THE LIGHT, AND HATETH HIS BROTHER,
IS IN DARKNESS EVEN UNTIL NOW.

December 17 (Day 351), Memory Verse #960
I John 2:15:

LOVE NOT THE WORLD, NEITHER THE THINGS THAT ARE IN THE WORLD.
IF ANY MAN LOVE THE WORLD, THE LOVE OF THE FATHER IS NOT IN HIM.

December 18 (Day 352), Memory Verse #961
I John 2:17:

AND THE WORLD PASSETH AWAY, AND THE LUST THEREOF:
BUT HE THAT DOETH THE WILL OF GOD ABIDETH FOR EVER.

December 18 (Day 352), Memory Verse #962
I John 3:1:

BEHOLD, WHAT MANNER OF LOVE THE FATHER HATH BESTOWED UPON US,
THAT WE SHOULD BE CALLED THE SONS OF GOD:
THEREFORE THE WORLD KNOWETH US NOT, BECAUSE IT KNEW HIM NOT.

December 19 (Day 353), Memory Verses #963 to #965
I John 3:16-18:

16. **HEREBY** PERCEIVE WE THE LOVE OF GOD,
BECAUSE HE LAID DOWN HIS LIFE FOR US:
AND WE OUGHT TO LAY DOWN OUR LIVES FOR THE BRETHREN.

17. **BUT** WHOSO HATH THIS WORLD'S GOOD,
AND SEETH HIS BROTHER HAVE NEED,
AND SHUTTETH UP HIS BOWELS OF COMPASSION FROM HIM,
HOW DWELLETH THE LOVE OF GOD IN HIM?

18. **MY** LITTLE CHILDREN, LET US NOT LOVE IN WORD,
NEITHER IN TONGUE; BUT IN DEED AND IN TRUTH.

December 20 (Day 354), Memory Verses #966 & #967
I John 3:23-24:

23. **AND** THIS IS HIS COMMANDMENT,
THAT WE SHOULD BELIEVE ON THE NAME OF HIS SON JESUS CHRIST,
AND LOVE ONE ANOTHER, AS HE GAVE US COMMANDMENT.

24. **AND** HE THAT KEEPETH HIS COMMANDMENTS DWELLETH IN HIM,
AND HE IN HIM. AND HEREBY WE KNOW THAT HE ABIDETH IN US,
BY THE SPIRIT WHICH HE HATH GIVEN US.

December 20 (Day 354), Memory Verse #968
I John 4:4:

YE ARE OF GOD, LITTLE CHILDREN, AND HAVE OVERCOME THEM:
BECAUSE GREATER IS HE THAT IS IN YOU, THAN HE THAT IS IN THE WORLD.

December 21-22 (Days 355-356), Memory Verses #969 to #974
I John 4:7-12:

7. **BELOVED,** LET US LOVE ONE ANOTHER: FOR LOVE IS OF GOD;
AND EVERY ONE THAT LOVETH IS BORN OF GOD, AND KNOWETH GOD.

8. **HE** THAT LOVETH NOT KNOWETH NOT GOD; FOR GOD IS LOVE.

9. **IN** THIS WAS MANIFESTED THE LOVE OF GOD TOWARD US,
BECAUSE THAT GOD SENT HIS ONLY BEGOTTEN SON INTO THE WORLD,
THAT WE MIGHT LIVE THROUGH HIM.

10. **HEREIN** IS LOVE, NOT THAT WE LOVED GOD, BUT THAT HE LOVED US,
AND SENT HIS SON TO BE THE PROPITIATION FOR OUR SINS.

11. **BELOVED,** IF GOD SO LOVED US, WE OUGHT ALSO TO LOVE ONE ANOTHER.

12. **NO** MAN HATH SEEN GOD AT ANY TIME.
IF WE LOVE ONE ANOTHER, GOD DWELLETH IN US, AND HIS LOVE IS PERFECTED IN US.

December 23 (Day 357), Memory Verse #975
I John 4:15:

WHOSOEVER SHALL CONFESS THAT JESUS IS THE SON OF GOD,
GOD DWELLETH IN HIM, AND HE IN GOD.

December 23 (Day 357), Memory Verses #976 & #977
I John 4:18-19:

18. THERE IS NO FEAR IN LOVE; BUT PERFECT LOVE CASTETH OUT FEAR:
BECAUSE FEAR HATH TORMENT.
HE THAT FEARETH IS NOT MADE PERFECT IN LOVE.

19. WE LOVE HIM, BECAUSE HE FIRST LOVED US.

December 24 (Day 358), Memory Verse #978
I John 5:12:

HE THAT HATH THE SON HATH LIFE;
AND HE THAT HATH NOT THE SON OF GOD HATH NOT LIFE.

December 24 (Day 358), Memory Verses #979 & #980
I John 5:14-15:

14. AND THIS IS THE CONFIDENCE THAT WE HAVE IN HIM, THAT,
IF WE ASK ANY THING ACCORDING TO HIS WILL, HE HEARETH US:

15. AND IF WE KNOW THAT HE HEAR US, WHATSOEVER WE ASK,
WE KNOW THAT WE HAVE THE PETITIONS THAT WE DESIRED OF HIM.

II JOHN

December 25 (Day 359), Memory Verses #981 & #982
On Christmas Day, you may also want to read Matthew 2 and Luke 2.
II John verses 5-6:

5. ...LOVE ONE ANOTHER.

6. AND THIS IS LOVE, THAT WE WALK AFTER HIS COMMANDMENTS...

III JOHN

December 25 (Day 359), Memory Verse #983
III John verse 2:

BELOVED, I WISH ABOVE ALL THINGS THAT THOU MAYEST PROSPER
AND BE IN HEALTH,
EVEN AS THY SOUL PROSPERETH.

December 25 (Day 359), Memory Verse #984
III John verse 11:

BELOVED, FOLLOW NOT THAT WHICH IS EVIL, BUT THAT WHICH IS GOOD...

Jude

December 26 (Day 360), Memory Verses #985 to #987
Jude verses 21-23:

21. KEEP YOURSELVES IN THE LOVE OF GOD,
LOOKING FOR THE MERCY OF OUR LORD JESUS CHRIST UNTO ETERNAL LIFE
(to bring you to eternal life, NIV).

22. AND OF SOME HAVE COMPASSION, MAKING A DIFFERENCE
(be merciful to those that doubt, NIV):

23. AND OTHERS SAVE WITH FEAR, PULLING THEM OUT OF THE FIRE;
HATING EVEN THE GARMENT SPOTTED BY THE FLESH.

December 27 (Day 361), Memory Verses #988 & #989
Jude verses 24-25:
(Jude's closing verses)

24. NOW UNTO HIM THAT IS ABLE TO KEEP YOU FROM FALLING,
AND TO PRESENT YOU FAULTLESS BEFORE THE PRESENCE OF HIS GLORY
WITH EXCEEDING JOY,

25. TO THE ONLY WISE GOD OUR SAVIOUR, BE GLORY AND MAJESTY,
DOMINION AND POWER, BOTH NOW AND EVER. AMEN

Revelation

December 28 (Day 362), Memory Verse #990
Revelation 1:8:

I AM ALPHA AND OMEGA, THE BEGINNING AND THE ENDING, SAITH THE LORD,
WHICH IS, AND WHICH WAS, AND WHICH IS TO COME, THE ALMIGHTY.

December 28 (Day 362), Memory Verses #991 & #992
Revelation 3:19-20:

19. AS MANY AS I LOVE, I REBUKE AND CHASTEN:
BE ZEALOUS THEREFORE, AND REPENT.

20. BEHOLD, I STAND AT THE DOOR, AND KNOCK:
IF ANY MAN HEAR MY VOICE, AND OPEN THE DOOR,
I WILL COME IN TO HIM, AND WILL SUP WITH HIM, AND HE WITH ME.

December 29 (Day 363), Memory Verse #993
Revelation 20:15:

AND WHOSOEVER WAS NOT FOUND WRITTEN IN THE BOOK OF LIFE
WAS CAST INTO THE LAKE OF FIRE.

December 29 (Day 363), Memory Verse #994
Revelation 21:1:

AND I SAW A NEW HEAVEN AND A NEW EARTH: ...

December 30 (Day 364), Memory Verse #995
Revelation 21:4:

AND GOD SHALL WIPE AWAY ALL TEARS FROM THEIR EYES;
AND THERE SHALL BE NO MORE DEATH, NEITHER SORROW, NOR CRYING,
NEITHER SHALL THERE BE ANY MORE PAIN:
FOR THE FORMER THINGS ARE PASSED AWAY.

December 30 (Day 364), Memory Verses #996 & #997
Revelation 21:22-23:

22. AND I SAW NO TEMPLE THEREIN:
FOR THE LORD GOD ALMIGHTY AND THE LAMB ARE THE TEMPLE OF IT.

23. AND THE CITY HAD NO NEED OF THE SUN, NEITHER OF THE MOON, TO SHINE IN IT:
FOR THE GLORY OF GOD DID LIGHTEN IT, AND THE LAMB IS THE LIGHT THEREOF.

December 31 (Day 365), Memory Verses #998 & #999
Revelation 22:13-14:

13. I AM ALPHA AND OMEGA,
THE BEGINNING AND THE END; THE FIRST AND THE LAST.

14. BLESSED ARE THEY THAT DO HIS COMMANDMENTS,
THAT THEY MAY HAVE RIGHT TO THE TREE OF LIFE,
AND MAY ENTER IN THROUGH THE GATES INTO THE CITY.

December 31 (Day 365), Memory Verse #1000
Revelation 22:17:

...AND WHOSOEVER WILL,
LET HIM TAKE THE WATER OF LIFE FREELY.

REVELATION 3:20:

BEHOLD, I STAND AT THE DOOR,
AND KNOCK:
IF ANY MAN HEAR MY VOICE,
AND OPEN THE DOOR,
I WILL COME IN TO HIM,
AND WILL SUP WITH HIM,
AND HE WITH ME.

PERSONAL NOTES

PERSONAL NOTES

PERSONAL NOTES

PERSONAL NOTES

_____
_____
_____
_____
_____
_____
_____
_____
_____
_____
_____
_____
_____
_____
_____
_____
_____
_____
_____
_____
_____
_____
_____
_____
_____
_____
_____
_____
_____

PERSONAL NOTES

PERSONAL NOTES

PERSONAL NOTES

PERSONAL NOTES

PERSONAL NOTES

_____

_____

_____

_____

_____

_____

_____

_____

_____

_____

_____

_____

_____

_____

_____

_____

_____

_____

_____

_____

_____

_____

_____

_____

_____

_____

PERSONAL NOTES

PERSONAL NOTES

RESOURCES

Study Bibles:

THE HARPER COLLINS STUDY BIBLE with the Apocryphal / Deuterocanonical Books, New Revised Standard Version: Wayne A. Meeks, General Editor; © 1993 by Harper Collins Publishers, Inc., New York, NY.

THE NIV STUDY BIBLE, New International Version: Kenneth Barker, General Editor; © 1995 by The Zondervan Corporation, Grand Rapids, Michigan; (The Holy Bible, New International Version © 1973, 1978, 1984 by International Bible Society).

THE REFORMATION STUDY BIBLE, New King James Version: R.C. Sproul, General Editor; © 1995 by the Foundation for Reformation, Thomas Nelson Publishers, Nashville, Tennessee.

RYRIE STUDY BIBLE, EXPANDED EDITION, King James Version: Charles Caldwell Ryrie, Th.D., Ph.D.; © 1986, 1994 by Moody Bible Institute, Chicago, Illinois.

ZONDERVAN KJV STUDY BIBLE, King James Version: Kenneth Barker, General Editor; © 2002 by Zondervan Publishers, Grand Rapids, Michigan.

Other Resources:

THE BIBLE MADE PLAIN AND SIMPLE, AN EASY TO UNDERSTAND GUIDE TO THE BIBLE: Mark Water, Author; © 1999 by Hunt and Thorpe, Text copyright by Mark Waters; Designed and produced by the Bridgewater Book Company, Ltd; Hendrickson Publishers, Inc., Peabody, Massachusetts.

Reader's Digest COMPLETE GUIDE TO THE BIBLE, An Illustrated Book-by-Book Companion to the Scriptures: Gayla Visalli, Editor; © 1998 by The Reader's Digest Association, Pleasantville, NY/ Montreal.

THE CONCISE BIBLE COMMENTARY, James M. Gray, D.D.; © 1999 by Hendrickson Publishers, Inc., Peabody, Massachusetts.

HOLMAN BIBLE DICTIONARY, Trent C. Butler, Ph.D., General Editor; © 1991 by Holman Bible Publishers, Nashville, Tennessee.

NAVE'S TOPICAL BIBLE, Orville J. Nave, Revised and compiled by Edward Viening, A.B., B.D.; © 1969 by Zondervan, Grand Rapids, Michigan

THE NEW STRONG'S EXHAUSTIVE CONCORDANCE OF THE BIBLE, James Strong, LL.D., S.T.D.; © 1995,1996 by Thomas Nelson Publishers, Nashville, Tennessee.

INDEX OF KEY MEMORY VERSES

BIBLICAL ORDER:

OLD TESTAMENT MEMORY VERSES

GENESIS (pages (pp) 11-17 & 255–256) **1:1,27-28; 2:3,24; 12:1-3; 18:14; 31:49**
EXODUS   (pp 18-23 & 256 -258) **3:14; 20:3-17; 33:14**
LEVITICUS (pp 24-25 & 258) **19:18, 20:7-8**
NUMBERS (pp 26 -29 & 258) **6:24-26; 32:23**
DEUTERONOMY   (pp 30-33 & 258-259) **4:39; 6:5; 10:12-13; 32:4; 33:27**
JOSHUA (pp 34-36 & 259) **1:9; 24:15**
JUDGES (pp 37 -40 & 259) **21:25**
RUTH   (pp 41 & 260) **1:16**
I SAMUEL (pp 42-47 & 260) **2:2; 12:24; 15:22; 16:7**
II SAMUEL (pp 48 -51 & 260-261) **22:29,31,34,47; 23:3-4**
I KINGS (pp 52-56 & 261) **2:3**
II KINGS   (pp 57–62 & 261) **17:35-37**
I CHRONICLES (pp 63–66 & 262) **4:9-10; 16:8-12,23-25,34; 22:19**
II CHRONICLES   (pp 67-74 & 263) **7:14; 16:9, 20:21**
EZRA   (pp 75 & 263) **7:10**
NEHEMIAH (pp 76 & 263) **8:10; 9:17**
ESTHER (pp 77 & 264) **4:14**
JOB (pp 78–79 & 264) **1:21; 5:17; 6:25; 19:25; 28:28; 37:14**
PSALMS (pp 80–94 & 265-276) **1:1-2; 5:3; 8:1; 12:6-7; 14:1; 18:2,30-33; 19:1,7-10,14; 22:1,14-18; 23:1-6; 24:1; 25:6-8; 27:1,14; 28:7; 31:5,24; 33:12; 35:9; 36:7; 37:4-5,7,23-24; 40:5; 42:1; 44:21; 46:1,10; 47:1,6-7; 49:17; 51:7,10,12; 53:1; 55:22; 56:3,11; 62:5-8; 67:1; 84:11; 86:5,11,15; 90:2,4,12; 91:2; 92:1-2; 94:12; 95:6-7; 100:1-5; 102:25; 103:1-2,12; 104:33-34; 111:10; 117:1-2; 118:8,22,24; 119:11,80,103,105,127; 121:1-8; 122:1; 130:5; 133:1; 136:1,5-9; 139:9-10,14,23-24; 141:3; 143:8; 144:15; 145:3; 150:1-6**
PROVERBS   (pp 95–100 & 276 - 281) **1:7; 2:3-5; 3:1-9,11-12; 4:18; 6:6,20-22; 9:10; 10:1,12; 11:30, 12:28; 14:21,30; 15:1,6,13,15-16,33; 16:3,24,32; 17:3,17,22; 18:7-8,10,12,15; 20:15; 21:2; 22:1,6; 23:7,17; 24:13-14; 25:11, 21-22; 27:2; 29:23,25-26; 30:5; 31:30**
ECCLESIASTES (pp 101-102 & 282) **3:1,17; 5:18-19; 7:1,20; 9:10; 12:1, 13-14**
SONG OF SOLOMON (pp 103 & 283) **2:4,16; 8:6-7**
ISAIAH (pp 104-115 & 283-287) **1:18; 2:4; 6:8; 7:14; 9:6-7; 11:6; 12:2-5; 25:8; 26:3; 33:15-16; 40:8,28-29,31; 41:4; 44:6 45:22; 49:23; 52:7; 53:3-9; 55:6,9; 61:10; 64:8**
JEREMIAH (pp 116-124 & 287-288) **9:23-24; 10:10,23-24; 17:7-10; 29:13; 31:31-34**
LAMENTATIONS (pp 125 & 289) **3:22-23,25,40-41; 5:19**
EZEKIEL (pp 126–132 & 289) **17:24; 18:30-32**
DANIEL (pp 133-134 & 290) **2:20,22; 12:3,10**
HOSEA (pp 135 & 290) **12:6; 13:4; 14:9**
JOEL (pp 136 & 291) **2:13,21,28**
AMOS (pp 137 & 291) **5:4,24**
OBADIAH (pp 138 & 291) **Verse15**
JONAH (pp 139 & 292) **2:9**
MICAH (pp 140-141 & 292) **4:2-3; 5:2; 6:8; 7:7-8,18**
NAHUM (pp 142 & 293) **1:7**
HABAKKUK   (pp 143 & 293) **2:4, 20; 3:18-19**
ZEPHANIAH (pp 144 & 293) **2:3; 3:17**
HAGGAI (pp 145 & 294) **1:13**
ZACHARIAH   (pp 146 & 294) **1:3; 9:9**
MALACHI (pp 147 & 294) **3:6-7; 4:2**

NEW TESTAMENT MEMORY VERSES

MATTHEW (pages (pp) 148-161 & 295 -303) **1:22-23; 3:10,17; 4:4,7,10,17,19; 5:1-12,13-18,39,44,48; 6:3-4,6,9-13,14-15,20-21,24-29,33-34; 7:1,5,7-8,12,14; 9:37-38; 10:32-33, 39; 11:28-30; 12:50; 13:12; 16:16,24-26; 17:20; 18:3-4,19-22; 19:14,26,30; 20:16,27-28; 21:22; 22:14,21,37-40; 23:11; 24:35,40,42; 25:13,21,29,40; 26:39,41; 28:19-20**

MARK (pp 162-168 & 303-305) **1:17; 2:27; 3:25,35; 4:24-25; 8:34-38; 9:23-24,35,37,40,50; 10:15,24,27,31,43-45; 11:25; 12:29-31; 13:31; 14:35-36; 16:15-16**

LUKE (pp 169–180 & 306-312) **1:37,46-48, 76-77; 2:1-20,52; 3:22; 4:4,8,12; 6:27-29,31,35-38,41,45; 8:21; 9:23,48; 10:2; 11:9-10,13; 12:15,31,34,40; 14:27,33; 15:7; 16:10,13; 17:6,33; 18:14,16-17,27; 19:10,26; 21:33; 22:42; 23:42-43; 24:5-6**

JOHN (pp 181-191 & 312-319) **1:1-5,10,12-14,29, 2:19; 3:3,16-18,30,36; 4:14,23-24,34-36; 5:24; 6:27,35,40,48,51,63; 7:37-38; 8:7,12,31-32,51,58; 9:39; 10:9-11,14-15,27-28,30; 11:25-26; 12:25,46; 13:14-15,34-35; 14:1-3,6,13-15,21,26-27; 15:5,12-13; 16:33; 17:5,11,20-21; 20:29,31; 21:16,25**

ACTS (pp 192–197 & 320 -321) **1:8; 2:21,24,38; 4:12; 5:29,41; 10:34-35,43; 16:31; 17:28; 20:35**

ROMANS (pp 198-204 & 321-325) **1:1,16-17; 2:4,11; 3:10,23; 5:1,8; 6:3-4,23; 8:1,3,6,15-17,28, 31,38-39; 10:9,13,17; 11:33-36; 12:1-2,5,10,14-15,18,20-21; 13:8-10; 14:12-13; 15:1**

I CORINTHIANS (pp 205 -210 & 325-328) **1:18,27,31; 2:9-10; 3:16; 4:2,4; 6:15,17,19-20; 8:1; 10:13,24,31; 12:4; 13:1-13; 14:33; 15:3-4,33,54-58**

II CORINTHIANS (pp 211-213 & 328-329) **1:3-4; 3:18; 5:7,15,17,21; 6:2; 9:7-8; 10:17; 12:10**

GALATIANS (pp 214-216 & 329-331) **2:16; 3:8,11,28-29; 5:13-14,16,22-23,25; 6:2,7,9-10**

EPHESIANS (pp 217-220 & 331-333) **1:4-5,22-23; 2:4-5,8-9,22; 3:19-21; 4:4-6,26,32; 5:2,21-22,25,31; 6:1-4,10-12,18**

PHILIPPIANS (pp 221-223 & 334-335) **1:3,21; 2:5-11; 3:8,14; 4:4,6-8,11,13,19**

COLOSSIANS (pp 224-225 & 335-336) **1:17; 2:8-9; 3:2,12-17**

I THESSALONIANS (pp 226-227 & 336-337) **4:16-17; 5:2,8,13-18,22**

II THESSALONIANS (pp 228 & 337) **3:13**

I TIMOTHY (pp 229-230 & 337-338) **1:5; 2:5-6; 3:16; 4:12; 5:8; 6:6-7,10-12,17-18**

II TIMOTHY (pp 231-232 & 339) **1:7-8,12; 2:15; 3:15-17; 4:7**

TITUS (pp 233-234 & 340) **1:2; 2:11-14; 3:4-7**

PHILEMON (pp 235 & 340) **Verses 4-5**

HEBREWS (pp 236 –239 & 341-342) **1:1-3; 4:12,14-16; 9:27; 10:23-25, 38; 11:1,6; 12:1-2 12:6; 13:1-2,8**

JAMES (pp 240–242 & 343-344) **1:5,12-13,17,22,26; 2:8,17,26; 3:17-18; 4:7-8,11,17; 5:12,16**

I PETER (pp 243-244 & 345-346) **1:15,22,24-25; 2:2,24-25; 3:8,12,15; 3:18; 4:8-9; 5:5,7**

II PETER (pp 245 & 346) **1:5-9; 3:8**

I JOHN (pp 246 -248 & 347-349) **1:7,9; 2:1-3,6,9,15,17; 3:1,16-18,23-24; 4:4,7-12,15,18-19; 5:12,14-15**

II JOHN (pp 249 & 349) **Verses 5-6**

III JOHN (pp 249 & 349) **Verses 2, 11**

JUDE (pp 250 & 350) **Verses 21-23, 24-25**

REVELATION (pp 251-254 & 350 -351) **1:8; 3:19-20; 20:15; 21:1,4,22-23; 22:13-14**

ALPHABETICAL ORDER:

ACTS (pages [pp] 192–197 & 320 -321) **1:8; 2:21,24,38; 4:12; 5:29,41; 10:34-35,43; 16:31; 17:28; 20:35**

AMOS (pp 137 & 291) **5:4,24**

I CHRONICLES (pp 63–66 & 262) **4:9-10; 16:8-12,23-25,34; 22:19**

II CHRONICLES (pp 67-74 & 263) **7:14; 16:9; 20:21**

COLOSSIANS (pp 224-225 & 335-336) **1:17; 2:8-9; 3:2; 3:12-17**

I CORINTHIANS (pp 205 -210 & 325-328) **1:18,27,31; 2:9-10; 3:16; 4:2,4; 6:15,17,19-20; 8:1; 10:13,24,31; 12:4; 13:1-13; 14:33; 15:3-4,33,54-58**

II CORINTHIANS (pp 211-213 & 328-329) **1:3-4; 3:18; 5:7,15,17,21; 6:2; 9:7-8; 10:17; 12:10**

DANIEL (pp 133-134 & 290) **2:20,22; 12:3,10**

DEUTERONOMY   (pages [pp] 30-33 & 258-259) **4:39; 6:5; 10:12-13; 32:4; 33:27**

ECCLESIASTES (pp 101-102 & 282) **3:1,17; 5:18-19; 7:1,20; 9:10; 12:1, 13-14**

EPHESIANS (pp 217-220 & 331-333) **1:4-5,22-23; 2:4-5,8-9,22;   3:19-21; 4:4-6,26,32; 5:2,21-22,25,31; 6:1-4,10-12,18**

ESTHER   (pp 77 & 264) **4:14**

EXODUS   (pp 18-23 & 256 -258) **3:14; 20:3-17; 33:14**

EZEKIEL   (pp 126–132 & 289) **17:24; 18:30-32**

EZRA   (pp 75 & 263) **7:10**

GALATIANS (pp 214-216 & 329-331) **2:16; 3:8,11,28-29; 5:13-14,16,22-23,25; 6:2,7,9-10**

GENESIS (pp 11-17 & 255 -256) **1:1,27-28; 2:3,24; 12:1-3; 18:14; 31:49**

HABAKKUK (pp 143 & 293) **2:4,20; 3:18-19**

HAGGAI   (pp 145 & 294) **1:13**

HEBREWS   (pp 236 –239 & 341-342) **1:1-3; 4:12,14-16; 9:27; 10:23-25, 38; 11:1,6; 12:1-2,6; 13:1-2,8**

HOSEA   (pp 135 & 290) **12:6; 13:4; 14:9**

ISAIAH   (pp 104-115 & 283-287) **1:18; 2:4; 6:8; 7:14; 9:6-7; 11:6; 12:2-5; 25:8; 26:3; 33:15-16; 40:8,28-29,31; 41:4; 44:6 45:22; 49:23; 52:7; 53:3-9; 55:6,9; 61:10; 64:8**

JAMES (pp 240–242 & 343-344) **1:5,12-13,17,22,26; 2:8,17,26; 3:17-18; 4:7-8,11,17; 5:12,16**

JEREMIAH (pp 116-124 & 287-288) **9:23-24; 10:10,23-24; 17:7-10; 29:13; 31:31-34**

JOB   (pp 78–79 & 264) **1:21; 5:17; 6:25; 19:25; 28:28; 37:14**

JOEL (pp 136 & 291) **2:13,21,28**

JOHN   (pp 181-191 & 312-319) **1:1-5,10,12-14,29, 2:19; 3:3,16-18,30,36; 4:14,23-24,34-36; 5:24; 6:27,35,40,48,51,63;   7:37-38;   8:7,12,31-32,51,58;   9:39;   10:9-11,14-15,27-28,30; 11:25-26; 12:25,46; 13:14-15,34-35;   14:1-3,6,13-15,21,26-27; 15:5,12-13; 16:33; 17:5,11,20-21; 20:29,31; 21:16,25**

I JOHN   (pp 246 -248 & 347-349) **1:7,9; 2:1-3,6,9,15,17; 3:1,16-18,23-24; 4:4,7-12,15,18-19; 5:12,14-15**

II JOHN (pp 249 & 349) **Verses 5-6**

III JOHN   (pp 249 & 349) **Verses 2, 11**

JONAH   (pp 139 & 292) **2:9**

JOSHUA (pp 34 -36 & 259) **1:9; 24:15**

JUDE (pp 250 & 350) **Verses 21-23, 24-25**

JUDGES (pp 37 -40 & 259) **21:25**

I KINGS (pp 52-56 & 261) **2:3**

II KINGS (pp 57–62 & 261) **17:35-37**

LAMENTATIONS (pp 125 & 289) **3:22-23,25,40-41; 5:19**

LEVITICUS (pp 24-25 & 258) **19:18; 20:7-8**

LUKE   (pp 169–180 & 306-312) **1:37,46-48, 76-77;   2:1-20,52;   3:22;   4:4,8,12;   6:27-29,31,35-38,41,45;   8:21;   9:23,48;   10:2;   11:9-10,13;   12:15,31,34,40;   14:27,33;   15:7;   16:10,13;   17:6,33; 18:14,16-17,27; 19:10,26; 21:33; 22:42; 23:42-43; 24:5-6**

MALACHI (pp 147 & 294) **3:6-7, 4:2**

MARK   (pp 162-168 & 303-305) **1:17; 2:27; 3:25,35; 4:24-25; 8:34-38; 9:23-24,35,37,40,50; 10:15,24,27,31,43-45; 11:25; 12:29-31; 13:31; 14:35-36; 16:15-16**

MATTHEW   (pp 148-161 & 295 -303) **1:22-23; 3:10,17; 4:4,7,10,17,19;   5:1-12,13-18,39,44,48; 6:3-4,6,9-13,14-15,20-21,24-29,33-34; 7:1,5,7-8,12,14; 9:37-38; 10:32-33, 39; 11:28-30; 12:50; 13:12; 16:16,24-26;   17:20; 18:3-4,19-22;   19:14,26,30;   20:16,27-28;   21:22;   22:14,21,37-40;   23:11; 24:35,40,42; 25:13,21,29,40; 26:39,41; 28:19-20**

MICAH   (pp 140-141 & 292) **4:2-3; 5:2; 6:8; 7:7-8,18**

NAHUM   (pp 142 & 293) **1:7**

NEHEMIAH   (pp 76 & 263) **8:10; 9:17**

NUMBERS   (pp 26 -29 & 258) **6:24-26; 32:23**

OBADIAH   (pp 138 & 291) **Verse 15**

I PETER   (pp 243-244 & 345-346) **1:15,22,24-25; 2:2,24-25; 3:8,12,15,18; 4:8-9; 5:5,7**

II PETER   (pp 245 & 346) **1:5-9; 3:8**

PHILEMON   (pp 235 & 340) **Verses 4-5**

PHILIPPIANS (pp 221-223 & 334-335) **1:3,21; 2:5-11; 3:8,14; 4:4,6-8,11,13,19**

I PETER 1:24-25:

24. ...THE GRASS WITHERETH, AND THE FLOWER THEREOF FALLETH AWAY:

25. BUT THE WORD OF THE LORD ENDURETH FOREVER...

Hebrews 4:12:

For the word of God is quick,
and powerful,
and sharper than any
twoedged sword,
piercing even to the dividing
asunder of soul and spirit,
and of the joints and marrow,
and is a discerner of the
thoughts and intents
of the heart.

Deposit God's Word in your memory bank, and you will draw interest for life!

Author of quote unknown

Quick Order Form for BIBLE IN A NUTSHELL
Available in PAPERBACK and E-BOOK!!

Receive the SPECIAL DISCOUNT price of $19.95 (paperback) when paying by check or money order, filling out this form, and mailing to the following address:

HIS LIGHT Publications, P.O. Box 1666, Easley, S. C. 29641   USA

— Credit card orders for PAPERBACK and E-BOOK can be taken online at www.Bibleinanutshell.com or www.trafford.com.

— Look for future editions in hardback and with the option of other Bible versions.

<u>Note</u>:   ALL ORDERS by bookstores, distributors, wholesalers, or other resale purchasers should be directed to:
TRAFFORD Publishing, Inc.
TOLL-FREE (US and Canada) 1-888-232-4444 or 250-383-6864, FAX 250-383-6804
East Coast Office: 5804 Jolly Roger Court, New Bern, NC, 28560-9767
West Coast Office: Suite 6E - 2333 Government St., Victoria BC V8T 4P4
http://www.trafford.com

Name: _____

Mailing Address: _____

City: _____ State: _____ Zip: _____

E-mail address: _____

Telephone: _____ FAX: _____

<u>ITEM ordered</u>: <u>Paperback (U.S. $19.95)</u>   Quantity ___   Total Price this line $ _____
<u>Sales Tax</u>: <u>S.C. addresses</u> — ADD $1.20 sales tax for each $19.95 order. $ _____
<u>Shipping and Handling</u>: <u>U.S. Orders</u> — ADD $6.00 S/H + $2.00 S/H each additional book.
<u>International Orders</u> — ADD $16.00 S/H U.S. currency + $4.00 S/H each additional book. $ _____

<u>Total</u>: $ _____

Total Amount enclosed: _____

Enclosed is: ☐ Check   ☐ Money Order   **(Do not send cash)**
All orders will be shipped via USPS book rate, unless otherwise requested.
Expect 2-3 week delivery. Contact Trafford Publishing, Inc. for rush orders.

☐ **I would like information on using** <u>Bible in a Nutshell</u> **for fundraisers in my church.**
   Larger discounts are available when ordering 50 or more copies.

ISBN 1553951O5-O

9 781553 951056